THE BELL CURVE DEBATE

THE BELL CURVE DEBATE

DEBATE

History, Documents, Opinions

EDITED BY

Russell Jacoby and Naomi Glauberman

TIMES 𝕿 BOOKS

RANDOM HOUSE

Published in the United States by Times Books, a division of
Random House, Inc., New York, and simultaneously in Canada by
Random House of Canada Limited, Toronto.

Owing to space limitations, permission acknowledgments for
previously published material can be found on pages 683-688

Library of Congress Cataloging-in-Publication Data
The bell curve debate: history, documents opinions/
edited by Russell Jacoby and Naomi Glauberman.—1st ed.
p.   cm.
Included bibliographical references and index.
ISBN 0-8129-2587-4
1. Bell Curve Debate, 1995.   I. Jacoby, Russell   II. Glauberman,
Naomi.

Manufactured in the United States of America

9 8 7 6 5 4 3 2

First Edition

Contents

ACKNOWLEDGMENTS

THIS PROJECT was conceived by Tim Mooney, marketing manager of Times Books, and expertly guided with great skill and enthusiasm by Steve Wasserman, editorial director of Times Books. Our thanks to both of them. We also want to thank Laura Taylor and Nancy Inglis of Times Books. Numerous people aided us in tracking down pertinent documents and readings. We want to particularly thank Willy Forbath of the UCLA Law School and Linda Maisner and June H. Liebert of the UCLA Law School library for indispensable assistance in putting together this collection. We also received help from Richard Geiger of the *San Francisco Chronicle* library. At varied moments Dianne McKinney, Jackie Pine, Brian Morton, Carol Oblath, Katya Slive, Chuck Reich and, of course, Sam and Sarah Jacoby played decisive roles: our thanks to them.

Introduction

In 1969 a University of California psychologist Arthur R. Jensen published an essay entitled "How Much Can We Boost IQ and Scholastic Achievement?" Jensen doubted much could be done. Programs designed to compensate for cultural and economic deprivation have "failed"; they misinterpreted genetic differences as environmental. The article, which included a bell curve showing the distribution of "intelligence," raised a firestorm of responses; within two years well over a hundred appeared. In a 1978 list of a decade's most cited social science articles Jensen's ranked sixth.[1]

Amid the controversy appeared a lengthy defense of Jensen called "IQ" written by a Harvard psychologist. "The data on IQ and social-class differences," concluded this 1971 *Atlantic Monthly* essay, shows that we are creating "an inherited system of stratification. The signs point to more rather than less of it in the future."[2] Over twenty years later Richard J. Herrnstein, the author of "IQ," published with Charles Murray a fat volume that expands his 1971 article, itself a gloss of Jensen's 1969 argument. The book? *The Bell Curve.*

Is this—to use a favorite Americanism—déjà vu all over again? Like the Jensen piece, *The Bell Curve* elicited a torrent of articles, many hundreds within months of its publication. Few seem to be able to resist its pull; even those who detest the book have been drawn to it. *The Bell Curve* is no longer just a book; it is a phenomenon, a gale in the zeitgeist.

Many want to dismiss *The Bell Curve;* it should not be done. A serious book that gains several hundred thousand readers within months of publication deserves serious attention. For better or worse—and many think for worse—the book has struck a chord. To be sure, hype and salesmanship prepared the way. Advance copies were kept from reviewers, who might have dampened enthusiasm. The book wound up on the front covers of *Newsweek, The New Republic,* and *The New York Times Book Review.* Is this a case of a big book garnering big attention or big attention begetting a big book?

The Bell Curve gives a sophisticated voice to a repressed and illiberal sentiment: a belief that ruinous divisions in society are sanctioned by nature itself. For many readers the graphs and charts of *The Bell Curve* confirm a dark suspicion: the ills of welfare, poverty, and an underclass are less matters of justice than biology. The visceral support for Herrnstein and Murray arises from the endless accounts of crime, which note the arrested never knew a father, the mother is on welfare, and the many siblings are either just entering or leaving prison. *The Bell Curve* taps the frustration provoked by relentless stories of sixteen-year-old mothers pushing baby carriages while the state pays the bills. Many Americans conclude these people cannot figure out anything, except how to reproduce and get welfare, and warrant nothing.

This reaction is both common and ashamed of itself. It is embarrassed because it flagrantly contradicts an official egalitarianism to which almost everyone in American society gives lip service; it is common because the grievous social decay seems both worsening and irreversible, prompting many to return to ideas of biology and race they never abandoned. The more society looks like the jungle it actually is, the more people trade in ideas of blood and breeding. The primitivism of advanced society gives rise to advanced primitivism. When a book comes along that ratifies these ancient and new ideas, readers line up.

The popularity of *The Bell Curve* puts an odd spin on the authors' pose as feckless seekers of truth who are bucking liberal conformism. They embellish the myths of our time, which hardly seems courageous. Indeed, one of their favorite put-downs is "elite wisdom," as if wisdom is popular and they are its agents. Yet they not only address but celebrate "the cognitive elite." *The Bell Curve* is a feel-good book for high achievers. Herrnstein and Murray regularly toast their readers as the best and the brightest. "In all likelihood, almost all of your friends and professional associates belong in that top Class I slice [of intelligence, i.e., the very bright]." How do they know? You're reading their book.

While some critics deny it, *The Bell Curve* has something to say, not about race but about a new elitism the authors both champion and bemoan. Herrnstein and Murray's observation that top universities, once clubs for wealthy mediocrities, are stepping-stones for a new talented elite is worth considering. Their skewing of a liberal hypocrisy that self-righteously denounces and ardently pursues elitism is apt. Their fear that "the smart and the rich" increasingly withdraw from a corroding society by way of gated communities, private schools, and insulated lives is hardly misplaced. Their worries of a future where the poor, the misfit, and the witless are shunted off to "high-tech" reservations cannot be discounted.

Yet something tempers their qualms. Do they dread this future or desire it—and even promote it? In his previous book, *Losing Ground*, Murray championed "vouchers," direct payments from the state to parents who could bypass public education. In *The Bell Curve*, Herrnstein and Murray suggest ending special education programs and government aid for neighborhoods. "Government policy can do much to foster the vitality of neighborhoods by trying to do less for them." These ideas play well to Americans who have never warmed to government, but they are less the solution to the crisis than its prehistory.

The extraordinary response to *The Bell Curve* suggests that it touches an open nerve. The book bespeaks a society that is losing confidence in its own egalitarian and democratic promise. As the prospect dims, society taps biology for answers. Nowadays this is everywhere. Not a month goes by without an announcement that researchers have discovered the genetic or chemical source of some human ill or tendency. Usually everyone applauds. *Time* magazine envisions "a lab test for suicide" because scientists can measure certain chemicals in the brain, identifying "those people with a biological predisposition to self-destruction."[3]

The point is not to negate or belittle the genetic or chemical research; it is to understand its limits. The findings do not tell us, for instance, why Americans are heavier this decade than last or why intelligence thrives in well-funded suburban schools and withers in run-down inner-city schools. What does a gene pool that hardly alters from generation to generation illuminate of these configurations? Not much.

Almost a century ago, the American sociologist Charles H. Cooley settled accounts with Francis Galton, the founder of eugenics, the "science" to improve the human race. Cooley took up the issue why "genius" does not appear to be equally distributed among groups and races. He did not find convincing the biological or genetic explanation. Cooley's reflections, which we include in Chapter 6, breathe of unsurpassed good sense.

> Suppose a man, having plowed and cultivated his farm, should take in his hand a bag of mixed seeds . . . and walk straight across his land, sowing as he went. All pieces on his path would be sown alike: the rocks, the sandy ground, the good upland soil . . . but

there would be great variety in the result when harvest time came around. In some places nothing would come up at all. In the sand perhaps only the beans would flourish . . . while some generous soils would allow a variety of plants to grow side by side in considerable vigor.

For Cooley, the seed bag is mankind, the seeds are genius and talent, and the soil—some cultivated, some rocky, and some abandoned—represent the very diverse historical conditions. "Something like this, I think, is the case with a stock of men passing through history." Amen.

THE FOLLOWING pages chew over, and often chew up, *The Bell Curve.* They constitute a complete response to Herrnstein and Murray, taking up the argument, the evidence, and the research. We also provide essential documents and readings from earlier stages of the debate. We have selected the best pieces from all quarters. Most of the current contributions—not all—are sharply critical of *The Bell Curve:* this reflects the weight of published opinion. We should note that our efforts to include an extract from *The Bell Curve* or an essay by Charles Murray were rebuffed by the author and his publisher.

We have organized the readings straightforwardly in two parts with the first, "Hue and Cry: The Debate" dealing with the current controversy and the second, "Root and Branch: The History," covering its past. The second part surveys earlier stages of the debate over intelligence, inheritability, and race from the mid-nineteenth century to the 1970s. Throughout, our editorial deletions, mainly restricted to historical material in the second part, are marked so: [. . .].

In Chapter 1 we open with the longer reviews that take up *The Bell Curve.* In Chapter 2, we turn to a series of essays that explore the political and institutional roots of *The Bell Curve* research; the media response to the debate; and the IQ controversy as it has played out in East Asia and Ireland. In Chapter 3 we select a series of shorter pieces—opinions and testimonies—provoked by the book. In Chapter 4 we offer a selection of conservative commentary and critiques, including six contributions to the *National Review* symposium on *The Bell Curve.* Another symposium that appeared in *The New Republic* will be part of a Basic Books volume.[4] We close the first part with a sampling of editorials from around the country.

In the second part we move from *The Bell Curve* to the larger history of the issues of inherited intelligence. We proceed roughly chronologically, with selections in Chapter 6 from Francis Galton, who founded the field of eugenics in the 1860s, from Karl Pearson, a follower of Galton, and from Charles H. Cooley, the American sociologist who wrote one of the first and most searching criticisms of Galton.[5] We also include an extract from the 1911 *Encyclopaedia Britannica* entry on "The Negro."

In Chapter 7 we turn to the World War I period and open with three recent pieces that outline the rise of eugenics in the United States, the origins of IQ testing, and the response to these tests by black intellectuals. We also include a number of key documents, namely extracts by Lewis B. Terman and Carl C. Brigham, two of the principals who promoted intelligence testing; Lothrop Stoddard, an American writer and eugenist, who, drawing on the results of these tests, feared the decline of intelligence; and Walter Lippmann, the journalist who questioned the tests, the testers, and their conclusions. We close this chapter with Horace Mann Bond, an educator who criticized the army intelligence tests.

In our last chapter we take up the immediately preceding debate to *The Bell Curve*, the arguments kicked off in the late sixties and early seventies by Arthur Jensen. We include a piece by Jensen, which restates his 1969 position; an abridged version of Richard Herrnstein's classic defense of the Berkeley professor; and three responses—all of which raise issues that are virtually identical to those discussed today.

That may be the problem. The return of this dispute testifies to an intellectual life moving in circles because society moves in circles. The intractable poverty of the late 1960s becomes the implacable poverty of the 1990s and gives rise to notions we have seen before. Halfhearted social policies doomed to failure engender social policies confirming failure. The idea of equality is again shelved as unworkable and untrue.

One notion should be dispatched. The belief in equality hardly denies differences in talents, skills, and intelligence among people. "To criticize inequality," wrote R. H. Tawney in his *Equality*, a wonderful tonic to *The Bell Curve*, "and to desire equality is not, as sometimes suggested, to cherish the romantic illusion that men are equal in character and intelligence."[6] It is, however, to cherish a society that eliminates inequalities founded on social and economic injustices.

Today the just society is distant. Revitalized ethnic and racial myths sanction inequalities based not on talent or ability but group membership and test scores. All is not lost, however. The idea of equality is not only continuously discarded, but continuously rediscovered. "I used to think there were smart people and dumb people," states Russell Thomas, a black high school basketball player profiled in Darcy Frey's *The Last Shot*, "but that's not true. Everybody's got the same brain. . . . But you got to practice. That's how your mind starts to expand and mature."[7]

Notes

1. Jensen's article and a bibliography of the first responses can be found in Arthur R. Jensen, *Genetics and Education* (New York: Harper & Row, 1972). The article originally appeared in *Harvard Educational Review* and with the original replies can be found in *Environment, Heredity, and Intelligence, Harvard Educational Review*, Reprint Series No. 2 (1969). See generally William H. Tucker, *The Science and Politics of Racial Research* (Urbana: University of Illinois Press, 1994), pp. 195–233.

2. Richard J. Herrnstein, "IQ," *Atlantic Monthly,* September 1971, p. 64.

3. Christine Gorman, "Suicide Check," *Time,* November 28, 1994, p. 65.

4. *The New Republic* symposium appeared on October 31, 1994.

5. It is important to realize that eugenics in its inception was not a province for crackpots and racists. Many eugenists saw themselves as liberals and progressives, even socialists. They wanted to improve the human species, regulating human reproduction in the same way they wanted to regulate the economy. Pearson considered himself a socialist. "We may even say that Socialism is the logical outcome of the law of Malthus," stated Karl Pearson in "The Moral Basis of Socialism," in his *The Ethic of Freethought* (London: T. Fisher Unwin, 1888), p. 336. Many feminists fighting for birth control rights, like Margaret Sanger, enthusiastically supported eugenics. "To Breed a Race of Thoroughbreds" was a slogan of Sanger's American Birth Control League. See Diane Paul, "Eugenics and the Left," *Journal of the History of Ideas,* 45 (1984): 567–590; Linda Gordon, *Woman's Body, Woman's Right: A Social History of Birth Control in America* (New York: Penguin Books, 1977), especially pp. 274–290; and Donald K. Pickens, *Eugenics and the Progressives* (Nashville: Vanderbilt University Press, 1968).

6. R. H. Tawney, *Equality* (New York: Barnes & Nobles, 1965), p. 57. *Equality* was first published in 1931, and revised variously through 1952.

7. Darcy Frey, *The Last Shot: City Streets, Basketball Dreams* (New York: Houghton Mifflin, 1994), p. 70.

HUE AND CRY:
THE DEBATE

I
REVIEWS AND ARGUMENTS

MISMEASURE BY ANY MEASURE

Stephen Jay Gould

THE BELL CURVE, by Richard J. Herrnstein and Charles Murray, subtitled "Intelligence and Class Structure in American Life," provides a superb and unusual opportunity to gain insight into the meaning of experiment as a method in science. The primary desideratum in all experiments is reduction of confusing variables: we bring all the buzzing and blooming confusion of the external world into our laboratories and, holding all else constant in our artificial simplicity, try to vary just one potential factor at a time. But many subjects defy the use of such an experimental method—particularly most social phenomena—because importation into the laboratory destroys the subject of the investigation, and then we must yearn for simplifying guides in nature. If the external world occasionally obliges by holding some crucial factors constant for us, we can only offer thanks for this natural boost to understanding.

So, when a book garners as much attention as *The Bell Curve*, we wish to know the causes. One might suspect the content itself—a startlingly new idea, or an old suspicion newly verified by persuasive data—but the reason might also be social acceptability, or even just

Stephen Jay Gould is a professor of zoology at Harvard University; he is author of *The Mismeasure of Man, Hen's Teeth and Horse's Toes*, and many other works. This review appeared in *The New Yorker*, November 28, 1994, entitled "Curveball."

plain hype. *The Bell Curve*, with its claims and supposed documentation that race and class differences are largely caused by genetic factors and are therefore essentially immutable, contains no new arguments and presents no compelling data to support its anachronistic social Darwinism, so I can only conclude that its success in winning attention must reflect the depressing temper of our time—a historical moment of unprecedented ungenerosity, when a mood for slashing social programs can be powerfully abetted by an argument that beneficiaries cannot be helped, owing to inborn cognitive limits expressed as low IQ scores.

The Bell Curve rests on two distinctly different but sequential arguments, which together encompass the classic corpus of biological determinism as a social philosophy. The first argument rehashes the tenets of social Darwinism as it was originally constituted. "Social Darwinism" has often been used as a general term for any evolutionary argument about the biological basis of human differences, but the initial nineteenth-century meaning referred to a specific theory of class stratification within industrial societies, and particularly to the idea that there was a permanently poor underclass consisting of genetically inferior people who had precipitated down into their inevitable fate. The theory arose from a paradox of egalitarianism: as long as people remain on top of the social heap by accident of a noble name or parental wealth, and as long as members of despised castes cannot rise no matter what their talents, social stratification will not reflect intellectual merit, and brilliance will be distributed across all classes; but when true equality of opportunity is attained, smart people rise and the lower classes become rigid, retaining only the intellectually incompetent.

This argument has attracted a variety of twentieth-century champions, including the Stanford psychologist Lewis M. Terman, who imported Alfred Binet's original test from France, developed the Stanford-Binet IQ test, and gave a hereditarian interpretation to the results (one that Binet had vigorously rejected in developing this style of test); Prime Minister Lee Kuan Yew of Singapore, who tried to institute a eugenics program of rewarding well-educated women for higher birth rates; and Richard Herrnstein, a co-author of *The Bell Curve* and also the author of a 1971 *Atlantic Monthly* article that presented the same argument without the documentation. The general claim is neither uninteresting nor illogical, but it does require the validity of four shaky premises, all asserted (but hardly discussed or defended) by Herrnstein and Murray. Intelligence, in their formulation, must be depictable as a single number, capable of ranking people in linear order, genetically based, and effectively immutable. If any of these premises are false, their entire argument collapses. For example, if all are true except immutability, then programs for early intervention in education might work to boost IQ permanently, just as a pair of eyeglasses may correct a genetic defect in vision. The central argument of *The Bell Curve* fails because most of the premises are false.

Herrnstein and Murray's second claim, the lightning rod for most commentary, extends the argument for innate cognitive stratification to a claim that racial differences in IQ are mostly determined by genetic causes—small differences for Asian superiority over Caucasian, but large for Caucasians over people of African descent. This argument is as old as the study of race, and is almost surely fallacious. The last generation's discussion centered on Arthur Jensen's 1980 book *Bias in Mental Testing* (far more elaborate and varied than anything presented in *The Bell Curve*, and therefore still a better source for grasping the argument and its problems), and on the cranky advocacy of William Shockley, a Nobel Prize–winning physicist. The central fallacy in using the substantial heritability of within-group IQ (among whites, for example) as an explanation of average differences between groups (whites versus blacks, for example) is now well known and acknowledged by all, including Herrnstein and Murray, but deserves a re-statement by example. Take a trait that is far more heritable than anyone has ever claimed IQ to be but is politically uncontroversial—body height. Suppose that I measure the heights of adult males in a poor Indian village beset with nutritional deprivation, and suppose the average height of adult males is five feet six inches. Heritability within the village is high, which is to say that tall fathers (they may average five feet eight inches) tend to have tall sons, while short fathers (five feet four inches on average) tend to have short sons. But this high heritability within the village does not mean that better nutrition might not raise average height to five feet ten inches in a few generations. Similarly, the well-documented fifteen-point average difference in IQ between blacks and whites in America, with substantial heritability of IQ in family lines within each group, permits no automatic conclusion that truly equal opportunity might not raise the black average enough to equal or surpass the white mean.

Disturbing as I find the anachronism of *The Bell Curve*, I am even more distressed by its pervasive disingenuousness. The authors omit facts, misuse statistical methods, and seem unwilling to admit the consequences of their own words.

THE OCEAN of publicity that has engulfed *The Bell Curve* has a basis in what Murray and Herrnstein, in a recent article in *The New Republic* (October 31, 1994), call "the flashpoint of intelligence as a public topic: the question of genetic differences between the races." And yet, since the day of the book's publication, Murray (Herrnstein died a month before the book appeared) has been temporizing, and denying that race is an important subject in the book at all; he blames the press for unfairly fanning these particular flames. In *The New Republic* he and Herrnstein wrote, "Here is what we hope will be our contribution to the discussion. We put it in italics; if we could, we would put it in neon lights: *The answer doesn't much matter.*"

Fair enough, in the narrow sense that any individual may be a rarely brilliant member of an averagely dumb group (and therefore not subject to judgment by the group mean), but Murray cannot deny that *The Bell Curve* treats race as one of two major topics, with each given about equal space; nor can he pretend that strongly stated claims about group differences have no political impact in a society obsessed with the meanings and consequences of ethnicity. The very first sentence of *The Bell Curve*'s preface acknowledges that the book treats the two subjects equally: "This book is about differences in intellectual capacity among people and groups and what those differences mean for America's future." And Murray and Herrnstein's *New Republic* article begins by identifying racial differences as the key subject of interest: "The private dialogue about race in America is far different from the public one."

Furthermore, Herrnstein and Murray know and acknowledge the critique of extending the substantial heritability of within-group IQ to explain differences between groups, so they must construct an admittedly circumstantial case for attributing most of the black-white mean difference to irrevocable genetics—while properly stressing that the average difference doesn't help in judging any particular person, because so many individual blacks score above the white mean in IQ.

Quite apart from the rhetorical dubiety of this old ploy in a shopworn genre—"Some of my best friends are Group X"—Herrnstein and Murray violate fairness by converting a complex case that can yield only agnosticism into a biased brief for permanent and heritable difference. They impose this spin by turning every straw on their side into an oak, while mentioning but downplaying the strong circumstantial case for substantial malleability and little average genetic difference. This case includes such evidence as impressive IQ scores for poor black children adopted into affluent and intellectual homes; average IQ increases in some nations since the Second World War equal to the entire fifteen-point difference now separating blacks and whites in America; and failure to find any cognitive differences between two cohorts of children born out of wedlock to German women, reared in Germany as Germans, but fathered by black and white American soldiers.

THE BELL CURVE is even more disingenuous in its argument than in its obfuscation about race. The book is a rhetorical masterpiece of scientism, and it benefits from the particular kind of fear that numbers impose on nonprofessional commentators. It runs to eight hundred and forty-five pages, including more than a hundred pages of appendixes filled with figures. So the text looks complicated, and reviewers shy away with a knee-jerk claim that, while they suspect fallacies of argument, they really cannot judge. In the same issue of *The New Republic* as Murray and Herrnstein's article, Mickey Kaus writes, "As a lay reader of *The Bell Curve*, I'm unable to judge fairly," and Leon Wieseltier adds, "Murray, too, is hiding the hardness of his politics behind the hardness of his science. And his science, for all I know, is soft. . . . Or so I imagine. I am not a scientist. I know nothing about psychometrics." And Peter Passell, in *The New York Times:* "But this reviewer is not a biologist, and will leave the argument to experts."

The book is in fact extraordinarily one-dimensional. It makes no attempt to survey the range of available data, and pays astonishingly little attention to the rich and informative history of its contentious subject. (One can only recall Santayana's dictum, now a cliché of intellectual life: "Those who cannot remember the past are condemned to repeat it.") Virtually all the analysis rests on a single technique applied to a single set of data—probably done in one computer run. (I do agree that the authors have used the most appropriate technique and the best source of information. Still, claims as broad as those advanced in *The Bell Curve* simply cannot be properly defended—that is, either supported or denied—by such a restricted approach.) The blatant errors and inadequacies of *The Bell Curve* could be picked up by lay reviewers if only they would not let themselves be frightened by numbers—for Herrnstein and Murray do write clearly, and their mistakes are both patent and accessible.

While disclaiming his own ability to judge, Mickey Kaus, in *The New Republic,* does correctly identify the authors' first two claims that are absolutely essential "to make the pessimistic 'ethnic difference' argument work": "(1) that there is a single, general measure of mental ability; (2) that the IQ tests that purport to measure this ability . . . aren't culturally biased."

Nothing in *The Bell Curve* angered me more than the authors' failure to supply any justification for their central claim, the sine qua non of their entire argument: that the number known as *g*, the celebrated "general factor" of intelligence, first identified by the British psychologist Charles Spearman, in 1904, captures a real property in the head. Murray and Herrnstein simply declare that the issue has been decided, as in this passage from their *New Republic* article: "Among the experts, it is by now beyond much technical dispute that there is such a thing as a general factor of cognitive ability on which human beings differ and that this general factor is measured reasonably well by a variety of standardized tests, best of all by IQ tests designed for that purpose." Such a statement represents extraordinary obfuscation, achievable only if one takes "expert" to mean "that group of psychometricians working in the tradition of *g* and its avatar IQ." The authors even admit that there are three major schools of psychometric interpretation and that only one supports their view of *g* and IQ.

But this issue cannot be decided, or even understood, without discussing the key and only rationale that has maintained *g* since Spearman invented it: factor analysis. The fact that Herrnstein and Murray barely mention the factor-analytic argument forms a central indictment of *The Bell Curve* and is an illustration of its vacuousness. How can the authors base an 800-page book on a claim for the reality of IQ as measuring a genuine, and largely genetic, general cognitive ability—and then hardly discuss, either pro or con, the theoretical basis for their certainty?

Admittedly, factor analysis is a difficult mathematical subject, but it can be explained to lay readers with a geometrical formulation developed by L. L. Thurstone, an American psychologist, in the 1930s and used by me in a full chapter on factor analysis in my 1981 book *The Mismeasure of Man*. A few paragraphs cannot suffice for adequate explanation, so, although I offer some sketchy hints below, readers should not question their own IQs if the topic still seems arcane.

In brief, a person's performance on various mental tests tends to be positively correlated—that is, if you do well on one kind of test, you tend to do well on the other kinds. This is scarcely surprising, and is subject to interpretation that is either purely genetic (that an innate thing in the head boosts all performances) or purely environmental (that good books and good childhood nutrition boost all performances); the positive correlations in themselves say nothing about causes. The results of these tests can be plotted on a multidimensional graph with an axis for each test. Spearman used factor analysis to find a single dimension—which he called *g*—that best identifies the common factor behind positive correlations among the tests. But Thurstone later showed that *g* could be made to disappear by simply rotating the dimensions to different positions. In one rotation Thurstone placed the dimensions near the most widely separated attributes among the tests, thus giving rise to the theory of multiple intelligences (verbal, mathematical, spatial, etc., with no overarching *g*). This theory (which I support) has been advocated by many prominent psychometricians, including J. P. Guilford, in the 1950s, and Howard Gardner today. In this perspective, *g* cannot have inherent reality, for it emerges in one form of mathematical representation for correlations among tests and disappears (or greatly attenuates) in other forms, which are entirely equivalent in amount of information explained. In any case, you can't grasp the issue at all without a clear exposition of factor analysis—and *The Bell Curve* cops out on this central concept.

As for Kaus's second issue, cultural bias, the presentation of it in *The Bell Curve* matches Arthur Jensen's and that of other hereditarians, in confusing a technical (and proper) meaning of "bias" (I call it S-bias, for "statistical") with the entirely different vernacular concept (I call it V-bias) that provokes popular debate. All these authors swear up and down (and I agree with them completely) that the tests are not biased—in the statistician's definition. Lack of S-bias means that the same score, when it is achieved by members of different groups, predicts the same thing; that is, a black person and a white person with identical scores will have the same probabilities for doing anything that IQ is supposed to predict.

But V-bias, the source of public concern, embodies an entirely different issue, which, unfortunately, uses the same word. The public wants to know whether blacks average 85 and whites 100 because society treats blacks unfairly—that is, whether lower black scores record biases in this social sense. And this crucial question (to which we do not know the answer) cannot be addressed by a demonstration that S-bias doesn't exist, which is the only issue analyzed, however correctly, in *The Bell Curve*.

THE BOOK is also suspect in its use of statistics. As I mentioned, virtually all its data derive from one analysis—a plotting, by a technique called multiple regression, of the social behaviors that agitate us, such as crime, unemployment, and births out of wedlock (known as dependent variables), against both IQ and parental socioeconomic status (known as independent variables). The authors first hold IQ constant and consider the relationship of social behaviors to parental socioeconomic status. They then hold socioeconomic status constant and consider the relationship of the same social behaviors to IQ. In general, they find a higher correlation with IQ than with socioeconomic status; for example, people with low IQ are more likely to drop out of high school than people whose parents have low socioeconomic status.

But such analyses must engage two issues—the form and the strength of the relationship—and Herrnstein and Murray discuss only the issue that seems to support their viewpoint, while virtually ignoring (and in one key passage almost willfully hiding) the other. Their numerous graphs present only the form of the relationships; that is, they draw the regression curves of their variables against IQ and parental socioeconomic status. But, in violation of all statistical norms that I've ever learned, they plot *only* the regression curve and do not show the scatter of variation around the curve, so their graphs do not show anything about the strength of the relationships—that is, the amount of variation in social factors explained by IQ and socioeconomic status. Indeed, almost all their relationships are weak: very little of the variation in social factors is explained by either independent variable (though the form of this small amount of explanation does lie in their favored direction). In short, their own data indicate that IQ is not a major factor in determining variation in nearly all the social behaviors they study—and so their conclusions collapse, or at least become so greatly attenuated that their pessimism and conservative social agenda gain no significant support.

Herrnstein and Murray actually admit as much in one crucial passage, but then they hide the pattern. They write, "It [cognitive ability] almost always explains less than 20 percent of the variance, to use the statistician's term, usually less than 10 percent and often less than 5 percent. What this means in English is that you cannot predict what a given person will do from his IQ score. . . . On the other hand, despite the low association at the individual level, large differences in social behavior separate groups of people when the groups differ intellectually on the average." Despite this disclaimer, their remarkable next sentence makes a strong causal claim. "We will argue that intelligence itself, not just its correlation with socioeconomic status, is responsible for these group differences." But a few percent of statistical determination is not causal explanation. And the case is even worse for their key genetic argument, since they claim a heritability of about 60 percent for IQ, so to isolate the strength of genetic determination by Herrnstein and Murray's own criteria you must nearly halve even the few percent they claim to explain.

My charge of disingenuousness receives its strongest affirmation in a sentence tucked away on the first page of Appendix 4, page 593: the authors state, "In the text, we do not refer to the usual measure of goodness of fit for multiple regressions, R^2, but they are presented here for the cross-sectional analyses." Now, why would they exclude from the text, and relegate to an appendix that very few people will read, or even consult, a number that, by their own admission, is "the usual measure of goodness of fit"? I can only conclude that they did not choose to admit in the main text the extreme weakness of their vaunted relationships.

Herrnstein and Murray's correlation coefficients are generally low enough by themselves to inspire lack of confidence. (Correlation coefficients measure the strength of linear relationships between variables; the positive values run from 0.0 for no relationship to 1.0 for perfect linear relationship.) Although low figures are not atypical for large social-science surveys involving many variables, most of Herrnstein and Murray's correlations are very weak—often in the 0.2 to 0.4 range. Now,

0.4 may sound respectably strong, but—and this is the key point—R^2 is the square of the correlation coefficient, and the square of a number between zero and one is less than the number itself, so a 0.4 correlation yields an r-squared of only .16. In Appendix 4, then, one discovers that the vast majority of the conventional measures of R^2, excluded from the main body of the text, are less than 0.1. These very low values of R^2 expose the true weakness, in any meaningful vernacular sense, of nearly all the relationships that form the meat of *The Bell Curve*.

LIKE SO MANY conservative ideologues who rail against the largely bogus ogre of suffocating political correctness, Herrnstein and Murray claim that they only want a hearing for unpopular views so that truth will out. And here, for once, I agree entirely. As a card-carrying First Amendment (near) absolutist, I applaud the publication of unpopular views that some people consider dangerous. I am delighted that *The Bell Curve* was written—so that its errors could be exposed, for Herrnstein and Murray are right to point out the difference between public and private agendas on race, and we must struggle to make an impact on the private agendas as well. But *The Bell Curve* is scarcely an academic treatise in social theory and population genetics. It is a manifesto of conservative ideology; the book's inadequate and biased treatment of data displays its primary purpose—advocacy. The text evokes the dreary and scary drumbeat of claims associated with conservative think tanks: reduction or elimination of welfare, ending or sharply curtailing affirmative action in schools and workplaces, cutting back Head Start and other forms of preschool education, trimming programs for the slowest learners and applying those funds to the gifted. (I would love to see more attention paid to talented students, but not at this cruel price.)

The penultimate chapter presents an apocalyptic vision of a society with a growing underclass permanently mired in the inevitable sloth of their low IQs. They will take over our city centers, keep having illegitimate babies (for many are too stupid to practice birth control), and ultimately require a kind of custodial state, more to keep them in check—and out of high-IQ neighborhoods—than to realize any hope of an amelioration, which low IQ makes impossible in any case. Herrnstein and Murray actually write, "In short, by *custodial state*, we have in mind a high-tech and more lavish version of the Indian reservation for some substantial minority of the nation's population, while the rest of America tries to go about its business."

The final chapter tries to suggest an alternative, but I have never read anything more almost grotesquely inadequate. Herrnstein and Murray yearn romantically for the good old days of towns and neighborhoods where all people could be given tasks of value, and self-esteem could be found for people on all steps of the IQ hierarchy (so Forrest Gump might collect clothing for the church raffle, while Mr. Murray and the other bright ones do the planning and keep the accounts—they have forgotten about the town Jew and the dwellers on the other side of the tracks in many of these idyllic villages). I do believe in this concept of neighborhood, and I will fight for its return. I grew up in such a place in Queens. But can anyone seriously find solutions for (rather than important palliatives of) our social ills therein?

However, if Herrnstein and Murray are wrong, and IQ represents not an immutable thing in the head, grading human beings on a single scale of general capacity with large numbers of custodial incompetents at the bottom, then the model that generates their gloomy vision collapses, and the wonderful variousness of human abilities, properly nurtured, reemerges. We must fight the doctrine of *The Bell Curve* both because it is wrong and because it will, if activated, cut off all possibility of proper nurturance for everyone's intelligence. Of course, we cannot all be rocket scientists or brain surgeons, but those who can't might be rock musicians or professional athletes (and gain far more social prestige and salary thereby), while others will indeed serve by standing and waiting.

I closed my chapter in *The Mismeasure of Man* on the unreality of *g* and the fallacy of regarding intelligence as a single-scaled, innate thing in the head with a marvellous quotation from John Stuart Mill, well worth repeating: "The tendency has always been strong to believe that whatever received a name must be an entity or being, having an independent existence of its own. And if no real entity answering to the name could be found, men did not for that reason suppose that none existed, but imagined that it was something particularly abstruse and mysterious."

How strange that we would let a single and false number divide us, when evolution has united all people in the recency of our common ancestry—thus undergirding with a shared humanity that infinite variety which custom can never stale. E pluribus unum.

APOCALYPSE NOW?

Alan Ryan

*T*HE BELL CURVE is the product of an obsession, or, more exactly, of two different obsessions. Richard Herrnstein—who died on September 24, 1994—was obsessed with the heritability of intelligence, the view that much the largest factor in our intellectual abilities comes in our genes. He was also convinced that there had been a liberal conspiracy to obscure the significance of genetically based differences in the intelligence of different races, social classes, and ethnic groups, and that all manner of educational and economic follies were being perpetrated in consequence. Charles Murray—who is energetically and noisily with us still—is obsessed with what he believes to be the destructive effects of the American welfare state.

The result of their cooperation is a decidedly mixed affair. The politics of *The Bell Curve* are at best slightly mad, and at worst plain ugly. Its literary tone wobbles uneasily between truculence and paranoia. Its intellectual pretensions are often ill founded. For all that, anyone who has an interest in the philosophy of science and a taste for public policy will enjoy much of *The Bell Curve;* it is full of interesting,

Alan Ryan teaches politics at Princeton University. His new book, *John Dewey and the High Tide of American Liberalism*, will be published in 1995. This article was published in *The New York Review of Books*, November 17, 1994.

if dubiously reliable, information, and it offers the always engaging spectacle of two practical-minded men firmly in the grip of irrational passion.

Richard Herrnstein's passion was the conviction that each person has a fixed or nearly fixed quantum of "cognitive ability," the intelligence whose quotient constitutes your IQ. Herrnstein began his career as a disciple of the behaviorist psychologist B. F. Skinner, and therefore as a devout environmentalist. Then he fell in love with "Spearman's *g.*" Charles Spearman was a turn-of-the-century British Army officer and statistician who thought that people possess varying amounts of general intelligence—or *g*—and invented statistical techniques to discover which intelligence tests most directly tap into this basic ability.

Skeptics have always said that *g* explains nothing: the fact that the performance of individuals on different tests is closely correlated, and predicts their success in school work and some occupational settings, is important and interesting. Talk of *g* adds nothing to the fact of the correlation. Herrnstein, however, was no skeptic in this matter. At the first mention of *g* he confesses that "its reality . . . was and remains arguable." But eleven pages later, he claims that *g* sits at the center of the mind's capacities "as an expression of a core mental ability much like the ability Spearman identified at the turn of the century," while eight pages on, after a further bout with the skeptics, he announces that it is universally accepted that "there is such a thing as a general factor of cognitive ability on which human beings differ."

Does it matter? Only to the extent that it reinforced Herrnstein's fascination with ethnicity. The more you think that talk of IQ is talk of a mysterious something that possesses the same reality as visible qualities like skin color or the curliness of the hair, the more obvious it will seem that ethnic groups that differ in such visible qualities must differ in intelligence too. By the same token, it bolsters the extraordinary fatalism that infuses *The Bell Curve:* once you discover that the average IQ of people in jail is 93, it's easy to believe that people with too little *g* are more or less doomed to social dysfunction. How other countries of the same ethnic composition as white America manage to commit fewer murders and yet jail far fewer of their citizenry remains for ever inexplicable. Conversely, a certain skepticism about what there is to IQ besides being good at certain sorts of tests may make us less superstitious about its importance.

CHARLES MURRAY is intoxicated by an apocalyptic vision of the American future, nicely summarized as "The Coming of the Custodial State." The anxieties about the widening inequality produced by the American economy are ones that Mickey Kaus and Robert Reich long ago familiarized us with, but they are here run through Murray's wilder and darker imaginings to yield a vision of an incipient semifascist future that neither of them would recognize.[1] American society is increasingly partitioned into a high-IQ, ever more affluent, upper caste, a hard-pressed middle class, and a cognitively underprivileged underclass, whose criminality threatens the rest of us and whose unchecked breeding threatens to dilute the pool of talent, and so alarmingly on. The well-off migrate to enclaves of comfortable housing, which are walled-off, well-policed, and equipped with decent schools; the underclass are shut away in urban slums. The struggling middle class feels trapped.

The elite may hold liberal views and they may be willing to pay for help to the poor, but they will not live among them. The middle class have neither money to spend on the underclass nor tolerance of its ways. They will insist on coercive policing and a more punitive welfare system, and will want the underclass kept in whatever "high-tech and more lavish version of the Indian reservation" it takes to keep them from preying on the respectable. The end result, Murray argues, is catastrophe: a version of the welfare state in which the incompetent have their lives managed without their consent. "It is difficult to imagine the United States preserving its heritage of individualism, equal rights before the law, free people running their own lives, once it is accepted that a significant part of the population must be made permanent wards of the state." This is a eugenicist, and not (in the usual sense) a racist, nightmare, for Murray believes that the bottom 10 percent of the white population is headed for the degradation that already afflicts the black urban underclass. The people he affectionately describes as "white trash" will need as much looking after as their black counterparts.

So far as I can see, none of Murray's anxieties about the direction of American domestic policy depends on the truth of Richard Herrnstein's ideas about the ontological status of *g*, and none of Herrnstein's

---

[1] Mickey Kaus, *The End of Equality* (Basic Books, 1992), cited in *The Bell Curve*, p. 524; Robert Reich, *The Work of Nations* (Knopf, 1991), cited p. 529. I ought to note that Kaus himself describes Murray's views in general as "alien and repellent," *The New Republic*, October 31, 1994, p. 4.

claims about intelligence support Charles Murray's ideas about social policy. Murray himself seems to recognize this: "Like other apocalyptic visions, this one is pessimistic," he says, "perhaps too much so. On the other hand, there is much to be pessimistic about." That statement is a bit casual when it is used as the basis of social prophecy; there always has been much to be pessimistic about, but not much of it licenses the expectation of the imminent extinction of American civil liberties. For all the scientific apparatus with which they are surrounded, Murray's fears are closer to the ravings of Rush Limbaugh's audience than to Tocqueville's anxieties about "soft despotism."

Herrnstein and Murray don't explicitly contradict each other, to be sure, but Murray was hostile to the welfare state long before he encountered Herrnstein; and Herrnstein's views on intelligence are in principle consistent with the politics of almost any persuasion from socialist to libertarian. Socialists might think that ineradicable differences in IQ should be met by making sure that the less clever were compensated with more education than the gifted, and with income supplements to make up for their difficulties in the competitive marketplace; libertarians might think we should treat such differences as the luck of the draw, no more worthy of treatment than the accident that makes some of us better baseball players than others. Between trying to obliterate their effects and letting them make whatever difference they make in the labor market, there are innumerable further alternatives.

Herrnstein and Murray have many common enemies—Head Start, open door immigration, unwed mothers, lax ideas about sexual morality, and the "dumbing down" of American secondary education—but *The Bell Curve* is very much not the work of one mind. Indeed, each of the authors is in more than one mind on more than one issue.

FOR ALL ITS ODDITIES, *The Bell Curve* is a fluent piece of work. It is a still more fluent piece of publicity-seeking. The authors have tried to have their cake and eat it, and they have succeeded in a big way. They—this is largely Murray's achievement—claim to be frightened that they will stir up terrible controversy, but they have advertised their fears in such a way as to do just that. They insist that they have no urge to stir up racial dissension or give comfort to racists, but then say that their findings only reflect what people already think in their heart of hearts—which is, that blacks and white trash are born irremediably dumb, that black Americans have been overpromoted in the academy, that smarter white workers have been displaced by incompetent black ones at the behest of the federal government. A disagreeably wheedling tone is an unsurprising feature of such arguments.

There is a good deal of genuine science in *The Bell Curve;* there is also an awful lot of science fiction and not much care to make sure the reader knows which is which. What catches the eye of reviewers and reporters are Herrnstein's gloomy predictions about the declining intelligence of the American population, and Murray's prediction of imminent fascism. Fewer readers will notice the authors' throwaway admissions that these predictions are highly speculative, and only loosely rooted in the data they assemble. Take the connection between the fact that illegitimacy rises as IQ declines, and Murray's fears about the imminent collapse of the liberal state. It is, for a start, quite impossible—as is readily acknowledged by the authors—that the rising rate of illegitimate births in both the black and white American populations should in the first instance have had much to do with intelligence.

The rate remained almost stable between 1920 and 1960, at about 5 percent of all births, then took off sharply in the early 1960s to reach 30 percent in 1990. Herrnstein and Murray say, "If IQ is a factor in illegitimacy, as we will conclude it is, it must be in combination with other things (as common sense would suggest), because IQ itself has not changed nearly enough in recent years to account for the explosive growth in illegitimacy." They then evade the obvious implication that their obsession with IQ is largely irrelevant. They say "some of these 'other things' that have changed in the last three decades—broken homes and the welfare system being prime suspects—interact with intelligence, making it still more likely than before that a woman of low cognitive ability will have a baby out of wedlock." True, but largely beside the point; the social pressures they mention make it more likely that women of *any* degree of cognitive ability will have a baby out of wedlock. If the pressures operate more powerfully on women of lower intelligence, we want to know why this is so.

The interesting question is not one of genetics but one of changes in the culture; it is not what has happened to the intelligence of the mothers that needs explaining, but what happened in the early 1960s that so altered the incentives to have babies later rather than earlier and in wedlock rather than out. (It must mean something that divorce rates rose at the same speed during the same years.) That is the sociologist's territory, not the psychometrician's, and too often *The Bell Curve* relies on Herrnstein's real distinction as a psychologist to prop up what is essentially armchair sociology. A sociologist would at least wonder why the welfare system should be one of the "prime suspects" in the rising rate of illegitimacy when it has been *decreasingly* generous over the past thirty years; and a sociologist would at least notice that other Western societies such as Britain and the Netherlands have experienced rising illegitimacy rates, too. None of this suggests we ought not to worry about the propensity of the less clever to get pregnant out of wedlock, but it does suggest that we ought to attend to the real complexities of the social environment in which all this takes place.

Again, all readers will grasp the authors' insistence that Head Start programs haven't worked; fewer will notice that those failures are more partial than the authors say, and that the failures provide a better argument for seeking programs that work than they do for *The Bell Curve*'s conclusion that we should abandon the attempt to raise the IQs of the disadvantaged and devote virtually all our attention to the highly intelligent. The fashion in which such programs have failed is not analyzed with the scrupulousness one might wish. In essence, *The Bell Curve*'s data suggest that Head Start and other preschool programs can raise children's IQs quite sharply for a short period; once the children are in a regular school, their IQ scores drift back to something like the level they began at. For a believer in *g*, this is evidence that in the long run the quantum of cognitive ability, whatever it might be, simply reveals itself.

Someone who wanted to draw the opposite conclusion might think that the data only show that there is no cheap, one-shot environmental fix for deprivation. Environmental fixes are possible, but they take much longer to work, or where they work quickly, they need to be repeated so that they keep working. It may well be that a much more extensive transformation of the child's environment than Head Start and preschool programs can offer is needed to effect lasting changes in intelligence. There are suggestive data about the impact of adoption on the children of low-IQ mothers that might make one believe that is the case. If it is true, however, it provides an argument for affirmative action that renders *The Bell Curve* irrelevant from start to finish; for it suggests that one purpose in creating a larger black (or whatever) middle class is to create a better environment for the next generation and its descendants. The true beneficiaries of affirmative action on this view would be the children and the grandchildren of the people promoted today.

That could be quite wrong; it might be that the only effective environmental fix would be a national health service that gave babies a better prenatal and perinatal environment. It might even be that Charles Murray's "custodial state" would have to get into the act to insist that the mothers of children who are at risk should use such care. What one can certainly say is that the failure of Head Start to live up to its backers' most extravagant hopes is neither a knock-down argument for genetic determinism nor any sort of argument for abandoning the disadvantaged. Herrnstein and Murray argue elsewhere in *The Bell Curve* that American secondary education has "dumbed down" bright children, and so imply—what they elsewhere admit—that bad environments at least have an effect. After several hundred pages of this, one begins to wonder just what Herrnstein and Murray do believe other than that any old argument against helping the disadvantaged will do.

THE SHEER REPETITIVENESS of its tables, graphs, and bar charts eventually dulls *The Bell Curve*'s impact for the conscientious reader; but Herrnstein and Murray do not expect—and perhaps do not really want—most of their readers to work their way through all 845 pages of their text.[2] They say they want to make the reader's life easy. For readers whose minds go blank at the mention of multiple regression, they provide a wonderfully lucid appendix on "Statistics for People Who Are Sure They Can't Learn Statistics." For readers in a

---

[2] It is already becoming clear that the air of dispassionate scientific curiosity that they are at such pains to maintain is at odds with the eccentricity of some of their sources. J. Philippe Rushton's bizarre *Race, Evolution and Behavior* is treated as the work of a serious scholar; but Rushton's view is essentially that sexuality and intelligence are inversely related, or, as Adam Miller reported him as saying, "it's a trade-off; more brain or more penis. You can't have everything" (*Rolling Stone*, October 20, 1994). For what it's worth, the recent report on American sexual behavior suggests that he's wrong; Ashkenazi Jews have higher IQs and more active sex lives than anybody else. Richard Lynn is described as a "leading scholar of racial and ethnic differences," and no mention is made of his fondness for the theories of Nordic superiority that were the common coin of early twentieth-century scientific racists.

particular hurry, they summarize their claims in some forty pages of italicized text spread across their twenty-two chapters.

Their main claims can be boiled down further still. They are essentially these: America is today a "meritocracy" in the sense that the best predictor of success in life is IQ; the various institutions that pass children up the ladder to success increasingly select the brightest children to train for entry to the best colleges, the best professional schools, and the most rewarding occupations. Where once the alumni of Harvard and Princeton were socially rather than mentally smarter than their peers, the students of the best colleges are today almost off the scale—inside the top 1 percent of their age group. Nor does IQ represent the result of training, or parental advantage; the social standing of our parents is a less reliable predictor of our future economic success and failure than our IQ—it's good to have well-off parents *and* brains, but if you can have only one, take the brains.

More intriguingly, most indicators of our ability to function successfully in society correlate to a significant degree with IQ. Very few students with an average or above average IQ fail to complete high school; conversely, the students who fail to complete high school usually do so because they find it intellectually beyond them; unsurprisingly, they have higher levels of long-term unemployment, both when they are able-bodied and because they are more likely to be sick. Men with lower IQs show up disproportionately in prison, and that is not because the dim crooks get caught, since self-reported but otherwise undetected crime is also largely committed by the less bright. Crime, of course, is mainly a male activity, and *The Bell Curve* duly acknowledges that what IQ explains is which men are more likely to commit offenses, not why men do and women (generally) don't. Herrnstein and Murray's interest in women is mostly an interest in their propensity to produce children out of wedlock, to go on welfare, and to have difficult children. As ever, the less bright have higher rates of illegitimacy and less amenable children, and to nobody's surprise stay longer on welfare.

As for our relations with one another, the clever marry later, breed later, and stick together; the less bright marry in haste and repent in haste, or at any rate are twice as likely to get divorced within five years. One thing to remember in the face of all this—and usefully insisted on by the authors—is that IQ differences do not account for *much* of the difference in the fate or behavior of people; in statistical terms, IQ rarely accounts for as much as a fifth of the difference between one person and another, and usually for much less. The only thing with which IQ correlates very closely is our performance on tests that measure the same skills that IQ tests measure—which in a world full of lawyers and economists and scientifically trained professionals is surely likely to create a high-IQ caste of what Robert Reich labeled "symbolic analysts." Intelligence tests test for just that kind of intelligence. To the extent that other personal characteristics are involved in what happens to us, the impact of IQ is less. The importance of *any* contribution of IQ to the causation of social problems, however, is that when we are dealing with very large numbers it makes a difference whether we think the population we are dealing with is averagely bright, especially bright, or rather dim.

For readers who are convinced that any discussion of the heritability of intelligence is fundamentally, if covertly, a discussion of the inferior mental capacities of black Americans, Herrnstein and Murray seem at first to provide some measure of reassurance. All these gloomy results about the damage done by having lower intelligence than the average come from an analysis of the experiences of white Americans in the 1980s. Most of the data which Herrnstein and Murray use come from the National Longitudinal Survey of Labor Market Experience of Youth (NLSY), a study of some 12,500 Americans who were between fourteen and twenty-two in 1979 when the survey began, and whose progress has been followed ever since.

Its usefulness to Herrnstein and Murray is that "only the NLSY combined detailed information on the childhood environment *and* parental socioeconomic status *and* subsequent educational and occupational achievement *and* work history *and* family formation *and*—crucially for our interests—detailed psychometric measures of cognitive skills." The sample was used by the federal government to reassess its intelligence tests, so it fortuitously provides data on measured intelligence as well as on everything else that correlates with success and failure in the labor market. The NLSY covers all ethnic groups, but the first twelve chapters of *The Bell Curve* stick to the distribution of intelligence across the white American population in that sample. Only then do Herrnstein and Murray turn to the discussion of ethnic differences in IQ.

OF COURSE, as the hubbub in the press suggests, the reassurance is less than skin deep; as soon as ethnic differences have been identified—the one that swamps all others is that the mean IQ of African Americans is 85 as against 100 for white Americans—the reader is in for two hundred pages of familiar complaints against affirmative action policies. Before we move on to these, some other findings are worth a brief look. The most familiar will be the fairly well-confirmed discovery that just as African Americans are one "standard deviation," i.e., 15 percent, less good than white Americans at tests of analytical and spatial intelligence, so East Asians—especially the Hong Kong Chinese—are anything up to one standard deviation better. If the white American average is set at 100, the black American average is 85, and the East Asian average 111–115. Ashkenazi Jews have similar scores to East Asians, but the scores of Oriental Jews in Israel show an embarrassing contrast.

Herrnstein and Murray don't dwell at length on the implications of their views for the social difficulties of black Americans, but they hardly need to. Once they have piled up the statistics on the disadvantages attendant on having an IQ much below 100, the case is made. Where they concentrate their attention is on the two related questions, whether we can do anything to raise IQ, and whether affirmative action policies in education and employment are worth the candle. In brief, their answer to both questions is no.

The greater part of the argument against remedial education is their argument against Head Start and analogous programs. But that argument, as we have seen, can be used to suggest that the programs should be more intensive, not abandoned. They acknowledge the possibility in principle of eugenicist programs, but flinch at the thought of putting into the hands of government the power to dictate such matters as who may and may not produce children—William Shockley gets a passing mention as someone who enjoyed shocking people by suggesting that we might pay the poor to be sterilized and might set up sperm banks to pass on the genes of geniuses (he contributed to a privately organized sperm bank: there is no record of the results). But Shockley is dismissed as excessively eccentric. Whether his proposal to pay the poor to be sterilized is more eccentric than Murray's proposal to abolish welfare payments and face the short-term consequences for the hapless children on the receiving end of the change, readers will judge for themselves.

AFFIRMATIVE ACTION greatly preoccupies Herrnstein and Murray. Oddly enough in discussing it, they back away from an insistence on the genetic determination of IQ. All that matters is that IQ predicts performance at work and in the academy, and cannot be increased by short-term educational and environmental enrichment. In academic matters, they are much bothered by the probability that the SAT scores of black students at the best universities are anything up to 200 points lower than those of their white peers, with obvious consequences for the clustering of black students among the least successful and therefore least happy members of the college community. Herrnstein and Murray argue that we do such students no favor by putting them in a situation where they are anxious in school and possess an undervalued credential when they leave.

Nor are Herrnstein and Murray any happier about affirmative action in employment. They launch a two-pronged attack. The first is to demonstrate that although the raw income data suggest that black Americans earn less than white Americans, the picture changes when we add in the distribution of intelligence. At this point, we find that black Americans earn relatively more than white Americans—that is, relative to their IQs. What you might call "dollars per IQ point" comes out in favor of African Americans. If your notion of justice is that people should be paid according to their IQs, then this is unjust. On the other hand, you might think that what matters is overall efficiency; and Herrnstein's other argument is that affirmative action damages efficiency. Given even halfway plausible assumptions, of course, it must do so; if IQ predicts competence, anything that makes us appoint people on some basis other than IQ produces some degree of incompetence. Old-fashioned class biases were denounced by British socialists precisely because they helped the incompetent to keep out the competent. Herrnstein advertises himself as an enthusiast for that view.

There is a lot to be said on both sides. In a highly competitive society like ours, it may be true that affirmative action causes anxiety in, say, the student who gets into a place like Princeton or Harvard with SATs well below those of his or her white peers. But this anxiety doesn't seem to affect athletes or "legacies," i.e., the children of alumni—groups whose presence at such places Herrnstein is surprisingly happy about—which suggests that even if this generation of black students does less well in strictly academic terms than their white peers, there are better ways of reducing their anxieties than refusing to admit them in the first place. The same thought applies in employment. It may be that there are many black Americans struggling with jobs they cannot deal with and many white colleagues muttering about them under their breath. It may also be that these are the labor pains of a different sort of society from the one we have had for the past three centuries.

THIS, HOWEVER, throws one back on the fundamental question raised by *The Bell Curve*—how seriously we should take its science. Is there an intelligence gap between black and white Americans that no passage of time and no social policy can close? If there were, would anything follow about the social policies a humane society should adopt? The answer seems to be that there is good reason to believe that there is a gap, but no conclusive reason to believe that it is unshrinkable; if there were, it would have a good many implications about the need to balance the search for efficiency against the desire for a more humane social order—but it would not dictate how we struck the balance and it would introduce no moral novelties into the calculation. In particular a belief in the importance of inherited differences in IQ need not encourage apocalyptic conservatism.[3]

It is an under-remarked feature of arguments over the inheritability of intelligence that an obsession with the presumed incapacities of the poor, the children of the slums, the bastard offspring of dim servant girls, and all the rest was once characteristic of reformers and sexual radicals as much as of anxious conservatives. The unwillingness of the contemporary liberals and the left to think eugenically has everything to do with racism being disgusting and not much to do with logic. In 1916 Bertrand Russell condemned the inner city as a site of "race suicide," but meant only that the slums produced large numbers of undernourished, unfit, and ineducable children. It was a common hope of birth control pioneers that wanted children would be fitter and brighter children.

---

[3] Readers of Christopher Jencks's *Rethinking Social Policy* (Harvard University Press, 1991) will recall his skepticism about affirmative action, and readers of *Who Gets Ahead?* (Basic Books, 1979) will recall his patient demonstration of the role of IQ differences in explaining income differentials. They will also recall that Jencks remains a cautious liberal, a class of person whose existence Herrnstein and Murray simply cannot comprehend.

The label "eugenics" itself was coined by Darwin's cousin, Sir Francis Galton, to describe a program for improving the British stock. Nor was the idea foreign to the Fabians. It is not an ignoble hope that as the welfare state improves the physical health of the citizenry it will also make them brighter, more alert, more interested in their surroundings and themselves. One could fear that the most likely end result would be *Brave New World*, with its Alphas, Betas, and Gammas, but that would not be because eugenic science was disgusting, but because the science would be used by the wrong people for the wrong reasons. It is surely true that an interest in the connections between heredity and intelligence need not be malign. After all, our interest in hereditary disease usually stems from the wish to help the sufferers. One can readily imagine a benign educational program that addresses the different strengths and weaknesses of students more intelligently than contemporary schooling does. But if a concern for inherited intelligence or the reverse need not be driven by panic and superstition, it usually has been.

IN THE UNITED STATES, fear of new immigrants rather than optimism about the chances of raising the level of the whole population always seems to have driven the discussion; and fears of the "dilution" of the "pure-bred" white stock by Jewish or Negro blood were the common coin of academic discussion throughout the first forty years of this century. Herrnstein misrepresents this past and the complaint against it. He says that Stephen Jay Gould's famous attack on psychometrics in *The Mismeasure of Man* was unfair to the military psychologists of World War I and to the psychologists on Ellis Island, whom Gould accused of announcing that on first testing 80 percent of the Jews, Hungarians, Italians, and Russians were feeble-minded, and that even on re-analysis, 50 percent were so. "The intelligence of the average 'third class' immigrant is low," said H. H. Goddard, "perhaps of moron grade." Gould, in essence, claimed that research into the supposed racial differences in intelligence was driven by panic and prejudice, and resulted in absurd findings. Herrnstein responds that the psychologists were looking only for mental defectives, and naturally reported cases of mental deficiency.

This, as Herrnstein knows, won't wash in the case of Carl Brigham, the Canadian military psychologist who came to the United States in World War I and stayed to become professor of psychology at Princeton and a leading figure in the work of the Educational Testing Service and the development of the SAT. Herrnstein diverts the argument from the point at issue by claiming that Brigham's book, *A Study of American Intelligence,* had less influence on the Immigration Restriction Act of 1924 than Gould supposed. But that is not the point. Brigham was a leading figure in World War I intelligence testing for the American Army, and Brigham held, and popularized, exactly the views that Gould complained of. Brigham knew that many people thought Jews were clever; having examined large numbers of Russian-born Americans in the war, he thought he knew better. His army sample was "at least one-half Jewish," he thought, and they "had an average intelligence below those from all other countries except Poland and Italy." Taking Negro draftees as his reference, he discovered that 39 percent of the Russian-born were below the Negro average, 42.3 percent of the Italian-born, and 46 percent of the Polish-born. This was not an eccentric's vision of the world but the respectable psychometrics of the day.[4]

Brigham's estimates of the cognitive inferiority of black Americans were, as this would suggest, much greater than Herrnstein's—in which case, the unclosable gap has been closing. Even Brigham acknowledged that putting black Americans in a different environment made a difference to their tested intelligence; and other interwar studies confirmed Brigham's finding that northern blacks did better on his tests than southern blacks. Some even found that northern blacks scored higher on many tests than southern whites. None of this proves that there is no inbuilt difference in cognitive abilities between different human groups, though it is hard to believe that anything of the sort would follow the haphazard lines of self-reported ethnicity. What it does suggest is that either relative cognitive abilities change more rapidly than Herrnstein believed or that our estimates of them are less reliable than he thought.

ONE OTHER THING it suggests is that we should worry less than Herrnstein did about the danger that American intelligence is declin-

---

[4] Gould gives a perfectly clear account of H. H. Goddard's search for mental defectives on pp. 158–174 of *The Mismeasure of Man* that does nothing to exculpate him. Perhaps more to the point, Goddard himself came to think his work had been scientifically worthless and politically dangerous, as did Carl Brigham half a dozen years after *A Study of American Intelligence* (Princeton University Press, 1923).

ing. Herrnstein was an old-fashioned "deteriorationist," squarely in the Brigham tradition.

> When people die, they are not replaced one for one by babies who will develop identical IQs. If the new babies grow up to have systematically higher or lower IQs than the people who die, the national distribution of intelligence changes. Mounting evidence indicates that demographic trends are exerting downward pressure on the distribution of cognitive ability in the United States and that the pressures are strong enough to have social consequences.

Other evidence, also quoted by Herrnstein, suggests that intelligence levels are generally rising. As usual where the evidence points in both directions, Herrnstein and Murray urge us to accept the more frightening scenario.

Herrnstein's fears were partly those that recently alarmed Sir Keith Joseph, Mrs. Thatcher's former education minister. In Britain as elsewhere, the cleverer members of the population have fewer children than the less clever. If *g* is handed down in the genes, there will be less to go round in each generation. Even if each clever woman had as many children as each less clever woman, there would still be deterioration; the less clever have their children earlier, producing three generations of less bright children, while their intellectual superiors produce two. But Herrnstein also shared Brigham's more American anxieties: the wrong sort of immigrants have been flooding into the country. Small numbers of bright East Asians were no match for large numbers of less bright Latino and Caribbean migrants. Herrnstein knew that his critics would retort that all this was said about the Poles, the Russians, and the Italians a century ago; all he could say in reply was that this time the anxiety was justified.

The latent contradiction of *The Bell Curve*'s politics emerges when one contrasts Herrnstein's enthusiastic defense of meritocracy with Murray's final fantasy of a world in which we live in "clans" that are high on self-regard and cheerfully ignore the existence of cleverer and less clever people in the world. Herrnstein essentially wants the world in which clever Jewish kids or their equivalent make their way out of humble backgrounds and end up running Goldman Sachs or the Harvard physics department, while Murray wants the Midwest in which he grew up—a world in which the local mechanic didn't care two cents whether he was or wasn't brighter than the local math teacher. The trouble is that the first world subverts the second, while the second feels claustrophobic to the beneficiaries of the first. The authors are united only in their dislike of the mostly unnamed liberals who have been hostile to Herrnstein's obsessions with race and to Murray's obsessions with the welfare system. In short, *The Bell Curve* is not only sleazy; it is, intellectually, a mess.[5]

---

[5] I am indebted to Nicholas Lemann for a long and helpful conversation while I was preparing this review.

BLACKTOP BASKETBALL AND *THE BELL CURVE*

Gregg Easterbrook

Y EARS AGO, hoping to persuade *The Washington Monthly* to hire me, I quit a decent job in Chicago and moved to Washington. Unemployed and low on money, I lived in a seedy neighborhood behind the Navy Yard in Southeast D.C. Because the editor of the magazine unaccountably took his time in acknowledging my merit as an applicant, to blow off steam I played basketball on the local court several hours each day. I was the only white player in the game, accepted at first as a charity case. After a few weeks on the blacktop, however, I was startled to discover other players wanting me on their team. After two months of daily basketball, I found myself able to hold my own in one-on-one matches against the hot players from nearby Eastern High School. I was squaring my shoulders for accurate jump shots, ducking under other players for lay-ups—the sorts of coordinated, classy-looking moves I had never been able to do before and have not been able to do since.

It would hardly be a wild guess that practice had improved my game, and that lack of practice has since eroded it. Charles Murray and the late Richard Herrnstein would say, however, I had suddenly acquired basketball genes. Then just as suddenly, I lost them!

Gregg Easterbrook, a contributing editor of *The Washington Monthly*, *Atlantic Monthly*, and *Newsweek*, is author of the forthcoming *A Moment on the Earth*. This article appeared in *The Washington Monthly*, December 1994, as "The Case Against the Bell Curve."

Page after page of obstruent data and marching columns of Pearson correlations in the new book *The Bell Curve* by Murray and Herrnstein, which holds that success in life is mainly determined by inherited IQ and that statistically significant differences in inherited intellect exist among the races, imply that the issues at play in the IQ dispute are so sophisticated only readers of high intelligence can grasp them. This isn't so. Most common-sense aspects of the IQ debate are more significant than the statistical motes and jots—and being much better understood, are a sounder basis for social policy. The complex statistical claims of *The Bell Curve* have received extensive notice in initial reactions to the work. In the end the book's common-sense faults are more telling. Blacktop basketball offers an entry point for understanding why.

The reverse of the notion that blacks are born with less intelligence than whites is that blacks are born with more athletic potential. Well-meaning people who believe that whites are smarter than blacks often quickly add, "But look at how gifted blacks are physically," citing the undeniable black dominance of basketball. Yet if blacks have superior innate athletic ability, why are hockey, tennis, and many other lucrative sports largely dominated by whites? As the writer Farai Chideya will show in a forthcoming book, of the approximately 71,000 Americans who earn livings from sports (broadly defined to include golfers, skaters, and so on), only 10 percent are black.

A likely explanation for black success in basketball is not some mystically powerful jumping gene—natural selection may have favored strength and size in people, but what are the odds it ever favored jumping?—but that many blacks practice the sport intensely. For good or ill, thousands of black kids spend several hours per day through their youth playing basketball. By the time age eighteen is reached, it shows: In general, blacks are really good at basketball. Meanwhile, hockey and tennis are usually practiced in youth by whites, who in turn dominate these sports.

In all the complex arguments about inheritability and environment in IQ, the mundane, common-sense question of practice time is often overlooked. Other things being equal, what you practice is what you're good at. As Charles Darwin once wrote to his cousin Francis Galton, founder of the eugenics movement: "I have always maintained that, excepting fools, men [do] not differ much in intellect, only in zeal and hard work."

As a long-time basketball-league participant and a mediocre small-college football player, I have spent a notable portion of my life being knocked down, run past, and otherwise outperformed by black athletes. None ever struck me as possessing any mystical genetic athletic ability, though it may be that as a group they hold some small edge over whites. What often does strike me as a black basketball player in a pick-up game hits his shot and I miss mine is the thought: "He's taken that shot maybe five million times in his life, and I've taken it maybe five thousand." It's safe to say that if there had been no color barrier to college basketball in the 1940s and 1950s, blacks would not have dominated in those years, because at that time few blacks practiced basketball as much as the best white players of the period. By coincidence, the week before *The Bell Curve* was published, the "Science Times" section of *The New York Times* ran a prominent article on new research showing that the most accomplished violinists and other artistic performers spend significantly more time practicing than the less accomplished—though presumably they enjoy the advantage of genetic gifts. There seemed to me a pellucid connection between this research and the Herrnstein-Murray thesis.

Another missed connection concerns a 1990 flap at the University of California at Berkeley. There, a tenured anthropologist, Vincent Sarich, began to say that black success in basketball proved the inherited basis of talent, which in turn supported the view that whites could inherit superior mental faculties. Sarich's argument is revealingly faulty: He would tell classes that "There is no white Michael Jordan . . . nor has there ever been one." Actually there *was* a white Michael Jordan—the late Pete Maravich. Maravich scored much more than Jordan in college and had the same league-leading scoring average in the NBA, 31 points per game. Maravich had the same ability as Jordan to throw the no-look pass, to dunk in ways that appeared to defy certain laws of physics, and so on. Jordan became a sports legend because his college and pro teams were champions; this happened because Jordan was a highly disciplined defensive performer and an astute judge of the court situation. Maravich, in contrast, became something of a standing joke, even to sportswriters eager for white stars, because his teams always lost. Maravich was a hopelessly selfish performer, inert on defense and he never passed up a shot. The comparison between Jordan and Maravich both defies the stereotype of the white player as disciplined and the black player as the gunner, and undermines the notion of black genetic dominance generally.

So if white kids as a group spend more time practicing schoolwork, should we then be surprised that they score better on school-related tests? Herrnstein and Murray acknowledge that 150 hours of extra study will raise the typical student's SAT score by 40 points—a common-sense confirmation that scholastic practice makes for scholastic success. True, the score-boosting effects of extra study on SAT tests reach a plateau beyond which further practice adds little. Yet seeing that behavior (study time) alters brain-test outcome, and then concluding as *The Bell Curve* does that brain performance is mainly genetic, is an inverted form of the logic that Stalin's favorite scientist, Trofim Lysenko, employed to contend that genetic characteristics are acquired during a person's life. That many white kids may spend more hours studying than many black kids may well be an argument that some minority parents are negligent in compelling their children to hit the books. But this is an argument about environment, not inheritance.

It is not racist for Herrnstein and Murray to study whether there are differences in inherited IQ. Some commentators have attempted to reject *The Bell Curve* out of hand on grounds of racism, and thereby avoid dealing with its discomfiting contentions. Yet obviously people talk about the mental abilities of various groups, usually in whispers; better to talk about this in the open. For this reason, in my affiliation with *The Atlantic Monthly,* I favored that magazine's publication of some of Herrnstein's earlier work. I agreed with the decision of *The New Republic* to put an excerpt from *The Bell Curve* on its cover. And I am glad Herrnstein and Murray (the principal author) wrote *The Bell Curve,* which is not a racist work, though it is fantastically wrongheaded. Bringing the arguments about race, inheritance, and IQ out into the open in Murray's straightforward writing style is a useful service—especially because the more you know about this line of thought, the less persuasive it becomes.

Now, other objections to *The Bell Curve,* concentrating on those not already raised by other commentators:

• *The Hollywood corollary.* Perhaps black overrepresentation in basketball is essentially a fluke telling nothing about the general relationship between practice and achievement. Yet consider that blacks are also overrepresented in several performing arts, notably singing and comedy. Is this because they have superior singing and joking genes? It's hard to imagine why natural selection would have favored DNA for human song. On the other hand, African Americans as a group have spent generations learning various forms of performance. Most African culture is oral; and until recent decades, owing both to discrimination and poverty, when American blacks wanted entertainment they had to entertain each other. That is, they practiced song and comedy, and they got good at it.

• *Is everybody too dumb to know who's smart?* In *The Bell Curve* there are numerous assertions that society has handicapped itself by failing to favor the smart. For instance, the book asserts that the American economy loses as much as $80 billion per year because a 1971 Supreme Court decision bars most forms of workplace IQ testing. High-IQ workers are more productive, Herrnstein and Murray say; promoting them would increase productivity. But if high-IQ employees are more productive, that should be self-evident to employers regardless of tests. Are employers so dumb they don't promote the productive workers? On a common-sense basis, society has long been attuned to what can be accomplished by the smart, and almost always rewards this already.

• *The Hiram College contradiction.* Early in *The Bell Curve* comes a section describing how in the fifties the freshman class at Harvard was not composed exclusively of the brightest of the bright; many were slow-witted kids entering on Dad-um's alumni connections. This was actually to the good, Murray writes, because it meant that many bright kids who otherwise would have been consolidated at Harvard instead had no choice but to attend Hiram or Kenyon or some other school, distributing IQ throughout society. These days, *The Bell Curve* says, owing to accurate SAT testing (which is now quite accurate, but only so far as it goes), Harvard gets the brightest of the bright, withdrawing the "cognitive elite" into a small, isolated world. This, the book says, is bad.

Yet later, in a section assailing affirmative action (*The Bell Curve* really despises affirmative action), Murray says that offering special admissions consideration to minority students is awful because it denies some worthy white students entry slots in the top schools. But isn't the effect that a percentage of smart kids end up at Hiram and Kenyon, distributing IQ throughout society? When some smart white kids were denied admission to Harvard because the sons of the landed had a special deal—in other words, when there was a patrician system that favored the affluent—that was great, according to *The Bell Curve*. Now that some smart white kids are denied admission to Harvard because the sons and daughters of *poverty* have a special deal—the new system no longer rigged in favor of the affluent—that's offensive, according to the same book.

• *Those inherited differences that have been confirmed are small.* It's obvious that there exist inheritable physical differences among racial groups. But all such differences are too minor to mean anything, except as sources of the many forms of prejudice. Perhaps there are inherited mental differences among racial groups, but the observed pattern in physical differences suggests any mental differences would also be too minor to matter in practical terms. For instance, African Americans are on average about an inch and a half taller than Caucasian Americans. This distinction is real but just too small to make a difference except in highly competitive situations like, say, entry into the small number of slots in the National Basketball Association: There, a competition between two players of otherwise equal skills might end in the taller being selected. Similarly, suppose there really are on average a few points of difference between whites and blacks in IQ. This is too little to matter in practical terms, except in highly competitive situations like, say, entry into the small number of clerkships to the Supreme Court, where an extra margin of IQ might carry the day.

• *If this stuff is really true, it's whites that ought to feel inferior.* The same IQ tests that Murray says show blacks one "standard deviation" (in this case, very roughly 15 percent) less smart than whites show white children duller than Asian-American children by almost the same margin. Simple-minded me might say that is mainly because of the phenomenal (probably excessive) study time many Asian-American parents impose on their kids. But if genes are the IQ destiny that *The Bell Curve* asserts, shouldn't whites be maneuvering to protect themselves against Asians, given that Asians already outnumber Caucasians worldwide? Instead, nearly all of the book's prescriptive material focuses on reasons to retaliate politically against blacks: end affirmative action, shift money from compensatory education programs like Head Start to programs for the "gifted" (that is, white students), scale back welfare.

• *What's the mechanism?* All human beings are physically similar because they share a line of descent and have all been subject to about the same "selection pressure" from evolution. For there to be significant inherent mental differences among racial groups, there would have to have been significantly different selection pressure. Scientists call this the "What's the mechanism?" question. Any researcher claiming to have found a substantial genetic difference among similar creatures is expected to propose a selection mechanism by which the differential arose.

Early in *The Bell Curve* controversy, *The New York Times* ran an op-ed article asserting that from an evolutionary standpoint, differential intellect among human groups could not have evolved in fewer than "hundreds of thousands of years." This is weak science: Most recent discoveries tend to support the notion that natural selection can operate relatively quickly in geologic terms. So differential intellect is not precluded. Yet neither Herrnstein and Murray nor any credentialed believer in the brain-gene theory has suggested how, on an evolutionary basis, black and white intelligence DNA could have diverged significantly.

The sole researcher asserting a hypothesis in this category is J. Philippe Rushton, a psychologist at the University of Western Ontario. *The Bell Curve* makes a point of praising Rushton as "not . . . a crackpot." But a crackpot is precisely what Rushton is. He believes that among males of African, European, and Asian descent, intellect and genital size are inversely proportional, and that evolution dictated this outcome in an as-yet-undetermined manner. Sound like something the sixteen-year-olds at your high school believed? That should not stop Rushton or any researcher from wondering if there might have been different selection pressures on different racial groups. But Rushton's "research" methods, defended by *The Bell Curve* as academically sound, are preposterous. For instance, Rushton has conducted surveys at shopping malls, asking men of different races how far their ejaculate travels. His theory is the farther the gush, the lower the IQ. Set aside the evolutionary absurdity of this. (Are we to presume that in pre-history low-IQ males were too dumb to find pleasure in full penetration, so their sperm had to evolve rocket-propelled arcs? Give me a break.) Consider only the "research" standard here. Is it possible that one man in a hundred actually knows, with statistical accuracy, the average distance traveled by his ejaculate? Yet *The Bell Curve* takes Rushton in full seriousness.

• *Are the natives doltish as well as restless?* Herrnstein and Murray note that not only do African-Americans score somewhat below white Americans on IQ tests but tribal black Africans score significantly low even in pure-logic tests designed to correct for language differences. (Mazes and so on.) Though many claims of cultural bias are exaggerated by the we're-all-victims lobby, here IQ tests would be expected to be of little reliability, considering the gulf between cultures as different as those of the United States and tribal Africa. Yet *The Bell Curve* takes the low scores of tribal Africans in earnest, implying this proves the existence of an entire continent of morons.

Just what mechanism of selection pressure would have caused this wide disparity? The authors do not say, gliding past this and all other complications of genetic science. More, they make a tee-hee implication, citing IQ scores among South African "coloureds," that American blacks are smarter than African blacks because of interbreeding with whites. Objection One: If black-white interbreeding in North America were substantial enough to transfer the presumed white intellect to the black gene pool, would not the same process have transferred the presumed black athletic gifts to the white gene pool, leading to an NBA dominated by guys named Blaine and Todd? Objection Two: Though geologic time would probably not be required for differential intellect to arise if a selection mechanism could be shown, a couple of centuries seems insufficient. That is, unions between whites and blacks since colonial times would be unlikely to account for African-Americans doing substantially better on IQ tests than tribal black Africans. The exposure of African-Americans to an educational system teaching (as it should) book-based culture would, on the other hand, explain it pretty neatly.

• *Geneticists don't claim genes explain IQ.* "The people who say intelligence is genetic are the ones with no training in genetics," says Evan Balaban, a former professor of evolutionary biology at Harvard and now a fellow at The Neurosciences Institute, a research organization. Murray is a social scientist; Herrnstein was a psychologist. Balaban continues: "Any serious biologist would be horrified by the idea of using the little we know about genes as the basis for social policy. Current genetic research cannot even explain how basic body parts form." Nearly all contemporary discoveries about human genetics concern only markers or genes associated with protein coding, vastly less complicated than a developmental trait like intellect.

Troy Duster, a sociologist at the University of California at Berkeley who has studied the history of claims of inherited intellectual inferiority, notes that, "Since the turn of the century the people making political assertions about population genetics always reason backwards from the phenotype [observed trait] to the presence of a gene. This is the reverse of the way molecular biology reasons. Since molecular biologists have discovered genes for diseases like cystic fibrosis and Tay Sachs, the public has begun to believe biologists already understand the human genome. People like Herrnstein and Murray use the halo effect of that belief to give their views a sheen of modern genetics, when in truth their assertions run counter to what can be supported by modern genetics." I called prominent molecular biologists at Harvard, MIT, Penn State, Stanford, and the University of Washington, and all asserted that the notion of a traceable gene line for intelligence has no grounding in present research.

Telling in this regard is *The Bell Curve*'s misunderstanding of Mendelian genetics. The authors treat inheritance from parents as if it could be charted in straight lines: Smart parents A beget smart kids B, etc. This is a common blunder. Trait-inheritance charts more often look like zigzags, as phenotypes bounce around among offspring and may skip entire generations. Two red-haired parents may have two brunette children, each of whom in turn have one red- and one black-haired child, and so on. Herrnstein and Murray allude in a few sentences to the common outcome that the children of very bright parents may be only somewhat above average in intellect, but otherwise depict IQ as reliably passed through the generations in straight-line fashion. If IQ does pass down generations in straight lines, then the cause must be mainly the environment families create, since genetic traits don't express so predictably.

• *Nonsense dysgenics.* A substantial doom section of *The Bell Curve* is devoted to "dysgenics," the reverse of eugenics—the fear that high fertility rates among those of low mental prowess will swamp society with dumbness. At least since Malthus, this has been a belief of the privileged classes whose concerns Murray and Herrnstein hold foremost. It was the central fear of Darwin's cousin Galton, and was a reputable paranoia among the educated in the United States as recently as the years when the Nazi use of eugenics became known. Even Norman Thomas, the most important American socialist of this century, in the thirties denounced the high rate of fertility among "those of a definitely inferior stock."

Yet during the very century in which, *The Bell Curve* says, dysgenics has run wild globally, overall scores on IQ tests have consistently risen by decade, among blacks as well as whites. Now, how can it be that overall IQ scores are going up, yet society simultaneously is being swamped by fertile dullards? One possible explanation is that in decrying high fertility rates among low-achieving inner-city women (a problem, to be sure, though first for the women themselves), *The Bell Curve* conveniently overlooks a parallel social phenomenon: the rise of the American black middle class. Today, for every one African-American whose life pattern fits the dysgenic nightmare, there are roughly two following the eugenics prescription—moving out of the city, having smaller families, advancing financially and scholastically. Black middle class school achievement trails comparable white numbers, but a small trailer effect seems easily explained as a remnant of segregation.

Herrnstein and Murray say little about the black middle class, a significant group which for good or ill is busily embracing suburban American norms. The authors can't deal with this factor because not only would it foul up claims of dysgenics; dealing with it forces you to confront the fact that many studies show children's IQs tend to be higher in smaller families. This is what might be expected, as other things being equal, smaller families offer children more attention and have better social and economic circumstances. That's er, ahem, nurture rather than nature, which falls outside the desired conclusion of *The Bell Curve.*

• *Spin disguised as scholarship.* The most disquieting aspect of *The Bell Curve* is its insistence on phrasing as detached data analysis what is in truth an ideological argument about social policy. Ideology regarding social policy is fine, but should be presented as such. The authors of *The Bell Curve* adopt a weary tone of "we hate these conclusions, yet as scientists we are driven to them by impartial reading of neutral data." The data they offer as impartial has, however, been elaborately scrunched to fit the desired ideological boxes.

The book's main artifice in this regard is to present the work of those researchers who do conclude that IQ is mainly inherited and is the main determinant of life outcomes (there are a few such researchers, with full credentials), then describe their studies as generally accepted or no longer seriously contested by other researchers. This is duplicitous. Most academic researchers now accept the notion that IQ tests have become reasonably fair and reasonably predict performance in school. Beyond that there exists a fantastic range of opinions about what the tests really tell you. Many credentialed academic "psychometricians" (students of IQ) come to conclusions dramatically at odds with what Herrnstein and Murray think about IQ, genes, and mental determinism, Robert Sternberg of Yale probably standing as the leading example. *The Bell Curve* makes passing reference to the existence of prominent academics who would reject its thesis, but in the main represents to readers that few researchers now contest the notion that IQ rules. This borders on intellectual dishonesty.

• *Spin disguised, period.* Murray's work on *The Bell Curve* was underwritten by a grant from the Bradley Foundation, which the *National Journal* in 1993 described as "the nation's biggest underwriter of conservative intellectual activity." Bradley is a respectable foundation about whose financial support no author need apologize. But Bradley backs only one kind of work: that with right-wing political value. For instance, Bradley is currently underwriting William Kristol, a former adviser to President Bush and director of the Project for a Republican Future. *The Bell Curve* identifies Murray as a "Bradley Fellow" but gives readers no hint of the foundation's ideological requirements. Telling readers this would, needless to say, spoil the book's pretense of objective assessment of research.

Slipping down the slope from the respectable Bradley Foundation, Herrnstein and Murray praise some research supported by the Pioneer Fund, an Aryan crank organization. Until recently, Pioneer's charter said it would award scholarships mainly to students "deemed to be descended from white persons who settled in the original 13 states." Pioneer supports Rushton and backed the "Minnesota Twins" study, which purports to find that identical twins raised apart end up similar right down to personality quirks. The Aryan crank crowd has long been entranced by the Minnesota Twins project, as it appears to show that genes for mentation are entirely deterministic. Many academics consider the protocols used by the Minnesota Twins study invalid.

Lesser examples of disguised ideological agenda are common in *The Bell Curve*. For example, at one point Murray presents an extended section on problems within the D.C. Police Department, saying their basis lies in "degradation of intellectual requirements" on officer hiring exams. Information in this section is attributed to "journalist Tucker Carlson." No one who lives in Washington doubts its police department has problems, some of which surely stem from poor screening of applicants. But who is the source for the particularly harsh version of this problem presented in *The Bell Curve*? "Journalist Tucker Carlson" turns out to be an employee of the Heritage Foundation; he is an editor of its house journal *Policy Review*. Heritage, for those who don't know it, has a rigid hard-right ideological slant. Its *Policy Review* is a lively and at times insightful publication, but anyone regarding its content as other than pamphleteering would be a fool. The article *The Bell Curve* draws from lampoons the intelligence of D.C. police officers because some cases have been dismissed owing to illegible arrest records. And just how many high-IQ white doctors have unreadable handwriting? If an article in *Policy Review* were an impartial source of social science observations, Murray would simply come out and say where his citation originates. Instead he disguises the source, knowing full well its doctrinaire nature.

• *Even the worst-case claimed by the brain-gene believers just doesn't sound so bad.* Herrnstein and Murray estimate that intelligence is 60 percent nature, 40 percent nurture. Since genes get the majority number here, to them this clinches the argument for inborn intellectual determinism.

But think about this worst-case—intelligence as 40 percent nurture. "Forty percent variability based on environment would make intelligence an exceptionally pliant trait," Balaban says. It's known, for example, that better nutrition can improve height—but only by a few inches, about a 5 percent swing based on the potential range of human statures. If IQ swings by 40 percent owing to circumstances and life experiences, then human society has more control over intelligence than virtually anything else in its genetic inheritance. Thus, even *The Bell Curve*'s own contentions would seem solid ground upon which to support further attempts to improve the school and home environments of underprivileged children.

In the end, *The Bell Curve* should be seen not as racist or violating a taboo, but simply as an attempt to torment data to make it support a right-wing agenda. That's fine so far as it goes: Right-wing ideas have as much claim on society's attention as any other kind, and some of the conclusions Herrnstein and Murray offer are surely correct ones. (They're surely correct, for example, in contending that in most cases small, stable, "legitimate" parents-wedded families are in the best interests of the child.) It is essential, however, that *The Bell Curve* be seen as a tract advocating a political point of view, not a detached assessment of research. In that regard two final common-sense objections to the book are particularly strong:

• *You don't have to be real smart to grasp test-score convergence.* For decades black scores on IQ and aptitude tests have been converging upward toward white scores, even as white scores rise. Exceptionally high intelligence is not required to theorize that this is happening because of improved educational opportunity.

The Bell Curve makes a passing mention of black IQ score increases, calls them encouraging, then quickly switches back to doom pronouncements about genetic determinism and the feeble-mindedness of minorities and the poor. Anything more than a passing mention of black IQ test convergence would have kicked the chair out from under the premise of Herrnstein and Murray's tract. If someday black scores stop rising toward white scores, that might be alarming. But this hasn't happened yet, and until it does all the marching data in *The Bell Curve* and similar works will contain a huge common-sense defect.

• *Even if* The Bell Curve *were right about genes, then it's still wrong about policy.* It turns out that since IQ testing became common, approximately in the 1920s, the scores of American blacks have shifted upward by about two "standard deviations"—that is, about twice as much positive shift as the negative gulf Herrnstein and Murray find between whites and blacks today. But then almost every American group's IQ score has upshifted by about two standard deviations in recent decades. Blacks, whites, yellows, reds, browns: According to IQ testing, we're all getting smarter dramatically fast. The explanation would seem obvious—quality and quantity (especially number of years of schooling) of education has gone up for everybody, so everybody now does better on tests of educational aptitude. Herrnstein and Murray reject this view, saying it must be mainly genes.

Suppose they're right. If rising IQ levels are mainly genetic, then some evolutionary force must be propelling genus *Homo* in the direction of more DNA for brainpower. Modern society rewards education and mental prowess, so evolution may now be rewarding the same. (Genes do not change during life, but changing circumstances influence which genes are deemed fit and passed to offspring—this is the definition of selection pressure.) Thus if *The Bell Curve* is correct about intellect being mainly genetic, then some aspect of modern social circumstances and government policy must be encouraging or at least neutral to a fantastic wave of improvements in the human genetic endowment for IQ.

Yet *The Bell Curve* concludes by calling for drastic changes in social circumstances and government policy—the very forces which, in Herrnstein and Murray's analysis, seem to be causing natural selection to favor IQ as never before. The book ends up mired in such illogic either because its authors do not understand the science of genetics on which they pretend to premise their case, or have produced what should properly be seen as an unusually lengthy promotional brochure for a rather unattractive political package.

THE MEDIAN IS THE MESSAGE

Ellen Willis

*T*HE BELL CURVE, Charles Murray and the late Richard J. Herrnstein's 845-page monument to hierarchy, is really two books. One of them is a media event designed to fill a conspicuous gap in public discourse—while the figures on crime and "illegitimacy" have served to release sensitive white people from their pesky inhibitions about calling blacks violent and hypersexual, in recent years there has been no comparable statistical outlet for the sentiment that blacks are dumb. The other, which has received about as much attention as 845-page monuments usually get, is a polemic about the intelligentsia or, as the authors call it, the "cognitive elite." The first book presents IQ as the preeminent criterion of social worth; the second attacks intelligence as the chief prerequisite of social power. If these arguments sound contradictory, they nonetheless converge in a paradoxical vision: invoking the authority of science, *The Bell Curve* rejects the whole enterprise of modernity.

Conservatives are perennially tempted by the illusion that vexing social conflicts can be settled by exposing their opponents' aspirations to the dry air of "the facts." (While radicals are by no means immune to this impulse, it's harder to marshal facts in defense of a social system

Ellen Willis teaches journalism at New York University and is a contributing editor of *The Village Voice*. This article was published in *The Village Voice*, November 15, 1994.

that doesn't yet exist.) Twenty years ago Steven Goldberg thought he could prove the "inevitability of patriarchy" by citing studies that linked aggression with testosterone and concluded that men were innately more aggressive than women—a line of argument that, so far as I can tell, has had no effect on sexual politics except to inspire mock diagnoses of "testosterone poisoning." Ten years ago right-to-life activists imagined that the expansion of scientific knowledge about fetal development would have to change people's minds about abortion. Now *The Bell Curve*'s revival of decades-old claims about IQ— that there is such a thing as a quantifiable general intelligence; that IQ tests measure it accurately and objectively; that it is largely genetic, highly resistant to change, and unevenly distributed among races; that high IQ correlates with economic and social success, low IQ with the abject condition and aberrant behavior of the poor—is supposed to tell us what to do about social equality, namely abandon the idea as quixotic. Yet to argue about the meaning of IQ—as about the humanity of fetuses or the nature of sexual difference—is really a way of defusing anxiety by displacing onto impersonal "scientific" dispute a profound clash of interests and worldviews, with all the yearning, hatred, and fear that clash entails. If I bought the authors' facts, I would still be allergic to their politics. I don't advocate social equality because I think everyone is the same; I believe that difference, real or imagined, is no excuse for subordinating some people to others. Equality is a principle of human relations, not Procrustes' bed.

In fact, Murray and Herrnstein tacitly recognize that science is not the key issue here. In recounting the history of the IQ debate, they focus less on the substance of the argument ("To prove our case, taking each point and amassing a full account of the evidence for and against, would lead us to write a book just about them. Such books have already been written") than on the struggle to prevail as conventional wisdom. As they tell it, their view of intelligence and IQ testing was taken for granted until it ran into the dogmatic egalitarianism of the sixties and seventies. Then for purely ideological reasons, the left attacked Arthur Jensen's research attributing the failure of remedial education programs to the lower IQ scores of black kids, as well as Herrnstein's early work on the link between IQ and class status; they and their allies were driven out of the public arena by intimidating demonstrations and intellectual antagonists like Stephen Jay Gould;

but although the latter "won the visible battle," discussion of the significance of IQ continued offstage, in the "cloistered environment" of the academy. The clear implication of this tale of exile is that with the rightward shift in the nation's politics, it's time for the return.

In short, *The Bell Curve* is not about breaking new intellectual ground, but about coming up from underground: "we have become convinced," Murray and Herrnstein declare, "that the topic of genes, intelligence, and race in the late twentieth century is like the topic of sex in Victorian England. Publicly, there seems to be nothing to talk about. Privately, people are fascinated by it." I can't quarrel with this point. The idea that black brains are genetically inferior to white brains did not fade from public view simply because white people were convinced by Stephen Jay Gould's eloquent arguments. Rather, the gap between Americans' conscious moral consensus for racial equality and the tenacious social and psychic structures of racism was papered over with guilt and taboo. Many opponents of racism thought they were doing their moral duty by shouting down the Jensens and the Herrnsteins, driving them underground. But this literal enforcement of taboo was only a crude reflection of a much more widespread process of self-censorship.

I don't mean that the moral consensus of the post-civil-rights era wasn't genuine. I mean that morality isn't enough, that it can't forever keep the lid on contrary feelings rooted in real social relationships that have not been understood, confronted, or transformed. Commenting on *The Bell Curve* in *The New Republic*, John B. Judis indignantly points out that the taboo Murray and Herrnstein are so proud of violating was a reaction against Nazism: "It's not the taboo against unflinching scientific inquiry, but against pseudo-scientific racism. Of all the world's taboos, it is most deserving of retention." The problem, though, is that taboos can never truly vanquish the powerful desires that provoke them. For some decades after the Holocaust, there was a moratorium on open anti-Semitism in Europe and America; it didn't last. So long as hierarchy is a ruling principle of our culture, a basic fact of everyday life, the idea of black inferiority cannot be transcended, only repressed. And in an era when an ascendant global capitalism is creating a new worldwide class structure—when the language of social Darwinism is increasingly regarded as a simple description of reality—genetic determination of social status is an idea whose time has come back.

The most intense public fixation on IQ since Forrest Gump began with Murray's picture on the cover of *The New York Times Magazine*, its headline a classic self-fulfilling prophecy: THE MOST DANGEROUS CONSERVATIVE. "Over a decade," the cover type continued, "Charles Murray has gained ground in his crusade to abolish welfare. But now, with his contentious views on IQ, class and race, has he gone too far?" Jason DeParle's profile was critical of Murray's views. But the real message of the article lay in its existence, its prominence, and the assumption embedded in its presentation: that *The Bell Curve* has pushed the American public debate to a new and daring frontier, with all the disreputable glamour such an undertaking implies—and, incidentally, has outflanked Murray's crusade to abolish welfare, which is now respectable (hasn't Clinton all but endorsed it?).

Subsequent coverage has continued in this vein, shouting through sheer volume and visibility that *The Bell Curve* is a serious work whose thesis, however unpalatable, must be reckoned with. *Newsweek*'s cover story features a Janus-like white face and black face turned away from each other (is it my imagination, or does the black face look a little like O. J. Simpson?) on either side of the headline IQ: IS IT DESTINY? The front page of *The New York Times Book Review*—which includes in the same issue *The Bell Curve* and a number of other books that make biological-determinist arguments—asks, "How Much of Us Is in the Genes?" (Note the ubiquitous question as ass-covering device. Is it destiny? Hey, we're not saying it is, we're not saying it isn't.) *The New Republic*'s cover, in huge type, simply reads RACE & IQ; virtually the entire issue is devoted to an article by Murray and Herrnstein, based on material from the book, and nineteen (!) replies. Murray's TV appearances and countless op-eds hammer the theme home: attention must be paid.

While the *TBR* review was cautiously sympathetic, much of the mainstream commentary—the daily *Times, Time, Newsweek, New York*, even John Leo in *U.S. News & World Report*—has been hostile to the book. (In *The New Republic*, where most of the staff opposed publishing the Murray-Herrnstein essay, the rebuttals not only took up more space than the essay itself, but actually preceded it in the magazine.) Some of it notes that *The Bell Curve*'s thesis is not new but a rehash of ideas with a long and dubious pedigree. Despite Murray's policy credentials and the enormous impact of his 1984 book *Losing Ground* on the welfare debate, it would not have been an implausible reaction if editors had rolled their eyes at his getting in bed with the IQ crowd, if they'd felt the kind of embarrassment one feels when, say, a respectable intellectual joins a religious cult; instead, their dominant emotion seems to be fear of being or being called a censor. I can't help suspecting that that fear has less to do with a healthy respect for debate than with the cultural unconscious of a white, educated middle class projecting onto an Evil but Courageous book its own tabooed racial feelings.

Not coincidentally, the media's treatment of *The Bell Curve* has centered obsessively on race and virtually ignored class, which is the book's main subject (its subtitle is "Intelligence and Class Structure in American Life"). Murray and Herrnstein clearly invited this reaction, not only by including a section on race and repackaging it for *The New Republic,* but by devoting so much space to their dire view of the underclass—while they warn of an "emerging white underclass," elsewhere in the book, as in public conversation generally, the word is code for "black." Still, it seems peculiar that journalists, certified members of *The Bell Curve*'s "cognitive elite," should have so little comment on its analysis of their own class status. Their silence is one more piece of evidence that even as economic restructuring makes class an issue in more and more people's lives, Americans stubbornly resist talking about it. It strikes me, in fact, that blackness has become as much a code for "underclass" as the other way around—that when whites treat middle-class black men in suits and ties like potential muggers and rapists, what they fear is being engulfed and tainted by lower-classness. It's a truism that poor whites embrace racism so they can see the lower class as safely Other. But in the new, anarchic world order, the specter of downward mobility haunts us all.

The Bell Curve's class analysis goes like this: At an earlier time, when social classes were sorted out by birth and there were many fewer specialized occupations that demand high intelligence, cognitive ability was distributed fairly evenly throughout the class structure. Now equal opportunity—particularly equal access to higher education— and the shift toward a high-tech, knowledge-based economy have made intelligence the main agent of class stratification. (If you're tempted to tune out right here—equal opportunity? what are they talking about?—bear with me. The argument gets more interesting.)

As the brainy rise to the top and the dull-witted sink to the increasingly miserable bottom, social proximity makes people ever more likely to mate within their own cognitive group (a tendency exacerbated by feminism, which encourages educated men in high-IQ jobs to marry similarly situated women). That accelerates the process of IQ stratification, since (to quote one of the summaries for the cognitively impaired that precede each chapter), "as America equalizes the circumstances of people's lives, the remaining differences in intelligence are increasingly determined by differences in genes."

The intellectual meritocracy they see emerging—while "in many ways an expression of what America is all about"—worries Murray and Herrnstein. They worry that the cognitive elite (CE) is coalescing "into a class that views American society increasingly through a lens of its own." Smart people are socialized in similar ways and isolated from the TVtabloidtalk-radio culture of ordinary Americans. They have exploited the increasing reach of the federal government since the 1960s to impose their values on the rest of society. And now, as the rich get brighter and the bright get richer, a scary confluence looms: "Do you think," the authors ask rhetorically, "that the rich in America already have too much power? Or do you think the intellectuals already have too much power? . . . just watch what happens as their outlooks and interests converge." A probable consequence, in the authors' view, is that a large class of smart, affluent people (10 to 20 percent of the population) will wall itself off from the rest of society, particularly from the threatening underclass, withdrawing from public institutions and preferring to pay for its own private services. Still clinging to its belief in the welfare state, even as it loses faith that the poor can improve their condition, this class will most likely use its power to institute "the custodial state"—"an expanded welfare state for the underclass that also keeps it out from underfoot."

How to avoid this dystopia? What people need, *The Bell Curve* argues, is a "valued place" in the social order. In traditional societies, people across the cognitive spectrum attained this "valued place" through work, community, and family. As occupations that don't require a high IQ lose prestige and earning power, it is harder and harder for the dull to find a valued place at work. This makes community and family all the more important, yet these sources of valued place have also been undercut. And much of the blame for this situation rests on, you guessed it, the CE's misguided attitudes and values. For one thing, "the federal domination of public policy that has augmented the cognitive elite's political leverage during the last thirty years . . . has had the collateral effect of stripping the neighborhood of much of the stuff of life." This hasn't bothered the CE because its members aren't centered in a geographic community but are oriented to the nation and the world; "they may read about such communities in books" but don't believe they really exist. Furthermore, the CE is now running American society by rules that people with low or even ordinary IQs find too difficult to follow. These rules are based on the idea that "complicated, sophisticated operationalizations of fairness, justice, and right and wrong are ethically superior to simple, black-and-white versions." They are the kind of rules "that give the cognitive elite the greatest competitive advantage," since "deciphering complexity is one of the things that cognitive ability is most directly good for."

One example is bureaucratic regulations that confound everyone from "a single woman with children seeking government assistance" to "a person who is trying to open a dry-cleaning shop." The callous CE doesn't care that "they are complicating ordinary lives. It's not so complicated to them." Another problematic area is morality. Society should make it easy for dullards to be virtuous by making simple rules about crime and punishment that everyone agrees on and enthusiastically enforces. Crime in such a society would consist of "a few obviously wrong acts"; punishment would be swift and sure. But the CE with its complicated rules and moral ambiguities has produced a confusing system where the bad guys don't always lose, and worse, people don't always agree on what's bad. Similarly, the CE's sexual revolution has made it more difficult for the dull "to figure out why marriage is a good thing, and, once in a marriage . . . to figure out why one should stick with it through bad times." Marriage is satisfying to the extent that society unequivocally upholds it as an institution; the CE has mucked things up, not only by supporting the right to sex and procreation outside marriage, but by demanding legal and social recognition of nonmarital relationships.

This broadside against the *clercs* has little glitches (solicitude for the poor single mother stymied by those pointy-head rules for getting government assistance sits oddly with Murray's resolve to abolish the assistance along with the rules), middle-sized contradictions (the increasing reliance of the affluent on private rather than public services, which the authors view with alarm, is a direct result of the governmental shrinkage they champion), and gaping holes. Take the supposed ruling coalition of the rich and the smart, which lumps together the titans of the global marketplace with people like me. Since I belong to the CE if anyone does (skipped a grade in junior high school, graduated from a Seven Sisters college, work in not one but two knowledge industries, managed to get through *The Bell Curve* with a minimum of cheating), how come I'm not running the World Bank?

In the real world, intellectuals and techies not directly tied into the production of wealth are fast following blue-collar workers into redundancy. Technology eliminates intellectual along with manual labor; white-collar jobs migrate to countries whose newly educated classes are willing to work at lower rates; obsession with the bottom line translates into suspicion of any intellectual work whose productivity can't be easily measured. Companies are shedding managers and replacing engineers and computer programmers with machines. The job markets in the academy and the publishing industry are dismal, support for artists and writers even scarcer than usual, the public and nonprofit sectors—hotbeds of cognitive elitism—steadily shrinking. Nor are card-carrying CE members exempt from the pervasive trend toward employment of part-time, temporary, and benefit-free workers. Wealth is increasingly concentrated at the top and, last I looked, still handily outstrips other sources of power.

Still, I do have something in common with the Walter Wristons, the Rupert Murdochs, the venture capitalists in Eastern Europe—that deeply suspect tropism for locating the center of our lives beyond the neighborhood. Like genetic theories of racial inferiority, antipathy toward intellectuals and capitalists on the grounds of their rootless cosmopolitanism is a recurring theme among reactionaries whose loyalties are more aristocratic than bourgeois. And for all the authors' lip service to the American ideals of meritocracy and equal opportunity (as opposed to equal results), their vision of the good society is essentially feudal: it's that old chestnut the organic community, where there is "A Place for Everyone" (a chapter heading) and all cheerfully accept their place, while a kindly but firm paternal ruling class runs things according to rules even the darkies can understand. Equality of opportunity unleashes the disruptive force of intelligence, deposes the organic hierarchy, and rends the social fabric. In effect, *The Bell Curve* restates a core belief of unreconstructed conservatives (not the free-market kind): that the Enlightenment ruined culture.

Yet Murray and Herrnstein, themselves part of the elite they decry, are nothing if not free marketeers; despite their suggestion that the rich are too powerful, their targets are government and culture, not the economic system. On the surface, this doesn't make sense: do they seriously imagine that capitalism can somehow be divorced from its cosmopolitan character and that if only the government and the CE would get out of the way, community and family would provide the underclass with a "valued place"? But a deeper logic is at work here. Murray and Herrnstein don't really object to the power of wealth; they're merely willing to appeal to resentment of the rich to bolster their argument against intellectuals and their subversive ways. Who after all is the *you* they're addressing with those rhetorical questions? Clearly, "the average American," whom the authors regard as "an asset, not part of the problem," and who, they imply, would do fine were it not for the oppressively powerful cognitive elite and the burdensome underclass its policies have nurtured. By this route, *The Bell Curve*'s aristocratic outlook merges seamlessly with right-wing populism.

But that's not all. A psychopolitical quiz: What mythic, menacing figure combines in one package excessive wealth and power, rootlessness, and subversive intellect? *The Bell Curve* says nothing about Jews except that "Ashkenazi Jews of European origins" have higher IQ scores than other ethnic groups. Nonetheless, just as the book's insistence on racial difference will bring the eugenics nuts out of the woodwork—despite the authors' protests that that's not what they meant at all—I'd guess that its attack on intelligence will find its way into the arsenal of anti-Semites.

The Bell Curve, with its dry academic tone and its pages of statistics, is not in itself a powerful book. But it rides a powerful wave of emotion—the frustration of a middle class that, whatever its IQ scores, see its choices narrowing, its future in doubt. Rejecting the moral taboos of the left to flirt with the shameless brutality of the right feels like a hit of freedom. But like all drugs, it wears off, leaving the underlying problem untouched. The danger is that Americans will seek out more and bigger doses. The irony is that real radicalism is still the greatest taboo of all.

CLEVER ARGUMENTS, ATROCIOUS SCIENCE

John Carey

A T THE CORE of the American psyche is the belief that hard work, education, and perseverance can overcome any disadvantage of wealth, background, or class. It may even be true. The history of the United States is filled with individuals rising from rural poverty or immigrant ghettos to gain affluence, political power, or Nobel prizes.

These successes are even more striking given the public prejudices arrayed against many of these people. After the great wave of immigration from eastern and southern Europe in the early 1900s, for instance, a *Denver Post* columnist warned that New York City had become "a cesspool" of "immigrant trash." Social scientists "proved" that the new Americans, many of them Jewish, would drag down the nation's average intelligence, since they scored lower on IQ tests.

But a funny thing happened on the way to the future. Within decades, the "trash" was not only rising through society but also was showing remarkable gains in the supposedly fixed measure of IQ. In fact, Jews now score some 10 points higher than the white average.

Consider another group of "new" Americans, the newly freed blacks of the late 1800s. Historians say they shared the immigrants' belief in education as the path to advancement. By World War I, Northern

John Carey is a regular contributor to *Business Week*. This review originally appeared in *Business Week*, November 7, 1994.

blacks were outscoring Southern whites on Army IQ tests. Haverford College's Roger Lane has found that black literacy rates in Philadelphia quadrupled in the 1890s. Rising achievement led to blacks' first major political demand—that the city award jobs based on written exams.

But even though blacks performed better than white rivals on the tests, achievement didn't open doors. Philadelphia refused to hire accordingly, leaving "trained black doctors working as bellhops," says Lane. "As a result, the hunger for education got beaten out."

These facts are only hinted at in *The Bell Curve*, the controversial new book by conservative American Enterprise Institute Fellow Charles Murray and late Harvard psychologist Richard J. Herrnstein. The authors admit "immigrants have sometimes shown large increases" in IQ, and that a lack of education can cause poor test performance. But their thesis is exactly the opposite: IQ scores, they say, are largely immutable and represent innate intelligence.

The ranks of the cognitively inferior, they assert, are disproportionately filled with blacks, Latinos, and today's immigrants. And that's a serious disadvantage, because low IQ—not education or opportunity—is the key factor underlying problems ranging from poverty and criminal behavior to out-of-wedlock births and being a bad parent. "Success and failure . . . are increasingly a matter of the genes that people inherit," the authors warn. That people can get ahead by plain hard work is "no longer true."

Worse, they add, growth of the dumb population may already be dragging America down. All of this is "uncomfortable" truth that the authors purport to be bravely revealing. To deny it, they say, is to cave in to political correctness.

There are grains of truth—and much cleverness—in this argument. People differ in a wide range of talents and abilities, and being smart is unquestionably an advantage. Moreover, the authors deserve credit for venturing provocative statements about social problems. They argue persuasively that many schools fail to challenge students, that affirmative action has undermined the perceived legitimacy of college degrees for minorities, and that America is increasingly split between haves and have-nots.

But *The Bell Curve*'s message—that IQ is destiny—is not just politically incorrect, it's a breathtakingly wrongheaded interpretation of the underlying science. In fact, there's a grim sport for sharp-eyed readers in spotting the weak links, misrepresentations, and logical inconsistencies that riddle the supposedly objective analysis of the data.

Consider the book's assertion that IQ scores reflect fundamental cognitive ability and can be equated with "maturity . . . and personal competence." That's a huge reach. A number of social scientists, brusquely dismissed by the authors, say intelligence is many-faceted and that IQ represents but one component. Yale's Robert J. Sternberg, for example, has constructed tests to measure "practical intelligence"—how well people deal with real-life situations. Scores on these tests predict job performance better than IQ tests—and scores don't differ among ethnic groups. What does IQ really represent? As the authors themselves point out, it seems to measure thinking speed.

Murray and Herrnstein forget to note other uncomfortable truths. Most of their key data come from a long-term study of some 12,000 people who once took an Armed Forces aptitude exam. But Pentagon scientists who administer it say the test isn't even an IQ test. Scores rise with the amount of schooling test-takers have, notes Bernard M. Baruch College's June O'Neill, who uses the test to study such issues as workplace discrimination. So it's no surprise that scores predict school performance.

Those who probe the statistics will find that many of the book's claims for the predictive power of IQ are dubious at best. If the average IQ of the United States drops just three points, the authors warn, poverty will jump 11 percent, crime 13 percent, and single motherhood 8 percent. But that assumes that all these measures change with every point difference in IQ. In fact, such negative outcomes rise only with increases in the number of people with very low scores—borderline retarded and below. Even then, they rise only modestly. For the vast majority, big differences in IQ lead to virtually no difference in such key measures as income. After all, the average IQ difference between any pair of siblings is 13 points, about the same as the black/white spread.

Even if we suspend reason and accept the book's belief in IQ, *The Bell Curve* founders on contradictions. Social scientists agree that IQ scores of all groups have risen some 15 points in the last forty years—and the gap between whites and blacks has narrowed. So how can Murray and Herrnstein argue that growing social ills are partly caused by an increase in dumb folks? They admit that disadvantaged children adopted into more affluent and stable families can show big increases in IQ. So why do they insist IQs can rarely be changed? How can they say coaching doesn't raise scores over the long term, then dismiss a big long-term increase in a Milwaukee program as merely a product of coaching? And how can they denigrate the college degrees earned by blacks who matriculate despite lower SAT scores without saying that whites with the same SAT scores—the disadvantaged, perhaps, or children of alumni—are equally undeserving?

What's more, when it comes to key facts such as the high rate of blacks on welfare, the authors have to admit IQ isn't the explanation. They concede, for example, that data suggest "that blacks differ from whites or Latinos in their likelihood of being on welfare for reasons that transcend both poverty and IQ."

There are two inescapable conclusions. One is that IQ scores are not destiny, especially for the vast majority of us—of whatever color—who are not retarded. The other is that *The Bell Curve* is a house of cards constructed to push a political agenda—an attack on affirmative action, the welfare system, and schools that fail the gifted. Those views deserve airing. As Herrnstein and Murray argue, a forthright discussion of these issues might even lead to better social policy.

But to couch their opinions as scientific truth is downright dangerous. *The Bell Curve* could trigger insidious discrimination. A century ago, doors closed on people striving for a better life just because of the color of their skin. Now, the slamming will be justified on the grounds of lower intelligence. That's not the kind of America we want to create.

SKIN-DEEP SCIENCE

Jim Holt

A MONG THE IDEAS that have harmed mankind, one of the most durable and destructive is that the human species is divided into biological units called races and that some races are innately superior to others. At the moment this notion is being resurrected yet again, in a new and seemingly objective guise, by several prominent social scientists. Their argument goes like this. Blacks perform more poorly on IQ tests than whites, so they must be less intelligent. The IQ scores of children correlate with those of their parents, so intelligence must be at least partly governed by genes. Therefore, the IQ difference between blacks and whites has a genetic component that cannot be eliminated by society. A highly sophisticated version of this reasoning can be found in an incendiary new book called *The Bell Curve* by Charles Murray, a fellow of the American Enterprise Institute, and Richard J. Herrnstein, a professor of psychology at Harvard who recently died of cancer.

The topic of racial differences in intelligence today is like the topic of sex in Victorian England, the authors submit. Among friends—in the office, locker room, and dormitory—people say things that would

Jim Holt writes frequently about science and technology for *The New York Times, The Wall Street Journal,* and other publications. This article first appeared in *The New York Times,* October 19, 1994, as "Anti-Social Science?"

be considered racist if uttered in a public forum. "As the gulf widens between public discussion and private opinion," they write, "confusion and error flourish."

What the authors fail to mention is that it is social scientists like them who have been responsible for much of the "confusion and error." Psychometry—the measurement of mental faculties like intelligence—has a long and farcical history, one driven by irrational convictions about racial superiority. Among its discoveries over the last century and a half are that Jews are not really very smart, that Mediterranean peoples are genetically inferior to Nordic ones, and that the average mental age of white U.S. enlistees in World War I was thirteen.

That such findings can now be seen to be nonsense does not, of course, mean that the conclusions like those in *The Bell Curve* should be dismissed out of hand, for genuine science sometimes sprouts from the manure of pseudoscience and quackery. But it does suggest that we should be extremely skeptical of claims that whites are on average smarter than blacks, that Japanese and Chinese are smarter than whites, and that these differences are writ immutably in our genes. It also suggests that we should take a look at what the natural sciences—biology and genetics, as against the more dubious field of psychometry—have to say about racial differences.

And here is what we learn when we do. First, the human species most likely arose only a hundred thousand years or so ago—the day before yesterday in evolutionary time. That means that any differences among the races must have emerged since then. Superficial adaptations like skin color can evolve very quickly, in a matter of several thousand years. Changes in brain structure and capacity take far longer—on the order of hundreds of thousands of years. Moreover, there is no evidence for such changes since *Homo sapiens* first appeared on the fossil record. Innate differences in intelligence among the races have simply not had enough time to evolve.

Second, genetic diversity among the races is minuscule. Molecular biologists can now examine genes in different geographical populations. What they have found is that the overwhelming majority of the variation observed—more than 85 percent—is among individuals within the same race. Only a tiny residue distinguishes Europeans from Africans from Asians. This means that Patrick Buchanan has more in common genetically with many Xhosas and Outer Mongolians than he does with, say, Prince Charles.

Mr. Murray and Mr. Herrnstein respond by insisting that "some ethnic groups nonetheless differ genetically for sure, otherwise they would not have differing skin colors or hair textures. . . . The question remaining is whether the intellectual differences overlap the genetic differences to any extent." But with hundreds of human genes now mapped, it has become apparent that patterns of variation in the outwardly visible traits by which we distinguish the races are independent of those in other genetically determined traits. Biologically speaking, a person's color reveals very little indeed about what's beneath his skin.

So, while all men may not be created equal when it comes to cognitive abilities, it would seem that all races are. How then do we account for the sizable gap in measured IQ (some 15 points on average) that seems to separate American blacks and whites?

Mr. Murray and Mr. Herrnstein are adept at rebutting many of the conventional explanations for the discrepancy—that IQ tests are culturally biased, that poverty and racism alone are to blame. They and many fellow researchers have gone to heroic lengths to disentangle nature from nurture, striving to show that environmental factors explain only a small part of the racial gap. But they have not gone far enough. Perhaps that is owing to their rather naive understanding of the relation between genes and the physical embodiment of IQ, the brain. Genes encode only a sketchy blueprint of our cortical hardware. Even identical twins, who are exact genetic clones of each other, have somewhat dissimilar brains at birth—a consequence of the different patterns of stimulation they were exposed to in the womb, which give rise to different neuronal connections.

The importance of this prenatal "hard-wiring" for a child's future intellectual prospects is only beginning to be appreciated. What is amply known, though, is that African-Americans are enormously disadvantaged when it comes to the quality of prenatal care they receive; a black mother is three times as likely as a white mother to have a low-birth-weight baby. This is one environmental effect (and a correctable one) that, to the social scientist, looks like a matter of genetics.

Of all the interracial comparisons of intelligence that have been made over the years, only one effectively controlled for differences in pre- and postnatal care. That was a 1961 study of the out-of-wedlock offspring of black and of white U.S. soldiers and German mothers during the Allied occupation. The very small IQ difference observed actually favored the black children. Put this together with adoption studies showing that an early move from a deprived home to an advantaged one can boost a child's IQ by 20 points, and the conviction expressed in *The Bell Curve* that public policy is impotent to redress IQ inequalities begins to betray a lack of imagination, if not will.

Are racial differences in intelligence natural, innate, and unchangeable, as some social scientists like to believe? Or can such differences be made to shrink and ultimately disappear with a better understanding of how the early environment determines the formation of our cognitive apparatus, as the conclusions of natural scientists seem to indicate? I am putting my money on the natural scientists. After all, at least one occupational study has shown that they have the higher IQs.

SCHOLARLY BRINKMANSHIP

Howard Gardner

DESPITE its largely technical nature, *The Bell Curve* has already secured a prominent place in American consciousness as a "big," "important," and "controversial" book. In a manner more befitting a chronicle of sex or spying, the publisher withheld it from potential critics until the date of publication. Since then it has grabbed front-page attention in influential publications, ridden the talk-show waves, and catalyzed academic conferences and dinner table controversies. With the untimely death of the senior author, psychologist Richard Herrnstein, attention has focused on his collaborator Charles Murray (described by *The New York Times Magazine* as "the most dangerous conservative in America"). But this volume clearly bears the mark of both men.

The Bell Curve is a strange work. Some of the analysis and a good deal of the tone are reasonable. Yet the science in the book was questionable when it was proposed a century ago, and it has now been completely supplanted by the development of the cognitive sciences and neurosciences. The policy recommendations of the book are also exotic, neither following from the analyses nor justified on their own

Howard Gardner is a professor of education and co-director of Project Zero at Harvard University; his new book, *Leading Minds*, will be published in 1995. This review appeared in *The American Prospect*, Winter 1994, titled "Cracking Open the IQ Box."

terms. The book relies heavily on innuendo, some of it quite frightening in its implications. The authors wrap themselves in a mantle of courage, while coyly disavowing the extreme conclusions that their own arguments invite. The tremendous attention lavished on the book probably comes less from the science or the policy proposals than from the subliminal messages and attitudes it conveys.

Taken at face value, *The Bell Curve* proceeds in straightforward fashion. Herrnstein and Murray summarize decades of work in psychometrics and policy studies and report the results of their own extensive analyses of the National Longitudinal Survey of Labor Market Experience of Youth, a survey that began in 1979 and has followed more than 12,000 Americans aged 14–22. They argue that studies of trends in American society have steadfastly ignored a smoking gun: the increasing influence of measured intelligence (IQ). As they see it, individuals have always differed in intelligence, at least partly because of heredity, but these differences have come to matter more because social status now depends more on individual achievement. The consequence of this trend is the bipolarization of the population, with high-IQ types achieving positions of power and prestige, low-IQ types being consigned to the ranks of the impoverished and the impotent. In the authors' view, the combined ranks of the poor, the criminal, the unemployed, the illegitimate (parents and offspring), and the uncivil harbor a preponderance of unintelligent individuals. Herrnstein and Murray are disturbed by these trends, particularly by the apparently increasing number of people who have babies but fail to become productive citizens. The authors foresee the emergence of a brutal society in which "the rich and the smart" (who are increasingly the same folks) band together to isolate and perhaps even reduce the ranks of those who besmirch the social fabric.

Scientifically, this is a curious work. If science is narrowly conceived as simply carrying out correlations and regression equations, the science in *The Bell Curve* seems, at least on a first reading, unexceptional. (My eyebrows were raised, though, by the authors' decision to introduce a new scoring system after they had completed an entire draft of the manuscript. They do not spell out the reasons for this switch, nor do they indicate whether the results were different using the earlier system.) But science goes far beyond the number-crunching stereotype; scientific inquiry involves the conceptualization of problems, decisions about the kinds of data to secure and analyze, the consideration of alternative explanations, and, above all, the chain of reasoning from assumptions to findings to inferences. In this sense, the science in *The Bell Curve* is more like special pleading, based on a biased reading of the data, than a carefully balanced assessment of current knowledge.

Moreover, there is never a direct road from research to policy. One could look at the evidence presented by Herrnstein and Murray, as many of a liberal persuasion have done, and recommend targeted policies of intervention to help the dispossessed. Herrnstein and Murray, of course, proceed in quite the opposite direction. They report that efforts to raise intelligence have been unsuccessful and they oppose, on both moral and pragmatic grounds, programs of affirmative action or other ameliorative measures at school or in the workplace. Their ultimate solution, such as it is, is the resurrection of a world they attribute to the Founding Fathers. These wise men acknowledged large differences in human abilities and did not try artificially to bring about equality of results; instead, Herrnstein and Murray tell us, they promoted a society in which each individual had his or her place in a local neighborhood and was accordingly valued as a human being with dignity.

The Bell Curve is well argued and admirably clear in its exposition. The authors are, for the most part, fair and thorough in laying out alternative arguments and interpretations. Presenting views that set a new standard for political incorrectness, they do so in a way that suggests their own overt discomfort—real or professed. Rush Limbaugh and Jesse Helms might like the implications, but they would hardly emulate the hedges and the "more in sorrow" statements. At least some of the authors' observations make sense. For example, their critique of the complex and often contradictory messages embodied in certain governmental social policies is excellent, and their recommendations for simpler rules are appropriate.

Yet I became increasingly disturbed as I read and reread this 800-page work. I gradually realized I was encountering a style of thought previously unknown to me: scholarly brinkmanship. Whether concerning an issue of science, policy, or rhetoric, the authors come dangerously close to embracing the most extreme positions, yet in the end shy away from doing so. Discussing scientific work on intelligence, they never quite say that intelligence is all-important and tied to one's genes; yet they signal that this is their belief and that readers ought to embrace the same conclusions. Discussing policy, they never quite say that affirmative action should be totally abandoned or that childbearing or immigration by those with low IQs should be curbed; yet they signal their sympathy for these options and intimate that readers ought to consider these possibilities. Finally, the rhetoric of the book encourages readers to identify with the IQ elite and to distance themselves from the dispossessed in what amounts to an invitation to class warfare. Scholarly brinkmanship encourages the reader to draw the strongest conclusions, while allowing the authors to disavow this intention.

IN A TEXTBOOK published in 1975, Herrnstein and his colleague Roger Brown argued that the measurement of intelligence has been the greatest achievement of twentieth-century scientific psychology. Psychometricians can make a numerical estimate of a person's intelligence that remains surprisingly stable after the age of five or so, and much convergent evidence suggests that the variations of this measure of intelligence in a population are determined significantly (at least 60 percent) by inheritable factors. As Herrnstein and Murray demonstrate at great length, measured intelligence correlates with success in school, ultimate job status, and the likelihood of becoming a member of the cognitively entitled establishment.

But correlation is not causation, and it is possible that staying in school causes IQ to go up (rather than vice versa) or that both IQ and schooling reflect some third causative factor, such as parental attention, nutrition, social class, or motivation. Indeed, nearly every one of Herrnstein and Murray's reported correlations can be challenged on such grounds. Yet Herrnstein and Murray make a persuasive case that measured intelligence—or, more technically, g, the central, general component of measured intelligence—does affect one's ultimate niche in society.

But the links between genetic inheritance and IQ, and then between IQ and social class, are much too weak to draw the inference that genes determine an individual's ultimate status in society. Nearly all of the reported correlations between measured intelligence and societal outcomes explain at most 20 percent of the variance. In other words, over 80 percent (and perhaps over 90 percent) of the factors contributing to socioeconomic status lie beyond measured intelligence.

One's ultimate niche in society is overwhelmingly determined by non-IQ factors, ranging from initial social class to luck. And since close to half of one's IQ is due to factors unrelated to heredity, well over 90 percent of one's fate does not lie in one's genes. Inherited IQ is at most a paper airplane, not a smoking gun.

Indeed, even a sizable portion of the data reported or alluded to in *The Bell Curve* runs directly counter to the story that the authors apparently wish to tell. They note that IQ has gone up consistently around the world during this century—15 points, as great as the current difference between blacks and whites. Certainly this spurt cannot be explained by genes! They note that when blacks move from rural southern to urban northern areas, their intelligence scores also rise; that black youngsters adopted in households of higher socioeconomic status demonstrate improved performance on aptitude and achievement tests; and that differences between the performances of black and white students have declined on tests ranging from the Scholastic Aptitude Test to the National Assessment of Educational Practice. In an extremely telling phrase, Herrnstein and Murray say that the kind of direct verbal interaction between white middle-class parents and their preschool children "amounts to excellent training for intelligence tests." On that basis, they might very well have argued for expanding Head Start, but instead they question the potential value of any effort to change what they regard as the immutable power of inherited IQ.

The psychometric faith in IQ testing and Herrnstein and Murray's analysis are based on assumptions that emerged a century ago, when Alfred Binet devised the first test of intelligence for children. Since 1900, biology, psychology, and anthropology have enormously advanced our understanding of the mind. But like biologists who ignore DNA or physicists who do not consider quantum mechanical effects, Herrnstein and Murray pay virtually no attention to these insights, and as a result, there is a decidedly anachronistic flavor to their entire discussion.

Intoxication with the IQ test is a professional hazard among psychometricians. I have known many psychometricians who feel that the science of testing will ultimately lay bare all the secrets of the mind. Some believe a difference of even a few points in an IQ or SAT score discloses something important about an individual's or group's intellectual merits. The world of intelligence testers is peculiarly self-contained. Like the chess player who thinks that all games (if not the world itself) are like chess, or the car salesman who speaks only of horsepower, the psychometrician may come to believe that all of importance in the mind can be captured by a small number of items in the Stanford-Binet test or by one's ability to react quickly and accurately to a pattern of lights displayed on a computer screen.

Though Herrnstein deviated sharply in many particulars from his mentor B. F. Skinner, the analysis in *The Bell Curve* is Skinnerian in a fundamental sense: It is a "black box analysis." Along with most psychometricians, Herrnstein and Murray convey the impression that one's intelligence simply exists as an innate fact of life—unanalyzed and unanalyzable—as if it were hidden in a black box. Inside the box there is a single number, IQ, which determines vast social consequences.

OUTSIDE the closed world of psychometricians, however, a more empirically sensitive and scientifically compelling understanding of human intelligence has emerged in the past hundred years. Many authorities have challenged the notion of a single intelligence or even the concept of intelligence altogether. Let me mention just a few examples. (The works by Stephen Ceci and Robert Sternberg, as well as my own, discuss many more.)

Sternberg and his colleagues have studied valued kinds of intellect not measured by IQ tests, such as practical intelligence—the kind of skills and capacities valued in the workplace. They have shown that effective managers are able to pick up various tacit messages at the workplace and that this crucial practical sensitivity is largely unrelated to psychometric intelligence. Ralph Rosnow and his colleagues have developed measures of social or personal intelligence—the capacities to figure out how to operate in complex human situations—and have again demonstrated that these are unrelated to the linguistic and logical skills tapped in IQ tests.

Important new work has been carried out on the role of training in the attainment of expertise. Anders Ericsson and his colleagues have demonstrated that training, not inborn talent, accounts for much of experts' performances; the ultimate achievement of chess players or musicians depends (as your mother told you) on regular practice over many years. Ceci and others have documented the extremely high degree of expertise that can be achieved by randomly chosen individuals; for example, despite low measured intelligence, handicappers at the racetrack successfully employ astonishingly complex multiplicative models. A growing number of researchers have argued that while IQ tests may provide a reasonable measure of certain linguistic and mathematical forms of thinking, other equally important kinds of intelligence, such as spatial, musical, or personal, are ignored (this is the subject of much of my own work). In short, the closed world of intelligence is being opened up.

Accompanying this rethinking of the concept of intelligence(s), there is growing skepticism that short paper-and-pencil tests can get at important mental capacities. Just as "performance examinations" are coming to replace multiple-choice tests in schools, many scientists, among them Lauren Resnick and Jean Lave, have probed the capacities of individuals to solve problems "on the scene" rather than in a testing room, with pencil and paper. Such studies regularly confirm that one can perform at an expert level in a natural or simulated setting (such as bargaining in a market or simulating the role of a city manager) even with a low IQ, while a high IQ cannot in itself substitute for training, expertise, motivation, and creativity. Rather than the pointless exercise of attempting to raise psychometric IQ (on which Herrnstein and Murray perseverate), this research challenges us to try to promote the actual behavior and skills that we want our future citizens to have. After all, if we found that better athletes happen to have larger shoe sizes, we would hardly try to enlarge the feet of the less athletic.

SCIENTIFIC UNDERSTANDING of biological and cultural aspects of cognition also grows astonishingly with every passing decade. Virtually no serious natural scientist speaks about genes and environment any longer as if they were opposed. Indeed, every serious investigator accepts the importance of both biological and cultural factors and the need to understand their interactions. Genes regulate all human behavior, but no form of behavior will emerge without the appropriate environmental triggers or supports. Learning alters the way in which genes are expressed.

The development of the individual brain and mind begins in utero, and pivotal alterations in capacity and behavior come about as the result of innumerable events following conception. Hormonal effects in utero, which certainly are environmental, can cause a different profile of cognitive strengths and limitations to emerge. The loss of certain sensory capacities causes the redeployment of brain tissue to new functions; a rich environment engenders the growth of additional cortical connections as well as timely pruning of excess synapses. Compare a child who has a dozen healthy experiences each day in utero and after birth to another child who has a daily diet of a dozen injurious episodes. The cumulative advantage of a healthy prenatal environment and a stimulating postnatal environment is enormous. In the study of IQ, much has been made of studies of identical and fraternal twins. But because of the influences on cognition in utero and during infancy, even such studies cannot decisively distinguish genetic from environmental influences.

Herrnstein and Murray note that measured intelligence is stable only after age five, without drawing the obvious conclusion that the events of the first years of life, not some phlogiston-like g, are the principal culprit. Scores of important and fascinating new findings emerge in neuroscience every year, but scarcely a word of any of this penetrates the Herrnstein and Murray black-box approach.

PRECISELY THE SAME kind of story can be told from the cultural perspective. Cultural beliefs and practices affect the child at least from the moment of birth and perhaps sooner. Even the parents' expectations of their unborn child and their reactions to the discovery of the child's sex have an impact. The family, teachers, and other sources of influence in the culture signal what is important to the growing child, and these messages have both short- and long-term impact. How one thinks about oneself, one's prospects in this world and beyond, and whether one regards intelligence as inborn or acquired—all these shape patterns of activity, attention, and personal investments in learning and self-improvement. Particularly for stigmatized minorities, these signals can wreck any potential for cognitive growth and achievement.

Consider Claude Steele's research on the effects of stereotyping on performance. African-American students perform worse than white students when they are led to believe that the test is an intellectual one and that their race matters, but these differences wash out completely when such "stereotype vulnerable" conditions are removed.

To understand the effects of culture, no study is more seminal than Harold Stevenson and James Stigler's 1992 book *The Learning Gap: Why Our Schools Are Failing and What We Can Learn from Japanese and Chinese Education*. In an analysis that runs completely counter to *The Bell Curve*, Stevenson and Stigler show why Chinese and Japanese students achieve so much more in schools than do Americans. They begin by demonstrating that initial differences in IQ among the three populations are either nonexistent or trivial. But with each passing year, East Asian students raise their edge over Americans, so that by the middle school years, there is virtually no overlap in reading and mathematics performance between the two populations.

Genetics, heredity, and measured intelligence play no role here. East Asian students learn more and score better on just about every kind of measure because they attend school for more days, work harder in school and at home after school, and have better-prepared teachers and more deeply engaged parents who encourage and coach them each day and night. Put succinctly, Americans believe (like Herrnstein and Murray) that if they do not do well, it is because they lack talent or ability; Asians believe it is because they do not work hard enough. As a Japanese aphorism has it, "Fail with five hours of sleep; pass with four." Both predictions tend to be self-fulfilling. As educator Derek Bok once quipped, Americans score near to last on almost all measures save one: When you ask Americans how they *think* they are doing, they profess more satisfaction than any other group. Like Herrnstein and Murray, most Americans have not understood that what distinguishes the cultures is the pattern of self-understanding and motivation, especially the demands that we make on ourselves (and on those we care about) and the lessons we draw from success and failure—not the structure of genes or the shape of the brain.

LIKE MURRAY'S earlier book *Losing Ground*, *The Bell Curve* views most recent governmental attempts at intervention as doing more harm than good and questions the value of welfare payments, affirmative action programs, indeed, any kind of charitable disposition toward the poor. To improve education, Herrnstein and Murray recommend vouchers to encourage a private market and put forth the remarkable proposal that the government should shift funds from disadvantaged to gifted children. And while they do not openly endorse policies that will limit breeding among the poor or keep the dispossessed from our shores, they stimulate us to consider such possibilities.

Nowhere did I find the Herrnstein and Murray analysis less convincing than in their treatment of crime. Incarcerated offenders, they point out, have an average IQ of 92, eight points below the national mean. They go on to suggest that since lower cognitive aptitude is associated with higher criminal activity, there would be less crime if IQs were higher. But if intelligence levels have at worst been constant, why did crime increase so much between the 1960s and 1980s? Why have crime rates leveled off and declined in the last few years? Does low IQ also explain the embarrassing prevalence of white-collar crime in business and politics or the recent sudden rise in crime in Russia? Astonishingly, no other influences, such as the values promoted by the mass media, play any role in Herrnstein and Murray's analysis.

Considering how often they remind us that the poor and benighted at society's bottom are incapable through no fault of their own, Herrnstein and Murray's hostility to efforts to reduce poverty might seem, at the very least, ungenerous. But, at the book's end, the authors suddenly turn from their supposed unblinking realism to fanciful nostalgia. Having consigned the dispossessed to a world where they can achieve little because of their own meager intellectual gifts, Herrnstein and Murray call on the society as a whole to reconstitute itself: to become (once again?) a world of neighborhoods where each individual is made to feel important, valued, and dignified. They devote not a word to how this return to lost neighborhoods is to be brought about or how those with low IQs and no resources could suddenly come to feel worthwhile. It is as if we were watching scenes from *Apocalypse Now* or *Natural Born Killers,* only to blink for a minute and to find the movie concluding with images from a situation comedy or *Mr. Rogers' Neighborhood.*

PERHAPS THE MOST troubling aspect of the book is its rhetorical stance. This is one of the most stylistically divisive books that I have ever read. Despite occasional avowals of regret and the few utopian pages at the end, Herrnstein and Murray set up an us/them dichotomy that eventually culminates in an us-*against*-them opposition.

Who are "we"? Well, we are the people who went to Harvard (as the jacket credits both of the authors) or attended similar colleges and read books like this. We are the smart, the rich, the powerful, the worriers.

And who are "they"? They are the pathetic others, those who could not get into good schools and who don't cut it on IQ tests and SATs. While perhaps perfectly nice people, they are simply not going to make it in tomorrow's complex society and will probably end up cordoned off from the rest of us under the tutelage of a vicious custodial state. The hope for a civil society depends on a miraculous return of the spirit of the Founding Fathers to re-create the villages of Thomas Jefferson or George Bailey (as played by Jimmy Stewart) or Beaver Cleaver (as played by Jerry Mather).

How is this rhetorical polarization achieved? At literally dozens of points in the book, Herrnstein and Murray seek to stress the extent to which they and the readers resemble one another and differ from those unfortunate souls who cause our society's problems. Reviewing the bell curve of the title, Herrnstein and Murray declare, in a representative passage: "You—meaning the self-selected person who has read this far into this book—live in a world that probably looks nothing like the figure. In all likelihood, almost all of your friends and professional associates belong to that top Class I slice. Your friends and associates who you consider to be unusually slow are probably somewhere in Class II."

Why is this so singularly off-putting? I would have thought it unnecessary to say, but if people as psychometrically smart as Messrs. Herrnstein and Murray did not "get it," it is safer to be explicit. High IQ doesn't make a person one whit better than anybody else. And if we are to have any chance of a civil and humane society, we had better avoid the smug self-satisfaction of an elite that reeks of arrogance and condescension.

Though there are seven appendices, spanning over 100 pages, and nearly 200 pages of footnotes, bibliography, and index, one element is notably missing from this tome: a report on any program of social intervention that works. For example, Herrnstein and Murray never mention Lisbeth Schorr's *Within Our Reach: Breaking the Cycle of Disadvantage*, a book that was prompted in part by *Losing Ground*. Schorr chronicles a number of social programs that have made a genuine difference in education, child health service, family planning, and other lightning-rod areas of our society. And to the ranks of the programs chronicled in Schorr's book, many new names can now be added. Those who have launched Interfaith Educational Agencies, City Year, Teach for America, Jobs for the Future, and hundreds of other service agencies have not succumbed to the sense of futility and abandonment of the poor that the Herrnstein and Murray book promotes.

When I recently debated Murray on National Public Radio, he was reluctant to accept the possibility that programs of intervention might dissolve or significantly reduce differences in intelligence. If he did, the entire psychometric edifice that he and Herrnstein have constructed would collapse. While claiming to confront facts that others refuse to see, they are blind to both contradictory evidence and the human consequences of their work. Herrnstein and Murray, of course, have the right to their conclusions. But if they truly believe that blacks will not be deeply hurt by the hints that they are genetically inferior, they are even more benighted—dare I say, even more stupid—than I have suggested.

It is callous to write a work that casts earlier attempts to help the disadvantaged in the least favorable light, strongly suggests that nothing positive can be done in the present climate, contributes to an us-against-them mentality, and then posits a miraculous cure. High intelligence and high creativity are desirable. But unless they are linked to some kind of a moral compass, their possessors might best be consigned to an island of glass-bead game players, with no access to the mainland.

INNUMERACY

K. C. Cole

T HERE IS A DIRECT correlation, mathematicians have found, between children's achievement on math tests and shoe size. A clear signal that big feet make you smarter? And what about the striking link, documented in the early part of this century, between increasing pollution and rising birthrates in the Los Angeles Basin? Does breathing bad air make people fertile? And what, for that matter, should be made of studies that connect skin color with IQ scores? Does that mean that race can make you dumb or smart?

Certainly that is what the authors of *The Bell Curve*—Charles Murray of the American Enterprise Institute and the late Richard Herrnstein of Harvard—would have us believe. Their controversial book trots out an arsenal of mathematical artillery to bolster their proposition that intelligence is mostly inherited, that blacks have less of it, and that little can be done about it. Reviewers—not to mention readers—have admitted to shell shock in the face of such a barrage of statistics, graphs, and multiple regression analysis. And surely numbers cannot lie. Or so most people believe.

K. C. Cole is a science writer for the *Los Angeles Times*. Her article, in slightly abridged form, appeared on the front page of the *Los Angeles Times* on January 4, 1995, entitled "Statistics Can Throw Us a Curve."

Mathematicians, however, know better. Correlation, they say, does not necessarily mean causation. Correlation means only that one thing has a relationship with another. Causes sometimes can get lost in a tangled web of competing factors so impenetrable that even sophisticated mathematical sifting fails to sort them out.

Individual studies showing one result can be contradicted by larger studies analyzing the same data. Background statistical noise drowns out signals as readily as radio static garbles one's favorite song. To top it all, some scientists even suggest that humans ultimately may be ill suited for seeing through the veil of statistics to the real relationships of cause and effect. These numerical obfuscations explain, among other things, why studies can indicate one day that oat bran lowers cholesterol, and a few years later, show that it has no more effect than good old refined wheat.

The stories told in numbers have profound effects on the design of personal and social agendas. Sometimes statistical correlations point the way to significant findings that result in major policy changes. For example, the correlation between lung cancer and smoking motivated scientists to find direct causal links.

But misinterpreting statistics—even inadvertently—is an old problem that goes far beyond matters of race and IQ. In fact, it's difficult to find an area of life where it doesn't apply. "The truth is, you can make a correlation between almost anything," said Temple University mathematician John Allen Paulos, whose research revealed the connection between feet and ability in math. "It's the mystique of precision." Psychologist and statistician Rand Wilcox of the University of Southern California concurred: "Correlation doesn't tell you anything about causation. But it's a mistake that even researchers make."

Indeed, correlations may be nothing more telling than coincidence. Or timing. For example, studies routinely reveal a strong statistical link between divorced parents and troubled adolescents. But it is also true that adolescents are attracted to trouble no matter what parents do. *The Bell Curve*, some experts say, is a more complex variation on this theme. "It's quite possible that two things move together, but both are being moved by a third factor," Stanford statistician Ingram Olkin said.

Paulos points out that almost anything that correlates with high IQ is also associated with high income. This conclusion comes as no surprise, given that affluent parents can more easily afford better schools, more books, and computers and generally raise more healthy, better-nourished children. Studies of IQ and race, experts say, may mask the stronger relationship between white skin and wealth. "The most reasonable argument against *The Bell Curve*," Paulos said, "is that disentangling these factors may be impossible."

Medical studies are rife with correlations that may or may not be meaningful. Several years ago, according to Wilcox, a study concluded that Japan's low-fat diet was correlated with a high incidence of stomach cancer compared with U.S. rates. "The speculation was that our high-fat diet somehow prevented stomach cancer," Wilcox said. "Then it turned out that it wasn't the low-fat diet [that contributed to cancer]. It was soy sauce."

Mark Lipsey of Vanderbilt University is involved in a study of the relationship between alcohol use and violent behavior. "People believe that alcohol is causative," he said. "But the research base is not adequate to support that conclusion. It may be that the same kind of people who are prone to violence are prone to alcohol abuse." Sometimes a seemingly causal factor is a "proxy" for something else, he said. Many gender differences fall into this category. A number of studies show differences in the math abilities of boys and girls. "It's obviously not the gonads," he said. "It would be hard to link that with math ability."

Instead, some experts say, society has a way of subtly prodding each sex in a certain direction. Racing Hot Wheels, for example, teaches boys about velocity, momentum, and spatial relationships, while playing house teaches girls to be passive. Teachers encourage boys to be more analytical, girls to be "good."

Even studies of twins that purport to prove inheritance of behavioral characteristics may be explainable by other factors. Genetics may not be the main reason that identical twins raised apart seem to share so many tastes and habits, said Richard Rose, a professor of medical genetics at Indiana University. "You're comparing individuals who grew up in the same epoch, whether they're related or not," said Rose, who is collaborating on a study of 16,000 pairs of twins. "If you asked strangers born on the same day about their political views, food preferences, athletic heroes, clothing choices, you'd find lots of similarities. It has nothing to do with genetics."

Comparing more than one factor always complicates the issue. When one is dealing with income, age, race, IQ, and gender, the effects of these co-variants, as the statisticians call them, can be almost insurmountable. Impressive-sounding statistical methods such as multiple regression analysis are said to eliminate this confusion by controlling for certain variables, erasing their effects. To see what effect shoe size really has on math scores, one might control for the influence of grade level, which always would confuse the results; only a comparison of children in the same grade would be meaningful. But mathematically erasing influences that shape life as pervasively as race, income, and gender is far more difficult. "There are lots of ways to get rid of [these variables]," Wilcox said, "but there are also a million ways that [the methods] can go wrong."

The Bell Curve overflows with statistical analyses that purport to control for numerous variables. The income difference between blacks and whites wouldn't be so extreme, the authors argue, if only the IQs of blacks were as high as those of whites. Using regression analysis, they control for IQ, effectively seeing what would happen if it were equal for both groups. This mathematical manipulation, the authors say, reduces the difference between poverty rates for blacks and whites by 77 percent, an impressively precise statistic. This suggests, they say, that income differences are primarily the result of IQ rather than of a family's economic status.

But mathematicians like Stanford's Olkin take a more skeptical view of what it means to control for anything. "It's a bad term because it can mean many different things," he said. "It can help you predict, but it doesn't help you determine causality." Knowing who goes to church in a community, he said, can help predict who gets burglarized—because "people who go to church frequently leave their [home] doors open. But it doesn't mean that you cause burglaries by going to church." Even if the statisticians could somehow unweave this web, "it's still just glorified correlation," Paulos said. "You still don't know anything about causes."

The best analysis of what they see as the statistical sleight of hand in *The Bell Curve*, Olkin and other experts said, was done by Harvard professor Stephen Jay Gould, who has written volumes about attempts to subvert science for the purpose of "proving" that one race, gender, or ethnic group is superior. Gould argues that the way *The Bell Curve* uses multiple regression analysis to "prove" the strong correlation between IQ and poverty violates all statistical norms. In particular, he said, the graphs in *The Bell Curve* do not show the strength of these correlations, which turn out to be very weak. "Indeed, very little of the variation in social factors," he said, is explained by either IQ or parents' socioeconomic status. Although *The Bell Curve*'s authors acknowledge in the book that some of the correlations are weak, they say they are strong enough to use as a basis for their conclusions about race and intelligence.

Comparing groups—as *The Bell Curve* compares blacks and whites—complicates the matter even further. Because you can't compare everyone in one group with everyone in another, most studies compare averages. And "average" is about the slipperiest mathematical concept ever to slide into popular consciousness.

Let's say the payroll of an office of fifteen workers is $1,977,500—and the boss brags that the average salary is about $131,833. But what if the boss takes home $1 million, pays her husband $500,000 as vice president, and pays two other vice presidents $200,000 each? That means the average salary of the other workers is far less. Yet nothing is technically wrong with the math.

Rather, something is wrong with the choice of "average." In this case, using the average known as the arithmetical "mean" (dividing the total by the number of workers) disguises gross disparities. The median (the salary of the person in the middle of the range of employees) would provide the more realistic "average"—$10,000. One could also use the mode, or most common number in the list—$5,000.

A bell curve plots the so-called normal distribution of probabilities. In a perfect bell curve, the mean, median, and mode coincide, so it does not matter which "average" is used. In plotting IQ scores, for example, the vast majority of people are in the middle of the curve, with the Forrest Gumps and Albert Einsteins almost alone on the tails. But the assumption that the distribution is normal is "almost never true," Wilcox said. "And if you violate that assumption ever so slightly, it can have an unusually large impact. I could draw a curve that would look exactly like [the perfect bell curve], but it could have a very different meaning." The difference of fifteen points between the mean IQs of blacks and whites, as proposed in *The Bell Curve*, could be very misleading, Wilcox said. "The median could be a lot smaller," he said. "Even the title—*The Bell Curve*—is a red flag, because it assumes a perfectly normal distribution. And no group is normal. If you have one unusual person, that can have an unusually large impact."

Recently, statisticians have discovered yet another reason to use caution in reviewing studies. A technique known as meta-analysis—an analysis of analyses that pools data from many studies on the same subject—can produce results that apparently contradict many of the individual studies. Hundreds of studies concluded that delinquency prevention programs did negligible good. But a meta-analysis by Lipsey showed a small but real positive effect: a 10 percent reduction in juvenile crime. At the same time, he found that "scare 'em straight" programs led to higher delinquency rates compared with those of control groups.

Meta-analysis works, Lipsey explained, by clearing the background "noise" that comes from doing research in the real world, instead of in a laboratory. A teenager could have a bad memory or decide he doesn't trust the interviewer; or the interviewer could have an off day. Even objective measures such as arrest records have statistical noise, Lipsey said. "That may vary from officer to officer. It's not just a function of how the kid does." Sampling errors are common, he said. "From the luck of the draw, you get a group of kids that is particularly responsive or resistant. And all those quirks come through in that study." Individual studies, amid this buzz, may not find a statistically significant effect. By pooling data with meta-analysis, however, "the noise begins to cancel out," Lipsey said. "Suddenly you begin to see things that were in the studies all along but were drowned out."

Another dramatic reversal in the story numbers tell came in a meta-analysis released in April 1994 on school funding's effect on pupil performance. Previously, studies suggested that pouring money into teacher salaries and smaller class size made a negligible difference. But when Larry Hedges of the University of Chicago reviewed several dozen studies conducted between 1954 and 1980, he found that money made a big difference. "People who didn't want to pay more for schools used to cite studies showing that funding didn't make any difference," he said. "So these results were very influential."

In the end, a correlation is no more than a hint that a relationship might exist. Without a plausible mechanism—that is, a way that one thing might cause another—it's practically useless. Therefore, it's unlikely that the surge in Wonderbra sales caused the recent Republican election sweep, even though the trends were closely linked in time. On the other hand, studies linking rising teenage obesity to increased hours of TV viewing at least offer a way to get from cause to effect without straining credibility.

The Bell Curve, critics say, ultimately sinks under the absence of a realistic mechanism for linking race to IQ. Evolution is too slow and the differences between races are too muddled and too small to account for the apparent statistical divergence, according to Gould and others. To do the kinds of experiments necessary to prove the link in humans would be unthinkable, said mathematician William Fleishman of Villanova University. Such research would have to involve random mating and perfectly controlled environments. "Here we seem to have these highly heritable traits," he said. "But what is it we know about what's really important to the successful education of young children?" Every correlation, he said, should come with an automatic disclaimer. "There's a big logical fallacy here. What you need is a mechanism. But the numbers can be oh so seductive."

Curiously, the very reason that people are prone to jump to conclusions based on tenuous correlations may have something to do with humans' genetic endowment, according to Paul Smith, who has been analyzing social statistics since the early 1970s. "You and I don't have a statistical facility in our brains," said Smith, who is at the Children's Defense Fund. "We are primates evolved to gather fruit in the forest and when possible to reproduce, and I think it's marvelous that we can do what we do.

"But we have to exercise almost intolerable discipline to not jump to conclusions. There might be a banana behind that leaf, or it might be the tiger's tail. The one who makes the discrimination best and moves fastest either gets the banana or gets away from the tiger. So this leaping to conclusions is a good strategy given that the choices are simple and nothing complicated is going on.

"But at the level of major social policy choices, [jumping to conclusions] is a serious concern."

In fact, humans as a species are notoriously bad at certain kinds of mathematical reasoning. It's not unusual for people to think they have to invoke psychic powers when only probability is at work. How many people do you have to put into a room to all but guarantee that two will share a birth date? Answer: two dozen should do nicely. (This seems counterintuitive because we automatically think how many people it would take to match our own birthday; when any matched pair is possible, the probability shoots up sharply.)

The size of your sample can also have a wildly deceptive effect. You might be impressed, for example, if I told you that half the cars on my street were BMWs—until you learned that there are only two cars on my street.

Scientists and mathematicians, curiously enough, tend to be wary of data for just these reasons. Social scientists might do well to acquire a similar skepticism, statistical experts say. Especially when more than a banana is at stake. Or as the late physicist Richard Feynman put it: Science turns out to be "a long history of learning how to not fool ourselves."

LIES, DAMNED LIES, AND STATISTICS

Leon J. Kamin

W ITHIN TWO MONTHS of its publication, 400,000 copies of *The Bell Curve* were in print, and Rep. Newt Gingrich of Georgia was elected Speaker of the House of Representatives. Those two events probably represent a correlation, rather than cause and effect, but the book and the congressman have a good deal in common. They let us know, up front, where they are coming from and where they are headed—which turn out to be the same place. We are going back, if they have their way, to a country familiar to Ebenezer Scrooge and Oliver Twist, and to a landscape dotted with orphanages and almshouses.

The publicity barrage with which the book was launched might suggest that *The Bell Curve* has something new to say; it doesn't. The authors, in this most recent eruption of the crude biological determinism that permeates the history of IQ testing, assert that scientific evidence demonstrates the existence of genetically determined differences in intelligence among social classes and races. They cite some 1,000 references from the social and biological sciences, and make a

Leon J. Kamin is professor of psychology at Northeastern University; he is author of *The Science and Politics of IQ*, and with R. C. Lewontin and Steven Rose of *Not in Our Genes*. This is an expanded version of a review that appeared in *Scientific American*, February 1995.

number of suggestions for changing social policies. The pretense is made that there is some logical, "scientific" connection between evidence culled from those cited sources and the authors' policy recommendations. Those policies would not be necessary or humane even if the cited evidence were valid. But I want to concentrate on what I regard as two disastrous failings of the book. First, the caliber of the data cited by Herrnstein and Murray is, at many critical points, pathetic—and their citations of those weak data are often inaccurate. Second, their failure to distinguish between correlation and causation repeatedly leads Herrnstein and Murray to draw invalid conclusions.

I'LL DEAL FIRST, at some length, with an especially troubling example of the quality of the data on which the authors rely. They begin their discussion of racial differences in IQ by assuring us that they "will undertake to confront all the tough questions squarely," and they caution us to "read carefully" as they "probe deeply into the evidence and its meaning." That tough, deep probing leads them to ask, "How Do African-Americans Compare with Blacks in Africa on Cognitive Tests?" Their reasoning is that low African-American IQ scores might be due either to a past history of slavery and discrimination or to genetic factors. Herrnstein and Murray evidently assume that blacks reared in colonial Africa have not been subjected to discrimination. Thus, if low IQ scores of African-Americans are a product of discrimination rather than genes, black Africans should have higher IQs than African-Americans; or so Herrnstein and Murray reason.

To answer the question they have posed, Herrnstein and Murray rely on the authority of Richard Lynn, described as "a leading scholar of racial and ethnic differences," from whose advice they have "benefited especially." They state that Lynn, who in 1991 reviewed eleven African IQ studies, "estimated the median black African IQ to be 75 . . . about ten points *lower* [emphasis added] than the current figure for American blacks." This means, they conclude, that the "special circumstances" of African-Americans cannot explain their low average IQ relative to whites. That leaves genetics free to explain the black-white difference.

But why do black Americans have higher scores than black Africans? Herrnstein and Murray, citing "Owen 1992" in support, write that "the IQ of 'coloured' students in South Africa—of mixed racial background—has been found to be similar to that of American blacks." The implication is clear: the admixture of Caucasian and African genes, taking place in America as well as in South Africa, boosts "coloured" IQ some ten points above that of native Africans. But the claims made about African and coloured IQ levels cannot withstand critical scrutiny.

Lynn's 1991 paper describes a 1989 publication by Ken Owen as "the best single study of Negroid intelligence." That 1989 Owen study compared white, Indian, and black pupils on the "Junior Aptitude Tests"; no coloured pupils were tested. The mean "Negroid" IQ in this "best" study was, according to Lynn, 69. That was also, Lynn wrote, "around the median" IQ found in the eleven studies of "Negroid populations." He therefore suggested 70 as "the approximate mean for pure Negroids." I forbear to comment on Lynn's conclusion that half of all Africans are mentally retarded. (Herrnstein and Murray calculated the median of the eleven studies as 75, and took that value to represent average African IQ. I would like to believe that they added five IQ points to Lynn's estimate because they found 70 to be a ludicrously implausible figure, but I have no supporting evidence.)

But Owen did not in fact assign "IQs" to any of the groups he tested. He merely reported test score differences between groups in terms of standard deviation units. The IQ figure of 69 was concocted by Lynn out of those data. There is, as Owen made clear, no reason to suppose that the low test scores of blacks had much to do with genetics: "language played such an important role and the knowledge of English of the majority of black testees was so poor" that some of the tests proved to be "virtually unusable." The tests assumed that the Zulu pupils were familiar with such things as electrical appliances, microscopes, and "Western type of ladies' accessories." The original plan of research had been to draw the black sample from the same metropolitan areas as the whites and Indians. That was not possible, "owing to the unrest situation," so a black sample was obtained in KwaZulu.

In 1992 Owen reported on a sample of coloured students that had been added to the groups he had tested earlier. A footnote in *The Bell Curve* credits "Owen 1992" (the reference does not appear in the book's bibliography) as showing that South African coloured students have an IQ "similar to that of American blacks"—i.e., about 85. That statement does not accurately characterize Owen's findings.

The test used by Owen in 1992 was the "nonverbal" Raven's Progressive Matrices, thought to be less culturally biased than most other IQ tests. He was now able to compare the performance of coloured students with that of the whites, blacks, and Indians in his 1989 study, since the earlier set of pupils had taken the Matrices as well as the Junior Aptitude Tests. The black pupils, recall, had poor knowledge of English, but Owen felt that instructions for the Matrices "are so easy that they can be explained with gestures."

In any event, Owen's 1992 paper again does not assign "IQs" to the pupils. The mean number of correct responses on the Matrices (out of a possible 60) is given for each group: 45 for whites, 42 for Indians, 37 for coloureds, and 28 for blacks. The test's developer, John Raven, always insisted that Progressive Matrices scores cannot be converted into IQs. The several standardizations of his test indicate only what raw score corresponds to what percentile score. The Matrices scores, unlike IQs, are not symmetrically distributed around their mean (no "bell curve" here). There is thus no meaningful way to convert an average of raw Matrices scores into an IQ, and no comparison with American black IQ is possible.

The percentile score to which the average raw score of a sample corresponds is not the same quantity as the average percentile score of the tested individuals. The skewed distribution of Matrices scores virtually guarantees that, in any sample with a reasonable spread of scores, those two quantities will differ considerably. Further, in Europe and America the average Matrices score has been increasing by about one standard deviation per generation; should one compare African scores to early (low) Western norms or to more recent (high) ones? These considerations did not prevent Lynn from converting average Matrices scores to percentile scores based on an unspecified Western standardization, and then, using the bell curve, transforming the percentile scores to "IQs."

To illustrate what Lynn has done, consider a small "thought experiment." We travel to Africa and give the Matrices test to a large number of children, all aged 13.5. Half of the children have raw scores of only thirteen correct answers, because they do not get the point and are merely guessing on the multiple choice test. The other half do get the point, and all have raw scores of 56. The British standardization of 1979 indicates that those two raw scores fall at the 1st and 99th percentiles, respectively. Thus the average percentile score of the children is 50, corresponding to the exact center of the bell curve. The center of the bell curve, of course, implies an average IQ of 100. But Lynn would seize upon the fact that the average *raw* score was 34.5. That score corresponds to the 8th percentile in the standardization sample. Lynn, consulting the bell curve, would observe that the 8th percentile of a normal distribution corresponds to an IQ of 79, and would report that figure as the average Negroid IQ. Herrnstein and Murray would believe him; he is, after all, their expert.

The remaining studies cited by Lynn, and accepted as valid by Herrnstein and Murray, tell us little about African IQ, but do tell us something about Lynn's scholarship. Thus, one of the eleven entries in Lynn's table of the intelligence of "pure Negroids" indicates that 1,011 Zambians, tested with the Progressive Matrices, had a low average IQ of 75. The source for this quantitative claim is given as "Pons, 1974; Crawford Nutt, 1976." A. L. Pons did test 1,011 Zambian copper miners, whose average number of correct responses was 34. Pons reported on this work orally; his data were summarized in tabular form in a paper by D. H. Crawford-Nutt. Lynn took the Pons data from Crawford-Nutt's paper and converted the number of correct responses into a bogus average IQ of 75. But Lynn chose to ignore entirely the substance of Crawford-Nutt's paper, which reported that 228 black high school students in Soweto had an average of 45 correct responses on the Matrices—*higher* than the mean of 44 achieved by the same-aged white sample on whom the test's norms had been established, and well above the mean of Owen's coloured pupils. We should note that seven of the 11 studies which Lynn did choose to include in his "Negroid" table reported only average Matrices raw scores. The cited IQs are Lynn's inventions. The other studies used tests more clearly dependent on cultural content.

Lynn had earlier, in a 1978 paper, summarized six studies involving African pupils, most again based on the Matrices. The arbitrary "IQs" concocted by Lynn for those six studies ranged between 75 and 88, with a median of 84. There was almost no overlap between the studies selected for inclusion by Lynn in his 1978 and 1991 "summaries." Five of the studies cited in 1978 were omitted from Lynn's 1991 table, by which time African IQ had in his expert judgment plummeted to 69.

I will not mince words. Lynn's distortions and misrepresentations of the data constitute a truly venomous racism, combined with scandalous disregard for scientific objectivity. But to anybody familiar with Lynn's work and background, this comes as no surprise. Lynn is widely known to be an associate editor of the vulgarly racist journal *Mankind Quarterly;* his 1991 paper comparing the intelligence of "Negroids" and "Negroid-Caucasoid hybrids" appeared in its pages. He is a major recipient of financial support from the nativist and eugenically oriented Pioneer Fund. It is a matter of shame and disgrace that two eminent social scientists, fully aware of the sensitivity of the issues they address, take as their scientific tutor Richard Lynn, and accept uncritically his surveys of research. Murray, in a newspaper interview, asserted that he and Herrnstein had not inquired about the "antecedents" of the research they cite. "We used studies that exclusively, to my knowledge, meet the tests of scholarship." What tests of scholarship?

WHATEVER those tests might be, Herrnstein and Murray are not rigorous in applying them, even to the work of reputable scholars. To support their assertion that high IQ is a "preventative" against crime, they cite a Danish study based upon 1,400 boys. That study, they say, reported that sons whose fathers had a "prison record" were six times more likely to have a "prison record" themselves than were sons of fathers with "no police record of any sort." That fact is scarcely surprising, and is open to many different interpretations. But Herrnstein and Murray call attention to a further alleged fact. The sons of fathers with prison records can be regarded as being at "high risk" for imprisonment themselves. Among such high-risk sons, those who had "no police record at all" had IQs 13 points higher than those who "had a police record." Thus, according to Herrnstein and Murray, it is only the less bright among the sons of jailed criminals who themselves acquire police records.

That is not, however, what the Danish study reported. For a *father* to be classified as "severely criminal" he had to have received "at least one prison sentence." That one sentence placed his son into the high-risk category. For a *son* to be classified as "seriously criminal," two quite different definitions were employed by the researchers. To calculate the rate of "serious criminal behavior" among sons, the son—

like the father—need only have received one prison sentence. It was by use of that definition that high-risk sons were six times more likely to be seriously criminal (jailed) than were sons of fathers with no police record. But *to be included among the "seriously criminal" sons whose IQs were studied,* the son had to have received "at least one jail sentence plus an additional offense." With that new definition, the noncriminals among the high-risk sons had a higher IQ than the criminals; no such difference existed among low-risk sons. The 13-point IQ difference cited by Herrnstein and Murray is thus not simply between high-risk sons with and without "a police record."

There is no explanation given by the researchers as to why the definition of sons' criminality was changed when making the IQ analyses. The consequence of the change is that in calculating IQ scores, a son who is merely sentenced to prison for one rape is not counted as a criminal. To earn that designation he will have to rack up a parking ticket as well. To one steeped in the research literature of social science, a possible explanation for this unusual definition of criminality suggests itself. Perhaps if the definition of criminal for the IQ analyses were the same as that used for determining high risk, the data would not support the hypothesis tested by the research. That may not have been the case in this instance; but arbitrary post facto categorizing of data is not unheard of in science.

We should note in any event that most of the "additional offenses" which, when added to a jail sentence, qualified an at-risk son to be IQ tested could not have been very serious. Fully 57 percent of the 1,400 sons had such minor offenses on their records, in the absence of any jail sentence. Parking tickets and littering seem like reasonable candidates. What does a high IQ protect a high-risk Danish son against—committing rape or parking illegally? I don't know, and neither did Herrnstein and Murray.

HERE IS ANOTHER example of mis-citation in *The Bell Curve,* this time part of the effort to convince readers that blacks are less intelligent than whites. Herrnstein and Murray maintain that "smarter people process [information] faster than less smart people," and that reaction time, requiring "no conscious thought," indexes an underlying "neurologic processing speed . . . akin to the speed of the microprocessor in a computer." "Reaction time" is the time elapsing between onset of a signal light and a subject's lifting a finger to initiate a required response; "movement time" is the additional time needed to execute the response. Herrnstein and Murray report, "In modern studies, reaction time is correlated with the *g* factor in IQ tests. . . . Movement time is much less correlated with IQ. . . ." The cognitive processing, they explain, is measured by reaction time, while movement time measures "small motor skills." The work of Arthur Jensen is cited as follows: "The consistent result of many studies is that white reaction time is faster than black reaction time, but black movement time is faster than white movement time." White men can't jump, but they have faster computer chips inside their heads.

The cited Jensen paper (1993) presents data for blacks and whites, for both reaction and movement time, for three different "elementary cognitive tasks." The results are not, despite Herrnstein and Murray's contention, "consistent." Blacks are reported to have faster movement times on only two of the three tasks; and they have faster *reaction times* than whites on one task, "choice reaction time." Simple reaction time merely requires the subject to respond as quickly as possible to a given stimulus each time it occurs. Choice reaction time requires him/her to react differently to various stimuli as they are presented in an unpredictable order. Thus it is said to be more cognitively complex, and to require more processing, than simple reaction time. When Jensen first used reaction time in 1975 as a measure of racial differences in intelligence, he claimed that blacks and whites did not differ in simple reaction time, but that whites, with their higher intelligence, were faster in choice reaction time. He repeated this ludicrous claim incessantly, while refusing to make the raw data of his study available for inspection. Then, in a subsequent 1984 paper, he was unable to repeat his earlier finding in a new study described as "inexplicably inconsistent" with his 1975 results. Now, in the still newer 1993 study cited by Herrnstein and Murray, Jensen reports as "an apparent anomaly" that (once again!) blacks are slightly faster in choice reaction time than whites. Those swift couriers, Herrnstein and Murray, are not stayed from their appointed rounds by anomalies and inconsistencies. Two out of three is not conclusive. Why not make the series three out of five?

To anybody who has ever watched a professional basketball game, the idea that blacks are incapable of making quick choices about how to respond to complex and changing visual displays will not be very convincing. How can scientists talk themselves into believing such a thing? But then, how can they talk themselves into believing that half of all Africans are mentally retarded? The answer to such questions doesn't require much thought. Murray, complaining to *The Wall Street Journal* that his book had been "blatantly misrepresented," blamed "the American preoccupation with race." Indeed.

I TURN NOW to a revealing example of Herrnstein and Murray's tendency to ignore the difference between a mere statistical association (correlation) and a cause-and-effect relationship. They lament that "private complaints about the incompetent affirmative-action hiree are much more common than scholarly examination of the issue." They proceed to a scholarly and public discussion of "teacher competency examinations." They report that such exams have had "generally beneficial effects," presumably by weeding out incompetent affirmative-action hirees. That positive view of standardized tests for teachers is not shared by those who argue that, since blacks tend to get lower scores, the tests are a way of eliminating competent black teachers. But Herrnstein and Murray assure us that "teachers who score higher on the tests have greater success with their students."

To support that claim they cite a single study by a couple of economists who analyzed data from a large number of North Carolina school districts. The researchers obtained average teacher test scores ("teacher quality") and average pupil failure rates for each district. They reported that a "1% increase in teacher quality . . . is accompanied by a 5% decline in the rate of failure of students." That is, there were fewer student failures in districts where teachers had higher test scores. But it does not follow from such a correlation that hiring teachers with higher test scores will reduce the rate of student failure. The same researchers found that "larger class size tends to lead to improved average [pupil] performance." Does it follow that increasing the pupil-to-teacher ratio will improve student performance? That policy recommendation might please many taxpayers, just as firing teachers with lower test scores would please some. But neither policy follows logically from the observed correlations.

To understand why, consider the following. The average proportion of black students across the school districts was 31 percent. Suppose— it does not stretch the limits of credibility—that there was a tendency for black teachers (who have lower test scores) to work in districts with large proportions of black pupils (who have higher failure rates). That nonrandom assignment of teachers to classrooms would produce a correlation between teacher test scores and pupil failure rates—but one cannot then conclude that the teacher's test score has any causal relation to student failure. To argue that, we would have to show that for a group of black teachers (and for a separate group of white teachers) the teachers' test scores predicted the failure rates of their students. There was no such information available either to the original researchers or to Herrnstein and Murray.

What about the surprising finding that high pupil-teacher ratios are associated with good pupil performance? There's no way to be certain, but suppose deprived black children tended to be in small, de facto segregated rural schools, whereas more privileged whites were in larger classrooms. Would cramming more pupils into the rural schools promote academic excellence? There is a general and important lesson buried in this example: the arithmetical complexity of the multitude of correlations and logistic regressions stuffed into the Herrnstein-Murray volume does not elevate their status from mere associations to causes and effects.

THE CONFUSION between correlation and causation permeates the largest section of *The Bell Curve*, an interminable series of analyses of data gathered from the National Longitudinal Survey of Labor Market Experience of Youth (NLSY). Those data, not surprisingly, indicate that there is an association within each race between IQ and socioeconomic status (SES). Herrnstein and Murray labor mightily in an effort to show that low IQ is the cause of low SES, and not vice versa. Their argument is decked out in all the trappings of science—a veritable barrage of charts, graphs, tables, appendices, and appeals to statistical techniques that are unknown to many readers. But on close examination, this scientific emperor is wearing no clothes.

The NLSY survey included more than 12,000 youngsters who were aged fourteen to twenty-two when the continuing study began in 1979. The respondents and/or their parents at that time provided information about their educations, occupations, and income, and answered other questions about themselves. Those reports are the basis for classifying the childhood SES of the respondents. The teenagers also took the

Armed Forces Qualification Test, regarded by psychometricians as essentially an IQ test. As they have grown older, the respondents have provided more information about their own schooling, unemployment, poverty, marital status, childbearing, welfare dependency, criminality, parenting behavior, etc.

Herrnstein and Murray pick over these data, trying to show that it is overwhelmingly IQ—not childhood or adult SES—that determines worldly success and the moral praiseworthiness of one's social behaviors. But their dismissal of SES as a major factor rests ultimately on the self-reports of youngsters. That is not an entirely firm basis. I do not want to suggest that such self-reports are entirely unrelated to reality. We know, after all, that children from differing social class backgrounds do indeed differ in IQ; and in the NLSY study the young peoples' self-reports are correlated with the objective facts of their IQ scores. But comparing the predictive value of those self-reports to that of quantitative test scores is playing with loaded dice.

Further, the fact that self-reports are correlated with IQ scores is, like all correlations, ambiguous. For Herrnstein and Murray, the relation of their index of parental SES to the child's IQ means that high-SES parents—the "cream floating on the surface of American society"—have transmitted high quality genes to their offspring. But other interpretations are possible. Perhaps, for example, the kinds of people who get high test scores are precisely those who are vain enough to claim exaggerated social status for themselves. That tendency could artificially inflate correlations of IQ both with parental SES and with self-reports of success, distorting all tests of the relative predictive power of SES and IQ. That may seem far-fetched to some readers, but it is clearly a logical possibility. The choice between alternative interpretations of statistical associations cannot be based upon logic alone. There is thus plenty of elbow room for ideological bias in social science.

THE CORE of the Herrnstein-Murray message is phrased with a beguiling simplicity: "Putting it all together, success and failure in the American economy, and all that goes with it, are increasingly a matter of the genes that people inherit." The "increasing value of intelligence in the marketplace" brings "prosperity for those lucky enough to be intelligent." Income is a "family trait" because IQ, "a major predictor of income, passes on sufficiently from one generation to the next to constrain economic mobility." Those at the bottom of the economic heap were unlucky when the IQ genes were passed out, and will remain there.

The correlations with which Herrnstein and Murray are obsessed are of course real: the children of day laborers are less likely than the children of stockbrokers to acquire fortunes or to go to college. They are more likely to be delinquent, to receive welfare, to have children outside of marriage, to be unemployed, and to have low-birth-weight babies. The children of laborers have lower average IQs than children of brokers, and so IQ is also related to all these phenomena. Herrnstein and Murray's intent is to convince us that low IQ causes poverty and its attendant evils—and not, as others might hold, vice versa.

For eight dense chapters they wrestle with data derived from the white respondents in the NLSY survey, attempting to disentangle the roles of IQ and of SES. They employ a number of quantitative tools, most prominently logistic regression—a technique that purports to specify what would happen if one variable is "held constant" while another variable is left free to vary. When SES is statistically "held constant" by Herrnstein and Murray, IQ remains related to all the phenomena described, in the obviously predictable direction. When IQ is held constant, the effect of SES is invariably reduced, usually very substantially, and sometimes eliminated.

There are a number of criticisms to be made of the ways in which Herrnstein and Murray analyze the data, and especially so when they later extend their analyses to include black and Hispanic youth. But for argument's sake, let us now suppose that their analyses are appropriate and accurate. We can also grant that, rightly or wrongly, disproportionate salaries and wealth accrue to those with high IQ scores. What then do the Herrnstein-Murray analyses tell us?

The SES of one's parents cannot in any direct sense "cause" one's IQ to be high or low. Family income, even if accurately reported, obviously cannot directly determine a child's performance on an IQ test. But income and the other components of an SES index can serve as rough indicators of the rearing environment to which a child has been exposed. With exceptions, a child of a well-to-do broker is likely to be exposed to book-learning earlier and more intensively than a child of a laborer. And extensive practice at reading and calculating does affect, very directly, one's IQ score. That is one plausible way of interpreting the statistical link between parental SES and a child's IQ.

The significant question is not whether the Herrnstein-Murray index of SES is more or less statistically associated with success than is their measure of IQ. Different SES measures, or different IQ tests, might substantially affect the results they obtained; other scholars, using other indices and tests, have gotten quite different results. The significant question is, why don't the children of laborers acquire the skills that are tapped by IQ tests?

Herrnstein and Murray answer that the children of the poor, like their laborer parents before them, have been born with poor genes. Armed with that conviction, they hail as "a great American success story" that after "controlling for IQ," ethnic and racial discrepancies in education and wages are "strikingly diminished." They reach this happy conclusion on the questionable basis of their regression analyses. But the data, even if true, would allow another reading. We can view it as a tragic failure of American society that so few black and low-SES children are lucky enough to be reared in environments that nurture development of the skills needed to obtain high IQ scores. For Herrnstein and Murray it is only fair that the race should go to the swift, and the swift are those blessed with good genes and high IQs. The conception that we live in a society that hobbles most of the racers at the starting line does not occur to them.

THE CONFIDENCE that Herrnstein and Murray appear to place in the ability of logistic regressions to interpret the social world seems excessive. To many readers that statistical procedure will be unknown, and thus beyond the reach of critical evaluation. That in turn will lead many to misunderstand the apparently simple charts scattered through the volume. The problem can be illustrated by a chart on page 322, captioned: "After controlling for IQ, blacks and Latinos have substantially higher probabilities than whites of being in a high-IQ occupation." The top panel of the chart indicates that "For a person of average age (29) before controlling for IQ," the probability of being in such an occupation is 5 percent for whites, 3 percent for blacks, and 3 percent for Latinos. The surface appearance, that blacks and Latinos are discriminated against, is misleading; logistic regression will demonstrate that.

The bottom panel of the chart shows that "for a person of average age and average IQ for people in high-IQ occupations (117)," the probability of being in such an occupation is 10 percent for whites, 26 percent for blacks, and 16 percent for Latinos. These adjusted probabilities arise from using regression to "hold IQ constant," statistically, at the average value of NLSY respondents in high-IQ occupations (lawyers, doctors, et cetera). The insight afforded by the regression analysis is powerful. Those relatively rare blacks and Latinos who have IQs of 117, far from being discriminated against, are more likely than whites with the same high IQ to be in the high-income professions. Maybe affirmative action has degenerated into reverse racism.

The chart does not tell us the actual number, or actual proportions, of NLSY whites, blacks, and Latinos in the professions. The regression analysis has fitted a smooth curve through a cloud of actual data points. The probabilities in the chart have been read off from that idealized ("best-fitting") curve. We do not know how closely the curve fits the real data. We do know that since IQs as high as 117 are relatively rare, the curve at that point is based largely on extrapolating from the much more numerous data points at lower IQ levels. That extrapolation is pretty much an act of faith. How much so can be illustrated by a few simple and rough calculations.

There were 3,022 blacks in the total NLSY sample. The respondents were about equally distributed across eight different ages, with the same racial mix at all age levels. We can thus calculate that the sample of 29-year-olds (the top panel of the chart) contained about 378 blacks. The regression analysis predicts that 3 percent of them (about 11 people) should be in the professions. But it also tells us (the bottom panel) that among 29-year-old blacks with the necessary IQ (117 or higher), the probability of being in a profession skyrockets to 26 percent. We know that the average IQ of blacks in the NLSY sample was 86.7, with a standard deviation of 12.4. That enables us to calculate (the bell curve again) that 2.78 of the black 29-year-olds in the sample should have IQs of 117 or higher. The regression analysis informs us that fully 26 percent of those 2.78 blacks (0.72 of a black) are predicted to be in the professions. Murray is right; we are losing ground. Before the days of affirmative action, an entire token black was par for the course.

THE BELL CURVE's basic thesis is that "intelligence and its correlates—maturity, farsightedness, and personal competence—are important in keeping a person employed and in the labor force." That kind of theory is not new, and psychometricians are especially prone to it. Raymond Cattell, described as "one of most [sic] illustrious psychometricians of his age," wrote during the Great Depression that "Unemployment—persistent unemployment—has unfortunately been regarded as a purely economic problem when in fact it is fundamentally a psychological one." The stress on psychological factors encourages Herrnstein and Murray to speculate on why, even if matched for IQ, blacks are more likely than whites to be unemployed. They raise "the possibility of ethnic differences in whatever other personal attributes besides IQ determine a person's ability to do well in the job market. We do not know whether ethnic groups differ on the average in these other ways.... We will not speculate further along these lines here." This tease encourages the reader to follow the authors into the locker room, where such speculations are routinely entertained. Professor Cattell was less shy about speculating in public. He wrote that the Negro race "has contributed practically nothing to social progress and culture (except in rhythm, sensitiveness to which is revealed by tests to be constitutionally better in the negro than the European)." Too bad that rhythm doesn't count for much in the job market.

Tests of cognitive ability, unlike tests of rhythm, are claimed by Herrnstein and Murray to be excellent predictors of "job productivity." Thus an employer concerned with the bottom line would do well to hire, no matter what the job, those applicants with high IQ test scores: "the smart busboy will be more productive than the less-smart busboy...." But how do we measure the "productivity" of an employee? The vast majority of studies "validate" the predictive power of IQ tests by demonstrating that supervisors assign higher ratings to workers with high test scores. That fact, of course, tells us that supervisors think highly of workers with high test scores—most of whom share various traits (whiteness is one of them) with most supervisors. It does not necessarily tell us that high-IQ workers are more productive.

There is also an extensive research literature which demonstrates that workers with high IQs possess more "job knowledge," as assessed by written multiple-choice tests. High-IQ workers are also more likely to pass written qualifying examinations given at the end of training courses for particular jobs. But again, these facts do not demonstrate that—once on the job—high-IQ workers are really more productive.

There have been some studies, many conducted by the military, in which the criterion for job productivity has involved actual work samples, or "hands-on" tests. Maier and Hiatt, in a technical report cited by Herrnstein and Murray, explain that "hands-on job performance tests have intrinsic validity because of their high fidelity to the skills required to perform job tasks. . . . [they] are the benchmark measure for evaluating the job relatedness of surrogate measures of job performance, such as written tests, ratings, and grades."

With an understanding of how psychologists measure job productivity, we can now follow Herrnstein and Murray as they grapple with the problem of whether experience on the job can "make up for less intelligence." They conclude that "the difference in productivity associated with differences in intelligence diminishes only slowly and partially. Often it does not diminish at all. The cost of hiring less intelligent workers may last as long as they stay on the job." To arrive at this bleak conclusion, they cite only two studies (both in the military) which used work samples or hands-on tests. Their description of one study is false; their description of the other study is accurate, but incomplete.

Herrnstein and Murray assert that Schmidt et al. studied armor repairmen, armor crewmen, supply specialists, and cooks "extending out to five years of experience and using three different measures of job performance." They indicate that the researchers found high-IQ workers to begin at higher levels, and to continue to outstrip low-IQ workers by the same amount, in all jobs, for all measures, for five years. That much is basically true, but it obscures an important fact. In all measures—work samples, job knowledge tests, and supervisory ratings—both high- and low-IQ workers improved steadily with experience. Thus, in work sample scores, a low-IQ worker after two years was about as productive as a high-IQ worker after one year of experience. Facts of that sort are not irrelevant to the productive utilization of "human capital."

But more; despite Herrnstein and Murray's claim that the study extended out to five years, 194 of the 1,457 workers had had more than five years of experience. The work sample scores of such highly experienced low-IQ workers had completely caught up to those of equally experienced high-IQ workers! The supervisory ratings of the experienced low-IQ workers were actually higher than those of high-IQ workers, although a substantial gap remained in "job knowledge" tests. These embarrassments were explained away by the study's authors with an appeal to "a fluke of sampling error," and an assertion that "findings in the highest experience group are suspect."

The second military study cited by Herrnstein and Murray is that of Maier and Hiatt. That study was described, accurately enough, as finding that a difference favoring high-IQ workers persisted over time when "job knowledge" was the criterion, but disappeared when a work sample was the measure. The data in fact indicated that, for both ground radio repairers and automotive mechanics, high-IQ workers initially outscored low-IQ workers on both hands-on and written tests. But after four or five years of experience, the low-IQ workers actually did better on the hands-on test than those with high IQs! On the written test of "job knowledge," low-IQ workers showed no sign whatever of catching up to the superior multiple-choice testing skills of their high-IQ betters. Maier and Hiatt concluded that the military's IQ test was "a valid predictor of job performance as measured by hands-on tests," but that the content validity of hands-on tests "is sensitive to job experience." That is a psychometrician's way of saying that after a few years on the job the correlation between IQ and worker productivity was actually slightly negative.

This military research, I think, has a genuine and deep meaning. The kinds of people who don't do well on standardized tests have some trouble catching on to job requirements in the early going; but with experience their actual work performance catches up to that of their more academically talented peers. Their problem appears to be that even when they are doing the job excellently, they have no "job knowledge." They don't *know* how to do the job, they just *do* it; or at least they can't write down what they do know. That, in the view of Herrnstein and Murray, is sufficient reason to consign them to unemployment.

In the world of *The Bell Curve*, the importance and the explanatory power of IQ are ubiquitous. Before the advent of IQ tests, "gossip about who in the tribe was cleverer" was "a topic of conversation around the fire since fires, and conversation, were invented." Among Bushmen of the Kalahari, "the best hunters score above their tribal average on IQ tests." Faced with the choice, it is "better to be born smart [than] rich."

Herrnstein and Murray note that among blue-collar workers who tell researchers that they have dropped out of the labor force because of physical disability or injury, low IQ is common. Why? "An answer leaps to mind: The smarter you are, the less likely that you will have accidents." That answer leapt to mind before the thought that low-IQ workers, in minimum wage jobs, have little incentive to remain in the labor force. Dull young women lack the "foresight and intelligence" to understand that the welfare system offers them a bad deal. Welfare might be a bad deal for Herrnstein and Murray, but I am not so sure that single mothers on welfare haven't figured out *their* odds pretty accurately.

A low-IQ woman is likely to have a low-birth-weight baby because she "never registers the simple and ubiquitous lessons about taking care of herself" when pregnant. Her problem is not that she has no prenatal care; it is that she has "difficulty in connecting cause and effect." People who have low IQs, according to *The Bell Curve*, commit crimes because, lacking foresight, the threat of prison does not deter them; further, they cannot "understand why robbing someone is wrong." Then what is to be made of the fact that although "very dull" young males are stopped by the police, booked for an offense, and convicted of an offense less often than "normal" males, they are nevertheless jailed more than twice as often? "It may be . . . that they are less competent in getting favorable treatment from the criminal justice system. The data give us no way to tell." Perhaps not, but some hints are available. There is no doubt that O. J. Simpson is "competent"; but his ability to hire high-priced lawyers is not irrelevant to the treatment he will receive from the criminal justice system.

THE BELL CURVE, near its closing tail, contains two chapters concerned with affirmative action, in higher education and in the workplace. To read those chapters is to hear the second shoe drop. The rest of the book, I believe, was written merely as a prelude to its assault on affirmative action. The vigor of the attack is astonishing.

Affirmative action "cannot survive public scrutiny." It is based on "the explicit assumption that ethnic groups do not differ in . . . abilities." Hiring and promotion procedures "that are truly fair . . . will produce . . . racial disparities," and "employers are using double standards for black and white applicants . . . because someone or something . . . is making them do so. . . ." The "degradation of intellectual requirements" in recruiting police has affected "police performance on the street." We learn that a veteran of the Washington, D.C., police force has heard "about people in the academy who could not read or write." And a former instructor saw "people diagnosed as borderline retarded graduate from the police academy." These anecdotes take their place among the politically potent folk tales about welfare queens driving Cadillacs.

Herrnstein and Murray contribute to the genre by describing a black student who "it was reported, received a straight grant of $85,000, plus $10,000 in annual travel budgets, from one of Harvard's competitors in minority recruiting." Their cited source for this tale is the *Harvard University Gazette*. The account in that journal quotes a Harvard admissions officer as having learned, through "an informal poll," of an African-American student who was offered "a grant of $85,000 over four years, plus an additional $10,000 each summer for travel and *research*" [emphasis added]. When I asked that admissions officer for specific details, he replied that the principle of confidentiality prevented him from answering. He did, however, cite as a relevant "minority scholarship" the Angier B. Duke scholarships awarded by Duke University. Inquiry at Duke established that these are not "minority scholarships." They are full tuition, four-year scholarships awarded each year, without regard to need, to the sixteen most outstanding applicants to Duke. They include support to travel for summer study at Oxford University in England. This seems the likely source of *The Bell Curve*'s saga about the Willie Horton of the Ivy League.

Now, at long last, Herrnstein and Murray let it all hang out: "affirmative action, in education and the workplace alike, is leaking a poison into the American soul." Having examined the American condition at the close of the twentieth century, these two philosopher-kings conclude, "It is time for America once again to try living with inequality, as life is lived. . . ." This kind of sentiment, I imagine, lay behind the conclusion of *New York Times* columnist Bob Herbert that "the book is just a genteel way of calling somebody a nigger." Herbert is right. The book has nothing to do with science.

WITH *THE BELL CURVE* proper behind us, I want now to consider one of the more pernicious effects of its publication. The enormously successful marketing of the book by its publisher and by the

American Enterprise Institute has served to legitimize as "scholarship" overtly racist works which only a year or two ago were widely regarded as outside the mainstream of academic respectability. The *New York Times* science reporter, Malcolm Browne, appropriately chose to review the Herrnstein and Murray volume together with recent books by J. Philippe Rushton (*Race, Evolution, and Behavior*) and by Seymour Itzkoff (*The Decline of Intelligence in America*). Browne, in lumping the books together, assured readers of the *Times* that "the government or society that persists in sweeping their subject matter under the rug will do so at its peril." We can only hope, perhaps naively, that exposure to the light of critical scrutiny might have some antiseptic effect against the scholarship of writers like Rushton and Itzkoff.

Rushton has written that human evolution has produced three major races—Mongoloids, Caucasoids, and Negroids. These races are said to differ, in the same rank ordering, with respect to a large number of correlated physical and behavioral traits, all related to "reproductive strategies." Those traits—all of which Rushton believes to be encoded in the genes of the different races—include intelligence, brain size, penis size, nurturing one's young, frequency of sexual intercourse, number of offspring, law-abidingness, sexual hormone levels, the tendency to have low-birth-weight babies, and altruism. For these and other traits Negroids are said to be at one end of a continuum, far removed from Caucasoids. Mongoloids are at the other end of the continuum, but close to Caucasoids. The Rushton portrait of Negroids—stupid, small brains, big penises, sexually licentious, criminal, spawning lots of low-birth-weight babies for whom they will not care—strikes a responsive chord in America; David Duke was almost elected governor of Louisiana.

Herrnstein and Murray grant that "Rushton paints with a broad brush," but write of his "detailed and convincing empirical reports of the race differences," and declare that his "work is not that of a crackpot or a bigot. . . . As science, there is nothing wrong with Rushton's work in principle. . . ." I'll mention just a couple of the empirical details that Herrnstein and Murray found convincing. Rushton asserts that blacks have larger penises than whites. Presumably this scholar's understanding of human sexuality includes the belief that big penises are more likely to engage in intercourse and to produce babies than are small penises. To demonstrate that blacks have big penises, Rushton cited just two sources—some casual observations by an anonymous French army surgeon in Africa writing in 1898, and some unpublished data from Kinsey's study of American sexual behavior. The volunteer male subjects in the Kinsey study were asked to measure their own penises. The proportion of black subjects complying with that request was significantly smaller than the proportion of whites. The few blacks who did comply—scarcely a random sample of blacks—claimed slightly larger penis sizes than the many whites who responded.

To demonstrate that black genes produce unbridled sexual behavior, as well as big genitals, Rushton reported that a significantly higher proportion of black than of white interviewees had told Kinsey that the female partner tended to have more than one orgasm per act of intercourse. To assert this as a fact Rushton—unknown to his readers—had to lump together the responses of male and female interviewees, which had been tabled separately by Kinsey. The actual data were that 18 percent of black males, but only 8 percent of black females (!), claimed that the female had multiple orgasms; among whites, the proportion making that claim was 9 percent of both males and females. The data as published by Rushton indicated simply that 13 percent of blacks and 9 percent of whites reported multiple female orgasms. That evidently qualifies in the eyes of Herrnstein and Murray as a "detailed and convincing report of the race differences." What would Rushton have to write before *The Bell Curve*'s authors would conclude that he is a crackpot or a bigot?

Predictably, Rushton's theorizing has excited the prurient interest of Herrnstein and Murray's psychometric expert, Richard Lynn. "The high rate of sexual activity in Negroids," Lynn has suggested, may be caused by a high level of the male sex hormone, testosterone. The "crucial supporting evidence" for the notion that blacks have an oversupply of testosterone is the fact that "Negroids have higher rates of cancer of the prostate than Caucasoids . . . an important determinant of cancer of the prostate is the level of testosterone." The chain of reasoned evidence is: prostate cancer is caused by testosterone; blacks tend to have prostate cancer; therefore blacks must have lots of testosterone; the abundance of testosterone makes blacks sexually active; that causes them to produce lots of babies, for whom they will not provide, and who will become criminals and/or welfare cases. It's all in the genes.

This train of reasoning can be headed off at the pass. To show that testosterone causes prostate cancer (a view not widely shared in medical circles), Lynn cites a paper by Ahluwalia et al. That paper, Lynn writes, reported "higher levels of testosterone in patients with prostatic cancer than in healthy controls." That claim, like Rushton's claim about multiple female orgasms, does not quite tell the whole truth. Ahluwalia et al. reported that black prostate patients in the United States had higher testosterone levels than did control subjects. But among blacks in Nigeria, control subjects had higher testosterone levels than did prostate patients! Testosterone appears to cause prostate cancer in America, while protecting Nigerians from the same affliction.

What about the next claim, that blacks are more prone than whites to develop prostate cancer? That again is partially true—but not in the sweeping racial sense that Lynn intends. Lynn reprints some age-standardized incidence rates of prostate cancer for "Negroids" and "Caucasoids" in seven American cities. Those statistics and others had been gathered by the International Union Against Cancer. There was variation from city to city, but in each case African-Americans had about twice the incidence of whites. The highest white rate was 59.7 per 100,000 population, in Hawaii (Lynn erroneously attributes that rate to Hawaiian "Negroids"); the lowest black rate was 72.1, in New Orleans.

The paper from which Lynn copied (or tried to copy) those figures contains other relevant statistics. The rate in Senegal was 4.3—the lowest rate, except for Japan and Shanghai, among the thirty-odd countries for which data were given. The rates in Jamaica and (then) Rhodesia were 28.6 and 32.3—still far below the rates of both black and white Americans. Follow-up studies by the International Union reported a rate of 9.7 in Nigeria. In the Cape Province of South Africa, the rate for whites was a low 23.2; for Bantus it was 19.2, and for Africans in Natal 23.2. The facts are well known to every serious scholar concerned with prostate cancer: American blacks have an alarmingly higher rate of prostate cancer than American whites, but black Africans have a much lower rate than either American blacks or whites. These facts do not lend themselves to the racist interpretations advanced by Herrnstein and Murray's psychometric expert, Richard Lynn. To admit Lynn and Rushton into the scientific mainstream—I'll say it bluntly—is a betrayal of science. To say this out loud is not to advocate what Malcolm Browne describes as a "shroud of censorship imposed upon scientists and scholars by pressure groups." It is a simple defense of truth and integrity in science. Herrnstein and Murray's defense of Rushton's racist claptrap—"we expect that time will tell whether it is right or wrong in fact"—is couched in the tones of moderation and reason. In my view both the work and its defense are contemptible.

THE WORK by Itzkoff, and its echoes in *The Bell Curve*, could (and should) have been written seventy years ago; in fact, it was. Browne summarizes Itzkoff's views with entire accuracy: "the least intelligent, least educable, poorest, most politically apathetic and abusive contingent of the population is reproducing faster than the smart, rich, politically active and nurturing contingent . . . this has fueled a dysgenic trend: America's collective smartness is being diluted, gravely endangering the nation's ability to compete economically." Herrnstein and Murray similarly bemoan the alleged propensity for the cognitively least able to reproduce excessively; and worse yet, once more guided by "Richard Lynn's computations," they conclude that America's "immigrants in the 1980s came from ethnic groups that have [IQ] scores significantly below the white average. . . ."

The same phenomena had seized the attention of Carl C. Brigham in 1923. Brigham, convinced that excessive breeding by the lower classes must produce a decline in "American intelligence," analyzed the mental test scores of foreign-born draftees into the American army during World War I. Those data indicated that immigrants from southern and eastern Europe, and Russia ("our army sample of immigrants from Russia is at least one half Jewish"), had appallingly low IQs. Brigham advocated, and Congress enacted, laws to minimize the proportion of immigrants admitted from southern and eastern Europe. He warned that "racial admixture" in America "is infinitely worse than that faced by any European country today, for we are incorporating the negro into our racial stock, while all of Europe is comparatively free from this taint. . . . The decline of American intelligence will be more rapid than the decline of the intelligence of European national groups, owing to the presence here of the negro." Brigham looked forward to "the prevention of the continued propagation of defective strains in the present population." He, and these views, were not outside the mainstream of psychological science in 1923; Brigham went on to become secretary both of the American Psychological Association and of the College Entrance Examination Board, where he developed the Scholastic Aptitude Test.

Malcolm Browne, commenting on the books by Herrnstein and Murray, by Rushton, and by Itzkoff, suggests that "the authors . . . may have softened their agendas somewhat to parry the expected fury of liberal critics, fellow academics and hostile mobs. . . . it is hard to believe that these writers would oppose a eugenically motivated program designed to influence patterns of reproduction." The notion that these writers labor under a "shroud of censorship" imposed by "pressure groups," or that the lavishly endowed American Enterprise Institute trembles before the expected fury of liberal critics, academics, and hostile mobs, seems out of touch with what is really happening in America. What, other than "a eugenically motivated program," is the Herrnstein-Murray recommendation to end welfare aid to unmarried mothers with dependent children?

The specter of dysgenesis has haunted psychometrics since its inception; no material facts are capable of dislodging that specter. Raymond Cattell, then in England, wrote an entire book in 1937 on *The Fight for Our National Intelligence*. The fact that intelligence, measured by IQ, was inherited was self-evident; the only opposition to that view came from "enemies of democracy" and "people primarily political in outlook." While Hitler swept Europe before him, Cattell—that "most illustrious" psychometrician—explained that since "intelligence tests point to significant differences between races," it was "people racially in a temporarily awkward tactical position" who opposed the findings of the IQ testers.

The tendency of the lower classes to breed excessively, and of the upper classes to restrict their fertility, must surely—unless counteracted—lead to a decline in "national intelligence." Cattell, joined by virtually all the leading psychometricians of the time, confidently predicted that national surveys would show a decline in average IQ of some 1.5 points per decade. When national surveys showed instead that there had been an *increase* in average IQ over time, psychometricians concluded that the test used in the surveys (the Stanford-Binet) was an imperfect measure of "innate" intelligence. Whatever imperfect tests might indicate, actual intelligence *had* to have declined.

That psychometric tradition of heads-I-win-tails-you-lose has been carried forward intact by Herrnstein and Murray. They acknowledge that James Flynn has demonstrated that across the world intelligence as measured by IQ tests has been increasing dramatically over time. Thus an average contemporary youngster, taking an IQ test that had been standardized twenty years ago, would have a considerably higher than average IQ score. Perhaps, Herrnstein and Murray suggest, "Improved health, education, and childhood interventions may hide the demographic effects. . . . Whatever good things we can accomplish with changes in the environment would be that much more effective if they did not have to fight a demographic head wind." Their conviction that "something worth worrying about is happening to the cognitive capital of the country" is unshakable. Imagine the heights that America could scale if a Ph.D. in social science were a prerequisite for the production of offspring! With environmental advantages working exclusively upon such splendid raw material, no head winds would delay our arrival at Utopia. And we would sell more autos to the Japanese.

That is the kind of brave new world toward which *The Bell Curve* points. Whether or not our country moves in that direction depends upon our politics, not upon science. To pretend, as Herrnstein and Murray do, that the 1,000-odd items in their bibliography provide a "scientific" basis for their reactionary politics may be a clever political tactic, but it is a disservice to and abuse of science. That should be clear even to those scientists (I am not one of them) who are comfortable with Herrnstein and Murray's politics. We owe it to our fellow citizens to explain that the reception of their book had nothing to do either with its scientific merit or the novelty of its message.

SERMON AS SCIENCE

Peter Passell

C HARLES MURRAY, best known for attacking welfare, and Richard Herrnstein, an experimental psychologist who argued that intelligence is largely in the genes, built public careers as the dark angels of social science. And with the publication of *The Bell Curve*, their reputations have apparently been secured: The 845-page tract has driven liberal editorial writers to rug-chewing and led the editors of *The New Republic* to elicit seventeen separate rebuttals.

The idea behind *The Bell Curve*, as many readers must know by now, is that IQ is destiny, determining how individuals get along in school, jobs, and social relations. Since little can be done to raise "cognitive ability," the argument goes, little can be done to change the socioeconomic pecking order. This is a grim message, the authors acknowledge, but someone must deliver it. "There can be no real progress in solving America's social problems," Mr. Herrnstein and Mr. Murray explain, "when they are as misperceived as they are today."

Not everyone has been charmed by the pair's appeal to sweet reason. Indeed, some critics have been inclined to hang the defendants without a trial: merely entertaining the idea that IQ tests predict eco-

Peter Passell is a writer for *The New York Times*. This article originally appeared in *The New York Times*, October 27, 1994, as "It's a Grim Message: Dummies Fail More Often."

nomic performance, they believe, breeds complacency about racism because just one black American in six scores above the average for whites. That is unfortunate, for the authors' look at the nexus between measured intelligence and life outcomes is the most original and interesting part of the book. The analysis deteriorates sharply when it moves on to the question of whether intelligence can be raised through government intervention, and the implications for public policy if it cannot. Indeed, what begins as provocative research on the plight of the losers in a meritocracy ends in a sloppily reasoned rationale for letting them eat cake.

Look again at that unpalatable first premise. Standardized tests of intelligence have been widely condemned for cultural bias, and their use as sorting devices has been discouraged by the courts as well as by liberal opinion. But whatever the tests measure, Mr. Herrnstein and Mr. Murray correctly remind us that the scores predict success in school for ethnic minorities as well as for whites. What works in predicting school performance apparently also works for predicting success on the job. Even when other key variables (education, parents' social class) are accounted for, scores on one widely administered examination, the Armed Forces Qualification Test, are a potent factor in predicting differences in later earnings. It seems that the growing role of intelligence in determining economic productivity largely accounts for the widening gap between rich and poor.

If all this rings a (different) bell, go to the head of the curve. A number of commentators, including Secretary of Labor Robert B. Reich, have fretted in public about the unhealthy consequences of rewarding citizens according to their skills when so many have so few skills. The authors of *The Bell Curve* go much further, however, slipping a moral dimension into the argument. They say intelligence also predicts crime rates, welfare dependence, poor parenting, and indifference to civic responsibility. And they cleverly trump their race-conscious critics by looking solely at the evidence of differences among whites.

Unlikely as this direct link between intelligence and character may seem, the analysis is scientifically respectable. What comes next, though, is heavily compromised by ideology. Since they say IQ is the key to success, they agree it would be tempting to give the dullards a helping hand. But, alas, they conclude, a better society cannot be built on good intentions and taxpayers' money alone. "For the foreseeable future," they write, "the problems of low cognitive ability are not going to be solved by outside interventions to make children smarter."

Why not? Efforts to raise intelligence through improved childhood nutrition, the authors explain, have been inconclusive. The measurable benefits of preschool enrichment programs dissipate when the youngsters return to the mean streets. A week's worth of prepping for the SATs raises average math scores by only 25 points.

Note the disconnect here: The ambiguous evidence from America's on-again, off-again efforts to cope with the consequences of poverty and racial prejudice hardly squares with the authors' deeply pessimistic conclusion. But a belief in genetic determinism would explain it. And while they never make a fuss about heredity, they don't bother to conceal it. It is "beyond significant technical dispute," they write, that "cognitive ability is substantially heritable, apparently no less than 40 percent and no more than 80 percent."

Does that put the authors beyond the scholarly pale? Many biologists think so, dismissing the possibility that a group characteristic as complex as heritable intelligence could have diverged so sharply between races in what amounts to a single tick of the evolutionary clock. But this reviewer is not a biologist, and will leave the argument to experts.

It takes less expertise to analyze the Herrnstein-Murray policy prescription. With society increasingly dominated by its meritocratic elite, they predict the winners will create a "custodial state" in which the underclass will be stripped of rights and responsibilities. "We have in mind a high-tech and more lavish version of the Indian reservation for some substantial minority of the nation's population," they write. And what is the alternative that follows from their full and frank discussion of the plight of those not fortunate enough to have been born in Lake Wobegon? They would give the losers a chance to "find valued places in society."

All Mr. Herrnstein and Mr. Murray seem to have in mind, however, is getting Big Brother off the backs of the intellectually challenged. Simpler economic rules, they say, would free the underclass from regulation and taxation intended to protect the perquisites of the elite. Clearer rules about the vices of crime and dependence would provide disincentives for theft, violence, and procreation outside marriage. Decentralization of government responsibility to the neighborhood level would help restore community (racial?) pride and traditional values.

If this seems a bit underwhelming, join the crowd. After wading through a long, quasi-academic examination of the statistical links between intelligence, character, race, and poverty, the reader's reward is a hoary lecture on the evils of the welfare state.

At least Rush Limbaugh has a sense of humor.

DANGEROUS, BUT IMPORTANT

Richard Nisbett

RICHARD HERRNSTEIN and Charles Murray have written an important and ultimately dangerous book on intelligence and achievement that has far-reaching implications for our society. It's important, because at least in the public arena, it will be used to frame the controversial debate on intelligence and social problems for a long time to come. But it's also dangerous because the two authors bluntly argue that blacks are intellectually inferior to whites, and the cause is in our genes. That assertion is not only wrong but irresponsible. Crucial questions about intelligence and social problems should be debated, but those will now, alas, be distorted by the authors' spurious thesis.

There are, in fact, several points raised in their book, *The Bell Curve* that, while not universally agreed upon by social scientists, would be accepted at least in qualified forms by most. One is that intelligence, as measured by IQ tests, matters. People with higher IQ scores get themselves into higher status occupations, are rated as more proficient, make more money, and are less likely to commit crimes or go on welfare. A second point is that IQ is going to matter more and more for sta-

Richard Nisbett is Distinguished University Professor of Psychology and director of the Culture and Cognition Program at the University of Michigan, Ann Arbor. This article originally appeared in *Newsday*, October 23, 1994, as "Warning: Dangerous Curves Ahead."

tus and income in the future, partly because jobs at the top end are getting more complex and partly because such jobs require more "credentializing," which may be unrelated to real talent, but is related to the ability to get high IQ scores and get into the right schools.

The consequence of this is that we may be moving toward a Latin American type of economic structure, in which an elite, in our case a "cognitive elite," gets a higher and higher fraction of the wealth. Some policy implications flow from this; for example, we ought to be looking for ways to reduce income gaps between the elite and the less skilled. Why not go to the source of this problem and try to improve the intelligence of those at the bottom? Partly, according to Herrnstein and Murray, because IQ is to a substantial extent fixed and inherited. Then, for no obvious reason other than to render their book incendiary, Herrnstein and Murray go on to argue that it is not merely individual differences in IQ that are partly genetic in origin, but the average IQ difference between blacks and whites as well.

How big is the IQ difference between the races? Herrnstein and Murray give the value of 15 points, roughly the difference between an average lawyer or engineer and an average tradesman or data manager. If the 15-point difference between the races were largely genetic in origin and could not be overcome by educational intervention, then blacks would forever and increasingly be condemned to having lower status, lower pay. But do they really mean this?

Yes, they do. They argue that the average IQ of children born to low IQ parents (whether white or black) cannot be significantly altered by anything society can do. This conclusion is based in good part on the results of Head Start and similar programs. Such programs typically begin when a youngster is three or four and end when school starts. The best of these programs actually produce a 7- or 8-point gain initially, but as Herrnstein and Murray correctly note, this gain is mostly lost over time. Yet that doesn't mean these programs are useless. In fact it seems the problem is that children are not kept in enriched environments. On the contrary, they are returned to home and school and community environments that are not designed to sustain the IQ gains.

Suppose children from homes likely to be disadvantaged are reared in middle- or upper-class environments? What does this do for IQ? The best estimates (and they are not very firm ones) range from a gain of about 6 points to a gain of about 20 points! In short, there is every reason to believe that sustaining the enrichment does indeed sustain the IQ gains. Of course, not everyone can be adopted by well-to-do parents. So can anything practical be done after the preschool period to produce or sustain intellectual gains and reduce the gap between advantaged and disadvantaged?

Astonishingly, Herrnstein and Murray do not review the evidence here. Yet we know that drastic change can be produced in inner-city schools. Dr. James Comer of the Yale Psychiatry Department set up programs in two inner-city schools that were the poorest in academic achievement among the thirty-five or so schools in the New Haven system. Within a few years, the two schools were among the top five in achievement. The key to his program was to involve mothers in their children's education by making the school an attractive place to be and to involve them in their children's education.

Comer's success is by no means unique. In his campaign, President Clinton made much of similar elementary education programs for the inner city that produce achievement above the national norms. Herrnstein and Murray can scarcely claim that these successes had not been drawn to their attention. By the time students reach age seventeen, Murray is now saying in public, nothing at all can be done to reduce the gap between the genetically and environmentally deprived and their luckier fellows. Here again, the good news is ignored. At the University of Michigan, where I teach, and many others, educational experiments have succeeded in dramatically improving the performance of African-American students in particular types of courses, as well as improving overall grade-point averages and increasing retention rate. These programs are relatively low cost and, incidentally, seem to benefit white students as well—though not by as much.

We also know that very early interventions—before the first year of life—can affect IQ even many years after termination of the programs. And we know that interventions for high school age youth can have significant effects. The authors cite this evidence but challenge it with nitpicking technicalities that they don't apply to evidence in support of their position.

In short, Herrnstein and Murray would have the reader believe that nothing can be done educationally even though the consensus of knowledgeable social scientists is that a great deal can be done. The same puzzling inversion of the implications of evidence is found when they review the literature on reducing the gap between black and white IQ and intellectual achievement. Herrnstein and Murray imply that the gap has remained steady at fifteen points over many generations, but in fact almost all the evidence, much of it familiar to Herrnstein and Murray, points to a reduction in recent years. The degree of convergence found ranges from one or two points to seven or eight— that is half the difference in a period of roughly the last twenty years. A reasonable estimate, based on the best evidence, might be that blacks have reduced the gap by three or four points in the last twenty or twenty-five years. At this rate, the gap would be gone by the middle of the next century.

But Herrnstein and Murray argue that the difference probably won't continue at the present rate. They assert that the increase in black ability scores on tests such as the Scholastic Assessment Test (essentially a measure of IQ for the college-bound) is coming only at the "low end" of the range—much as improved diet can increase the height of malnourished children but not that of children who are already adequately fed. And yet they themselves admit that there has been more than a 35 percent increase in the percentage of black students receiving scores in the highest ranges of the SAT between 1980 and 1990! (The rate of improvement of the high end has continued to be substantial since 1990 for blacks, while it has stagnated for whites.) The improvement in black SAT scores is dismissed on the grounds that relatively few blacks had high scores on the SAT in 1980, so the gains are not very important. This argument is as specious as it sounds. The increase in the number of extremely talented blacks is sure to have significant consequences for society. The book is full of such distortions and eccentric interpretations of evidence that are not shared by most experts, while evidence that undermines the conclusions of the authors is missing or dismissed on technical grounds.

So why is the book receiving favorable attention in the media, even about the portions of it dealing with race and the alterability of IQ and intellectual achievement? I suspect that the authors have tapped into deeply rooted anxieties about our society and that many people assume that Herrnstein and Murray are courageously forcing the public to address some painful truths that other social scientists are not willing to face or to discuss. Yet, in truth, the genetic basis for IQ differences between the races is not much discussed by social scientists because few believe the evidence has sufficient credibility to make it worth talking about. By contrast, the issue of alterability is much discussed by social scientists because new successes are being discovered all the time. There is a sort of courage to be found in *The Bell Curve*, but fortunately not of the kind that scholars generally display.

A DYSTOPIAN FABLE

Michael Stern

*T*HE BELL CURVE is already riding a tidal wave of controversy
that has moved it off the book page to the front page, from a technical debate in the psychology journals over the validity of its evidence
to the vitriolic political judgments of the culture wars. That's exactly
where it belongs.

The book has heft and footnotes, and the authors have credentials—Richard Herrnstein held a chair of psychology at Harvard University before his recent death, and Charles Murray is a fellow at the
American Enterprise Institute and author of *Losing Ground,* an influential assault on the welfare state. But *The Bell Curve* is no more a scientific treatise than were *A Modest Proposal* or *Mein Kampf.* It's a
pseudoscholarly dystopia, a nonfiction Brave New World misrepresented by its authors and their allies as disinterested scholarship.

Despite its length and many tables, graphs, and statistical appendixes, *The Bell Curve* is readily accessible. Its prose is clear and forceful,
and its arguments carefully translated from psychometrics to plain-
English examples. The authors' views and policy recommendations
are explicit, if not the ideological sleight of hand that has transformed

Michael Stern, a former journalist and English professor, is a lawyer for General Magic,
Inc., in Silicon Valley. This review was published in the *San Francisco Chronicle*, November 6, 1994, as "Exploring the Bell Curve Furor."

debatable assumptions and suspect research into the purported "facts" that are used to support them. The core "fact" on which the book is based is this: There is such a thing as "general intelligence," or *g*, that can be precisely measured in all cultures in the same way, and that is accurately reflected by IQ scores. *G* is predominantly inherited and is thus largely independent of social status or educational level. Therefore, different racial and ethnic groups have different distributions of intelligence—the mean IQ for whites is 100, for blacks 85, for example—because of their genetic makeup. Because "high cognitive ability is generally associated with socially desirable behaviors, low cognitive ability with socially undesirable ones," "dull" people are more likely to be poor, divorced, criminals, welfare mothers of illegitimate children, bad parents, and so on.

The authors conclude that American society is being stratified into a self-segregated "cognitive elite" of wealthy, successful business and technical professionals and a rapidly breeding, disproportionately black underclass of the stupid, who are becoming incapable of dealing with the ever-more-complex world around them. "People in the bottom quartile of intelligence are becoming not just expendable in economic terms; they will sometime in the not-too-distant future become a net loss. . . . For many people, there is nothing they can learn that will repay the cost of education." While this process cannot be reversed, they argue, its effects—especially the anger of the cognitively advantaged over all of the money and rhetoric being wasted on the incurably dumb—can be mitigated. First, the authors suggest, social policies that have exacerbated the "dumbing down" of America must change: eliminate welfare for unwed mothers, who, because of their own genetic inferiority, presumably have the dullest kids; permit IQ testing for job placements and eliminate affirmative action in all cases except where minority applicants have high IQs; cut back Head Start and other ineffectual attempts to remedy genetic inequality with education; and devote federal and state funds to educating those with high enough IQs to deserve it.

Second, they argue, a moral transformation of society must occur, so that all people, even those with minimal intelligence, can earn a "valued place" in the world (as, in their preferred example, did farm laborers in pre-industrial America) by being diligent, obedient workers and strict parents. If not, they argue, the cognitive elite will handle the underclass by consigning it to an authoritarian "custodial state," a "high tech and more lavish version of the Indian reservation." Herrnstein and Murray purport to abhor the coming of the custodial state, but in fact the only logical conclusion to their arguments about the heritability of intelligence is eugenics—for the state to encourage reproduction by the most fit (those with high IQs) and to discourage or prevent reproduction by the unfit (the "cognitively disadvantaged").

That's where the issue about the validity of the "facts" arises. "G is one of the most thoroughly demonstrated entities in the behavioral sciences," the authors state. This is, quite simply, nonsense. As Stephen Jay Gould and James Fallows, among many others, have pointed out, the very idea of a bell curve for intelligence is a self-fulfilling prophecy. The first intelligence testers assumed that responses to their questionnaires would follow a "normal" distribution in the form of a bell curve; if they didn't, the questions were changed until they did. Nothing in the way standardized intelligence tests are produced has altered since.

Further, the idea of a single, generalized form of "intelligence" that can be precisely measured does not command the universal assent in the field that Herrnstein and Murray claim for it. Indeed, it's not even mainstream. Modern genetics and neuroscience propound the notion that human intellectual capabilities are the product of interactive domains of different sorts of cognitive abilities that are variously enabled or impeded by the cultural tools available to individuals, with only very general hereditary constraints at the upper and lower bounds.

Even for those inclined to be more charitable about psychometrics, *The Bell Curve* should give pause in yet another sense: its ahistoricism. At the beginning of the Industrial Revolution, as Gertrude Himmelfarb has shown in *The Idea of Poverty*, the Victorians began to wonder if the new urban poor, whose blasphemy, alcoholism, promiscuity, and crime were rampant in the streets of London and Birmingham, constituted a new "race," a breed apart from "normal" humanity. *The Bell Curve* really operates on this level. It's a fable masquerading as social science. There's no more validity to the authors' division of society into cognitive segments under a bell curve of IQ score distributions than to H. G. Wells's extrapolation of the class structure of London circa 1900 to the bowers of the Eloi and the caves of the Morlocks in *The Time Machine*.

Once the book is understood on those terms, we can get on with the real debate—about the proper distribution of wealth and power in a society founded on a concept of equality that is being increasingly contested in terms of results rather than just opportunities—and leave the pseudoscience to the crackpots.

THE HEART OF THE MATTER

Joe Chidley

W HATEVER THE OTHER merits of *The Bell Curve,* read-ability is not one of them. In its 845 pages, Harvard University psychologist Richard J. Herrnstein and political scientist Charles Murray mount a near-overwhelming assault of statistics, charts, theoretical constructs, and correlation values. But despite its density, the book has become a publishing phenomenon in the United States, where in the weeks since its release it has set off a firestorm of debate. The major points of Herrnstein and Murray's argument have ramifications beyond America's borders: they go to the heart of race, class, and the value that society places on human beings.

Simply stated, Herrnstein and Murray say that IQ (short for "intelligence quotient," as rated on standardized tests) is a determining factor in success or failure in life. Because the marketplace increasingly values jobs requiring high intelligence, smart people are winning an increasing share of wealth and power in society. Conversely, people of low intelligence account disproportionately for America's social ills—poverty, unemployment, welfare dependency, illegitimacy, and crime. That stratification of society, the authors argue, demands a radical shift

Joe Chidley is an associate editor of *Maclean's* in Toronto. This article appeared in *Maclean's*, November 28, 1994, as "The Brain Strain."

in American social policy. Not surprisingly, that shift is to the right—Murray is a conservative ideologue—and the authors' prescription calls for the abolition of welfare, an end to affirmative action programs and a reassessment of such government projects as Head Start, which provides a preschool education for disadvantaged kids.

The Bell Curve's most controversial thesis lies in its handling of the thorny issue of intelligence and race. Herrnstein and Murray claim that blacks, on average, are less intelligent than whites, citing as evidence the fact that African Americans typically score about 15 points lower than white Americans on standard IQ tests. Asians—at least those from Japan, China, "and perhaps Korea"—are smarter than whites, typically scoring about three points higher on IQ tests. And then the crux of their argument: the authors contend that between 40 and 80 percent of cognitive ability is genetic, and therefore heritable. That, they maintain, means that blacks score lower on IQ tests, on average, at least in part because they are born that way—that is, they are born "dull." And try as one might, the authors argue, efforts to improve cognitive ability through better education or better living conditions will always have limited returns because of the genetic factor. But the scientific community remains sharply divided on the heredity of intelligence—especially when it is linked to race. "To geneticists, classifications based on skin color give us groupings that are biologically meaningless," wrote David Suzuki in a recent *Toronto Star* column criticizing *The Bell Curve*. "For a trait as complex as intelligence, there is lots of room to manipulate environmental conditions that affect it."

Not surprisingly, J. Philippe Rushton, a psychologist at the University of Western Ontario, is among Herrnstein and Murray's supporters. After all, in his new book, *Race, Evolution and Behavior*, Rushton states even more emphatically the alleged link between race and intelligence. Of *The Bell Curve*, he told *Maclean's:* "I think it's a superb book, and superb scholarship. It has the potential to alter the way we look at human beings."

To others, however, that very potential is worrisome, to say the least. And while it is difficult for the lay reader to argue with the data *The Bell Curve* compiles from a wide array of sources, its underlying assumptions have been widely questioned. Among the more compelling—and contentious issues raised:

• *Can intelligence be measured?* Central to Herrnstein and Murray's argument is their belief in an entity known as *g*, for "general intelligence." That is a "unitary mental factor," the product of statistical analyses of IQ test scores made by former British army officer Charles Spearman in 1904. Tests of IQ, like any standardized test of academic achievement, measure general intelligence to some degree and, the authors say, the scores match "whatever it is that people mean when they use the word intelligent or smart in ordinary language."

They claim that *g* and the validity of IQ tests are issues that are now "beyond significant technical dispute" among psychometricians—hardly surprising given that psychometricians, by definition, are people in the business of measuring cognitive ability as if it were quantifiable. As Herrnstein and Murray acknowledge, however, some dissent remains. Howard Gardner, a Harvard psychologist whom *The Bell Curve* authors dub "a radical," dismisses the concept of *g* and argues instead that there are many types of intelligence—linguistic, musical, logical-mathematical, spatial, bodily kinesthetic, and so-called personal intelligence based on social skills. Gardner's theory seems more consistent with actual human experience: how does one measure the "intelligence" of Michael Jordan's magical maneuvers on the basketball court, of Charlie Parker's inspired improvisations on the saxophone?

• *What is the influence of socioeconomic factors on IQ scores?* Herrnstein and Murray spend more than half their book arguing that socioeconomic performance and intelligence are linked—people who score better on IQ tests, they say, tend to do better in life, both socially and financially. At this point, a chicken-and-egg argument presents itself. Rather than IQ leading to socioeconomic success or failure, it could also be the case that IQ is a measure of a group's socioeconomic history—that is, an ethnic group may score low because the tests measure ability to function in a political or economic system that excludes it from full participation. Catholics in Northern Ireland, for instance, have scored lower than Protestants. In South Africa, blacks have scored lower than the mixed-race "Coloured," who scored lower than whites—a scale that seems to follow the three groups' relative status under apartheid. In passing, Herrnstein and Murray mention that blacks in the South generally score lower than blacks in the northern states. Is that coincidence? Or do the IQ tests, as many critics argue, simply validate

socioeconomic inequalities—and in this case demonstrate that northern blacks have integrated more fully into white American society?
What effect does a history of slavery, racism, and poverty have on self-
esteem? And what effect does self-esteem have on motivation in a test
situation? In other words, it is impossible to "factor out" socioeconomic
history in any comparison of racial differences.

• *What effect does culture have on intelligence?* Herrnstein and Murray
say that IQ tests today have no significant cultural biases. But other
critics, such as outspoken Philadelphia cultural historian Camille
Paglia, author of *Sexual Personae*, contend that background has deeper
implications. "What they're calling IQ is Apollonian logic—cause and
effect—that the West invented," she told *Maclean's*. "It's Eurocentric.
It produced all of modern technology and science. Anyone who wants
to enter into the command machinery of the world, as I hope many
aspiring African Americans do, must learn that style. It is a very narrow
style—like chess. But to identify that narrow thing with all human
intelligence is madness. It is folly."

• *Even if everything Herrnstein and Murray claim were true, so what?*
The authors frequently caution readers not to draw real-life conclusions from their statistical analyses. "We cannot think of a legitimate
argument why any encounter between individual whites and blacks
need be affected by the knowledge that an aggregate ethnic difference
in measured intelligence is genetic instead of environmental," they
write. That might seem disingenuous—what is the point of arguing for
broad racial differences if they have no meaning to individuals?

The Bell Curve is not only a scientific treatise, however: it is also an
exercise in polemics. In the more readable sections of the book, it is
clear that the authors are concerned more with arguing than investigating. In 1971, Herrnstein, the psychologist of the duo, published an
article in *The Atlantic* magazine making roughly the same points about
genetics, IQ, and social standing as *The Bell Curve* does. The article
met with wide opprobrium from the media, and Herrnstein was
branded a racist. In that sense, *The Bell Curve* can be seen as his last
salvo in an ongoing academic debate.

The book's analysis and conclusions are consistent with the concerns of the American conservative movement that Murray represents.
Witness the authors' rating of test subjects on a dubious standard that
they themselves invented, something called "The Middle-Class Val-

ues Index." Consistent, too, is the alarmist tone: if something is not done—and soon—the welfare state will become a "custodial state" for "dull" people, a "more lavish version of the Indian reservation."

It is hard not to wonder why Herrnstein and Murray spent so much gray matter formulating arguments that are part and parcel of two already well-established ideologies. One—which argues that some people, usually the rich, have an intrinsically greater value to society than others—is called elitism. The other—which holds that some people, because of their color, are inferior to others—is called racism.

II
SOURCES AND POLEMICS

TAINTED SOURCES

Charles Lane

F OR ALL THE SHOCK VALUE of its assertion that blacks
are intractably, and probably biologically, inferior in intelligence
to whites and Asians, *The Bell Curve* is not quite an original piece of
research. It is, in spite of all the controversy that is attending its publication, only a review of the literature—an elaborate interpretation of
data culled from the work of other social scientists. For this reason, the
credibility of its authors, Charles Murray and Richard J. Herrnstein,
rests significantly on the credibility of their sources.

The press and television have for the most part taken *The Bell
Curve*'s extensive bibliography and footnotes at face value. And, to be
sure, many of the book's data are drawn from relatively reputable academic sources, or from neutral ones such as the Census Bureau. Certain of the book's major factual contentions are not in dispute—such as
the claim that blacks consistently have scored lower than whites on IQ
tests, or that affirmative action generally promotes minorities who
scored lower on aptitude tests than whites. And obviously intelligence
is both to some degree definable and to some degree heritable.

The interpretation of those data, however, is very much in dispute.
So, too, are the authors' conclusions that little or nothing can or should

Charles Lane is a senior editor of *The New Republic*. This essay appeared in *The New York Review of Books* titled "Tainted Sources," December 1, 1994.

be done to raise the ability of the IQ-impaired, since so much of their lower intelligence is due to heredity. Murray and Herrnstein instead write sympathetically about eugenic approaches to public policy (though they do not endorse them outright). It is therefore interesting that Charles Murray recently expressed his own sense of queasiness about the book's sources to a reporter from *The New York Times:* "Here was a case of stumbling onto a subject that had all the allure of the forbidden," he said. "Some of the things we read to do this work, we literally hide when we're on planes and trains. We're furtively peering at this stuff."[1]

What sort of "stuff" could Murray mean? Surely the most curious of the sources he and Herrnstein consulted is *Mankind Quarterly*—a journal of anthropology founded in Edinburgh in 1960. Five articles from the journal are actually cited in *The Bell Curve*'s bibliography (pp. 775, 807, and 828).[2] But the influence on the book of scholars linked to *Mankind Quarterly* is more significant. No fewer than seventeen researchers cited in the bibliography of *The Bell Curve* have contributed to *Mankind Quarterly*. Ten are present or former editors, or members of its editorial advisory board. This is interesting because *Mankind Quarterly* is a notorious journal of "racial history" founded, and funded, by men who believe in the genetic superiority of the white race.[3]

Mankind Quarterly was established during decolonization and the U.S. civil rights movement. Defenders of the old order were eager to brush a patina of science on their efforts. Thus *Mankind Quarterly*'s avowed purpose was to counter the "Communist" and "egalitarian" influences that were allegedly causing anthropology to neglect the fact of racial differences. "The crimes of the Nazis," wrote Robert Gayre, *Mankind Quarterly*'s founder and editor-in-chief until 1978, "did not, however, justify the enthronement of a doctrine of *a-racialism* as fact, nor of egalitarianism as ethnically and ethically demonstrable."[4]

Gayre was a champion of apartheid in South Africa, and belonged to the ultra-right Candour League of white-ruled Rhodesia.[5] In 1968, he testified for the defense at the hate speech trial of five members of the British Racial Preservation Society, offering his expert opinion that blacks are "worthless."[6] The founders of *Mankind Quarterly* also included Henry E. Garrett of Columbia University, a one-time pamphleteer for the White Citizens' Councils who provided expert testimony for the defense in *Brown* v. *Board of Education;*[7] and Corrado

Gini, leader of fascist Italy's eugenics movement and author of a 1927 Mussolini apologia called "The Scientific Basis of Fascism."[8]

Mainstream anthropologists denounced *Mankind Quarterly*. "It is earnestly hoped that *The Mankind Quarterly* will succumb before it can further discredit anthropology and lead to even more harm to mankind," G. Ainsworth Harrison wrote in a 1961 article in *Man*, the journal of Britain's Royal Institute of Anthropology.[9] Božo Skerlj, a Slovene anthropologist who had survived Dachau, resigned in protest from his post on the editorial advisory board of *Mankind Quarterly*, saying that he had joined unaware of the journal's "racial prejudice."[10] Undaunted, *Mankind Quarterly* published work by some of those who had taken part in research under Hitler's regime in Germany. Ottmar von Verschuer, a leading race scientist in Nazi Germany and an academic mentor of Josef Mengele, even served on the *Mankind Quarterly* editorial board.[11]

Since 1978, the journal has been in the hands of Roger Pearson, a British anthropologist best known for establishing the Northern League in 1958. The group was dedicated to "the interests, friendship and solidarity of all Teutonic nations." In 1980, Pearson resigned from the ultra-right World Anti-Communist League in a struggle with members who said he was too far to the right.[12] But *Mankind Quarterly* didn't change. Pearson published eugenically minded attacks on school integration by two American academics, Ralph Scott and Donald Swan, who were alleged to have pro-Nazi affiliations; reports on a sperm bank in which geniuses have deposited their superior genetic material; elaborate accounts of the inherited mental inferiority of blacks; and the fact that Jews first came to South Africa because its gold and diamonds were "attractive" to them.

Pearson's Institute for the Study of Man, which publishes *Mankind Quarterly*, is bankrolled by the Pioneer Fund, a New York foundation established in 1937 with the money of Wickliffe Draper. Draper, a textile magnate who was fascinated by eugenics, expressed early sympathy for Nazi Germany, and later advocated the "repatriation" of blacks to Africa. The fund's first president, Harry Laughlin, was a leader in the eugenicist movement to ban genetically inferior immigrants, and also an early admirer of the Nazi regime's eugenic policies.[13]

The Pioneer Fund's current president, Harry Weyher, has denied any Nazi or white supremacist connections. But the fund's current agenda remains true to the purpose set forth in its charter of 1937: "race betterment, with special reference to the people of the United States." In a letter in 1989, the fund proposed that America abandon integration, on the grounds that "raising the intelligence of blacks or others still remains beyond our capabilities."[14] The fund not only underwrites *Mankind Quarterly* and many other Pearson publications, but has also provided millions of dollars in research grants to sustain the "scholars" who write for it and serve on its editorial board.[15]

Which brings us back to Murray and Herrnstein. They cite in their book no fewer than thirteen scholars who have benefited from Pioneer Fund grants in the last two decades—the grants total more than $4 million. Many of *The Bell Curve*'s sources who worked for *Mankind Quarterly* were also granted Pioneer money.[16]

Most of *The Bell Curve* does not explicitly address the relationship between race, genes, and IQ—as Murray has taken great pains to point out. Rather, the book couches its arguments about the impact of IQ on social behavior in terms of class, mostly using examples drawn from data on whites. But in view of the characteristic overlaps between race and class in American society, the insinuation is that all the connections between social pathology and low IQ which the authors find for whites must go double for blacks. It is only after one factors in their argument that IQ itself is mostly inherited (however hedged that argument may be), that the racial connotations of their policy prescriptions become evident.

And many of *The Bell Curve*'s most important assertions which establish causal links between IQ and social behavior, and IQ and race, are derived partially or totally from the *Mankind Quarterly*–Pioneer Fund scholarly circle. The University of California's Arthur Jensen, cited twenty-three times in *The Bell Curve*'s bibliography, is the book's principal authority on the intellectual inferiority of blacks. He has received $1.1 million from the Pioneer Fund.[17] To buttress Jensen's argument, Murray and Herrnstein draw on a book edited by University of Georgia psychologist R. Travis Osborne (the book, co-edited by former *Mankind Quarterly* editorial advisory board member Frank McGurk, is also cited by Murray and Herrnstein as an authority on the link between low IQ and criminality: pp. 277, 339). Osborne, the recipient of $387,000 from Pioneer, once testified as an expert witness for plaintiffs in a federal suit to overturn the *Brown* v. *Board of Education* decision.[18]

Other scholars who have received substantial amounts of money from Pioneer include Robert A. Gordon, a Johns Hopkins sociologist cited by Murray and Herrnstein on the causal link between low IQ and black criminality (pp. 321, 327, and 338); Linda Gottfredson of the University of Delaware, cited on the disproportionate representation of lower-IQ blacks in the professions; and University of Pennsylvania demographer Daniel Vining, Jr., a former *Mankind Quarterly* editorial advisory board member, cited on incipient "dysgenesis," or biological decline, in America, owing to the falling birthrate among the most intelligent members of society.[19]

THE TAINTED FUNDING of some of the scholars Murray and Herrnstein cite does not by itself invalidate those scholars' findings. After all, history is full of examples of scientists who were pilloried as crackpots in their own times but are hailed as geniuses today. However shocking it may be that some of Murray and Herrnstein's sources have chosen to affiliate themselves with such organizations, their work— and those parts of *The Bell Curve* that draw upon it—must be judged on the scholarly merits.

Take the case of Richard Lynn. A professor of psychology at the University of Ulster in Coleraine, Northern Ireland, Lynn was particularly influential in guiding the two authors of *The Bell Curve* through their review of the literature. In the book's acknowledgments, they say they "benefited especially" from the "advice" of Lynn, whom they identify only as "a leading scholar of racial and ethnic differences" (pp. xxv, 272).

Lynn is an associate editor of *Mankind Quarterly*, and has received $325,000 from the Pioneer Fund.[20] One of his articles expressed support for the view that "the poor and the ill" are "weak specimens whose proliferation needs to be discouraged in the interests of the improvement of the genetic quality of the group, and ultimately of group survival."[21] He has also written that the genetic mental superiority of the Jews may be a happy Darwinian byproduct of "intermittent persecutions which the more intelligent may have been able to foresee and escape."[22]

Lynn's work is cited twenty-four times in *The Bell Curve*'s bibliography.[23] It is used to support three important claims: that East Asians have a higher average IQ than whites; that most immigrants come from groups with subpar IQs; and that the IQ score of blacks in Africa is "substantially below" the American black average. Each of these seemingly discrete claims has a key role in the formulation of *The Bell Curve*'s broader suggestions about the relationship among race, heredity, IQ, and social structure.

The assertion about inferior black African intelligence has particularly far-reaching implications. If it can be shown that low IQ predicts social ills such as crime, poverty, and unstable families, current views of Africa and of the sources of its tragic problems would have to be significantly revised. The finding would also support the claim that the IQ superiority of whites is genetic, because the African-American edge over blacks in Africa could be attributed to their admixture of white genes. (Murray and Herrnstein note pointedly that South African "coloureds" have about the same IQ as American blacks.) And lagging African IQ could also be taken to refute the claim that black Americans' lower IQ is a legacy of racism—assuming, as Murray and Herrnstein put it, that "the African black population has not been subjected to the historical legacy of American black slavery and discrimination and might therefore have higher scores" (p. 288).

SETTING UP their discussion of Lynn's data, Murray and Herrnstein contend that the comparison between black Americans and black Africans is a valid exercise because IQ scores have been found to predict job and school performance of black Africans as well as those of black Americans (p. 288). They also attribute the paucity of published estimates of an overall average IQ score for blacks in Africa to the fact that these scores have been extremely low—the implication being that researchers are reluctant to publish such politically incorrect findings (p. 289).

These assertions are based on a highly selective reading of the article Murray and Herrnstein cite to support them: a comprehensive 1988 review titled "Test Performance of Blacks in Southern Africa," by the South African psychologists I. M. Kendall, M. A. Verster, and J. W. V. Mollendorf (p. 289). The main point of these three researchers' argument is to question sweeping comparisons such as the one Lynn attempts, and Murray and Herrnstein repeat. The three South African psychologists write:

It would be rash to suppose that psychometric tests constitute valid measures of intelligence among non-westerners. The inability of most psychologists to look beyond the confines of their own culture has led to the kind of arrogance whereby judgments are made concerning the "simplicity" of African mental structure and "retarded" cognitive growth.[24]

Given the host of environmental and cultural factors that hamper black Africans' test performance, they also say, "one wonders whether there is any point in even considering genetic factors as an additional source of variance between the average performance levels of westerners and Africans."[25]

Nevertheless, Murray and Herrnstein venture an estimate of African IQ, drawn mainly from an article by Lynn that appeared in *Mankind Quarterly* in 1991. It should be noted, for a start, that the authors of *The Bell Curve* misreport Lynn's data. They say he found a median IQ of 75 in Africa (p. 289). But in his article, "Race Differences in Intelligence: The Global Perspective," Lynn said that the mean African IQ—not the median—was 70.[26]

In any event, how did Lynn arrive at his number? First, he assembled eleven studies of the intelligence of "pure African Negroids," drawn from different tests of several different peoples and widely varying sample sizes in the years from 1929 to 1991. Then, he decided which was the "best": a 1989 study from South Africa. In this test, he says, 1,093 sixteen-year-old black students (who had been in school for eight years and were therefore familiar with pencil-and-paper tests) scored a mean of 69 on the South African Junior Aptitude Test. Finally, Lynn rounded this result up to 70, and declared it a valid approximation of black IQ in the continent of Africa as a whole.[27]

This methodology alone invites skepticism. But Lynn also seems to have misconstrued the study. Its author, Dr. Ken Owen, told me his test was "not at all" an indication that intelligence is inherited. He blamed the low performance of blacks on environmental factors such as poorer schooling for blacks under apartheid and their difficulty with English. Owen said his results "certainly cannot" be taken as an indication of intelligence among blacks in Africa as a whole.[28]

Lynn further defends his choice of 70 as a "reasonable" mean for Africa on the grounds that 70 was the median of the average IQ scores reported in the eleven studies he had found. This statistical artifact aside, his list of studies is dubious. It includes what he calls "the first good study of the intelligence of pure African Negroids": an experiment in 1929 in which 293 blacks in South Africa were given the U.S. Army Beta Test, and got a mean score of 65.[29]

The test was administered by M. L. Fick, whom Kendall, Verster, and Mollendorf call an "extreme protagonist" of the view that blacks are inherently inferior to whites.[30] The Beta test, which was developed for illiterate recruits in the U.S. military, shows blatant cultural bias. One question presents a picture of people playing tennis without a net; respondents are supposed to sketch in the net to get full credit. In 1930, just a year after the Beta test was given in South Africa, C. C. Brigham, who had been its leading proponent in the United States, finally admitted that the test was invalid for non-Americans. Lynn does not mention this fact.[31]

Far from refuting the thesis that the legacy of racism is to blame for black Americans' lower IQ scores vis-à-vis whites, as Murray and Herrnstein contend, Lynn's data actually support it (to the extent they have any meaning at all). Of Lynn's eleven studies, five were conducted in South Africa under apartheid (and one in the Belgian Congo in 1952).[32] If any country oppressed black people more than the United States, it was South Africa. Indeed, as the modern South African psychologists now acknowledge, one of the main uses of IQ tests under apartheid was to provide "scientific" justification for that system.

The assertion of an East Asian IQ advantage over whites, though essentially a success story, also plays a subtle, but crucial, supporting role in *The Bell Curve*'s overall argument about the connections among IQ, social achievement, and race. Coming before the discussion of black-white differences, it helps prepare the reader to accept racial categories as units of social analysis. It also conforms to readers' preconceptions, shaped both by the media and by everyday experience, about the amazing brilliance of Asian immigrants and their offspring.

The authors would seem to be on firmer ground invoking Lynn here, since his specialty is the inherited mental superiority of East Asians, or "Mongoloids," as he refers to them. In *Mankind Quarterly*, he has contended that the Japanese "have the highest intelligence in the world."[33] In an article in *Nature* in 1982, Lynn claimed the Japanese enjoy a ten-point IQ advantage over European whites, and that this difference is growing. He suggested that this helps to explain the post-war economic miracle in Japan.[34]

But two American psychologists, Harold W. Stevenson and Hiroshi Azuma, pointed out in a rebuttal in *Nature* that the Japanese sample Lynn used was made up of children of relatively well-off urban parents—a fact Lynn failed to disclose in his article. Lynn's result was thus fatally flawed: he had tried to compare this socially skewed sample with a much broader and more representative American one.[35] Murray and Herrnstein's sole mention of this is a footnote: "For a critique of Lynn's early work, see Stevenson and Azuma 1983" (p. 716).

At the opening of their section headed "Do Asians Have Higher IQs Than Whites?" Murray and Herrnstein seem to be struggling to salvage some meaning from Lynn's data. The basic problem is the enormous difficulty of drawing conclusions about the relative intelligence of people who come from vastly different civilizations. They cite a string of Lynn's comparisons that suggest East Asians are superior, but eventually back off, conceding that the various test results he has assembled are not really comparable. Finally, the authors note: "Given the complexities of cross-national comparisons, the issue [of relative East Asian-white-black intelligence] must eventually be settled by a sufficient body of data obtained from identical tests that are comparable except for race" (pp. 272–274).

Murray and Herrnstein write that they "have been able to identify three such efforts." In the first, they say, "samples of American, British, and Japanese students ages thirteen to fifteen were administered a test of abstract reasoning and spatial relations"—the British and American students did far worse than the Japanese, naturally. In the second "set of studies," they write, nine-year-olds in Japan, Hong Kong, and Britain, drawn from comparable socioeconomic populations, were administered the Ravens Standard Progressive Matrices. Once again, the British children lost out by "well over half a standard deviation" (p. 274).

Only by checking the footnotes (at the back of the 845-page book) can readers discover that the author of both these studies is Richard Lynn. With regard to the first case, *The Bell Curve*'s text leaves the impression that the tests were conducted with similar samples in the three countries at more or less the same time. This is not quite what happened, as one learns from reading the 1987 *Mankind Quarterly* article from which these data are drawn. Lynn and his assistants gave the test in 1985 to 178 Japanese children. The tiny sample was not checked to reflect the social makeup of Japan as a whole (some 57 percent of the test-takers were boys). The test-givers merely showed up at two schools, one rural and one urban, and gave the tests to whoever was present. Lynn then compared this result to results from an American test that had been given thirteen years earlier to 64,000 subjects screened for their representativity, and to the results of a test given in 1978 to a similarly representative sample of 10,000 students in Britain. His conclusion that Japanese children do better was arrived at by distributing extra points among the three groups to "adjust" for the time lag among the three tests.[36]

The second "set of studies" is in the same 1991 *Mankind Quarterly* article in which Lynn presented his claims about "pure African Negroids." He says that a group of 118 Hong Kong nine-year-olds scored a 113 IQ, a sample of 444 Japanese children got a 110 IQ, and a sample of 239 British children got a 100 IQ. He asserts that all three samples were "representative" and drawn from "typical public primary schools," as Murray and Herrnstein report. But in the article Lynn does not explain how he assured the "representativity" of the samples, or the "typicality" of the schools.[37]

Murray and Herrnstein then go on to describe a third set of studies done by Harold Stevenson in Minnesota. In contrast to their seeming circumspection about Lynn's identity, they mention Stevenson's name in the main text of the book. As they note, he "carefully matched the children on socioeconomic and demographic variables"—and found no difference at all between the IQs of Japanese, Taiwanese, and American children (pp. 274–275).

"Where does this leave us?" Murray and Herrnstein then ask. On the one hand, we have two methodologically dubious studies by Lynn, a professor who believes, as he wrote in the *Mankind Quarterly* article, that "the Caucasoids and the Mongoloids are the only two races that have made any significant contribution to civilization."[38] On the other hand is a rigorous study by a social scientist with no known axe to grind, who finds no IQ disparity between whites and Asians. But Murray and Herrnstein portray this as a debate among a large number of contentious and equally reputable experts. "We will continue to hedge," they write; and simply split the difference. They venture that East Asian IQ exceeds that of whites by three points, a figure which "most resembles a consensus, tentative though it still is" (pp. 276).

By the time Murray and Herrnstein get around to talking about immigrants, their "tentative consensus" on the East Asian–white IQ gap has grown by two points, and hardened into a datum firm enough to be factored into immigration policy. Drawing, once again, on Lynn's 1991 article in *Mankind Quarterly*, they assign East Asians a mean IQ of 105, whites 100, "Pacific" populations a score of 91, and blacks 84. Without reference to Lynn or any other source, Murray and Herrnstein give "Latinos"—a designation empty of meaningful "racial" content—a mean IQ of 91. They give no data on IQs of South Asians and Middle Eastern people, who supplied 11 percent of the immigrants in the 1980s. They're just "omitted from the analysis," as the authors put it. From this hodgepodge of assumptions Murray and Herrnstein produce the "basic statement" that 57 percent of legal immigrants in the 1980s came from ethnic groups with average IQs less than that of American whites, and therefore the mean for all immigrants is probably below that of all native-born Americans (pp. 359–360).

Even if their "basic statement" is true, it says nothing at all about the scores of the individuals who actually did immigrate to the United States. Thus Murray and Herrnstein must deal with the common-sense notion that immigrants generally represent the brightest and most energetic members of their former societies, by virtue of their willingness to get up and go to the United States. This the authors try to do by citing numbers from the National Longitudinal Survey, or NLSY. They find that foreign-born NLSY members had a mean IQ ".4 standard deviation" lower than the rest of the NLSY sample (p. 360).

But the NLSY began in 1979, as a survey of people who were fourteen to twenty-two years old at the time, and have then been re-examined and re-interviewed each succeeding year. Thus it has no bearing at all on people who arrived in the United States after 1979, when immigration from the third world reached its height—as Murray and Herrnstein themselves report. (Probably for this reason, the sample did not include a statistically significant percentage of East Asians.) The authors also acknowledge that the slightly poorer IQ performance of those Latino immigrants who were interviewed in the NLSY probably reflects their weak command of English. That normally improves in a few years, and IQ rises along with it. Finally, Murray and Herrn-stein find that foreign-born blacks in the NLSY score five points higher than native-born blacks (p. 360)—a fact they are utterly at a loss to explain, perhaps because some of the immigrants must have come from Africa, and they have just finished alleging that black Africans are even stupider than American blacks.

"Nonetheless," Murray and Herrnstein assert, "keeping all of these qualifications in mind, the kernel of evidence that must also be acknowledged is that Latino and black immigrants are, at least in the short run, putting some downward pressure on the distribution of intelligence" (pp. 360–361). One hundred eighty-nine pages later, this strained contention is used to justify their inclination toward a more eugenically minded—and, hence, restrictive—U.S. immigration pol-icy. Yet other than Lynn's flawed survey, and their own bald assertion that Latinos have a mean IQ of 91, there is no "kernel of evidence" of the kind they refer to (p. 360).

MURRAY AND HERRNSTEIN aren't answerable for every belief of every member of the racialist crowd they rely on for so much of their data. (And they didn't get any money from Pioneer.) Still, there are two matters on which their book and the intellectual mission of the men who founded *Mankind Quarterly* overlap: both sought to restore the scientific status of race, and to reintroduce eugenic think-ing into the public policy debate.

The more pertinent issue here is full disclosure, or what used to be called intellectual honesty. Just as Murray blushingly covered some of his materials on the Delta shuttle, so *The Bell Curve* tiptoes around facts that might have an inconvenient influence on its readers' evaluation of the book's sources and data—not to mention the judgment of its authors in choosing those sources. Geoffrey Cowley of *Newsweek*, in a sympathetic review of the book, pronounced its scholarship "over-whelmingly mainstream."[39] Would he have done so if Murray and Herrnstein had provided a full account of the provenance of their data? Indeed, would this heavily marketed book have achieved the same sales success and as much respectful press attention if it had leveled with readers about all of its sources?

There is no way to isolate the scholarship of Richard Lynn, and that of the other *Mankind Quarterly* contributors, from their racial and political views. Social science is not so easily insulated from ideology, as Murray and Herrnstein are quick to emphasize when railing against their critics. The scholarly subcultures on which the authors of *The Bell Curve* depend for information are hardly less biased than those they are summoned to rebut. The bias of the *Mankind Quarterly* contributors, however, is much nastier. And as we have seen, some of the scholars Murray and Herrnstein rely on distort the evidence, which in key cases does not support *The Bell Curve*'s contentions.

NOTES

1. Jason DeParle, "Daring Research or Social Science Pornography?" *The New York Times Magazine*, October 9, 1994, p. 51.
2. Richard J. Herrnstein and Charles Murray, *The Bell Curve* (Free Press, 1994).
3. According to the bibliography of *The Bell Curve*, and to back issues of the *Mankind Quarterly*, the seventeen are W. J. Andrews, Cyril Burt, Raymond B. Cattell (eight citations), Hans J. Eysenck, Seymour Itzkoff, Arthur Jensen (twenty-three citations), Richard Lynn (twenty-four citations), Robert E. Kuttner, Frank C. J. McGurk (six citations), C. E. Noble, R. Travis Osborne (three citations), Roger Pearson, J. Philippe Rushton (eleven citations), William Shockley, Audrey Shuey, Daniel Vining (three citations), and Nathaniel Weyl. The ten who are or were either editors or members of the editorial board are: Cattell, Eysenck, Itzkoff, Kuttner, Lynn, McGurk, Noble, Pearson, Shuey, and Vining.
4. Robert Gayre, "The Mankind Quarterly Under Attack," *The Mankind Quarterly*, Vol. 2, No. 2 (October–December 1961), p. 79. Emphasis in original.
5. Michael Billig, *Die Rassistische Internationale* (Frankfurt: Neue Kritik, 1981), p. 101. This is the German edition of Billig's 1979 book *Psychology, Racism, and Fascism* (Birmingham, England: A. F. and R. Publications/Searchlight, 1979).
6. Billig, *Die Rassistische Internationale*, p. 97.
7. Billig, *Die Rassistische Internationale*, pp. 103–104, and Adam Miller, "Professors of Hate," *Rolling Stone*, October 20, 1994, p. 113. Garrett also wrote in 1961 that "Hitler's persecution of the Jews has greatly oversensitized the American Jew toward anything which smacks of racial distinction. The preoccupation of the Jews with racial matters today is evident in the activities of various Jewish organizations. Most of these belligerently support the equalitarian dogma which they accept as having been 'scientifically' proven." *Mankind Quarterly*, Vol. 1, No. 4 (1961), p. 256.
8. Billig, *Die Rassistische Internationale*, p. 104.
9. G. Ainsworth Harrison, "The Mankind Quarterly," *Man*, September 1961, p. 164.

10. Božo Skerlj, "Correspondence," *Man*, November 1960, pp. 172–173.

11. Billig, *Die Rassistische Internationale*, p. 106; Stefan Kuehl, *The Nazi Connection: Eugenics, American Racism, and German National Socialism* (Oxford University Press, 1994), pp. 102–103.

12. Kuehl, *The Nazi Connection*, p. 4; Miller, "Professors of Hate," p. 113; and Tim Kelsey and Trevor Rowe, "Academics 'were funded by racist American trust,' " *The Independent*, March 4, 1990, p. 4.

13. Kuehl, *The Nazi Connection*, p. xv passim.

14. Kuehl, *The Nazi Connection*, p. 6; Miller, "Professors of Hate," p. 114; and Kelsey and Rowe, "Academics 'were funded by racist American trust.' "

15. Miller, "Professors of Hate," Kuehl, *The Nazi Connection*, pp. 9, 10, and Kelsey and Rowe, "Academics 'were funded by racist American trust.' " See also copies of federal form 990-PF tax returns filed by the Pioneer Fund, which are available on microfiche at The Foundation Center, Washington, DC.

16. The numbers were derived by cross-checking the Murray-Herrnstein bibliography with Kuehl, Billig, Miller, and Kelsey, back issues of *Mankind Quarterly*, and copies of federal form 990-PF filed by the Pioneer Fund.

17. Miller, "Professors of Hate," p. 114.

18. Miller, "Professors of Hate," p. 113.

19. Miller, "Professors of Hate," p. 114, and the federal 990-PF forms filed by the Pioneer Fund at The Foundation Center. Vining is also thanked in the book's acknowledgments. The amounts of the Pioneer Grants are often in the hundreds of thousands of dollars over several years. Another major recipient, J. Philippe Rushton of Canada's University of Western Ontario, is cited eleven times in *The Bell Curve* bibliography, and receives a two-page mention in the book's appendix (pp. 642–643) defending his highly controversial work. Rushton believes that blacks have been selected by evolution to have low intelligence. They have small heads, large genitalia, and other supposed racial features, because they developed in the warm savannah and jungle climates of Africa, where natural selection favored a reproductive strategy of high birthrates and low parental investment. In other words, Rushton believes that black people are genetically programmed to be irresponsible parents; he has also written that this genetic predisposition to sexual excess explains why so many blacks have AIDS.

20. Miller, "Professors of Hate," p. 114.

21. Richard Lynn, "Civilization and the Quality of Population," *Journal of Social, Political and Economic Studies*, Vol. 16, No. 1 (Spring 1991), p. 123. This is another Roger Pearson publication.

22. Richard Lynn, "Orientals: The Emerging American Elite?" *Mankind Quarterly*, Vol. 31, Nos. 1 and 2 (Fall/Winter 1990), p. 189.

23. Six of the Lynn articles cited by Murray and Herrnstein appeared in *Personality and Individual Differences*, a British journal edited by Hans J. Eysenck.

Eysenck is the recipient of $250,000 in Pioneer grants and a frequent contributor to *Mankind Quarterly*. In 1990, two years after the University of London barred Eysenck from taking any more funds from Pioneer, Lynn channeled $30,000 from one of his Pioneer grants to Eysenck. All told, eighteen of *The Bell Curve*'s bibliographical citations are from Eysenck's journal. See Pioneer Fund's 990-PF forms at The Foundation Center, and Kelsey and Rowe, "Academics 'were funded by racist American trust.' "

24. I. M. Kendall, Mary Ann Verster, and J. W. Von Mollendorf, "Test Performance of Blacks in Southern Africa," in S. H. Irvine and J. W. Berry, editors, *Human Abilities in Cultural Context* (Cambridge University Press, 1988), p. 328.

25. Kendall, Verster, and Mollendorf, "Test Performance of Blacks in Southern Africa," p. 326.

26. Richard Lynn, "Race Differences in Intelligence: A Global Perspective," *The Mankind Quarterly*, Vol. 31, No. 3 (Spring 1991), p. 255 passim.

27. Lynn, "Race Differences in Intelligence: A Global Perspective," p. 272.

28. Interview with the author.

29. Lynn, "Race Differences in Intelligence: A Global Perspective," p. 272.

30. Lynn, "Race Differences in Intelligence: A Global Perspective," p. 267; Kendall, Verster, and Mollendorf, "Test Performance of Blacks in Southern Africa," p. 300.

31. Steven Jay Gould, *The Mismeasure of Man* (Norton, 1981), p. 233.

32. Lynn, "Race Differences in Intelligence: A Global Perspective," p. 269.

33. Richard Lynn, Susan L. Hampson, and Saburo Iwakawi, "Abstract Reasoning and Spatial Abilities Among American, British and Japanese Adolescents," *The Mankind Quarterly*, Vol. 27, No. 4 (Summer 1987), p. 379.

34. Lynn, "IQ in Japan and the United States shows a growing disparity," *Nature*, Vol. 297 (May 20, 1982), pp. 222–223.

35. Harold Stevenson and Hiroshi Azuma, "IQ in Japan and the United States," *Nature*, Vol. 306 (November 17, 1983), pp. 291–292.

36. Lynn, "Abstract Reasoning and Spatial Abilities Among American, British, and Japanese Adolescents," pp. 400 and 401.

37. Lynn, "Race Differences in Intelligence: A Global Perspective," pp. 275, 278.

38. Lynn, "Race Differences in Intelligence: A Global Perspective," p. 284.

39. Geoffrey Cowley, "Testing the Science of Intelligence," *Newsweek*, October 24, 1994, p. 56.

THE CURIOUS LAIRD OF NIGG

Magnus Linklater

N<small>UMBER</small> O<small>NE</small> Darnaway Street is one of the grander houses in the West End of Edinburgh's New Town. Today it is divided into flats. But thirty years ago it was the town residence of Lieutenant Colonel Robert Gayre of Gayre and Nigg, KCN, GCMM, KCL, KCCI, Hon. KMV, GCLJ, MA, DPhil, DPolSc, Dsc. Goodness knows what half the initials mean, but he is, by his own account, Chief of the Clan Gayre, a Knight of St. Lazarus, has collected six knighthoods, three international Grand Crosses and is a colonel of the honorary kind thanks to the state militias of Alabama and Georgia. He also claims to be a world expert on race, ethnology, genetics, and inherited characteristics.

Colonel Gayre is still alive, aged eighty-seven, and living a reclusive life in Minard Castle near Inveraray in Argyll, where his colorful past is reflected in armorial decorations, heraldic memorabilia and portraits of popes, kings, ancestors, and himself. He is an eccentric, but not exactly a lovable one. For he has, throughout most of his life, sought to publicize views on race and intelligence which are not only widely discredited today, but have branded him an extremist in the eyes of most mainstream academics.

Magnus Linklater, former editor of *The Scotsman*, is a regular columnist for *The Times* of London, where a slightly abridged version of this piece, titled "The Barmy Laird of Nigg," appeared on November 23, 1994.

The reason why the Colonel is once again, in his twilight years, under scrutiny, is because of the magazine he founded and edited back in 1960 in the top flat of Number 1 Darnaway Street. *The Mankind Quarterly*, devoted to the study of ethnology, genetics, and racial history, has survived ever since and though its base has moved from Edinburgh to Washington, D.C., it still exerts an insidious influence in the minefield that is anthropology today.

In a recent issue of the *New York Review of Books*, Charles Lane reveals that it is the *Mankind Quarterly* that provided the main source material for *The Bell Curve*, a book that has stirred controversy in America by asserting that blacks are biologically inferior in intelligence to whites and Asians. Written by Charles Murray and Richard J. Herrnstein it not only presents a bleak picture of growing inequality but argues that little or nothing can be done to raise the ability of those with "impaired" IQs since so much of their lower intelligence is due to heredity.

The Bell Curve derives much of its claimed authority from a mass of impressive-looking footnotes and an apparently authoritative bibliography. But what Lane discovered as he trawled through them was how much the book relied on research carried originally in the *Mankind Quarterly*. Five of its articles are cited in the book, and no fewer than seventeen researchers listed in the bibliography have contributed to it. Ten are present or former editors or members of its editorial advisory board. Lane found this interesting because, in its field, *Mankind Quarterly* is known as a journal of "racial history," founded and funded by men who believe in the genetic superiority of the white race.

In its time it has run articles by most of those who make up the demonology of the right in matters of race and intelligence: Cyril Burt, Raymond Cattell, H. J. Eysenck, Arthur Jensen, Richard Lynn, J. Philippe Rushton, and William Shockley among them. From the outset it attracted controversy, partly because of the thrust of its central argument, partly because of the nature of some of its contributors. Leafing through early issues one comes across a steady stream of articles with titles like "The Emergence of Racial Genetics," "The Evolutionary Basis of Race Consciousness," "North-South Dichotomy," and endless variations of IQ tests demonstrating the underachievement of Negroes in comparison to their white counterparts. Time after time the conclusion is reached that integration of different races is counterproductive because it drags whites down to the level of blacks to the detriment of both.

Lane has looked closely at some of the magazine's contributors and advisers. They included Corrado Gini, leader of fascist Italy's eugenics movement and author of a 1927 apologia for Mussolini called "The Scientific Basis of Fascism"; Ottmar von Verschauer, a leading race scientist in Nazi Germany and an academic mentor of Josef Mengele; the present editor, Roger Pearson, a British anthropologist who was forced to resign from the ultra-right World Anti-Communist League because its members considered he was too far to the right.

And, of course, Gayre himself. He was always careful to argue that he was not a proponent of white supremacy and was entirely hostile to Nazism. But in Volume Two of the *Mankind Quarterly*, responding to attacks on his journal, he revealed his colors: "The crimes of the Nazis," he said, "did not justify the enthronement of a doctrine of a-racialism as fact, nor egalitarianism as ethnically and ethically demonstrable . . . in respect of some characters, various stock will be superior to others, in other characters inferior." This was demonstrated, he wrote, by different IQ tests. Some were more suitable for "the genius of the Black races, such as those which gave due credit in the field of humour, music, art, ability to live a community life, a feeling for emotional religious expression or physical ability in boxing, running, and much else. It would be very surprising if Negroes did not prove themselves superior to Europeans in these respects." Whites, on the other hand, excelled in matters involving the intellect. They should be allowed to develop separately. It is not surprising to learn that Gayre was an early champion of apartheid.

I first heard of Robert Gayre in relatively innocent circumstances when he objected strongly in the early sixties to the use by my father of his family name in a novel called *The House of Gair*. He threatened legal action, then announced he would be sailing north in his motor yacht to pay a visit to our family home in Nigg on the Cromarty Firth. He was, he said, the hereditary laird of Nigg, as certified by Scotland's chief herald, the Lord Lyon King at Arms. In the event neither writ nor yacht arrived.

Four years later, in 1968, he was locked in legal action against the *Sunday Times* which had revealed that Gayre had been prosecuted, though acquitted, under the Race Relations Act for distributing material "likely to stir up racial hatred." He had been handing out a pamphlet attacking liberal integrationist policies which were "turning Britain into a mongrelised and Communist-dominated slum."

The exchanges in court reported by the *Sunday Times* were revealing. At one point Gayre told his defense counsel: "Nearly all our foresight and acquisitiveness is due to the high development of the temporal lobes. This is not anything like so developed in the Negro race, and as a result they are feckless, they are not worried about the future—and they do not suffer from ulcers as a consequence."

As the *Sunday Times* pointed out, this was not only offensive but inaccurate on every score, and there was no lack of experts to say so. Gayre, stung by the rebuke, brought a costly libel action which he lost, not least perhaps because the jury listening to his arguments on race and intelligence concluded that they were fairly barmy.

Barmy they may have been, but harmless they probably were not. Despite the regular demolition of academic views which, when taken to their extreme, are venomously racist, the beast survives. Twenty-six years on, the *Mankind Quarterly* which Gayre founded is still in publication, and still churning out its unlovely views. Judging by the awful success of *The Bell Curve*, it seems that there is still an appetite for the maverick views of the Chief of Clan Gayre.

INSIDE THE PIONEER FUND

John Sedgwick

I N THE THIRTY-SIX YEARS that Harry F. Weyher has headed the Pioneer Fund, he had never met with a member of the press until I had lunch with him in the summer of 1994. This reclusiveness is somewhat surprising, given that the Pioneer Fund— a small, right-wing outfit that subsidizes research into racial differences, much of which puts blacks in a highly unfavorable light—must be the most controversial organization of its size in America. It has set off localized media explosions practically everywhere it has gone for the past quarter century. A few years ago, for instance, a grant recipient named J. Philippe Rushton, a professor of psychology at the University of Western Ontario, declared that blacks as a race could be characterized by low intelligence, high criminality, and extreme sexuality. That view was considered so abhorrent that the Ontario premier called for his firing, Rushton was investigated by the police for possible violations of Canadian laws against hate propaganda, and he was obliged to deliver his lectures by videotape after the university could no longer vouch for either his safety or that of his students. Other such Pioneer-related incidents have occurred in recent years at the University of Delaware, Smith College, the University of Min-

John Sedgwick is a contributing writer to *GQ* and a contributing editor of *Newsweek*. This article was published in *GQ* as "The Mentality Bunker," November 1994.

nesota, the City College of New York and the University of London, in England.

It was probably appropriate that when Weyher did emerge from the shadows, he chose to meet me for lunch at his club—the Racquet & Tennis Club, one of New York's toniest, a virtually all-white-male bastion on Park Avenue. Attuned to pedigrees, Weyher (pronounced "wire") had somehow divined that I am a Harvard graduate, and he apologized for not taking me to the Harvard Club, to which he also belongs. But there had been too much "noise" there lately, he said, referring to the boisterous crew of striking staff members, mostly black and Hispanic, that has gathered outside the front entrance for months now. He imagined that I would find the Racquet Club most congenial.

Weyher himself, at seventy-three, doesn't play much tennis anymore. A courtly southerner, he is a little stooped with age, but as we settled ourselves into our chairs in the vast dining room, his face bore a sly, attentive expression. Club rules forbid bringing out pens and paper at the tables, which poses obvious difficulties for a reporter; I'd also had to check my bag with my notebook and tape recorder at the door. Weyher fumbled in his pocket and produced a small, rather elegant leather notepad with several sheets of paper. "You can write a few things on that," he said with his North Carolina accent, redolent of tobacco fields on hot summer afternoons. "Just don't be too conspicuous."

Conspicuousness has always been an issue for the Pioneer Fund. Founded in 1937, it controls only $5 million of an endowment left by an eccentric Massachusetts textile heir named Wickliffe Draper upon his death in 1972, but it has gotten quite a bang for its relatively few bucks. Weyher himself attributes this to the fund's fiscal restraint. The fund maintains no office and pays no employees. It is run on a voluntary basis by Weyher out of his Fifth Avenue law office, with the occasional assistance of four unpaid directors.

More likely, it is the nature of the Pioneer Fund's activities that has made the impact. Broadly speaking, the Pioneer Fund advocates the cause of hereditarianism—in common terms, the notion that it is nature, not nurture, that determines our fates. That notion may appear to be a dry, academic proposition until you understand its implications, especially its racial ones. According to the fund's operating premise, intelligence is largely inherited, and one's class standing is an inevitable result of that inherited IQ. Further, Pioneer would contend, low IQ leads to criminality and to dangerous sexual licentiousness. Not surprisingly, given these questionable premises, the fund's directors maintain that African Americans are at the bottom of most socioeconomic measures not because of traumas they have faced as a race but largely because they are genetically deficient. By positing that the races are inherently unequal because of their respective IQ scores, the Pioneer Fund dismisses one of our nation's central tenets, the unifying idea that opens the Declaration of Independence and that Lincoln reaffirmed at Gettysburg: "All men are created equal."

At this point, the Pioneer Fund grantees are so closely allied that they might qualify as a race themselves. They know each other, support each other, study with each other, publish each other, cite each other's books and, in one case, have even been married to each other. To list these recipients is to know the Pioneer Fund. The notorious Berkeley psychologist Arthur Jensen was one grantee. Weyher calls him "a giant in the profession," and Jensen returns the favor by praising the fund for its "important contribution" to genetic research. Jensen set off a national firestorm with his 1969 essay in the *Harvard Educational Review* arguing that compensatory educational programs for blacks were useless, since blacks were intellectually inferior to whites for largely genetic reasons. To Weyher's sorrow, the fund never did provide money to Jensen's intellectual descendent, the late Richard Herrnstein, whose controversial last book, *The Bell Curve*, cowritten with Charles Murray, was recently published. "We'd have funded him at the drop of a hat," said Weyher, "but he never asked." The fund did give a grant to William Shockley, a Nobel Prize–winning physicist and the coinventor of the transistor, who took Jensenism, as it came to be called, one step further, recommending the establishment of a fund to pay what he termed "intellectually inferior" people to allow themselves to be sterilized. Weyher has always denied that Shockley made any such proposal, ascribing its wide currency to a bit of misreporting that was broadly disseminated through the Nexis computer database—a tactic that he often uses to counter the many bits of unpleasantness that have involved the Pioneer Fund over the years. But in fact, Shockley, besides mentioning the idea on several talk shows, made this recommendation in a letter he sent to members of the National Academy of Scientists on April 16, 1970. He suggested that $1,000 be paid for each point below 100 IQ and noted that "$30,000 [placed] in trust for a 70 IQ moron of twenty-child potential . . . might return $250,000 to taxpayers in reduced costs of mental retardation care." Weyher calls Shockley a "great humanitarian," acknowledging only that he could be "bullheaded."

While such extremists have certainly had their effect, it is the mainstream research paid for by the fund that has yielded the greatest return for the cause. The Pioneer Fund has been the largest single supporter of Thomas Bouchard's now-famous Minnesota study of twins reared apart, having contributed $500,000 to the effort over ten years. "We couldn't have done this project without the Pioneer Fund," Bouchard told me. Bouchard's team astounded the public with tales of the frequently uncanny similarities in twins raised separately. There were, for example, the sisters who both wore seven rings, leaving environmentalists grasping for explanations, such as that both women wanted to show off their elegant fingers. While Bouchard has published in refereed journals, he seems to have had his greatest impact in the mainstream press, which gloried in such anecdotes, invariably failing to note the many more differences that had been overlooked. Still, when the authors of a book called *The IQ Controversy* asked experts in issues involving heredity what evidence they'd found most convincing, a majority listed the twins studies, of which Bouchard's is by far the best-known. Indeed, Bouchard's research may well have paved the way for the current resurgence in hereditarian lines of inquiry that has, for example, led to the enormous public receptivity to news of the "discoveries" of the genes for alcoholism, homosexuality and schizophrenia, reports that were later either retracted or mired in qualifications. His work has encouraged deceptively simple, low-cost biological solutions, such as issuing Norplant implants to inner-city teenage girls, to complicated social problems. It has marshaled support for the current Human Genome Project—at $3 billion, the largest biological study ever undertaken—which is designed to locate and identify each of the 100,000 genes in the human body. And, more broadly, the Pioneer Fund's racial hereditarianism provides a frightening angle on much of the news of the day: the calamities in Rwanda and Haiti, the population issues recently raised at the United Nations conference in Cairo, even the O. J. Simpson murder case. In tilting public consciousness toward nature and away from nurture, in sum, the Pioneer Fund grants have ultimately caused us to think differently about ourselves and about one another.

On the political front, the fund's hereditarianism forms a kind of dogma that leads it to venture well away from strictly scientific topics to shape the larger debate over policy implications. Weyher freely admits that he would like to eliminate what he calls "Head Start–type" programs. But, to judge by the grants that it has made, the fund's administrators are also interested in limiting immigration, stopping busing, reversing integration, and ending affirmative action. Given this agenda, it is not surprising that the Pioneer Fund has links to the far right. Thomas Ellis, a long-time political adviser to Jesse Helms, was a fund director for four years in the seventies and is, in Weyher's words, "a very good friend." In 1985, Weyher's law firm, Olwine, Connelly, Chase, O'Donnell & Weyher, handled a suit against CBS for the Ellis-founded right-wing group Fairness in Media when it attempted to take over the network, although Weyher insists he had nothing to do with that litigation. The Pioneer Fund has also made grants to the Coalition for Freedom, which described itself in one register of foundations as "establishing a Jesse Helms Institute for Foreign Policy and American Studies."

Weyher has been approached many times by reporters, but he has not always been very cooperative with them. One team recently came to interview him at his New York office. "They harassed me a lot," Weyher recalled. "But you could see what they were doing. They were going to get me there and then ask me 'When did you last have lunch with Adolf Hitler?' and then photograph me with my mouth open." He had his secretary send them away. The producers of *Inside Edition* were more persistent. Unable to get in to see him at his office, they dispatched a camera crew to his apartment building to interview his startled neighbors. "They showed my building on the programs, and then they showed clips from the Holocaust of dead bodies as far as you could see," Weyher said.

With me, he seemed to be completely unconcerned that he might be in the presence of an enemy. He went on quite happily about the 450-page genealogy of the Weyher family that he had spent several years compiling, expressing mild distress at finding no particularly distinguished ancestors and many who were able to sign their names in county registers only with an X. He discussed his own rise from the tiny tobacco-farming town of Kinston, North Carolina, which he left for the University of North Carolina and, ultimately, Harvard Law School. In fact, the only time he reacted powerfully was when he got me talking about my own Harvard years, and he extracted from me the information that I had graduated magna cum laude. The light that suddenly came into his eyes nearly illuminated the room. "Well, good for you," he said solemnly. "You are one of the elite."

I FIRST GOT WIND of the Pioneer Fund from a sociologist who told me that if I wanted to find out about it, I should call historian Barry Mehler at Ferris State University, in Big Rapids, Michigan: He had done more investigating into it than anyone else. When I called Mehler, he would not talk to me until he could verify my identity. He explained that private investigators had been calling his friends, identifying themselves as reporters and asking probing questions about him. He assumed they were from the Pioneer Fund. Mehler must have assured himself that I was legitimate, because I soon received in the mail a number of articles he had written about the fund. When I called him back, however, he was still reluctant to speak to me. "They have threatened litigation," he said, "although they have never carried through on it. Still, the threat is there." He did explain that he'd looked into the fund because he saw it as laying a pseudoscientific rationale for the Fascist resurgence in Europe and for the rise of racist demagogues like David Duke and Tom Metzger in this country. As a Jew, he was especially unnerved by such developments. Then he returned to the hazards that he faced: "Look, I'm getting midnight phone calls. I'm getting harassing letters. I'm the subject of an ongoing investigation. That's my reward for every blow that I strike against them. I don't slough this stuff off. The work I do, I pay for in a certain amount of anxiety for myself and my family."

Asked about Mehler, Weyher quickly grew irritated. "This fella is a historian, or so he says. He has all kinds of stuff about Nazis and Fascists and innuendo, and sometimes simply false things that are very often irrelevant to the whole field. He throws it around, and the media picks it up. It's exciting, it's titillating, and the denial of it kinda adds fuel to it." Did he put a private investigator on Mehler? "In a very limited situation," he said. He claimed he had an operative tape a press conference that Mehler held after he lost his job at the University of Illinois. "It was the funniest press conference you ever heard," Weyher said. "They fired him because of affirmative action. Mehler said, 'But I'm Jewish!' And they said, 'But you're white.' He was outraged." Weyher sounded delighted.

"Harry got the whole story wrong," Mehler replied when I asked about Weyher's charges. "I wasn't fired from anywhere." He couldn't have been fired by the University of Illinois because he never worked there; nor has he ever held a press conference. He did once give a lecture on academic racism at the YMCA near Ferris State, where he is an associate professor, in which he mentioned that the school had wanted to save his position for a minority applicant for reasons of affirmative action but instead ended up hiring two people: himself and a black woman.

In his published material, Mehler is extremely hard-hitting, several times linking the Pioneer Fund historically to the Nazi program of racial purification. The Pioneer Fund grantees have retaliated by publishing their own investigations of Mehler's past, slamming him in one lengthy account as "an excellent example of a political activist operating from the security of the academic world."

The ultimate result of all this mudslinging is unclear, but the lesson is unmistakable. One enters the sphere of the Pioneer Fund as one enters a centrifuge. It quickly pushes everything to extremes.

THIS PAST WINTER, Oxford University Press published *The Nazi Connection*, a book that draws on some of Mehler's research to link the Pioneer Fund to the Nazi supremacists of the 1930s. The author notes that one founding director of the Pioneer Fund called himself "honored" to have received an honorary degree from the Nazi-tainted University of Heidelberg in 1936, well after the Nazi racial purification campaign was under way, and another wrote admiringly of the campaign a year later.

Since then, the Pioneer Fund has flirted with enough undesirables that the Nazi aura has never been entirely dispelled, even though, as Weyher repeatedly points out, many of the past and current directors fought against the Nazis in World War II. For example, when Donald Swan, a recipient of a $6,000 Pioneer Fund grant in the seventies, was investigated for mail fraud in 1966, the police discovered a small arsenal of illegal weapons and a large stash of racist literature, plus some Nazi flags, a German helmet, and several photographs of himself with, according to the New York *Daily News*, "members of George Lincoln Rockwell's neo-Nazi organization." And in 1978, grant recipient Roger Pearson organized a World Anti-Communist League conference that included a rogues' gallery of authoritarians, neofascists, racial hierarchists, and anti-Semites, according to *The Washington Post*'s detailed report on the meeting. Among them were Giorgio Almirante, a leader in Benito Mussolini's government, who was then the party chief of the Movimento Sociale Italiano-Deutra Nazionale, which *The Post* described as "the principal neo-fascist party of Italy"; and Willis Carto, head of Liberty Lobby, an ultraconservative organization that publishes *Spotlight,* featuring classified ads for Ku Klux Klan T-shirts and cassettes of Nazi marching songs. The Mexican delegation passed out an article attacking the NBC miniseries *Holocaust* as "another gigantic campaign of Jewish propaganda to conceal their objectives of world domination."

Pearson was assisted in running the conference by Earl Thomas, a former American Nazi Party storm trooper. At one point during the proceedings, Pearson noticed two men distributing what *The Post* termed "anti-Jewish tracts," as well as reprints from the *Thunderbolt,* a newspaper of the avowedly racist National States Rights Party (NSRP). Pearson asked them to leave, though not before telling them that he was "sympathetic with what you're doing." He added: "But don't embarrass me and cut my throat." As they left, he asked them to "give [his] regards" to NSRP chief Edward Fields, *The Post* reported.

This is all certainly repugnant, but it is doubtful if it makes the Pioneer Fund itself a tool of the Nazis any more than the fund's environmentalist opponents are the Communist stooges the fund grantees invariably accuse them of being. Instead, it simply demonstrates the heavy politics of the nature-versus-nurture debate, by which those emphasizing "nature" are embraced by the hard right, while those embracing "nurture" make their friends on the left. In its search for companionship, the Pioneer Fund frequently finds itself in repellent company. But to call the administrators of the present-day Pioneer Fund "Nazis" is to miss the point. If anything, such staunch hereditarians are royalists. Like kings, they believe that the most important things in life are settled by birth.

This elitist theme emerges quite clearly in the heritage of the Pioneer Fund, which grew out of the eugenics movement of the early part of this century. Eugenics, which proposed cultivation of what was then termed the "germ plasm" to produce a superior strain of humanity, encouraging the breeding of the "fit" and discouraging the reproduction of the "unfit," was inspired by Charles Darwin's theories about the evolution of species. It was Darwin's polymath cousin Francis Galton who coined the movement's name—from the Greek, meaning "of good stock"—in 1883.

The idea of eugenics is reviled today, ever since the Nazis appropriated its notions of racial hygiene. Nevertheless, the philosophy was endorsed by a great number of the social elite, including such luminaries as Theodore Roosevelt, Winston Churchill, John D. Rockefeller Jr., Lady Ottoline Morrell, and even the young F. Scott Fitzgerald, through the thirties. Eugenics inspired Alfred Binet to create his famous intelligence test—a basis for the standard IQ test and the dreaded SATs—as a first step toward weeding out what was then called the "feebleminded." And eugenics prompted the Italian criminologist Cesare Lombroso to try to identify a criminal "type" on the basis of certain physical features. It is amazing, in retrospect, that the socially prominent backers of the eugenics movement—and they were nearly all from the upper middle class—were so unaware, or so unconcerned, that the criteria they set for eugenic perfection were invariably ones best met by themselves. One does not have to be a Marxist to see the class-bound tinge to these precepts, as the upper classes were inevitably exalted by all eugenics programs and the lower class decried. Indeed, the Catholic Church was a staunch opponent of the movement, in part because so many of its followers were the poor immigrants who were on every American eugenicist's hit list.

In the United States, the movement led to the Immigration Act of 1924, which sharply restricted the admittance of certain out-of-favor ethnicities, especially those of Eastern and Southern Europe, for almost exactly the same reasons put forth by current Pioneer Fund grant recipients: They supposedly dilute the country's genetic strength. Eugenicists have always been preoccupied with the breeding habits of populations they consider inferior, and this obsession reached its zenith in the early thirties, as no less than thirty American states adopted laws requiring the sterilization of individuals bearing "undesirable" traits. According to *In the Name of Eugenics*, by Daniel Kevles, as a result of these laws, as many as 20,000 people had been forcibly sterilized in the United States by the time of World War II.

The most famous of them was Carrie Buck, who, after giving birth in the early 1920s to a baby girl named Vivian, was found to have a mental age of nine years, making her, in the terminology of the day, a "moron." Since her mother scored lower still, Carrie was subject to sterilization under a Virginia law that required it in cases of second-generation mental deficiency. The man to give the case its scientific impetus was Harry H. Laughlin, superintendent of the Eugenics Record Office, tireless critic of immigrants and author of *Eugenical Sterilization in the United States*. Without taking the trouble even to meet Buck, Laughlin testified that her feeblemindedness had been inherited. In his view, she belonged to "the shiftless, ignorant, and worthless class of anti-social whites of the South." The case ultimately went to the Supreme Court, where Laughlin's views prevailed, eight to one. Vivian died of an intestinal disorder while she was still in elementary school. According to Kevles, her teachers considered her "very bright."

Harry Laughlin became one of the four founding directors of the Pioneer Fund. Another was Frederick Osborn, the scion of a New York mercantile family and nephew of Henry Fairfield Osborn, then the director of the American Museum of Natural History. The younger Osborn was secretary of the American Eugenics Society, and, while he was a force for moderation in that effort, he expressed his admiration for Nazi eugenic sterilization in 1937. By that year, with the alarming news of the Nazi program starting to filter back from Europe, the steam had begun to run out of the eugenics cause—which may have been what spurred industrial heir Wickliffe Draper, along with Laughlin and Osborn, to start the Pioneer Fund.

The clubby overtones of the fund's charter are unmistakable. It lists its first purpose as aiding "parents of unusual value as citizens," and then defines those parents as ones whose children "are deemed to be descended predominantly from white persons who settled in the original thirteen states prior to the adoption of the Constitution of the United States. . . ." (The phrase "white persons" was amended to "persons" in 1985.) The ancestral requirements, not surprisingly, were met by the board of directors, which Weyher describes as "really blue chip." Laughlin could trace his lineage back to sometime before the Revolutionary War, and even now, Harry Weyher can hardly contain himself when describing Draper's distinguished forebears, who included two governors and two Civil War generals, one on each side. "He had the background where you'd expect he'd be something," Weyher said.

It is not quite clear what Draper was, however. Independently wealthy, he traveled widely, hunted big game in Africa and took part in an archaeological expedition to search for evidence of early man.

Above all, he seems to have been a war buff. In World War I, he fought first for the British, then for the Americans. He was an unpaid newspaper correspondent during the Spanish Civil War and served as an intelligence observer stationed in northern India in World War II.

One of Draper's first acts after establishing the fund was to try to earmark money to encourage army pilots to have multiple children in order to boost the country's genetic stock, but he soon abandoned the idea. Instead, he concentrated on the fund's second purpose: to conduct research into "racial betterment." The term was changed in 1985 to "human race betterment," but the racial component cannot so easily be concealed. It was the 1954 *Brown* v. *Board of Education* decision desegregating the nation's public schools that drew Harry Weyher into the organization. Although that decision is now generally hailed as a landmark in the development of civil rights in America, Draper instinctively regarded it as anathema, and the young Weyher shared that view.

Draper had come to Weyher in search of some fresh blood for the fund. He'd asked around at the prominent New York law firm Cravath, Swaine & Moore, as well as at the smaller firm established by John Marshall Harlan, a Pioneer Fund director who would later become a Supreme Court justice. Weyher worked at Cravath as an associate, and he'd joined with Harlan on a crime-commission project. "My name floated back to Draper from both those sources," said Weyher. Draper asked him if he had "an open mind" about the Supreme Court's *Brown* decision. "I said that's right," Weyher told me. In truth, Weyher's mind was more than open, it was positively keen on Draper's point of view. "That decision was supposed to integrate the schools and everybody said we'd mix 'em up and the blacks' scores would come up," Weyher said. "But of course they never did. All *Brown* did was wreck the school system." Before long, Draper had signed Harry Weyher on as the president of the Pioneer Fund.

And he had his man. Weyher supported the work of Audrey Shuey, whose "Testing of Negro Intelligence" was the first study to pursue a scientific basis for the idea that blacks are intellectually inferior to whites. In a kind of apostolic succession, Shuey provided the scientific underpinnings for Arthur Jensen, who in turn brought Thomas Bouchard into the Pioneer fold, and together, Jensen and Bouchard led the Pioneer Fund to Philippe Rushton.

PHILIPPE RUSHTON was an obscure academic at the remote University of Western Ontario when he set off what amounted to an intellectual stink bomb at the annual meeting of the American Association for the Advancement of Science in San Francisco in 1989. It was here that he propounded his theory comparing blacks, whites and Asians, by which blacks trailed whites, who in turn trailed Asians, on various supposed measures of desirability, including intelligence, sexual restraint, social organization and something he called "maturational delay," which included the age of first intercourse and the age of death.

Wholesale comparisons between races are always of dubious value and motive, and for Rushton to subject much of the world's population to his own kind of thumbs-up/thumbs-down ranking compounded his problems. As one might expect, the media jumped all over him. The geneticist David Suzuki took on Rushton in a televised debate. Two weeks later, Rushton went on *Geraldo*. "I felt my views were being very badly distorted through the media," Rushton explained to me. It was likely the first time in history that anyone turned to Geraldo Rivera to sort out a scientific debate. As a condition for appearing on the show, Rushton required that he be joined by other "knowledgeable behavioral geneticists." Barry Mehler was one, and Jerry Hirsch of the University of Illinois was another. The conversation quickly got bogged down in charges and countercharges, so Geraldo dismissed the other geneticists and brought out some black activists, and then popped the big question about the sole area where, according to Rushton, black men are definitely superior—penis size. A verbal brawl erupted. As Rushton remembered it, "the situation deteriorated into name-calling and so on." What names? "The usual—'racist,' 'Nazi.' I don't recall."

In the weeks after the show, the cacophony grew louder. Besides calling for Rushton's firing, Ontario premier David Peterson declared his work to be "highly questionable, destructive, and offensive to the way Ontario thinks." The widely read *Toronto Star* went after the "Nazi" Pioneer Fund for sponsoring such research; later, it ran a cartoon depicting Rushton wearing a Ku Klux Klan hood. After a police investigation, the Ontario attorney general decided not to prosecute Rushton for hate propaganda but, in a parting salvo, dismissed his ideas as "loony." Picketers set up shop outside Rushton's classroom. The university recalled too well an incident just a few months before in which a psychopath had murdered fourteen female economics students at the Ecole Polytechnic in Montreal before killing himself. Western considered having Rushton teach in a "portable," a kind of trailer, since that could be easily defended by police. It settled on having him teach by videotape, a procedure that he reluctantly followed for three months, until the uproar finally subsided.

IT IS HARD to know how to respond to research like Rushton's. The University of Western Ontario decided to hold its nose and let Rushton proceed, which was probably wise. Censorship is a game that more than one can play. No matter how repugnant most people might find his ideas, Rushton has had them published repeatedly in respected, peer-reviewed journals and has received a Guggenheim Fellowship, among other honors. "When I say that Rushton's academic record is sterling, I'm not kidding," said Emoke Szathmary, a former dean of social sciences at the University of Western Ontario, who had headed the committee that decided Rushton's professional fate. Still, this seems to have given Rushton delusions about how his work would play in public. Possibly Rushton enjoys the martyr's role, now that he has gotten a chance to play it. One might think that his *Geraldo* experience would have soured him on talk shows, but he followed it with self-aggrandizing appearances on *Donahue* and the national cable show *Jane Wallace*. "Do you know of even Nobel Prize winners who compare themselves to Galileo?" Szathmary asked me. "Philippe Rushton does."

More dangerously, Rushton and his Pioneer Fund confreres suffer from a blindness to the historical context of their work, as if they thought that blacks had never before been called stupid, untrustworthy, and oversexed. "Think of an equivalent topic for scientific inquiry, like 'Are Jews Pushy?' " said Nicholas Lemann, author of *The Promised Land*, the award-winning study of African-American northern migration in the twentieth century. "Is this an issue that should be put out on the table?" Race relations are so fragile that it is impossible to discuss them without immense tact and a great deal of caution, two qualities that Rushton clearly lacks. When explaining his work to me, he did not gloss over his thoughts on differences in penis size, as I thought he might have, but rather recounted them in some detail. Besides being inflammatory, the topic of penis size may very well be irrelevant to the issues of male fertility that Rushton is exploring. As Szathmary, herself a population biologist, pointed out, "I would think that the size of the testicles, since they are the sperm-producing organ, would be a more direct measure of male fertility than the penis, which is only the object that delivers the sperm."

In a sense, Rushton's work is the natural culmination of that of so many of the Pioneer Fund hereditarians, as they circle around the great imponderable of racial differences. While comparative reproductive rates are a matter of concern for the hereditarians, they are bothersome to the rest of us, largely because of the so-called dysgenic trend involved—the notion that blacks are somehow dragging down the national IQ, and that the more blacks there are, the lower it goes. The essential issue, then, centers on race and IQ. With this, of course, the hereditarians press two of the hottest buttons in the culture.

The debate over racial differences in intelligence is so gnarled and thorny and intricate, it is nearly impossible for a layperson to evaluate the many conflicting claims. Indeed, that is one of the difficulties in addressing the issue at all, since experts on race are rarely experts on intelligence, experts on intelligence are rarely experts on race, and experts on genetic inheritance are rarely experts on either. And in this, no amount of expertise is ever enough. There is, for example, lingering controversy about whether there even is such a thing as IQ. Stephen Jay Gould argued in his celebrated *Mismeasure of Man* that the concept was, in effect, a result of social scientists' physics envy, their determination to give an impossible abstraction a number in hopes of capturing something real. Gould called this "reification," and he derided it at some length. Hereditarians counter that, real or not, and whatever the cause-and-effect relationship, IQ does correlate rather decidedly with socioeconomic success. As for IQ's genetic component, enough twins studies have been done by now that most experts agree that heritability accounts for somewhere in the vicinity of 50 percent to 70 percent of intelligence, with 60 percent the most likely figure, which of course still leaves ample room for environmental influence.

On the racial side of the question, it is hard to know what to make of the very premise of "race" these days. Technically, a race is genetically isolated, but that is hardly the case in a world that is growing more intermixed by the hour. Arthur Jensen concedes that the mingling of the races necessarily leads to a "dilution" of any race-related genetic effects. Now, most categorization is done purely on a cultural basis. If one thinks of oneself as black, one is.

If anything, "race," in the sense that the Pioneer Fund grantees use the term, might well be a measure of the cultural bias against it. The very terms "Asian," "white," and "black" carry a lot of baggage. And this is important, for, as Harvard biologist Richard Lewontin has pointed out, heritability measures only the genetic variability of a population within a comparable group. It does not measure differences between noncomparable groups, and that is the crux of the debate over racial characteristics. Statistically, blacks do seem to lag behind whites by about fifteen points on most IQ tests. But are blacks and whites comparable groups? If not, to attribute any IQ differential to deficient genes is a stretch. Jensen himself has wondered if there is an "X" factor to account for blacks' lower average performance on IQ tests. It shouldn't be hard to find, in a country where blacks are far more likely than whites to grow up poor, fatherless, malnourished, badly educated, and victimized by crime and drugs. Then there is the matter of racism in America, which, like the bloodstains on the hands of Lady Macbeth, cannot be washed away.

It is important to realize that, even with a genetic basis, IQ scores vary over time for individuals, and they shift markedly for groups. Rushton lauds Chinese-Americans for their average IQ of 107, but tests showed that those Chinese who had immigrated to America after World War II trailed the white average of 100 by a point or two, according to James Flynn, a professor of political science at the University of Otago in New Zealand and the author of several scholarly books on the IQ controversy. Yet these Chinese immigrants then proceeded to outpace Americans socioeconomically—55 percent of them became professionals, compared with 30 percent of whites—and their IQ scores have since risen. "If IQ fully determined life's outcomes, then what the Chinese did is quite impossible," said Flynn. The Chinese, however, had the benefit of what Flynn termed a "dynamic work ethic"; they were entrepreneurial and abstemious, as well. Flynn noted that a study of black and white children of American GIs stationed in Germany—where their economic status is equivalent—suggests that there isn't anything especially deficient about being black once environments have been equalized.

Of all the branches of science, the field of behavioral genetics—the area for much of the Pioneer Fund's research into race and intelligence—is generally regarded as the most dubious, in large part because it is so prone to personal prejudices about the individuals under examination. Too often, the behavioral geneticist's conclusions merely reflect his assumptions. Garbage in, as they say, garbage out. "People always come into behavioral genetics with some bias, and it may reflect their social bias," Jonathan Beckwith, a professor of genetics at the Harvard Medical School, told me. "At the extreme, you get racists doing research of this sort." Like Philippe Rushton? I asked. "When I said 'racist,' that's the first person I thought of," he replied. "From everything I know, it's quite clear where his starting bias is."

Because of its pure-science aura, genetics can easily be used as a cover for what are essentially political arguments. "One group of people is arrogating to themselves the ability to decide who is superior to whom," Beckwith said. "And I object to that." Besides, he argued, even if the heritability of a trait like intelligence is 70 percent, environmental factors can still affect it drastically, just as a drought can extinguish a corn crop, whatever its genetic programming. "Whether intelligence is genetic or environmental, you are still faced with a political and social decision about how to deal with any disparity in mental ability," he concluded. "That's the real question: Is society going to devote the resources to improving the situation?"

THE PIONEER FUND faced a crisis of survival in 1991. That year, a dispute over two grant recipients, Linda Gottfredson and Jan Blits, came to a head at the University of Delaware. Previously, uproars over fund grants only tangentially concerned Pioneer. This time, as Gottfredson told me, "the Pioneer Fund was the issue." As an anguished letter to the school's president from a linguist named William Frawley put it, "I . . . find it very difficult to believe that the University of Delaware, with its avowed goals of multicultural sensitivity, racial tolerance, and the promotion of minority education, could continue to accept money from the Pioneer Fund." How could Delaware truly be committed to affirmative action? "I saw it as a make-or-break business for me and for the fund," Gottfredson said. "If they could pick me off on account of my funding, if there were a precedent for cutting off funding, it would gradually kill the fund by disabling the people doing the work."

Gottfredson and Blits received their grant to investigate "race-norming," the practice by which minorities' score on federal job examinations are compared only to those of applicants from their own ethnicity, not to the entire pool of applicants. As a result, black scores are artificially inflated, giving blacks what Gottfredson and Blits believed was an unfair advantage. Congress ultimately agreed, and the practice was eliminated in the Civil Rights Act of 1991. Gottfredson and Blits believe that they were attacked precisely because of their success in the political arena. Perhaps, but in its published records, the university seemed to be principally preoccupied with the ugly history of the Pioneer Fund, chiefly the racial orientation as expressed in its original charter and as evidenced by numerous grants since. As is typical where the fund is concerned, the debate quickly became overheated. At one point, the University of Delaware African American Coalition took out an ad in a local paper accusing Gottfredson of genocide, and it organized a sit-in of her class. Seeing how much was at stake, Harry Weyher himself made a rare public appearance to testify on behalf of the fund. Nevertheless, the university ruled that, while Gottfredson could keep her grant, future Pioneer money was not welcome on campus as long as the fund "remains committed to the intent of its original charter and to a pattern of activities incompatible with the university's mission." Barry Mehler found that impressive. "For a university to say 'We don't want your money,' that's amazing," he said. "Usually all they say is 'Is it green?' "

Gottfredson and Blits declared that the ruling violated their academic freedom, and, with the assistance of University of Delaware trustee and former Republican presidential candidate Pete du Pont, they secured the services of an attorney to appeal the decision to a federal arbitrator. In the end, the arbitrator sided with Gottfredson and Blits for reasons that had little to do with the Pioneer Fund. The arbitrator declared that, in violation of the university's "own standards for procedural fairness," the university had inquired into the "substantive nature" of Gottfredson's work, and therefore the ban on accepting Pioneer Fund money should be lifted.

SO THE PIONEER FUND has survived—at least for the time being. It may soon spend itself out of existence. The fund is now running through $500,000 a year, regardless of the income on the investments that Morgan Guaranty has selected for it. "It seemed to make more sense to spend the money than to save it," Weyher said, "so we spent it. Once it's gone we'll just quit." If the stock market stays flat, the Pioneer Fund could be depleted in ten years.

Or it could literally die out. This is, after all, a fund administered by five very old men—a kind of politburo of powerful geriatrics. At seventy-three, Weyher is the youngest by about a decade. One of the other four, Randolf Speight, is a former partner at Shearson Lehman who now devotes himself to playing croquet in Bermuda. Another, former investment banker John B. Trevor, has dedicated himself to carrying on the policies of his father, anti-immigration advocate John B. Trevor Sr. Another is Karl Schakel, whom Weyher describes as an "international farmer." "He has seen civilization," Weyher said cryptically. "We didn't have to educate him."

The full effects of these cumulated years were not fully apparent to me until Harry Weyher proudly led a little tour of the Racquet Club after lunch. We got a bit lost in the maze of the upper floors but finally made our way first to the racquets court, with walls and floor of slate, then to the room for court tennis, a rare, antique game that was also played at Henry VIII's Hampton Court and precious few other places. "Somebody once told me that if I played court tennis, I'd immediately be ranked eighteenth in the world," Weyher joked. He had been intrigued by the possibility but declined nevertheless. He showed me the odd felt-covered ball, a hybrid of a tennis ball and a baseball, and the peculiar lopsided racquet, which looked like an old wooden tennis racquet that had been left out in the rain.

If the Pioneer Fund had a headquarters, it would be a place like this. No less than the Racquet Club, the Pioneer Fund is a club. It has its musty charter, its lily-white members, its smug exclusivity, its foolish lore. Unlike the Racquet Club, however, the Pioneer is trying to foist its principles on the country. Happily, the country continues to lumber on in fitful pursuit of the ideals of its founders. With luck, the Pioneer Fund will someday be as much a relic as court tennis.

PROFESSORS OF HATE

Adam Miller

M ICHAEL LEVIN'S OFFICE is difficult to find. His door
is not marked with a nameplate—the only one missing in the
halls of the philosophy department at the City College of New York.
The door itself is a slightly brighter shade of blue than the others; later
I learn that it has been repainted to cover the swastikas and ethnic
slurs that had been scrawled across it.

Levin is the professor who made headlines in the early 1990s with
public pronouncements that blacks are genetically less intelligent than
whites. What the sinewy fifty-one-year-old teacher calls his "five minutes of fame" peaked with a 1990 speech at a largely black Brooklyn,
New York, university campus. Before a crowd of about two hundred,
Levin announced that given high black crime rates, whites should fear
and avoid blacks. "Blackness is a sign of danger," proclaimed the balding, bespectacled professor.

The police ought to consider "blackness" a criterion for just cause
in a stop and search, Levin continued, adding that "some forms of
racism are justified." Violence erupted as about fifty members of the
audience stormed the stage. When it was over, nine students had been

Adam Miller is working on a book on eugenics. This article was originally published in
Rolling Stone, October 20, 1994.

arrested, five cops had been injured, and Levin had made a solitary side-entrance escape. "I liken Levin coming here to a KKK member burning a cross in your backyard," said one student who was there.

The riot is now a memory, but Levin has little interest in rewriting his past—or re-imagining his future. He is mostly untroubled by his status as a self-described pariah at City College, a campus where minority students form a majority. "I'm probably very deficient as a human being in that I have no desire or need to be liked by anybody," he says. "With rare, rare exceptions, being disliked by people just doesn't bother me."

Levin's apparent isolation is somewhat deceiving. He's not really so alone. While some in the New York media cast him as a crackpot working on the fringe of academia, there was a fact that they missed, and he didn't point it out. Levin belongs to a community of academics who share many of his unproved and inflammatory ideas about race. An even better-kept secret is that these professors, tenured at such private institutions as Smith College, Johns Hopkins University, and the University of Pennsylvania, as well as state schools in California, Delaware, and Georgia and the University of Western Ontario, in Canada, also share a common source of financial support: a fifty-seven-year-old nonprofit foundation called the Pioneer Fund.

From an office in New York City, the Pioneer Fund dispenses about $1 million a year to academics, most of whom do research related to establishing a genetic basis for racial differences in intelligence and personality. The fund also supports the work of scholars like Levin, who analyze and discuss the political implications of those differences. But the most important agenda for the Pioneer Fund has been the same since its founding: a movement known as eugenics.

Eugenicists believe that humans—like cattle and canines—should be bred selectively. They usually consider intelligence, which they believe is genetically passed on from parents to children, to be the most valuable human attribute. They also believe that smarter people have fewer children. So they reason that unless they get the bright to have more children and the dull to have fewer, human intelligence will not evolve. Instead it will deteriorate until the species fails to meet the demands of its environment and falters into extinction.

The eugenics movement was created by Englishmen in the late nineteenth century. They used it to try to control reproduction among the Irish, who were thought to threaten Anglo-Saxon society with their low intelligence and high birthrate. In the early twentieth century the idea of genetic management caught on in the United States, where Italians, Asians, and especially Jews were identified as the oversexed and slow-witted. The partnership of eugenics and political power reached full flower with the rise of Germany's Third Reich. For a time it seemed that Adolf Hitler might accomplish his goal of creating a world in which the biologically worthy would breed prodigiously and the unworthy would be kept from contaminating the gene pool.

Since then eugenics has largely fallen out of favor, recognized for the most part as a vehicle for racism. From time to time, however, a highly visible proponent like the late William Shockley of Stanford University, who proposed sterilizing welfare recipients, stumbles into public view, but for the most part, the work goes on quietly, almost stealthily.

Today's eugenicists—many of them gathered under the Pioneer Fund's umbrella—focus their attention on blacks and Latinos, although a fixation with Jews still persists among the most rabid, who, like Hitler, believe the "colored races" are being used to genetically undermine whites so that Jews can take over the world. Under various guises, Pioneer Fund researchers have promoted many of the same policies for tailoring the gene pool as did their Nazi precursors. To limit mixing with the unworthy, Pioneer Fund grant recipients have lobbied for restrictive immigration policies and promoted various forms of segregation. To rid the world of "undesirables"—and their potential offspring—some grant recipients have suggested sterilization or even extermination.

A PIONEER FUND colleague calls him "a provocateur," and though sitting in a chair in his Manhattan apartment, Michael Levin seems coiled, ready to pounce. "I do enjoy the cut and thrust," says the native New Yorker, who dresses with an academic's disdain in dated tan twill flares, a well-worn undershirt, and cheap white tennis sneakers. "I like a fight, and I rise to the occasion."

Levin proved it when his university took steps against him after his racial views were publicized in 1990. The New York media cast him as a foil to fellow City College professor Leonard Jeffries, a black supremacist. New York governor Mario Cuomo denounced Levin. Students picketed and disrupted his classes. But when school administrators tried to limit his contact with students and to challenge his tenure, he sued and won on the basis of academic freedom. (Like Levin, few Pioneer-paid professors whose views are similarly controversial make known their racial interests before receiving tenure's protections.) By then the press and public had lost interest, and no one noticed that in 1991, Levin received his first support check from the Pioneer Fund.

Levin's work begins with the fact that—on average—blacks score 15 points lower than whites do on standardized IQ tests. He rejects claims that the tests are culturally biased or that the gap results from oppression and its effects. He insists that reasonable analysts now agree the difference is mostly genetic.

This certainty is by no means shared by other scholars. "I see no evidence of a genetic difference in intelligence between blacks and whites," says University of Pennsylvania psychology professor and former department chairman Henry Gleitman. "As a colleague of mine has said, 'Given the trickiness of the data, concluding it does exist is like standing up in a crowded theater and yelling, "Fire . . . maybe." ' I can't believe a fair-minded psychologist wouldn't know this."

There is not even a consensus on what IQ tests measure. Many experts say they reflect only a small part of human know-how. Harvard University education professor Howard Gardner says there are at least seven types of intelligence. He developed tests that measure them and found that many people who score well on his tests do not excel on IQ tests.

But racial differences in intelligence are a given for Levin, and based on this questionable conclusion, he makes policy recommendations on affirmative action, school integration, housing policy, welfare reform, and as he demonstrated in Brooklyn, criminal justice. He does not expound on his views in his philosophy courses, he says, but would volunteer them if an appropriate context came up.

"I'm interested in innocence for whites, and the genetic hypothesis is evidence for the defense," Levin says. "It undercuts affirmative action, the basis for which is the great black claim on the American consciousness that 'We're down, and you owe us for what you did to us with slavery and Jim Crow.' Race differences show whites aren't at fault for blacks being down, and making whites pay for something they're not responsible for is a terrible injustice. Eliminating affirmative action is the first step. Next—please, yes, if only—eliminate the Civil Rights Act."

Levin believes the U.S. Supreme Court erred when it ordered American schools to be integrated. "Let's go back to 1954 and tell a story," he says, sounding now every bit the professor. "Blacks are not doing well, and everyone said, 'Well, if we just had equal education, that'll change, just like it did for Italians, Jews, the Irish.' Instead blacks got more antisocial, and whites fled. Now it's 1994 and [it's] even worse. The reason is two basic and unalterable black characteristics: less intelligence and greater proneness to violence."

Levin sweeps his hands to indicate the bareness of his co-op apartment. He complains bitterly that after paying for private school for his sons, ages fourteen and eleven, he has nothing left for furnishings or new paint. "It's a horrible, sadistic thing that Washington tells whites, 'You have to send your kids to school with blacks so they can beat them up,'" Levin says. "Don't white kids have any rights? It's terrible to make them go to school with blacks, who are intellectually inferior and misbehave in class. You know, my son is transferring to [a very selective public high school] in the fall. They've got a special program for blacks. I just hope they leave him alone."

"Have you been left alone?" I ask.

"I've been mugged so many times," Levin says wearily. "The whole bit: knives, guns. Blacks just have fewer inhibitions, a greater readiness to express anger, an impulsiveness. It fuels this incredible idea that you see something you want and shoot somebody to get it. What do they do that for? Because the alternative—to work and save—is not psychologically available."

Levin says blacks are now taking these alleged shortfalls beyond shared schools and streets and into white America. "They turned projects into dope dens and shooting galleries, so now the government decides the only way it'll work is if they're scattered into white communities. This is an implicit admission that—left to themselves—blacks will form societies whites would find intolerable and that it takes whites to prop them up."

Levin's recommendation echoes like a mantra: "End welfare. . . . End welfare."

"What would that do?" I ask.

"The country is being overrun by people who don't work and have illegitimate children," Levin says. "[Ending welfare] would simply be ceasing to subsidize them. That would automatically have a very excellent demographic effect."

"Eugenics," I say.

"There's nothing wrong with eugenics," Levin says. "It's a perfectly respectable idea. I think it may be making a comeback."

Levin's family history would seem to make him an unlikely candidate for such views. Around the turn of the century, his grandparents fled czarist pogroms against Jews in Russia. Members of Levin's family were killed in the Holocaust. And this son of a short-order cook—educated at Michigan State and Columbia universities—is happily married to a Latino immigrant whom he calls his best friend. Margarita Levin, now a professor of philosophy at Yeshiva, met her husband when she took one of his courses at City College, long an educational mecca for New York's poor and its recent immigrants.

Despite this multicultural background, Levin remains fixated on race differences. "That's the crisis facing America," he says. "No one wants to talk about it or support research on it but the Pioneer Fund. When the history of the twentieth century is written, it'll be among its heroes."

Levin, who is a very accomplished classroom instructor, seems to be unaware of either the Pioneer Fund's past or the beliefs of some of the company he's keeping. In the next few hours I read aloud to him from material about the foundation and by fellow Pioneer Fund recipients. I quote a 1966 passage by fund recipient Roger Pearson. "If a nation with a more advanced, more specialized, or in any way superior set of genes mingles with, instead of exterminating, an inferior tribe, then it commits racial suicide," wrote Pearson, a journeyman academic turned publisher who has taught at the universities of Maryland and Southern Mississippi and Hampden-Sydney College, in Virginia, as well as Queens College, in Charlotte, N.C. "[Without] elimination of the unfit, evolution amongst the higher forms does not, in fact, take place. . . . [If] we follow the dictates of the eugenicist, there is the hope always that some sound stock will survive."

Levin, who has had frequent contact with Pearson and whose wife approves of the man's courtly manners, suddenly looks dismayed. And then his face registers a change, as if a switch had been thrown in his thinking, and his doubts are cast aside.

"Let me ask you a question, and I really don't know the answer," he says. "Suppose you see a racial crisis coming in the United States that nobody wants to talk about. Everybody wants to pretend everybody is Bill Cosby and Mary Tyler Moore. And the only guy besides you who can see this is like a freight train going 90 mph to a bridge that's out is Josef Mengele. Do you join forces with him to try to stop the train?"

THE ELEVATOR DOORS open and students and professors stream into the maze of halls. I separate from the crowd at the psychology-department directory, and I read: J. PHILIPPE RUSHTON RM. 6434. As I take what turns out to be a long walk to his office, I wonder if Rushton—like Michael Levin—seeks insulation from heated student reactions to his views. For Rushton, who has been teaching for more than ten years at the University of Western Ontario, in London, these views are found in what a Pioneer Fund colleague calls his "bold theory of racial differences." But critics call his hypothesis a pseudoscientific justification for a "racial pecking order," with blacks on the bottom, whites in the middle and Asians on top.

Rushton's office is open but unoccupied, and I sit down to wait for him. His publications lie in neat piles on a shelf. I leaf through one in which he describes the reproductive strategies that different life forms use in their evolutionary struggles. He claims that less evolved organisms—such as blacks—fight for survival by coupling promiscuously, flooding the environment with offspring for whom they provide little care and many of whom die. He says more evolved forms—such as Asians—wage their battle through monogamous relationships, producing few children upon whom they lavish care and many of whom survive. Whites, he says, fall in between.

Perhaps most striking is Rushton's focus on sexual characteristics, including breast, buttock and genital size, all of which he says are largest in blacks, middling in whites and smallest in Asians. Rushton pays particular attention to penis size, which he says is an evolutionary adaptation to blacks' indiscriminate sexuality. "Where ejaculates from more than one male occur in the vicinity of ova, sperm competition often leads to enlarged penises and testes to make deeper and more voluminous ejaculations possible," Rushton writes.

"Hullo," Rushton says. The accent is British Empire, cultured but of indeterminate origin. He is a natty dresser and despite the heat, the tall fifty-year-old wears a sweater knotted over his shoulders. We exchange pleasantries, and, raising the paper I'm reading, I ask which reproductive strategy will prove the most successful.

"In the short term the small brained will appear to be winning, because they can produce three offspring for every one the big brained produce," Rushton says, warming to his subject. "But the minute you introduce selection pressures, the small brained will cease to be competitive and will crash, while the big brained will have the intelligence to adapt. But that's in the long run, which isn't any help to the big brained in New York City today."

Rushton says he has concentrated lately on brain size, which he claims is directly related to race, head size, and intelligence. "Next time you see the North Korean president [the late Kim Il Sung] and his aides on television, just look at their heads and compare them to Jimmy Carter's and the white dignitaries' in the audience. Then when you see some high-speed runners from, say, Kenya, look at their heads. If you can't see the difference, I'd be surprised."

But what some notice is Rushton's bias. C. Loring Brace, a renowned University of Michigan anthropologist who has amassed a vast database of head measurements, says there's no significant difference in head size among races—in fact, he doesn't believe in the concept of race—and no connection between brain size and intelligence. "[Rushton] uses selected pickings to reach a predetermined conclusion," Brace says. "When you take [his work] apart and look at the pieces, it completely collapses. It's not science, it's racism."

Tired of being slammed for his "selected pickings" from others' data, Rushton began producing his own. At a local mall, he used Pioneer money to pay 150 participants—a third were black, a third were white, a third were Asian—to complete a form with questions asking, for example, how far each subject could ejaculate and "How large [is] your penis?" His university subsequently reprimanded him for not having the project pre-approved. Rushton says approval for off-campus experiments had never before been required. "A zoologist," he says, "doesn't need permission to study squirrels in his back yard."

Rushton gained even greater notoriety when he published a paper tying high black HIV-infection rates to his theory of reproductive strategies. He suggested that "Negroids" are genetically programmed for sexual behavior that spreads the deadly virus. Dr. Robert Gallo, one of the first scientists to identify HIV, denounced Rushton, who struck back, producing an invitation to an AIDS conference in China as proof that his HIV research is respected. But a reporter discovered that the invite was one of 600 spit from a computer mailing list. The organizers of the trip—for which attendees had to pay their own way—subsequently rescinded their invitation.

Rushton's troubles didn't stop there. He has been threatened and assaulted. The university gave him a bodyguard to escort him to class. He was nearly prosecuted under Canada's hate-crime laws, has had politicians call for his firing and now faces a suit by students who charge that his teachings violated their civil rights.

Rushton describes student protests against him: "They have a large number of blacks parading the halls with bullhorns, shouting, banging on the walls. If four or five skinheads with swastika armbands showed up outside my class, there would be tanks on campus to get them off and into jail. If you've got, quote, disadvantaged groups, a band of blacks and left wingers, the university will cave in."

Eventually school officials ordered that Rushton teach by videotape. "This was for my own safety and the safety of my students," he says.

I ask Rushton about claims that he's describing a racial hierarchy. "I object to the use of the terms *superior* or *inferior*," says Rushton, who has repeatedly denied being a racist. "People are always saying, 'Oh, you say whites are superior to blacks.' Even if you take something like athletic ability or sexuality—not to reinforce stereotypes or some such thing—but, you know, it's a trade-off: more brain or more penis. You can't have everything."

Stanford University professor Marcus Feldman, whose work Rushton has cited, is an expert on the theory of reproductive strategies. This theory is "absolutely inapplicable" to comparisons within species, Feldman said on a Canadian radio show called *Quirks and Quarks*. Rushton doesn't come across as a scientist but as "someone who has an ax to grind. . . . [His work] has no content. It's laughable."

"I guess my upbringing led me to believe there really were genetically based class, ethnic, and racial differences," says Rushton, who spent four years in an all-white South African elementary school before his father, who owned a construction business, moved the family to England, where Rushton later attended the University of London. "So when I went to university and found out, supposedly, there were not [differences], it came as a surprise. And I came to the conclusion they really did exist after all."

Rushton's conclusions have not only made him an object of peer ridicule, they have also led those whom he mentored to reject him. "I had a graduate student from China," Rushton says. "Curiously enough he didn't think Chinese are more intelligent. His parents were furious with him for working with me and told him to stop. He brought in editorials from Vancouver newspapers from 1911 or 1907—whenever Canada passed a law forbidding Orientals to immigrate from China. And the reason, the newspapers said, is the Oriental is a much harder worker and unfair competition for the decent working white man."

How would you feel, I ask, if your work was used for similar ends?

"I don't see anything wrong with research on immigration policy and population policy overall," Rushton says. "People often describe world population as out of control. That very soon touches the nerve of race differences in reproduction. Population policy touches on who's going to reproduce. It touches on eugenics."

Rushton insists he's uninterested in applications for his research. But a 1986 article in *Politics and the Life Sciences* indicates otherwise. In it, Rushton connects Nazi Germany's military prowess to the purity of its gene pool. He suggests that white supremacists' opposition to abortion is a genetic impulse against a procedure that may add to what they perceive to be the demographic threat of black and Latino immigration and fertility. He details how humanist, egalitarian, and anti-racist ideas support these population shifts that endanger "North European" civilization. And he implies eugenics could change this.

I mention my interviewing population-studies professor Daniel Vining Jr., a Pioneer colleague whose work Rushton has cited. Vining had a stroke nine years ago that left him seriously disabled. I'm describing how difficult it is for him to speak when Rushton's measured manner evaporates.

"I met him at a conference a few years ago, and it was hard talking to him with politeness for two minutes," Rushton says. "He was inappropriately insistent. He refused to allow me to go, almost like he wanted to practice [speaking] on me or something like that. I was thinking, 'Go practice with your wife or somebody else like you, don't practice on me.' But he insisted. Sort of childish—like he wanted to take all the attention. I think he grabbed my hand or something, and I thought, 'Who the hell are you, grabbing my hand?'"

Later I read Rushton the Pearson "exterminating" passage that shook Levin.

"Why should I pass value judgments on other people's political opinions?" says Rushton, a Pearson acquaintance.

"So you wouldn't agree with that?"

"For God's sake, I just told you. Why should I pass value judgments on other people's political opinions? I'm terminating this [interview] right now."

IN 1937 the Pioneer Fund was founded by Wickliffe Draper, whose New England textile fortune started the fund's endowment and helps finance it today. Harry Laughlin, the first president of the fund, was a well-known eugenicist who in 1924 was instrumental in pushing through legislation blocking U.S. entry to Jews fleeing pogroms in Russia. Before Congress, he testified that IQ data proved that 83 percent of Jewish immigrants were born feeble-minded and therefore were a threat to the nation's economy and genetic makeup. Laughlin subsequently lobbied to keep these barriers in place, successfully cutting off sanctuary for Jews seeking refuge from the Third Reich.

In 1922, Laughlin also wrote the Model Eugenical Sterilization Law, which was adopted in one form or another by thirty states and resulted in the forced sterilization of tens of thousands of people in the United States. The law also served as the basis for the Nazi program that resulted in the forced sterilization of at least 2 million people. For his contributions to eugenics, Laughlin received an honorary degree from the University of Heidelberg, in Germany, in 1936. The Nazis' scientific adviser for the extermination of the handicapped notified Laughlin of the award. In 1937, Laughlin obtained a Nazi film praising eugenic cleansing and offered screenings to 3,000 U.S. high schools. There were 28 takers. Third Reich newspapers celebrated this success. The Pioneer Fund's founder, Draper, took a special interest in this project as well as in efforts to promote black repatriation.

Current Pioneer Fund treasurer John B. Trevor Jr. maintains multiple interests of his own. In addition to thirty-five years of foundation duties, he was a long-time official of the Coalition of Patriotic Societies, which in 1942 was named in a U.S. Justice Department sedition indictment for pro-Nazi activities. Trevor was the group's treasurer in 1962 when it called for the release of all Nazi war criminals and announced its support for South Africa's "well-reasoned racial policy."

Pioneer officials later organized the Draper Committees, officers of which included Rep. Francis Walter of Pennsylvania, the author of highly restrictive immigration legislation. The Draper project took as a counsel New York attorney Harry Weyher, who has for many years

been the Pioneer Fund president. The Draper project financed research on new uses for isolysin, a chemical used to determine whether
blood types could mix in a transfusion. Some believed blacks' alleged
inferiority was blood borne, and blood banks' refusals to separate holdings by race might result in whites being compromised by black blood,
a variation on the dreaded miscegenation.

In *Brown* v. *Board of Education of Topeka*, the 1954 U.S. Supreme
Court case in which the court ordered school integration, Columbia
University psychology professor and future Pioneer Fund director
Henry Garrett was a featured witness for the segregationists. Garrett, a
pamphleteer of the White Citizens Councils, which has been referred
to as a "white-collar Klan," testified that school integration would be a
disaster. He said that blacks' genetically inferior intelligence would
require leveling the curriculum, which would leave whites bored and
blacks frustrated. In an unsuccessful suit brought to reverse *Brown*,
University of Georgia psychology professor emeritus R. Travis Osborne
played a role similar to Garrett's. Now an octogenarian, Osborne was for
years the recipient of Pioneer stipends.

Thomas Ellis, a North Carolina lawyer and Jesse Helms adviser
who served on the Pioneer Fund board from 1973 to 1977, also opposed *Brown*, writing, "The eventual goal of this [school integration]
movement is racial intermarriage and the disappearance of the Negro
race by fusing into the white."

With the Civil Rights Act of 1964, the floodgates of integration
opened—at least in law—and the Pioneer Fund entered a new era.
Having failed to keep the dam intact, certain foundation recipients
now sought to provide a basis for erecting smaller, subtler barriers to
integration. A 1969 article by University of California at Berkeley
educational psychology professor Arthur Jensen, who has received
more than $1 million in Pioneer funds, argued that black students'
poor academic performance was due to irreversible genetic deficiencies, so programs like Head Start were useless and should be replaced
by vocational education. The claim drew an avalanche of academic
rebuttals, and then the media took over. *Newsweek* headlined its piece
BORN DUMB?

More recently some fund recipients have been shown to have associations that are remarkably similar to the Nazi ties of Laughlin and
Draper, the fund's key players at its inception. University of Northern

Iowa educational-psychology professor Ralph Scott had another life as a vice president of the pro-Nazi German-American National Congress, which was led by a Holocaust denier. In the mid-seventies, Scott used some of his Pioneer money to barnstorm the country in opposition to busing, a court-ordered path to integration.

Scott's work caught the eye of University of Southern Mississippi anthropology professor Donald Swan, another Pioneer Fund recipient. Swan's idea was that blacks are a more primitive species than whites. In 1966 he was arrested for mail fraud after a raid on his home during which police found a cache of weapons, Nazi memorabilia, a photo of him with American Nazi Party members and reams of racist, anti-Semitic and anti-Catholic literature.

When Swan died, Pioneer Fund money was used to purchase and transfer his library to Roger Pearson, who left academia in the late seventies and took over the American chapter of the ultra-conservative World Anti-Communist League. A man who has reportedly claimed a role in hiding Josef Mengele (the Third Reich doctor known as the "Angel of Death," who performed brutal experiments on live concentration-camp prisoners) from Nazi hunters, Pearson was soon removed by the international organization in reaction to his efforts to pack the league with Nazis and their sympathizers. He now runs an array of organizations that publish books and journals; many of these organizations have been Pioneer Fund–sponsored outlets.

A recent Pearson publication that reflects other troubling connections and views is the collected works of the late William Shockley, the Pioneer-supported Stanford University engineering and mathematical-science professor whose Bonus Sterilization Plan turned heads in the 1970s and '80s. Under the plan, the government would offer cash incentives to welfare recipients with below-average IQs who agreed to be sterilized—$1,000 for every point below the white mean of 100. Various Pioneer professors had early contact with Shockley. Levin, while still in his twenties, regularly phoned Shockley, and Rushton sought input on his work from Shockley.

Pioneer grant recipient and Johns Hopkins University sociology professor Robert Gordon recently called for a campaign to convince those with low IQs to breed less. Gordon's research yokes race to intelligence, juvenile delinquency, and criminality, all of which he deems genetic.

Gordon's former wife, University of Delaware educational studies professor Linda Gottfredson, was for many years the only woman receiving Pioneer funding, Gottfredson, whose work has been embraced by the white supremacist National Alliance and the David Duke–edited National Association for the Advancement of White People magazine, argues that low black representation in high-status schools and jobs is due to blacks' inferior intelligence, which she says undermines the justification for quotas.

As a private, nonprofit foundation, the Pioneer Fund must declare how its funds are disbursed but is under no obligation to identify its patrons. About $5 million in the fund's investment portfolio, together with donations, trusts and other revenues, produces about $1 million in annual income, most of which is distributed in relatively small pieces to about twenty recipients a year, including Seymour Itzkoff of Smith College and Richard Lynn of the University of Ulster, in Northern Ireland.

The tax-exempt organization is run by five long-time directors and operates from a Third Avenue location not far from the Manhattan law offices of Harry Weyher. Weyher, who refused numerous requests for an interview, has repeatedly denied that the foundation has any white-supremacist aims or Nazi ties.

DANIEL VINING, JR., a fifty-year-old University of Pennsylvania population-studies professor, sits immobile, his legs and wheelchair tucked under his long office desk.

"I had a stroke," Vining grunts, straining visibly to force each syllable from his mouth. "It didn't impair my brain—not the thinking portion anyway."

Vining, who is ruddy, rail thin, and bent forward at the waist, has little fine motor control of his mouth. He has some handle on his body, but his pipestem arms flail wildly at times, arcing through air, then banging against his sunken chest. In his work, which he began before he became disabled, Vining compiles evidence that the higher someone's IQ, the fewer children he or she will have. He believes IQ reflects intelligence and that intelligence is largely inherited. So he concludes humanity is becoming progressively less intelligent.

"Those are the facts," Vining rasps thickly.

As part of this work, Vining evaluates eugenic practices as they are carried out today in countries like Singapore and China. He proposes that lowering the birthrates of the United States' poor, who he suggests are less intelligent than the country's rich, would help reverse the theoretical slide in intelligence.

"Demographers don't talk or write much about population quality," writes Vining in the *Journal of Social, Political and Economic Studies*, which is a Pearson publication. "In my view, this silence is not because American demographers deem the subject unimportant but rather because of its association in so many persons' minds with eugenics and the interest shown in the latter by National Socialists."

In his article titled "The Demographic Decline of Homo Occidentalis," which appeared in another Pearson publication, *Mankind Quarterly*, Vining wonders whether such stances among white intellectuals can be seen "as a kind of pacific maneuvering of an aging, demoralized, sterile people before the onslaught of . . . reproductively more vigorous races in the pathetic hope that the writers themselves will be spared."

Faculty colleagues and school administrators exude a grimness when the subject of certain Pioneer professors comes up. If possible, the work of people like Vining, Rushton, and Levin is swept under the rug, and they are ignored and avoided. Because they are tenured, however, there is very little that an administration can do, as City College of New York found out with Levin. These professors are academia's dirty secret.

Associate professor of regional sciences Stephen Gale is chair of Vining's department and also his faculty colleague at the University of Pennsylvania. "Whether I want Dan to continue doing this kind of work or whether I think it is an embarrassment doesn't matter," Gale says, measuring his words carefully. "At the university we have academic freedom, which gives him the right to research whatever he chooses."

But is that research racist? I ask.

"I'm not going to tell you whether I think Dan is a prejudiced man," says Gale. "He may be."

Vining was born in Arkansas and grew up near Charlottesville, Virginia, the home of the University of Virginia, where his father has taught economics. There were childhood visits from family friends like Thorsten Veblen, a scholar famed for his publication *Theory of the Leisure Class*. While school-integration battles raged back home, Vining studied in northeastern boarding schools. During the early 1960s he was at Yale and Princeton.

Vining enlisted in the Marines and saw combat as an officer in Vietnam. He returned from the war uninjured, married an Asian woman, and became a professor at Penn in 1974. An athletic man his whole life, he was known around campus for his intense game of squash. One day while mowing his lawn, he collapsed.

"There was no warning at all," Gale says of the stroke. "It was an act of God."

During our halting discussion, Vining mentions the similarities between his work and that of another recipient of Pioneer support, Garrett Hardin, a professor emeritus of biological sciences at the University of California at Santa Barbara. "We're both interested in human population growth," Vining says.

Hardin, who has served on the boards of two Pioneer-funded groups that seek to restrict non-European, primarily Latino immigration on eugenic grounds, has written on the matter of philanthropy from a eugenic point of view. I hand over an excerpt of his work to Vining.

"Consider the matter of charity," writes Hardin, who in his most recent book thanked Pioneer president Weyher for his encouragement. "When one saves a starving man, one may thereby help him to breed more children. . . . Every time a philanthropist sets up a foundation to look for a cure for a certain disease, he thereby threatens humanity eugenically. . . . It is difficult, on rational grounds, to object to the sterilization of the feebleminded. . . . [But] more spectacular results could be obtained by preventing the breeding of numerous members of the subnormal classes higher than the feebleminded."

Isn't he saying, I ask Vining, that the poor, sick, or ignorant are genetically flawed and should be removed from the gene pool?

Vining twists in his wheelchair but is silent.

I pull out stills from the Nazi eugenics film that Laughlin hoped would raise America's consciousness. The movie, which depicts the handicapped living in luxurious institutions on the taxpayers' tab, was an opening gambit by the Third Reich in desensitizing the public to eugenic measures. First to hit the slippery slope would be the most vulnerable, those whose deformities and incapacities seem to make them almost another species.

Vining, his patrician features distorted by the stroke that erased a piece of his brain, grasps a photo. His eyes dart over a grainy black and white of a man identified as a "pinhead," a condition in which a person is born with the part of the brain that controls involuntary functions but not the portion for reasoning. "Many idiots are deep under the animal," reads the caption.

The individual featured in the photograph, who the filmmakers supposed would elicit the viewer's disgust, looks confused, uncomprehending. Vining, trapped in his wheelchair, hands shaking but eyes steady, understands all too well. Without raising his head, Vining speaks.

"I probably would have been exterminated myself," he says.

THE RUSHTON FILE

Irving Louis Horowitz

A<small>N ARTICLE</small> in *Rolling Stone* (October 20, 1994) by Adam Miller called J. Philippe Rushton a "professor of hate," someone who "takes money from an organization with a terrible past" (the Pioneer Fund, a foundation said to have an orientation toward eugenics). He is accused of being "obsessed with intelligence and genetics" to the point of having "racist" attitudes by Jeffrey Rosen and Charles Lane in *The New Republic* symposium on IQ (October 31, 1994). They single out Rushton for linking ethnocentricism to genetic factors; this in turn subjects him to the broad brush of being, along with Richard J. Herrnstein and Charles Murray, "Neo-Nazis" in *Newsweek* (October 24, 1994). In a *Chronicle of Higher Education* (October 26, 1994) critiquing Herrnstein and Murray's *The Bell Curve* it is clear that Rushton is central to their negative imputations. To be sure, in a thoughtful and sympathetic early review of the Rushton book in *The National Review* (September 12, 1994), Mark Snyderman warned of the barrage to come. "Philippe Rushton has written his own epitaph. Any genetic

Irving Louis Horowitz is the Hannah Arendt Distinguished Professor of Sociology and Political Science at Rutgers University. Among his many books are *The Rise and Fall of Project Camelot* and *Science, Sin, and Scholarship.* He is also editorial director and president emeritus of Transaction Publishers, the publisher of J. Philippe Rushton's *Race, Evolution, and Behavior.* This article originally appeared in a slightly longer form as "The Rushton File: Racial Comparisons and Media Passions" in *Society,* January–February 1995.

predisposition toward the defense of one's race only adds to the near impossibility of rational response to the scientific study of race in a world that has seen the Holocaust and racial subjugation. . . . Rushton's work may be ignored by the fearful, damned by the liberals, and misused by the racists. It is unlikely to be truly understood by anyone." Subsequent events have proved Snyderman prophetic; although Malcolm Brown's review in *The New York Times Book Review* made a valiant effort at understanding and empathy.

Beyond slogans and slurs, what is the "flap" over IQ about? Why does it elicit this broad-ranging discussion of the nature of social research in contemporary society? In particular, why does Philippe Rushton and *Race, Evolution, and Behavior* elicit such animus? After all, at one level, Rushton's book might be perceived as a small blip in the larger discourse on the status of intelligence and its racial correlates. Such a jaundiced view misses the point. Scandals over specific scholars or books become public issues because in some special way, in this instance through surrogates, they mirror larger themes and concerns of the century. And since this is the time of social science and ours the century of moral self-consciousness, the linkages of public policy and social research are as inevitable as they are at times misplaced.

Such issues go to the heart of media interest. Debates among social scientists permit the media to evince concern without expressing partisanship. Sensing that racial rifts seemingly grow over time, rather than diminish in direct proportion to a closure in the income gaps between the races, the media seek some way to tap deep public unease over volatile issues such as racial disparities in welfare receipts, criminal activities, drug intakes (euphemistically addressed as substance abuse), and the intimacies of personal behavior, without appearing to adopt a clear position of their own. They wish to respond to larger white racial dismay about black attitudes, and to do so without giving offense to minority views. In such a context, the work of someone like Rushton is a godsend. The media can point to independent, scholarly data sets, without taking sides or making claims.

In such a context, the media drives the data as much as the data drives the media. Attention to racial elements in intelligence is hardly unprecedented. In the 1960s there was the work of the late William Shockley, in the seventies that of Arthur Jensen, and in the 1980s that of a group of people much closer to media studies, such as Stanley Rothman. These individuals sought media attention as a mechanism for making their policy views known. The fact is that for a nondiscussible subject, the issue of race and genetics has been rather widely examined. The sequence has typically been to break out of the narrow professional journal literature first in a major book, or sometimes articles in general interest magazines. The next step is the widespread publication of reviews and commentary in newsprint form, followed in quick order by cover stories in news weeklies, radio and television talk shows, and the conversion of the whole communication chain into an object of news unto itself. Behind the information curtain is generous support from funding agencies with special interests in publicizing issues of racial imbalance and inheritance. Indeed, a review of major figures in psychology supported by the Pioneer Fund, ranging from Jensen to Rushton, indicates a more than casual interest in those who work the area of racial genetics. Such foundations measure success as much by media coverage as by scientific results.

Rushton's book, *Race, Evolution, and Behavior,* became a tagalong to the more popularly written and widely publicized book by Herrnstein and Murray, *The Bell Curve: Intelligence and Class Structure in American Life.* Rushton became like Zelig of Woody Allen's movie by the same name: a minor but very noticeable player peeking out and waving at the crowd as the totalitarian leaders of Nazi Germany and Fascist Italy worked the crowds. Rushton's book is no less convincing or less worthy, but the media's pickup of Rushton was as much an effort to create a sense of widespread academic contagion as a desire to investigate a deviant professional literature.

Media attention to Rushton was also fueled in part by the death of Herrnstein just weeks before *The Bell Curve* was published. Charles Murray has cachet as a journalist and conservative, but Herrnstein's death left an unmet need for a social science type who eschewed politics and policy. In addition, the networks competed with each other over coverage of this issue: CBS, NBC, CNN, ABC, all felt compelled to follow the lead of the major print media. Spreading Charles Murray too thin was undesirable; having someone like Rushton, articulate, composed, soft-spoken, and reminiscent of an Edwardian don, suited media requirements for foil and fop just fine.

Equally fascinating is the ripple effect within media life. While the television networks reach the masses, the news weeklies reach the television networks, informing them of what is hot and what is not, what is in and what is out. Thus, the fact that within one month in the autumn of 1994, we witnessed feature articles on intelligence and the IQ controversy in *Newsweek, Time,* and *U.S. News & World Report,* a symposium in *The New Republic,* not to mention review essays in *The New York Times, The Washington Post,* and *The Chronicle of Higher Education,* indicates the continued potency of the written word. The dirty little secret of media impact is that the print media supply the brains while the television and radio media supply the audience and the sound bites.

This is heady wine for people like Murray, who live on media glitz and foundations that covet media blitz. After all is said and done, both share concerns with the policy consequences of genetic differentiation. Although Philippe Rushton denies any such populist concerns, his desire to encourage attention to his work remains undeniable. In part, this is a normal impulse. Any author wants an audience. The media provide this missing link. For Rushton such attention is both a potent form of redemption and a revocation of years of obloquy from attacks on his scholarship and person at his home base, the University of Western Ontario. That in itself becomes a media "story," one that Rushton is not reticent to discuss, if for no other reason than to prevent his name from being tarnished.

Media interest is ultimately fixated on policy concerns, not empirical information. For broadcast journalism nothing is more deadly than a recitation of statistical tables. But that is precisely the world in which Rushton lives, and, he repeatedly asserts, the one in which he wants to live. Consequently, in interview and debate formats, Rushton comes off either as evasive or unconvincing. He becomes a pawn in the hands of the media rather than a shaper of events, a tool rather than a teacher. This is not to pass moral judgment on media activities in areas of race relations but rather to note that the impulses that lead the media to a Rushton, and for that matter, a Rushton to the media, are at loggerheads, preventing social science from serving as an instrument of enlightenment on the basic issues of the day.

Thus, Rushton was able to attract attention in a round of dismaying radio and television appearances, including the Geraldo Rivera show on NBC, Connie Chung for CBS, and several radio talk shows on WWOR and WMCA. Rushton was able to attract attention and certainly gain a larger readership than is usual for a scholarly treatise in psychology. But in simplifying his discussion of the genetic bases of racial differentiation among Mongoloid, Negroid, and Caucasoid "races," he opened the door to questions about what the larger public should do, if anything, with this assumption. Further, Rushton was unable or unwilling to enter into a policy discourse that might satisfy either a conservative or radical agenda. From Rushton's viewpoint, this is precisely what sets his work apart from, and puts it at a higher level than, that of others who share his approach. The difficulty is that such a self-evaluation does not still charges of racism and bias. In the absence of any policy agenda of his own, the policy agendas of others ranging from laissez-faire ideas of doing nothing for the poor to racialist policies of liquidation, have now been ascribed to him.

In Canada, the announcement of publication of *Race, Evolution, and Behavior* may have stimulated renewed efforts to oust Rushton from his academic post. The Canadian context of the Rushton file provides a national and a university framework for media interest in Rushton. For example, in August 1991, a group of nineteen students asked the Ontario Human Rights Commission to investigate charges of human rights abuses by Rushton on the basis of the 1981 Human Rights Code and, specifically, Ontario's policy on race relations, which states in part that "All doctrines and practices of racial superiority are scientifically false, morally reprehensible, and socially destructive, and are contrary to the policies of this government, and are unacceptable in Ontario." The complainants, while denying the racial categories adduced by Rushton, nonetheless declared that they were "Caucasian, black, and East Indian in origin." Evidently, those seeking Rushton's ouster in 1991 as a "racist who infected the learning environment at the University of Western Ontario" were not above utilizing his categories in so doing. They also sought action against the university on the grounds that by letting Rushton present his data, the university permitted actions that were "thereby aggravating the humiliating and degrading effect of Rushton's and their actions." The university response was difficult and courageous. George Pedersen, the president of the university, made it plain that academic freedom would be maintained, and that vigilante acts against Rushton would not be tolerated. His statement deserves attention as an affirmation of what a university is about. Its essential distinctions between professor and university are equally applicable to author and publisher.

The principle of academic freedom is not new. It has been in force in all universities in North America for several decades. Academic freedom provides a university community with the protection that must accompany independent research and the publication of its results. Academics frequently express ideas that are at odds with other views within the university, and sometimes with the views of society or government. Academic freedom ensures that such ideas can be expressed without fear of interference or repression from university administrators, politicians or others.

It is the essence of a university that independent research should be undertaken; this frequently involves highly controversial issues and sometimes highly controversial results and interpretations. It is a matter of historical record that members of the academic community, faculty and students alike, evaluate such results and interpretations. Conclusions are either sustained or refuted. The basis of this process is that the university must remain the center of such free intellectual inquiry and interchange.

In the specific instance that has occasioned this debate, the question has arisen concerning the relationship between the conclusions of Professor Philippe Rushton and the views of his University. The question can be addressed directly and succinctly: there is *no* relationship between Professor Rushton's conclusions and any position which the University itself might take on the issues involved. In other words, in his capacity as a researcher and scholar, Professor Rushton does not represent the views of The University of Western Ontario. The University deplores bigotry, intolerance, and racism in any form. To abrogate academic freedom would be to invoke those very attitudes which the principle of academic freedom itself rejects.

Since Canada, unlike the United States, has neither a Bill of Rights to protect the individual against government intrusion, nor a historical tradition of republicanism rather than royalism of both the British and French sorts, Pedersen's words are heartening for their commitment to academic freedom, as well as a sobering reminder to those who would shut down debate on race or any other subject of legitimate scholarship and research.

RACE IS HARDLY a new subject for American social science. Indeed, some of our earliest books were little else than warmed-over justifications for slavery. Books with titles like *Sociology of the African Negro* were among the very first to present racism as an ideology. After the Civil War, discussions about race were taken up in anthropology; and the tradition persisted through Carleton S. Coon and his works on *The Origin of Races* in 1962, and *Racial Adaptations* twenty years later. Coon promulgated a multiregional hypothesis in which racial differences were attributed to races emerging at different times in evolutionary history, with distinctive physiological characteristics and adaptations to climate and temperature.

The nineteenth-century debates over nature versus nurture brought the issue of race and ability to the fore in ways not dissimilar to the present flap over the Rushton and Herrnstein-Murray books. Oddly enough, this earlier phase involved Charles Darwin's cousin, Francis Galton—who was a pioneer in the eugenics movement. For Galton, the number of famous men a race produces is largely due to hereditary factors; genius and fame were said to go hand in hand. Not surprisingly, in Galton's view Anglo-Saxons were the world's most superior group. Galton's studies had the unintended effect of mobilizing sociologists into a response. In his essay of 1897, "Genius, Fame, and the Comparison of Groups" published in *Annals of the American Academy of Political and Social Science*, Charles Horton Cooley cut Galton to the quick. He noted that golden ages of creativity, peopled as they were with famous figures, could not be explained by sudden hereditary changes. "Every race probably turns out a number of greatly endowed men many times larger than the number that attains fame." Cooley concluded that "by greatly endowed I mean with natural abilities equal to those that made men famous in other times and places. The question which, if any, of these geniuses are to achieve fame is determined by historical and social conditions." Many social scientists continued to argue the case for heredity *and* society; nature *and* nurture.

By so doing, sociologists and anthropologists vacated the field of race differentiation in favor of studies of racial hierarchies. The emphasis shifted from biological to social causes of varied levels of achievement, focusing on opportunity, income, employment, housing, and schooling. The high point in the social scientific use of race as a conceptual tool may well have been the work of Gunnar Myrdal in economics, Arnold Rose in sociology, and Kenneth Clark in social psychology that emerged in the juridical framework of the *Brown* v. *Board of Education of Topeka* decision of 1954. This cemented a relationship between juridical decision making and social science research that persists to this day. Notably, this relationship is influenced by a strong impulse toward egalitarianism, as evident in contemporary sociology and anthropology: in sociology it derives from its roots in social welfare; in the case of anthropology from a strong bias in favor of cultural relativism, and conversely, a denial of ethical or behavioral superiority of one culture over another. This is clearly characteristic in the classical works of Franz Boas, Bronislaw Malinowski, Margaret Mead, and Ruth Benedict.

The egalitarian impulse, while theoretically modified over the past half century, continues to inform attitudes toward race within these two social sciences. Despite recent breast-beating among the experts, blaming themselves for everything from failure to predict that blacks would become social actors in their own right to the inability to render a meaningful picture of black innovators in their own culture, the support rendered by sociologists and anthropologists to black-white equity is incontestable. This impulse is at times misplaced. Sometimes researchers will dampen, even suppress, the racial variable, if its inclusion "distorts" normal curves and representative samples. Recently, a colleague of mine who did a study on children's attitudes toward work and the labor process simply discarded all the data he had on race, since attitudes of black children were radically at variance with those of white children. As a result, a study with a perfectly fascinating potential for helping us understand racial differences regarding work became a pedestrian examination of different attitudes among white children. This is unfortunately all too common, and may explain why we are so unprepared for a book that tackles issues of race with respect to a wide range of factors, as does Rushton's *Race, Evolution, and Behavior.*

The history of psychology with the subject of race is quite different from that of sociology and anthropology. From Abram Kardiner's work on the neurotic basis of explosive aggression to more familiar efforts to isolate genetic factors in black educational underachievement, the focus on individual behavior rather than social conditioning points to major differences in the orientations, philosophies, and goals of each social science. While one might arguably claim that psychologists are no less partisan to the cause of black equity, the concepts they utilize, from "black rage" to the linkage of racial frustration to racial aggression lend themselves to meliorative approaches at the policy level. The extension of laboratory techniques to field research, when played out on a racial canvas, also provides psychologists with a range of risky analogues between the animal and human kingdoms that sociologists and anthropologists have generally abandoned.

The social sciences cut at least two ways with respect to the democratization process. Done with integrity, social science analysis can and often does serve the cause of democracy. On the other hand, social science research has supported the most evil forms of dictatorship, such as the German Nazi use of demographers to chart concentrations of Jewish people in urban centers like Berlin, Vienna, and Warsaw so that genocide could be committed efficiently and with minimum disruption of the economic order. How and when social research becomes a tool for human liberation or for human decimation is itself a subject worthy of independent consideration. More to the point, the question of how data generated by social research plays out on a larger social canvas is rarely addressed directly in the literature.

Many of the impulses that inspire individuals to enter the social sciences have their roots in moral issues of the most politically worthwhile sort. Indeed, deprived of such a moral base, I suspect that the social sciences would be far less hospitable or attractive; I know it would be for me. As Max Weber and a few courageous individuals of earlier years well appreciated, the problem is less with the word *social* than with the word *science*. For whatever else science is or does, it requires that the chips fall where they may. And for social science, that cuts both ways, making such research morally despicable or personally engrossing depending on one's point of view.

The fascination of these tough social science "cases" is as much about moral fiber as it is about scientific rigor. Once again, we have in J. Philippe Rushton an unusual person with a history of stubbornly pursuing the study of racial differentiation despite a most inhospitable intellectual climate. In his capacity as professor of psychology at Western Ontario University, Rushton has felt the lash of student protests, the threat of censorship, menacing legal actions to remove him from his tenured post, and the summary rejection of manuscripts and articles, at times under duress and after such material had already been accepted for publication.

WITHOUT WISHING to dampen enthusiasm for the book, or to repeat what Rushton says, or what reviewers claim that Rushton says, it might be useful to summarize the major scientific statements and empirical claims made in *Race, Evolution, and Behavior*.

First, race is a meaningful biological category, and not just a sociological construct. While a notion of three broad racial categories may be oversimplified, it provides a framework for analysis that holds up on a series of measures and over a wide spectrum of nations and regions.

Second, examinations of such disparate data as brain size, intelligence, sexual activity, law-abiding propensities, and social organization skills show such powerful variations between the races over time and space that differences can hardly be dismissed or reduced to environmental conditioning.

Third, such a key variable as crime indicates intense asymmetry: black assaults against whites, black violence unleashed against other blacks, strong racial patterns in assaults such as rape and homicide, indicate something more than economic deprivation.

Fourth, intelligence quotient studies all point in the same broad direction: while environmental impact is real, the differentials in "educational achievement" remain substantial, up to 15 percent between whites and blacks, and 5 percent between whites and Asians—with the latter having the advantage. Intelligence is seen as related to speed of maturation, temperament, health, and longevity, and as a result to patterns of behavior as such.

Fifth, race has been found to have strong "effects" on learning propensities, independent of social class. This signifies that a range of considerations from mental illness to sexual behavior cannot be reduced to class analysis.

Sixth, the physical properties of races differ, so that indicators ranging from penis size to testosterone level and cranial capacity exist; which, in turn, one can infer are directly related to concepts of the self, temperament, sexuality, aggression, altruism, and value judgments.

Seventh, human beings form themselves into hierarchies of dominance, with those at the top of the hierarchy exhibiting higher levels of whatever traits make for success in a specific culture and in turn to gain greater than equal share of whatever scarce resources are available. This might be termed the neo-Darwinian strain in Rushton's thinking.

Eighth, given the degree to which social organization varies with fertility, people who live within interpersonal social systems in one context frequently seek out each other for friendship and marriage. This might be termed the primary-group effect in Rushton's analysis.

Ninth, and finally, people create cultures compatible with their genotypes. Thus such tendencies rooted in genetic makeup not only relate to each other, but also to sociopolitical attitudes, that is, to macro questions of order vs. freedom, and demographic trends that occur in the sweep of history.

Clearly, Rushton's work goes considerably beyond these main points, and his evidence, marshaled from a study of sixty racial variables presented in five times that number of tables, raises serious concerns about the extent to which genetic factors determine behavior. This is not to say that Rushton proceeds through his tables mechanically, but it does indicate a lifetime of concern about the more exacting importance of race in the competition of consensus and conflict in North America.

Rushton and the study of race and IQ has long had his *scientific* critics. Alvin Poussaint detects a self-fulfilling mode in white prejudices against blacks. Stephen Jay Gould sees the tendency to emphasize broad statistical averages as pseudo-science disguising social prejudice. Urie Bronfenbrenner argues that nature and nurture ought not to be seen as polarized extremes; rather the heritability factor moves up when environmental conditions improve. David Perkins of the Harvard educational school and Leon Kamin of Princeton and now Northeastern, postulate different types of intelligence (neural, experiential, and reflective), and thus the improbability of effectively using intelligence tests as even a crude measure of mental capability.

Since many critics in this most recent discussion of IQ have focused on the Herrnstein-Murray book, they tend to aim wide of the mark of the concerns targeted by that "obscure professor of psychology, Philippe Rushton," so called by Michael Lind in *The Washington Post*. But in this dismissive attitude, Rushton's claims that the scientific situation has been sacrificed on the altar of ideology tend to be confirmed. Given the accuracy of that charge, I should like to cite my own concerns.

THE DIVISION of mankind into three races is far too simplistic to admit of statistically significant correlations. The neat fifty-fifty split between hereditary and environmental factors possesses little operational potential. (For what it is worth, Herrnstein-Murray place the ratios at 40 percent environment and 60 percent hereditary.) At times Rushton appears to diffuse criticism by admitting the existence of environment; at other times, he writes with a certainty that suggests human behavior is a function of gene transplants.

IQ researchers' notion of a general intelligence, accepted by Rushton, is much too broad; implications as to the limits of pedagogic correctives are drawn much too narrowly. Some experiments, such as those of twins raised by separate sets of parents, produce sufficiently distinctive learning curves as to cast doubt on genetic determinations. However, it is clear that many major studies do support hereditarian assumptions.

It is not at all clear that test results involving blacks are radically different from those involving other Americans when measured at microscopic levels. Thus, in cases of twins raised in separate households, with different income levels, the actual disparities that can be traced to genetic rather than environmental conditions tend to be randomly distributed.

One must be concerned that observation of differences too readily slips into the language of superiority and inferiority. Thus Rushton is too ready to be dismissive of African cultural achievements and too celebratory of European standards of culture and learning. European highs are taken for granted. European lows (such as technological murder) are less well defined. This is not to say that genocide is exclusively a European invention, as we can see by recent events in Cambodia and Rwanda. However, the preponderant evidence is that such matters as depravity and bestiality are not confined to any single race.

There are problems of analysis that are simply not covered. For example, if Asians score highest on intelligence measures today, then why was the development of science stymied so thoroughly in China, despite a substantial initial lead in a variety of areas of discovery and technology? We are not able to extend over time racial disparities. However, if standardized tests uniquely determine or define achievement, than the huge advantage of the West over China in the classical period should not be so evident. On the other hand, if such a breakdown of science is a function of China's political experience, then can one not with equal vigor argue that such environmental factors are also at work in defining levels of African achievement?

An additional dilemma exists in identifying brain size with intelligence. In examining its form and function the brain per se is one of the smallest units in the nervous system. Few contemporary studies of the anatomy and functions of the human nervous system, or studies of nervous diseases and disorders, relate brain size to intelligence. Rushton's own data display such small variances along a racial axis that it is difficult to draw broad inferences. While it is true that the human nervous system differs from other mammals chiefly in the enlargement and elaboration of the cerebral hemisphere, studies do not offer a conclusive picture of intelligence capacities in human racial types as a direct consequence of brain size or weight.

Despite appeals to hundreds of tests and sixty distinctive variables, we seem to be in a realm of a more indeterminate physiological universe than the racially determined one Rushton offers. There is a reductionistic appeal to a single variable to explain various aspects of behavior, and the result is more problematic than predictive. For example, what does one do with the idea of Asians having lower sexual drives than Africans? This may or may not correlate with intelligence, but it certainly does not explain the huge birthrates in China over time. To be sure, the ability of the Chinese to develop policies that sharply reduce its birthrate indicates the strength, not weakness, of environmental factors.

If by hard science in contrast to soft science we mean the ability to define explanation by prediction, what might be called the Reichenbach standard of positivism, Rushton's fair-minded admission that his racial categories hardly define specific levels of accomplishment by individual black people casts doubt on the aggregate worth of his data. Levels of achievement may differ by racial category, but it is simplistic to explain such differences as genetically defined.

Having said this, it must be strongly stated that Rushton emerges from the pages of his work as a vigorous opponent to all forms of racial genocide or solutions based on experimental tampering with the human species. There are no notions of eugenics guiding his work, as was common among academics at the start of the twentieth century. Moreover, he is emphatic "that it is totalitarianism in the service of fanaticism that causes people to be murdered, not theories of human nature." But certainly these theories have been uniformly adopted by totalitarian regimes as a mobilizing force in underwriting ethnic supremacy and racial separatism throughout the century.

While it might be true, as Rushton claims, that "there are no necessary policies that flow from race research," it remains the case that some forms of totalitarianism have historically adopted racial doctrines to justify everything from medical experimentation on human beings to mass murder ostensibly for the greater goal of the improvement of the human species. In such cases, the unnatural selection of indicators rather than the natural adaptation of gene pools to particular environments determines and defines human performance.

It is not quite the case that the situation in intelligence research is the same as in physics, from which came Enrico Fermi's warning, which Rushton repeats, that "whatever Nature has in store for mankind, unpleasant as it may be, men must accept." For it is precisely the indeterminate status of social behavior in contrast to the determinate behavior of atomic matter that distinguishes social from physical sciences. To speak of racial difference as assisting our sense of human diversity is fine. To assume that such differences somehow measure human success or failure is less convincing.

The "Darwinian Perspective" is less one of evolutionary differentiation than one of social adaptation to precisely the global village to which Rushton pays homage. The drawing together of races, the factor of intermarriage, the growing secularization of cultures, all point to a decline in the racial factor as a unitary variable of analysis. On the other hand, fundamentalism of all sorts, the revival of religious and linguistic separations, the emergence of exclusionist doctrines of superiority among the former colonial peoples, do indeed point to a continuation of race and ethnicity as a dividing line, if not a detriment. But all of these *social* (in contrast to *behavioral*) factors are obscure footnotes to the Rushton approach. In this, he is not alone. An entire cluster of researchers has aligned itself to reductionist schemes as a way of doing scientific business. All social science that seeks answers in single variables must be held to strict accountability, for analytical no less than ideological and valuational reasons.

THE CONTRADICTIONS in Rushton's thinking were essentially brought about by himself. By a steady, unyielding claim that he is operating only at the level of empirical data, his strong suit turned into a public relations weakness. With an increasing number of public appearances, ranging from network extravaganzas on Cable NBC with Geraldo Rivera, radio superchannel shows on WWOR, and the Connie Chung show on CBS, the discussion quickly changed from the empirical information to the policy consequences of Rushton's line of reasoning, and here Rushton fell short. In effect, Rushton wanted to have it both ways. Had he declined a vast array of public appearances, in a climate of intense racial feelings, he might have carried off the positivist vision of scientific behavior: "Here are the data on the subject of race and intelligence. Do with it as you will." Rushton might then have claimed the mantle of objectivity and avoided the censure that has dogged him from the start of his research work.

By accepting a round of radio, television and newsweekly interviews—often with individuals less than kindly disposed to his information, or how it was derived—Rushton placed himself in a policy environment, or at least in an environment that cried out for remedial action. Charles Murray understood this well in his approach, which can readily be summarized as a combination of Adam Smith in economics and Darwinian sociobiology. But Rushton does not claim, either in his book or in his appearances, that remedial measures like Head Start or a variety of affirmative action measures are total failures. Indeed, since he admits to a fifty-fifty relationship of inheritance to environment he would be hard put to make this claim. He might have warded off criticism by taking the policy bull by the horns to begin with.

For example, it might have been quite feasible to say that the set of data on racial differentiation is real unto itself, and that the same data sets used by Herrnstein-Murray are used by Rushton. But it is just as reasonable to claim the reverse from the data. Far from leading to the belief that educational and cultural remedies do not work, or work only marginally, and hence should be cut or eliminated, one might just as reasonably argue that the data compel one to reassess the problems of black inheritance no less than black environment, and that the support levels should be doubled, even tripled, as a serious approach to closing the gap in measures of health, education, work, and environment.

Since Rushton credits environment with being 50 percent of the explanation of racial differentiation, one could argue that working double time and twice as hard on that end of the scale could offset supposed genetic variabilities. In that way, a liberal rather than conserva-tive policy analysis might be derived from the data. That Rushton chose not to do this, but instead insists that he operates only at a level of fact, and that the facts do not support the idea that such programs as Head Start change intelligence quotients, only disarms him, and makes him vulnerable to the charge that he—along with Charles Murray—really believes that no sort of remedial policies have long-term merit.

One of the calamities of pure positivism in the social sciences has been the erection of a high wall between information and policy. Yet, the public demand for remedies, if not solutions, to major social prob-lems like crime and drug addiction, cannot be slaked by a mere recita-tion of data showing the racial disparities of such things as incarceration. And of course, the notion of a social science cannot be served by its reduction to a behavioral science. And on this, the historic problems of psychology themselves become problematic, in the research environ-ment no less than in the larger system.

Rushton's work stems from a tradition in which one measures dif-ferences in intelligence and behavior between cats and dogs, between mice and monkeys. In the animal kingdom, given the absence of a the-ory of improvement or a belief in correction (or at least not much of one without human assistance) one can argue the positivist cause with some persuasiveness. But the same sort of measures when applied to human variabilities collapse precisely on the shoals of humanity as such. That is to say, policy is intrinsic to the very nature of social science.

The incapacity of the author of *Race, Evolution, and Behavior* to draw out its policy-making implications is a liability, and his recourse to bald empiricism serves to weaken his larger claims. Far from stand-ing on the solid bedrock of fact, Rushton finds himself mired in the sands of speculation. In the nature of the democratic impulse of West-ern societies, Rushton would have served his interests better by avoid-ing media pitfalls and asserting, as he tries to do, the empirical base of his research data. He would have done even better by fashioning a set of policy options that might flow from the nature of such data.

On the other hand, if Rushton insists on remaining true to his posi-tivist proclivities, to which he is entitled, then his travels on the media and lecture circuit become of dubious merit. To enter the larger fray of racial politics armed with the slim pickings of psychological tests is a bold, if not suicidal thing to do. Such tests prove to be a mighty small instrument on which to play new chords. For example the *fact* that black on white crime is sixty times greater than white on black crime may *in part* be a function of disproportionate economic holdings of blacks and whites, as much as supposed incivilities of black people. That holdings of wealth are no less in evidence as differentials in measures of intelligence can be adduced as an argument against a hereditary vision. This is especially the case, since Rushton readily, even happily, admits a 50 percent environmental conditioning; just how Rushton and his associates allocate proportions in this nurture-nature mix remains wide open.

Not only Rushton as an individual but the science of psychology as a whole, must come to terms with these issues in a far bolder sociological way than they have in the past. What we are faced with in the furor over Rushton's work is no less dangerous ground for social science as a whole than are racial attitudes in particular. It represents a return to older struggles between psychologism and sociologism. There is no point in denying the strength of the data indicating racial and ethnic differentiation. There is great point in asserting that such differentiation points to a need for, rather than avoidance of, policy analysis, to help us to understand the sources of decision making and implementation.

OVER THE YEARS, I have engaged in a hybrid activity that might best be described as the journalistic investigation of social science "scandals." Indeed, I think it fair to say that my reputation in part rests on the frank discussion of the Department of Defense use of social science as civic action in *The Rise and Fall of Project Camelot*, the ideological struggles over a social science component in an agency known for its contributions to physics, chemistry, and mathematics in my article on *Struggle in Paradise: The Institute of Advanced Studies*, the cogitations of the social sciences in relation to marginal religious movements that were examined in *Science, Sin, and Scholarship: The Politics of the Unification Church*, and the struggles between individual conscience and the collective anthropological will in my examination of the Mosher Case at Stanford University in which a student of modern China was denied his doctorate for daring to raise the ethics of infanticide as official policy in Maoist China. There have been other, arguably less important papers that I wrote on social science in federal agencies—especially in wartime conditions.

In this peculiar matter of the Rushton file, and as head of Transaction Publishers [the publisher of Rushton's *Race, Evolution, and Behavior*], this lifelong professional concern with the "scandals" of the field, comes together with equally lifelong publishing considerations. So the stuff of analysis is at least in part the substance of self-evaluation. In this connection, I must draw attention to two cases in which advertisements for *Race, Evolution, and Behavior* were rejected. The first instance involved *The American Spectator*, an erstwhile "conservative" publication that informed our publisher of a problem and later a decision not to accept the Rushton advertisement. John Funk, in a pair of sad letters he wrote to Transaction [and here I paraphrase], stated that "*The American Spectator* is declining the opportunity to publish the advertisement for *Race, Evolution, and Behavior*." As a policy, they do not comment as to reasons for a rejection. He claimed to be simply carrying out the policies and duties of his position. A second letter from Mr. Funk indicated that he made the case before his editorial people, but it was not enough to carry the day. Clearly, this decision was made by the editorial directors of *The American Spectator*, and as a result, I wrote to R. Emmett Tyrrell, Jr., who, whatever his politics, always struck me as a courageous individual. In this instance, a long letter (and two follow-up letters) was met by silence. The contents warrant partial reproduction:

> I am not dogmatic on such editorial concerns, and indeed, appreciate the anguish that goes into all such supposedly cut-and-dried decisions about publishing advertising materials for specialized publics such as those we serve. We come then to Professor Rushton's book.
>
> The advertisement lists no fewer than eight distinguished psychologists and educators who are enthusiastic about the quality of scholarship involved in this book. It is also plainspoken on what the book is about, and the position it takes on racial differentiation with respect to sixty variables related to everything from cranial size to intelligence, crime and sexual behavior. If anything, its findings celebrate Asian achievements, with Europeans occupying an intermediate position, and people of African background at the low end of the scale.
>
> It may well turn out that this sort of analysis is a crock. Indeed, not a few psychologists have heatedly claimed just that. By the

same token, we are publishers of a wide-ranging series of books on the African presence in Asia and Egypt, with claims of African origins in science and culture. These too have had their detractors (not a few of which have been published in *Society*, by the way). Scholarship is an uneven and rocky road. While for the most part, issues of such fundamental antipathies do not occur, it is precisely the safeguarding of just those works which dare to tread on dangerous ground that need the most protection.

The decision by *The American Spectator* to reject a paid advertisement for *Race, Evolution, and Behavior* will not make issues of genetics and race dissolve. Only by the fullest exploration of the issues raised by Rushton will we arrive at a higher ground. But for a journal as fiercely concerned with political truths as yours to spurn a priori, publication of such a statement indicates that your affection for scientific truths may not be equally great.

My letter went on to indicate that in the nearly four thousand titles that Transaction has published over the years, not a single one has been recalled for faulty scholarship; although many have been sharply criticized. But the decision to accept or reject advertisements should be taken with caution, not only on professional but on civil libertarian grounds. Despite this letter, more an appeal in retrospect, and two subsequent letters, our concerns have been met by stony silence.

A second case had to do with the scholarly journal, *Evolutionary Anthropology*, which also rejected the advertisement. It was assumed that the journal editor, John G. Fleagle, had decided against publication of the advertisement—and Rushton wrote to the journal protesting its cancellation. At the same time, I wrote to the publishers of this journal, John Wiley & Sons, also protesting this decision. It is a tribute to the qualities of Wiley as a great independent American publishing house, that its vice-president acknowledged that the decision to cancel the advertisement was made in the publishing house, not in the editorial room. More important, upon review, the vice-president and general manager of Wiley decided to rescind its decision, acknowledge its error, and move ahead with publication of the advertisement. Wiley's letter requires reproduction, not only for its candor, but to provide a sense of the everyday nature of the struggle for a free press in social science as in other areas of life:

I have your recent letter regarding an advertisement for J. Philippe Rushton's book *Race, Evolution, and Behavior.* You are quite correct in your observation that freedom of the press must be practiced with respect to advertising as well as editorial matters. While there are appropriate limits to the application of that freedom—FDA restrictions on pharmaceutical advertising and the rejection of phone-sex ads in scholarly journals come to mind—advertising a scholarly book, however controversial, from a scholarly publisher in a scholarly journal hardly transgresses such limitations.

I have therefore instructed our advertising department to run the advertisement on receipt of Transaction's insertion order for a paid advertisement. You might want to assure Professor Rushton that the decision to reject the advertisement was made here and not by the scientific editor of the journal. It is not Wiley's policy to engage in the suspension of "the free and unfettered exchange of ideas" in any form, but we do make mistakes. You and Professor Rushton have my apologies for this one.

The task of a professional publisher in social and behavioral science is not to stand in absolute judgment, but to offer the latest information and best theory available on subjects of general concern and professional competence. Transaction has published a series of ten titles by my dear colleague at Rutgers, Ivan Van Sertima. In a nutshell, he uniformly claims the priority of discovery and the centrality of the black race in the creation of culture, science, and institution-building in places as far apart as North Africa and Central Asia.

The work of Professor Van Sertima has generated significant discussion and criticism, sometimes even in the pages of *Society*. Thus, Mary Lefkowitz, in the March–April 1994 issue, argues that the idea of Greek indebtedness to Egyptian sources is untrue and fraudulent, and that some of this misinformation (although not explicitly referring to Van Sertima's works) deserves "a place on the shelf of hate literature . . ." This is the same sort of rhetoric that one hears—in reverse—with respect to the Rushton book.

That the writings of Rushton, and a few earlier efforts on the IQ controversy, have generated a similar brand of heated rhetoric is hardly the sort of intellectual outcome that should occasion surprise in the current climate of academic divisiveness. Nor must one presume that the truth is somewhere in between, or that the claims made on the "left" by Van Sertima are either more or less correct than those made by Rushton on the "right." Indeed, it is the belief of these scholars that they are not speaking in ideological tongues, but reciting plain truths that others seek to avoid.

These opinions are sufficiently reasonable and thought-provoking to merit review in the court of scholarly opinion. But I must confess not to be persuaded by either position. Indeed, I am far less concerned with staking claims for racial superiority—whether based on ancient history or modern genetics—than I am with finding a way to reach racial comity, so that American, and world, society can move ahead in concert. To what end is the research on theories of superiority to be put? This, it seems to me, is a reasonable question that cannot be dodged by claims that a specific theory is empirically or historically grounded and hence not subject to policy scrutiny.

If this is indeed the case, then we have a right to inquire why figures at both ends of the racial spectrum seek out media fame and public notoriety by appearing on many radio and television broadcasts, granting interviews to a variety of hysterical media personalities, and lecturing on circuits in which academic substance gives way to ideological ballast—either stated frankly, or surreptitiously, and hence less convincingly, as a function of analysis.

It might well be the case that in a generation it will be determined that environmental techniques and remedies have failed of their purpose. But since Rushton argues that environmental-genetic factors are a statistical toss-up, the argument for accelerating support to African Americans in need cannot be rejected out of hand or in parlor-talk fashion. I find that many of the new breed of genetic psychobiologists have not pursued the implications of their work, preferring by inference to let the data speak for itself, when in policy terms, data does no such thing. What in fact takes place is a deterministic rendition of data. Pessimism becomes the overarching leitmotif. Race differentiation is somehow held to be immutable, like the sun rising or the earth traveling about the sun in its proper orbit. It is this sense of the *physics* of race relations that undermines claims to objectivity. It is appropriate for an author to limit his field of analysis and interpretation. It is rather less proper for an author to ignore the limits of his data.

The position of a social science should be unequivocal in the presentation of information: to support unpleasant and innovative opinions even when they go against the grain of current prejudices at the core of liberal society. But the tasks of social science are also to make clearer the limits of the evidential basis of such thinking, and to insist upon a public acknowledgment of policy consequences by those who invite public notoriety—not on the basis of their evidence, but on the implications of what they write. These are a complex set of factors to digest, much less to operationally implement. It is precisely this set of relationships that the modern university must juggle. It is precisely this set of relationships that elevates social science above and beyond empiricism in theory or racism in practice. For these reasons, Professor Rushton is and must be considered a valued member of both the academic and scientific communities to which he contributes. We need to be reminded that those truths held to be self-evident are those which are most in need of reexamination.

THEORIES OF EAST ASIAN SUPERIORITY

Barry Sautman

W ESTERN PSYCHOLOGISTS first floated theories of East Asian superiority in the late 1970s,[1] when Japan emerged as a world-class economic power. The theories claim higher innate intellectual and behavioral qualities for East Asians.[2] Before the dawn of the "Pacific Asian Century," such claims would have had marginal implications.[3] The context is now very different. It is estimated that the combined gross domestic product of East Asia—4 percent of the world economy in 1960—will rise to 33 percent by 2010.[4] With the ascent of East Asia contrasted to slow growth or perceived crises elsewhere,[5] endorsements of theories of East Asian superiority by prominent personages take on increased political salience.[6]

In a 1993 interview with an Australian business magazine, Lee Kuan Yew, Singapore's strongman for the past thirty-five years, compared the superior work ethic of Chinese in Singapore to that of Singapore Indians and wondered aloud about a genetic basis.[7] The following year, Lee stated during a tour of Australia that its people lacked the drive to compete with East Asians, who are "specially geared for scholarship and high performance."[8] To a U.S. journal in

Barry Sautman is an assistant professor at the Hong Kong University of Science and Technology. This article has not previously been published.

1994, Lee asserted that because the genetic link between East Asians and fellow "Mongoloid" Native Americans was severed by the mixture of the former with Central Asians and the migration of the latter across the Bering Straits, East Asians now enjoy a superior "neurological development" and culture.[9]

Lee is a social Darwinist who admits to prejudices against non–East Asians.[10] His statements epitomize a long adherence to the views of "hereditarian" psychologists, many of whom now posit a hierarchy of intellect with East Asians on top, whites in a close intermediate position, and others at the base.[11] Lee is the patriarch of a mini-state, but is admired by East Asian leaders. His views carry weight all out of proportion to his power.[12]

Senior minister Lee has not been alone among East Asian leaders in this racial worldview. In 1986, Japanese prime minister Yasuhiro Nakasone told a meeting of his party that

> So high is the level of education in our country that Japan's is an intelligent society. Our average [IQ] score is much higher than those of countries like the U.S. There are many blacks, Puerto Ricans and Mexicans in America. In consequence, the average score over there is exceedingly low.[13]

When criticism from the United States followed these remarks, Nakasone issued a "clarification" indicating that he had intended to praise the remarkable achievements made by Americans despite the presence of minorities.[14] Several other Japanese politicians have since made deprecatory comments about Americans generally and African Americans particularly.[15] Malaysia's prime minister Mahathir bin Mohammed has also long adhered to a theory of East Asian superiority, but with a twist. Convinced of the genetic inferiority of his own Malay people vis-à-vis Malaysian Chinese (allegedly brought on by more inbreeding among Malays),[16] he has concluded that tight control is needed to avoid Chinese economic dominance turning into political hegemony.[17]

While less famous than Hans Eysenck, Britain's foremost race difference theorist and the mentor of J. Philippe Rushton and Arthur Jensen,[18] University of Ulster psychologist Richard Lynn is a prolific proponent of theories of East Asian intellectual superiority. His 1977 study broke with past showings of equal IQ scores for Asians and whites and estimated mean Japanese IQ at 106.6, as against the United States mean of 100, or 110 for Japanese born in the 1960s. Lynn regarded this as the highest mean IQ ever recorded for a nationality and thought it likely of genetic origin.[19]

While Lynn regarded Japanese as exhibiting IQs above Americans and Britons, he then held that other East Asians were only on a par with northern Europeans.[20] Lynn did, however, compare IQ scores among Chinese and Malay boys in Singapore,[21] noting a 14 point difference (Chinese, 110; Malays 96, against an outdated British norm) comparable to that between U.S. whites and blacks. He concluded that Singapore's prosperity is owed mainly to high Chinese intelligence, despite the Chinese having been born into relative poverty. This, he argued, shows that low IQ in certain groups is responsible for their poverty, and not the reverse.

In 1980, Lynn compared Japanese children's IQ scores with those of Ulster children given a translation of a test standardized in Japan and one standardized in the United States.[22] Conversion of the Japanese scores into their equivalents on the U.S. tests using the Ulster data showed a mean Japanese IQ of over 110. Lynn argued that this result and high scores by East Asians in other national settings disconfirm contentions that U.S. IQ tests favor white middle-class Americans and that variations in intelligence among ethnic groups are caused by environmental factors.[23]

Headlines were made in the English-speaking world and Japan when Lynn presented data in 1982 indicating that young Japanese have a mean IQ of 111, compared to 100 for whites.[24] He noted that while 2 percent of the U.S. population have 130+ IQs, 10 percent of Japanese reach this level and 77 percent have IQs above the United States mean. Lynn argued that this gap was not due to superior education in Japan because it already appears in six-year-olds. Differences had also widened in the twentieth century, with a 7-point rise in the last generation. Lynn concluded that its "IQ advantage may have been a significant factor in Japan's outstandingly high rate of economic growth."[25]

Lynn's theories of East Asian intellectual superiority continue to be discussed by the North American media,[26] while in Japan varied attitudes toward these studies have been evinced.[27] In the United States the theory has been promoted in journals widely read in business and political circles. *Fortune* magazine writer Daniel Seligman has been particularly vigorous in promoting Lynn's theories.[28]

The work of James Flynn and other scholars who question Lynn's findings receive less public exposure. Flynn pointed out that researchers[29] have found sampling biases in Lynn's data that indicate a rough parity between the "full-scale" IQs of Japanese and U.S. whites.[30] Most important, he noted large gains in U.S. and Japanese IQs in a generation. He showed even greater single-generation IQ gains—without any evidence of extraordinary achievement—in other countries.

Flynn argued that because IQ tests give nonsense results when used to rank generations over time, they have explanatory power only in a context of cultural homogeneity. Since "races" have greater cultural differences than do two generations within the same culture, but the magnitude of between-generation score gaps at least match those between races, Lynn's findings cannot be measures of between-race intelligence differences.[31] Asian-American IQ scores, for example, have been higher than white scores because the former were scored against obsolete norms. Whites of an earlier generation are outscored, but because of IQ gains over time, present-day whites are not.[32]

Harold Stevenson and Hiroshi Azuma argued that Lynn's Japanese samples were biased for higher socioeconomic status (SES) and urban residence and that the subtests used differed for Japan and the United States.[33] In a 1985 study, a team led by Stevenson reported no IQ difference between children in Minneapolis and Sendai, Japan.[34]

Lynn recognized the massive IQ score gains in Japan and Western countries,[35] but unlike Flynn regarded these not as artifacts that discredit the tests as direct measures of intelligence, but as increases in intelligence due mainly to improved nutrition[36] and largely unnoticed because they were nonverbal.[37] He also did not accept the claim that genetic factors caused a disparate IQ gain between Americans and Japanese because class-based birthrate differentials led to a fall in IQs in the post-war West, while Japanese birth rates were less dysgenic.[38] His rejection of this hypothesis allowed Lynn to offer his own theory, one in which East Asian superiority is more primordial.

In an essay on the "intelligence of the Mongoloids,"[39] Lynn again asserted that *g* is higher for Japanese than for whites[40] and imputed to

Taiwan and Hong Kong Chinese and Asian-Americans the same higher overall intelligence and pattern of relatively low verbal scores and very high visuospatial scores claimed for the Japanese.[41]

Lynn argues that these differences are "genetically programmed" and explicable through evolutionary theory. Because the Ice Age was most severe in Northeast Asia, higher intelligence was needed for survival among archaic Northeast Asians than among early Europeans—not to speak of Africans. Besides improved g, Northeast Asians required better visuospatial abilities because of their reliance on hunting, as opposed to gathering. Enhanced visuospatial abilities, located in the right cerebral cortex of the "Mongoloid brain," took place at the expense of verbal abilities sited in the left cerebral cortex.[42]

Lynn and University of Hong Kong psychologist Jimmy Chan have made clear why they regard the putatively higher intellectual ability of East Asians as significant:

> The theoretical interest of the apparently high means obtained by Oriental peoples on tests of intelligence and educational attainment lies in the difficulties it presents for theories which seek to explain the low scores of other ethnic minorities in the United States in terms of test bias, discrimination or low incomes per head. All these factors operate equally against the Oriental peoples but apparently without detrimental effects.[43]

In short, Lynn and Chan argue that a showing that East Asians in societies less affluent than those of whites nonetheless have superior intelligence means that lower scores among other peoples of color are not related to poverty.[44]

Lynn sought a third source of evidence of race differences in intelligence in "contributions to civilization"—discoveries and inventions made by the brightest individuals in populations with high average intelligence. He reproduced twenty-one criteria, set out by Baker,[45] by which early civilizations are to be judged and claimed that "Caucasoids" developed all twenty-one of these in Sumer, Crete, the Indus Valley, and ancient Egypt. Amerindians developed ten or less in Mayan and Aztec society. "Negroids" and Australian aborigines achieved almost no "criteria of civilization." Because they escaped glaciation 24,000 to 10,000 years ago, Africans and Southeast Asians never independently developed settled agriculture, written language, arithmetic, astronomy, etc.[46]

Lynn claims that in the past 2,000 years, "discoveries that constitute developed peoples have been made only by the Caucasoid and Mongoloid peoples." Mongoloids were marginally ahead in the first 1,600 years of this period, but Caucasoids dominated the next 500, only to meet with a recent challenge from Japan. Citing a list of 1,500 scientific and technological discoveries compiled by Asimov[47] that Lynn alleges shows that all useful inventions were made by whites or East Asians, he concludes:

> Who can doubt that the Caucasoids and the Mongoloids are the only two races that have made any significant contribution to civilization. . . . Whatever criteria are adopted, the Caucasoids and the Mongoloids are the two most intelligent races and the historical record shows that this has been the case for approximately the last 5,000 years.[48]

Lynn also argues that it is "beyond dispute that brain size and intelligence are positively correlated in man"[49] and cites studies of the brain sizes of various populations, most using head circumference as a measure that he claims show a striking resemblance to racial differences in intelligence.[50]

Lynn's "global" and "evolutionary" perspectives were laid out in his house organ, *Mankind Quarterly*,[51] where he argued that there are two co-equal superior races. Because Lynn sees East Asians and whites as enjoying long-standing genetic advantages not amenable to environmental reordering,[52] he infers that "Sinic" and "Western" civilizations will continue to be twin jewels of humanity. This position is shared by an even more outspoken exponent of a racial worldview, University of Western Ontario psychologist J. Philippe Rushton.

The race differences theories Rushton propounded in the 1980s went unnoticed outside academia until he presented a paper at the American Association for the Advancement of Science meeting of 1989. The AAAS paper added little to what Rushton had written before, but as it was presented before a key scientific body, much media attention was accorded its conclusions. These were that (1) the progression of evolutionary development has been from blacks to whites to East Asians; (2) East Asians will eventually outdistance whites in economic and scientific accomplishment; and (3) blacks are most at risk from AIDS because "r-selectivity" leads to multiple sexual partners.[53]

Criticism of Rushton was immediate. The Canadian geneticist David Suzuki termed his theories "ridiculous" and "dangerous," and the UWO student council challenged his right to teach them. The premier of Ontario called for Rushton's dismissal. The provincial police investigated him for possible violations of a law forbidding incitement to race hatred, but the attorney general declined to prosecute. Demonstrations against Rushton were held on and off the UWO campus and in 1989–90 he was failed in a peer review, a decision overturned by the university senate. He was also required, for security reasons, to teach one course via videotape in the fall of 1990.[54] In late 1994, a complaint to the Ontario Human Rights Commission lodged against Rushton by students was still pending.[55]

Rushton is more willing than other race differences exponents to promote the most controversial of his ideas in the most public manner. Lynn holds almost identical views, but sets forth the most politically charged of these only in *Mankind Quarterly*. With the long history of protest against his theory of genetically based black intellectual inferiority, Arthur Jensen is the most careful to present his theories of a racial hierarchy of intellect.

A professor of psychology at the University of California at Berkeley, Jensen is the man behind the eponym Jensenism, a term synonymous with race differences theory since he hypothesized in a 1969 article that genetic factors may be strongly implicated in black-white "intelligence differences."[56] Jensen is the leading U.S. hereditarian and has greatly influenced Lynn and Rushton. In recent years he has turned more to studying the differences between Chinese- and Anglo-American children.

While academic and media attention has focused on Jensen for a quarter-century because of his conclusions that American blacks are on average intellectually inferior to whites,[57] his view that Asian-Americans are on average intellectually superior dates back almost as far. In a 1973 work, Jensen wrote that Chinese-American and Japanese-American children equal or exceed whites in the most heavily *g*-loaded and nonverbal IQ tests, despite having lesser environmental advantages. Genetic factors account in part for this "average intellectual superiority."[58]

He also presaged Rushton by stating that race differences in reactivity to stimuli of neonates and the rate of multiple births suggest a "developmental continuum" reflecting differing evolutionary ages for the races. Jensen hypothesized that East Asians may be the most recently evolved and developed "race" and blacks the least, with whites "more or less intermediate."[59]

In a later appreciation of Rushton's work, Jensen cited twenty-two variables among which reliable race/g correlations can be shown, including brain size, criminality, and others central to Rushton's argument.[60] He noted in an article in the Hong Kong Teachers' Association journal that the most highly overrepresented group among the intellectually gifted in the United States are Asians, while blacks, Hispanics, and Amerindians are underrepresented.[61]

From behind a patina of "disinterested science," proponents of race differences theories project an image of apoliticism[62] and accuse opponents of pursuing an ideological agenda.[63] At the same time, they are linked with ultra-rightist political forces and do draw policy implications from their theories.[64] For example, Rushton, who holds that "All social problems in the world are related to ethnicity," has speculated that genetic similarity theory suggests that the Nazi army was effective in battle in World War II because it was racially homogeneous, while the U.S. army was ineffective in Vietnam because it was racially mixed. He has also averred that the "Anglo-Saxon world's" alliance with Japan and antipathy toward the then-existing Soviet Union was contrary to natural, gene-based sympathies.[65]

Race differences theorists are funded by forces that promote an ideology of racial hierarchy. They in turn provide these forces with scientized arguments. Much of their money comes from the Pioneer Fund, founded in 1937 by Wycliffe Draper, a textile-machinery magnate. Co-founder Harry Laughlin, a eugenics expert for the U.S. House of Representatives Immigration Committee, was instrumental in 1924 in convincing Congress to limit immigration to northern Europeans and later distributed films touting Nazi eugenics programs. The fund's original purpose was to encourage the propagation of descendants of the whites of pre-independence America.

Apart from academics, the fund aids political organizations and activists. The most favored ($1 million as of 1993) is the Federation of American Immigration Reform (FAIR), which advocates sharply reducing immigration into the United States. Its board has included prominent politicians and was recently consulted on immigration policy by California Governor Pete Wilson. Its leader in the 1980s and current board member, Dr. Joe Tanton, has made clear that his concern is with "third world" immigration,[66] as has board member Garrett Hardin, a University of California at Santa Barbara human ecologist.

Hardin fears an immigrant invasion of the United States and praises Japan's efforts to avoid multiculturalism. He received $29,000 from the fund to write a recent book that associates immigration with decay and violence and explicitly endorses ethnocentrism. The book was also funded by the Laurel Foundation, distributor of Jean Raspail's *Camp of the Saints*, a novel lauded by Hardin that fantasizes about the destruction of the "white race" in France through an immigrant invasion. Hardin's own book has been glowingly reviewed by Paul Fromm, a Canadian neo-Nazi with connections to Rushton.[67] FAIR in turn praises those financed by the fund as "reputable, distinguished scientists associated with America's major universities."[68]

Foremost among individual activists financed by the fund is the British anthropologist Roger Pearson.[69] With Hans Gunther, the leading Nazi anthropologist, Pearson founded the Northern League in 1958. Intended to foster "Teutonic" solidarity, it has had close ties with a variety of neo-Nazi organizations. In a 1966 work, Pearson stated that "if a nation with a more advanced, more specialized or in any way superior set of genes mingles with, instead of exterminating, an inferior tribe, then it commits racial suicide."[70] Moving to the United States in the 1960s, Pearson taught at several colleges (becoming dean at one), worked with the ultrarightist Liberty League,[71] served as an aide to U.S. Senator Jesse Helms, formed a U.S. chapter of the World Anti-Communist League (WACL) composed of neo-Nazis, became president of the University Professors for Academic Order, and received a letter of praise from President Reagan.[72]

Pearson's main link to theories of East Asian superiority, however, has been as a publisher. He formerly edited the Pioneer Fund–financed *Mankind Quarterly*, founded in 1960 by the British anthropologist R. Gayre. A long-time associate of Nazis, Gayre contrasted black "leisure" with white and East Asian "dynamism." Many *Mankind Quarterly* editors have had pro-Nazi backgrounds—e.g., Baron Otmar von Verschuer, ex-eugenics director at Berlin's Kaiser Wilhelm Institute from 1942 to 1945 and a devotee of studies of twins and the inheritance of intelligence and behavior.[73] Esyenck has been an "Honorary Advisor" of *Mankind Quarterly*, just as Jensen has been on the advisory board and written articles for its German counterpart, *Neue Anthropologie*, a journal replete with connections to Nazism. Pearson became chief editor of *Mankind Quarterly* in the late 1970s and Lynn was made an associate editor. Lynn now effectively runs *Mankind Quarterly*, while Pearson edits *The Journal of Social, Political and Economic Studies*, a Fund-financed house organ of race differences theorists and other ultrarightists.[74]

The political linkages of the Western proponents of East Asian superiority mark them as associated with ultrarightism generally, and neo-Nazism specifically. These links have not marginalized them in political discourse in the West. Indeed, a quarter century after emerging in Jensen's 1969 article, their arguments about race differences have moved from the pages of the many respected journals in which Lynn, Rushton, Jensen and others publish to centers of policy discussion in the United States.

Race differences activists maintain overt political linkages, while the theorists claim to steer clear of politics, but say they must take their friends as they find them. The use of their work as the ideological underpinnings of racist activism is so predictable, however, that it must be presumed that this result is intended. Because they can be advanced as explanations for the existing racial hierarchy, theories of East Asian superiority have now diffused from the margins to the general mainstream. In contrast, theories of black superiority ("melanism"), which are at odds with the existing racial hierarchy, can enter only the black mainstream.[75]

How far beyond the West these theories have diffused and how deeply they reinforce pre-existing indigenous views are open questions. East Asians cannot have the same political links as Western proponents of East Asian superiority. They can and often do have equally race-based worldviews and must be held to the same standard of responsibility.[76] Theories of superiority, created in the West with the assistance of East Asians, may already be falling on fertile ground in the East.

East Asian adherents of theories of racial hierarchy may project that East Asians and whites will be allies against their intellectual and behavioral inferiors. The idea of biracial hegemony has a history of more than a century in East Asia. The Chinese writer Tang Caichang (1867–1900) put it thus: "Yellow and white are wise, red and black are stupid; yellow and white are rulers, red and black are slaves; yellow and white are united, red and black are scattered." Late nineteenth century Japan saw a wave of advocacy of intermarriage with Westerners.[77] A recent large-scale study of Asian-Americans, many of whom were born in East Asia, found that they were generally more racially prejudiced than whites against other U.S. minorities and perceived less social distance between themselves and whites than other "racial" groups.[78]

It is reported that "the Japanese" are "fascinated with IQ studies because they score five points higher on average than Caucasians."[79] There are also signs of government favor in the reports by official news agencies of studies claiming higher intelligence for East Asians.[80] If theories of East Asian superiority are discussed in elite circles in East Asia, some effect on policy-makers can be presumed, both from the fact that the latter are drawn from these same elites and from the examples of states outside the region that have informally incorporated the idea of racial hierarchy in their statecraft.[81]

Theories of East Asian superiority are now an integral prop of Western proponents of race differences studies. To many observers, these ideas seem like anachronisms dressed up in the contemporary garb of evolutionary psychology. Brain size comparisons and an imputed relationship between physical type and criminal propensities were the stuff of the Victorian era. As late as the early 1980s, even Jensen ridiculed the idea that anyone would want to resurrect such antediluvian precepts— and then proceeded to himself revive the notion that IQ is correlated with speed of reaction, a theory abandoned around 1900.[82]

The revival of late-nineteenth-century racism at the end of the twentieth century would also have been thought out of the question not long ago. In fact, as Adolph Reed, Jr., observes, a whole set of Victorian ideas are back in style. "Scientific racism has made a major comeback in its sociohistorical guise, with 'culture' as a stand-in for race."[83] Compare, for example, the conclusions drawn by Lynn, Rushton, or Jensen and those of the Victorian-era scholar Frederic Farrar:

> The grand qualities which secure the continuous advance of
> mankind, the generalising power of pure reason, the love of per-
> fectibility, the desire to know the unknown, and, last and great-

est, the ability to observe new phenomena and new relations—these mental faculties seem to be deficient in all the dark races.[84]

Even if it is recognized that scientized race concepts thought dead not long ago affect domestic social policy in the West, it may not seem conceivable that theories of East Asian superiority can actually influence world politics. It was not in the Victorian era, however, but within living memory that an advanced European state and an advanced East Asian state espoused anti-egalitarianism generally and racial superiority specifically, attempting to reduce to vassalage neighbors they judged inferior.

NOTES

1. There are scattered earlier references. See, e.g., Ellsworth Huntington, "Geographical Environment and Japanese Character," *Journal of Race Development* 2 (1912), pp. 260; Thomas Garth, *Race Psychology: A Study of Racial Mental Differences* (New York: McGraw-Hill, 1931), pp. 76–77, 244–245; Anne Anastasi, *Differential Psychology: Individuals and Group Differences in Behavior* (New York: Macmillan, 1937), p. 508. Until the 1960s, most U.S. psychologists held that Asian-Americans and whites had the same intelligence level. See James Coleman, *Equality of Educational Opportunity* (Washington: U.S. Office of Education, 1966); E. E. Werner, "Ethnic and Socioeconomic Status Differences in Abilities and Achievements Among Pre-School and School Age Children in Hawaii," *Journal of Social Psychology* (*JSP*) 75 (1968), pp. 43–59.

2. The term East Asians is used for convenience. The theories refer only to northeast Asians and the theorists conceive of southeast Asians as the intellectual inferiors of northeast Asians.

3. World War II assertions of Japanese superiority over other Asians were implicit in home-front propaganda and explicit in government documents. See John Dower, *War Without Mercy: Race and Power in the Pacific War* (New York: Pantheon Books, 1986), pp. 264–265, 277, 284–285, 288. There were no assertions of East Asian or Japanese superiority to whites. Indeed, Japanese war heroes were "Caucasianized" in propaganda. Ibid., pp. 208–210.

4. C. Wallace, "Asia's Tigers Flex Their Muscles," *Los Angeles Times* (*LAT*), May 28, 1994, p. A1.

5. See, e.g., Kishore Mabhubani, "The Dangers of Decadence: What the Rest Can Teach the West," *Foreign Affairs* (*FA*) 72:4 (September/October 1993), pp. 10–14, and Malaysian analysts Noordin Sopiee, "Need for World to Rein in Cultural Arrogance"; and Karim Raslan, "Crisis of Confidence Afflicts the West," in *Business Times* (*BT*), April 27, 1994, p. 15.

6. Reactions to claims of superiority emanating from East Asia emerged in the Western media in 1993–94. See, e.g., Jim Hoagland, "Troubling Signs of a Sense of Cultural Superiority," *Washington Post* (*WP*), March 21, 1994, p. 5; Gerald Segal, "This Rhetoric About Clashing Civilizations Can Only Hurt Asia," *International Herald Tribune* (*IHT*), October 6, 1993, p. 6.

7. B. Gomez, "Culture Vital for Country's Success: LKY Tells Aussie Magazine," *BT* (Singapore), June 26, 1993, p. 2. Compare Richard Lynn, "Educational Achievements of Asian Americans," *American Psychologist* (*AP*) 46:8 (August 1991), pp. 875–876, in which a leading proponent of racial differences in intelligence considers the possibility that Asians have a genetic predisposition for working hard for long-term goals.

8. "Resource-Rich Australia Needs to Become More Competitive," *Straits Times*, April 19, 1994, p. 26.

9. Fareed Zakaria, "Culture Is Destiny," *FA*, 73:2 (1994), p. 118.

10. Lee Kuan Yew, "What Kind of New Order in East Asia?" *New Perspectives Quarterly* (*NPQ*) (Winter 1992), p. 7; H. McDonald, "Bricks and Babies," *Far Eastern Economic Review* (*FEER*), September 6, 1990, p. 25; M. Leifer, "Triumph of the Will," *FEER*, November 15, 1990, pp. 27–28; Ian Buruma, "Uncivilized Values," *Sunday Telegraph* (*ST*), May 8, 1994, p. 31.

11. On Lee's familiarity with the work of "race differences" theorists, see Chan Chee Khoon and Chee Heng Leng, "Singapore 1984: Breeding for Big Brother," in Institute for Social Analysis, *Designer Genes: IQ, Ideology, and Biology* (Pelaing Jaya, Malaysia: INSAN, 1984), pp. 4–14; Steven Jay Gould, "Singapore's Patrimony and Matrimony," *Natural History* 93 (May 1984), pp. 22. Lee is in turn admired by the theorists. See, e.g., Richard Herrnstein, "IQ and Failing Birthrates," *The Atlantic* 263:5 (May 1989), p. 72.

12. On Lee's international influence, see Eric Jones, "Asia's Fate: A Response to the Singapore School," *The National Interest* (*NI*) (Spring 1994), pp. 18–28.

13. W. Wetherall, "Nakasone Promotes Pride and Prejudice," *FEER*, February 19, 1987, pp. 86–87.

14. T. McCarthy, "Cult of Uniqueness Makes the Japanese Rude to Foreigners," *Independent*, January 26, 1992, p. 10.

15. "Government Hits Politician's Slander of Blacks," *Kyodo*, March 19, 1993; "Loose Talk from Japan," *LAT*, January 23, 1992, p. A4.

16. Ironically, one hereditarian psychologist has argued that inbreeding decreases general and verbal intelligence, but increases visuo-spatial abilities, the very "intelligence" that other hereditarians find in abundance in Chinese. Arthur Jensen, "Effects of Inbreeding on Mental-Ability Factors," *Personality & Individual Differences* (*P&ID*) 4 (1983), pp. 71–87. An environmentalist has found no convincing evidence of inbreeding depression on IQ. Leon Kamin, "Inbreeding Depression and IQ," *Psychological Bulletin* (*PB*) 87 (1980), pp. 469–478.

17. Mahathir bin Mohammed, *The Malay Dilemma* (Singapore: Asian Pacific Press, 1970), pp. 24–31; Christopher Hitchens, "Race Relations in Malaysia," *Nation* 246:1 (January 9, 1988), p. 6.

18. See, e.g., H. J. Eysenck, "The Nature of Cognitive Differences Between Blacks and Whites," *Behavioral and Brain Sciences* (*BBS*) 8 (1985), p. 229 ("There is a general decline of IQ mean scores, ranging from the Mongoloid peoples, particularly the Chinese and the Japanese, through Northern European Caucasoids and their descendants, to Southern European Caucasoids and Indians, to Malays and Negroid groups"). See also his remarks on the superior IQs of Asian-descended children in H. Eysenck, "Science, Racism and Sexism," *Journal of Social, Political and Economic Studies* (JSPES) 16 (Summer 1991), pp. 217–250.

19. R. Lynn, "The Intelligence of the Japanese," *Bulletin of the British Psychological Society* (*BBPS*) 30 (1977), pp. 69–72.

20. R. Lynn, "Ethnic and Racial Differences in Intelligence: International Comparisons," in R. Travis Osborne et al., eds., *Human Variation: The Biopsychology of Age, Race and Sex* (New York: Academic Press, 1978), pp. 261–286.

21. R. Lynn, "The Intelligence of the Chinese and Malays in Singapore," *Mankind Quarterly* (*MQ*) 18 (1977), pp. 125–128.

22. R. Lynn and J. Dziobon, "On the Intelligence of the Japanese and Other Mongoloid Peoples, *P&ID* 1 (1980), pp. 95–96.

23. See also Philip Vernon, *The Abilities and Achievements of Orientals in North America* (New York: Academic Press, 1982), p. 67, which concludes that there are strong arguments for admitting that genetic factors are involved in mental differences between whites and East Asians. Ibid., pp. 272–273. Vernon's study was financed by the Pioneer Fund discussed below. Ibid., p. xiii.

24. R. Lynn, "IQ in Japan and the United States Shows a Growing Disparity," *Nature* 297 (1982), pp. 222–223; P. Hilts, "Young IQs in Japan Rising Smartly," *WP*, June 13, 1982, p. A14; "The Japanese are the Brainiest People in the World . . ." *Reuters*, December 6, 1982; R. Cowen, "Are People Smarter in Japan?" *Christian Science Monitor* (*CSM*), June 16, 1982, p. 16.

25. See also Daniel Vining, "Fertility Differentials and the Status of Nations: A Speculative Essay on Japan and the West," in Raymond Cattell, ed., *Intelligence and National Achievement* (Washington: Institute for the Study of Man, 1983), pp. 100–141. Vining, a University of Pennsylvania demographer, holds that the Japanese have been "empirically observed to be the best fit for life and work" in a modern economy and adduces a causal relationship between their high IQ and high economic productivity. Ibid., p. 117.

26. See, e.g., E. McGrath, "Confucian Work Ethic; *Time*, March 28, 1983, p. 52; E. Bowen, "Nakasone's World Class Blunder," *Time*, October 6, 1986, p. 66; "Italian Commission Investigates the Safety of Sensual Kissing," *Chicago Tribune* (*CT*), March 25, 1992; Douglas Birch, "Controversial Research Says Asians Are Smarter Than Whites," *Vancouver Sun* (*VS*), April 25, 1992, p. B7.

27. See Saburo Iwawaki and P. E. Vernon, "Japanese Abilities and Achievements," *Human Abilities in Cultural Context* (Cambridge: Cambridge University Press, 1988), pp. 358–384; C. Allen, "Gray Matter, Black-and-White Controversy," *Washington Times* (*WT*), January 13, 1992, p. 4.

28. D. Seligman, "Japanese Brains" *Fortune*, May 3, 1982, p. 77; "The Drama Backstage, How Japan Got Smarter..." *Fortune*, July 12, 1982, p. 17; "Some Think Smarter Than Others," *Fortune*, October 12, 1987, p. 228; "The Emperor's Brain," *Fortune*, March 14, 1988, p. 163; "Is America Smart Enough? IQ and National Productivity," *National Review* 43:6 (April 15, 1991), pp. 24+; Peter Brimelow, "Gambler Dan," *Forbes*, February 1, 1993, pp. 86+; *The IQ Debate in America* (Birch Lane Press, 1992).

29. See M. Mohs, "IQ: New Research Shows that the Japanese Outperform All Others in Intelligence Tests. Are They Really Smarter?" *Discovery* (September 1982), pp. 19–24, and Stevenson and Azuma, discussed below.

30. "Now the Great Augmentation of American IQ," *Nature* 301 (1983), p. 655; "Japanese IQ," *Nature* 308 (1984), p. 222; "The Rise and Fall of Japanese IQ," *BBPS* 40 (1987), pp. 459–464.

31. J. Flynn, "Massive IQ Gains in 14 Nations: What IQ Tests Really Measure," *Psychological Bulletin* (*PB*) 101:2 (1987), pp. 171–191; "Japanese Intelligence Simply Fades Away," *The Psychologist* 9 (1988), pp. 348–350; "Race and IQ: Jensen's Case Refuted," in Sohan Modgil, ed., *Arthur Jensen: Consensus and Controversy* (New York: Falmer, 1987), pp. 221–232; "The Ontology of Intelligence," in John Forge, ed., *Measurement, Realism and Objectivity: Essays on Measurement in the Social and Physical Sciences* (Dordrecht: Reidel, 1987), pp. 1–40; "Causal Factors in Generational IQ Gains," *Nature* 328 (1987), p. 765.

32. J. Flynn, "Rushton, Evolution, and Race: An Essay on Intelligence and Virtue," *The Psychologist* 9 (1989), pp. 363–366. Re-normed tests have halved the US black-white gap. Ken Vincent, "Black/White IQ Differences: Does Age Make the Difference?" *Journal of Clinical Psychology* (*JCP*) 47:2 (1991), pp. 266–270.

33. Harold Stevenson and Hiroshi Azuma, "IQ in Japan and the United States," *Nature* 306 (November 17, 1983), pp. 292–293.

34. H. Stevenson et al., "Cognitive Performance of Japanese, Chinese and American Children," *Child Development* (*CD*) 56 (1985), pp. 718–734. See also H. Stevenson et al., *Contexts of Achievement: A Study of American, Chinese and Japanese Children* (Chicago: University of Chicago Press, 1990), pp. 4–5; H. Stevenson and J. Stigler, *The Learning Gap* (New York: Summit Books, 1992); F. Butterfield, "Why Asians are Going to the Head of the Class," *New York Times* (*NYT*), August 3, 1986, p. 18; Stanley Sue and Sumie Okazaki, "Asian-American Education Achievements: A Phenomenon in Search of an Explanation," *AP* 45:8 (August, 1990), pp. 913–920; David Geary et al., "Loci of Ability Differences Comparing Children from China and the United States," *Psychological Science* (*PS*) 3:3 (May 1992), pp. 180–185.

35. R. Lynn and S. Hampson, "The Rise of National Intelligence: Evidence from Britain, Japan and the USA," *P&D* 7:1 (1986), pp. 23–32. Lynn nevertheless argued that rises in national scores are not mainly due to improved education and cultural environment. Lynn et al., "A Long-term Increase in the Fluid Intelligence of English Children," *Nature* 328 (August 27, 1987), p. 797.

36. See R. Lynn, "A Nutrition Theory of the Secular Increases in Intelligence: Positive Correlations Between Height, Head Size and IQ," *British Journal of Educational Psychology (BJEP)* 59 (1989), pp. 372–377; "The Role of Nutrition in Secular Increases in Intelligence," *P&ID* 11:3 (1990), pp. 272–285; "New Evidence on Brain Size and Intelligence: A Comment on Rushton and Cain and Vanderwolf," *P&ID* 11:8 (1990), pp. 795–797.

37. R. Lynn, "Differential Rates of Secular Increase of Five Major Primary Abilities," *Social Biology (SB)* 27:1–2 (1990), pp. 137–141.

38. See, e.g., Vining, op. cit., p. 131. Lynn is nevertheless convinced that there is a negative association between fertility and intelligence which at some point will cause increases in intelligence to start to decline. R. Lynn and C. Pagliari, "The Intelligence of American Children Is Still Rising," *Journal of Biosocial Science (JBS)* 26 (1994), pp. 65–67.

39. R. Lynn, "The Intelligence of the Mongoloids: A Psychometric, Evolutionary, and Neurological Theory," *P&ID* 8:6 (1987), pp. 813–844. For a critique, see Frederic Weizmann et al., "Scientific Racism in Contemporary Psychology," *International Journal of Dynamic Assessment and Instruction* 1:1 (Fall 1989), pp. 81–93.

40. See also R. Lynn, "Japan: Land of the Rising IQ. A Reply to Flynn," *BBPS* 40 (1987), pp. 464–468, in which Lynn places the g range for Japanese between 103.4 and 107.5 and again concludes that "the high level of Japanese intelligence has played a significant role in the brilliant successes of Japanese industrialists." Ibid., p. 465.

41. Compare Thomas Sowell, "Race and IQ Reconsidered," in T. Sowell, ed., *Essays and Data on American Ethnic Groups* (New York: Urban Institute, 1978), pp. 203–238, where the median IQ of Chinese-Americans in the 1970s is shown as 108, comparable to 109 and 110 mean IQs shown for Irish- and Polish-Americans.

42. R. Lynn, "The Intelligence of the Mongoloids . . ." See also Craig Nagoshi and Ronald Johnson, "Cognitive Abilities Profiles of Caucasian v. Japanese Subjects in the Hawaii Family Study of Cognition," *P&ID* 8:4 (1987), pp. 581–583. Lynn's cold climate theory of the origins of superior races is redolent of the proto-Nazi postulation of a hyperborean origin of the "Aryans." See Jocelyn Goodwin, *Arktos: The Polar Myth in Science, Symbolism and Nazi Survival* (Grand Rapids: Phanes Press, 1993).

43. Chan and Lynn, op. cit., p. 461.

44. Curiously, Lynn elsewhere has argued that nutritional differences may be responsible for much of the black-white IQ score gap. R. Lynn, "Nutrition and

Intelligence," in *Biological Approaches to the Study of Human Intelligence* (Norwood, N.J.: Ablex, 1993), pp. 243–258.

45. John R. Baker, *Race* (Oxford: Oxford University Press, 1974). Baker, an Oxford zoologist, was active in the "raciological" International Association for the Advancement of Ethnology and Eugenics. IAAEE's secretary was Donald Swann, a University of Southern Mississippi professor with links to neo-Nazis. T. Kelsey and T. Rowe, "Academics 'Were Funded by Racist American Trust,'" *Independent*, March 4, 1990, p. 4. Baker and Swann also advised *Neue Anthropologie*, a publication associated with neo-Nazis. Baker's work claiming that Africa has been devoid of invention is relied upon by race differences theorists and much praised by Jensen. See Michael Billig, *Psychology, Racism, and Fascism* (Birmingham: Searchlight Books, 1979), Chap. 4; Barry Mehler, "The New Eugenics: Academic Racism in the U.S. Today," *Science for the People* 15:3 (May/June 1983), pp. 18–23; Arthur Jensen, *Straight Talk About Mental Tests* (New York: Free Press, 1981). The idea of blacks as incapable of invention was central to Victorian thought. See James Belich, *The Victorian Interpretation of Racial Conflict: The Maori, the British and the New Zealand Wars* (Montreal: McGill-Queen's, 1986), pp. 323–327.

46. R. Lynn, "The Evolution of Racial Differences," pp. 111–112. Compare this view with that of K. Knox, *Races of Man* (Philadelphia: Lea & Blanchard, 1850), p. 263, that "The Jew has no monumental history. He never had any literature, science, or art; he has none yet."

47. Isaac Asimov, *Chronology of Science and Discovery* (London: Grafton Books, 1989).

48. Lynn, "Evolution of Racial Differences," pp. 280–284.

49. Compare John Lorber, "Is Your Brain Really Necessary?" *Archives of Disease in Childhood* 53:10 (1978), pp. 834, which details cases of hydrocephalus—i.e., gross underdevelopment of brain size—where individuals were normal or even brilliant.

50. R. Lynn, "The Evolution of Racial Differences," pp. 114–116. In 1994, Lynn also concluded that men are more intelligent than women based upon their supposedly larger brain sizes. J. Burne, "Sex War on the Brain," *Observer*, September 18, 1994, p. T85.

51. There is a house organ for race differences psychologists, *Personality & Individual Differences*, co-edited by Hans and Sybil Eysenck. Its board includes Hans son Michael Eysenck, Lynn and his frequent collaborator Susan Hampson, Jensen and Professor Shigehisa of Tokyo Kasei-Gakuin University, another collaborator.

52. In comparing head sizes and correlating these with intelligence, Lynn notes that the black children are slightly taller than whites and concludes that it is not likely that differences in nutrition are responsible for the differences in head size. "The Evolution of Racial Differences," p. 114.

53. J. P. Rushton, "Contributions to the History of Psychology: Evolutionary Biology and Heritable Traits (with Reference to Oriental-White-Black Differences): The 1989 AAAS Paper," *PR* 71 (1992), pp. 811–821.

54. D. Suzuki, "Defence of Rushton 'Right' Is Propping up Faculty Work," *Toronto Globe & Mail*, February 11, 1989; R. Dolphin, "Race and Behavior," *Macleans*, February 13, 1989, p. 44; Barry Gross, "The Case of Philippe Rushton," *Academic Questions* 3:4 (1990), pp. 35–46; "Passages," *Macleans* (May 28, 1990), p. 6; L. Ainsworth, "Rushton Objects to Teaching by Video," *Toronto Star* (*TS*), August 22, 1990, p. A9; "Rushton Must Work in Secret to Foil Protestors," *TS*, September 11, 1990, p. A9; J. Wilkes, "Western's New Rules on Racism Criticized," *TS*, September 21, 1990, p. A12; J. Deverell, "Rushton Says Job Safe Despite Race Theory," *TS*, October 3, 1990, p. A19; P. Adamick, "Rushton to Return to Classes on January 3, University Decides," *TS*, December 20, 1990, p. A26; J. Armstrong, "Student Racism Protest Disrupts Legislature," *TS*, March 22, 1991, p. A5; P. Adamick, "Rushton Foes Planning Human Rights Action," *TS*, May 24, 1991.

55. Robin Abscarian, "What They Don't Tell You About Research," *Los Angeles Times*, August 16, 1994, p. E1.

56. A. Jensen, "How Much Can We Boost IQ and Scholastic Achievement?" in *Environment, Heredity, and Intelligence* (Cambridge, Mass.: Harvard Educational Review, 1969), p. 82.

57. See, e.g., Raymond Fancher, *The Intelligence Men: Makers of the IQ Controversy* (New York: Norton, 1985), pp. 185–201, James R. Flynn, *Race, IQ and Jensen* (London: Routledge & Kegan Paul, 1980); S. Mogdil and C. Mogdil, *Arthur Jensen: Consensus and Controversy* (Lewes, UK: Falmer Press, 1987).

58. A. Jensen, *Educability and Group Differences* (London: Methuen & Co., 1973), pp. 60, 252–253, 289, 304–305, 312, 317. See also Jensen's 1975 letter, quoted in Jayjia Hsia, *Cognitive Assessment of Asian Americans* (Los Alamitos, Calif.: National Center for Bilingual Research, 1981), p. 5, describing his unpublished research comparing IQ test results of Berkeley "Japanese and Chinese" children to those of whites.

59. Jensen, *Educability and Group Differences*, pp. 289–290.

60. A. Jensen, "Sociobiology and Differential Psychology: the Arduous Climb from Plausibility to Proof," Joseph Royce and Leendert Mos, *Annals of Theoretical Psychology* (New York: Plenum Press, 1984), pp. 49–58. See also A. Jensen and S. N. Sinha, "Physical Correlates of Human Intelligence," in P. A. Vernon, ed., *Biological Approaches to the Study of Human Intelligence* (Norwood, N.J.: Ablex, 1993), pp. 139–242, which praises a study that concludes that the cranial capacities of Asians exceed those of Europeans, which exceed those of Africans.

61. A. Jensen, "New Findings on the Intellectually Gifted," *New Horizons* 30 (1989), pp. 73–80.

62. See, e.g., William Rees-Moog, "Why Science Must Be Free to Breach Taboos," *Independent*, June 10, 1991, p. 19, where Rushton is termed "a respected professor of psychology who may well be mistaken but on the face of it is acting in good faith." Barry Gross, "The Case of Philippe Rushton," *Academic Questions* 3:4 (1990), p. 45, fn. 13, has noted that "some forty-five academics, some of international reputation, have written in support of Rushton. Even among those who disagree with his theory there is strong support for its scientific character and competence."

63. See, e.g., A. Jensen, *Bias in Mental Testing* (London: Methuen, 1980), Chap. 1, where Jensen both accuses his opponents of being ideologically motivated and defends mental tests on the ground that they point up the folly of affirmative action. Some critics of "biologism" are socialists. See Richard Lewontin, Steven Rose, and Leon Kamin, *Not in Our Genes: Biology, Ideology, and Human Nature* (New York: 1984). Others range across the political spectrum and include at least one well-known conservative. See Thomas Sowell, *Race and Culture: A World View* (New York: Basic Books, 1994), Chap. 6. For an argument that race differences theory is not value-free, see Anne Harrington, "Studying Race-Differences, or the Problem of 'Value-Free' Science," *Psychologische Beitrage* 32 (1990), pp. 151–156.

64. See, e.g., Arthur Jensen, "Mental Ability: Critical Thresholds and Social Policy," *JSPES* 17 (1992), pp. 171–182. Jensen argues that about one-fourth of blacks and one-twentieth of whites are below the threshold of normal intelligence and should be given "incentives" to reduce their birthrate.

65. Rushton in *London Free Press*, January 13, 1990, reproduced in Frederic Weizmann et al., "Eggs, Eggplants and Eggheads: A Rejoinder to Rushton," *CP* 32:1 (1991), pp. 43–50; J. P. Rushton, "Gene Culture Coevolution and Genetic Similarity Theory: Implications for Ideology, Ethnic Nepotism and Geopolitics," *Politics and the Life Sciences* 4 (1986), pp. 144–148.

66. Politicians on FAIR's board have included a former U.S. senator, an ex–U.S. attorney general, a former governor, and an ex–New York City mayor. *State News Service*, June 23, 1989; J. Cohen, "Media Help Shut the Door to Immigrants," *Cleveland Plain Dealer*, August 7, 1993, p. 6B; P. McDonnell, "FAIR at Forefront of Push to Reduce Immigration," *LAT*, November 24, 1993, p. A1; S. Ferriss, "FAIR," *San Francisco Chronicle* (*SFC*), December 12, 1993, p. A1; A. Lewis, "The Politics of Nativism," *NYT*, January 14, 1994, p. A29; Crawford, op. cit., pp. 158–159. In "Immigration and Criminality in the U.S.A.," *JSPES* 18 (1993), pp. 217–234, Tanton confines his discussion of criminal gangs to those composed of Asians, Africans, Latin Americans, and Jews.

67. G. Hardin, *Living Within Limits: Ecology, Economics, and Population Taboos* (New York: Oxford University Press, 1993), pp. 296, 306; Crawford, op. cit., pp. 158–159; Paul Fromm, "Living Within Limits," *JSPES* 18 (Fall 1993), pp. 367–370; G. Caplan, "Classroom No Place for Teacher with Racist Views," *TS*,

May 3, 1992, p. B3; C. Mallan, "Top Trustee Mum on Racial Remark by Peel Teacher," *TS*, October 10, 1991, p. MA1; J. Hall, "Teacher's 'Scalp Them' Remark Faces Board Probe," *TS*, September 27, 1991, p. A6; P. Small, "Racist Comment Prompts Ejections," *TS*, September 25, 1991, p. A10; Miller, loc. cit.

68. FAIR, "Questions and Answers Regarding the Federation for American Immigration Reform and One of Its Many Foundation Supporters," *PR Newswire*, September 15, 1994.

69. Pearson has received at least $787,000. Miller, loc. cit.

70. Quoted in Miller, op. cit., p. 109.

71. Billig, op. cit., Chap. 2; Benno Muller-Hill, *Murderous Science* (New York: Oxford University Press, 1988); Barry Mehler, "The New Eugenics: Academic Racism in the U.S. Today," *SFP* 15:3 (May/June 1983), pp. 18–23.

72. Craig Pyes, "Private General," *New Republic* 193 (September 30, 1985), p. 11; I. Hilton, "Obituary: Roberto d'Aubuisson," *Independent*, February 22, 1992, p. 46; "Controversial Publisher—Racial Purist Uses Reagan Plug," *Wall Street Journal*, September 24, 1984, p. 1; Kuhl, op. cit., p. 110, fn. 6; Mehler, "Rightist on the Rights Panel," *Nation*, May 7, 1988, pp. 640–661; Mehler, "The New Eugenics," p. 19; *Independent*, March 4, 1990; J. Sedgwick, "The Mentality Bunker," *GQ*, November 1994.

73. On von Verschuer, see Benno Muller-Hill, *Murderous Science: Elimination by Scientific Selection of Jews, Gypsies, and Others, Germany 1933–1945* (Oxford: Oxford University Press, 1988), passim; *Independent*, January 9, 1994, p. 2; Kuhl, op. cit., p. 113, fn. 39; Kristie Macrakis, *Surviving the Swastika: Scientific Research in Nazi Germany* (New York: Oxford University Press, 1993), pp. 125–130; Robert Proctor, "Nazi Biomedical Policies," in Arthur Caplan, *When Medicine Went Mad: Bioethics and the Holocaust* (Totowa, N.J.: Humana Press, 1992), p. 28. Verschuer's protegé Josef Mengele regularly sent body parts to Verschuer from the Auschwitz extermination camp.

74. Billig, op. cit., Chaps. 3–4, *Independent*, March 4, 1980, p. 4. The *JSPES* board includes Garrett Hardin.

75. On melanism, the theory that blacks are superior because they have higher levels of melanin in their skin and brains, see Bernard Ortiz de Montellano, "Melanism, Afrocentricity, and Pseudoscience," *Yearbook of Physical Anthropology* 36 (1993), pp. 33–58; Barry Mehler, "African-American Racism in the Academic Community," *Review of Education* 15 (1992), pp. 341–353. The most prominent melanist is now feted by mainstream African-American organizations, including those of black psychologists, the prime movers behind "melanism." See "Dr. Frances Cress-Welsing Lectures on Race at Penn," *Ethnic Newswatch* 110:30 (March 23, 1993) p. 5-A; E. Whitford, "Afrocentrist Professor Will Speak Here Today," *Atlanta Constitution*, April 2, 1992, p. D4.

76. Some East Asian psychologists may compare mean IQs because they know there is an interest in the West. See, e.g., Houcan Zhang, "Psychological Mea-

surement in China," *International Journal of Psychology* 23 (1988), pp. 101–117, reporting a test of 5,000 urban Chinese with a revised British IQ test that produced a norm slightly higher than the UK norm and similar to that of Hong Kong. Others collaborate with and promote the theories of Lynn, Rushton, etc., despite their links to racist activists. See, e.g., Jimmy Chan, "Chinese Intelligence," in Michael Bond, ed., *Handbook of Chinese Psychology* (in press); J. Chan, "Heredity and Environment Implications for Teaching," *New Horizons* No. 33 (1992), pp. 39–45. Note also that *Psychologia: An International Journal of Psychology in the Orient* includes Eysenck on its advisory board.

77. Quoted in Frank Dikotter's excellent "Racial Identities in China," *China Quarterly* 138 (June 1994), p. 407; Chitoshi Yanaga, *Japan Since Perry* (Westport, Conn.: Greenwood, 1949), p. 97.

78. National Conference, *Taking America's Pulse: The Full Report of the National Conference Survey on Inter-Group Relations* (New York: National Conference, 1994).

79. C. Allen, "Gray Matter, Black-and-White Controversy," *WT,* January 13, 1992, p. 4.

80. "Shanghai Children Rank High in IQ Tests," *Xinhua,* December 22, 1985, based on "Shanghai Ranks High in IQ Tests," *Beijing Review* No. 51, December 23, 1985, p. 29, reporting summary of article in *Kexue Guanli Yanjiu* (Scientific Management Study) indicating that Shanghai children ranked higher than U.S. children in seven of twelve IQ subtests. "Women Have Smaller Brains Than Men: Scholar," *Central News Agency* (Taiwan), reported Rushton's findings on larger mean brain sizes among Asian-Americans.

81. See, e.g., George Shepher, *The Study of Race in American Foreign Policy* (Denver: University of Denver, 1969); Walter Crocker, *The Racial Factor in International Relations* (Canberra: Australian National University, 1956).

82. A. Jensen, "The Debunking of Scientific Fossils and Straw Persons," *Contemporary Education Review* 1:2 (1982), pp. 121–135; "Old Chestnut, New Thoughts," *Economist,* December 26, 1992, p. 33.

83. Adolph Reed, Jr., "The New Victorians," *Progressive* 58:2 (February 1994), pp. 20–22. See also A. Reed, "Look Backward," *Nation,* November 28, 1994, pp. 654–662; A. Reed, "Intellectual Brown Shirts," *Progressive,* December 1994, pp. 15–17.

84. Frederic Farrar, "The Aptitude of Races," reprinted in Michael Biddiss, ed., *Images of Races* (New York: Holmes & Meier, 1979), p. 151.

IRELAND'S "LOW" IQ: A CRITIQUE

Ciarán Benson

T HERE HAS BEEN little analysis of the assertions, especially the most recent ones by Richard Lynn (1979), concerning the low Irish IQ. The consequence has been that even amongst relatively well-informed groups in Ireland, such as University students, there lingers the belief that it has been 'scientifically' shown that the Irish have an unusually low IQ.

In Chapter 10 of *Intelligence: The Battle for the Mind*, H. J. Eysenck (1981) asserts that 'It is commonly believed that certain national, racial and cultural groups are more intelligent than others', and he goes on to claim that 'There is little debate about the actual existence of such differences: they have been demonstrated on quite large samples many times and seem to be very much in line with popular belief' (p. 74). Indeed, as this paper will try to show, Eysenck and Richard Lynn have contributed to popular belief as the authors of a modern myth that the Irish have a low IQ. Their particular myth stands merely as the most recent in a long line of such myths which derive their vitality from the nature of the political rela-

Ciarán Benson is professor of psychology and chair of the department of psychology, University College, Dublin. His most recent book is *The Absorbed Self: Pragmatism, Psychology and Aesthetic Experience*. This article originally was published as "Ireland's Low IQ: A Critique of the Myth," in *The Irish Journal of Psychology*, VIII, 1987.

tionship between Ireland and its larger neighbour (cf. Curtis, 1971 and Curtis, 1984).

I T   W A S   I N his *Race, Intelligence, and Education* (1971, pp. 47, 127, 142) that Eysenck first made his reference to the low Irish IQ. His explanation in terms of the brightest Irish being the ones with the initiative to emigrate, with the less bright being left behind, was later challenged by McGonigle and McPhilemy (1974a, 1974b). In his 1981 book he affirms that he 'will simply state the facts of the case and leave interpretation to the reader' (p. 74). Three pages on come the particular set of 'facts' which refer to the Irish and which are presented under the heading 'The British Experience'. The empirical heart of this section is the work of Lynn (1979). While acknowledging Lynn in the text, Eysenck omits any mention of Lynn in his list of references, thus making checking difficult. (There is a similar curious absence of reference to Eysenck by Lynn in *his* paper). 'Re-analysing large quantities of figures', writes Eysenck, 'Richard Lynn arrived at the Distribution pictured in Figure 23. (Figure 1 in the present paper). London and South-East England have the highest mean IQ score (102), and the Republic of Ireland the lowest (96). This difference of 6 points is highly significant, from a practical as well as a statistical point of view' (p. 78). Eysenck affirms that Lynn's main explanation for these differences is in terms of selective migration from an impoverished cultural environment, and he overlooks the fact that Lynn's conceptions of culture and environment seem rather crude. For example, in his paper 'Ethnic and racial differences in intelligence: International comparisons' (in Osborne *et al.*, 1978), Lynn reviews studies which looked at mean IQ scores of 'developed' and 'less developed peoples' and writes of one investigation thus:

> This argument is advanced among others by Berry (1966) in comparing the intelligence test scores of Eskimos with those of lower SES Scotsmen living in Scotland. He argues that this group is most appropriate for comparative purposes because the members are reared in a relatively unsophisticated environment like that of the Eskimos. The lower SES classes in Scotland have mean IQs in the range of 85–100, which is only a bit higher than the IQ Range of Eskimos. Thus the argument runs, if we take Northern

European Caucasoids brought up in a similar environment to Eskimos, the IQ Difference is reduced. Therefore, the innate intelligence must be approximately the same (p. 278).

Lynn does not even question the idea of equating the environment of Eskimos with that of working class Scotsmen, and he misses the point that Berry's study was not of IQ but of perceptual skills.

In *Race, Intelligence, and Education*, Eysenck (1971) also claimed the average Irish IQ was about 15 points lower than the average English IQ (p. 127). He derived this difference from Macnamara's (1966) study on the effects of bilingualism amongst Irish schoolchildren. As part of that study Macnamara had administered the Jenkins Nonverbal Reasoning Test to 1,083 Irish schoolchildren. It was no part of Macnamara's intention to make IQ comparisons between Irish children and others, let alone with an English adult population. Macnamara was disturbed by the apparently very poor performance of Irish schoolchildren on the Jenkins test and devoted considerable space to the issue in his book. A main hypothesis was that Irish children were not as test-wise as their English or American counterparts, as degree of familiarity with tests is certainly known to influence performance. In a letter to the *Bulletin of the British Psychological Society* Macnamara (1972) pointed out that Eysenck had interpreted his findings 'in a sense which I explicitly rejected in that book *Bilingualism and Primary Education*. Lest there be any misunderstanding, I wish to dissociate myself from his interpretation of my findings'. In his reply to Macnamara, Eysenck (1972) claimed, without adducing evidence, that Macnamara's proffered explanations in terms of environmental causes could only account for a small proportion of the differences observed. Also, Eysenck contended that 'This conviction (of an Irish inferiority in IQ to the English) is strengthened by the fact that other writers, using non-verbal tests, found similar differences'. The reference here is to research by Ian Hart *inter alios*.

In his 1971 paper in *The Irish Journal of Psychology*, Hart reported that 'Irish people tend to score extremely low on such tests as the Cattell Culture Fair Test of Intelligence' (p. 30). But Hart's study was not designed to be a study of national IQ. What Hart found was that the mean test performance of 126 male Dublin voters on a twenty-minute test of their ability to perceive relationships within spatial patterns of different types, was lower than the mean of the North American standardization sample. There is the question of whether Cattell's test is 'culture fair'. Moreover, Hart was aware of the possible impact on performance of practice and general test sophistication. He concluded that from the difference between his small, unrepresentative sample of Dublin men and a North American (not English) norm group 'it would be precipitate at this stage to consider the implications of a low national IQ . . .' (p. 34).

The next chapter in this story came when Enda Byrt and Peter Gill decided to standardize Raven's Progressive Matrices and the Synonym Selection subtest of the Mill Hill Vocabulary Test on a national sample of Irish primary schoolchildren. In September 1972 they and student colleagues tested 3,695 children aged 6–13 years in 82 schools in 25 counties. In March 1975 *The Education Times* published an extensive and detailed article by Byrt and Gill entitled 'Eysenck and the Irish IQ: The evidence that proves him wrong' (pp. 12–13). In the first half of this article they attacked the basis of Eysenck's assertions about the low Irish IQ, and then they presented the results of their work as evidence to the contrary. Their main conclusion was that 'The performance of Irish schoolchildren does not differ significantly from that of British schoolchildren when samples are matched as closely as possible' (p. 13). Comparing the 1972 Irish results with Raven's 1940 Ipswich sample they concluded that 'No significant difference exists for ages 8–11 or for ages 6–8', but they did find a significant drop in the scores of 12- and 13-year-olds (p. 12). This they explained in terms of a 'piling-up' of less able pupils in sixth classes, when their academically more able peers had transferred to postprimary schools. However, questions arise about the validity of comparing 1972 Irish data with 1940 Ipswich data, and also about the differences between the 1972 Irish sample and the latest, 1979 British sample on Raven's Standard Progressive Matrices (Raven et al., 1983).

IN 1979 Lynn published in *The British Journal of Social and Clinical Psychology* a paper entitled 'The social ecology of intelligence in the British Isles'. It referred to a brain drain from Ireland. Since no critical appraisal of this article appeared in any Irish journal or, apart from Kirby's (1980, 1982a, 1982b) papers, in any British journal, the critique that follows, focusing on the 'facts' as presented by Lynn, seems overdue.

'The social ecology of intelligence in the British Isles' is a paper in three parts. The first deals with what the author calls the distribution of intelligence in the British Isles. The second part deals with the relation of 'population IQ' to various social and economic factors, and the last part treats of supposed causes of regional differences. Parts two and three assume the validity of the 'facts' established by part one. The central data are the mean IQs for the various regions as given in Figure 1.

FIGURE 1. STANDARD REGIONS OF ENGLAND, WALES, SCOTLAND AND IRELAND SHOWING MEAN POPULATION IQS. (FROM LYNN, 1979, P. 4, TABLE 1)

Figure 1 features the 'overall mean' IQ data from Table 1 and the findings of one study in Northern Ireland and one study in the Republic of Ireland.

TABLE 1. REGIONAL IQS DERIVED FROM THREE STUDIES, THEIR OVERALL MEANS, AND RESULTS OF A COGNITIVE MEASURE BY DAVIE ET AL. (1972). (FROM LYNN 1979, P. 2, TABLE 1).

REGION	VERNON NAVY	VERNON ARMY	DOUGLAS	OVERALL MEAN IQ	DAVIE ET AL.
London–South Eastern	101.9	103.0	101.5	102.1	7.34
Eastern	102.1	101.7	101.4	101.7	7.35
East-West Ridings	101.6	101.2	100.6	101.1	7.14
Southern	100.0	101.5	101.2	100.9	7.38
North Midland	100.6	101.5	100.3	100.8	6.99
North Western	101.2	98.1	101.5	100.3	7.12
Northern	99.8	99.6	99.7	99.7	7.11
South Western	98.2	101.4	99.1	99.6	7.12
Wales	98.5	97.9	98.8	98.4	7.24
Midland	98.6	97.2	98.4	98.1	6.91
Scotland	97.3	96.6	98.1	97.3	6.73

The unwary reader might assume that the source studies which formed the basis of Lynn's and Eysenck's arguments were explicitly designed to study these particular IQ questions. In *not one* of the cited studies was this so. Indeed in some cases, notably Vernon (1951), the studies presented data in support of exactly those 'environmental' explanations—such as test sophistication effects, practice and training effects—which Lynn and Eysenck so curiously dismiss as explanations for the small, and, as will become clear, unsubstantiated regional and national differences which they allege. There is no reference at all to Macnamara's (1972) rebuttal of Eysenck. Nor is there any reference at all to Byrt and Gill's (1975) scathing and detailed attack on Eysenck's position.

In his Table 1, which is also Table 1 in this paper, Lynn used the regional divisions employed by the Registrar General pre-1965. Since the main studies from which Lynn derived his British 'regional IQs' were two by Vernon (1947 and 1951) and since each Vernon study divided Britain into different numbers of regions, Lynn had to transform Vernon's data. He did this by giving 'the mean IQ of its group' to each county and then re-combining the counties into the regions distinguished by the Registrar General pre-1965. Information, which would militate against Lynn's proposition, has been lost in the process. Take his conclusion that the London–South Eastern and the Eastern regions had the highest 'population IQs' whereas, in the U.K., Scotland had the lowest. Even a superficial examination of Vernon's data (1951, Table III, p. 127) reveals that Scotland is in fact divided into two regions; 'g' for Scotland East and North Counties is given by Vernon as 99.6 which is higher than 'g' for Wales, Lancashire, Warwick, Staffs. and Salop. On the other hand 'g' for Glasgow and South-West Scotland is 93.7. Lynn then proceeds to make the classic aggregation error. He simply adds 99.6 and 93.7, divides by 2 and gets the figure of 96.6 for Scotland. So Lynn's method obscures precisely those inconsistencies within regions which favour 'environmental' explanations of test performance variations in terms of social class differences, family size, schooling differences, test sophistication differences, etc., all of which were considered in the Vernon papers.

It is not at all clear how Lynn arrived at the column of figures which he gives in Table 1 for 'Vernon Navy' (Vernon, 1947). What is clear is that Vernon used Raven's Progressive Matrices with a 20-minute time limit. Now Raven (1942) said of his test: 'matrix test mental ages should not be used like Binet mental ages for the calculation of intelligence quotients' (p. 145). And Vernon (1951) warns:

> ... recent investigations by myself and others have forced me to
> the conclusion that, while intelligence tests are admirable instru-
> ments for practical purposes such as educational and occupational
> selection and guidance within any one cultural group, they can-
> not be regarded as sufficiently pure measures of innate ability to
> be employed in comparisons between different groups such as
> races or nations, nor for genetic studies (p. 125).

Lynn ignored all this and blithely aggregated disparate data from three studies in his comparison of 11 British regions for intelligence. The first study (Vernon, 1947) presents Progressive Matrices data on nearly 90,000 male candidates for the Royal Navy. The second study (Vernon, 1951) presents data in terms of an index 'g' (derived from a combination of tests such as Arithmetic-Mathematics, Verbal Ability,

Clerical, Non-Verbal Intelligence) for about 10,000 national service recruits, male and mostly aged 18. Neither was a representative random sample and the deficiencies of each were pointed out by Vernon. The third study was a longitudinal study of 5,000 boys and girls born in March 1946 and assessed at ages 8, 11 and 15 using unspecified tests. The heterogeneous data from these three studies provide the first three columns of Table 1 and from these Lynn derives the 'overall mean IQ' for each British region by simply adding across columns and dividing by 3, completely ignoring the fact that the data were derived from different tests applied to non-random samples of different sizes drawn from different populations at different times. Therefore, all of the British 'regional IQs' given in the table and on the map are misleading.

While not using their data in his calculations because 'the standard deviation is not given', Lynn presents data from Davie et al. (1972) as the last column in Table 1 and asserts it confirms the other three studies. However, in the Davie et al. study children were given what Lynn describes as 'a copying design test similar to the subtest in the Stanford-Binet' (p. 3). Results are not given in terms of IQ scores at all but in terms of percentages of children 'good' at copying geometric designs. (See Figure 2.) Davie et al. clearly never intended their test to be regarded as an IQ test. It was included by them 'principally in order to identify those with perceptual or perceptual/motor difficulties'. The results of the copying designs test as given by Davie et al. (1972) are shown in Figure 2.

From this figure it can be seen that Wales, Eastern, and London and Southern Eastern regions all contain 26 percent of the children with good design copying performances. However, after Lynn's conversion of the data, Wales now comes out at 7.24, below the 7.35 and 7.34 for the other two regions. One could grant that these are trivial differences, were it not for the fact that the evidence which Lynn adduces to link the data from Davie et al. with the other three studies appears to be a *rank* order correlation coefficient. Before Lynn's conversion, Wales would have tied ranks with the other two regions. Also, all of the points from the Davie et al. study which would contradict Lynn's argument, such as that design copying performance is clearly related to socio-economic class and that regions differ in the mix of classes they contain or that Scotland had far and away the highest proportion of 'good' readers in this same study (Davie et al., p. 109), are completely ignored.

FIGURE 2. PERCENTAGES OF CHILDREN WITH 'GOOD' DESIGN COPYING SCORES BY REGION OF BRITAIN. (FROM DAVIE ET AL., 1972, P. 108, FIGURE 33).

SCOTLAND
19%

NORTHERN
23%

EAST
AND WEST
RIDINGS
25%

NORTH
WESTERN
23%

NORTH
MIDLAND
21%

MIDLAND
19%

WALES
26%

EASTERN
26%

28%

LONDON
AND
SOUTH
EASTERN 26%

SOUTH
WESTERN
24%

SOUTHERN

In a paper reviewing twenty-five years of research on pupil achievement in Northern Ireland, Wilson (1973) discusses how differences in the relative weight which similar types of school systems attach to objectives can account for differences in performance between children from each system. He also argues that cultural and home differences account, in part, for variations in performance on standardized tests. This is all by way of explaining the differences which researchers in Northern Ireland have found over a long period of time between scholastic achievement of children there and the standardized test norms. Ignoring such explanations, Lynn uses that same paper by Wilson to calculate a 'population IQ' for Northern Ireland. Wilson's study was conducted in 1970 on over 2,000 boys and girls in each of two age groups. Seven-year-olds were given a Moray House Picture Test, and ten-year-olds were given tests of verbal and non-verbal ability. Lynn takes the means of the children on each of these tests (see column c, Table 3, Wilson, 1973, p. 110), adds them up and divides by 3. This is how he gets a mean 'population IQ' for Northern Ireland of 96.7.

Lynn derives the Republic of Ireland's mean IQ from data provided by Gill and Byrt (1973). In their standardization of Raven's Standard Progressive Matrices on Irish children, they reported an overall mean difference of 3 points between the performance of Irish children and that of the British standardization samples. On that basis, and noting that the Irish children were approximately two months older than the British children, Lynn arrived at 96 as his 'working estimate of mean IQ in the Republic of Ireland' (Lynn, 1979, p. 5).

In effect, Lynn compared a 'corrected' mean score on a test of one type of non-verbal ability given to a sample of 6- to 13-year-old Irish children in 1972 with a wrongly calculated index score derived from unrepresentative samples of young men during the Second World War whose scores on a variety of different types of tests were aggregated with those of boys and girls who took two unspecified tests in the 1950s and 1960s. On such a foundation rests Lynn's finding of a difference of 6 IQ points between the Republic of Ireland and London and South Eastern England which Eysenck claims to be 'highly significant from a practical as well as a statistical point of view' (Eysenck, 1981, p. 78).

Such being the 'facts' on which the low Irish IQ myth is based, there is really no need to pursue the critique any further.

ACKNOWLEDGMENTS

The author gratefully acknowledges permission to reprint from the following:

Figure 1 and Table 1. From R. Lynn (1974), *British Journal of Social and Clinical Psychology*, 18, pp. 2 and 4. © British Psychological Society. Also permission of Professor R. Lynn.

Figure 2. From Davie, R., Butler, N., Goldstein, H. (1972), *From Birth to Seven*, p. 108. © National Children's Bureau. Also permission of Longman.

REFERENCES

Byrt, E., and Gill, P. (1975). Eysenck and the Irish IQ: The evidence that proves him wrong. *The Education Times*, 3, 12, 12–13.

Curtis, P. Jr. (1971). *Apes and Angels: The Irishman in Victorian Caricature*. Newton Abbot: David & Charles.

Curtis, L. (1984). *Nothing but the Same Old Story: The Roots of Anti-Irish Racism*. London: Greater London Council.

Davie, R., Butler, N., and Goldstein, H. (1972). *From Birth to Seven*. London: Longman.

Eysenck, H. J. (1971). *Race, Intelligence and Education*. London: Temple Smith.

Eysenck, H. J. (1972). Letter of reply to John Macnamara. *Bulletin of the British Psychological Society*, 25, 86, 79.

Eysenck, H. J. and Kamin, L. (1981). *Intelligence: The Battle for the Mind*. London: Pan Books.

Gill, P. E. and Byrt, E. (1973). The standardisation of Raven's Progressive Matrices and the Mill Hill Vocabulary Scale (Synonym Selection) for Irish schoolchildren aged 6 to 12 years. Unpublished MA thesis, University College, Cork.

Gould, S. J. (1981). *The Mismeasure of Man*. New York: Norton.

Hart, I. (1971). Scores of Irish groups on the Cattell Culture Fair Test of Intelligence and the California Psychological Inventory. *Irish Journal of Psychology*, 1, 30–35.

Kirby, A. (1980). A critical comment on 'The social ecology of intelligence in the British Isles'. *British Journal of Social Psychology*, 19, 333–336.

Kirby, A. (1982a). Public issue or private achievement; a further comment on the issue of the social ecology of intelligence and educational attainment. *British Journal of Social Psychology*, 21, 63–67.

Kirby, A. (1982b). A final response to Lynn on the existence of a social ecology of intelligence. *British Journal of Social Psychology*, 21, 341–342.

Lynn, R. (1978). Ethnic and racial differences in intelligence: International comparisons. In R. T. Osborne et al. (eds), *Human Variation: The Biopsychology of Age, Race and Sex*. New York: Academic Press, pp. 261–286.

Lynn, R. (1979). The social ecology of intelligence in the British Isles. *British Journal of Social and Clinical Psychology*, 18, 1–12.

McGonigle, B. and McPhilemy, S. (1974a). Genesis of an Irish myth. *Times Higher Educational Supplement*, No. 152, p. 13.

McGonigle, B., and McPhilemy, S. (1974b). Dispelling the mist around an Irish myth. *Times Higher Educational Supplement*, No. 158, p. 14.

Macnamara, J. (1966). *Bilingualism and Primary Education: A Study of Irish Experience*. Edinburgh: University Press.

Macnamara, J. (1972). Letter re H. J. Eysenck. *Bulletin of the British Psychological Society*, 25, 86, 79.

Osborne, R. T., Noble, C. E., and Weyl, N. (eds) (1978). *Human Variation: The Biopsychology of Age, Race and Sex*. New York: Academic Press.

Raven, J. C. (1942). Standardization of Progressive Matrices, 1938. *Medical Psychology*, 19, 137–50.

Raven, J. C., Court, J. H., and Raven, J. (1983). *Manual for Raven's Progressive Matrices and Vocabulary Scales*. London: Lewis.

Vernon, P. E. (1947). The variations of intelligence with occupation, age and locality. *British Journal of Statistical Psychology*, 1, 52–63.

Vernon, P. E. (1951). Recent investigations of intelligence and its measurement. *Eugenics Review*, 43, 125–137.

Wilson, J. (1973). Pupil achievement in Northern Ireland primary schools: Twenty-five years of findings and issues. *Irish Journal of Education*, 7, 102–116.

III
OPINIONS AND TESTIMONIES

A LONG TRADITION

E. J. Dionne, Jr.

I F   Y O U   H A D any doubts that Americans live in a time of deep
pessimism about the possibilities of social reform, the revival of
interest in genetic explanations for human inequality ought to resolve
them. This is a recurring pattern in American history. Whenever the
social reformers are seen as failing, along come allegedly new theories
about how the quest for greater fairness or justice or equality is really
hopeless because people and groups are, from birth, so different, one
from another. The social reformer is dismissed as a naive meddler in
some grand "natural" process that sorts people out all by itself.

That is the real significance of the appearance of and interest in *The
Bell Curve*, by the late Richard J. Herrnstein and Charles Murray. The
implicit argument of the book is that if genes are so important to intelligence, and intelligence is so important to success, then many of the
efforts made in the past several decades to improve people's life
chances were mostly a waste of time. Mr. Herrnstein and Mr. Murray
never quite say that. Their book and their article summarizing it in a
recent issue of *The New Republic* are full of careful hedges aimed at sav-
ing them from being charged with crude racism or determinism.

E. J. Dionne, Jr. is a writer for *The Washington Post*. This article originally was published as
"Race and IQ: Stale Notions," in *The Washington Post*, October 18, 1994.

On the one hand, they cite data showing persistently large differences between the IQ scores of blacks and whites (and smaller ones between whites and Asians). But they then assert that it is, of course, wrong to attribute to any given individual the characteristics that the data associate with their race. They produce an 845-page book on race, class, genes and IQ, and then assert that "the fascination with race, IQ, and genes is misbegotten"—as if their book would not increase the level of fascination with race, IQ, and genes.

But let us accept their goodwill and their caveats. The real problem here is with the authors' claims that making the argument they are making requires enormous courage; that this argument represents some sort of breakthrough; and that "it doesn't much matter" whether "the black-white difference in test scores is produced by genes or the environment." Mr. Herrnstein and Mr. Murray assert that they are taking on "a taboo issue." They argue that the question is "filled with potential for hurt and anger," but that it is "essential that people begin to talk about this in the open."

But who will be hurt and who will be angry? Surely it does not require great courage to make arguments that will reassure the well-educated and well-off that they hold their high positions because they are on the whole smarter than everybody else. If you deserve to be at the top, you needn't trouble yourself over whether those who aren't have been relegated to their positions through bad luck or discrimination or other forms of injustice. Mr. Herrnstein and Mr. Murray say they support "some sort of redistribution" for the poor. But they also "urge generally" that welfare be ended because it encourages "low-IQ" women to have babies.

They are in a long tradition. Every time arguments about genes or intelligence have arisen in American politics, it has been to blunt the drive for "some sort of redistribution." That is why their argument is not new. One need only revisit the historian Richard Hofstadter's fine book *Social Darwinism in American Thought*. He showed how similar theories—holding that "nature would provide that the best competitors in a competitive situation would win"—have been used for nearly a century to thwart social change. Social Darwinism, Mr. Hofstadter wrote, "gave strength to attacks on reformers and on almost all efforts at the conscious and directed change of society."

Before Mr. Murray and Mr. Herrnstein there was William Graham Sumner, who wrote eighty years ago that "the millionaires are the product of natural selection, acting on the whole body of men to pick out those who can meet the requirement of certain work to be done." Sure, these people "get high wages and live in luxury, but the bargain is a good one for society." Why? Because, said Mr. Sumner, "there is the intense competition for their place and occupation," and "this assures us that all who are competent for this function will be employed in it."

The Herrnstein-Murray argument is thus not a brave breakthrough but a flashy repackaging of a repeatedly discredited fashion. Thus was pseudoscience about racial differences used to justify the end of Reconstruction and the reimposition of a segregated caste system on the American South.

So the focus on nature or nurture really does matter. Of course, all of us are inescapably a product of both genes and environment. But the issue of which factors to emphasize in explaining what is happening to a society is not, finally, a "scientific" question, because the "science" of the matter is utterly crude, to the extent that it exists at all. Mr. Herrnstein and Mr. Murray say that estimates of whether IQ is inheritable range from 40 percent to 80 percent. This is science? Even if a figure as high as 40 or 60 percent were accurate, that leaves a huge amount of room for environmental factors that can be affected by the conscious choices of individuals and their government. And all of this begs the question of how important intelligence should be in ordering the rewards that a society offers, as against other virtues such as hard work, risk-taking, loyalty, or concern for others.

The Herrnstein-Murray book is not a "scientific" book at all but a political argument offered by skilled polemicists aimed at defeating egalitarians. It is gaining attention because social reformers have not done such a good job of it lately and because it is a lot easier to blame somebody else's genes or brain cells than to improve a society. Mr. Murray's critics should oppose him but resist vituperation, lest they suggest that they are afraid of what he is saying. There is nothing to fear in these stale notions, provided they are understood as such. What does need to be worried about, and changed, is a political climate so pessimistic that offerings such as these come to be taken as "science."

THE TRUTH ABOUT ASIAN AMERICANS

Margaret Chon

W HEN I WAS in college, I applied to the Air Force ROTC program. I thought I would save my parents the expense of paying
tuition and also learn to fly an airplane. I was given the most complete
physical of my life (confirming, among other things, that I was too near-
sighted to fly a kite, much less a plane). And I took an intelligence test.
When I reported back to the ROTC staff, they looked glum. What is it?
I thought. Did the physical turn up some life-threatening defect?

It turns out I had gotten the highest test score ever at my school,
higher than the engineering and pre-med students who had kept me at
the bottom of the bell curve in calculus. Rather than feeling pleased
and flattered, I felt like a sideshow freak. The recruiters were not
happy either. I think our reactions had a lot to do with the fact that I
did not resemble a typical recruit. I am a woman of East Asian, specifically Korean, descent. Also, I probably looked like a hippie. They did
not want me in ROTC no matter how "intelligent" I was.

The caricature of the superintelligent Asian is part of what drives
Charles Murray and the late Richard J. Herrnstein's book, *The Bell*

Margaret Chon, an associate professor of law at Syracuse University, writes about the
intersections of technology, culture, and law. This article appeared in *New York Newsday*,
October 28, 1994, under the title "About Asian Americans: False Flattery Gets Us
Nowhere."

Curve. In it, they rely on a number of statistical studies to make claims about the superior intelligence of certain groups—specifically Asian Americans—and the inferior intelligence of others, including African Americans. Because I am supposedly smarter than any previous ROTC candidate at my college, I'll explain why Asian Americans are not more intelligent than other people and, more important, why Murray and Herrnstein do a disservice to Asian Americans by promoting us as the superhuman race.

The authors make a mountain of a claim out of a molehill of evidence. Only two studies sampled Asians in America, and they were inconclusive. Five other studies compared Asians in Asia to white Europeans or white Americans. A scientist who is testing for the effects of genes independently of environment could not think of a worse study than one which compares groups in radically different cultures. People in different countries are going to have different environments, regardless of socioeconomic status. Comparing Asians in Asia to whites in America is like comparing apples to oranges—not to mention the fact that IQ is to intelligence as apples are to zebras. In lawyer's language, Murray and Herrnstein have not met their burden of proof: They have not demonstrated an IQ difference between Asians and whites in America.

So why do Murray and Herrnstein insist that Asians are smarter?

Because they need to find an Asian-white IQ difference. Once they establish a superhuman or "good" minority, then there can't be any racism in their research. If two white males admit that Asians are smarter than whites, then the rest of us might as well accept the inevitable: There are subhuman or "bad" minorities.

Asian Americans must not allow themselves to be misused in the service of Murray and Herrnstein's political agenda. To do so would just exacerbate two problems that we already face in the United States. First, painting Asian Americans as superintelligent just lets America pretend we don't exist. Social service agencies ignore us because we don't need help. Governments ignore us because we've already made it. Schools won't recruit us because we do so well on the SATs. Yet Asian Americans have inadequate access to culturally and linguistically appropriate voter assistance, health care, and job training. Asian-American households are less wealthy than white ones. Asian Americans occupy substandard housing projects and attend underfunded public schools. And at least thirty Asian Americans died in 1993 as a result of homicides in which racial animus was suspected or proven. Asian Americans, of all intelligence levels, face discrimination based on accent and appearance.

Second, the false flattery allows Murray and Herrnstein to taunt and provoke other minority groups. Using the myth of the superhuman Asian, they drag us into the racialization of American politics, creating an Asian buffer between black and white America. This strategy turns our pluses into negatives, our intelligence into cunning. We are perceived as fanatic, clannish kamikazes who threaten to overtake the local or world economy. That makes us targets of misunderstanding, hatred, and violence. After all, the accumulated rage of the black community cannot reach Beverly Hills or Bronxville, but it can make itself felt at Korean grocery stores in South Central Los Angeles and Flatbush.

Asian Americans seem almost invisible, except when there is a grocery store boycott—or when we're touted as the model minority. Unfortunately, Asian Americans are just visible enough to be misused in the social science pornography that is *The Bell Curve*.

FOR WHOM THE BELL CURVE REALLY TOLLS

Tim Beardsley

R ARELY DO 800-page books crammed with graphs reach best-seller lists. *The Bell Curve*, an inflammatory treatise about class, intelligence, and race by the late Richard J. Herrnstein, a psychology professor at Harvard University, and political scientist Charles Murray of the American Enterprise Institute, is an exception. The book's deeply pessimistic analysis of U.S. social woes, together with its conservative policy prescriptions, has hit a nerve. Publishing *The Bell Curve* may have been a calculated political move on the part of its authors. As the country lurches to the right, many people will be seduced by the text's academic trappings and scientific tone into believing its arguments and political inferences well supported. Those readers should think again.

The Bell Curve depicts a frightening future in which, absent strong corrective measures, a "cognitive elite" will live in guarded enclaves distant from the dull masses. Opportunities for the underclass will become limited as tolerance evaporates. Strict policing will be widely accepted, and racial hostility will likely spread. The least intelligent

Tim Beardsley has a D. Phil. in zoology from Oxford University. He worked as a staff writer for *Nature*, the British science journal, before joining the board of editors of *Scientific American*. This article appeared in *Scientific American*, January 1995, as "For Whom the Bell Curve Really Tolls."

denizens of this dystopia will be consigned to a "high-tech and more lavish version of the Indian reservation." This apocalyptic vision is presented as the consequence of unpalatable, undeniable "facts" about inheritance and intelligence. But the thesis rests on curiously twisted logic. Its authors have been highly selective in the evidence they present and in their interpretation of ambiguous statistics. The work is "a string of half-truths," states Christopher Jencks, a sociologist at Northwestern University.

The arguments stem from the same tradition of biological determinism that led, not so long ago, to compulsory sterilizations in the United States and genocide elsewhere. The notion is that individuals' characteristics are both essentially fixed by inheritance and immune to alteration by the environment. Efforts to help those who are unfortunate by reason of their genes are unlikely to be rewarded. Solutions, therefore, should include those Murray has long advocated: abolish welfare, reduce affirmative action, and simplify criminal law.

Herrnstein and Murray produce data suggesting that intelligence—as assessed by a high IQ score—is increasingly important to economic success. They also argue that people who have low scores—including disproportionate numbers of blacks—are more likely than others to fall prey to social ills. The two accept evidence from studies of twins reared apart that there is a large heritable component to IQ scores: they estimate it to be 60 percent. The writers declare themselves agnostic on the question of whether racial differences in IQ scores are genetic, although they are clearly inclined to favor that possibility.

Herrnstein and Murray countenance that just because a trait has a heritable origin does not mean it is unchangeable. Nearsightedness is one example of an inherited, modifiable condition. But they decide, on the basis of a questionable look at the data, that "an inexpensive, reliable method of raising IQ is not available." This conclusion is used to justify an attack on programs aimed at helping society's most vulnerable: the authors prefer to let the genetically disadvantaged find their own level. Evidence that does not accord with Herrnstein and Murray's way of thinking—such as the observation that IQ scores worldwide are slowly increasing—is acknowledged then ignored.

Leaving aside the substantial and unresolved issue of whether a single number can adequately summarize mental performance, *The Bell Curve* plays fast and loose with statistics in several ways. According to Arthur Goldberger, an econometrician at the University of Wisconsin who has studied genetics and IQ, the book exaggerates the ability of IQ to predict job performance. Herrnstein and Murray assert that scores have an impressive "validity" of about 0.4 in such predictions. They report that the Armed Forces Qualification Test, an IQ surrogate, has a validity of 0.62 at anticipating the success of training for mechanical jobs. Yet many of the measures used to assess validity include supervisors' ratings, which are subject to bias, Goldberger notes. Furthermore, the validities that the duo see as so revealing are in fact hypothetical quantities that no employer would expect to find in prospective employees. "It's really bad stuff," Goldberger says.

Other correlations that the writers establish between social ills and low IQ scores are equally suspect. Herrnstein and Murray put great weight on comparisons between the ability of IQ scores and parental socioeconomic status to predict what will happen to young people. Yet the measures of socioeconomic status they use cannot ensure that homes are equally stimulating. The point is crucial because numerous studies have demonstrated that early childhood surroundings have a large role in molding IQ scores—certainly more studies than have indicated a significant role for heredity. Consequently, conclusions about the dominance of IQ cannot be taken at face value. Leon Kamin, a psychologist at Northeastern University and well-known critic of research on intelligence, maintains that interactions between genes and environment make attempts to weigh nature against nurture "meaningless."

Herrnstein and Murray's hereditarian bias is also obvious in their account of a study of a hundred children from varying ethnic backgrounds who were adopted into white families. The study got under way in the 1970s. At age seven, the black and interracial children scored an average of 106 on IQ tests—considerably better than the national average of black children and close to levels scored by white children. A decade later researchers Sandra Scarr of the University of Virginia and Richard A. Weinberg of the University of Minnesota found that the IQs of the black children had declined to 89, whereas those of white adoptees had fallen from 112 to 106. Scarr and Weinberg concluded that racially based discrimination at school probably explained the drop in the black youngsters' scores. Jencks agrees: "The results are perfectly consistent with the difference being due to something in the early home environment and, for older kids, their experience in school." But Herrnstein and Murray interpret the findings differently: "Whatever the environmental impact may have been, it cannot have been large."

The Bell Curve's most egregious failing, however, may be its bleak assessment of educational efforts to improve the intellectual performance of children from deprived backgrounds. Herrnstein and Murray cast a jaundiced eye over Head Start and other more intensive efforts for at-risk youngsters—projects that have been claimed to produce long-lasting gains in IQ, a possibility that would not square well with biological determinist thought. Herrnstein and Murray downplay such results, noting that such interventions are too expensive to be widely used. The only one they are enthusiastic about is adoption, which, paradoxically, they accept as having a clearly positive effect on IQ. "Their treatment of intervention wouldn't be accepted by an academic journal—it's that bad," exclaims Richard Nisbett, a psychology professor at the University of Michigan. "I'm distressed by the extent to which people assume [Murray] is playing by the rules."

Jencks is also unhappy with the book's conclusions about education. "Herrnstein and Murray are saying Head Start didn't have a profound effect. But that doesn't tell us that we couldn't do a lot better if we had a different society," he says. "In Japan, for example, children learn more math than they do in the U.S. because everybody there agrees math is important."

Scarr, who accepts a substantial role for heredity in individual IQ differences, insists that efforts to boost intellectual functioning in disadvantaged youth can deliver results. "There's no question that rescuing children from desperately awful circumstances will improve their performance," she notes. Scarr also points out that ameliorating a child's environment may reduce social problems, regardless of its effect on IQ. "The low-IQ group deserves a lot more support than it is getting," she argues. "Other societies manage not to have the same levels of social ills as we do." Edward F. Zigler, a prominent educational psychologist at Yale University, asserts that "in terms of everyday social competence, we have overwhelming evidence that high-quality early education is beneficial."

Therein lies the fatal flaw in Herrnstein and Murray's harsh reasoning. Even though boosting IQ scores may be difficult and expensive, providing education can help individuals in other ways. That fact, not IQ scores, is what policy should be concerned with. *The Bell Curve*'s fixation on IQ as the best statistical predictor of a life's fortunes is a myopic one. Science does not deny the benefits of a nurturing environment and a helping hand.

A TRIUMPH OF PACKAGING

David M. Kutzik

A MAINLY WHITE "cognitive elite" rules America, and African Americans, Latinos, and working-class whites are destined to be left in the dust. Too bad, but they're just inferior genetically. So say Charles Murray and Richard J. Herrnstein in their new and much-debated book, *The Bell Curve*. Not to appear white supremacist, the authors point out that Asian Americans post higher IQ scores on the average than whites, claiming that their scores reflect the Asian "ethnicity's" genetically superior "nonverbal" capacity. Yet Chinese Americans provide the clue to what is wrong with this reasoning. During the 1920s, IQ testers pegged the Chinese at the bottom of the intelligence pile: average IQ between 65 and 70. By the 1950s, Chinese Americans were scoring almost on a par with whites and twenty years later they were scoring higher than whites.

The question is why.

Are we to believe that some magic mutation made the Chinese-American gene pool more intellectually powerful? Or is the increase in IQ explainable in terms of a variety of sociological factors on the wings of which a significant proportion of this formerly impoverished and

David M. Kutzik is on the faculty of the Center for Applied Neurogerontology at Drexel University and is writing a book on IQ testing and racism. This article was published as "Bell Curve Doesn't Deserve the Fuss" in *The Philadelphia Inquirer,* November 1, 1994.

undereducated ethnic group is today solidly upper middle class and successful in high-end "cognitive elite" occupations?

That African Americans score on the average fifteen points less than whites on IQ tests is a fact well known to all who have studied the literature. A fact also known to those who have studied the history of IQ is that up until the mid-1920s, women lagged behind men by a similar point spread. The tests were redesigned to be "unbiased," thereby equalizing their scores.

This second fact, lost on Herrnstein and Murray, was the main reason why the Supreme Court of California banned IQ tests as an educational placement tool. The court concluded that until the tests are adjusted in relation to non-white and non-middle-class groups, as they were in relation to women, the tests will continue to discriminate against these groups.

Also overlooked by the authors is an extensive body of literature on the irrelevance of IQ to creativity and productivity in different "cognitive elite" professions. Although it is true that, on the average, scientists, lawyers, and engineers score higher than blue-collar workers, differences in IQ within these professional groups seem to have no impact on the individual's contribution to the field—high-IQ mathematicians are no more successful than low-IQ mathematicians. The explanation offered by researchers is that IQ is in no way connected to creativity and that the kind of intelligence it measures is too narrow to predict success within occupations. Behavioral and cognitive scientists studying human intelligence over the past dozen years have reached the consensus that IQ is only one very small part of the human intelligence puzzle.

The real problem with intelligence test scores is revealed by way of analogy: IQ tests are to intelligence what crossword puzzles are to literary creativity. In other words, being able to do well on a Sunday-morning puzzle may be correlated with knowledge of world literature, but such knowledge is not causally connected with the ability to write a novel. In a manner typical of hereditarians, Herrnstein and Murray blur the distinction between correlation and causation and conclude that society is destined to be dominated by a racially (read "genetically") superior elite of the highly intelligent, and that the ideals of equality are at best unfounded and at worst dangerous.

Their spiritual father is Sir Francis Galton, who more than a century ago demonstrated that the 714 most eminent men in England were related to each other through a network of some 50 or so families. Did Galton conclude that he was looking at a hereditary ruling class? No. Galton concluded that he had proved these families were of superior racial worth, achieving their position solely on the basis of their inherited intelligence. Galton was the first to statistically "prove" the relationship between intelligence, heredity, and social class. He was also the first to apply the normal (i.e., "bell") curve to heredity and intelligence. Galton called his science "eugenics" and launched hereditarian research as a political movement to weed out the racially inferior and promote the procreation of the superior.

The Bell Curve is just the latest example in a long history of what's known in the trade as "Galtonesque hereditarianism." The media frenzy ballyhooing the appearance of *The Bell Curve* is quite an orgy of advertising. It cannot be "news" because there is nothing really "new" in *The Bell Curve*, other than packaging.

The real news story is how and why a media campaign fit for a president has cast the authors, and their scientific racism, into the spotlight. The real news story is precisely how this book has hit the covers of magazines, the editorial pages, and the talk shows with such perfect timing. And the truly big story is that this book will be taken so seriously by so many of the "cognitive elite" as an ideological basis for a more openly racist ultraconservative agenda.

THROWING A CURVE

Bob Herbert

I N M O N T C L A I R , New Jersey, where I grew up in the 1950s
and 1960s, there was an elderly woman named Mildred Maxwell
who would greet the periodic outbursts of segregationists and other
racial provocateurs with the angry and scornful comment "There isn't
a hell hot enough for that man and his ideas." Mrs. Maxwell comes to
mind whenever I think (angrily and scornfully) about Charles Murray
and his book *The Bell Curve*, a scabrous piece of racial pornography
masquerading as serious scholarship.

Mr. Murray fancies himself a social scientist, an odd choice of profession for someone who would have us believe he was so sociologically
ignorant as a teenager that he didn't recognize any racial implications
when he and his friends burned a cross on a hill in his hometown of
Newton, Iowa. In a *New York Times Magazine* article by Jason DeParle,
Mr. Murray described the cross-burning as "dumb." But he insisted, "It
never crossed our minds that this had any larger significance."

Oh, no. Of course not.

Now, in middle age, Mr. Murray gets his kicks by thinking up ways to
drape the cloak of respectability over the obscene and long-discredited

Bob Herbert is a columnist for *The New York Times*. This column appeared in *The New York Times*, October 27, 1994, as "Throwing a Curve."

views of the world's most rabid racists. And so *The Bell Curve*, written with Richard Herrnstein, who recently died, promotes the view that blacks are inherently inferior to whites.

It's an ugly stunt. Mr. Murray can protest all he wants, his book is just a genteel way of calling somebody a nigger.

The book shows that, on average, blacks score about fifteen points lower than whites on intelligence tests, a point that was widely known and has not been in dispute. Mr. Murray and I (and many, many others) differ on the reasons for the disparity. I would argue that a group that was enslaved until little more than a century ago; that has long been subjected to the most brutal, often murderous, oppression; that has been deprived of competent, sympathetic political representation; that has most often had to live in the hideous physical conditions that are the hallmark of abject poverty; that has tried its best to survive with little or no prenatal care, and with inadequate health care and nutrition; that has been segregated and ghettoized in communities that were then red-lined by banks and insurance companies and otherwise shunned by business and industry; that has been systematically frozen out of the job market; that has in large measure been deliberately deprived of a reasonably decent education; that has been forced to cope with the humiliation of being treated always as inferior, even by imbeciles—I would argue that these are factors that just might contribute to a certain amount of social pathology and to a slippage in intelligence test scores.

Mr. Murray says no. His book strongly suggests that the disparity is inherent, genetic, and there is little to be done about it.

Most serious scholars know that the conclusions drawn by Mr. Murray and Mr. Herrnstein from the data in *The Bell Curve* are bogus. The issue has been studied ad nauseam and the overwhelming consensus of experts in the field is that environmental conditions account for most of the disparity when the test results of large groups are compared.

The last time I checked, both the Protestants and the Catholics in Northern Ireland were white. And yet the Catholics, with their legacy of discrimination, grade out about fifteen points lower on IQ tests. There are many similar examples. Scholars are already marshaling the evidence needed to demolish *The Bell Curve* on scientific grounds. But be assured that when their labors are completed and their papers submitted, they will not get nearly the attention that *The Bell Curve* has received.

A great deal of damage has been done. The conclusions so disingenuously trumpeted by Mr. Murray were just what millions of people wanted to hear. It was just the message needed to enable whites to distance themselves still further from any responsibility for the profound negative effect that white racism continues to have on all blacks.

Mildred Maxwell is no longer with us. I wish she were. Just once I would like to hear her comment on Charles Murray and his book.

BORN TO LOSE

DeWayne Wickham

I WAS BORN to dirt-poor parents and grew up in poverty. For twenty years, I lived in federally subsidized housing in an inner-city neighborhood where just about everyone needed some form of government assistance to survive. My first-semester grades in high school ranged from a 30 in geometry to a 63 in music. I was kicked out of one high school, denied admission into two others, and finally dropped out of a fourth. At eighteen, I was deeply mired in the social abyss from which Charles Murray says African Americans cannot escape.

If Murray, co-author of *The Bell Curve*—a book that soon will replace the white hood and sheet as the most pernicious symbol of resistance to the push for racial equality—had his way, people like me would be written off. He believes that economic success is tied to intelligence—which, he says, is largely inherited. In other words, it's bad genes, more than a bad environment, that locks people into inner-city ghettos or rural poverty. Murray's prescription is to replace affirmative action programs with a "survival of the fittest" acceptance of the inevitability of their fate.

DeWayne Wickham is columnist for *USA Today* and author of *Fire at Will*, a collection of columns. His autobiography, *Woodholme,* will be published in 1995. This piece was carried by Gannet News Service, October 24, 1994, titled "Living Proof That Author of 'Bell Curve' Is Wrong."

Charles Murray is the linear successor to Arthur Jensen and William Shockley, two psychologists who raised similar arguments in the 1960s. Had they succeeded, I never would have escaped the ghetto. And if Murray accomplishes what Jensen and Shockley could not, he will deal a deadly blow to the millions of African Americans who now live in poverty.

Eventually, I changed my environment, earned a high school GED, and went on to get two college degrees—in each case with higher cumulative averages than most of my white classmates. Murray says people are poor because they are inherently, and irreversibly, stupid. I'm living proof that he is wrong.

Publicly, Murray pines for a return to the mythical good old days when people in this country went as far in life as their "abilities and energies" would take them. When was that?

Certainly not during the 246 years slavery was legal in this country. Nor can he be talking about the 99 years following abolition, when the force of law was used to lock black people out of the American main-stream. For all that time, race was a major factor in determining how opportunities were meted out in this country. The truth is, this is not a color-blind society, nor has it ever been. Sure, we're a lot closer today to it than we were 100 or even 50 years ago, but we still have a long way to go to get there.

Privately, I suspect, Murray wants to beat a path back to the time when success in life was determined largely by skin color. He denies this, but that's the modus operandi of today's bigots. They cloak their racism in an appeal for a return to a meritocracy that never existed, or disguise their chauvinism in disingenuous complaints about reverse racism. Like the Ku Kluxers of old, they seek to create a neo-slavery America in which black people are at the lowest rung of a caste system that whites sit atop.

Murray would never say that, but he implies as much. In his book, Murray says many blacks languish in poverty, crime, and an overre-liance on government handouts because they are genetically dumb. As a group, he says, we are a lower form of human than whites and Asians. And then, having established this premise, he argues the government is wasting money trying to improve the lives of the black underclass.

Murray doesn't want to reform welfare, he wants to end it. He doesn't want to slash the number of births to unwed mothers so much as he'd like to do a little social engineering by discouraging child-bearing by poor women with low intelligence. He wants to massage immigration laws to favor the educated. And he wants to do away with job discrimination laws because they force employers to give people with low IQs a fair chance at earning a paycheck. He says he has science on his side, but I think he stands a lot closer to Jim Crow than Albert Einstein.

BRANDED

Gary Earl Ross

T HE CONTROVERSY over race and intelligence lies sleeping beneath the surface of American consciousness like a sea monster that awakens every two or three decades to molest passing ships. The monster is dormant until summoned by a magic spell or, in the absence of magic, "scientific" certainty. The latest numerical necromancy, *The Bell Curve* by Charles Murray and the late Richard Herrnstein, is presently gathering its share of media attention. At 845 pages of complex statistics and intellectual argument, the book is already being summarized so that the reach of its ideas will exceed its grasp on readers. It will be remembered for a single assertion—that, genetically, blacks are intellectually inferior to whites.

That belief is certainly an old one and has been reinforced by both religion and science in the past. Slavery apologists noted that blacks bore "the mark of Cain" and were thus destined to baseness. Nineteenth-century naturalists measured skulls and body parts and lung capacity to reinforce white superiority. Belief in black inferiority was dragged so far into the twentieth century by discriminatory cus-

Gary Earl Ross, an associate professor at the Buffalo Educational Opportunity Center, is preparing a collection of his previously published short stories and is writing a novel. This essay was published in *The Buffalo News*, November 26, 1994, titled "The Insidiousness of the Bell Curve."

toms, public school textbooks, media stereotypes, standardized test-ing, and a host of other social variables that the nation's embrace of racial equality is less than forty years old. Indeed, African-American culture itself is comparatively young, its connection to its cultural antecedents having been severed by slavery.

The first time I learned I was from intellectually inferior stock, I was seated in a Buffalo public high school psychology class. In response to a question, the teacher said, almost offhandedly, that blacks generally scored lower than whites on intelligence tests. One of only two or three blacks in the class, I felt especially visible that day, as if I had been flat-tened between glass slides and slipped under a microscope.

The following year, when I was a college freshman, the Arthur Jensen–William Shockley controversy erupted. Though I felt equally visible among the handful of blacks on campus, I argued passionately instead of sinking into my seat. But at seventeen and eighteen, I knew only the passion. Now, at forty-three, I have more fundamental ques-tions with which to challenge biological determinism.

If belief in inequality is four hundred years old—or ten times the age of the nation's belief in equality—doesn't it stand to reason that American culture has been so biased by an undercurrent of racism that anything that addresses race is necessarily tainted? What are the cumulative effects of systemic racism on the intellectual development of the African-American child? What are the effects of growing up in a culture of freedom still in its infancy? Of enduring poverty and dimin-ished expectations? How do such factors as higher levels of smoking in African-American homes, lead-based paint, and fatty diets born of scrap-fed slave traditions influence the ability to take a test? How does belief in what social scientists accept as truth—that black IQ scores are lower—influence the writers of IQ tests? For that matter, how signifi-cant is IQ? Is it the only true intelligence? If not, why aren't the others measured with the same dogged intensity?

My own history suggests the limitations of IQ testing. When I was in grammar school, according to my cumulative record, my IQ was 94. In junior high it was 114, then 127 in high school, and finally 133 on a Mensa-style test I took for fun several years ago. A spread of nearly 40 points is well outside the range of statistical error, yet I could easily have been categorized, counseled, and conditioned to fulfill the expec-tations of a first- or second-grade test I have no memory of taking.

IQ tests don't measure talent or creativity or interpersonal skills. Their failure to do so is what makes *The Bell Curve* so insidious. In calling for an end to social redress of inequities, Murray and Herrnstein elevate IQ testing to an importance that justifies the racist's perceptions of "those people" and "their troubles." Scientific sanctioning of such ideas consigns me and every other African American to a human scrap heap, a writhing black mass of problem people. It will not matter to the casual passerby that I have published prose and poetry or taught two thousand students or been listed in several *Who's Who* publications. Mine will simply be another dark face in the pile.

TIMING IS EVERYTHING

Salim Muwakkil

T HE REPUBLICAN electoral revolution of November 1994 arrived on the heels of a controversy about race and intelligence provoked by Charles Murray and Richard Herrnstein's already infamous book, *The Bell Curve*. The two contemporary events may seem unconnected, but as cultural portents they form a dangerous tandem that could easily escalate the level of racist discourse in the United States.

While pundits and political psychologists have used terms like anger, frustration, and exasperation to explain the electorate's boisterous mood, the word "xenophobia" does a better job of gauging the national sentiment. Issues from immigration to crime to welfare reform all have racial dimensions that tie very much into the mood of the American moment. And, of course, this is not just an American moment—xenophobia is all the rage in Europe as well.

The Bell Curve further poisons this already poisonous atmosphere, suggesting that social success or failure is largely a function of IQ, and that IQ is a function of genetics. Since blacks have a lower aggregate IQ than whites, the authors contend, it is no mystery why they suffer disproportionate miseries, generation after generation.

Salim Muwakkil is a senior editor at *In These Times,* where this article originally appeared on November 28, 1994, entitled "Dangerous Curve."

Of course, this argument is nothing new; it formed a cultural context that justified chattel slavery and the commodification of Africans. Murray, a fellow at the American Enterprise Institute, and his deceased co-author both are amateurs in the fields of race and genetics (Murray has a degree in political science and Herrnstein was trained in psychology). But a lack of professional expertise has seldom deterred some of the Western world's finest minds—David Hume, Immanuel Kant, Benjamin Franklin, and Thomas Jefferson among them—from expressing similarly Afrophobic ideas in their respective eras.

What is particularly significant about *The Bell Curve* is its timing. Rarely has a book come out at a more propitious political moment. (Murray's *Losing Ground,* which argued for a cold turkey withdrawal of welfare benefits during the middle of the Reagan administration, was similarly well timed.) While Murray loudly denies a political motive for writing *The Bell Curve,* the controversial volume makes the same point he has been pushing for years: welfare-state policies aggravate rather than ameliorate social problems. The new book's conclusions inevitably attack the notion that social policies can promote economic justice. Programs designed to alter the natural dominance of the "cognitive elite" are useless, the book argues, because the genes of the subordinate castes invariably doom them to failure.

In recent years polls increasingly have revealed that many white Americans feel that programs like affirmative action and racial set-asides have gone too far and are unfairly affecting them. Programs once heralded as part of a compassionate social safety net are now demonized as part of a socialistic welfare state. *The Bell Curve* sanctifies those tendencies and provides a respectable cover of science. The economic status quo, it argues, is simply a ratification of genetic justice.

"[Murray and Herrnstein's] argument is racism, pure and simple," says Dr. Steve Jones, a geneticist at University College in London and author of the award-winning book *Language of the Genes.* "They've hijacked false genetics to push an ideological agenda." *The Bell Curve* is an 845-page bundle of data, compiling a number of previously published studies. But many geneticists who have reviewed the book condemn the authors' selective use of contested data.

"It is already becoming clear that the air of dispassionate scientific curiosity that [Murray and Herrnstein] are at such pains to maintain is at odds with the eccentricity of some of their sources," writes Alan

Ryan in *The New York Review of Books*. Ryan denounces Murray and Herrnstein's treatment of J. Philippe Rushton's "bizarre" book, *Race, Evolution, and Behavior,* as the work of a serious scholar.

Rushton is a Canadian psychologist who has argued that Asians have larger brains for their body size, smaller penises, lower sex drives, and a stronger work ethic than Caucasians. He argues that Caucasians have a similar relationship to blacks. Murray and Herrnstein's use of sources like Rushton and of white supremacist writers like Richard Lynn illuminates their ideological links to the Pioneer Fund, a shadowy group that has been trying for many years to resurrect the eugenic ideas that were discredited by the Nazi horror.

Though neither Murray nor Herrnstein have received any money from the group, they rely on the findings of several fund recipients. The Pioneer Fund is a small right-wing organization founded in 1937 to fund research on racial differences and the importance of heredity. According to the fund, it is nature, not nurture, that guides an individual's fate. This belief is called hereditarianism and it posits, essentially, that African Americans are at the bottom of most socioeconomic measures because they are genetically deficient. Pioneer subsidizes those researchers whose work reinforces these general principles.

Arthur Jensen, the notorious Berkeley psychologist who triggered controversy with a 1969 essay in *Harvard Educational Review* arguing that blacks were intellectually inferior to whites for genetic reasons, won a Pioneer Fund grant. So did William Shockley, the late Nobel Prize–winning physicist and co-inventor of the transistor, who urged the establishment of a fund to pay "intellectually inferior" people to allow themselves to be sterilized.

Certainly, discussion about the influence of biology on human nature has become more respectable since the seventies, when the left uniformly condemned such speculation as providing fuel for racist demagogues. Recent advances in genetic research have shown genes to have powerful determinative effects. But such revelations have provided cover for the unscientific and formerly discredited theories of eugenicists. According to Troy Duster, author of *Backdoor to Eugenics* and director of the Institute for the Study of Social Change at the University of California at Berkeley, we should be worried about using revolutionary breakthroughs in molecular biology to support ideas of genetic determinism.

"We can screen an individual's genes at the molecular level to see who's at risk for devastating medical disorders like Tay-Sachs, sickle-cell anemia, and cystic fibrosis," says Duster, who is black. "And these breakthroughs have created an unjustified halo effect for geneticists trying to explain behavior."

Duster appreciates the quandary posed by that medical progress. On the one hand, there is much value in the insights afforded by genetic mapping, and simply to protest those methods for their racist potential is unreasonable. But on the other hand, as Duster points out, there are responsible "critics who have been portrayed as naysayers and paranoids, or know-nothing Luddites who would put their heads in the sand or try to stop the machinery of progress."

Ideas of genetic determinism historically have provided "scientific" justification for stigmatizing various groups besides blacks, including Asians and Eastern and Southern European immigrants. Duster fears that if the general public accepts the notion that there are genetic propensities for violence or other social pathology and fails to understand the need for safeguards against abuse, then genes could easily be used as a rationalization for the political oppression—and worse—of African Americans and other minorities.

Many of those other minorities are also on the Pioneer Fund's hit list. The group helps to subsidize the Federation for American Immigration Reform (FAIR), which backs immigration restriction and campaigned for California's Proposition 187. The fund also supports an English-only advocacy group called U.S. English. Not surprisingly, the fund looks disparagingly on affirmative action and coercive integration. In general, much of its program coincides with the views of the most nativist and xenophobic elements of the conservative movement.

Thus it's no surprise to find that the Pioneer Fund has links to those right-wing political forces who made large gains in the midterm elections. Thomas Ellis, who is a close confidant of Sen. Jesse Helms (R-NC), is a former Pioneer Fund director. The fund itself has made grants to a right-wing group called the Coalition for Freedom that has established a "Jesse Helms Institute for Foreign Policy and American Studies."

These are heady days for the Pioneer Fund. Many legislators who favor its political agenda are now ascendant in Congress, and the popular press has magnified the significance of its hereditarian arguments with the publicity surrounding *The Bell Curve*. For example, a review of the Murray-Herrnstein book in *The New York Times Book Review* also featured two other books with largely the same theme. One of them was Rushton's *Race, Evolution, and Behavior,* the volume Alan Ryan has dismissed as "bizarre." Though the Pioneer Fund hasn't subsidized either Herrnstein or Murray, its director, Harry Weyher, has expressed strong support for their conclusions.

And *The Bell Curve* boils those conclusions down to this: those with the lowest intellectual levels are outbreeding the brightest population, and since intelligence is largely inherited, this country is losing the cognitive base essential for coping with national problems. Perhaps the most damaging aspect of the book's argument is the conclusion that remedial attempts to boost the intelligence of certain groups are fruitless. That argument can't help but be reassuring to an electorate demanding that the government be less concerned with the social safety nets that have aided many urban blacks in our resource-starved postindustrial cities. If, as *The Bell Curve* argues, social pathology is a function of genes, then the crisis in black America is impervious to social remediation.

But such arguments also set the stage for a vigorous resistance from those groups deemed genetically incapable. The confluence of *The Bell Curve* and the Republican revolution has provoked an increase in organizing activity in African-American communities around the country. And the rabid anti-immigration sentiment unleashed by the battle over California's Proposition 187 has triggered a groundswell of Latino protest.

The convergence of the agendas of the political right and the advocates of hereditarianism has created the potential for a coalition of opposition that may turn out to be the silver lining in this stormy era.

INTELLECTUAL BROWN SHIRTS

Adolph Reed, Jr.

I N *THE NEW YORK TIMES MAGAZINE*, Charles Murray recently tried to defend himself against charges that he doesn't like women by jovially recalling his romps as a consumer in the Thai sex trade during his old Peace Corps days. In the profile, part of the media blitz accompanying publication of his book, *The Bell Curve: Intelligence and Class Structure in American Life*, Murray recoiled elaborately from characterizing his partners as prostitutes. (He prefers "courtesans" or "ladies of the evening," perhaps seeking to preserve to the end his illusion that he was not simply buying the sexual services of women who provided them because they were exploited, oppressed, and quite likely enslaved.)

It is certainly understandable that Murray—who, despite a Harvard/MIT pedigree, basically knocked around doing nothing special until the threshold of middle age, when in an epiphany he discovered the novel truth that people with power and privilege really are superior and that everyone else is defective—would avoid the "p" word. You know, like Dracula and mirrors.

Adolph Reed, Jr., teaches history and political science at Northwestern University; he is the author of two forthcoming books, *Fabianism and the Color Line: The Political Thought of W.E.B. Du Bois* and *Stirrings in the Jug: Black Politics in the Post-Segregation Era*. This article appeared in *The Progressive*, December 1994.

The Bell Curve is a vile, disingenuously vicious book by two truly odious men, Murray and Richard Herrnstein, the Harvard psychologist known outside the academy—like his Berkeley counterpart, Arthur Jensen—for a more than twenty-year crusade to justify all existing inequality by attributing it to innate differences in intelligence. Murray's epiphany led to *Losing Ground*, in which he argued that the source of poverty among black Americans in particular, the so-called urban underclass, is the attempt to alleviate poverty through social provision. The welfare system, he argued, provides perverse incentives that encourage indolence, wanton sexual reproduction, and general profligacy.

Appropriately for a book bearing a 1984 publication date, *Losing Ground* proposed that the best way to help the poor, therefore, is simply to eliminate all social support. A regimen on the good old-fashioned model of root, hog, or die would shape up that lazy human dreck on pain of extermination. This argument made him the Reagan administration's favorite social scientist and pushed him into a seat on the standing committee of the politburo of the social policy industry.

Imagine the celebrity of Thomas Malthus (maybe even an American Express commercial or a Nike endorsement?) if he could come back into a world with computers that do multiple regression analysis.

As their title implies, Murray and Herrnstein contend that the key to explaining all inequality and all social problems in the United States is stratification by a unitary entity called intelligence, or "cognitive ability"—as measured, of course, by "IQ." This claim has resurfaced repeatedly over the last seventy-five years only to be refuted each time as unfounded class, race, and gender prejudice. (See, for instance, Stephen Jay Gould's *The Mismeasure of Man*.) Yet *The Bell Curve* advances it with the same deluge of statistical and logical sophistries that has driven its predecessors.

Murray and Herrnstein reject a substantial body of scholarship discrediting the idea that there is some single thing identifiable as "intelligence" that can be measured and assigned numerical rank. Instead, they see rigid IQ stratification operating through every sphere of social life.

But *The Bell Curve* adds two new wrinkles. First is the claim that IQ stratification is becoming ever more intense and central in a supposedly postindustrial world that requires and rewards cognitive ability over all else. Second, they shy away from expressing the strength of their eugenic convictions, the memory of the Nazi death camps having not yet faded. Instead of direct endorsement of extermination, mass sterilization, and selective breeding, which nonetheless implicitly shadow the book, Murray and Herrnstein propose a world in which people will be slotted into places that fit their cognitive ability.

The effect will be to end resentment from and against those who seek more than their just deserts. Of course, we'll have to have controls to make sure that dullards do what is best for them and don't get out of line. But that price is necessary to avoid continuing the social breakdown that will eventually force the cognitive elite, increasingly merged with the intellectually ordinary petite bourgeoisie, to mobilize in self-defense and use its superior intelligence to establish itself as an oligarchic caste. We may, that is, have to destroy democracy to save it.

The Bell Curve is—beneath the mind-numbing barrage of numbers—really just a compendium of reactionary prejudices. Despite their insistence that it is not so reducible, the authors frequently infer "cognitive ability" from education or simply class position. For example, corporate CEOs must have high IQs, the authors decide, for how else could they have risen to lead large complex organizations?

IQ shapes farsightedness, moral sense, the decisions not to get pregnant, to be employed, not to be a female head of household, to marry and to remain married to one's first spouse (presumably the divorced and remarried Murray has an exemption from this criterion), to nurture and attend to one's offspring, etc.

Simply being stopped but not charged by the police becomes evidence of an IQ-graded tendency to criminality. (White men who never have been stopped have an average IQ of 106; those who have been schlep along at 103.) Instructively, they restrict their analysis of white criminality to a male sample and parenting to a female sample. "Parents" = mothers. And while they examine abuse and neglect of children among this female sample, spousal abuse is mentioned nowhere in the book, much less considered a discrete form of male criminality.

The analysis of supposed white variation in IQ, though, is ultimately a front to fend off charges of racism. What really drives this book, and reflects the diabolical power of the Murray/Herrnstein combination, is its claim to demonstrate black intellectual inferiority. They use IQ to support a "twofer": opposition to affirmative action, which only overplaces incompetent blacks, and contention that black poverty derives from the existence of an innately inferior black underclass. (They actually waffle on their key claim, that IQ is inherited and fixed by nature, but, having granted in passing that it may not be, they go on to treat it as immutable.)

As has been conventional to a stream of racism claiming scientific justification since Thomas Jefferson, Murray and Herrnstein feign a posture of neutral, if not pained, messengers delivering the indisputable facts. Since the book's publication, Murray has insisted that he and Herrnstein in no way want to be associated with racism, that the book is not even about race, which is the topic of only one of the book's twenty-two chapters. Beneath his distinctively sibilant piety, here, as elsewhere, Murray is a liar.

In addition to the infamous Chapter 13, "Ethnic Differences in Cognitive Ability," three others center on arguments about black (and, to varying degrees, Latino) inferiority. The very next chapter, "Ethnic Inequalities in Relation to IQ," is a direct attempt to explain existing racial stratification along socioeconomic lines as the reflection of differences in group intelligence. The other two chapters in Part III seek to pull together claims about racial differences in intelligence and behavior. Those four chapters set the stage for the book's only two explicitly policy-driven chapters, "Affirmative Action in Higher Education" and "Affirmative Action in the Workplace," both of which are about initiatives directed toward blacks and slide into stoking white populist racism with hypothetical cases of poor or working class whites shunted aside in favor of underqualified, well-off blacks.

Murray's protests suggest something about his views of race, however. *The Bell Curve* makes a big deal of restricting the eight chapters of Part II to discussion of whites alone. Whites, presumably, are also a "race," as much as blacks, Latinos, and Asians are. Therefore, well over half the book is organized consciously around race as a unit of analysis. Moreover, the theme of racially skewed intelligence runs through the entire book. And how could it be otherwise in a book whose point is that the society is and must be stratified by intelligence, which is distributed unequally among individuals and racial groups and cannot be changed in either.

Despite their attempts to insulate themselves from the appearance of racism, Herrnstein and Murray display a perspective worthy of an Alabama filling station. After acknowledging that genetic variations among individuals in a given race are greater than those among races, they persist in maintaining that racially defined populations must differ genetically in significant ways, otherwise they wouldn't have different skin color or hair texture.

Most tellingly, however, they attempt explicitly to legitimize the work of J. Philippe Rushton, the Canadian psychologist who resuscitates classic nineteenth-century scientific racism in its most literal trappings—measuring cranial capacities, brain weights, and penis sizes to argue for racially separate rates and patterns of evolution. They announce self-righteously that "Rushton's work is not that of a crackpot or a bigot, as many of his critics are given to charging." This about a man who attempts racial rankings on "Criteria for Civilization" (only "Caucasoids," naturally enough, have met all the twenty-one criteria on his checklist) and "Personality and Temperament Traits," in addition to erect penis size (by length and circumference, no less) and who computes an "Interbreeding Depression Score" to help clarify his statistical findings!

The Rushton connection reflects a particularly revealing and sinister aspect of the Herrnstein/Murray collaboration. It is embedded in the intellectual apparatus of the cryptofascist right. The central authorities on whom they rely for their claims about IQ, race, and heredity are nearly all associated with the Pioneer Fund, an ultrarightist foundation that boasts of having been almost entirely responsible for funding IQ and race and heredity research in the United States in the last twenty years, and much of it worldwide. (Rushton, along with almost everyone else who writes jacket blurbs for his book, is a major recipient of Pioneer grants.)

The Fund is also deeply implicated in the movement to restrict immigration (see Ruth Conniff, "The War on Aliens" in the October 1993 issue of *The Progressive*) and has helped bankroll California's nativist Proposition 187. Wealthy American eugenicist racists created the Fund in the 1930s, as Stefan Kuhl recounts in *The Nazi Connection: Eugenics, American Racism, and German National Socialism*, to " 'improve the character of the American people' by encouraging the procreation of descendants of 'white persons who settled the original thirteen colonies prior to the adoption of the constitution.' "

Professor Barry Sautman of the Hong Kong University of Science and Technology notes that this international network of racist scholars, quite like Herrnstein and Murray, recently has converged around tentative claims that Asians, especially Northeast Asians, rank above

whites on the scale of competence. The researchers hold up this thesis, which is gaining adherents among Asian reactionaries, as a way of
deflecting charges of racism.

What makes this international vipers' nest so dangerous is that
many of its members have maintained academic respectability. Rushton, for instance, as recently as 1988 won a Guggenheim Fellowship.
Others routinely do contract research for the U.S. military. Most hold
respectable university appointments. I can't account for the others'
legitimacy because their academic precincts are far enough away from
mine that I don't have a sense for the protocols that govern them or
what other kinds of scholarship they may do.

But Murray is a different matter. He has been an intellectual Brown
Shirt since he first slithered into public life. He has neither changed
nor done anything else that might redeem his reputation as a scholar.
We can trace his legitimacy to the spineless opportunism and racial and
ideological bad faith of the liberals in the social-policy establishment.
They have never denounced him. Instead, across the board they have
acquiesced in his desire to be seen as a serious and careful, albeit conservative, scholar. They appear on panels with him and engage him as
a fellow worker in the vineyard of truth. They have allowed him to set
the terms of debate over social welfare and bend over backward not to
attack him sharply. Take a look, for instance at the first chapter of
William Julius Wilson's catechism of liberal underclass ideology, *The
Truly Disadvantaged*, and compare the way that Wilson treats liberal
and left critics of the culture of poverty notion and the way he treats
Murray.

Indeed, their response to *The Bell Curve* should give us important
insight into just how bankrupt the new technicians of dispossession
are. There's not much reason for optimism on this score. In July 1994,
Daniel Patrick Moynihan announced at his Senate Finance Committee hearing on welfare reform that we could be witnessing the
processes of "speciation" at work among the inner-city poor. And he
did so with the assent of Secretary of Health and Human Services
Donna Shalala, and her two world-class liberal poverty-researcher
undersecretaries, Mary Jo Bane and David Ellwood (the originator of
the "two years and off" policy who, incidentally, shows up in *The Bell
Curve*'s acknowledgments). Just how different is that from Rushton or
the Aryan Nation or the old White Citizens Council?

BREAKING RANKS

Hugh Pearson

W HEN I WAS in the third grade an idea caught on among two of my fellow African-American classmates and me as we walked back and forth from our predominantly white elementary school adjacent to the small black middle-class enclave in which we lived in Fort Wayne, Indiana. The year was 1966, and it was character-ized by news accounts of a dynamic twenty-five-year-old named Stokely Carmichael, a leader of the Student Nonviolent Coordinating Committee (SNCC), who was popularizing something called Black Power.

If you believed in Black Power and you were a male, you stopped cutting your hair close to the scalp. You started wearing sunglasses, even in the dark. You took a liking to black leather jackets and black turtleneck sweaters. And, most important, you put on a black leather glove and began balling your hand into a fist, then raising your fist above your head in a salute as you repeated the mantra, "Black Power!" After the youthful activists in SNCC erroneously concluded that as a result of their failure to gain power in Mississippi and Alabama the electoral avenues to power were closed off to blacks,

Hugh Pearson is an editorial writer for *The Wall Street Journal*, and is the author of *The Shadow of the Panther: Huey Newton and the Price of Black Power in America*. His piece origi-nally appeared in *The Wall Street Journal*, November 23, 1994.

something first uttered by the recently assassinated Malcolm X was added to the slogan: "By Any Means Necessary!"

That addendum ushered in a youthful romanticism with guns, and large-scale black support for the 1967 riots in Newark and Detroit. Other SNCC leaders such as H. Rap Brown fanned the flames, encouraging violence in places like Cambridge, Maryland. Simultaneously Huey Newton's Black Panthers dazzled us with their rifles, berets, leather-jacketed military formations, and impressive drills. And hundreds of thousands of black youths became convinced that the society we were to enter as adults held no future for us.

Schoolwork, my two Black Power chanting elementary-school classmates and I decided, was for white people. Our take on Black Power meant not only that we were supposed to stop excelling in "the white man's school," but that we were to glorify one segment of the black community. The Black Panthers called them the lumpen proletariat.

They said that the lumpen proletariat, who constituted the poorest and least-skilled blacks, were the noblest of us all. So my two classmates and I reasoned that our middle-class families—particularly ones like mine in which my father was a physician—weren't truly black. How could my father be? Every time I used the English language improperly, he corrected me. The lumpen proletariat had their own speech patterns. Every time he took me to the barbershop and I attempted to let my hair stay put, he insisted that it be cut short. To my young mind he wasn't "acting black."

It wasn't long before, due to the Ds and occasional Fs on my report cards, my third-grade teacher began calling home insisting that I be held back from promotion to the fourth grade.

Black Power sloganeering be damned, thought my father. The idea that a violent American revolution could be pulled off by blacks was foolish. The notion that excelling in school meant "acting white" was beyond silly. To my father, the naive youthful behavior encouraged by the Black Power movement could only popularize once again the racist belief the civil rights movement originally set out to destroy: that blacks were a different species of human from whites.

And now the threat that that belief will become popular is presented once again. Only this time it comes from a new book written by a pair of white researchers. *The Bell Curve* by Charles Murray and Richard Herrnstein argues that, on average, black IQs are naturally lower than white IQs, raising the possibility that the nation will witness something that has never happened before. Black and white weariness due to the issue of race could combine with conclusions drawn from the book by certain decision makers to induce a national retreat from commitment to equal opportunity.

However, if read closely enough with a clear eye for reality, *The Bell Curve* could contain the ingredients for a different response. The authors discuss something called the Flynn Effect, in which over time IQ scores tend to drift upward among groups of people, a phenomenon that could only be due to improvements in the environment overriding any possible genetic basis for IQ performance. According to the Flynn Effect, over time the average IQ scores among a nation's population have been shown to increase by as much as one point per year, posting gains comparable to the fifteen points separating black and white IQ averages today. The only catch is that the authors argue it's doubtful the fifteen-point gap in average IQ scores between blacks and whites will be closed, since the Flynn Effect will happen equally among blacks and whites.

Apparently the authors didn't observe the educational environment among large numbers of black youths closely enough. Even today numerous black students tell of being made to feel uncomfortable if they apply themselves and get good grades. Such a tactic is the legacy of the type of behavior I experienced in the sixth grade.

My father ignored my third-grade teacher's advice, and I was not held back from promotion to the fourth grade. Neither was I held back from promotion to the fifth or sixth grades, despite my poor report cards. By the time I reached the sixth grade I was determined to enter junior high school at the highest level of the tracking system. So I applied myself in class and registered the greatest improvement in test scores of any student in my predominantly white school, only to hear a black classmate say, "I guess you think you're like the white students now."

That a black child would think that way about excelling academically underscores the indelible damage done to my classmates by the Black Power movement, though the movement also left many of us with a lasting racial pride. However, in the long run, the damage may have outweighed that benefit. Plenty of rap music performers have picked up where the Black Power movement left off, as they promote the notion among black youths that there is a unique black language and way of seeing the world that need only be defended to outsiders with the simple phrase: "It's a black thing. You wouldn't understand." So instead of applying themselves in English and math, thousands of black youths dedicate their energy to scratching records, mixing samples of music, and using their voices to create staccato rhymes.

Energy and industriousness that create an entire new window of economic opportunity should, on the one hand, be admired. Yet on the other hand, like black accomplishment in professional basketball, rap delivers the skewed message to black youths that their hopes and dreams need only be applied in a few limited directions. It signals that diversity of ambition and industry is "a white thing that blacks wouldn't understand."

The magnitude of the problem suggests that turning such attitudes around could more than make up for any natural environmental improvement that will occur among other youths through the Flynn Effect. A concerted effort to do so could mean that within fifteen years the fifteen-point gap in black and white IQ averages would be closed.

The question is whether our society will commit to such a turn-around. At the moment that doesn't appear likely. We're too balkanized, too determined to read what we wish to read into research findings, a tendency that is seen in the authors of *The Bell Curve*. Because our Constitution is dedicated to providing equal opportunity rather than a road map to the creation of a caste society, turning this situation around is the first step needed if we are to glean anything useful from a book like *The Bell Curve*.

DEFINING RACE

Steven A. Holmes

A S T H E C O N V E R S A T I O N about race and racism swells to a cacophony of accusations, defenses, and rationalizations, one question seems not to have been addressed: what do we mean by race, anyhow?

At first blush the answer seems self-evident. There are black people, and yellow people and white people and red people, aren't there? Everyone knows that. But in recent years there is a surprising lack of agreement among scientists over the popular notions of what constitutes a racial group. And even in their book, *The Bell Curve*, which suggests that differences in intelligence between races are a matter of inheritance, Richard J. Herrnstein and Charles Murray, duck the question. "The rule we follow here is a simple one," they write, "to classify people according to the way they classify themselves." That might be a fine standard for measuring racial disparities in housing, income or employment. But when it's applied to biology, things get murky. Racial categories, especially in the United States, are often more poetry than science. American blacks almost invariably have some white ancestry, so their classification has more to do with politics and culture than with genes.

Steven A. Holmes is a reporter for *The New York Times*. This article originally appeared as "You're Smart If You Know What Race You Are" in *The New York Times*, October 23, 1994.

Take, for example, Lani Guinier, the University of Pennsylvania Law School professor whose nomination to run the Justice Department's Civil Rights Division was withdrawn last year. She refers to herself as an African American, like her father. But she also notes that her mother is Jewish. Is she, for the purposes of empirically measuring inherited racial differences, a light-skinned black or a dark-skinned Jew?

In the Herrnstein-Murray methodology, a group is the sum of decisions by millions of individuals on where to place themselves. But that can change substantially with the political and social climate. The Census Bureau notes that the number of Native Americans rose by 72 percent from 1970 to 1980 and by 38 percent from 1980 to 1990. The jump is clearly more the result of heightened Indian pride than an impossibly large increase in Indian pregnancies.

The problem is giving second thoughts to the federal government. The Office of Management and Budget is considering changing the racial classifications used on federal forms, including the census. Any change, such as adding a category of "mixed race," could have many ramifications in areas like voting rights and allocation of federal funds. Those looking to science to help clarify the issue may have to search elsewhere. In a 1985 survey of physical and cultural anthropologists, 50 percent agreed that there is such a thing as race, biologically speaking, and 41 percent disagreed. "That's a revolution," said Leonard Lieberman, a professor of sociology and anthropology at Central Michigan University, who conducted the study. "Here is a concept around which this discipline had its beginnings. But now there is no longer a consensus."

Few scientists doubt that there are genetic differences between groups, but many say any division of *Homo sapiens* into four or five discrete groups is arbitrary. Take skin color, the most commonly cited racial trait. Does it help science distinguish among the sub-Saharan Africans, the people of southern India, and the aboriginal people of Australia? All have dark skin. But the three are considered to be of different races.

Some of the other genetic similarities between peoples make for interesting groupings. Jared Diamond, a professor of physiology at the UCLA School of Medicine, notes that only Eastern European Jews and French Canadians are genetically predisposed to Tay-Sachs disease. Does that make them a racial group? Likewise, the gene that produces sickle-cell anemia is relatively common among Africans, the people of the Arabian Peninsula, and southern India. But it is rare among Northern Europeans and the Xhosa people of South Africa. Does that make Nelson Mandela and Bjorn Borg racial kin? "We have information about far more similarities and differences among people based on traits other than skin color," Professor Diamond said. "But traditionally we have classified people by what we can actually see."

Anthropologists who defend the notion of race argue that while skin color may not be the best determinant, people who trace ancestry to the same geographic neighborhood and have similar inherited characteristics ought to be considered a single group. "Races refer to geographically separated portions of species that are distinguishable by inherited characteristics," said Vincent Sarich, a professor of anthropology at the University of California at Berkeley. "That in no sense says that, therefore, all human variations need be explained racially."

It is hardly a wonder that some scientists feel the best way to approach the concept of race is not to. "Historically, the word has been used in so many different ways that it's no longer useful in our science," Douglas Ubelaker, a physical anthropologist and a curator with the Smithsonian Institution's National Museum of Natural History, said recently in *Discover* magazine. "I choose not to define it at all. I leave the term alone."

TOO CLEVER BY HALF

The Economist

H ERE IS A CHALLENGE: find a man who can create a sensation big enough to displace O. J. Simpson in the headlines and on the covers of magazines. The first person who leaps to mind is probably not a balding, right-wing social scientist employed at a Washington think-tank. But Charles Murray, a fellow of the American Enterprise Institute, has a proven knack for making himself the talk of the nation. His latest, greatest splash is his second within a year.

"Every once in a while the sky really is falling," Mr. Murray wrote twelve months ago, as a prelude to a devastating analysis of America's figures for out-of-wedlock births—"the single most important social problem of our time," he argued, because it drove everything else. He revelled in alarming statistics. For blacks, illegitimacy had reached 68 percent of births in 1991, for blacks in inner cities it was typically higher than 80 percent, and although the figure for whites was still only 22 percent, it was closely related to poverty and on a rising path that threatened to lead to a white underclass.

The Murray formula for sensation-making was thus established. Be interesting (the illegitimacy story was certainly that). Be outrageous (Mr. Murray's cure for the problem: abolish welfare and build orphan-

This unsigned article appeared in *The Economist*, October 22, 1994.

ages). And be timely (the government was in the process of putting together its proposals for welfare reform and President Clinton, while disagreeing with Mr. Murray's suggested solution, praised him for setting out the problem so well).

Now Mr. Murray has repeated the formula, to even more stunning effect, with a new book, *The Bell Curve: Intelligence and Class Structure in American Life,* co-written by Richard Herrnstein, a Harvard psychology professor who died in September 1994. The ensuing fuss has mobilized an army of columnists and catapulted the book's theme to the cover of *Newsweek* and other magazines. At the *New Republic,* whose recent issue carried an eleven-page extract along with sixteen pages of rebuttals by a score of writers, the decision to give Mr. Murray such play caused apoplexy. His admirers praise him for daring to air controversial arguments and publicize uncomfortable evidence; his detractors accuse him of dangerous pseudoscience.

Like a dentist who hits a raw nerve and then coolly keeps on drilling, Mr. Murray writes with deceptively soothing, white-coated reasonableness as he inspires the inevitable outcry. His argument is that American society is increasingly stratified according to people's intelligence. A few decades ago, he says, people of high intelligence (or "cognitive ability," as measured in IQ tests) were scattered through a wide range of jobs. But the democratization of higher education and the march of technology have led to a highly efficient sorting process which has produced a striking concentration of bright people in a few high-earning, high-status occupations. Meanwhile, at the other end of the intelligence distribution—the "bell curve" of the book's title—a large and self-perpetuating crowd of the dimmest people, the swelling underclass, is stuck in poverty.

In this triumph of meritocracy, the clever folk (or "cognitive elite") are increasingly isolated from the rest, intermarrying, sending their children to private schools, living in secure enclaves. The dim caste festers and breeds. Mr. Murray conjures up the prospect of a "custodial state" in which a substantial minority of the population lives in "a high-tech and more lavish version of the Indian reservation."

So far, so consistent with some fairly commonplace warnings about America's widening inequalities and solidifying class structure. But Mr. Murray also argues that intelligence, rather than background or social status, is the most powerful determinant of poverty and of a swath of serious social problems, from crime to unemployment and welfare dependency. Most explosively, he claims that intelligence is substantially inherited (so there is nothing much that traditional social policy can do about it). In the Murray-Herrnstein view, racial differences in IQ scores—Asians as a group score somewhat higher than whites, while blacks score way below average—have very little to do with any cultural bias in the tests or environmental influences, and very much to do with genes. "Success and failure in the American economy, and all that goes with it," say the authors, "are increasingly a matter of the genes that people inherit."

It is this genetic and racial argument that has touched off the furor over the book. Hardly surprising, given the abhorrent uses to which analogous arguments have been put this century, from forced sterilization to apartheid, not to mention the Holocaust. In his pre-emptive defense, Mr. Murray surrounds his tale with caveats (the fascination with race is "misbegotten," the group averages are irrelevant to how individuals should be treated), while at the same time insisting that the sensitivity of the subject should not prevent important evidence from getting a proper airing.

Much of the evidence presented is indeed fascinating. It is intriguing to learn, for example, about the effects of the sharp increase in competition in the 1950s on the quality of students at Harvard, as measured by standard verbal tests: the average freshman in 1952 would have been in the bottom 10 percent of the incoming class by 1960. Eyebrows naturally rise at the information that whites with an IQ in the bottom 5 percent of the bell curve are fifteen times more likely to be poor than those in the top 5 percent, or that women in the bottom 5 percent are six times as likely to have an illegitimate child as those in the top 5 percent. It is certainly mind-concentrating that the average black person tests higher than only about 16 percent of whites. Remember the Murray formula for sensation-making. The first rule— tell an interesting story—is adhered to.

And so is the second rule—outrageousness. Mr. Murray well knows the explosiveness of the genetic-racial part of his argument, yet he bases it on little or no evidence. He admits that "the state of knowledge does not permit a precise estimate" of the degree of heritability of intelligence, so he opts for a "middling estimate" that about 60 percent is in the genes. Others would argue that the natural sciences permit a fairly exact estimate of the influence of genes on the ethnic differences in IQ scores: close to zero.

Mr. Murray may be wrong, besides, to assume that the cognitive elite will stay on top. Paul Krugman, an economics professor at Stanford, speculated recently that although tax lawyers may be replaced by computers, gardeners and house cleaners will still be essential. He added: "The high-skilled professions that have done so well in the last twenty years may be the modern counterpart of early nineteenth-century weavers, whose incomes soared after the mechanization of spinning, only to crash when technological revolution reached their own craft."

The flimsiness of Mr Murray's central pillars suggests that his work is less scientific than political. Re-enter the third rule of sensation-making, timeliness. If hereditary intelligence is crucial, much state intervention is pointless. Mr Murray argues against forlorn egalitarianism, whether in schools or in the workplace, and in favor of embracing stratification because "trying to pretend that inequality does not exist has led to disaster." The state, he insists, can help neighborhoods by withdrawing from them, should stop encouraging low-IQ women to have babies, should filter immigration by ability rather than by family.

This comes at a time when, as hundreds of vexed Washington politicians can attest as they campaign around the country, Americans are deeply disillusioned with government, and when a fed-up nation is groping for new answers. Along comes Mr Murray, pandering to popular prejudice and feeding one side of the ideological battle taking shape in America. Like it or no, Charles Murray and the zeitgeist make an awesome combination.

CORRELATION AS CAUSATION

David Suzuki

M ODERN LIFE is accompanied by familiar problems of violence, bigotry, poverty, alienation, and environmental degradation. But too often we deal with symptoms rather than getting at the
underlying roots of today's problems. Take environmental problems.
Once pollution has reached crisis levels, cleaning it up is often difficult
or impossible. But we have no way to mandate prevention of the production or release of pollutants in the first place. Or consider tubercu-
losis. Most of us have been exposed to the TB bacterium at some time
but never get the disease (I test TB-positive). Most people who
develop TB live on reservations or in slums and/or have AIDS. Discrimination and poverty are the real causes of TB, but it seems far easier to focus on the bacterium.

This is the context to consider the revived debate on the relative
roles of heredity and the environment in determining IQ scores in different races. It has been fueled by the recent publication of *The Bell
Curve* by two Americans, social scientist Charles Murray and psychologist Richard Herrnstein, and *Race, Evolution, and Behavior* by Canadian
psychologist Philippe Rushton. The books claim heredity is the major

David Suzuki is a Vancouver-based journalist, broadcaster, and author; his most recent
book is *Time to Change*. This article was published as "IQ Debate Treats Us As Cipher," in
the *Toronto Star*, November 12, 1994.

cause of the differences in average IQ test scores of black and white people.

It's a familiar rationale to justify eliminating programs for the disadvantaged—just blame the victims for having poor genes. More than twenty years ago, a president of the Canadian Medical Association recommended sterilization of welfare recipients before they receive welfare checks.

Lay people and scientists alike often fall into the trap of mistaking a correlation as causation. For example, there is a high correlation between nicotine-stained teeth and fingers with lung cancer. But that does not mean that stained fingers and teeth cause the disease. Yet correlations between an ethnic group and crime, poverty, or drug abuse are often claimed as causally based. Whatever IQ tests measure, heredity does influence the score achieved. And no one disputes the fifteen-point difference in average IQ scores between black and white populations. The question is, What causes that difference? Rushton, Murray, and Herrnstein are not geneticists. To geneticists, classifications based on skin color gives us groupings that are biologically meaningless. Besides, so long as society imposes such totally different social conditions and pressures on the basis of skin color, the cause basis for differences in IQ scores of blacks and whites can never be answered scientifically.

Even when a trait is genetically determined, its expression can be modified environmentally. Thus, genes that cause defects in response to high temperature or bright sunlight need not be expressed if the triggering conditions are avoided. And for a trait as complex as intelligence, there is lots of room to manipulate environmental conditions that affect it. Intelligence itself is an elusive entity. We claim it as a characteristic of our species, yet what intelligent creature, knowing air, water, soil, and biodiversity keep us alive, would behave as destructively as we do? Furthermore, there is no indication that levels of intelligence correlate with other important human traits of honesty, kindness, compassion, integrity, or generosity.

In any city, there are tens of thousands who have IQ scores above 120 or below 80. But what does that inform us about those people whose shared quality is a test score? They are just as liable to be stupid, greedy, ambitious, clever, bad, and good as people in any other group. The wonderful complexity and diversity of people cannot be encompassed by a single number or word. We are not ciphers. We do not deal with people as groups but as individuals with their own qualities and needs. Why waste time debating a question that can't be answered when there are things we can do? Discrimination and economic inequities underlie much of human poverty and misery and we can do something about changing the conditions if we stop trying to find excuses not to try.

You see, the way we deal with the disadvantaged defines who and what we are.

BLOOD SIMPLE

Carl Rowan

A YOUNG news executive here asked me, "What's your reaction to that *Bell Curve* book about the genetic inferiority of black people?"

I laughed. Confused, he said, "I thought you'd be angry and call it a dangerous book."

"It is useless, damaging, and dangerous in these times of deep racial troubles in America," I said.

I was laughing because I was reminded of the funny ways in which claims of black inferiority have graduated from the crude and comical to elitist pseudoscientific. I explained how, when I was in Mississippi just before and after the 1954 Supreme Court decision outlawing racial segregation in public schools, the defenders of Jim Crow never talked about genes; "Negro blood" was the feared substance.

A circuit judge, Tom P. Brady, was warning white people against "race mixin' " by asserting that "one drop of black blood thickens the lips, flattens the nose and puts out the lights of intellect." Brady said, "Whenever and wherever the white man has drunk the cup of black hemlock, whenever and wherever his blood has been infused with the blood of the Negro, the white man, his intellect and his culture have died."

Carl Rowan is a syndicated columnist. This column appeared in the *Buffalo News*, November 1, 1994, titled "Must We Go Through This Again?"

Then I recalled asking others who claimed blacks were inherently inferior how they explained the achievements of Ralph Bunche, Marian Anderson, and Jesse Owens. "Well, they must have some white blood in 'em" was the frequent reply. I was grimly amused by the contradictory assertions that one drop of "Negro blood" would destroy a white man, yet "some white blood" could lift an inferior black to greatness.

These crazy "blood" theories were not limited to backwoods bigots. The Reverend G. T. Gillespie, a leader in the Presbyterian church and president emeritus of Belhaven College, wrote an article, "A Christian View on Segregation," in which he said that the child of an interracial marriage would be weaker than either parent. He said that "the intermingling of breeding stock results invariably in the production of 'scrubs' or mongrel types, and the downgrading of the whole herd."

If educational, economic, and other public policies are to be based on the mumbo jumbo in *The Bell Curve* book, which says in effect that it is hopeless to try to lift blacks up to the level of whites, how do we now decide who is "black"? I know black children from black-Jewish marriages who are practicing Jews (or nominal Methodists), brilliant in the classroom and stars on the baseball, football, and soccer fields. Do they get a societal assumption that they are smart because they are half Jewish? Or do they get myriad denials of opportunity because they are genetically of some African descent, with the curved bell ringing out stupid cries that they somehow must be a trifle lower in intelligence?

I laughed at my Nashville colleague's question because I remembered going to New Orleans on New Year's Day in 1956 to see the first black play in the Sugar Bowl. Jim Crow hotel practices forced me to stay with a Negro family, one of very light-skinned people. One female in that family had been "passing" for years and was in fact married to one of the richest white men in New Orleans. She came to the family dinner alone and told me how she had recently been attacked by a little dog that tore her stockings. The dog's white owner had run out to apologize and offer new stockings, explaining, "I don't know what's wrong with Bitsy. She usually only attacks niggers."

That dog that discerned so much about the "blood" and genes of this "passing" woman might well have been the chief researcher for Charles Murray and the late Richard J. Herrnstein, authors of this dreadful book.

RESURGENT RACISM

Cynthia Tucker

W HEN I WAS growing up in Monroeville, Alabama, in the 1960s, I had a rosy view of the future. Though I lived under the lash of Jim Crow, I believed that America would change for the better until racism had been eradicated from the land—perhaps in my lifetime. Wasn't the Reverend Martin Luther King, Jr. ringing up victories at a rapid rate?

The future fooled me. Progress, I have learned, is no steady or certain thing. America has arrived at a time when racism is resurgent, intolerance increasing, hate crimes on the rise. We live in an era of backlash. The polls reflect a nation whose white citizens are tired of the black and brown poor, wary of immigrants, resentful of expanding civil rights. Blacks, for their part, are cynical about racial progress. The political climate is rife with cheap demagoguery and petty scapegoating. Welfare mothers, Mexicans, feminists, and gays top the hatemongers' hit list.

But there is no more telling indicator of political and social backlash than the recent publication of a book called *The Bell Curve*, which suggests that some racial groups are genetically predisposed to have higher IQs than others. It is racism in its most pernicious form. Actu-

Cynthia Tucker is the editorial page editor of *The Atlanta Journal and Constitution*, where this article was published, October 30, 1994, titled "Bell Curve Tolls Revival of Racisim."

ally, *The Bell Curve* leaps right over backlash; it appears out of a time warp. It recycles the pseudoscience of a century ago, when researchers, through such dubious methods as measuring the size of skulls and other body parts, concluded that northern Europeans were the smartest people on the planet.

A nineteenth-century intellectual dilettante named Francis Galton—who coined the term *eugenics*—beat Charles Murray and the late Richard J. Herrnstein to their thesis by more than a hundred years. As Pat Shipman points out in her book *The Evolution of Racism*, Galton, who was "convinced that the difference in human success simply reflected the quality of the breeding material," wrote *Hereditary Genius* in 1869. Science has come a long way since then, and those views have been widely discredited. But that did not stop Murray and Herrnstein from dredging them up under the guise of new research and analysis.

I have grown inured to the hateful harangues of radio talk-show hosts, the pointed racism of some politicians, the resentment so many whites harbor toward black progress. Still, I am stunned by *The Bell Curve*. This is an ugly piece of work with an even uglier agenda. Murray is the man who wrote *Losing Ground*, a conservative screed that blamed welfare benefits for creating a host of society's ills. While many of his conclusions have since been picked apart by more objective researchers, *Losing Ground*, published in 1984, nevertheless provided an intellectual underpinning for those who wished to abolish welfare.

Murray's latest book has a broader and more dangerous agenda. It provides a facile argument for those who would abandon efforts to help the less affluent. After all, if success is largely determined by biology, why bother with Head Start, Upward Bound, college remedial courses, prenatal care funds for the poor, or in-school free-meal programs?

Murray and Herrnstein concede that there are many blacks who are highly accomplished scholars and professionals. What they fail to acknowledge is that much of the current crop of black physicians, scientists, and lawyers would have been shut out of the economic mainstream were it not for the idealistic social programs started in the 1960s.

America does not have to go back to the future with Murray and Herrnstein. We can do better because we know better.

SO WHAT!

Tom Christie

M ISSING in the flurry of words responding to Charles Murray's and Richard Herrnstein's book, *The Bell Curve*, in which they suggest a racial IQ hierarchy (Asians and whites at the top, followed by Latinos and blacks), are these two: "So what!"

Although denunciations by everyone from Jesse Jackson to the social critic Mickey Kaus are understandable—and perhaps necessary to fend off Murray's pernicious Darwinian social agenda (for which the book was written)—there may be a more laissez-faire approach. I'm thinking of a comment by Bono, lead singer of the Irish rock band U2. "We Irish don't put people on the moon," he said, "but we've written some pretty good books." Ethnic pride, in other words, need not be based on rocket scientists—or intelligence quotient—alone.

A few years ago, a poll of the European Community found the Irish to be the happiest people in Europe. It didn't say who were the smartest. Nor do Murray and Herrnstein—though they note in passing that European Ashkenazi Jews score highest on IQ tests. But I'd hazard a guess that, in addition to the Ashkenazis, a number of European ethnic groups would outperform the Irish.

Tom Christie is a contributing editor of *Buzz*. This piece appeared as "IQ Furor? So What!" in the *Los Angeles Times*, November 20, 1994.

The Irish part of me can live with that, somehow, within the collective shadow thrown by the likes of William Butler Yeats, James Joyce, Samuel Beckett, George Bernard Shaw, and Oscar Wilde. There's so much to Ireland: the magical beauty of the land; the charm and poetry of its people, and what I would call their common intelligence—which seems to emanate from the intersection of simplicity and sophistication. (The result, of course, is profundity.) No statistically significant numbers of rocket scientists? So what?

Few of us, after all, have contributed anything notable to the modern technological world—not automobiles, PCs, televisions, fax machines, microchips, ATMs, VCRs, or on-line services. Moreover, most of us don't have a clue as to how these things even work. Yet we go on, blithely indifferent to most everything beyond what's for dinner. What Murray and Herrnstein are saying, though, in a book that might have been better titled "The Ultimate Revenge of the Nerds," is that the few who do know how these things work—and especially those who create them—are going to get richer and richer while the rest of us get poorer and poorer.

I can live with this, too. After all, I'm already living with the knowledge that baseball and basketball players are worth millions, that many CEOs are worth hundreds of millions, and that a fellow named Snoop Doggy Dogg has the Number 1 record in the country. Hey, go figure, it's the marketplace!

So I can also live with the notion that most computer scientists of the next century are likely to be Asian. As long as society, as a whole, benefits, and as long as their realm remains open to those who look like me, so be it. And so what.

What is far more difficult to live with, however, are the dangers inherent to such divisive studies—that one group lords it over and then uses it against another. If the authors know that Ashkenazi Jews score highest, do they also know how other European groups score, and aren't telling us? Imagine if someone compared European IQs by country or ethnic group. Imagine just how harmful this information would be to the community of nations now attempting to unify.

The T-shirt joke (Heaven is when the police are British, the cooks Italian, the mechanics German, the lovers French, and it's all organized by the Swiss; Hell is when the chefs are British, the mechanics

French, the lovers Swiss, the police German, and it's all organized by the Italians) would be rewritten—as it was in 1939.

But that, of course, is not going to happen. Because no Europeans are that stupid. Are they?

THE LIMITS OF IQ

William Raspberry

C HARLES MURRAY likes nothing better than to toss socio-logical stink bombs and then proclaim, with all his cherubic innocence: I had no *idea* it would smell like that! The innocence this time precedes official release of the newest stink bomb (written with the late Richard Herrnstein): *The Bell Curve: Intelligence and Class Structure in American Life.*

Murray and his co-author set out to examine a trend you might not have noticed as anything new and socially provocative: the isolation of the brightest Americans—and the dumbest—from the rest of the society. What is happening, *The Bell Curve* argues, is that more and more important jobs require more and more brains, that the possessors of these brains tend to marry among themselves, and that (braininess being heritable) the smart get smarter and more firmly in control. On the other end from this "cognitive elite," the dumb also marry among themselves. *Voilà!* The underclass.

Murray, who has been explaining himself in interviews (and also in a byline piece—excerpted from the book—that took most of the editorial page in a recent issue of *The Wall Street Journal*), seems not to notice that he has embraced largely discredited views regarding the

William Raspberry is a syndicated columnist. This column was published as "Is IQ Really Everything?" in *The Washington Post*, October 12, 1994.

heritability, measurability, and immutability of intelligence, or that he may be confusing brains with social advantage. And of course he had no *idea* his conclusion would sound racist.

The simple notion that both the poor and the well-off are members of what, to a significant degree, are self-perpetuating groups isn't much of a stink bomb. The olfactory offense is the contention that this self-perpetuation is IQ-based. Maybe there was a time early in the century when the intelligent were "scattered almost indistinguishably" among the rest of us, say Murray and Herrnstein in their *Journal* piece. No more. "In the job market today, as in the university, *IQ is the critical determining factor* [as] intelligence has become increasingly valuable to employers and workplaces, and salaries have become increasingly stratified by cognitive ability." (Emphasis added.) They then cite as evidence the widening wage gap between the average manufacturing employee and the average engineer. But how much of the gap is explained by the supposed superior cognition of the engineer? Might not the relative scarcity of engineers play some part? The superior education of the engineer? The decreasing influence of labor unions on wage structures? What led them to believe that "IQ is the critical determining factor"?

In fact it's not clear that they did believe it. Two paragraphs after their assertion, they posit an "X factor" to account for the residual wage difference not explained by education, experience, gender, and so on. And what might this X factor be? "It could be rooted in diligence, ambition, or sociability. Conclusive evidence is hard to come by, but we believe that it includes cognitive ability."

Well, that's quite a long (and common-sense) distance from IQ as the "critical determining factor." Even high-IQ authors can get confused. Of course diligence and ambition matter, and of course the predisposition to these traits is greatly influenced by family. It's a darn sight easier to be diligent and ambitious when you grow up with the evidence that diligence pays off. Sociability can be an important personal characteristic, but it can also, like "collegiality" and other such descriptives, be a matter of "fitting in." Do race and class and sex have nothing to do with whether one is deemed to "fit in" at the top levels of power, influence, and income?

The increasing bifurcation of the society may, as Murray and Herrnstein assert, be a fact. My problem is with their judgment that IQ is its principal driving force. Their charts and social-science jargon cannot obscure what experience teaches: the ordinarily intelligent sons and daughters of the well-off do better at those things the authors use as markers for success (income and position, for instance) than the bright children of the very poor. The "crucial determining factor" in my view is opportunity, a term that embraces access, family resources, and influence, non-family relationships, social environment and, still to too great a degree, sex, class, and race.

Murray knows that. Why is he at such pains to deny the widely accepted view that intelligence is more or less randomly distributed and to insist that IQ accounts for both wealth and poverty? Why doesn't he acknowledge what he surely must know: that members of Mensa (the high-IQ society) are no more likely than people of fairly ordinary brainpower to rise to the top ranks of leadership, professional distinction, or income?

Murray is very smart but also something of an intellectual daredevil. Maybe he wanted to prove that he is clever enough to get away with something that cost another smart guy, the late William Shockley, his credibility. Maybe he wanted to rationalize conservative indifference.

Or maybe he's just a balding fifty-one-year-old kid who loves to throw stink bombs.

THE IQ CULT

Brent Staples

EVERYONE KNOWS the stereotype of the fair-haired executive who owes the office with the view and the six-figure salary to an accident of birth—like relatives in the halls of power. What about merit, for heaven's sake? Why not give IQ tests, grant the best jobs to those who score well, and send the laggards to the mailroom?

That would never happen, nor should it. IQ scores in themselves tell you almost nothing. This was clearly explained by the Frenchman Alfred Binet, who invented the first usable IQ test in 1905. The test had one purpose: to help identify learning-disabled children who needed special schools. Binet warned that a "brutal pessimism" would follow if his test was ever mistaken as a measure of a fixed, unchangeable intelligence.

You wouldn't know it from the IQ worship in progress today, but using the tests to draw finer distinctions than Binet intended amounts to overreaching, if not scientific fraud. Most scientists concede that they don't really know what "intelligence" is. Whatever it might be, paper and pencil tests aren't the tenth of it.

The fair-haired executive gets a pass for other reasons entirely. First, because the world works more on insiderism and inherited

Brent Staples is an editorial writer at *The New York Times*, where this article was published, October 28, 1994, titled "The Scientific War on the Poor."

privilege than on "pure merit," whatever that might be. Second, because the charge of innate stupidity has historically been reserved for the poor.

That charge surfaced during the immigrant influx of the teens and 1920s, and again during the affirmative-action '60s and '70s—both times when America found "scientific" justifications of poverty very appealing. Misgivings about the "underclass" have made them appealing again. By way of example, consider Senator Daniel Patrick Moynihan's ludicrous claim that out-of-wedlock births in modern America amounted to the creation of a new species.

Alfred Binet's American imitators embraced "brutal pessimism" right away. In 1912, after Eastern and Southern Europeans began to outnumber Northern Europeans at Ellis Island, immigration authorities asked the psychologist Henry Goddard to do "quality control," through intelligence testing. Goddard and his colleagues believed that Nordic peoples were civilization's best and that the rest were genetically second-rate or worse. The test was merely a means of proving it. Not surprisingly, Goddard's testing of what he called a representative sample of immigrants showed that 80 percent of all Jews, Italians, and Hungarians and nearly 90 percent of Russians were "feeble-minded." As a result, hundreds each year were deported.

At the start of World War I, two million draftees were also tested. The results showed a gap between blacks and whites, but at the time, few were interested. The passion then was proving a connection between "mental deficiency" and national origin among white immigrants. The testers didn't bother with translation; non-English-speakers were instructed in pantomime.

Once again, British immigrants were classified as first-rate, with Poles, Italians, and Russians labeled stupid and undesirable. The data were published by the National Academy of Sciences in 1921, and contributed to the introduction of temporary limits on immigration. IQ hysteria also resulted in sterilization laws that were enforced only against the poor. The IQ believers worked with messianic zeal. Like many before him, the British psychologist Sir Cyril Burt went way beyond science in defense of his beliefs. Burt alleged that intelligence was so wired into the genes, so indifferent to environment, that identical twins reared apart had virtually identical IQ scores. Statisticians now agree that Burt made much of it up.

The IQ worshipers of today remain essentially unchanged from Goddard's time. Despite the impression that there is something new in *The Bell Curve*, its authors, Charles Murray and Richard Herrnstein, have merely reasserted the long-unproven claim that IQ is mainly inherited. The language is calmer, the statistical gimmicks slicker, but the truth remains the same: There exist no plausible data to make the case. Belief to the contrary rests mainly on brutal preconceptions about poverty, but also on a basic confusion between pseudoscience and the real thing.

A LARGE AND ENDURING MARKET

Nell Irvin Painter

A S I F W E H A D N ' T gone through this before, conservatives—this time Charles Murray and the late Richard Herrnstein—have announced that testable intelligence is social destiny. Their book, *The Bell Curve,* argues that people at the bottom of society are there inevitably, and thus all the money spent on welfare and food stamps is a total waste. There's nothing new here.

Thomas Jefferson, who lived as a gentleman thanks to his unpaid workforce, wrote in 1786 in "Notes on Virginia" that blacks had never uttered a subtle or profound thought. He thought that the fault lay in their nature, not their situation, and he disregarded evidence to the contrary. When the poet Phyllis Wheatley and the city planner Benjamin Banneker were brought to his attention, Jefferson denigrated the authenticity and quality of their work.

Francis Galton is the father of intelligence testing, and the main point of his first major work, *Hereditary Genius,* published in 1869, was evident in its title. Galton was a eugenicist, not a disinterested theorizer, and he wanted to make sure that those he saw as unfit did not have too many children.

Nell Irvin Painter teaches American history at Princeton University and is completing a biography of Sojourner Truth. This article, written for the Progressive Media Project, appeared in the *Miami Herald,* October 23, 1994, entitled "A History of Genes as Social Destiny."

Poor whites have long been a target of alarmists who proclaim the fundamental hereditability of intelligence and the too-rapid reproduction of people with low IQs. In 1877, the American sociologist Richard Dugdale published an influential study warning that one feeble-minded family, the Jukes, threatened to overrun upstate New York with its innumerable progeny. The late nineteenth and early twentieth centuries produced a bevy of white American Teutonists and Anglo-Saxonists, including the president of Columbia University, Nicholas Murray Butler; the Columbia political scientist, John W. Burgess; and the Boston Brahmin, Henry Cabot Lodge. These men argued that Teutons and Anglo-Saxons were naturally superior to the millions of southern and eastern immigrants arriving on our shores at the time.

Herbert Spencer, the father of Social Darwinism, who died in 1903, reached conclusions quite similar to those of our present-day conservatives: In the struggle for survival, the fittest would drive out the unfit. Spencer saw this as such a natural process that he opposed public education and all other "socialistic" institutions, including libraries, the post office, and poor relief that would delay the inevitable.

The mid-twentieth-century produced scientific racism and Nazism, which like earlier such notions, lost credence under close scrutiny and the horror of the Holocaust—one of the logical outcomes of this kind of thinking.

What's going on here? Hereditarian thinking is refuted time and again, but after a sabbatical, it returns to be taken seriously again. The attractiveness of hereditary logic in this country—which was built on racial, that is, hereditary, distinctions—is striking. Even though Richard Lewontin, Stephen Jay Gould, and other prominent scholars showed the speciousness of generalizations about hereditary intelligence in the 1970s and 1980s, the theory continues to find new life. The large and enduring market for this kind of argument tells us something disturbing about American culture.

The argument goes like this: (1) intelligence is hereditary and intractable; therefore, (2) welfare and food stamps ought to be abolished.

Even if the statistics were sound (which they're not), and even if the poor were threatening to outbreed the rich (which they're not), abolishing social welfare would not be a logical, sensible, or humane policy to follow.

Instead of further impoverishing the poor, we'd be much better off improving their lot, since higher incomes lower birthrates. This was the lesson of the population conference in Cairo. Rather than impose harsh population control measures, the conference recommended providing women with education and business opportunities so their fertility rates would fall. In the United States, as in other countries around the world, women who can look forward to fulfilling their larger ambitions have fewer children and make greater economic contributions than women who can look forward only to motherhood. If Murray and his cohorts are interested in more than punishing the poor, let them think of ways to help women reach all their goals.

LESSONS OF *THE BELL CURVE*

Christopher Winship

A T A R E C E N T   M E E T I N G of social scientists at the Harvard Business School, Richard Herrnstein's and Charles Murray's controversial book *The Bell Curve* came up. One group reported that in an earlier conversation they had thoroughly "trashed" it. Heads around the room nodded in approval. I asked the room at large—about twenty people—how many had actually read the book. Two raised their hands.

The condemnation of *The Bell Curve* in the media has been equally definitive, if presumably better informed. Most of the analysis has focused on the question raised in the book of whether IQ is hereditary and whether racial differences in IQ are predominantly due to environmental or genetic factors. The consensus appears to be that the book's argument is inherently racist and that Mr. Herrnstein (who died in September 1994) and Mr. Murray are academic charlatans.

Yet while their treatment of these issues has been justly criticized, much of *The Bell Curve* is not about race at all, and parts of it have been misrepresented. For example, a frequent assertion about *The Bell Curve* is that it argues that intelligence is essentially inherited. In fact,

Christopher Winship is a professor of sociology at Harvard University. This piece originally appeared in *The New York Times*, November 15, 1994, titled "Lessons Beyond the Bell Curve."

the authors make the weaker claim that, according to existing research, between 40 and 80 percent of intelligence is in the genes. They adopt the middle of this range, 60 percent, as reasonable. (If you think this amounts to arguing that intelligence is "essentially" inherited, ask yourself whether you would be "essentially" receiving the same pay if you received a 40 percent cut in salary.)

Mr. Herrnstein and Mr. Murray have been rightfully attacked for their shoddy and sometimes contradictory analysis of the relationship between race and intelligence. They acknowledge, for example, that there is no scientific way to determine even within broad ranges what proportion of the difference is due to environment and what proportion due to genes. After offering this critical warning, however, the authors conclude that the racial gap is more likely genetic than environmental—a divisive and irresponsible line of argument.

Yet, in spite of its serious flaws, *The Bell Curve* offers three potentially valuable insights that should not easily be dismissed. The first is that as a society we are becoming increasingly socially and economically stratified by level of cognitive ability. This is an observation that has been made by others from widely different political perspectives, including Secretary of Labor Robert Reich. The dramatic increase over the last two decades in the difference in incomes between high school and college graduates is strong evidence of this trend.

The second important assertion is that limited cognitive skills are strongly associated with myriad social problems. The authors find that among the poor, the unemployed, high schools dropouts, those in prison, women on welfare, and unwed mothers, 40 to 65 percent fall in the bottom 20 percent of measured IQ. Most of these groups, by the way, contain more whites than blacks. Indeed, seeking to sidestep the race question altogether, the authors restricted a large part of their analysis to whites. They find, as other social scientists have using the same data, that cognitive ability is a strong predictor of various social problems even when other factors such as family background are taken into account. Given the strong suggestion of a link between intelligence and behavior, isn't further study of a possible causal relationship needed?

The third important claim in *The Bell Curve* is that cognitive ability is largely immutable. Although the authors may well be overly pessimistic about the possibility of improving intellectual ability, surely we would be naive to think that simply increasing federal funding for early childhood education, say, or for job-training programs would be sufficient to compensate for the increasing gap between the highly educated and the barely literate in American society.

What are the consequences of ignoring such controversial but potentially important observations about our society? Twenty-nine years ago, Daniel Patrick Moynihan, then an aide in the Labor Department, wrote a report that argued for an aggressive social policy to address the rising number of out-of-wedlock births in the African-American community, then about 30 percent of the total. Today, nearly 70 percent of African-American children are born out of wedlock (as are 30 percent of white children, compared to about 12 percent in 1965). However valid the warning, after the report was published Mr. Moynihan and his defenders were denounced as racists and the African-American family became a taboo subject for scholars for the next twenty years. As we now try to grapple with the desperate situation of many black families in this country, we are missing two decades of research that could have informed current policy.

The furor about *The Bell Curve* risks the same perils. Many scholars are likely to back away from research on cognitive skills and social outcomes; others will be inclined to present only findings consistent with the thesis that IQ and race differences of any kind are largely environmentally determined. This is hardly an atmosphere conducive to objective, rigorous scientific study.

Few of the most controversial assertions in *The Bell Curve* can be shown with any certainty to be either true or false. Only better, more unbiased, and more sophisticated research can help us do this. We need to insure that neither the irresponsible statements in *The Bell Curve*—nor the media's vitriolic response to the book as a whole—prevents this research from being done. In an era of increasing stratification by level of ability and income, it is critical that we understand what the relationship is, if any, between intelligence and entrenched social problems if we are to develop sensible public policy.

RIGHT IS RIGHT

Elizabeth Austin

C HARLES MURRAY'S infuriating book, *The Bell Curve*, has all the earmarks of a nine-day wonder. Murray's theory that blacks, as a group, just aren't as smart as whites has conservatives licking their chops over Murray's argument that intelligence is bred in the bone, and that welfare programs targeted at improving the lot of inner-city blacks waste millions of federal dollars on a hopeless cause. Liberals are quaking in their Birkenstock sandals, fearful that Murray's status as the right's pet pundit will make this book the cornerstone of a return to Reaganism.

But as the weeks roll on, all of this hot air should blow Murray right off the national agenda. Real experts on the intricate connections between genetics and intelligence will expose the shaky underpinnings of Murray's research. Scholars will note that Murray's co-author, the late Richard Herrnstein, has been making these types of claims for more than a generation and that he has been debunked on a fairly regular basis. Soon the book will end up gathering dust on bookshelves nationwide. It will be cited only by white racists seeking to prove their superiority, and by black racists seeking evidence of whites' over-

Elizabeth Austin is a Chicago-based writer whose work has appeared in *Time, The Washington Post,* and other publications. This piece was first published in *The Chicago Tribune,* October 27, 1994, titled "Brains, Brawn, and Black Babies."

whelming prejudice and ill will. And Murray will be left to chortle all the way to the bank.

That's a shame. Because in two fundamental respects, Murray is absolutely right. Oh, certainly not in his contention that blacks are genetically inferior to whites when it comes to intelligence—an idea based largely on research that can most charitably be described as goofy. And his corollary, that blacks should therefore shift their focus away from intellectual pursuits and rely on sports, dance, and music to provide group self-esteem, is too condescending to require comment.

But Murray is correct when he says that intelligence has become increasingly critical to success in our society. Arnold Schwarzenegger and Michael Jordan aside, we reward brains much more highly than brawn. We now have machines that can dig ditches, but we still must hire a brain to decide where the ditch should go. And, sadly, some of Murray's figures on black IQ scores seem difficult to refute. There are far too many African Americans whose IQ scores are below where they should be.

That's not because of some tragic genetic mutation that occurred in Africa generations ago. It's stark evidence that the richest country in the world still can't manage to get decent health care to the people who need it, the most impoverished black mothers and their babies. Black women are two to three times more likely to have babies with low birth weights—under 5½ pounds. And babies who are dangerously small at birth are three times more likely to suffer mental retardation and other problems, medical studies show.

Low birth weight is an enormous problem. It's the leading cause of death among black infants, and it's blamed for a wide range of physical and mental difficulties for the children who survive. Yet from 1981 to 1991—not coincidentally, the decade during which Murray's "dismantle welfare" doctrine became fashionable among the right—the numbers of mothers who received no prenatal care at all increased by 50 percent. According to the Centers for Disease Control, the number of black infants whose weights at birth put them at risk for health problems grew to 134.9 out of every 1,000 live births. That compares with 57.8 out of every 1,000 live births for white mothers. Many babies are born too small because their mothers don't have access to good prenatal care so that they can protect their babies.

Low birth weight is just one of the many factors that can diminish a child's intelligence. If babies don't get adequate nutrition before they're born and in the critical year afterward, their brains don't get the building blocks they need to reach their full potential. And there are literally hundreds of diseases that, without good treatment, can blunt a child's mind for life.

Yet there's some real hope in all this. One major 1990 study found that low-birth-weight babies who get intensive education and training from birth to age three score nine points higher on IQ tests than similar babies who didn't get that extra help. That's the sort of number Murray ought to respect—and that, in good conscience, he ought to publicize. Because that number shows that IQ isn't decided by heredity alone. It's what geneticists call a "malleable" trait, something that can be deeply affected by the environment that surrounds a child, both before and after birth.

And those of us who believe that the lucky and privileged should help the unfortunate and oppressed owe a debt of thanks to Murray. By linking low IQs to crime, illegitimacy, unemployment, and welfare dependency, he's shown why it's in everyone's self-interest to try to raise IQs as much as possible, as quickly as possible. And that means spending more money on maternal and child health programs, early childhood education efforts, nutrition programs—all those things Murray has opposed in the past.

It's funny—one of the basic elements of an IQ test is the "if-then" question. It's a logic problem: If A exists, then what, logically, should follow?

With *The Bell Curve*, Murray has sketched a perfect if-then problem: If African-American children are not reaching their full potential because they lack access to the basic requirements of healthy life, and if their resulting problems, left untreated, cause huge societal problems, then what?

Murray's answer is to cut funding and give up. It makes me wonder about his IQ.

STRAIGHTENING OUT *THE BELL CURVE*

K. Anthony Appiah

EMERGE: Murray presents this as new, groundbreaking work. But isn't this actually a rather old argument?

APPIAH: Well, it depends on which argument. I think that the fuss has been about the question of whether the explanations have omitted differences in these test scores between blacks and whites. It's hereditary. The arguments about that have all been heard before. There's a little new data, but most of the data about heritability is, in fact, irrelevant to the question of the relation between black and white distributions on these scores.

EMERGE: How so?

APPIAH: There's an implicit argument [in the book] that's more implied than asserted that goes like this: "We have evidence for the heritability of IQ—among blacks and among whites. We have evidence that there's a difference between the average IQ of blacks and whites, so

K. Anthony Appiah is a professor of Afro-American studies at Harvard University and author of *In My Father's House: Africa in the Philosophy of Culture.* This interview was conducted by Harriet A. Washington for *Emerge* magazine, where it first appeared in the December/January 1994/1995 issue.

we have evidence that the explanation for the difference must be genetic, because IQ is highly heritable."

That sounds like a very good argument, but it's not. And the reason it's not a good argument is the following: Consider the population of India. The average height of the people in India is much lower than the average height of people in the United States.

Furthermore, the average height in India is highly heritable. The same is true in the United States. But the main reason for the difference between India and the United States is not heredity; it's nutrition. It could be the case that the major explanation for the differences in the [IQ] averages of the two populations is something completely environmental.

So there is something wrong with the structure of the argument if it supposes that because something is heritable within a group the explanation for the differences between two groups must also be hereditary.

EMERGE: So they are completely ignoring environmental factors.

APPIAH: I wouldn't say completely. But it seems to me that the book's rhetoric suggests that, "We can't do anything about it because 60 percent of the variance is explained by genetics." Well, that question has nothing to do with the race question. That's just a question about how heritable IQ is within groups, against a certain environment. I'm not convinced by their arguments.

EMERGE: What about their arguments about *g*?

APPIAH: Well, *g* is a number that comes out of a statistical analysis of these sorts of tests, and it is basically a statistical device for getting a factor that is common to many different tests. It's interesting that you can get this very stable statistical number, but it's not very psychologically interesting until you know something about what it means, about what psychological mechanisms produce these numbers.

And there is very little serious attention in their book, and indeed much too little attention in the whole field, to a theoretically interesting question: To the extent that there is a stable number here, what produces it? What mechanism?

Now, given the complexity of the cognitive skills intuitively involved in being what we call "smart," you might think that it was rather unlikely—and I certainly think it is unlikely—that the genetics of it, or the mechanisms, could be very simple. And may be very complicated. They may involve many factors, and it's rather unlikely that we'll get anywhere near a good model of any of that until we have a great deal more evidence.

So simply showing that 60 percent of the variation in a particular population against a certain background of environment can be explained by genetics doesn't tell you anything about what the genetics is that explains it. It just says, "Well, there's a genetic explanation somewhere."

Now, this is important for the policy questions. Murray draws what he portrays as a very reluctant conclusion, that a lot of the social policy questions are futile because the difference in intelligence he posits just can't be remedied.

On the narrow question, I just think that most of the data is just irrelevant. But let's suppose it were true. Let's forget about race. Let's just suppose that we're interested in what happens to white people because they have different IQs, and IQs play a big role in shaping what you can do, and that in turn plays a big role in shaping how much you earn and how much power you have. Suppose you think that there's this innate characteristic called *g*, which everybody has a value of at birth, and the final result of your *g*, which is the thing that actually determines how well you do in life, is determined 60 percent by your genes in the normal environment, on average. It does not follow from the fact that something is heritable that you can't do anything about it.

EMERGE: Give us an example.

APPIAH: The average age of death of people with sickle-cell anemia keeps going up. It's a hereditary condition. Why does the average age of death [in sickle cell cases] keep going up? Because the medicine gets better.

Also, short-sightedness is strongly hereditary. Does it matter? No. We can use glasses.

So the fact that something is genetic doesn't mean that you can't either affect its expression—and affecting its expression in the case of psychological characteristics might be done by educational things—or affect its effects, which is what we do with glasses. I don't stop you from being shortsighted. I just make it not matter anymore.

EMERGE: So even if there are some things that are true, the fact that something can be inherited does not mean that it's unchangeable?

APPIAH: Absolutely not.

EMERGE: You seem to be saying that, for black people, even in a worst-case scenario, some rather simple interventions might prove true.

APPIAH: I think, and this is important, whatever the explanation for the difference between blacks and whites is, if we understood more about the processes that shape our cognitive capacities, including whatever cognitive capacities are reflected in this number *g*, we could help lots of people to have greater potential . . . without interfering with any genetics. It might be done by improving nutrition. It might be done by changing elementary features of the way we educate children.

EMERGE: To what extent does IQ measure intelligence?

APPIAH: There is actually an example in the book where Murray and Herrnstein say that people who are very witty often don't have particularly high IQs. Now, they take that to be evidence that people who are witty aren't particularly intelligent. But you might take that as evidence that IQ doesn't measure intelligence.

EMERGE: Right.

APPIAH: Ordinarily we think of someone who is witty as intelligent. Then, the fact that this doesn't correlate, that would be grounds for supposing that you hadn't got something that we were after.

Nevertheless, there are cognitive skills that have to do with sort of symbolic processing and analysis, and you can sort of test for those. You have to ask what you want to use the tests for. Their argument is complicated because they say, "Yeah, you can design tests to correlate with various outcomes that you might be interested in, like whether somebody is going to get good grades in college, or whether they're going to get a Ph.D., or whether they're going to be a great lawyer." You can design tests like that. But they say, "If you then look at them, and their statistical analysis, there is a strong correlation between all of them, and most of them look like they're measuring *g* plus something else," where *g* is general intelligence.

Furthermore, most of them look like a large part of what they're measuring is this thing called "general intelligence." There is a risk here of treating something that is the product of many things as if it were one thing.

EMERGE: Is there a role for cultural values?

APPIAH: One of the things that happens in these sorts of models is that they treat it as if they were part of nature—things that are, in fact, the product of culture. If your way of measuring the adequacy of a test is to see how well it correlates with social success, then you're assuming that current society produces social success in a way that is just fine. If you think that there's something wrong with the way in which the society works, that the wrong people are successful, then you won't be very interested in the test that measures people's capacity to create in that kind of society.

So it isn't as if these tests are, in that sense, free of assumptions or evaluative assumptions in particular, because they do presuppose that there's something to the way in which success works in our kind of society. And this is particularly important when you're thinking about the race difference issue, because they sort of assume if you're seeing in the environment—that is, holding down average IQ for blacks in this country—if there is such a thing, if it were environmental, then all of the interventions that have gone on in the last few years would have removed it. But that presupposes that we know what it is in the environment that might be doing the damage.

EMERGE: Why is this book important?

APPIAH: Because these guys are basically putting fancy clothing on a hypothesis that lots of people believe anyway. There are things one could explore. I think that exploring them would have one not theoretical but practical benefit, which is that if we began to identify some of the environmental factors that were accounting for the difference, we could remove them.

EMERGE: What are some of the unwarranted assumptions *The Bell Curve* makes?

APPIAH: I do think that there is a kind of underlying ethical assumption, which is something like this: Smart people produce more and are worth more, and therefore, while it's sad that dumb people can't produce more, there's nothing to be done about it. None of that is obvious. [The authors] say, "Well, it's just a fact that smart people are worth more." But the answer is, "That's just a fact, given the current social arrangement." That's not the same as saying that they're worth more under any social arrangement.

And if you thought, for example, as I do, that inequality in outcome is undesirable, then instead of seeing the fact that some people are smart as children as grounds for spending more educational resources on them, you might think that you ought to spend more educational resources on people who will act smart.

EMERGE: Wasn't the original purpose of the IQ test to identify children who needed more attention?

APPIAH: The IQ test has lots of origins. There's a complicated history. But there is no reason why science shouldn't use IQ tests to help identify people who need special attention. In that practical way, I don't have any problem with these sorts of tests.

Low IQ is a disability, right? Like being born without a limb. We spend more on the education of people with physical disabilities than we do on the education of others. . . . Why? Because we care not just about maximizing the wealth of the nation, not just about profit, but about an issue of fairness. And if you grant [Murray and Herrnstein] the strongest premises you like, that 60 percent of the variance in IQ in our environment is hereditary, grant them that if we leave things as they are, that will mean that wealth will concentrate more in the hands of a very few. I say that's grounds for changing something.

EMERGE: How could we change such a scenario?

APPIAH: There are various things you could try and change. One of them is we could spend all of our time trying to make sure that people who are in the bottom quarter get more educational attention and more educational resources. But we also could make the system more progressive. To take it for granted that [because] these differences are substantially hereditary, there is nothing we can do about it, is just to misunderstand how much choice human beings have.

In the current environment, conservatives generally grant the naturalness of social difference or social inequality, and they do so sometimes by stressing heredity, as Murray and Herrnstein do.

EMERGE: Speaking of conservatives who are writing about race and intelligence, there's a Canadian, Philippe Rushton, who is writing about race and intelligence. Do you think that these books are presaging a new, nastier mood?

APPIAH: Oh, I think that the nastier mood has been coming along for quite a while. There are a lot of white people in this country who are not confident about their futures. There are problems ahead in the American economy. There are long-term problems already, some of which Murray and Herrnstein talk about. And so they are particularly likely to worry about anything that looks as though it might be getting in the way of getting the job. Any form of affirmative action for women or minorities looks like that.

And so there's a lot of resentment, even among people who are employed, because they're not sure how long they will be employed or how easy it will be for them to get a job again, or whether the job they get will have an income that is like the one they had before. And so I think there has been a lot of muttering going on for a while. In that sense, Murray's claim that they are simply talking about something that people are muttering about is perfectly right. And I think at this point it's as well, since they brought it up, to go through and see which things they're right about and which things they are wrong about.

I would say that insofar as it relates to the race question, there are a few things that they are fundamentally wrong about. They are wrong about the relevance of measures of heritability within groups in a certain environment, a series of questions of what the explanation is for differences between groups. And they are wrong in thinking that what's heritable is something you can do nothing about.

EMERGE: It seems as if they've totally ignored intermarriage, for want of a better term.

APPIAH: That's one of the reasons why the other biological question is about the evolution of these capacities. If you're interested in that, the relationship between the American blacks and whites is not the right relationship to look at. It's a very, very poor place to look.

EMERGE: Because there's a sharing of the gene pool?

APPIAH: There's enormous sharing, and it's more and more. But there has always been some, and on both sides. Between 5 and 20 percent of white Americans have African ancestry, depending on what figures you believe. So it's a very blurry thing.

EMERGE: Given some of the errors that the authors made, does this book deserve the consideration it has gotten in the media?

APPIAH: Well, they have the right to publish this stuff. I think it's kind of bizarre that this book has probably had more attention than many other books this year, because just by the ordinary professional standards of popularizing books of this sort, it contains fundamental methodological problems of a sort that already were pointed out when Richard Herrnstein published his original piece in *Atlantic Monthly* twenty years ago. And most of the best pointing out of those errors was done, in fact, by the population of biologists who said, "You don't understand how heritability works. You can't just take a mathematical model and plunk it down in an area that you don't have a good feel for."

If you look at the mathematical structures that are used to estimate heritability, you have to make rather substantial assumptions about the ways in which genetics and environment interact in order to get out the estimates that they use. There's a legitimate reason for skepticism about whether the book deserves attention.

EMERGE: What sort of results are likely if this is taken seriously by academics and the government?

APPIAH: Well, I don't think it will be. We'd have to start investigating the genetic differences between different parts of the white population. We'd start having to see whether the nineteenth-century hypothesis that the Irish are stupid can be empirically verified. And we'd have to see whether we can find statistical evidence of the relative superiority of the Nordic over the Mediterranean type. This would, of course, begin to demolish the constituency for this book. Because despite the fact that the main message of the book is that 98 percent of white people have no hope, people have focused on the fact that it says that 99.9 percent of black people have no hope.

This book says basically that our future lies in the hands of people with IQs in the 140s and 150s and 160s. These are people way out on the end of the curve. And they are a very, very small population. And, in fact, the book is [good] for the vanity of this group, because it keeps saying, "If you're reading this book, you're probably smart enough to be among the such and suches."

EMERGE: Is this changing how blacks and whites interact?

APPIAH: I'm black, at least as far as this country is concerned I'm black, and so some people don't tell me things that they think will upset me. But most of the people I have talked to about this think that there are moral and intellectual errors in this book of an unfortunate kind, the sort that need pointing out and correcting.

ON NOT GETTING IT

Roger E. Hernandez

I N T H E F U R O R about *The Bell Curve,* the new book that asserts
that blacks are genetically dumber than whites, few people have
paid attention to what authors Richard Herrnstein and Charles Murray
have to say about the group they call "Latinos." And what they say
shows such a lack of intellectual rigor, such slipshod scholarship, that it
calls into question everything else they say.

Most Americans don't understand that Hispanics—or Latinos, or
whatever the term might be—do not form a race. Hispanics may be of
any race. In the United States the largest Hispanic group traces its origins to Mexico, a country where most people are of mixed European
and Indian background. Yet in Mexico, as elsewhere in the Hispanic
world, there are people who are Asian, people who are white (mostly
Spanish, but also Jewish, Irish, Italian, and from almost every corner of
Europe that sent immigrants to the New World), people who are black,
and people who are every shade in between.

Herrnstein and Murray understand this. "The term Latino
embraces people with highly disparate cultural heritages and a wide
range of racial stocks," they write. "Add to that the problem of possi-

Roger E. Hernandez is a syndicated columnist for King Features Syndicate. This article
was published in the *Rocky Mountain News*, October 21, 1994, as "Hispanic Race Doesn't
Exist."

ble language difficulties with the tests, and generalizations about IQ become especially imprecise for Latinos."

So far so good. But with breathtaking disregard of what they just finished saying, they continue: "With that in mind, it may be said that their test results generally fall about one-half to one standard deviation below the national mean." In other words, (a) Hispanics are so racially diverse that testing their IQ reveals nothing about race and intelligence, and (b) forget what we just said: The Hispanic "race" is dumber than the national average.

The authors' explanation of the methodology that justified this contradiction is risible. "How are we to classify a person whose parents hail from Panama but whose ancestry is predominantly African? Is he a Latino? A black? The rule we follow here is to classify people according to the way they classify themselves."

Sounds nice and open-minded. The problem is that in a book that purports to analyze the links between race and intelligence, such a person must by necessity be classified as black, no matter how he identifies himself. What if Herrnstein and Murray's theoretical Panamanian had been of Chinese rather than African ancestry? Or what if he had been white? Or Indian? Would they all count together as "Latino"? If so, what racial group's intelligence is being measured? Obviously, averaging out the intelligence quotients of black, Asian, white, and Indian Panamanians yields a single figure that says nothing about any race.

The authors seem to accept this very simple principle only when it comes to non-Hispanics. The thought of lumping together North American Indians with non-Hispanic blacks, non-Hispanic whites, and non-Hispanic Asians—God forbid, they must have thought—did not occur to them. So why do it with Hispanics?

And what of the different white ethnicities among Hispanics? Who are smarter, Hispanics of Nordic stock or those of Spanish Mediterranean stock? What about the descendants of pre-Columbian peoples? A similar point could be made about non-Hispanics.

The book's conclusion about the intelligence of Hispanics is based on a premise so flawed it is unsustainable. That the authors could engage in such idiocies is enough to make one distrust the entire work.

MINORITY REPORT

Christopher Hitchens

A S A Y O U N G anthropologist conducting intense field studies in the controlled conditions of a male bonding and territorial boarding school, I made an observation that is only now being recognized as a contribution to primary research. There is, and there always has been, an unusually high and consistent correlation between the stupidity of a given person and that person's propensity to be impressed by the measurement of IQ. (These days you get the same thing, though represented along a shallower curve, if you test for susceptibility to the findings of opinion polls.) Was it not the boy at the back of the class, that prognathous dolt who, removing grimy digit from well-excavated nostril—the better to breathe through his mouth—would opine: "They're not as intelligent as us. Been proved, innit? *Scientific.*" (Sometimes the teensiest difficulty with that last word.) Thick and vicious white boys could derive obscure consolation from the fact that their *tribe*, at least, was rated the brightest or the brighter. And smart black and brown boys (who were, of course, always to be considered purely on merit) had to endure evaluations from teachers and prospec-

Christopher Hitchens is a columnist for *Vanity Fair* and writes the "Minority Report" column for *The Nation*. He is the author of several books, most recently *For the Sake of Argument: Essays and Minority Reports*. This article was originally published in *The Nation*, November 28, 1994.

tive employers who would, naturally, take no account of the fact that they "came from" tribes with hereditary intelligence deficits. All I needed to know about this nonsense I learned in public school. A society that takes it seriously is dumbing itself down.

More than that, it is missing the chance to throw the whole false antithesis of "nature versus nurture" into the necessary receptacle. As it happens, there *is* a revolution going on in the study of genetics, and the hereditarian IQ alchemists are choosing to greet it by gaping dully through the wrong end of a telescope.

Dispense with unnecessary assumptions at the start by recognizing that "natural" or heritable differences are environmental to begin with and are determined principally by climate, geography, and nutrition. Bear in mind Noam Chomsky's point that science takes no account of the nature/nurture distinction in its real work, and that "everybody knows that nature determines and that the environment modifies and that the only real question is by how much." Now consider the findings of genome science as they are unfolding.

I talked to Dr. William Haseltine, who runs Human Genome Sciences, Inc. This concern is by at least fivefold the largest holder of new information on genome and DNA properties in the world. (Haseltine may be familiar to some readers as one of the good-guy scientists in Randy Shilts's *And the Band Played On*.) His firm has recently identified the genes that predispose humans to colonic, ovarian, and uterine cancers. "We have gone in a relatively short time from identifying about 2 percent of human genes to more than 50 percent: That's from 2,000–3,000 to 60,000–70,000, and there are probably not more than 100,000. If the system is a transistor, we have gone from analyzing its circuit boards to breaking down its components. And only one-quarter of 1 percent of our basic genetic information can be ascribed to what we call 'racial' differences. It is the differences between individuals that are enormous and becoming better known. There are almost 15 million changes in the genetic code between one human and another."

In other words, scientific advance confirms that there is only one human "race," and that the individual possesses fantastic complexity and variety. But pseudoscience persists in its petty quest for the elusive *g* spot of quantifiable intelligence, and the result of the latter practice is that individuals become subsumed into lumpish, arbitrary categories. And the conservatives want to take credit for the brilliance of the second option! Let them have the "ice people" and the "sun people" and all the rest of the rubbish while the left emancipates itself from all versions of "ethnicity" and concentrates on what it should never have forgotten—what Gramsci called "the project of the whole man."

All societies that have tried to keep themselves "pure," from the Confucian Chinese through to the Castilian Spanish to the post-Wilhelmine Germans, have collapsed into barbarism, insularity, and superstition. And swiftly enough for us to be certain that the fall was no more connected to the genes than was the rise. There is no gene for IQ and there is no genetic or evolutionary timing that is short enough to explain histories or societies.

Or literatures. My pick-nose playmates may have gone on to father brilliant children, just as my cleverer ones often produced what they called "late developers." This is the best-observed "fact" about IQ testing. Charles Murray's policy would entail dropping the present and future gifted children of the underclass into the same midden as their parents—an irony in reactionary terms even if not in humane ones. Who cares to recall any member of the carefully tended Capulet family except Juliet? And why did Goya choose to paint a braying jackass, proudly pointing with a hoof to its family-tree portrait in which all the revered ancestors have the same long ears, thick muzzles, and cloven feet? In *The Scarlet Letter*, the brunt of the injustice and hypocrisy falls not merely upon the wronged Hester but upon the doubly wronged little Pearl. Mark Twain's *Pudd'nhead Wilson* has more about birth chances and life chances on a single page than do all the turgid and evasive chapters of Murray and Herrnstein's *Bell Curve*. Twain is also shrewder, as his nom de plume might imply, on twinship.

Linguistics, genetics, paleontology, anthropology: All are busily demonstrating that we as a species have no objective problem of "race." What we still do seem to have are all these racists. It's a shame that evolution moves so slowly, but though its mills may grind slowly, they grind exceeding small.

GET SMART

Mike Walter

A FEW YEARS AGO two research chemists announced they had achieved cold fusion in a glass jar. Later they were forced to abandon their claim under pressure from the makers of Alka Seltzer, who had established a previous patent on the process. Today we are challenged by perhaps a similar achievement in scientific research, *The Bell Curve*, an inquiry by Charles Murray and the late Richard Herrnstein into the meaning and measure of IQ as it relates to social stratification.

Now I must disclaim that I am not a professional chemist, though I can get most of the letters right in *ibuprofen* and *acetaminophen*. Likewise, I'm not a social scientist; but I do own a guinea pig (Mr. Booper) and have often thought of modeling myself on his behavior.

When cold fusion was the rage, I was a partisan. Who among us hasn't looked forward to the day when bath water everywhere would be self-reheating? But then the chemists were overruled by the physicists who pointed out, among other things, that the radiation given off by the cold fusion experiment should have killed the chemists. The physicists won the day and proceeded to turn off the cold fusion lights on their way out of the building.

Mike Walter is a software engineer. This article first appeared in *The Star Tribune* (Minneapolis), November 14, 1994, titled "Word Problems to Take Your Mind Off the Bell Curve."

I think we could use a couple of good physicists now, because some of the facts coming out of *The Bell Curve* tend themselves more to physics than to social science. Take those two factoids, for example, where Murray-Herrnstein's statistics show that blacks as a group exhibit a constant fifteen-point gap in IQ over time relative to whites; combined with the fact that both groups exhibit a three-point rise in IQ per decade. Let's turn these facts into a story problem of the kind found on aptitude tests and see what conclusions we come to:

> There are two trains, white and black, heading north from Baltimore to Boston. The white train is moving at constant velocity X and the black train is moving at constant velocity Y.
>
> The white train passes the Philadelphia station at noon and the New York station at 12:30. The black train passes the Philadelphia station at 12:15 and the New York station at 12:45. Which, then, is the correct relationship between the velocities of the white and black trains (velocities X and Y)?
>
> A. X < Y
>
> B. X = Y
>
> C. X > Y

The correct answer is B; the white and black trains are traveling at the same speed (let's say, for example, 3 kilometers per minute—or how about 3 IQ points per decade?).

Now here's the tricky part:

> Which train is the more powerful?
>
> A. White < Black
>
> B. White = Black
>
> C. White > Black
>
> D. Insufficient information

If you're a physicist, or maybe a ninth grader, the answer is D. We have no idea of the ultimate power of either train. If you're a social scientist, however, somehow the answer becomes C—the train farther along the track has the bigger engine, even though they're both traveling at the same speed.

To the physicist, this seems a strange conclusion. After all, if the white train stops for thirty minutes to take on mail and then takes off again at its original speed, it would then be behind the black train by as much as it was ahead of it earlier. Does this mean the white train has become less powerful?

Let's put this story in a more personal light. An evil scientist finds a way to put all white people to sleep for six decades. During this hibernation, the IQ of blacks rises three points per decade, or eighteen points. The IQ of whites stays the same. Now when the white group wakes up, it exhibits a persistent three-point IQ lag behind the black group. To the social scientist, this would constitute proof that whites are "genetically" inferior to blacks. A more historical perspective would reveal that genes had nothing to do with it.

There are many reasons why a racial group could become momentarily sidetracked in the course of history. Slavery rings a bell, or perhaps something less malicious like the uneven meting out of largesse during the Industrial Age. Yet I think even Mr. Booper would agree that as long as the IQs of both groups are growing at the same constant rate, we have no way of predicting the ultimate potential of either group. The issue then is not where are we in relation to each other, but where are we in relation to our potential? Perhaps whites have reached 80 percent of their potential whereas blacks have reached 75 percent of the very same potential.

Then it may also be true that sometime in the future all races will reach some unexceedable IQ limit, much the way a particle approaches the unexceedable velocity of light. Then it really won't matter who gets there first, because within a few decades that's where we'll all be, together, for the rest of time.

ETHNICITY, GENETICS, AND CUTENESS

(ADDENDUM TO RECENT FEARLESS FINDINGS)

Bruce McCall

H UMAN CUTENESS was not only never measured but was a virtually taboo subject in America up to and beyond Reconstruction. (Ulysses S. Grant's magisterial two-volume *Personal Memoirs* of 1885–86, for example, completely sidesteps it.) The authors of this impeccably fair-minded inquiry were therefore astonished, but not surprised, that 52 percent of white Americans in our meticulous study included the word "dimples" in their definitions of cuteness, while a similar number of African Americans did not. This is unsentimental science, in no way contradicted by the fact that the physiognomy of the average African American lends itself to no more and no fewer dimples than that of other clans or castes. To anticipate the firestorm of hysteria sure to be provoked in certain quarters by these findings: there are, of course, many cute African Americans. Looking out the window just now, we saw three.

But this is not the issue. It might more cogently be asked, Are federally funded dimple-awareness programs the answer? Emphatically no. Not as long as African Americans refuse to recognize the dimple—

Bruce McCall is a writer and illustrator. This article first appeared in *The New Yorker*, December 5, 1994.

as obvious, after all, as the declivity in the fatty areas on your face. Comparisons with cowlicks and wattles were found to be invalid, if not spurious; so much for ethnicity. Dimples aside, we found cuteness to be broadly multidimensional and omnifaceted. Basques, alone with their sheep for days at a time, have no fewer than six words for it, disproving the theory of a culturally imposed mind control.

Cuteness would appear to have been a free-floating "rogue factor," in psychometric parlance, within virtually all ethnic and racial categories, since at least the wedding of the Duke of Windsor and Wallis Warfield Simpson. It is worth noting, in this context, that on the same weighted scale that places her contemporary Betty Boop at 100 in perceived cuteness, the snobbish and pushy Mrs. Simpson scores a remarkable 72. Rogue factor, indeed. Cuteness has been known to occur even in societies where women seldom shave their legs. (See Laurel and Hardy's *The Bohemian Girl*, circa 1937.) The pioneer ethnometrician Miladovilovich's taunt, "Just show me a cute Herzegovinian and I'll eat the tassel on my fez," so eagerly trotted out by the proponents of cuteness-as-myth, can be easily discounted, but not here. More germane is the cute-face/cute-smile/cute-body trichotomy, dividing, we found, so sharply along the racial-cultural axis about to be delineated—come hell or high water—as to cut the fingers of the unwary.

Anomalies in any such sweeping study are sure to abound. For instance, 28 percent of immigrant male Sikh heads of household in the telltale 1890–1910 period took "cute smile" as a pretext for drawing

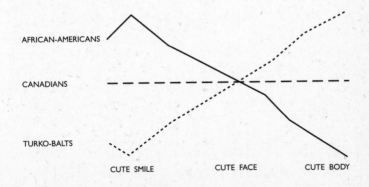

knives. That no one knows why should hardly be blamed on the authors, who are up front enough to admit that why the remaining 72 percent did not pull steel is also a statistical head-scratcher. This should not be interpreted to give high-IQ Asians cause for complacency. In the very next chapter, cuteness and its influence on the San Francisco Tong Wars of the early century will be all too clearly examined. So much for "environmental factors."

African-American cuteness would appear to vary little from norms already established for Hispanics, Inuits, Jews, and the like. We aren't advocating this, we're just reporting it. Whites the general reader will presumably already know about, since, according to standard demographics and Vegas odds, the general reader *is* white.

If nothing in this controversial study is comforting or nice, the authors can only borrow from the words of that latter-day avatar of the non-cute, Tina Turner, speaking for *The Ike and Tina Turner Revue*—and for tough-minded truth-seeking scientists everywhere—in saying, "We never, ever do nothing nice and easy."

Does this mean the authors aren't, personally, nice guys? That lies beyond the scope of this inquiry. We mean, you are, or aren't, a bigot. Nothing to do with us.

IV
CONSERVATIVE COMMENTARY
AND CRITIQUE

LEGACY OF RACISM

Pat Shipman

HUMAN INTELLIGENCE is an eel-like subject: slippery, difficult to grasp, and almost impossible to get straight. Charles Murray and the late Richard Herrnstein make a heroic attempt to lay before the public a topic of writhing complexity: the interaction of intelligence, class, and ethnicity in America. The authors have not succeeded wholly, either in presenting the information or in convincing this reader of their conclusions, but I must applaud them for the clarity and honesty of their attempt. Who else has had the audacity to try to teach a nation raised on factoids and ten-second sound bites to think in subtle terms of probabilities, correlations, and standard deviations?

The authors' conclusions are so unwelcome that many readers will find themselves, as I did, slogging slowly and carefully through each paragraph, poring over every footnote, making irritated notes to themselves to seek out this or that study from the original literature to satisfy their skepticism. The research that Herrnstein and Murray summarize is exquisitely sensitive to the way a question is framed, so

Pat Shipman, a paleoanthropologist, is the author of *The Evolution of Racism*. His article appeared in the *National Review*, December 5, 1994.

that the thinking reader cannot coast for even a paragraph without paying attention. But in the end, it all comes down to three questions: What do they say? Is it true? What should we do now?

Through summaries of myriad studies, the authors paint a vivid picture of the dark side of the American dream. The United States is the country of immigrants, the country where (at least in theory) name and family mean nothing and personal accomplishment is all. You can come to America with nothing, work hard, and rise to the top. This, Murray and Herrnstein show convincingly, is true *if* you are smart (and if, not incidentally, you are white). The consolidation of this meritocracy throughout this century has produced a class of smart, powerful, and wealthy individuals—the "cognitive elite"—who enjoy life at the high end of the bell curve.

But the shadowy inverse, rarely seen clearly, is also true: if you are not smart, you will fall to the bottom. The book tolls funereally, in chapter after careful chapter, ringing out the stunning relationship between low IQ and the tendencies to perform poorly in school; drop out of school; live in poverty; become dependent on welfare; bear children out of wedlock; go to jail; hold, perform badly at, and often lose menial jobs; achieve only a low socioeconomic status; earn little money; maintain households that score poorly in factors important in nurturing children; and even suffer disabilities that prevent working altogether. The land of golden opportunity inevitably offers the chance to fail abjectly as well.

In the latter part of the book, Herrnstein and Murray present the fearsome possibility that cognitive class and race are now coincident. They report data that, as a population, African Americans have a bell curve of IQ scores that is shifted to the lower side of the white mean. So do Africans, while East Asians have a bell curve of IQ scores shifted slightly to the right of the white curve. The authors are quick to observe that this does *not* mean that all blacks are stupider than all whites; there are many highly intelligent African Americans who perform as well as or better than their white counterparts on the various measures of achievement. Indeed, one of the brightest points in the book is the demonstration that the average annual incomes of blacks, Latinos, and whites of the same IQ fall within a few hundred dollars of each other. But there seem to be disproportionately more blacks at the lower end of the bell curve and thus disproportionately more caught in poverty, ignorance, helplessness, and depression. Furthermore, considerable data indicate that those at the lower end of the IQ scale, regardless of race, are breeding faster than those at the top. We seem trapped in a downward spiral of ever-increasing stupidity.

Having sounded the death knell, Herrnstein and Murray do not abandon their readers to this vision of doom. Since they find eugenics an abhorrent policy, they suggest we revise the affirmative-action laws to reap the economic benefits of a more intelligent and more productive work force; find a "valued place" and useful occupations for those who are not very smart; strengthen the bonds of community responsibility and interdependence by reintegrating the cognitive elite into the rest of society; and encourage breeding among the cognitive elite so that the intelligence of our nation as a whole is not swamped by the fertility of the less intelligent.

But is it true? Do the data Herrnstein and Murray report about black IQ support their conclusions about black intelligence?

Underlying their thesis are two crucial issues. First is the premise that intelligence—of whatever it may consist—can be measured accurately and reliably by various tests, including the familiar IQ test. Herrnstein and Murray discuss the debates over psychometric testing fairly and clearly, and conclude that IQ and other such measures do reflect the elusive quality or qualities we label "intelligence." This point is the basis for the authors' compelling argument for the existence of a cognitive elite and its dark twin. The second issue is the heritability of intelligence. Heritability does *not* mean the extent to which a particular trait, such as intelligence, is genetically determined. Rather, heritability is the faithfulness with which a trait's measured expression (or phenotype, like IQ) mirrors the underlying genetic basis (or genotype). Heritability is always time- and population-specific, which is why the heritability of intelligence in studies ranges from .4 to .8 (out of a maximum possible of 1.0). Some populations have a genuinely higher heritability for intelligence than others, which renders cross-population comparisons of IQ and its correlates problematic (as the authors know).

The point is that the value assigned to heritability indicates the amount of the variation in measured intelligence that can be explained by genetic factors; heritabilities of .4 to .8 thus explain from a modest 40 percent to a robust 80 percent of the observed variations in IQ within the samples studied. Statistically, both values may be highly significant, if the sample sizes are large enough. Yet even a heritability of .8 leaves a substantial portion of the variance in intelligence to be attributed to something non-genetic.

If African Americans have a lower heritability for intelligence, then their IQ scores are more heavily influenced by non-genetic factors. The authors reject the hypothesis that the mean IQ differences between blacks and whites are caused solely by environmental differences, commenting: "The *average* environment of blacks would have to be at the 6th percentile of the distribution of environments among whites, and the *average* environment of East Asians would have to be at the 63rd percentile of environments among whites, for the racial differences to be entirely environmental." This is the crux of the issue: *Could the prejudicial treatment of blacks in America during the last two hundred years have been so crippling as to produce a downshift of the mean IQ by some 15 points?* I find this thesis more plausible than do the authors, especially since most of the legislation outlawing racial discrimination is only about thirty years old. Little more than one generation ago, life was deeply different for blacks and whites in America, and social changes follow legislation slowly.

The issue cannot be resolved yet, but it deserves to be grappled with thoughtfully. I think Herrnstein and Murray missed an opportunity to examine the potential effects of prejudice on IQ and the other measures discussed here. They might have taken the circumstance of women and IQ as one way of establishing the *pattern* of changes that can be wrought by socialization. The advantage of looking at male-female differences (rather than racial or ethnic ones) is that men and women of the same racial background share the same gene pool; because it takes one of each sex to make a child, it is difficult to imagine how genes for high intelligence could become segregated in one sex or the other.

Today, it is acceptable and even admirable for white girls to be smart in school—at least until the age of twelve or thirteen, when school performance and girls' self-confidence plummet. In some segments of contemporary American society, females are encouraged to perform well all the way through college, with the critical drop-off point coming when the educated young woman wishes to enter graduate or professional school or obtain a job. The potency of the effect of discrimination over time can be seen by taking as an example the Johns Hopkins Medical School, a highly competitive professional school that trains many of the leaders of academic medicine in America. At its founding in 1892, the institution reluctantly agreed to admit women into every class on an equal footing with men—on pain of repaying a large financial contribution (plus accumulated interest) to a group of Baltimore women if the school ever failed in this undertaking. Yet not until 1994 did Hopkins Medical School have an entering class that was 50 percent (indeed slightly over 50 percent) female. Of the full professors at Hopkins who will teach this incoming class, only 11 percent are female: an indication of the environment for bright women who entered the system twenty to thirty years ago. Progress was very slow for the first ninety-odd years of Hopkins's history, accelerating rapidly in the last decade.

Data in *The Bell Curve* trace the outlines of a pattern of discrimination. The mean IQ score for females is about 2 points lower than for males (versus the 15 points that recurs in black-white comparisons), and the variance of scores—the scatter around the mean—is more restricted in females than in males. This suggests that part of the bell curve of female scores has been truncated; given the lower mean score, a reasonable hypothesis is that the upper end of the bell curve has been cut off. The correlates of IQ are also distorted by discrimination. Although IQ correlates highly with job status, job performance, and income among white males and working women, the correlation becomes meaningless with the inclusion of women throughout the range of IQ who are unemployed or denied employment.

Discrimination against blacks in America, until very recently, has been far stronger and more pervasive than that leveled at women, and its effects can be expected to be more dramatic. While the brightest and most determined blacks have succeeded—as have the brightest and most determined women—there has surely been a cost to everyone else. It will take further insightful analysis to determine just how great that cost has been. By opening the discussion and daring to educate their readers, Herrnstein and Murray have set the stage for such work.

As *The Bell Curve* suggests, whether low intelligence is fostered by genetic inheritance or nurtured by a culture of poverty, it is nonetheless passed from generation to generation. Herrnstein and Murray make some brave and radical suggestions, presented out of a genuine sense of responsibility and a fervent hope for a better future than the one our current policies will produce. Their prognosis is one we must take seriously, whether or not we accept their interpretations of the IQ data; and their prescription for social change, though daunting, is one we must listen to carefully. Ask not for whom *The Bell Curve* tolls; it tolls for all of us.

LIVING WITH INEQUALITY

Eugene D. Genovese

R ICHARD HERRNSTEIN and Charles Murray might not feel
at home with Daniel Patrick Moynihan and Lani Guinier, but they
should. However vast the differences between Mr. Moynihan's ill-fated
report on the black family, Miss Guinier's remarkable attempt to resurrect Calhoun's concurrent majority, and the message of *The Bell Curve*,
they have all been brave attempts to force a national debate on urgent
matters that will not go away. And they have met the same fate. Once
again academia and the mass media are straining every muscle to suppress debate. That the liberal and radical left is doing so in the name of
multicultural diversity merely proves that, contrary to the ignorant complaints of right-wingers, the left does have a sense of humor—of sorts.

The New York Times has led the way. The editors, apparently
appalled that their usually PC Sunday *Book Review* treated *The Bell
Curve* fairly, immediately launched a day-by-day campaign on their op-
ed page, in their letters-to-the-editor column, and in their own editorial space—a campaign marked not so much by gross distortion, puerile
reasoning, and "McCarthyite" slander as by flagrant lying about the
contents of the book.

Eugene D. Genovese is the author of numerous books, including *The Southern Tradition:
The Achievement and Limitations of an American Conservatism*. His article appeared in the
National Review, December 5, 1994.

So what else is new? But they may well accomplish their objective if conservatives and others committed to the rational discussion of burning issues rise to the defense of this thoughtful, challenging, and deeply flawed book by papering over its grave weaknesses, its carelessness, and its self-defeating tendencies. If the debate becomes polarized in that fashion, *The Bell Curve* may sell well, but its honorable larger purpose will be defeated.

The Bell Curve has much to offer. Its excellent analysis of the transformation of the American elite deserves high praise and a many-sided elaboration and critique, as do its cautious and modest proposals for reforms that, happily, do not fit any particular ideological pigeonhole. And the authors get three cheers for their ruthless exposure of the powers that be who cynically preach anti-elitism while they practice a sinister elitism that assaults our family life, educational institutions, and political culture. Whether we can build on the constructive efforts of *The Bell Curve* will depend heavily on our willingness to separate wheat from chaff and, especially, to challenge the book's incoherent treatment of race.

For incoherent it is. Herrnstein and Murray begin by rejecting "race" as a category that will not stand scientific analysis—as a category at best useless and at worst pernicious. They then go on for more than 800 pages to explore the ramifications of the category they have rejected. They use sleight of hand, speaking throughout of "ethnicity." Well then, why do they lump all blacks together? Where, apart from a few inadequate and unhelpful remarks, do we find an examination of the ethnic differences *among* blacks in, say, performance on IQ tests? And the same criticism could be extended to the treatment of whites, not all of whom might respond to other comparisons with the equanimity they show for comparisons involving blacks. Personally, I am pleased to be told that blacks are not as smart as Sicilians, but I would not recommend that anyone try to tell me that Sicilians are not as smart as WASPs or Jews.

Herrnstein and Murray insist that genetic endowment plays a significant role in intelligence—they do not, as mendacious critics charge, make it the whole story—and that IQ scores are in fact meaningful and must be taken into account. I find nothing here to have a kitten over, although, as I hope they would acknowledge, the state of scientific investigation should render all generalizations tentative and subject to further research. To be sure, liberal critics seem determined to suppress such research, lest it end in ideologically unpalatable findings. The trouble with suppression is that it will not work: sooner or later the truth will out. Still, Father Neuhaus and other conservatives may be excused for suggesting that civilized societies have always found it prudent to restrict the range of public discussion when it threatens to rend society to no good end.

And here the authors come close to a plunge into socially dangerous irresponsibility when they insist that blacks, considered not individually but as a group, have lower intelligence than whites. If race is an unsustainable category, and if we lump all blacks and all whites together in that unsustainable category, exactly what, we may ask, is the subject of this discussion?

Herrnstein and Murray slip into chilling naïveté, if not disingenuousness. Incredibly, they argue that whites need not be led into discrimination against individual blacks just because the collective IQ ratings of blacks fall below those of whites. Each person, they solemnly aver, should be taken as an individual and treated accordingly. What world do they live in? Do they seriously believe that any such sermon would, could, or should dictate the policy of employers with bills to pay, payrolls to meet, and profits to make? May I suggest that employers would have to be either saints or idiots not to be influenced by the collective statistics in choosing between competing individuals? The state could, of course, intervene to make employers act like saints or idiots, but Herrnstein and Murray advocate no such political program.

Conversely, do they seriously believe that the allegedly scientific demonstration of the inferiority of blacks as a group would not have devastating effects on the ability of black individuals to cope with the discrimination described at length in this book? Individual blacks would have to rise to heroic stature to resist such an assault on their self-confidence. And I do wonder if Herrnstein and Murray have reflected on the probability and consequences of the caste war between mulattoes and blacks that their argument invites. Once again, they may tell us that we must always be ready to face the truth bravely, but there is nothing brave, wise, prudent, or sensible in proclaiming a "truth" based on an unsustainable category of analysis that threatens society with civil war and threatens individuals with unspeakable and unnecessary pain in their everyday lives.

Given the explicit opposition of Herrnstein and Murray to racism and discrimination, given their no less firm commitment to the treatment of each person as an individual, and given their thoughtful proposals for improving the position of blacks in American society, how are we to understand their obsession with racial categories, the justification for which they reject at the outset? By proceeding as they have, they have done a disservice to themselves and to their salutary program of social reform by deflecting what should be a discussion of a wide variety of pressing problems onto terrain on which constructive discussion will be difficult to conduct. Which is too bad. For this is on balance a rich and valuable book, the constructive features of which far outweigh its mischievous nonsense.

The most valuable contribution of *The Bell Curve* lies in its exposure of the egalitarian swindle that is being promoted not only by a deranged left but also by an ideologically driven free-market right that reduces people to individual units in the manner of discrete commodities in the marketplace. (And be it noted: since free-market right-wingers also have a sense of humor—of sorts—they promote this twaddle while they preach family, religious, and community values, which the consumer choice and radical individualism of the marketplace have everywhere been undermining.) Herrnstein and Murray bluntly call upon us to learn—or, rather, relearn—to live with inequality. God bless them for it. But we dare not forget that it is inequality among individuals that remains the issue. It will take a maximum effort to bring a high-spirited American people, whose virtues do not include a readiness to accept authority or limits on what men may accomplish in this world, to a realistic appraisal of the narrow range within which it is sensible to speak of equality.

No such political effort will have a prayer without maximum intellectual clarity. The greater part of this infuriating book contributes manfully to that clarity. The lesser part—which is getting all the attention, thanks in part to the authors' obsession with a pointless, not to say destructive, sideshow—threatens to ruin the project. We must not let that happen.

PAROXYSMS OF DENIAL

Arthur R. Jensen

COMMENTING not as an advocate but as an expert witness, I can say that *The Bell Curve* is correct in all its essential facts. The graphically presented analyses of fresh data (from the National Longitudinal Survey of Youth) are consistent with the preponderance of past studies. Nowadays the factual basis of *The Bell Curve* is scarcely debated by the experts, who regard it as mainstream knowledge.

The most well-established facts: Individual differences in general cognitive ability are reliably measured by IQ tests. IQ is strongly related, probably more than any other single measurable trait, to many important educational, occupational, economic, and social variables. (Not mentioned in the book is that IQ is also correlated with a number of variables of the brain, including its size, electrical potentials, and rate of glucose metabolism during cognitive activity.) Individual differences in adult IQ are largely genetic, with a heritability of about 70 percent. So far, attempts to raise IQ by educational or psychological means have failed to show appreciable lasting effects on cognitive ability and scholastic achievement. The IQ distribution in two population groups socially recognized as "black" and "white" is represented by two largely overlapping bell curves with their means separated by

Arthur R. Jensen is professor emeritus of educational psychology at the University of California, Berkeley. His article appeared in the *National Review*, December 5, 1994.

about 15 points, a difference not due to test bias. IQ has the same meaning and practical predictive validity for both groups. Tests do not create differences; they merely reflect them.

The conjunction of these facts is a troubling picture to most people. And rightly so. The book's penultimate chapter ("The Way We Are Headed"), in the light of the chapters that precede it, probably leaves most readers depressed and disturbed, and it should. I, for one, am not all that comforted by the final chapter's remedial recommendations for public policy, entirely sensible though they may be. In the present climate, they have a slim chance of being realized. Yet one hates to believe there may be no morally acceptable, feasible, and effective way to mitigate the most undesirable social consequences of the increasing IQ stratification of the nation's population. The phenomenon itself is almost inevitable in a technological civilization. It is simply more salient when there are large subpopulations that differ in mean IQ. The "custodial society," which the authors portray as the worst scenario for public policy (and which their recommendations are intended to prevent), is hardly an agreeable resolution to most Americans. Yet at present it seems that is "the way we are headed."

The topic of race differences in IQ occupies only a fraction of *The Bell Curve* and is not at all essential to its main argument. All the socially important correlates of IQ are demonstrated in the white population sample. But the mass media have pounced exclusively on the race issue and, with a few notable exceptions, by and large have gone into paroxysms of denial, trashing the factual basis of *The Bell Curve* in every conceivable way, as if obeying a categorical imperative to inoculate the public against it.

Although social problems involving race are conspicuously in the news these days, too few journalists are willing or able to discuss rationally certain possible causes. The authors' crime, apparently, is that they do exactly this, arguing with impressive evidence that the implications of IQ variance in American society can't be excluded from a realistic diagnosis of its social problems.

The media's spectacular denial probably arises from the juxtaposition of the book's demonstrations; first, that what is termed "social pathology"—delinquency, crime, drug abuse, illegitimacy, child neglect, permanent welfare dependency—is disproportionately concentrated (for whites and blacks alike) in the segment of the population with IQs below 75; and second, that at least one-fourth of the black population (compared to one-twentieth of the white population) falls below that critical IQ point in the bell curve. Because the smaller percentage of white persons with IQs below 75 are fairly well scattered throughout the population, many are guided, helped, and protected by their abler families, friends, and neighbors, whose IQs average closer to 100. Relatively few are liable to be concentrated in the poor neighborhoods and housing projects that harbor the "critical mass" of very low IQs which generates more than its fair share of social pathology. The "critical mass" effect exists mostly in the inner city, which has been largely abandoned by whites. Of course thinking citizens are troubled. Thinking about possible constructive remedies strains one's wisdom.

But can any good for anyone result from sweeping the problem under the rug? Shouldn't it be exposed to earnest, fair-minded public discussion? Our only real fear, I think, should be that such discussion might not happen. Consideration of the book's actual content is being displaced by the rhetoric of denial: name calling ("neo-nazi," "pseudo-scientific," "racism," "quackery"), sidetracks ("but does IQ really measure intelligence?"), non sequiturs ("specific genes for IQ have not been identified, so we can claim nothing about its heritability"), red herrings ("Hitler misused genetics"), *ad hominem* attacks ("written in a conservative think tank"), falsehoods ("all the tests are biased"), hyperbole ("throwing gasoline on a fire"), and insults ("dishonest," "creepy," "indecent," "ugly").

The remedy for this obfuscation is simply to read the book itself. We should hope that President Clinton will do so before he speaks out on the subject again, or at least ask his science advisor's opinion of whether it is a serious work on important issues by qualified scholars. It would clear the air if the president asked the National Academy of Sciences to appoint a panel of experts to evaluate the factual claims of *The Bell Curve* and report its conclusions to the public. There is a precedent for such an action. Following the publication of my book *Bias in Mental Testing*, the NAS convened a panel of experts to examine the body of research it covered and issued a two-volume report confirming my main conclusions. A similar detailed examination of *The Bell Curve* seems warranted by the public's evident concern with the empirical substance of the argument and its meaning for the nation's future.

IS INTELLIGENCE FIXED?

Nathan Glazer

T HAT PEOPLE DIFFER in intelligence, that the more intelligent will do better at many things, that IQ tests (and a good
number of other similar tests) will give us a pretty good picture of how
people differ in intelligence—there is not much to object to in all of
this. Elaboration on these matters of common judgment makes up half
or more of *The Bell Curve*. Even this much has been found objectionable in the past, and will be found objectionable today, and by people
of, one assumes, high intelligence. Thus one federal judge in California has asserted, as a matter of law, that intelligence tests cannot be
used to place duller children in classes designed to help them, and
intelligence tests have been subjected to massive, book-length assault
by distinguished scientists because some of those who devised and
used them believed there were inherited differences in intelligence
among races.

On these matters Herrnstein and Murray are to me completely convincing. On more controversial matters, such as the notion that there
are substantial differences in intelligence among different groups
defined by a common inheritance and culture, they are also convincing

Nathan Glazer is co-editor of *The Public Interest*, professor of education and sociology
emeritus at Harvard University, and is the author of numerous books, including *The Limits of Social Policy*. His article appeared in the *National Review*, December 5, 1994.

to me. We take these differences in intelligence for granted in the case of families, and it stands to reason that such differences might also characterize larger groups that share some common features in genetic inheritance and culture. Otherwise we would have no explanation for the disproportionate presence of Jews and Asians in selective high schools and selective colleges, or the disproportionate presence of these groups in such occupations as medicine, law, and college teaching.

We could give a variety of explanations for these phenomena short of any reference to genes—for example, the disproportionate presence of persons of high education among immigrants from a number of Asian countries (some of these groups have a higher proportion of college graduates than do native Americans), or the high socioeconomic position they obtain on the basis of this education, and the background they are thus able to offer to their children; or the urban background of Jewish immigrants as contrasted with the predominantly peasant background of other immigrant groups that arrived here around the turn of the century. I would have preferred that Herrnstein and Murray had paid more attention to these differences as explanations of group differences in intelligence, owing to what has been made in the past of differences based on race. But on reflection, it hardly matters whether the differences are genetic or environmental; people can be brutal to those different from themselves regardless of the ultimate reasons for the difference.

On three further extensions of the argument, however, I would take issue with Herrnstein and Murray. First, how fixed are these differences? Second, are there interventions that could raise the test performance of persons and groups who score below average? Third, what about policies—that is, affirmative action—that set aside differences in performance in favor of group representation?

Herrnstein and Murray give some surprising data (surprising in the light of their argument that intelligence is fixed early and can't be changed appreciably through environmental intervention) on the degree to which differences between whites and blacks in performance on educational tests have been reduced in the past twenty years. The National Assessment of Educational Progress has been giving tests in science, mathematics, and reading to groups of school-children of different ages since 1969. The reductions in the differences between white and black performance in standard deviations (a crucial statistical measure of difference that will not be further explained here, but that Herrnstein and Murray explain admirably in the book) range from .12 to .44. As they write: "The overall average gap of .92 standard deviation in the 1969–1973 tests had shrunk to .64 standard deviation in 1990. The gap narrowed because black scores rose, not because white scores fell." There has also been a narrowing of the gap in SAT scores, they report.

I wonder why more is not made of this. After all, while we have tried to do a good deal, through various programs, to put more money into the education of low-achieving, mostly black inner-city children, this has not been an overwhelming national effort. Simultaneously there has been a drastic decline in the environment of many of these children—more drugs, more crime, more illegitimacy. If so much has been achieved with relatively little, why can we not expect further progress? Among all the wonderful charts in this book, it would have been interesting to see one mapping this reduction and extending it into the future.

One of the more intriguing data comes from a study of the children of black American servicemen and German women in Germany. There is no difference in IQ between these children and the children of white American servicemen and German women. This reminds one of the older literature, inspired by the desire to counter racism in the 1920s and 1930s, on the change possible in what were considered fixed racial characteristics. Fifty years ago, one read Otto Klineberg, who seemed to have given a fatal blow to theories of the fixity of intelligence by showing that blacks in the North scored higher on general intelligence tests than whites (or perhaps it was certain groups of whites) in the South. I would like to have seen what later research has done to this argument, but there is nothing on regional differences in intelligence in the book, and Klineberg is not in the massive bibliography.

Finally, on affirmative action Herrnstein and Murray tell us much that is not generally known but has been available for a long time— ever since Justice Powell, in his opinion in the *Bakke* case, contrasted Allan Bakke's scores on the Medical College Admission Test with the remarkably lower scores of those admitted under the affirmative-action program; ever since Thomas Sowell began making his powerful arguments on the too-large gap between black and non-black students in colleges that aggressively recruit the former; ever since Robert

Klitgaard, in his important book *Choosing Elites*, demonstrated how far down in the pool highly selective college and graduate programs have to reach to get substantial numbers of black students.

We know the story, but what is to be done? Once again, white students who feel they have been discriminated against by an affirmative-action program are suing an institution of higher education (the University of Texas Law School), and the Supreme Court will have to consider the matter. The documents in the case—no surprise—show that without the program of special preference, blacks would constitute only 1 to 2 percent of the class, a fraction of the number now enrolled. The degree of preference could be less, the amount of perceived unfairness reduced. But I do not see how a country that has struggled so long, and still struggles, to make blacks full and equal participants can take a purely meritocratic position on such matters. If higher education served only to qualify students to become theoretical physicists or Sanskritists, we could remain indifferent to group consequences of purely meritocratic selection. But it does considerably more than that. Group representation must be a consideration, and all we can do is argue about the details.

METHODOLOGICAL FETISHISM

Brigitte Berger

F OR ALL ITS WEALTH of data, skillful argumentation, and scope, *The Bell Curve* is a narrow and deeply flawed book. Murray and Herrnstein have fallen prey to a methodological fetishism that prevents them from adequately considering alternative, equally plausible inferences that can be drawn from the studies they marshal to buttress their conclusions.

The argument of *The Bell Curve* is carried out on two distinct, though in the authors' minds interrelated, levels. On the first, they discuss issues related to the rise of a "cognitive elite," a trend characteristic of *all* industrial societies, whose knowledge-driven economies offer fewer and fewer employment opportunities for people unable to operate in the type of occupations such economies require. On the second level, they argue that a more or less permanent underclass, characterized by the prevalence of low cognitive ability, is becoming a fixture of American society.

Both observations have been discussed here and abroad for some time. But by adding the dimension of race, a factor peculiar to American society, *The Bell Curve* carries the discussion in new directions. Race-determined cognitive ability, they argue, is the underlying real-

Brigitte Berger is a professor of sociology at Boston University. Her article appeared in the *National Review*, December 5, 1994.

ity driving a grisly sorting process that is dividing the nation. Caught in an epistemological paradigm in which psychological operations are reduced to genetic ones, they suggest that biology is destiny. No amount of camouflage or public and private efforts to create a level playing field, they imply, can prevent the inexorable slide of African Americans into a cognitive caste.

The question is not whether Murray and Herrnstein's argument is "racist"; the question is whether the empirically measured differences among racial groups reflect "intelligence." The tests do indeed measure *something*, but it is not "intelligence." Rather, they measure what I have called "modern consciousness," a set of intellectual skills that are particularly relevant to operating in the highly specialized worlds of modern technology and rationalistically organized bureaucracies. These core institutions of modern society are produced by, and in turn produce, peculiarly modern cognitive styles: the ability to operate on high levels of abstraction; to break reality down analytically into components; to keep multiple relationships in mind simultaneously; and, especially significant for IQ testing, to relate present tasks to possible future consequences. This last skill, by definition, can be achieved only on the basis of past experiences and habits of thought that individuals acquire during the earliest period of socialization, when a basic matrix of cognition develops.

Once one is willing to entertain this alternative explanation for the bulk of the data presented in this book, many things fall into place: the well-documented phenomenon of globally rising test scores as modernization progresses and, similarly, the "leveling off" of rising SAT scores among the most gifted students in already modernized countries; the much-noted capacity of East Asian students to outscore non–East Asians on the nonverbal part of IQ tests, which may be understood as attesting to the "cultural capital" of East Asians rather than their genetic superiority; the measured differences in IQ among siblings, known as the birth-order effect; the shift in scores when an individual moves from a rural to an urban setting or from one social class to another. The list could be expanded.

Murray and Herrnstein's methodological fixation blinds them to a different way of understanding these phenomena. The deficiency is especially conspicuous in their interpretation of the relatively low scores of African Americans as a group. While everyone would agree

that some individuals are smarter than others and that IQ is not as malleable as some have argued in the past, there is good evidence that
socialization practices (particularly in the early years) and factors of
family structure and interaction, of neighborhood and religion, help
shape an individual's cognitive structure. If one looks at the data presented in this book from the "modern consciousness" analytical framework, it becomes clear that African Americans, as a group, continue to
lead lives distant from the centers of modernity. Hence they have not
yet been fully initiated into the habits of thought underpinning the
operations of sophisticated technologies and organizational structures.
Yet there is no reason to suppose that this could not be changed
through the practices that help form modern consciousness.

When a methodological fetishism of the dimension manifested in
this book permeates the interpretation of individuals, groups, and social
life as a whole, the conclusions about what is to be done may indeed
look like those reached by Murray and Herrnstein. The authors conjure
up a future strangely at odds with everything I know both of them cherish, a future in which human efforts and virtues become ever more
insignificant. What remains is the triumph of pure intelligence. Looking at the future from the perspective I propose, however, one would
ask whether it is not likely that we, as a society, will come to put a premium on human qualities that have less to do with formal intelligence
than with an individual's capacity for, say, empathy, a sense of humor, or
religious commitment. What type of individuals, for example, will staff
the institutions of elder care that demography will increasingly require?
To put it succinctly: when I am about to die of Alzheimer's, I emphatically do not wish to be taken care of by Charles Murray.

The authors appear to believe sincerely that when everyone knows
his "place" in society (i.e., when individuals and groups accept their
genetic limitations), everything will be in balance. Yet a reliance upon
IQ as the ultimate arbiter in social policy could well make for sloth and
frivolity among all classes, with those at the top smugly certain that
they belong there, while the rest assume there is no point in making
any effort at all. If there is one thing more disturbing than a ruling class
based on privilege, it is a ruling class that believes it deserves its position by virtue of its intelligence. The one hopeful element of this scenario is that the cognitive elite, in its self-satisfied arrogance, would
become so lazy that its regime would not last long.

The implications of this book for American conservatives are, to my mind, quite simple. The worst thing for conservatives to do would be to become identified with the Murray-Herrnstein position. The "balkanization from the left" that conservatives have so valiantly fought for these past decades would be overshadowed by a specter of technological totalitarianism hardly consonant with visions of liberty and democracy.

DISPIRITED

Glenn C. Loury

R EADING HERRNSTEIN and Murray's treatise causes me
once again to reflect on the limited utility in the management
of human affairs of that academic endeavor generously termed social
science. The authors of *The Bell Curve* undertake to pronounce upon
what is possible for human beings to do while failing to consider that
which most makes us human. They begin by seeking the causes of
behavior and end by reducing the human subject to a mechanism
whose horizon is fixed by some combination of genetic endowment
and social law. Yet we, even the "dullest" of us, are so much more
than that.

Now, as an economist I am a card-carrying member of the social scientists' cabal; so these doubts now creeping over me have far-reaching
personal implications. But entertain them I must, for the stakes in the
discussion this book has engendered are too high. The question on the
table, central to our nation's future and, I might add, to the future success of a conservative politics in America, is this: Can we sensibly
aspire to a more complete social integration than has yet been
achieved of those who now languish at the bottom of American soci-

Glenn C. Loury is University Professor and professor of economics at Boston University.
His article appeared in the *National Review*, December 5, 1994.

ety? A political movement that answers no to this question must fail, and richly deserves to.

Herrnstein and Murray are not entirely direct on this point. They stress, plausibly enough, that we must be realistic in formulating policy, taking due account of the unequal distribution of intellectual aptitudes in the population, recognizing that limitations of mental ability constrain what sorts of policies are likely to make a difference and how much of a difference they can make. But implicit in their argument is the judgment that we shall have to get used to there being a substantial minority of our fellows who, because of their low intelligence, may fail to perform adequately in their roles as workers, parents, and citizens. I think this is quite wrong. Social science ultimately leads the authors astray on the political and moral fundamentals.

For example, in chapters on parenting, crime, and citizenship they document that performance in these areas is correlated in their samples with cognitive ability. Though they stress that IQ is not destiny, they also stress that it is often a more important "cause" of one's level of personal achievement than factors that liberal social scientists typically invoke, such as family background and economic opportunity. Liberal analysts, they say, offer false hope by suggesting that with improved economic opportunity one can induce underclass youths to live within the law. Some citizens simply lack the wits to manage their affairs so as to avoid criminal violence, be responsive to their children, and exercise the franchise, Herrnstein and Murray argue. If we want our "duller" citizens to obey our laws, we must change the laws (by, e.g., restoring simple rules and certain, severe punishments). Thus: "People of limited intelligence can lead moral lives in a society that is run on the basis of 'Thou shalt not steal.' They find it much harder to lead moral lives in a society that is run on the basis of 'Thou shalt not steal unless there is a really good reason to.' "

There is a case to be made—a conservative case—for simplifying the laws, for making criminals anticipate certain and swift punishment as the consequence of their crimes, and for adhering to traditional notions about right and wrong as exemplified in the commandment "Thou shalt not steal." Indeed, a case can be made for much of the policy advice given in this book—for limiting affirmative action, for seeking a less centralized and more citizen-friendly administration of government, for halting the encouragement now given to out-of-wedlock childbearing, and so on. But there is no reason that I can see to rest such a case on the presumed mental limitations of a sizable number of citizens. In every instance there are political arguments for these policy prescriptions that are both more compelling and more likely to succeed in the public arena than the generalizations about human capacities that Herrnstein and Murray claim to have established with their data.

Observing a correlation between a noisy measure of parenting skills, say, and some score on an ability test is a far cry from discovering an immutable law of nature. Social scientists are a long way from producing a definitive account of the causes of human performance in educational attainment and economic success, the areas that have been most intensively studied by economists and sociologists over the last half-century. The claim implicitly advanced in this book to have achieved a scientific understanding of the *moral* performance of the citizenry adequate to provide a foundation for social policy is breathtakingly audacious.

I urge Republican politicians and conservative intellectuals to think long and hard before chanting this IQ mantra in public discourses. Herrnstein and Murray frame their policy discussion so as to guarantee that its appeal will be limited to an electoral minority. Try telling the newly energized Christian right that access to morality is contingent on mental ability. Their response is likely to be, "God is not finished with us when he deals us our genetic hand."

This is surely right. We human beings are spiritual creatures; we have souls; we have free will. We are, of course, constrained in various ways by biological and environmental realities. But we can, with effort, make ourselves morally fit members of our political communities. If we fully exploit our material and spiritual inheritance, we can become decent citizens and loving parents, despite the constraints. We deserve from our political leaders a vision of our humanity that recognizes and celebrates this potential.

Such a spiritual argument is one that a social scientist may find hard to understand. Yet the spiritual resources of human beings are key to the maintenance of social stability and progress. They are the ultimate foundation of any hope we can have of overcoming the social malaise of the underclass. This is why the mechanistic determinism of science is, in the end, inadequate to the task of social prescription. Political science has no account of why people vote; psychology has yet to identify the material basis of religious exhilaration; economics can say only that people give to charities because it makes them feel good to do so. No analyst predicted that the people of Eastern Europe would, in Vaclav Havel's memorable phrase, rise to achieve "a sense of transcendence over the world of existences." With the understanding of causality in social science so limited, and the importance of matters of the spirit so palpable, one might expect a bit of humble circumspection from analysts who presume to pronounce upon what is possible for human beings to accomplish.

Whatever the merits of their social science, Herrnstein and Murray are in a moral and political cul-de-sac. I see no reason for serious conservatives to join them there. This difficulty is most clearly illustrated with the fierce debate about racial differences in intelligence that *The Bell Curve* has spawned. The authors will surely get more grief than they deserve for having stated the facts of this matter—that on the average blacks lag significantly behind whites in cognitive functioning. That is not my objection. What I find problematic is their suggestion that we accommodate ourselves to the inevitability of the difference in mental performance among the races in America. This posture of resignation is an unacceptable response to today's tragic reality. We can be prudent and hard-headed about what government can and cannot accomplish through its various instruments of policy without abandoning hope of achieving racial reconciliation within our national community.

In reality, the record of black American economic and educational achievement in the post-civil-rights era has been ambiguous—great success mixed with shocking failure. Myriad explanations for the failure have been advanced, but the account that attributes it to the limited mental abilities of blacks is singular in its suggestion that we must learn to live with current racial disparities. It is true that for too long the loudest voices of African-American authenticity offered discrimination by whites as the excuse for every black disability; they treated evidence of limited black achievement as an automatic indictment of the American social order. These racialists are hoist with their own petard by the arguments and data in *The Bell Curve*. Having taught us to examine each individual life first through a racial lens, they must now confront the specter of a racial-intelligence accountancy that suggests a rather different explanation for the ambiguous achievements of blacks in the last generation.

So the question now on the floor, in the minds of blacks as well as whites, is whether blacks are capable of gaining equal status, given equality of opportunity. It is a peculiar mind that fails to fathom how poisonous a question this is for our democracy. Let me state my unequivocal belief that blacks are, indeed, so capable. Still, any assertion of equal black capacity is a hypothesis or an axiom, not a fact. The fact is that blacks have something to prove, to ourselves and to what W. E. B. Du Bois once characterized as "a world that looks on in amused contempt and pity." This is not fair; it is not right; but it is the way things are.

Some conservatives are not above signaling, in more or less overt ways, their belief that blacks can never pass this test. Some radical black nationalists agree, arguing increasingly more openly now that blacks can never make it in "white America" and so should stop trying, go our own way, and maybe burn a few things down in the process. At bottom these parties share the belief that the magnitude of the challenge facing blacks is beyond what we can manage. I insist, to the contrary, that we can and must meet this challenge. I find it spectacularly unhelpful to be told, "Success is unlikely given your average mental equipment, but never mind, because cognitive ability is not the only currency for measuring human worth." This is, in fact, precisely what Herrnstein and Murray say. I shudder at the prospect that this could be the animating vision of a governing conservative coalition in this country. But I take comfort in the certainty that, should conservatives be unwise enough to embrace it, the American people will be decent enough to reject it.

THE MULTICULTURAL TRAP

Charles Krauthammer

"The black-white IQ difference (is) about 15 points
in the U.S. . . . ."

"In the United States, blacks of above-average
socioeconomic status have not averaged as high IQ
as whites of lower socioeconomic status."

"The question here is not whether [group] differences [in mental test performance] are cultural or
genetic in origin. The point is that they are real and
that their consequences are real."

S O T H I S is Charles Murray's heresy, the incendiary declarations
about race and IQ that have landed him and his co-authored
book, *The Bell Curve*, on the cover of *Newsweek*, *The New Republic*, and
The New York Times Magazine, and landed him in the liberal pantheon of
bigoted pseudoscience.

Charles Krauthammer is a contributing editor of *The New Republic* and a syndicated columnist. This column appeared as "Why Can't We Count People One by One?" in *The Washington Post*, October 23, 1994.

Well, no. The quotations above are from *Race and Culture* (chapter 6, "Race and Intelligence") published just two months before *The Bell Curve*. The author is Thomas Sowell, the Stanford economist and social scientist. Sowell is black. And his interest in ethnic differences in mental capacity is even broader than Murray's.

Starting with Cicero's observation twenty centuries ago that Britons were too stupid to make good slaves, Sowell offers a worldwide survey of ethnic differences in intelligence. They are ubiquitous. "Among Indians in colonial Malaya, for example, Tamils had higher scores than Gurkhas, and both had higher scores than Bengalis in Bengal." In math, he points out, ethnic Chinese school children outperform the English in Hong Kong, the Malays in Singapore, the Indonesians in Indonesia. In the United States, East Asians outperform whites.

With the phenomenon of ethnic IQ differences so universal, Sowell is quite relaxed about the American black-white difference. He notes (in a passage I purposely truncated above) that "the black-white IQ difference of about 15 points in the U.S. has been matched by the IQ difference between Sephardic and Ashkenazic Jews in Israel or between Catholics and Protestants in Northern Ireland."

Murray's *Bell Curve*, on the other hand, is more narrowly focused on ethnic differences in the United States. In particular, it marshals voluminous validation for the black-white IQ differences that Sowell and others have noted. For this, Murray has been subjected to fierce personal attack. To take an example almost at random, sociologist Alan Wolfe writes that "Murray and [co-author Richard] Herrnstein may not be racists, but they are obsessed by race. They see the world in group terms and must have data on group membership."

An interesting charge, given the fact that for the last two decades it is the very liberals who so vehemently denounce Murray who have been obsessed by race, insisting that every institution—universities, fire departments, Alaskan canneries—"must have data on group membership." It is they who have oppressively insisted that we measure ethnic "over-" and "underrepresentation" in every possible field of human endeavor. To take only the latest example, on September 26, 1994, the federal government proposed that banks making small business loans be required to ask the applicant's race and gender.

Not a month goes by when I do not get a survey of some sort in which I am asked to identify myself by race. (As a rule, I refuse.) Here is a liberal establishment forcing racial testing and counting for every conceivable activity, and when a study comes along which does exactly that for SATs and IQ, the author is pilloried for being obsessed by race.

In fact, Murray is obsessed by class. *The Bell Curve* is a powerful, scrupulous, landmark study of the relationship between intelligence and social class, which is what the book is mainly about. It is secondarily about differences among ethnicities (they are not addressed until Chapter 13), which is what the fuss is about.

I have two difficulties with the book. First, I see no reason to assume that group differences in intelligence (as opposed to individual variation) have anything to do with genes. The more plausible explanation is Sowell's: Ethnic differences in intelligence, which change over time (the British have come up smartly since Cicero), are due to culture, that part of the environment which, unlike socioeconomic status, is unmeasurable.

Second, I have trouble with Murray's recommendations about what to do with the fact of inequality. He offers a kind of conservative multiculturalism in which each ethnicity finds its honored niche in society according to its own areas of excellence and distinction.

I distrust all multiculturalism, liberal or conservative. The Balkans amply demonstrate the perils of balkanization. My answer is simpler: Stop counting by race. Stop allocating by race. Stop measuring by race. Let's return to measuring individuals. It seems hopelessly naive to propose this today. But it was not naive when first proposed by Martin Luther King, Jr. and accepted by a white society that was finally converted to his vision of color blindness. Instead, through guilt and intimidation, a liberal establishment has since mandated that every study of achievement in American life be broken down by race. *The Bell Curve* takes that mandate to its logical conclusion.

Enough. As both Murray and Sowell explicitly state, knowing the group score tells you nothing about the individual. Well, we have now seen the group score. Let's all go back to counting individuals. How many of Murray's critics will agree to that?

BACK TO THE FUTURE

Richard Lynn

A COCKTAIL of IQ, genetics, class, and race makes a heady brew, and readers of Richard Herrnstein and Charles Murray's book *The Bell Curve* dealing with these issues will not be disappointed. Both authors are social science heavyweights. Herrnstein is a professor of psychology at Harvard and Murray a political scientist at the American Enterprise Institute. They argue the case that low IQ plays a significant role in many important economic and social problems, including those of chronic unemployment, single motherhood, welfare dependency, and crime. To understand these problems fully, and to find the right solutions, we need to understand that low intelligence is a significant component of them.

Intelligence is measured on a scale on which the average of the population is 100 and 96 percent of the population fall within the range of 70, the upper threshold of mental retardation, and 130, roughly the lower threshold required to get a good honors degree. Two percent of the population fall in the IQ range of 0 to 70 and constitute the mentally retarded, while a further 2 percent fall in the range of 130 to 200 and constitute the intellectual elite. Virtually all the readers of this arti-

Richard Lynn is a professor of psychology at the University of Ulster in Coleraine. This review appeared in *The Times* (London), October 24, 1994, under the title "Is Man Breeding Himself Back to the Age of the Apes?"

cle will belong to this intellectual elite or be close to it. Don't imagine the rest of the population are like you. They aren't.

Herrnstein and Murray amass a wealth of evidence to show that the IQ levels of those who constitute the major social problems are substantially subnormal. To be precise, the average IQ of the mothers of illegitimate children is 88; of chronic welfare recipients, 85; of recidivist criminals, 80; and of the long-term unemployed, 77. Collectively, these social problem groups are known as the underclass, and the bottom line is that the underclass has an intelligence deficit.

The reason why low IQ is an important component of the underclass is easily understood. Intelligence is the capacity to think through the correct solution to problems, to learn quickly, and to plan one's life effectively. Those who are deficient do poorly at school, fail to acquire educational credentials and vocational skills, and are at high risk of ending up in the underclass.

The IQ deficit will not be easily solved. Intelligence is largely under genetic control. This means that the underclass is to a significant extent a genetic problem and will not be readily cured by the kinds of solution advocated by economists and politicians. Take chronic unemployment: the solution routinely advanced is more training in vocational skills. With an average IQ of 77, the chronic unemployed are not much above the level of mental retardation, and many of them are below this level. The brutal truth is that many of the chronic unemployed are mentally incapable of learning the skills increasingly required in advanced industrial economies. All they are capable of is unskilled labor, which is less and less in demand.

The future will be worse. For one thing, jobs will continue to become increasingly cognitively demanding, and the lumpen proletariat of low IQs unable to perform them will grow in numbers. Another problem is that the social classes are becoming increasingly differentiated in terms of intelligence. We have now reached the situation where at one extreme there is an intellectual elite that intermarries and produces high-IQ children. This elite hardly knows anyone with an IQ of less than 100. They have no experience of people with below-average IQs and no comprehension of the limited mental capacities of ordinary people, let alone of the intellectually subnormal.

Conversely, at the other social extreme there is an increasingly interbred low-IQ underclass which produces low-IQ children manifesting multiple social pathologies. This process is already familiar in British social science as the cycle of deprivation, although the research into the cycle activated by Sir Keith Joseph soft-pedaled any suggestion that genetic inadequacies might be involved.

Herrnstein and Murray are frank about this and argue that because intelligence is significantly under genetic control, the differentiation of the social classes has increasingly acquired a genetic basis brought about by the segregation of the genes for high intelligence in the higher social classes and the genes for low intelligence in the underclass. The threat to social cohesion posed by the underclass is exacerbated by racial division. In the United States the average IQ of blacks is 15 points below that of whites, and 16 percent of blacks have an IQ of below 70 and are mentally retarded, as compared with only 2 percent of whites. There are therefore many more blacks in the low IQ range being sucked into the underclass. Herrnstein and Murray have reached the conclusion, increasingly held by other experts in this field, that genetic factors are significantly involved in the low black IQ. Furthermore, the black underclass is growing in numbers, partly as a result of high fertility and partly through immigration. This means that the problem of the black underclass is likely to get worse in the future.

The authors' vision of the future is of Western societies becoming increasingly fractionated on the basis of intelligence. One of the major divisions will be between those who are sufficiently intelligent to work and an underclass lacking the requisite intelligence. The underclass will turn more and more to crime because it has little to lose. The crime problem will grow, and those who work will respond by moving to safe areas. Increasingly they will live in secure estates protected by fences and security guards, such as those which have sprung up in America. The heartlands of the underclass in the inner cities will be abandoned by everyone capable of working.

There is a further problem. There is one thing the underclass is good at, and that is producing children. These children tend to inherit their parents' poor intelligence and adopt their sociopathic lifestyle, reproducing the cycle of deprivation from generation to generation. The underclass has more children than the rest of society. This is another reason why it will expand in numbers and become increasingly troublesome.

It is a bleak analysis, but one convincingly documented and brilliantly expounded. The social threat of the growing underclass will not be easily solved, but at least in focusing on the low-IQ dimension Herrnstein and Murray have pinpointed an important constituent of the problem.

A MORAL IMPERATIVE

Douglas J. Besharov

I T S E E M E D L I K E a simple enough project. Christmas was coming and the local mall had jobs for gift wrappers. What better way for mothers on welfare to earn a few extra dollars? So a local job training program decided to give a group of welfare mothers a quick course in gift-wrapping before sending them off to apply for a job. It wasn't that easy. The first lesson was bows. The instructor asked the mothers to cut pieces of ribbon, each five inches long. The mothers quickly became confused—they did not know how to measure off the ribbon for cutting. There would be no jobs at the mall that season, because the mothers lacked the basic cognitive skills to wrap packages.

This true story illustrates a harsh reality: Long-term welfare recipients have extremely low cognitive abilities, at least as measured by traditional IQ tests. This is true for all races—the women at the training center just happened to be white. Almost 60 percent of women on welfare for five or more years are in the bottom 20 percent of intelligence, according to Richard Herrnstein and Charles Murray, authors of the controversial new book *The Bell Curve*.

Douglas J. Besharov, a resident scholar at the American Enterprise Institute, was the first director of the U.S. National Center on Child Abuse and Neglect. His most recent book is *Recognizing Child Abuse: A Guide for the Concerned*. This article first appeared in *The Washington Post*, October 23, 1994.

Herrnstein and Murray air social science's dirty little secret: IQ matters. As they document, using data for whites, high IQ is increasingly associated with economic and social success—and low IQ with poverty and a host of social problems, including out-of-wedlock births, welfare dependency, and crime. This undeniable reality is stunningly ignored by just about every program designed to address such problems. No wonder they fail.

The Bell Curve's unflinching recognition of racial differences in IQ test scores has, of course, generated the greatest controversy. African Americans, as a group, consistently score 15 points below whites, 85 versus 100. According to the authors, "The average white person tests higher than about 84 percent of the population of blacks."

But, what, exactly, is IQ? And how much of what we call IQ is attributable to inborn qualities and how much to environment and upbringing? This is, of course, the "nature" vs. "nurture" argument, which has been with us since before there were IQ tests. Reflecting the current scholarly consensus, Herrnstein and Murray say that "cognitive ability is substantially heritable, apparently no less than 40 percent and no more than 80 percent." For the purposes of their argument, they adopt a mid-range estimate of 60 percent heritability.

Especially in light of black-white differences in measured IQ, the issue of heritability is enormously significant. In response to charges that the book overstates the genetic component of IQ, Murray has recently written that it does not matter whether nature or nurture causes IQ differences, because either way, IQ is so difficult to raise. As evidence, Murray cites the failure of compensatory preschool and educational programs to raise IQs and to make meaningful changes in young people's lives. No clear-eyed reader of the research literature could deny these disappointing results.

But such programs hardly exhaust the possible interventions. Many linkages may exist between an individual's environment and his or her subsequently measured IQ, and these offer opportunities for intervention. Here are a few possibilities: What if IQ is affected by the mother's behavior during pregnancy?

In recent years, science has documented the importance of the fetal environment to later development. The message we try to give every pregnant woman is "Eat well, don't smoke cigarettes, don't drink alcohol and, most importantly, don't use illegal drugs like crack cocaine."

Prenatal exposure to cocaine results in newborns with smaller head circumferences, a sign of compromised brain development. All of these harmful behaviors are far more widespread among disadvantaged mothers. But they seem to afflict some racial minorities even more than economic statistics would suggest. In a recent survey, for example, Hispanic women were almost twice as likely to use cocaine while pregnant than were white women; African-American women were eleven times more likely to use cocaine. What if the first years of life are crucial?

In the first months of life, the number of synapses in the human brain increases twentyfold, from 50 trillion to 1,000 trillion. The absence of intellectual stimulation during this period is now believed to impose a permanent limit on the number of synapses, and therefore on intellectual potential. This phenomenon was demonstrated in a famous experiment in which the eyes of newborn kittens were covered for varying lengths of time. The longer their eyes were covered, the greater the permanent deficit in sight, not because their eyes were damaged, but because there were just fewer synapses in the areas of the brain responsible for processing visual images. As Jerry M. Wiener, chairman of the Department of Psychiatry at George Washington University Hospital and president of the American Psychiatric Association, explains: "What we call IQ is really the unfolding of innate abilities in response to environmental stimuli." Even smiling at a newborn may make a difference.

Again, it is disadvantaged families that are least likely to provide such cognitive cues. Numerous studies, for example, have described "lower-class child-rearing styles" as more angry and punitive, more humiliating, and less verbally interactive than middle-class child-rearing—and have correlated these differences to cognitive outcomes. These developmentally stunting child-rearing styles tend to disappear as families become more middle-class, but as Felton Earls, director of the Human Development and Criminal Behavior Program at Harvard University, explains, it can take two or three generations for the shift to occur. With so many African Americans only recently in the middle class, it should not be surprising that such behaviors have tended to linger on in what researchers consider middle-class households. What if preschool interventions could make a real change in a child's learning environment?

The Abecedarian preschool project in Chapel Hill, North Carolina, seems to have raised IQ scores by 16 points at the end of three years. Unlike Head Start, the Abecedarian project totally immersed children in a comprehensive developmental program that began within three months of birth—and provided nearly full-time care until they reached school age. Unfortunately, as the children got older—and they spent progressively less time under the influence of program staff—the gap between the experimental and control groups narrowed, to 7.6 IQ points at age five, and 4.6 points at age fifteen. "Other preschool proj-ects have also made improvements of 10 or more IQ points," notes Ron Haskins, who was the coordinator of the Abecedarian preschool project in the late 1970s, and is now the chief welfare specialist for House Republicans. "In all these projects, however, the initial IQ gains for the children in the program compared to those in the control group also shrank over time."

So we seem to be able to make early improvements in IQ; we just don't know how to make them stick. Some argue that this is the infa-mous "fade-out effect," with the children in the control group catching up with those in the program. It is just as possible, however, that other environmental factors, like neighborhood, had a supervening effect on the children in the program. What if good schools raise scores?

Forget about cultural bias in IQ tests. There is a bigger measure-ment problem. Most tests assess acquired knowledge as well as abstract thinking and problem solving, and that, of course, is where schools come in. A poor school environment, where discipline rather than learning is the first priority, could systematically depress test results. After all, if education does not matter, why are we so con-cerned about the quality of the schools where we send our children?

A change in the way schools teach could also narrow the black-white gap, according to Chester Finn, the founding partner and director of government relations for the Edison Project. "Conventional schools assume that all children learn one grade level a year, so they give both slow learners and quick learners the same 180 days of education. What if schools gave slow learners more time to learn? Would they do better? We cannot know until we try." What if neighborhoods dampen the desire of children to perform well? Young people are particularly sensitive to envi-ronmental influences. Sadly, many disadvantaged communities discour-age intellectual achievement. In African-American communities, some good students are ostracized for "acting white." That's one reason why so many of the parents who can do so move away from dysfunctional neighborhoods, and why so many of the parents who cannot leave do all they can to shield their children from neighborhood influences. Linda Burton, now a professor in human development at Pennsylvania State University, describes how she and her sisters were locked in their apartment after school to protect them from what was happening outside—and how the practice continues to this day in many inner-city neighborhoods. What if a child's entire neighborhood environment is improved dramatically?

We have a tantalizing suggestion from Chicago, where, as the result of the settlement of a housing discrimination lawsuit, *Gautraux* v. *the U.S. Department of Housing and Urban Development Chicago Housing Authority*, individual black families from housing projects could choose to participate in a program in which they would, by random assignment, be moved to either suburban white middle-class neighborhoods or to middle-class black ones within the city. Ninety-five percent of the black children who grew up in the suburbs graduated from high school and 54 percent went on to college, compared to 80 percent and 21 percent, respectively, of those who remained in the city. What if racial differences in IQ are the result of over two hundred years of slavery and more than a hundred more years of discrimination and oppression?

Since the 1950s, of course, black Americans have made major economic progress. Earnings for black men, for example, are now about 75 percent of those for white men, and the gap continues to close. But the figures for household wealth paint a much more dismal picture and show how far behind whites blacks still are: According to the Census Bureau, in 1988, the median net worth of white households was 10 times that of black and Hispanic ones, about $43,000 compared with about $4,000 and about $5,500, respectively.

But household wealth is not just money. It is also a form of stored human capital that has been built up over generations. It is what Roger Wilkins, the Robinson Professor of History and American Culture at George Mason University, describes as "the accumulated ease in dealing with the wider society." These stark disparities give a sense of the remaining gap in human capital between the races. Might not this legacy take many generations to erase? If so, perhaps carefully targeted education and affirmative action programs could succeed in giving this generation a jump start toward equality—thus permitting the next generation to reach its potential. Herrnstein and Murray are right in saying that there is no proven way to raise IQs on a consistent basis. Indeed, doing something about the environmental aspects of low cognitive ability may be more difficult than any of us suppose and raises troubling questions about parental behaviors and the performance of public institutions. But just asking these questions demonstrates why identifying the origins of IQ differences is so important.

If IQ matters as much as it seems to, and if IQ is substantially affected by the environment or, as is more likely, is the result of a complex interaction between genes and environment, then we are morally bound to keep plugging away until we find something that works to raise it.

RESTORATION MAN

Peter Brimelow

"MY POLITICAL aspiration," the American Enterprise Institute's Charles Murray tells *Forbes*, "is the restoration of the Jeffersonian republic."

Murray's critics may read his aspirations differently—and a good deal less charitably. For five years there has been fascinated speculation about his collaboration with Harvard's Richard J. Herrnstein (who died of lung cancer in September 1994). Herrnstein was one of the most honored academic psychologists in the country. Murray is one of the most influential social scientists, whose work has been accepted by conservatives and liberals alike.

Now these formidable talents were jointly taking on the most feared taboo of modern times: the links among intelligence, heredity, and some of the puzzling but apparently unstoppable pathologies raging in American society—such as crime, family breakup, the emergence of the underclass.

Finally, their long-awaited book *The Bell Curve: Intelligence and Class Structure in American Life* has appeared. It's massive, meticulous, minutely detailed, clear. Reading it gives you the odd sensa-

Peter Brimelow is a senior editor at both *Forbes* and *National Review*. His new book is *Alien Nation: Common Sense about America's Immigration Disaster*. This article was published in *Forbes*, October 24, 1994, as "For Whom the Bell Tolls."

tion of trying to swim in a perfectly translucent but immensely viscous liquid.

Like Darwin's *Origin of Species*—the intellectual event with which it is being seriously compared—*The Bell Curve* offers a new synthesis of research, some of which has been mounting insistently for years, and a hypothesis of far-reaching explanatory power.

But what about the Declaration of Independence—"All men are created equal"?

The ideal of equality was central to the American and the French revolutions. But is it to be taken as a literal statement about abilities?

Some would say yes, that, given the same opportunities, most people are pretty much alike.

But the reality is that guaranteeing equal opportunity does not produce equality of results. Some people are more disciplined than others, work harder—and, yes, are more intelligent. Some of the traits that make for worldly success can be acquired, but some are genetic, programmed in. Out of an erroneous, if well-meaning, overemphasis on egalitarianism, Herrnstein and Murray argue, we downplay the programmed-in part.

Psychometrics, the measurement of mental traits including intelligence, was a rapidly developing science earlier this century. But then came the savagery of Nazism. The pendulum swung. Any talk of inherent differences became taboo. In the last twenty years, as Herrnstein and Murray note, public repression of psychometrics reached its climax. Scientific popularizers like Leon Kamin and Stephen Jay Gould were able to proclaim not merely that intelligence was 100 percent determined by environment and a meaningless concept anyway but that any argument to the contrary was racist.

Herrnstein, tragically, is gone. But Murray still has a lot to lose. His 1984 book *Losing Ground* argued that Great Society programs had largely failed to help the poor and were actually stimulating illegitimacy. When it came out *Losing Ground* was bitterly assailed, but it has recently been enjoying a curious vindication as welfare reform becomes an ever hotter issue. Newspapers like *The New York Times* and *The Chicago Tribune* have noted his new acceptability. Even President Clinton mentioned Murray's work favorably in an interview with NBC's Tom Brokaw.

But isn't heredity discredited? Isn't intelligence a meaningless concept?

No, the authors argue forcefully. And they have many allies. The most extraordinary aspect of this extraordinary episode of intellectual regression is that psychometric research has continued, quietly, in ivory towers. And in the last twenty years every major objection to its findings has been rebutted.

The bizarre result: Surveys by psychologist Mark Snyderman and Smith College political scientist Stanley Rothman, published in their *IQ Controversy: The Media and Public Policy,* found a gulf between the consensus among experts in the field (cognitive scientists, behavioral geneticists) and the consensus among the "media elite" (key editors and journalists).

Basically, the experts believe that human intelligence can be measured; matters, a lot; differs by heredity (40 percent to 80 percent of IQ variation).

The media elite believe, and report, the opposite.

So what? It's a theoretical issue—what's it got to do with practical problems like crime and drugs?

A lot, Herrnstein and Murray argue. They believe that intelligence is highly predictive of how people will do in the world.

Consider two issues that have preoccupied the U.S. media: poverty and inequality.

• *Poverty.* For several decades the proportion of Americans living in poverty fell. It went from over half the population in 1939 to less than 15 percent in the late 1960s. Then—ironically, just as the Great Society programs to abolish poverty were kicking in—the decline stopped. Poverty has stayed stubbornly static for more than twenty years.

To avoid having their argument sidetracked by the race issue, Herrnstein and Murray looked at poverty among non-Hispanic whites. Their finding: A white individual's intelligence now predicts the likelihood of his being poor far better than whether or not he was born into poverty.

Among whites born into average socioeconomic conditions, but with IQs below 85, the probability of poverty in adulthood reached 26 percent—inner-city proportions. Conversely, among whites born into the very worst poverty, but with average intelligence, the probability of poverty in adulthood was only one in ten. About two-thirds of America's poverty-level population is white. Of that group, nearly two-thirds have IQs below 96.

Ironically, more equal opportunity means that differences in intelligence matter more than they once did. Born poor but smart, a child has a good—though not, of course, guaranteed—chance of rising in the world. Born middle class but dumb, he has a significant chance of descending in the world.

That was always somewhat true in the United States—shirtsleeves to shirtsleeves in three generations—but never to the degree it is today.

That's offensive—Murray and Herrnstein are saying that the poor deserve to be poor!

That's not at all what they say. But they do suggest that a good deal of poverty may be getting down to an intractable core, caused by personal traits rather than bad luck or lack of opportunity.

Which does not mean nothing can be done about poverty. Even most sub-75 IQ whites, after all, are still not poor. That's where environment comes in. Whites of below-average IQ who come from stable families are less likely to be in poverty than those born to unstable families. This suggests that people of below-average IQ are poverty-prone but are by no means destined for poverty. Note carefully: Herrnstein and Murray don't claim that IQ is the only thing that matters. A good home environment, nutrition, motivation, all still count. Unfortunately, Herrnstein and Murray demonstrate massively, these characteristics today are less likely to be present in families with low-IQ parents than in families with high-IQ parents.

• *Income inequality.* The economy is placing an increasing premium on skills. This process began well before the much-reviled Reagan Decade of Greed. There is more competition for brainpower and skills than for strong backs. And significantly, even within the "high-IQ professions," such as accountants, lawyers, physicians, Herrnstein and Murray show that individuals with superior IQ scores tend to earn significantly more.

Which suggests that income inequality cannot be eliminated simply by stuffing more schooling down the throats of those who, up until now, have been able to avoid it. The students must actually be able to use that schooling as well.

But why would this be happening now?

Apart from the economy's increasing premium on skills, education has become a much more efficient sorting mechanism.

In 1920, Herrnstein and Murray note, only about 2 percent of twenty-three-year-olds had college degrees. By 1990 the proportion had reached 30 percent. And the relationship between intelligence and college had become much closer. In the 1920s only one in seven of American youths with 110-plus IQs went directly to college. By 1990 it was four in seven. For the very highest IQs, college had become almost universal.

And the sorting continued within the college population. In the 1950s, for whatever reason—maybe it was the newly completed interstate highway system—a national market in higher education suddenly emerged. Admissions standards at Harvard and other elite colleges jumped dramatically, and decisively, as they spread their geographical nets more widely. And the average IQ of students at these elite colleges drew away from the average of college students overall, even though that had increased, too.

This, perhaps, would have pleased the Founding Fathers. And that's not counting sex. Despite reports to the contrary, love is not blind. Studies dating back to the 1940s show that the IQs of spouses correlate powerfully, almost as closely as that of siblings. More recent evidence suggests this "assortative mating" may be intensifying, as college graduates increasingly marry each other—rather than the boy or girl back home or someone met in church. No surprise, since the intelligent of both sexes are increasingly corralled together, on campuses and afterward in the "high-IQ professions."

The results are startling. The children of a typical Harvard-Radcliffe Class of '30 marriage, Herrnstein and Murray estimate, would have a mean IQ of 114; a third would be below 110—not even college material, by some definitions. But the children of a Harvard-Radcliffe Class of '64 marriage, after the admissions revolution, would have an estimated mean IQ of 124. Only 6 percent would fall below 110.

The American upper class, Herrnstein and Murray conclude, is becoming an upper caste. Society is stratifying according to cognitive ability. A "cognitive elite" is emerging at the top.

Americans can take a lot of pride in much of what this book describes. In one sense *The Bell Curve* is a description of how thoroughly the United States has realized the Founding Fathers' vision of equal opportunity for all.

Just look around. Who are the new American elite? They are, at least in part, drawn from every class, race, and ethnic background. The old domination of the so-called WASP class is over. Where once it was common to find mediocre people occupying high places by reason of birth, today it is much less so. The poor farm boy, the laundryman's children do not inevitably languish in their parents' social situation but have the opportunity to rise in the world.

If you doubt the American dream, read this book. Your eyes will be opened.

Isn't that great?

Well, yes, Herrnstein and Murray say, but . . .

The "but" is that the sorting process may be ending. Herrnstein and Murray argue that the "cognitive elite" may be increasingly isolated from the rest of society.

And the problems of the lower reaches of society, increasingly unleavened with intelligence, may become more chronic. Herrnstein and Murray, confining themselves first to the non-Hispanic white population, show that lower IQ is now more powerful than the socioeconomic status of parents in predicting an adult individual's likelihood of poverty, welfare dependency, dropping out of high school, unemployment, workplace injury (even when adjusted for type of occupation), divorce, illegitimacy and criminality.

Still, intelligence can't be that important. Look at all those rich businessmen in Kansas City with IQs of 106!

This comment was made recently by a prominent New York academic. But it just shows that, like many people, he hasn't thought through the way intelligence works in society.

Intelligence is distributed according to what statisticians call a "normal" (or "bell") curve. Most people are around the average of 100. Over two-thirds of the population are between 85 and 115. Very small numbers of people compose the extremes, or "tails." Five percent have IQs below 75. And 5 percent have IQs above 125.

This last is the group Herrnstein and Murray roughly define as the "cognitive elite." They estimate it at about 12.5 million Americans—out of a total population of nearly 260 million.

Two points are clear:

• Numbers fall off rapidly going up the IQ scale. Whatever snotty academics may think, Herrnstein and Murray report, the IQ of top executives is typically high—above the 115 average for college graduates.

But even if that rich Kansas City businessman really did have a 106 IQ, he would still be above 60 percent of the population.

- Life gets rarefied rapidly in the right tail of the bell curve. Paradoxically, the special cocoons in which society's winners live often confuse them about the critical role of intelligence. They see that success among their peers is not highly correlated with test scores. A chief executive realizes that he has many people working for him who are IQ-smarter than he or she is. It's almost a cliché today to say, "I'm where I am because I have a lot of people smarter than I am working for me." But people who say that forget that they themselves are probably well out there on the bell curve—their associates just happen to be a bit further out.

Basketball players might say that height doesn't matter much—if you're over seven feet tall.

Come on, everyone knows tests don't predict academic or job performance.

Everyone may "know" this, but it's not true. Tests actually work well. This is not to say that the highest-scoring person will necessarily be the best performer on the job. Performance correlates with test scores: It is not commensurate with them. So, overall, the best performers will be recruited from the pool of higher test scorers.

But what about cultural bias?

The argument that intelligence testing reflects white European cultural values was always shaky. Tests do predict performance (approximately) for everyone. And East Asians tend to outperform whites. Herrnstein and Murray estimate the mean East Asian IQ to be about three points above whites'. Is anyone arguing that the tests are biased against Caucasians?

Moreover, IQ appears to be reflected by an objective measure: neurologic processing speed, as measured in recent laboratory experiments that involve hitting buttons when lights flash.

But even if heredity is important, surely that environmental factor is enough to swamp it?

Not quite. Unlike the dominant intelligence-is-environment orthodoxy, the hereditarian position, as reported by Herrnstein and Murray, is actually very moderate: Everyone acknowledges that environment plays a role (20 percent to 60 percent) in determining intelligence.

But remember: We're talking about environment controlling 20 percent to 60 percent of the *variation*. The average variation between randomly selected individuals is 17 points. Equalizing environment, assuming a midpoint environmental influence of 40 percent, would still leave an average gap of nearly 10 points.

But haven't IQs increased over the years?

It's an apparently unkillable myth that IQ researchers once claimed that Jews and other immigrant groups in the 1900s were "feeble-minded." They weren't, and the testers never claimed it. But, yes, there has been a significant worldwide upward drift in average scores over the century—the so-called Flynn effect. One explanation: improvements in nutrition. Average height has increased similarly. As with IQ improvement, the increase in height is concentrated among individuals at the lower end of the range. Neither giants nor geniuses seem more common, but thare are fewer dwarfs and dullards. Wide and systematic variations, however, remain.

Don't compensatory programs like Head Start make a difference?

Not much, the authors say. Periodically there are optimistic press stories, but under careful scrutiny even the most expensive and ambitious programs have turned out to have little lasting effect, particularly on IQ.

What about Thomas Sowell? He's just argued in his new book Race and Culture: A World View *that improving environments will eventually overcome group IQ differences.*

Characteristically, *Forbes*'s pugnacious columnist, an economist at the Hoover Institution, has a position in the IQ debate that is distinctly his own. He agrees with Herrnstein and Murray that tests do predict individual performance and that ignoring their results is destructive for tester and testee alike. But he also thinks that environment determines much (although not all) cognitive ability. So he predicts that low-scoring groups will eventually improve with better social conditions.

Murray's response: Sowell's concept of "environment" must invoke extraordinarily subtle and pervasive cultural factors to explain why groups can live side by side for generations and still score differently. Sowell himself says it offers little opportunity for quick intervention and improvement. As a practical matter, Sowell and *The Bell Curve*'s authors are not so far apart as they might seem.

IQ isn't everything. The tests can't capture creativity, special talents . . .

Quite right, says Murray. He's a keen but not brilliant chess player, and says he wouldn't like to think his competitive rank reflects his IQ. (Which he says he doesn't know, but seems pleased with anyway.) Chess ability is correlated with, but is not at all commensurate with, general intelligence.

More generally, Murray argues, there's no reason any individual should regard an IQ score as a death sentence: Intelligence is only one of many factors contributing to success. Good personal habits, an ability to defer gratification, discipline, all these factors matter. Even without high IQ, individuals obviously can and do lead productive and satisfying lives.

So, what's the point of discussing IQ? There's nothing we can do about it.

In fact, *The Bell Curve* argues, social policy is already doing a lot about it—in a damaging and dangerous way.

• Welfare: "The technically precise description of America's fertility policy," the authors write, "is that it subsidizes births among poor women, who are also disproportionately at the low end of the intelligence distribution." They propose making birth control devices and information more widely available to poor people.

• Education: The impressive thing about America's education system, Herrnstein and Murray suggest, is not that 55 percent of sub-75 IQ whites drop out of high school—but that 45 percent graduate. The idea that everyone should complete high school is very new: As late as 1940, fewer than half of American seventeen-year-olds did so. However, that apparent progress among the less bright may have incurred a very high price. *The Bell Curve* demonstrates in a particularly closely argued passage that it has been achieved by focusing on the less able, a "dumbing down" that has resulted in sharply poorer performance among the most gifted children.

In 1993 over nine-tenths of federal aid to schools went to the "disadvantaged," meaning those with learning problems. Earmarked for the gifted: one-tenth of 1 percent. Herrnstein and Murray suggest a national scholarship program, to be awarded solely on merit.

• Adoption: Adopted children tend to do better than their natural siblings. Heredity still counts: They still tend to underperform their adoptive families. But this is an intervention that works—yet adoption is increasingly discouraged, particularly across racial lines.

• Affirmative action: There are high-IQ individuals of all races. But, exactly as Thomas Sowell has argued, young blacks and young people of other minority groups are the victims of college admissions officials blindly trying to fill quotas. This means they throw bright members of some minority groups into extremely competitive situations that neither they nor most whites can stand. Result: burnout.

Thus the average Harvard black student had an SAT score 95 points below the average Harvard white student—not because there aren't brilliant black kids but because Harvard overwhelms the quality of the black pool with its quota-based admission policies. This has the perverse effect of creating the illusion that minority kids cannot keep up.

Here's the rub: Some minority students over their heads at Harvard might do very well at other elite schools. The average black score at Harvard is about the same as the white average at Columbia, a fine school by any standard. By contrast, Asians appear to be held to a higher standard than everyone else at almost all the top schools.

"Whatever else this book does," said Herrnstein, showing his deep faith in the power of ideas, "it will destroy affirmative action in the universities." This may be hoping for too much. But remember that Murray's ideas about welfare were thought radical ten years ago.

This IQ stuff is too awful to think about.

Americans are optimists. They don't want to believe there are problems to which there are no solutions. The idea that IQ is destiny suggests a preordained universe that is uncongenial to us.

Ah, but there are things we can do, the authors say. What do they recommend?

Return to a society with "a place for everyone"—simpler rules, more neighborhood control, more direct incentives for virtue and disincentives for vice. A society where once again the cop on the beat is everyone's friend, where fortunate neighbors help unfortunate neighbors. A society that understands marriage is not just an inconvenient artifact but an institution that evolved to promote the care and nurture of children.

Thus, Herrnstein and Murray argue, people who disparage marriage and conventional morality are doing particular damage to the less intelligent portion of the population. Murphy Brown may be able to cope with being a single mother and even give her kid a good upbringing. But a poor woman with a relatively low IQ is less able to.

Herrnstein and Murray are not libertarian dreamers. They are critical of many past policies—state-sponsored segregation, for example. And they assume that government redistribution of income is here to stay. Indeed, in a society where the market puts increasing premiums on cognitive skills, they think that government should restore some balance by making routine jobs more attractive. Thus they express interest in such income-supplementing programs as Milton Fried-man's negative income tax.

But—they insist—the reality of human differences must be recognized. "What good can come of understanding the relationship of intelligence to social structure and public policy?" the authors write in their preface. "Little good can come without it."

V
THE PRESS SPEAKS OUT

THE BELLICOSE CURVE

Christian Science Monitor

*T*HE *BELL CURVE*, the hot new 845-page book by Charles Murray and Richard Herrnstein, comes from a cold and dark place in American thought. Subtitled "Intelligence and Class Structure in American Life," the book addresses issues of race, intelligence, and social policy "so sensitive," as the authors say, "hardly anybody writes or talks about them in public." Such "honesty," as these authors knew, ensured that when their book came out, people would talk about little else.

The book's thesis, openly Darwinian and behaviorist, is that "intelligence" is to a marked degree genetically inherited. More important to the authors, however, is their view that intelligence, or IQ, is "intractable"—that is, people can't be "smarter" than they are born to be, despite environment and education. If IQ determines economic success and social status, then it follows that social structures in America are "bound to be" inherited and unchangeable. All this has a clear racial undertone; the authors report that blacks score, in aggregate, fifteen points lower on IQ tests than whites.

"The Bellicose Curve" originally appeared as an unsigned editorial in *The Christian Science Monitor*, October 28, 1994.

The book then goes on to discuss the underclass, welfare, teenage mothers, and other admittedly very real problems. It offers a conservative attack on the liberal egalitarianism of the 1960s. *The Bell Curve* implies that such thinking distorts the "truth" about people's "differences," and that without "honest" talk about "less smart" people, we will not solve social problems.

This book does reflect a certain limited kind of truth, if one could see no sign of spiritual experience breaking in on what is so often defined as an uncompromisingly material world. But millions of people do find such evidence continually in their lives. What makes *The Bell Curve* such a disturbing piece of writing is its attempt to appease public thinking. It says to the American middle class: "Don't worry, those complicated feelings you have about prejudice or fear are nothing to be concerned about. It is really more honest to say that people aren't equal, and can't ever be."

The arguments have a friendly and responsible tone but are similar to right-wing views in Europe. They support ethnic bonding and nationalism. If such views seep into popular culture, "IQ" may be equated with "worth." Calling the book an abuse of science, the Union of American Hebrew Congregations stated: "As Jews, we know too well how these theories have been used against us . . . to justify hatred, discrimination, even murder and genocide." A Herrnstein associate told the *Monitor*, "If you take this seriously, eugenics is just around the corner."

With the family and social fabric already weak, and a need for a vision to show better ways of living together, are we to get wrapped up in genetic debates about who is smartest?

Even the notions of intelligence here are limited and skewed. They show nothing of the kinds of moral intuition, for instance, that scholars such as Carol Gilligan find. And under the criteria of *The Bell Curve*, such Americans as poet Robert Frost or Abraham Lincoln might not rate. The most intelligent people we know are quite suspicious of IQ, and of the wisdom of shaping social policy out of the Darwinian habits found and practiced in the academy. This newspaper is interested in civil intelligence, moral intelligence, and what early American theologian Jonathan Edwards called "spiritual sense." Sadly, *The Bell Curve* has little to say about these intangibles—so important for shaping any truly intelligent American future.

A HIGH IGNORANCE QUOTIENT

Boston Globe

W HAT DETERMINES a person's intelligence: genetics or life experience or both or something else? The question has been debated for years but has no definitive answer, because the human mind is too complex for definitive answers.

Everybody, particularly politicians, should remember this when the already controversial book by Harvard psychologist Richard Herrnstein and conservative political analyst Charles Murray is published this fall. Titled *The Bell Curve: Intelligence and Class Structure in American Life*, it takes the view that IQ is inherited. It will surely intensify the "nature vs. nurture" debate.

There's nothing wrong with intensifying intellectual debate. That's what makes academia interesting; let a thousand theories bloom. The danger here is that the theory could be used to justify regressive public policy.

Murray, a fellow at the American Enterprise Institute, has been an outspoken opponent of welfare and decries the growth of a "white underclass." Herrnstein's work equates low IQ with societal ills. "If you accept the correlation between crime and IQ," Herrnstein told *Globe* reporter Tony Flint, "then some people are genetically predisposed to

"A High Ignorance Quotient" was published as an unsigned editorial in *The Boston Globe*, August 10, 1994.

break the law. People on welfare on average have low IQs. The income distribution in this country is an echo of IQ distribution."

Such logic paints a world of "us versus them" and violates a basic tenet of democracy: that every person has a chance to succeed. A democratic government cannot cast aspersions in the plural—blaming the plight of welfare mothers, for instance, on their "stupidity." It must see these citizens as individuals, who come upon hard times for a variety of reasons and who need help getting back on their feet.

Americans who have risen from humble roots to lofty intellectual positions are legion: Abraham Lincoln, George Washington Carver, Maya Angelou, and Bill Clinton, to name a few. Every mind makes a unique journey. No one can or should draw a road map on the cradle.

DEAD-END CURVE

St. Louis Post-Dispatch

WRITERS CHARLES MURRAY and the late Richard Herrnstein have ignited a rather cruel and unfortunate debate about black-white superiority in their book *The Bell Curve*. It makes much of the fact that blacks on average score fifteen points below whites on IQ tests. Most of what they say about IQ tests isn't new and can be dismissed. Most scholars concede that the gap in what is known about intelligence is too wide to justify sweeping generalizations on the basis of IQ tests. Yet the authors sidestep this view in favor of appalling arguments about what these tests supposedly measure and what their results should mean for public policy.

Their arguments make clear that the real subject of *The Bell Curve* isn't IQ. That issue is merely a subterfuge. Behind the elaborate charts, numbers, and scientific jargon lies a poorly hidden agenda of eliminating welfare and other programs aimed at helping the poor. The authors try to make the case for this by saying low IQ scorers—make that blacks—are responsible for this nation's moral decline, its alarming poverty, its illegitimate births, street crimes, and welfare dependency.

Taking this racially tainted premise a step further, the authors argue that this group is dragging down the rest of society and, moreover, is

This appeared as an unsigned editorial titled "Charles Murray's Dead-End Curve," in *The St. Louis Post-Dispatch*, October 29, 1994.

beyond redemption in a high-tech age in which there are few places for those incapable of learning sophisticated skills. Hence, there's no point in wasting public resources to uplift these hopeless masses. At least the likes of Dan Quayle and William Bennett concede that there is hope even for those at the bottom, through better home foundations, schools, and spiritual underpinnings. *The Bell Curve*, on the other hand, amounts to the recycled idea that welfare is a waste. It skirts the real issue: Sufficient public-private investments in schools, housing, and above all, economic development programs could lift the very people the authors would write off. But such investments would be expensive, so the Murray-Herrnstein book takes the easy way out by scapegoating those who need the most help.

By framing their tired social policy ideas in the context of IQ scores, Mr. Murray and Mr. Herrnstein conceal the racism behind some of their thinking and give the anti-poor brigade in Congress respectable cover from which to attack welfare spending. But think of the message they would have sent to the impoverished underclass of European immigrants, who also had their share of illegitimate births and street criminals. Though some of these immigrants, too, were stigmatized for a time by IQ tests, America generally opened its arms to these new arrivals and made it easier for them to assimilate. Is it any wonder that they have done better than people whose ancestors were brought here involuntarily, were made to feel ashamed of their cultural roots, and have encountered racial hostility to this day?

Charles Murray is out of touch. He needs to get off his high, white horse for once and try to understand and appreciate the complexity of the black experience and get to know ordinary and exceptional blacks whose entry into the mainstream belies much of his theory. By his reasoning, many of these blacks would have been written off due to accident of birth or an impoverished upbringing.

WHAT'S AT STAKE

Buffalo News

T HE BEST ARGUMENT that intelligence levels are genetic comes from the fact that this society is ready to have the same debate all over again, long after we thought the useless idea had been put to rest. Evidently, we're not any smarter than our predecessors. That, of course, is not the argument made by sociologists Charles Murray and the late Richard Herrnstein in their inflammatory new book, *The Bell Curve*, or in the defense of it in *The New Republic*. In fact, given all of the qualifiers and rhetorical mollifiers, it's hard to figure out what argument Murray and Herrnstein are making. But once one sorts through the repetitious assertions and disclaimers, the pattern and their intent seem clear.

The authors are making one more attempt to bolster the case for genetic superiority simply by dint of repetition and assertion. It's as if they realize that simply by putting the topic back on the public agenda, they give the discredited notion new validity. That's why you can have the authors at one point citing research that seems to assert the validity of IQ tests as both accurate and relevant, even when controlling for environment. The next minute they are admitting that, "As of 1994, then, we can say nothing for certain about the relative roles

This unsigned editorial appeared as "IQ Debate Leads Nowhere, Except to Racial Animosity," in the *Buffalo News*, October 21, 1994.

that genetics and environment play in the formation of black-white differences in IQ."

Of course they can't. But if they have nothing certain to say, beyond what has already been hashed over, what are they adding to the debate? It's an argument that already has raged for decades and stems from the fact that different racial groups tend to get different results on IQ tests. The name of the book comes from the bell-shaped curves that show the typical distribution of test scores across a given population. Murray and Herrnstein graphically illustrate the scores of black and white test-takers with colorful charts showing what they cite as a significant difference of at least fifteen points in mean scores.

What they fail to show—for all the words they have written—is why that isn't a commentary on the tests and the social environments of those who take them, rather than on the test-takers themselves. Much of the evidence certainly points in that direction. Others have shown the bias inherent in most such tests and questioned both the scope and utility of whatever it is the tests measure. That is evidence these authors downplay or brush aside like a politician sticking to his stock campaign answer no matter what the question.

And of course, the authors—particularly Murray—are politicians without an office. For all of their innocent insistence that, in the end, such differences don't matter—that we don't judge ourselves or our friends by IQ—this is a political issue. It affects how society views its members and chooses to distribute its resources among them. That is what's at stake. And only a society that's not very bright would make any such decisions on the basis of Murray and Herrnstein's regurgitated, unproven speculation.

THE *BELL CURVE* AGENDA

New York Times

T HE BELL CURVE, a flame-throwing treatise on race, class, and intelligence by the late Richard Herrnstein and Charles Murray advances a grisly thesis: IQ, largely inherited and intractable, dictates an individual's success—an economic death knell for much of America's black population. The story has America increasingly divided by race and sliding inexorably into castes based on IQ. The book has already ignited bitter controversy, and that is no surprise. It declares settled what many regard as an unresolved argument over whether IQs have scientific merit. Moreover, Mr. Murray's record as a political ideologue who uses social science data to support his policy preferences touches a tender spot in American intellectual history on the issue of race and intelligence.

The notion that one group could be genetically superior to another has a long and sordid history in this country and abroad. Bigots purported to find "scientific" evidence that blacks, or American Indians, or Jews, to name three targets, were of inferior stock. Even supposedly objective scholars lent their talents to such racism. Individual readers can judge the authors' racial attitudes and data. The concern here is the governmental fallout of a book that aspires to set the agenda of

This unsigned piece appeared as an editorial in *The New York Times*, October 24, 1994.

social policy debate for the decade. What gives their sweeping generalities poignancy is an overlay of sophisticated statistical tools that create an aura of scientific certitude sure to intimidate ordinary citizens
from challenging the alarming conclusions.

That would be tragic. Though *The Bell Curve* contains serious scholarship, it is also laced with tendentious interpretation. Once unlike-
minded scholars have time to react, they will subject its findings to
withering criticism. At its best, the Herrnstein-Murray story is an
unconvincing reading of murky evidence. At its worst, it is perniciously
and purposely incendiary. The graphs, charts, tables, and data admit of
less dire conclusions. But less dire would not have put Mr. Murray on
the cover of newsmagazines, though it would have given America's disadvantaged a more accurate, hopeful glimpse of their future.

The authors argue that there is an underlying core to intelligence,
separate from individual talents or skills, that is well measured by IQ
tests. IQ scores are largely inherited, and after childhood, immutable.
In their view, high IQ leads to high income and respectable behavior.
Low IQ leads to social pathology—poverty, welfare dependency, out-
of-wedlock births, and crime. The book says low-IQ parents produce
large families, dragging average IQs lower. Its authors belabor the
well-known fact that the average IQ of blacks is fifteen points below
that of whites and dismiss arguments that these low test scores reflect
little more than biased testing. Their implication is that blacks are
trapped at the bottom of society.

But many experts reject these chilling conclusions. For starters, the
authors' statistical techniques are insufficiently powerful to distinguish the impact of IQ from talents or skills, some of which can be
taught. Here, terminology matters. Were Mr. Murray parading around
town with a story about skills, he would sound like everyone else who
has tried to explain the explosive increase in income inequality in the
last two decades. By blaming low IQ for poverty, he makes remediation look silly; by blaming skills for poverty, he would have invited
society to try. The first finding is obviously the more attractive for Mr.
Murray, who has built his career on arguing for the elimination of social
programs.

The authors give short shrift to explanations for low IQ scores that
are less bleak than their own. Some remedial programs have raised
IQs, even if temporarily. IQs for blacks, as well as whites, are moving

higher over time. Black educational achievement is catching up. And other countries do a better job integrating minorities in the economic mainstream than the United States does. One of the authors' key measures of innate intelligence, scores on the military's qualifying test, has been shown to be a product of education, an environmental factor. The issue is balanced interpretation. Mr. Murray has created an act of advocacy; he has not built a scientific case.

The Bell Curve presumes, but does not prove, that differences in genes account for 60 percent of the differences in the IQs of children. It is essential to note—which the authors do, but many of their critics do not—that group differences in IQ may have nothing to do with genes even if individual IQs are largely inherited. An example proves the point. Plants grown together under ideal conditions will achieve different heights based solely on individual genetic makeup. But lock half the plants in a dark closet and the difference in average height of the two groups will be due entirely to environment. So even if IQs are deemed to be largely inherited, that says nothing about the potential impact on IQ of altering prenatal care or aggressive early education.

Mr. Murray's findings are not wrong because they are ugly. They are wrong because they blind us to more compelling interpretations and because they ignore the huge gaps in understanding the precise nature of intelligence. What is right about the book was already well known: skills have taken on increasing importance in the economy and they are difficult to acquire. What is new about the book—the fixation on genes as destiny—is surely unproved and almost surely wrong: programs here and abroad produce measurable, if unspectacular, results. These sobering lessons were clear before *The Bell Curve* was published. They remain so afterward.

IQ AND SOCIAL JUSTICE

Los Angeles Times

A CENTURY AGO, the British statistician Karl Pearson argued that genetically inferior people were outbreeding superior ones and that the human species was degenerating by dysgenics. His thinking helped spawn the scientifically baseless eugenics movement that later led to the sterilization of thousands of "feeble-minded" people in the United States and Europe. Eugenics was perverted into the ultimate murderous evil by the Nazis to justify the Holocaust. Now comes a new wave of this old dysgenics to explain the woes of modern times. This time it is in the form of a provocative and deeply depressing new book that maintains that human intelligence is largely inherited and that blacks, on average, are intellectually inferior to whites, who in turn are slightly less intelligent than Asians.

The book is *The Bell Curve: Intelligence and Class Structure in American Life,* by the late psychologist Richard J. Herrnstein of Harvard and the political scientist Charles Murray of the American Enterprise Institute. In 845 pages of sharp rhetoric and dense statistics they argue that the United States is being polarized between an "emerging cognitive elite" and a low-IQ underclass destined, in disproportionate numbers, to lives of crime and welfare dependency. They see this "cognitive

This unsigned editorial was published in the *Los Angeles Times,* October 23, 1994.

partitioning" widening, and argue that affirmative action in education and jobs has only increased tensions among races without reducing differences in accomplishment. They call for cutbacks in welfare and other government programs to discourage people with low IQs from reproducing.

The Bell Curve has fueled a fierce new debate on a stale topic. It comes out at about the same time as two other books that, with differing rhetoric and purpose, make similar arguments. The two others are *The Decline of Intelligence in America: A Strategy for National Renewal*, by Seymour W. Itzkoff of Smith College, and *Race, Evolution, and Behavior: A Life History Perspective*, by J. Philippe Rushton of the University of Western Ontario. Certainly these scholars are right to discern a racially polarized class structure. Herrnstein and Murray argue for the primacy of IQ, rejecting contentions that differences in scores are rooted in cultural biases of tests.

But we are not convinced the science is adequate to distinguish the genetic component of IQ from environmental factors—such as historical discrimination, long-term poverty, and alcohol and drug abuse. IQ studies have long been plagued by methodological problems and even whiffs of fraud and racial politics. Nor does *The Bell Curve* deal adequately with the possibility that there are many kinds of intelligence other than the cognitive ability measured by IQ tests. And it is difficult to reconcile the Herrnstein-Murray argument with the expansion of an affluent black middle class in recent years.

However, we strongly oppose censoring such controversial research. And we denounce campus thought police who would harass scholars who dare to undertake it. Still, it must be asked: What is the real purpose of such research?

Herrnstein's and Murray's answer is that we need less social engineering by government and a "return to individualism," meaning less emphasis on group identification. The stress, they say, should be on "finding valued places if you aren't very smart." That was easier in past times, they argue, when the economy was agrarian and manual labor more valued. They say local neighborhoods rather than government should now assume responsibility for many social functions to "multiply the valued places that people can fill." In other words, in their words: "It is time for America once again to try living with inequality, as life is lived. . . ."

We find that a defeatist conclusion. Past studies attempting to link race and IQ have often given comfort to the forces of evil, stigmatizing large groups and legitimizing even murder. We see little chance of a resurgence of eugenics. But nothing is to be gained by resigning ourselves to a biological fate of two separate and unequal societies.

IQ IS NOT DESTINY

Business Week

T WO THINGS are absolutely true about *The Bell Curve*, the hot new book about IQ and achievement by Charles Murray and the late Richard J. Herrnstein. First, there is nothing new in the message. In the 1960s, physicist William B. Shockley advocated sterilization of people with low IQs, and psychologist Arthur R. Jensen scorned Head Start as useless because black kids were said to have inherited low IQs. Second, the importance of the book lies in its social context. America has a long history of turning to Darwinism and genetic explanations for inequality during times of economic dislocation. The 1990s certainly qualify.

So does the post–Civil War era, when capital and wealth were growing and recessions racked the middle and working classes. At that time of robber barons, political scientist William Graham Sumner was teaching at Yale University that "millionaires are a product of natural selection." The argument, of course, was that any kind of social or political change to increase fairness, opportunity, or equality for most people was hopeless. The implication is clear: Nature does the sorting, and attempts at change are naive.

This unsigned editorial appeared in *Business Week* as "In America IQ Is Not Destiny," October 31, 1994.

The 1920s and '30s—both decades of economic stress—saw a resurgence of genetic rationalization of inequality. The pseudoscience of eugenics, which started with British comparisons of brain size and intelligence in the nineteenth century, was first used as a justification for colonizing Africa. Blacks (and, indeed, women) were said to have smaller brains—ergo, less intelligence. Packaged as modern science before World War II, eugenics led to enforced sterilizations in the U.S. and all kinds of horrors in Germany.

Now come Murray and Herrnstein, purporting to break a putative taboo against speaking about IQ and race—a subject that has, in fact, been debated for over a century. Wrapped in an impenetrable fog of statistics, they argue that if intelligence is inherited and IQ is critical to success, efforts to improve people's opportunities in life are a waste of taxpayers' money: Do nothing because nothing can be done.

All this sounds like an attack on the tax-and-spend big-government liberals. And that it surely is. But it should be clearly understood that Murray's real dispute is with the American conservative tradition of equality of opportunity—not simply with equality of outcome. The true targets of *The Bell Curve* are Jack F. Kemp, William J. Bennett, and even Ronald Reagan. The heart of their conservative philosophy is to create a society of opportunity by replacing irrational incentives generated by bad government programs with market-based incentives. This would free all people to take their best shot.

But following Murray's logic, school vouchers and school choice are stupid policy options because letting parents move kids from bad schools to good ones won't improve their lives. IQ is baked in. Tax breaks and enterprise zones to promote urban business are pointless: High-IQ people will do well anyway, and low-IQ folks will fail even with help. Workfare for those on welfare is fated to fail because persons with low IQs don't benefit from work experience. Immigration is bad because it brings in people with low IQs, the same people who are said to compete unfairly against American workers in trade.

Biological determinism, which is what the Murray-Herrnstein book is all about, is anathema to the opportunity society. It opposes all market-based public-policy reform. Sure, IQ matters in achievement, but no more so than ambition, creativity, education, family, hard work, or character. The ultimate betrayal of the American ideal would be abandoning belief in the power of equality of opportunity.

ROOT AND BRANCH:
THE HISTORY

VI
ORIGINS AND IMPLICATIONS

HEREDITARY TALENT AND CHARACTER (1865)

Francis Galton

S O FAR AS BEAUTY is concerned, the custom of many countries, of the nobility purchasing the handsomest girls they could
find for their wives, has laid the foundation of a higher type of features
among the ruling classes. It is not so very long ago in England that it
was thought quite natural that the strongest lance at the tournament
should win the fairest or the noblest lady. The lady was the prize to be
tilted for. She rarely objected to the arrangement, because her vanity
was gratified by the *éclat* of the proceeding. Now history is justly
charged with a tendency to repeat itself. We may, therefore, reasonably
look forward to the possibility, I do not venture to say the probability,
of a recurrence of some such practice of competition. What an extraordinary effect might be produced on our race, if its object was to unite
in marriage those who possessed the finest and most suitable natures,
mental, moral, and physical!

Let us, then, give reins to our fancy, and imagine a Utopia—or a
Laputa, if you will—in which a system of competitive examination for
girls, as well as for youths, had been so developed as to embrace every

Francis Galton (1822–1911), an English scientist and cousin of Charles Darwin, was the
founder of eugenics, the study of methods to improve the inherited characteristics of the
race. His *Hereditary Genius* was published in 1869. This piece is excerpted from a two-part
essay that appeared in *Macmillan's Magazine*, XII (1865).

important quality of mind and body, and where a considerable sum was yearly allotted to the endowment of such marriages as promised to yield children who would grow into eminent servants of the State. We may picture to ourselves an annual ceremony in that Utopia or Laputa, in which the Senior Trustee of the Endowment Fund would address ten deeply-blushing young men, all of twenty-five years old, in the following terms:—

> "Gentlemen, I have to announce the results of a public examination, conducted on established principles; which show that you occupy the foremost places in your year, in respect to those qualities of talent, character, and bodily vigour which are proved, on the whole, to do most honour and best service to our race. An examination has also been conducted on established principles among all the young ladies of this country who are now of the age of twenty-one, and I need hardly remind you, that this examination takes note of grace, beauty, health, good temper, accomplished housewifery, and disengaged affections, in addition to noble qualities of heart and brain. By a careful investigation of the marks you have severally obtained, and a comparison of them, always on established principles, with those obtained by the most distinguished among the young ladies, we have been enabled to select ten of their names with especial reference to your individual qualities. It appears that marriages between you and these ten ladies, according to the list I hold in my hand, would offer the probability of unusual happiness to yourselves, and, what is of paramount interest to the State, would probably result in an extraordinarily talented issue. Under these circumstances, if any or all of these marriages should be agreed upon, the Sovereign herself will give away the brides, at a high and solemn festival, six months hence, in Westminster Abbey. We, on our part, are prepared, in each case, to assign £5,000 as a wedding-present, and to defray the cost of maintaining and educating your children, out of the ample funds entrusted to our disposal by the State."

If a twentieth part of the cost and pains were spent in measures for the improvement of the human race that is spent on the improvement of the breed of horses and cattle, what a galaxy of genius might we not create! We might introduce prophets and high priests of civilization into the world, as surely as we can propagate idiots by mating *crétins*. Men and women of the present day are, to those we might hope to bring into existence, what the pariah dogs of the streets of an Eastern town are to our own highly-bred varieties.

The feeble nations of the world are necessarily giving way before the nobler varieties of mankind; and even the best of these, so far as we know them, seem unequal to their work. The average culture of mankind is become so much higher than it was, and the branches of knowledge and history so various and extended, that few are capable even of comprehending the exigencies of our modern civilization; much less of fulfilling them. We are living in a sort of intellectual anarchy, for the want of master minds. The general intellectual capacity of our leaders requires to be raised, and also to be differentiated. We want abler commanders, statesmen, thinkers, inventors, and artists. The natural qualifications of our race are no greater than they used to be in semi-barbarous times, though the conditions amid which we are born are vastly more complex than of old. The foremost minds of the present day seem to stagger and halt under an intellectual load too heavy for their powers.

[...]

I have shown . . . that intellectual capacity is so largely transmitted by descent that, out of every hundred sons of men distinguished in the open professions, no less than eight are found to have rivalled their fathers in eminence. It must be recollected that success of this kind implies the simultaneous inheritance of many points of character, in addition to mere intellectual capacity. A man must inherit good health, a love of mental work, a strong purpose, and considerable ambition, in order to achieve successes of the high order of which we are speaking. The deficiency of any one of these qualities would certainly be injurious, and probably be fatal to his chance of obtaining great distinction. But more than this: the proportion we have arrived at takes no account whatever of one-half of the hereditary influences that form the nature of the child. My particular method of inquiry did not admit of regard being paid to the influences transmitted by the mother, whether they had strengthened or weakened those transmitted by the father. Lastly, though the talent and character of both of the parents might, in any particular case, be of a remarkably noble order, and thoroughly congenial, yet they would necessarily have such mongrel antecedents that it would be absurd to expect their children to invariably equal them in their natural endowments. The law of atavism prevents it. When we estimate at its true importance this accumulation of impediments in the way of the son of a distinguished father rivalling his parent—the mother being selected, as it were, at haphazard—we cannot but feel amazed at the number of instances in which a successful rivalship has occurred. Eight percent is as large a proportion as could have been expected on the most stringent hypothesis of hereditary transmission. No one, I think, can doubt, from the facts and analogies I have brought forward, that, if talented men were mated with talented women, of the same mental and physical characters as themselves, generation after generation, we might produce a highly-bred human race, with no more tendency to revert to meaner ancestral types than is shown by our long-established breeds of race-horses and fox-hounds.

It may be said that, even granting the validity of my arguments, it would be impossible to carry their indications into practical effect. For instance, if we divided the rising generation into two castes, A and B, of which A was selected for natural gifts, and B was the refuse, then, supposing marriage was confined within the pale of the caste to which each individual belonged, it might be objected that we should simply differentiate our race—that we should create a good and a bad caste, but we should not improve the race as a whole. I reply that this is by no means the necessary result. There remains another very important law to be brought into play. Any agency, however indirect, that would somewhat hasten the marriages in caste A, and retard those in caste B, would result in a larger proportion of children being born to A than to B, and would end by wholly eliminating B, and replacing it by A.

Let us take a definite case, in order to give precision to our ideas. We will suppose the population to be, in the first instance, stationary; A and B to be equal in numbers; and the children of each married pair who survive to maturity to be rather more than 2½ in the case of A, and rather less than 1½ in the case of B. This is no extravagant hypothesis. Half the population of the British Isles are born of mothers under the age of thirty years.

The result in the first generation would be that the total population would be unchanged, but that only one-third part of it would consist of the children of B. In the second generation, the descendants of B would be reduced to two-ninths of their original numbers, but the total population would begin to increase, owing to the greater preponderance of the prolific caste A. At this point the law of natural selection would powerfully assist in the substitution of caste A for caste B, by pressing heavily on the minority of weakly and incapable men.

The customs that affect the direction and date of marriages are already numerous. In many families, marriages between cousins are discouraged and checked. Marriages, in other respects appropriate, are very commonly deferred, through prudential considerations. If it was generally felt that intermarriages between A and B were as unadvisable as they are supposed to be between cousins, and that marriages in A ought to be hastened, on the ground of prudential considerations, while those in B ought to be discouraged and retarded, then, I believe, we should have agencies amply sufficient to eliminate B in a few generations.

I hence conclude that the improvement of the breed of mankind is no insuperable difficulty. If everybody were to agree on the improvement of the race of man being a matter of the very utmost importance, and if the theory of the hereditary transmission of qualities in men was as thoroughly understood as it is in the case of our domestic animals, I see no absurdity in supposing that, in some way or other, the improvement would be carried into effect.

It remains for me in the present article to show that hereditary influence is as clearly marked in mental aptitudes as in general intellectual power. I will then enter into some of the considerations which my views on hereditary talent and character naturally suggest.

I will first quote a few of those cases in which characteristics have been inherited that clearly depend on peculiarities of organization. Prosper Lucas was among our earliest encyclopædists on this subject. It is distinctly shown by him, and agreed to by others, such as Mr. G. Lewes, that predisposition to any form of disease, or any malformation, may become an inheritance. Thus disease of the heart is hereditary; so are tubercles in the lungs; so also are diseases of the brain, of the liver, and of the kidney; so are diseases of the eye and of the ear. General maladies are equally inheritable, as gout and madness. Longevity on the one hand, and premature deaths on the other, go by descent. If we consider a class of peculiarities, more recondite in their origin than these, we shall still find the law of inheritance to hold good. A morbid susceptibility to contagious disease, or to the poisonous effects of opium, or of calomel, and an aversion to the taste of meat, are all found to be inherited. So is a craving for drink, or for gambling, strong sexual passion, a proclivity to pauperism, to crimes of violence, and to crimes of fraud.

There are certain marked types of character, justly associated with marked types of feature and of temperament. We hold, axiomatically, that the latter are inherited (the case being too notorious, and too consistent with the analogy afforded by brute animals, to render argument necessary), and we therefore infer the same of the former. For instance, the face of the combatant is square, coarse, and heavily jawed. It differs from that of the ascetic, the voluptuary, the dreamer, and the charlatan.

Still more strongly marked than these are the typical features and characters of different races of men. The Mongolians, Jews, Negroes, Gipsies, and American Indians; severally propagate their kinds; and each kind differs in character and intellect, as well as in colour and shape, from the other four. They, and a vast number of other races, form a class of instances worthy of close investigation, in which peculiarities of character are invariably transmitted from the parents to the offspring.

In founding argument on the innate character of different races, it is necessary to bear in mind the exceeding docility of man. His mental habits in mature life are the creatures of social discipline, as well as of inborn aptitudes, and it is impossible to ascertain what is due to the latter alone, except by observing several individuals of the same race, reared under various influences, and noting the peculiarities of character that invariably assert themselves. But, even when we have imposed these restrictions to check a hasty and imaginative conclusion, we find there remain abundant data to prove an astonishing diversity in the natural characteristics of different races. It will be sufficient for our purpose if we fix our attention upon the peculiarities of one or two of them.

The race of the American Indians is spread over an enormous area, and through every climate; for it reaches from the frozen regions of the North through the equator, down to the inclement regions of the South. It exists in thousands of disconnected communities, speaking nearly as many different languages. It has been subjected to a strange variety of political influences, such as its own despotisms in Peru, Mexico, Natchez, and Bogota, and its numerous republics, large and small. Members of the race have been conquered and ruled by military adventures from Spain and Portugal; others have been subjugated to Jesuitical rule; numerous settlements have been made by strangers on its soil; and, finally, the north of the continent has been colonized by European races. Excellent observers have watched the American Indians under all these influences, and their almost unanimous conclusion is as follows:—

The race is divided into many varieties, but it has fundamentally the same character throughout the whole of America. The men, and in a less degree the women, are naturally cold, melancholic, patient, and taciturn. A father, mother, and their children, are said to live together in a hut, like persons assembled by accident, not tied by affection. The youths treat their parents with neglect, and often with such harshness and insolence as to horrify Europeans who have witnessed their conduct. The mothers have been seen to commit infanticide without the slightest discomposure, and numerous savage tribes have died out in consequence of this practice. The American Indians are eminently non-gregarious. They nourish a sullen reserve, and show little sympathy with each other, even when in great distress. The Spaniards had to enforce the common duties of humanity by positive laws. They are strangely taciturn. When not engaged in action they will sit whole days in one posture without opening their lips, and wrapped up in their narrow thoughts. They usually march in Indian file, that is to say, in a long line, at some distance from each other, without exchanging a word. They keep the same profound silence in rowing a canoe, unless they happen to be excited by some extraneous cause. On the other hand, their patriotism and local attachments are strong, and they have an astonishing sense of personal dignity. The nature of the American Indians appears to contain the minimum of affectionate and social qualities compatible with the continuance of their race.

Here, then, is a well-marked type of character, that formerly prevailed over a large part of the globe, with which other equally marked types of character in other regions are strongly contrasted. Take, for instance, the typical West African Negro. He is more unlike the Red man in his mind than in his body. Their characters are almost opposite, one to the other. The Red man has great patience, great reticence, great dignity, and no passion; the Negro has strong impulsive passions, and neither patience, reticence, nor dignity. He is warm-hearted, loving towards his master's children, and idolised by the children in return. He is eminently gregarious, for he is always jabbering, quarrelling, tom-tom-ing, or dancing. He is remarkably domestic, and he is endowed with such constitutional vigour, and is so prolific, that his race is irrepressible.

The Hindu, the Arab, the Mongol, the Teuton, and very many more, have each of them their peculiar characters. We have not space to analyse them on this occasion; but, whatever they are, they are transmitted, generation after generation, as truly as their physical forms.

What is true for the entire race is equally true for its varieties. If we were to select persons who were born with a type of character that we desired to intensify,—suppose it was one that approached to some ideal standard of perfection—and if we compelled marriage within the limits of the society so selected, generation after generation; there can be no doubt that the offspring would ultimately be born with the qualities we sought, as surely as if we had been breeding for physical features, and not for intellect or disposition.

Our natural constitution seems to bear as direct and stringent a relation to that of our forefathers as any other physical effect does to its cause. Our bodies, minds, and capabilities of development have been derived from them. Everything we possess at our birth is a heritage from our ancestors.

Can we hand anything down to our children, that we have fairly won by our own independent exertions? Will our children be born with more virtuous dispositions, if we ourselves have acquired virtuous habits? Or are we no more than passive transmitters of a nature we have received, and which we have no power to modify? There are but a few instances in which habit even seems to be inherited. The chief among them are such as those of dogs being born excellent pointers; of the attachment to man shown by dogs; and of the fear of man, rapidly learnt and established among the birds of newly-discovered islands. But all of these admit of being accounted for on other grounds than the hereditary transmission of habits. Pointing is, in some faint degree, a natural disposition of all dogs. Breeders have gradually improved upon it, and created the race we now possess. There is nothing to show that the reason why dogs are born staunch pointers is that their parents had been broken into acquiring an artificial habit. So as regards the fondness of dogs for man. It is inherent to a great extent in the genus. The dingo, or wild dog of Australia, is attached to the man who has caught him when a puppy, and clings to him even although he is turned adrift to hunt for his own living. This quality in dogs is made more intense by the custom of selection. The savage dogs are lost or killed; the tame ones are kept and bred from. Lastly, as regards the birds. As soon as any of their flock has learned to fear, I presume that its frightened movements on the approach of man form a language that is rapidly and unerringly understood by the rest, old or young; and that, after a few repetitions of the signal, man becomes an object of well-remembered mistrust. Moreover, just as natural selection has been shown to encourage love of man in domestic dogs, so it tends to encourage fear of man in all wild animals—the tamer varieties perishing owing to their misplaced confidence, and the wilder ones continuing their breed.

If we examine the question from the opposite side, a list of life-long habits in the parents might be adduced which leave no perceptible trace on their descendants. I cannot ascertain that the son of an old soldier learns his drill more quickly than the son of an artisan. I am assured that the sons of fishermen, whose ancestors have pursued the same calling time out of mind, are just as sea-sick as the sons of landsmen when they first go to sea. I cannot discover that the castes of India show signs of being naturally endowed with special aptitudes. If the habits of an individual are transmitted to his descendants, it is, as Darwin says, in a very small degree, and is hardly, if at all, traceable.

We shall therefore take an approximately correct view of the origin of our life, if we consider our own embryos to have sprung immediately from those embryos whence our parents were developed, and these from the embryos of *their* parents, and so on for ever. We should in this way look on the nature of mankind, and perhaps on that of the whole animated creation, as one continuous system, ever pushing out new branches in all directions, that variously interlace, and that bud into separate lives at every point of interlacement.

This simile does not at all express the popular notion of life. Most persons seem to have a vague idea that a new element, specially fashioned in heaven, and not transmitted by simple descent, is introduced into the body of every newly-born infant. Such a notion is unfitted to stand upon any scientific basis with which we are acquainted. It is impossible it should be true, unless there exists some property or quality in man that is not transmissible by descent. But the terms *talent* and *character* are exhaustive: they include the whole of man's spiritual nature so far as we are able to understand it. No other class of qualities is known to exist, that we might suppose to have been interpolated from on high. Moreover, the idea is improbable from a priori considerations, because there is no other instance in which creative power operates under our own observation at the present day, except it may be in the freedom in action of our own wills. Wherever else we turn our eyes, we see nothing but law and order, and effect following cause.

But though, when we look back to our ancestors, the embryos of our progenitors may be conceived to have been developed, in each generation, immediately from the one that preceded it, yet we cannot take so restricted a view when we look forward. The interval that separates the full-grown animal from its embryo is too important to be disregarded. It is in this interval that Darwin's law of natural selection comes into play; and those conditions are entered into, which affect, we know not how, the "individual variation" of the offspring. I mean those that cause dissimilarity among brothers and sisters who are born successively, while twins, produced simultaneously, are often almost identical. If it were possible that embryos should descend directly from embryos, there might be developments in every direction, and the world would be filled with monstrosities. But this is not the order of nature. It is her fiat that the natural tendencies of animals should never disaccord long and widely with the conditions under which they are placed. Every animal before it is of an age to bear offspring, has to undergo frequent stern examinations before the board of nature, under the law of natural selection; where to be "plucked" is not necessarily disgrace, but is certainly death. Never let it be forgotten that man, as a reasonable being, has the privilege of not being helpless under the tyranny of uncongenial requirements, but that he can, and that he does, modify the subjects in which nature examines him, and that he has considerable power in settling beforehand the relative importance in the examination that shall be assigned to each separate subject.

It becomes a question of great interest how far moral monstrosities admit of being bred. Is there any obvious law that assigns a limit to the propagation of supremely vicious or supremely virtuous natures? In strength, agility, and other physical qualities, Darwin's law of natural selection acts with unimpassioned, merciless severity. The weakly die in the battle for life; the stronger and more capable individuals are alone permitted to survive, and to bequeath their constitutional vigour to future generations. Is there any corresponding rule in respect to moral character? I believe there is, and I have already hinted at it when speaking of the American Indians. I am prepared to maintain that its action, by insuring a certain fundamental unity in the quality of the affections, enables men and the higher order of animals to sympathise in some degree with each other, and also, that this law forms the broad basis of our religious sentiments.

Animal life, in all but the very lowest classes, depends on at least one, and, more commonly, on all of the four following principles:— There must be affection, and it must be of four kinds: sexual, parental, filial, and social. The absolute deficiency of any one of these would be a serious hindrance, if not a bar to the continuance of any race. Those who possessed all of them, in the strongest measure, would, speaking generally, have an advantage in the struggle for existence. Without sexual affection, there would be no marriages, and no children; without parental affection, the children would be abandoned; without filial affection, they would stray and perish; and, without the social, each individual would be single-handed against rivals who were capable of banding themselves into tribes. Affection for others as well as for self, is therefore a necessary part of animal character. Disinterestedness is as essential to a brute's well-being as selfishness. No animal lives for itself alone, but also, at least occasionally, for its parent, its mate, its offspring, or its fellow. Companionship is frequently more grateful to an animal than abundant food. The safety of her young is considered by many a mother as a paramount object to her own. The passion for a mate is equally strong. The gregarious bird posts itself during its turn of duty as watchman on a tree, by the side of the feeding flock. Its zeal to serve the common cause exceeds its care to attend to its own interests. Extreme selfishness is not a common vice. Narrow thoughts of self by no means absorb the minds of ordinary men; they occupy a secondary position in the thoughts of the more noble and generous of our race. A large part of an Englishman's life is devoted to others, or to the furtherance of general ideas, and not to directly personal ends. The Jesuit toils for his order, not for himself. Many plan for that which they can never live to see. At the hour of death they are still planning. An incompleted will, which might work unfairness among those who would succeed to the property of a dying man, harasses his mind. Personal obligations of all sorts press as heavily as in the fulness of health, although the touch of death is known to be on the point of cancelling them. It is so with animals. A dog's thoughts are towards his master, even when he suffers the extremest pain. His mind is largely filled at all times with sentiments of affection. But disinterested feelings are more necessary to man than to any other animal, because of the long period of his dependent childhood, and also because of his great social needs, due to his physical helplessness. Darwin's law of natural selection would therefore be expected to develop these sentiments among men, even among the lowest barbarians, to a greater degree than among animals.

I believe that our religious sentiments spring primarily from these four sources. The institution of celibacy is an open acknowledgment that the theistic and human affections are more or less convertible; I mean that by starving the one class the other becomes more intense and absorbing. In savages, the theistic sentiment is chiefly, if not wholly, absent. I would refer my readers, who may hesitate in accepting this assertion, to the recently published work of my friend Sir John Lubbock, *Prehistoric Times*, pp. 467–472, where the reports of travellers on the religion of savages are very ably and fairly collated. The theistic sentiment is secondary, not primary. It becomes developed within us under the influence of reflection and reason. All evidence tends to show that man is directed to the contemplation and love of God by instincts that he shares with the whole animal world, and that primarily appeal to the love of his neighbour.

Moral monsters are born among Englishmen, even at the present day; and, when they are betrayed by their acts, the law puts them out of the way, by the prison or the gallows, and so prevents them from continuing their breed. Townley, the murderer, is an instance in point. He behaved with decorum and propriety; he was perfectly well-conducted to the gaol officials, and he corresponded with his mother in a style that was certainly flippant, but was not generally considered to be insane. However, with all this reasonableness of disposition, he could not be brought to see that he had done anything particularly wrong in murdering the girl that was disinclined to marry him. He was thoroughly consistent in his disregard for life, because, when his own existence became wearisome, he ended it with perfect coolness, by jumping from an upper staircase. It is a notable fact that a man without a conscience, like Townley, should be able to mix in English society for years, just like other people.

How enormous is the compass of the scale of human character, which reaches from dispositions like those we have just described, to that of a Socrates! How various are the intermediate types of character that commonly fall under everybody's notice, and how differently are the principles of virtue measured out to different natures! We can clearly observe the extreme diversity of character in children. Some are naturally generous and open, others mean and tricky; some are warm and loving, others cold and heartless; some are meek and patient, others obstinate and self-asserting; some few have the tempers of angels, and at least as many have the tempers of devils. In the same way, . . . by selecting men and women of rare and similar talent, and mating them together, generation after generation, an extraordinarily gifted race might be developed, so a yet more rigid selection, having regard to their moral nature, would, I believe, result in a no less marked improvement of their natural disposition.

Let us consider an instance in which different social influences have modified the inborn dispositions of a nation. The North American people has been bred from the most restless and combative class of Europe. Whenever, during the last ten or twelve generations, a political or religious party has suffered defeat, its prominent members, whether they were the best, or only the noisiest, have been apt to emigrate to America, as a refuge from persecution. Men fled to America for conscience' sake, and for that of unappreciated patriotism. Every scheming knave, and every brutal ruffian, who feared the arm of the law, also turned his eyes in the same direction. Peasants and artisans, whose spirit rebelled against the tyranny of society and the monotony of their daily life, and men of a higher position, who chafed under conventional restraints, all yearned towards America. Thus the dispositions of the parents of the American people have been exceedingly varied, and usually extreme, either for good or for evil. But in one respect they almost universally agreed. Every head of an emigrant family brought with him a restless character, and a spirit apt to rebel. If we estimate the moral nature of Americans from their present social state, we shall find it to be just what we might have expected from such a parentage. They are enterprising, defiant, and touchy; impatient of authority; furious politicians; very tolerant of fraud and violence; possessing much high and generous spirit, and some true religious feeling, but strongly addicted to cant.

We have seen that the law of natural selection develops disinterested affection of a varied character even in animals and barbarian man. Is the same law different in its requirements when acting on civilized man? It is no doubt more favourable on the whole to civilized progress, but we must not expect to find as yet many marked signs of its action. As a matter of history, our Anglo-Saxon civilization is only skin-deep. It is but eight hundred years, or twenty-six generations, since the Conquest, and the ancestors of the large majority of Englishmen were the merest boors at a much later date than that. It is said that among the heads of the noble houses of England there can barely be found one that has a right to claim the sixteen quarterings—that is to say, whose great-great-grandparents were, all of them (sixteen in number), entitled to carry arms. Generally the nobility of a family is represented by only a few slender rills among a multiplicity of non-noble sources.

The most notable quality that the requirements of civilization have hitherto bred in us, living as we do in a rigorous climate and on a naturally barren soil, is the instinct of continuous steady labour. This is alone possessed by civilized races, and it is possessed in a far greater degree by the feeblest individuals among them than by the most able-bodied savages. Unless a man can work hard and regularly in England, he becomes an outcast. If he only works by fits and starts he has not a chance of competition with steady workmen. An artisan who has variable impulses, and wayward moods, is almost sure to end in intemperance and ruin. In short, men who are born with wild and irregular dispositions, even though they contain much that is truly noble, are alien to the spirit of a civilized country, and they and their breed are eliminated from it by the law of selection. On the other hand, a wild, untameable restlessness is innate with savages. I have collected numerous instances where children of a low race have been separated at an early age from their parents, and reared as part of a settler's family, quite apart from their own people. Yet, after years of civilized ways, in some fit of passion, or under some craving, like that of a bird about to emigrate, they have abandoned their home, flung away their dress, and sought their countrymen in the bush, among whom they have subsequently been found living in contented barbarism, without a vestige of their gentle nurture. This is eminently the case with the Australians, and I have heard of many others in South Africa. There are also numerous instances in England where the restless nature of gipsy half-blood asserts itself with irresistible force.

Another difference, which may either be due to natural selection or to original difference of race, is the fact that savages seem incapable of progress after the first few years of their life. The average children of all races are much on a par. Occasionally, those of the lower races are more precocious than the Anglo-Saxons; as a brute beast of a few weeks old is certainly more apt and forward than a child of the same age. But, as the years go by, the higher races continue to progress, while the lower ones gradually stop. They remain children in mind, with the passions of grown men. Eminent genius commonly asserts itself in tender years, but it continues long to develop. The highest minds in the highest race seem to have been those who had the longest boyhood. It is not those who were little men in early youth who have succeeded. Here I may remark that, in the great mortality that besets the children of our poor, those who are members of precocious families, and who are therefore able to help in earning wages at a very early age, have a marked advantage over their competitors. They, on the whole, live, and breed their like, while the others die. But, if this sort of precocity be unfavourable to a race—if it be generally followed by an early arrest of development, and by a premature old age—then modern industrial civilization, in encouraging precocious varieties of men, deteriorates the breed.

Besides these three points of difference—endurance of steady labour, tameness of disposition, and prolonged development—I know of none that very markedly distinguishes the nature of the lower classes of civilized man from that of barbarians. In the excitement of a pillaged town the English soldier is just as brutal as the savage. Gentle manners seem, under those circumstances, to have been a mere gloss thrown by education over a barbarous nature. One of the effects of civilization is to diminish the rigour of the application of the law of natural selection. It preserves weakly lives, that would have perished in barbarous lands. The sickly children of a wealthy family have a better chance of living and rearing offspring than the stalwart children of a poor one. As with the body, so with the mind. Poverty is more adverse to early marriages than is natural bad temper, or inferiority of intellect. In civilized society, money interposes her ægis between the law of natural selection and very many of its rightful victims. Scrofula and madness are naturalised among us by wealth; short-sightedness is becoming so. There seems no limit to the morbific tendencies of body or mind that might accumulate in a land where the law of primogeniture was general, and where riches were more esteemed than personal qualities. Neither is there any known limit to the intellectual and moral grandeur of nature that might be introduced into aristocratical families, if their representatives, who have such rare privilege in winning wives that please them best, should invariably, generation after generation, marry with a view of transmitting those noble qualities to their descendants. Inferior blood in the representative of a family might be eliminated from it in a few generations. The share that a man retains in the constitution of his remote descendants is inconceivably small. The father transmits, on an average, one-half of his nature, the grandfather one-fourth, the great-grandfather one-eighth; the share decreasing step by step, in a geometrical ratio, with great rapidity. Thus the man who claims descent from a Norman baron, who accompanied William the Conqueror twenty-six generations ago, has so minute a share of that baron's influence in his constitution, that, if he weighs fourteen stone, the part of him which may be ascribed to the baron (supposing, of course, there have been no additional lines of relationship) is only one-fiftieth of a grain in weight—an amount ludicrously disproportioned to the value popularly ascribed to ancient descent. As a stroke of policy, I question if the head of a great family, or a prince, would not give more strength to his position, by marrying a wife who would bear him talented sons, than one who would merely bring him the support of high family connexions.

With the few but not insignificant exceptions we have specified above, we are still barbarians in our nature, and we show it in a thousand ways. The children who dabble and dig in the dirt have inherited the instincts of untold generations of barbarian forefathers, who dug with their nails for a large fraction of their lives. Our ancestors were grubbing by the hour, each day, to get at the roots they chiefly lived upon. They had to grub out pitfalls for their game, holes for their palisades and hut-poles, hiding-places, and ovens. Man became a digging animal by nature; and so we see the delicately-reared children of our era very ready to revert to primeval habits. Instinct breaks out in them, just as it does in the silk-haired, boudoir-nurtured spaniel, with a ribbon round its neck, that runs away from the endearments of its mistress, to sniff and revel in some road-side mess of carrion.

It is a common theme of moralists of many creeds, that man is born with an imperfect nature. He has lofty aspirations, but there is a weakness in his disposition that incapacitates him from carrying his nobler purposes into effect. He sees that some particular course of action is his duty, and should be his delight; but his inclinations are fickle and base, and do not conform to his better judgment. The whole moral nature of man is tainted with sin, which prevents him from doing the things he knows to be right.

I venture to offer an explanation of this apparent anomaly, which seems perfectly satisfactory from a scientific point of view. It is neither more nor less than that the development of our nature, under Darwin's law of natural selection, has not yet overtaken the development of our religious civilization. Man was barbarous but yesterday, and therefore it is not to be expected that the natural aptitudes of his race should already have become moulded into accordance with his very recent advance. We men of the present centuries are like animals suddenly transplanted among new conditions of climate and of food: our instincts fail us under the altered circumstances.

My theory is confirmed by the fact that the members of old civilizations are far less sensible than those newly converted from barbarism of their nature being inadequate to their moral needs. The conscience of a negro is aghast at his own wild, impulsive nature, and is easily stirred by a preacher, but it is scarcely possible to ruffle the self-complacency of a steady-going Chinaman.

The sense of original sin would show, according to my theory, not that man was fallen from a high estate, but that he was rapidly rising from a low one. It would therefore confirm the conclusion that has been arrived at by every independent line of ethnological research— that our forefathers were utter savages from the beginning; and, that, after myriads of years of barbarism, our race has but very recently grown to be civilized and religious.

ON BREEDING GOOD STOCK (1903)

Karl Pearson

T HERE ARE PROBABLY few persons who would now deny
the immense importance of ancestry in the case of any domestic
animal. The stud-books, which exist for horses, cattle, dogs, cats and
even canaries, demonstrate the weight practically given to ancestry
when the breeding of animals has developed so far that certain physical
characters possess commercial value. A majority of the community
would probably also admit to-day that the physical characters of man are
inherited with practically the same intensity as the like characters in cattle and horses. But few, however, of the majority who accept this inheritance of physique in man, apply the results which flow from such
acceptance to their own conduct in life—still less do they appreciate the
all important bearing of these results upon national life and social habits.
Nor is the reason for this—or better, one out of several reasons for this—
hard to find. The majority of mankind are more or less conscious that
man has not gained his pre-eminence by physique alone. They justly
attribute much of his dominance in the animal kingdom to those mental

Karl Pearson (1857–1936) was an English scientist and disciple of Francis Galton, about
whom he wrote a three-volume biography. This piece is excerpted from the Huxley Lecture for 1903, which appeared as "On the Inheritance of the Mental and Moral Characters
in Man, and its Comparison with the Inheritance of the Physical Characters." *Journal of
the Royal Anthropological Institute of Great Britain and Ireland*, 33 (1903).

and moral characters, which have rendered him capable of combining with his neighbours to form stable societies with highly differentiated tasks and circumscribed duties for their individual members.

Within such communities we see the moral characters developing apparently under family influences; the mental characters developing not only under home training, but under the guidance of private and public teachers, the whole contributing to form a complex system of national education. To use technical terms, we expect correlation between home influence and moral qualities, and between education and mental power, and the bulk of men too rashly, perhaps, conclude that the home and the school are the chief sources of those qualities on which social stability so largely depends. We are too apt to overlook the possibility that the home standard is itself a product of parental stock, and that the relative gain from education depends to a surprising degree on the raw material presented to the educator. We are agreed that good homes and good schools are essential to national prosperity. But does not the good home depend upon the percentage of innately wise parents, and the good school depend quite as much on the children's capacity, as on its staff and equipment?

It is quite possible to accept these views and yet believe that the moral and mental characters are inherited in either a quantitatively or a qualitatively different manner from the physical characters. Both may be influenced by environment, but the one in a far more marked way than the other. Since the publication of Francis Galton's epoch-making books, *Hereditary Genius* and *English Men of Science*, it is impossible to deny *in toto* the inheritance of mental characters. But we require to go a stage further and ask for an exact quantitative measure of the inheritance of such characters and a comparison of such measure with its value for the physical characters.

Accordingly some six or seven years ago I set myself the following problem: What is the quantitative measure of the inheritance of the moral and mental characters in man, and how is it related to the corresponding measure of the inheritance of the physical characters?

The problem really resolved itself into three separate investigations:—

(*a*) A sufficiently wide inquiry into the actual values of inheritance of the physical characters in man.

This investigation was carried out by the measurement of upwards of 1000 families. We thus obtained ample means of determining both for parental and fraternal relationships the quantitative measure of resemblance.

(b) A comparison of the inheritance of the physical characters in man with that of the physical characters in other forms of life.

This has been made for a considerable number of characters in diverse species, with the general result that there appears to be no substantial difference, as far as we have been able to discover, between the inheritance of physique in man, and its inheritance in other forms of life.

(c) An inquiry into the inheritance of the moral and mental characters in man.

This is the part of my work with which we are at present chiefly concerned, and I want to indicate the general lines along which my argument runs.

In the first place it seemed to me absolutely impossible to get a quantitative measure of the resemblance in moral and mental characters between parent and offspring. You must not compare the moral character of a child with those of its adult parents. You can only estimate the resemblance between the child and what its parents were as *children*. Here the grandparent is the only available source of information; but not only does age affect clearness of memory and judgment, the partiality of the relative is a factor which can hardly be corrected and allowed for. If we take, on the other hand, parents and offspring as adults, it is difficult to appeal to anything but the *vox populi* for an estimate of their relative moral merits, and this *vox* is generally silent unless both are men of marked public importance. For these and other reasons I gave up any hope of measuring parental resemblance in moral character. I confined my attention entirely to *fraternal* resemblance. My argument was of this kind. Regarding one species only, then if fraternal resemblance for the moral and mental characters be less than, equal to, or greater than fraternal resemblance for the physical characters, we may surely argue that parental inheritance for the former set of characters is less than, equal to, or greater than that for the latter set of characters.

In the next place it seemed impossible to obtain moderately impartial estimates of the moral and mental characters of *adults*. Who but rel-

atives and close friends know them well enough to form such an estimate, and which of us will put upon paper, for the use of strangers, a
true account of the temper, probity and popularity of our nearest?
Even if relatives and friends could be trusted to be impartial, the discovery of the preparation of schedules by the subjects of observation
might have ruptured the peace of households and broken down lifelong friendships. Thousands of schedules could not be filled up in this
manner. The inquiry, therefore, resolved itself into an investigation of
the moral and mental characters of *children*. Here we could replace the
partial parent or relative by the fairly impartial school teacher. A man
or woman who deals yearly with forty to a hundred new children,
rapidly forms moderately accurate classifications, and it was to this
source of information that I determined to appeal.

I would refer at once to an objection, which I think is not real, but
which I know will arise in the minds of some. It will be said that the
temper, vivacity and probity of children is not a measure of the like
qualities in the adult. The shy boy at school is not necessarily a shy
man on the floor of the House of Commons or confronting a native
race on the north-west frontier. Granted absolutely. But what we are
comparing is what that boy was at school, with what his brother and sis-
ter may have been. We can legitimately compare for purposes of
heredity a character of the larval stage of two insects, although that
character disappears entirely when both are fully developed as *imago*.

It is possible that some allowance ought to be made for changes
during the school period in the mental and moral characters, but I have
not found that those characters change very substantially in their percentages with the age of the school children, the bulk of whom lie
between 10 and 14. Accordingly, while the physical characters change
during the school period, it did not to a first approximation seem need-
ful to allow for age changes in the mental and moral characters. Such
changes may exist, but they do not appear to be so marked as to substantially influence our results.

[. . .]

Lastly, turning to the psychical character of man, to some the
greatest of all mysteries, we link it up to the physical. We see the man,
not only physically, but morally and mentally, the product of a long
line of ancestry. We realise that evolution and selection play no
greater, and play no less a part in the production of the psychical character than in the production of the physique of man. Once fully

realise that the psychic is inherited in the same way as the physical, and there is no room left to differentiate one from the other in the evolution of man. Realise all this, and two mysteries have been linked into one mystery, but the total mystery is no less in magnitude, and no more explicable than it was before. We know not why living forms vary, nor why either physical or psychical characters are inherited, nor wherefore the existence at all of living forms, and their subjection to the great principle of selective evolution. We have learnt only a law common to the physical and the psychical; we have not raised the one or debased the other, because in a world where the ultimate source of change is utterly inexplicable, whether you strive to perceive it through matter like a physicist, through the lower living forms like the biologist, or through man like the anthropologist, all terminology like higher and lower is futile. Where the mystery is absolute in all cases, there can be no question of grade.

But I would not leave you with a mere general declaration that all is mystery, that scientific ignorance of the ultimate is profound. Rather I would emphasize what I have endeavoured to show you to-night, that the mission of science is not to explain but to bring all things, as far as we are able, under a common law. Science gives no real explanation, but provides comprehensive description. In the narrower field it has to study how its general conceptions bear on the comfort and happiness of man. Herein, I think, lies especially the coming function of anthropology. Anthropology has in the first place to study man, to discover the sequence of his evolution from his present comparative stages and from his past history. But it cannot halt here; it must suggest how those laws can be applied to render our own human society both more stable and more efficient. In this function it becomes at least the handmaiden of statecraft, if indeed it were not truer to call it the preceptor of statesmen.

If the conclusion we have reached to-night be substantially a true one, and for my part I cannot for a moment doubt that it is so, then what is its lesson for us as a community? Why simply that geniality and probity and ability may be fostered indeed by home environment and by provision of good schools and well equipped institutions for research, but that their origin, like health and muscle, is deeper down than these things. They are bred and not created. That good stock breeds good stock is a commonplace of every farmer; that the strong man and woman have healthy children is widely recognized too. But we have left the moral and mental faculties as qualities for which we can provide amply by home environment and sound education.

It is the stock itself which makes its home environment, the education is of small service, unless it be applied to an intelligent race of men.

Our traders declare that we are no match for Germans and Americans. Our men of science run about two continents and proclaim the glory of foreign universities and the crying need for technical instruction. Our politicians catch the general apprehension and rush to heroic remedies. Looking round impassionately from the calm atmosphere of anthropology, I fear there really does exist a lack of leaders of the highest intelligence, in science, in the arts, in trade, even in politics. I do seem to see a want of intelligence in the British merchant, in the British professional man and in the British workman. But I do not think the remedy lies solely in adopting foreign methods of instruction or in the spread of technical education. I believe we have a paucity, just now, of the better intelligences to guide us, and of the moderate intelligences to be successfully guided. The only account we can give of this on the basis of the result we have reached to-night is that we are ceasing as a nation to breed intelligence as we did fifty to a hundred years ago. The mentally better stock in the nation is not reproducing itself at the same rate as it did of old; the less able, and the less energetic, are more fertile than the better stocks. No scheme of wider or more thorough education will bring up in the scale of intelligence hereditary weakness to the level of hereditary strength. The only remedy, if one be possible at all, is to alter the relative fertility of the good and the bad stocks in the community. Let us have a census of the effective size of families among the intellectual classes now and a comparison with the effective size of families in the like classes in the first half of last century. You will, I feel certain, find, as in the case of recent like censuses in America, that the intellectual classes are now scarcely reproducing their own numbers, and are very far from keeping pace with the total growth of the nation. Compare in another such census the fertility of the more intelligent working man with that of the uneducated hand labourer. You will, I again feel certain, find that grave changes have taken place in relative fertility during the last forty years. We stand, I venture to think, at the commencement of an epoch, which will be marked by a great dearth of ability. If the views I have put before you to-night be even approximately correct, the remedy lies beyond the reach of revised educational systems; we have failed to realize that the psychical characters, which are, in the modern struggle of nations, the backbone of a state, are not manufactured by home and school and college; they are bred in the bone; and for the last forty years the intellectual classes of the nation, enervated by wealth or by love of pleasure, or following an erroneous standard of life, have ceased to give us in due proportion the men we want to carry on the ever-growing work of our empire, to battle in the fore-rank of the ever intensified struggle of nations.

Do not let me close with too gloomy a note. I do not merely state our lack. I have striven by a study of the inheritance of the mental and moral characters in man to see how it arises, and to know the real source of an evil is half-way to finding a remedy. That remedy lies first in getting the intellectual section of our nation to realize that intelligence can be aided and be trained, but no training or education can *create* it. You must breed it, that is the broad result for statecraft which flows from the equality in inheritance of the psychical and the physical characters in man.

GENIUS, FAME, AND RACE (1897)

Charles H. Cooley

G ENIUS IS THAT aptitude for greatness that is born in a man; fame is the recognition by men that greatness has been achieved. Between the two lie early nurture and training, schools, the influence of friends and books, opportunities, and, in short, the whole working of organized society upon the individual. One is biological, the other social; to produce geniuses is a function of race, to allot fame is a function of history.

The question I propose to consider is, What is the relation between these two things? Does genius always result in fame? If not, why not, what determines whether it shall or shall not do so? These, in a general way, are the inquiries which suggest themselves, and which one would like to answer. I shall be well content if, without attempting to answer them fully, I can bring forward facts or reasoning that shall throw any light upon the matter whatever. That the question is a great one I think no one will doubt for a moment. It is a part of that larger question which is, from one point of view at least, the very root problem of soci-

Charles H. Cooley (1864–1929), an American social scientist, was a founder and first president of the American Sociological Society. He was a professor for many years at the University of Michigan, Ann Arbor, and wrote *Human Nature and Social Order* (1902) and *Social Organization* (1909). This piece is excerpted from the *Annals of the American Academy of Political and Social Science*, IX (1897), where it was published as "Genius, Fame, and the Comparison of Races."

ology, of history, perhaps of psychology, the question, that is, of the mutual relations between the individual and the social order, of how society makes the man and of how the man makes society. Although the "great-man-theory" of history, as taught by Carlyle and others, may not be entirely tenable, yet it is quite plain that recent studies in imitation, suggestion and the like have established more firmly than ever the fact of the momentous influence of remarkable men upon the progress of mankind.

One who wishes to work at this subject in as exact and verifiable a manner as its nature permits may well start, I think, from the writings of Francis Galton, and particularly from his great work on *Hereditary Genius*.* In this book the author, though concerned primarily with heredity, has found it necessary to his purpose to formulate roughly and to defend a theory of the relation between genius and fame. This theory, which I shall presently elucidate by ample quotations, may be stated, so far as it is capable of brief statement, somewhat as follows: Fame—on the whole, and reserving the right to allow for special conditions—is a sufficient test of genius. Fame can seldom be attained without genius, and genius as a rule achieves fame. Social conditions, though sometimes important and occasionally decisive, may on the whole be regarded as disturbing forces, not at all comparable in influence to natural capacity. This is so far the case that the number of illustrious men a race is capable of producing from a given population may be used as a criterion of the ability of the race, and upon this basis comparisons may justifiably be made between races so remote from each other as the ancient Athenians and the modern English.

I am led by a study of the facts in the case to uphold the following somewhat different theory—for which, however, I claim no originality. Every able race probably turns out a number of greatly endowed men many times larger than the number that attains to fame. By greatly endowed I mean with natural abilities equal to those that have made men famous in other times and places. The question which, if any, of these geniuses are to achieve fame is determined by historical and social conditions, and these vary so much that the production of great men cannot justifiably be used as a criterion of the ability of

* Galton's later writings contain, I think, no essential modification of the views set forth in *Hereditary Genius*.

races except under rare and peculiar circumstances hereafter to be specified.*

My view of the relation between genius and the social order may perhaps be made clear by the following comparison: Suppose a man, having plowed and cultivated his farm, should take in his hand a bag of mixed seeds—say wheat, rice, Indian corn, beans, and others—and should walk straight across his land, sowing as he went. All places on his path would be sown alike: the rocks, the sandy ground, the good upland soil, the rich mold in the hollows, the marshes, and whatever other sorts of soil there might be. All would be sown alike, but there would be a great variety in the result when harvest time came around. In some places nothing would come up at all. In the sand perhaps only the beans would flourish, in the marshes only the rice, and so on; while some generous soils would allow a variety of plants to grow side by side in considerable vigor. Something like this, I think, is the case with a stock of men passing through history. A good stock probably produces remarkable children with comparative uniformity, but of these only a few become famous men, and these few, instead of being evenly distributed, appear in groups, now of one sort, now of another, now of several sorts.

[. . .]

The reader can judge for himself whether it is not a fair description of Galton's theory to say that he holds social and historical conditions to be no more than disturbing forces in the career of genius. They may hasten or retard its success, but on the whole "few who possess very high abilities can fail in achieving eminence." That this is really his position must also be inferred from the fact that in another chapter, which I shall take up later, he estimates the comparative worth of different races on a basis of the number of great men they produce, with-

---

* Views more or less like this have been advanced by various writers; but I do not know that any one has treated the matter at length or answered Galton's arguments so much in detail as I have attempted to do in this paper.

Among the most important writings touching upon the subject are the article by Professor William James, entitled "Great Men, Great Thoughts, and the Environment," in the *Atlantic Monthly* for 1880, page 441, and the replies to it by John Fiske (1881, page 75) and Grant Allen (1881, page 371).

Lombroso's *Man of Genius* contains, of course, much interesting matter bearing on this question. See especially Part II.

out any attempt to compare their histories, or take account of their actual state of social development. Exceptions are here and there admitted, as, for instance, where he says that the Negroes in the United States have not had a fair chance to compete with the whites, but as to the general tenor of the book there can, I imagine, be no question.

Now let us first of all inquire what the facts and arguments quoted really show, supposing that we admit their general truth and reasonableness. They show that some men of genius can and do rise from a rather low rank of life—such as that in which d'Alembert passed his boyhood—and attain celebrity at an early age. This, I think, is nearly all that is shown: at any rate I wish to point out the following deficiencies in the reasoning:

1. It is not proved, or even claimed, except by inference, that there do not exist hindrances, greater than those surmounted by d'Alembert and others cited by Galton, which act as an effectual bar to genius. I shall give reasons for believing that such hindrances do exist, that they are effectual, and that they operate upon a large part of the population.

2. It is not shown, except by questionable *a priori* reasoning, that the ability to surmount ordinary social obstacles, proved to exist in certain cases, can be presumed to exist in men of genius as a class.

3. Finally, and most important omission of all, there is nothing to show that the ripening of genius into fame is not so far a matter of historical development—apart from the question of race—that race can at most be regarded as one of several equally important factors that must unite in the production of distinguished men. If this last be the case it follows that to estimate the worth of races merely by a count of famous men and without a comparison of their history and social organization, is a quite unjustifiable proceeding.

[. . .]

Is there, then, any form of social hindrance or disqualification that operates at all widely and effectually to prevent men of natural genius from achieving literary fame? I think there is at least one that has operated very widely and, so far as I can learn, quite effectually, namely, the circumstance of having been brought up without such an elementary education as consists in learning to read and write and having some access to good books.

In none of the cases cited by Galton of those who have attained to literary fame did the man in question fail to receive in his boyhood these simple tools by which all literary activity is carried on. Genius is wonderful, but not miraculous. A little suggestion, a little opportunity will go a great way with it—as Galton justly insists—but something of the sort there must be. A man can hardly fix his ambition upon a literary career when he is perfectly unaware, as millions are, that such a thing as a literary career exists. Between illiteracy and the ability to read a few good books there is all the difference between blindness and sight.

It is true that when reading and writing are generally diffused among the common people and recognized as necessary to any sort of advancement, a bright boy will manage to pick them up even when he has not been educated by his parents. But how recent the times and how few, even now, are the countries of which this can be said! Where whole classes of the people, or whole regions of the country know nothing of these difficult arts, how is a boy to get his start? How get that definite ambition that must go before any great achievement?

My opinion that an untaught childhood is an effectual bar to the development of literary genius does not, however, rest upon *a priori* arguments. Galton's list, as I have remarked, furnishes no example to the contrary. I have also, with the aid of Nichol's *Tables of European History*, prepared a list of about seventy of the most distinguished poets, philosophers and men of letters of Europe, consisting chiefly of those whose names are printed in large capitals by the authors of this work. Having examined the biographies of these men I find none who did not receive elementary instruction in his boyhood. In the few cases where men of letters have sprung from a class generally illiterate it appears that some special pains has been taken with their education. Thus the father of Burns "was at great pains to give his children a good education," and Bunyan, whose father was a tinker, "a settled and reputable man,"* says in his autobiography, "Notwithstanding the meanness and inconsiderableness of my parents it pleased God to put into their hearts to put me to school, to learn both to read and to write."

* Venables' *Life of Bunyan*, page 13.

The next question is whether this hindrance of illiteracy, which appears to have been effectual, has been felt by a large proportion of the population. Exact information upon this point cannot be had except for recent times, but the following statements are moderate and I have taken some pains to satisfy myself of their truth.*

Up to within the present century the great mass of the population of Europe, even in Protestant countries, was entirely illiterate. By the great mass I mean all but a rather small per cent, differing in different countries and nowhere precisely ascertainable.†

If we except France and Switzerland, the same is true of southern and eastern Europe at the present time. Spain, Russia and European Turkey are overwhelmingly illiterate. Italy is prevailingly so, though her condition in this respect is rapidly improving. The same may be said of Greece. In Austria-Hungary more than half of the army recruits are now returned as able to read and write; but we must remember that these are young men who have profited by recent reforms.

In England, where a powerful aristocracy and church establishment seem to have been, on the whole, hostile to the education of the common people, such education has been more backward than in any other large Protestant country.

[. . .]

There are other hindrances arising from social and economic conditions that operate effectually to prevent the development of natural ability. One of these, as I suppose everyone will admit, is underfeeding in childhood, or the subjection of children to premature and stunting labor. No breeder of horses would expect a colt, however excellent his parentage, to develop speed after having been put to the plow when two years old. Yet it is undeniable that something closely analogous happens to a considerable part of the children in countries so advanced as England and the United States. Mr. Galton has himself devised and brought into use methods of measuring large numbers of men which have recently been employed to determine the physical effects of nurture and environment. The most striking of these researches is perhaps the investigation by Spielmann and Jacobs of the comparative

---

* For information and references upon this point I am indebted to the kindness of Prof. B. A. Hinsdale.
† This was certainly the general fact. There may have been local exceptions.

measurements of Jews in the East and West Ends of London.* The West End Jews, who are a well-to-do class, did not differ much from Englishmen of the same class. Those from the East End, employed for the most part in sweat-shops upon the manufacture of cheap clothing, averaged more than three inches less in stature, and were inferior also in size of skull and in every particular covered by the measurements. The intellectual deterioration that goes with this cannot well be measured, but that it must exist will hardly be doubted.

In another paper, dealing with the ability of the Jews as compared with other races, Mr. Jacobs asserts that out of one and a half million of Jews living to fifty "only a little more than half a million can be said to have lived; the rest have but existed, and have been out of the running in the race for fame."

The biographies of men of letters seem to me to afford very small support to the theory that literary genius is independent of social hindrances. In going over the list already mentioned of seventy of the most distinguished European poets, philosophers and historians, I find that about two-thirds of them belonged by birth to the upper and upper middle classes, using the latter term rather broadly to include clergymen, advocates, well-to-do merchants and the like. Of the remainder nearly all came of the lower middle class, shopkeepers, prosperous handicraftsmen, etc., while the very few men who, like Burns, sprung from the peasantry, prove to have received an education uncommon in their class. It would seem, then, that if we divide mankind into these three classes, the number of famous men produced by each class is in something like inverse proportion to the total number in the class.

The only escape from these facts, for one who still believes that genius is superior to circumstance, is to assert that the lower classes are naturally as well as socially inferior, and this to such a degree that few or no men of genius are born in them. In our democratic days this will appear to most persons a monstrous supposition, and yet it may be supported by a plausible argument which ought, in fairness, to be stated.

The struggle for the best places in life operates, it may be said, as a sort of natural selection, by the working of which the ablest strains of men are continually finding their way to the top. Even in the most con-

* See their paper on "The Comparative Anthropometry of English Jews" in the *Journal of the Anthropological Institute*, 1890, p. 76.

servative societies there is always more or less penetration of social walls by men and families of uncommon energy. The natural effect of such a process is that hereditary ability becomes concentrated in the upper strata, and little or none is to be found anywhere else. To this might be added the argument already quoted from Galton, that since America, where education is diffused and opportunity open, does not produce more great writers than England, where social distinctions are comparatively fixed, we must conclude that democracy has no tendency to bring to light suppressed genius.

This view has some show of reason, and in fact it may be admitted that, for the cause mentioned, there is probably more unusual ability among the children of the well-to-do classes, in proportion to their number, than there is among those who have not made so good a place for themselves. But there is no proof that this superiority is very great, and when we see that a few men from the peasantry and the proletariat, having had instruction and opportunities unusual with their class, achieve literary fame, it seems reasonable to infer that if instruction and opportunity had been general the number of such men would have been correspondingly increased.

The argument derived from the United States is pertinent only if we assume that the failure of this country to produce a large number of famous writers cannot be explained by some historical cause, such as the inevitable preoccupation of the people with the material development of the country and its political organization. That it can be so explained is the general and defensible opinion with us, and I shall later offer some observations tending to confirm this view.

Moreover, if we take history as a whole, the proposition that democracy favors the development of genius will appear plausible, to say the least.* Athens and Florence, rich in famous men above all other places, were democracies when at the height of their glory, and ceased to be glorious soon after they ceased to be democratic. The great writers of the Augustan age were the product of the later days of the Roman Republic, and the time of Elizabeth was one of freedom and open opportunity compared with the times that preceded and followed it. The history of the Netherlands would also offer striking confirmation of the theory suggested.

* This topic is ably discussed in Bryce's *American Commonwealth*, Chaps. 107 and 108.

Freedom is certainly not the only cause of the appearance of great men, but it appears to be one of the causes, a favoring circumstance which has commonly united with other and more obscure conditions in the production of memorable groups of famous persons. It seems to me that if any conclusion upon this point is to be drawn from history it is the one opposite to that which Galton draws from the case of the United States. And if this fails, what other standing ground is there for the theory that genius is not suppressed by illiteracy and class distinctions?

The question how far genius can be helped or hindered by such differences of wealth and circumstance as are found within the educated classes of peoples as advanced as the English or the American, cannot be precisely determined because we have no way of knowing what a man might have done under different conditions. We cannot know what is in him until it comes out: if genius does not become fame we cannot be sure it was genius. There is no single, definite obstacle which, like illiteracy, is almost invariably efficacious; but what may help one may hinder another. In such a question more weight must be given to probability and the opinion of judicious observers than to anything else. Galton is very clear in his belief that these things do not materially affect the final result, that if a man of genius does not reach fame by one road he will by another. It is possible, however, that he does not do full justice to the considerations opposed to this view.

[. . .]

In estimating the importance of circumstance it should never be forgotten that "a favorable environment" is nothing fixed and definite, like social standing or wealth, but is different for every individual. That measure of struggle and disappointment which is only a wholesome and needed stimulus to one man, may drive another into dissipation, or wear out his body and mind with fruitless annoyance and anxiety. In the same way the wealth that may secure just the needed seclusion and materials for one, may keep another in lifelong indolence.

So much for those differences in education, nurture and opportunity that are found among the people of the same time and nation. Now how is it as between different countries and different times? Can it be shown that there are forces apart from race that cause genius to flourish here and droop there, which at one period foster the germs of greatness in a people until they yield a rich fruitage of accomplishment and fame, and at another wither and chill them into barrenness? Are such things as historical tendency and the spirit of the age sufficiently real and powerful to control the production of famous men?

If the affirmative of these questions can be established, it is clear that the whole plan of estimating the worth of races by their great men and with only incidental reference to their history falls to the ground. Such comparisons can be defended only upon the theory that race is the paramount factor.

I hope to show that history is quite as important as race in this matter; that while it is a function of race to turn out geniuses, historical forces determine how many of them shall be famous, and of what sort these shall be, that the appearance of great men in the past has been of a sort impossible to reconcile with the theory that such appearance is controlled by race alone.

Let me begin by giving the main argument and conclusions of Galton's chapter on "The Comparative Worth of Different Races."

In discussing this the first question considered is, What are the qualities which are needed in civilized society, and which may, therefore, be used as a test of the worth of races?

> They are, speaking generally, such as will enable a race to supply a large contingent to the various groups of eminent men, of whom I have treated in my several chapters. Without going so far as to say that this very convenient test is perfectly fair, we are at all events justified in making considerable use of it, as I will do, in the estimates I am about to give.

The comparison, then, is to be based upon the number and grade of the eminent men that a race produces, the supposition being that the distribution of ability is similar in all races, so that if the ablest men in a given race are superior in a certain degree to those of another race, the men of medium and low ability will be superior in like degree. It is like the inference of a zoologist, who, having only a single bone of an animal of known species, will compute approximately all the other dimensions.

> I know this cannot be strictly true, for it would be in defiance of analogy if the variability of all races were precisely the same; but, on the other hand, there is good reason to expect that the error intro-

duced by the assumption cannot sensibly affect the off-hand results for which alone I propose to employ it; moreover, the rough data I shall adduce, will go far to show the justice of this expectation.

Upon this basis Galton proceeds to compare the Negro race with the Anglo-Saxon, the Lowland Scotch and the English North-Country men with the ordinary English, and the English with the ancient Athenians.

The Negro race he finds to be about two grades below the Anglo-Saxon. This conclusion is based upon the fact that its greatest men, such as Toussaint l'Ouverture, appear to be at least that much inferior to the greatest men of the rival race, also upon the opinions of travelers who have had to do with African chiefs, and upon the large proportion of half-witted persons found among the blacks.

The Lowland Scotch and the English North-Country men are held to be "decidedly a fraction of a grade superior to the ordinary English," both because they produce more eminent men in proportion to their number, and because the well-being of the masses of the population is greater.

We now come to the Athenians.

> Of the various Greek sub-races, that of Attica was the ablest, and she was no doubt largely indebted to the following cause for her superiority. Athens opened her arms to immigrants, but not indiscriminately, for her social life was such that none but very able men could take any pleasure in it; on the other hand, she offered attractions such as men of the highest ability and culture could find in no other city. Thus, by a system of partly unconscious selection, she built up a magnificent breed of human animals, which, in the space of one century—viz., between 530 and 430 B. C.—produced the following illustrious persons, fourteen in number:
>
> Statesmen and Commanders.—Themistocles (mother an alien), Miltiades, Aristides, Cimon (son of Miltiades), Pericles (son of Xanthippus, the victor at Mycale). Literary and Scientific Men.—Thucydides, Socrates, Xenophon, Plato. Poets.—Aeschylus, Sophocles, Euripides, Aristophanes. Sculptor.—Phidias.

The population of Attica at the time she produced these men consisted, it seems, of about 90,000 native free-born persons, 40,000 resident aliens, and a laboring and artisan population of 400,000 slaves. Of these Galton holds that the first-mentioned alone are to be considered, the aliens and slaves being excluded, doubtless because they did not belong to the Athenian race.

> Now let us attempt to compare the Athenian standard of ability with that of our own race and time. We have no men to put by the side of Socrates and Phidias, because the millions of all Europe, breeding as they have done for the subsequent 2000 years, have never produced their equals. They are therefore two or three grades above our G—they might rank as I or J. But, supposing we do not count them at all, saying that some freak of nature acting at that time may have produced them, what must we say about the rest? Pericles and Plato would rank, I suppose, the one among the greatest of philosophical statesmen, and the other as at least the equal of Lord Bacon. They would, therefore, stand somewhere among our unclassed X, one or two grades above G—let us call them between H and I. All the remainder, the F of the Athenian race—would rank above our G, and equal to or close upon our H. It follows from all this, that the average ability of the Athenian race is on the lowest possible estimate, very nearly two grades higher than our own—that is, about as much as our race is above that of the African Negro. This estimate, which may seem prodigious to some, is confirmed by the quick intelligence and high culture of the Athenian commonalty, before whom literary works were recited, and works of art exhibited, of a far more severe character than could possibly be appreciated by the average of our race, the calibre of whose intellect is easily gauged by a glance at the contents of a railway book-stall.

This argument is so ingenious and the conclusion so startling that I propose to assume for a few moments that the method is sound—that it is practicable to compare peoples so widely different in almost every respect as the English and Athenians upon a basis of the number and grade of their eminent men—and inquire whether it is fairly applied, whether it does, after all, show such a preeminence on the part of the Greeks as Galton asserts. The only changes I propose to make are such as in my opinion tend to insure fair play between the contending nations.

As we allow Athens to choose her ground, so to speak, and rest her claims upon the age of Pericles, we ought surely to allow the same privilege to England. The brightest period in her history, having in view the number of her great men and of the population from which they were drawn, was undoubtedly the age of Elizabeth.

The population of the country at that period is not accurately known, but it appears to have been not greater than four and a half millions. Against this we have in Athens only about 90,000 free citizens, or but two per cent of the number of Englishmen.

I have already given reasons, however, for holding that in questions of fame the illiterate and overburdened poor should be counted out. Now among the free citizens of Athens there was no such class as this; although the government was democratic, so far as concerned those who shared in it, the citizens were really an aristocratic caste, ruling over a vast population of slaves. There were, on the average, four or five of these latter to every man, woman and child of the Athenian population, and even the poorest families had at least one slave to do the lower sorts of manual labor. The education of boys appears to have been nearly universal, and it was not a mere smattering of the elements, enabling the pupil to write his name or spell out laboriously a few paragraphs, but lasted from the age of seven to that of sixteen, and was often followed by more advanced studies. The three main divisions were gymnastics, music and letters, and the course as a whole appears to have been a thorough initiation into the culture of the Athenian people. This culture was, as all will admit, one peculiarly favorable to the development of literary and artistic genius.

I have not been able to find even an estimate of the number of English people that could read and write in the time of Elizabeth; but it was some small percentage of the population. Of course the upper and middle classes were feeling in some measure the general intellectual awakening that followed the revival of learning and the invention of printing, but culture was by no means general in any class and scarcely touched the common people. Froude says in his *Life of Bunyan,* "In those days there were no village schools in England; the education of the poor was an apprenticeship to agriculture or handicraft."

Without pretending to definite knowledge upon the matter I venture to suggest that it is at least a fair question whether more than two per cent of the people of England had such opportunities for culture that they can reasonably be classed, in this respect, with the free-born population of Athens.

Another circumstance in favor of the Athenians is, in my opinion, of almost equal importance. The development of literary and artistic genius is greatly stimulated by facility of access to great centres of culture, where one can come into contact with eminent men and their works, and gain an inspiration more personal and visible than can be gotten from books. It is in capitals, and there only as a rule, that literature and art are organized, communication and sympathy established among men of promise, and an "atmosphere" created.

Upon this point I shall take the liberty of quoting Goethe again. He has discussed the question at length, with his usual sagacity and amplitude of information. Take for instance this concerning Béranger, whom he is contrasting with Schiller.*

> On the other hand, take up Béranger. He is the son of poor parents, the descendant of a poor tailor; at one time a poor printer's apprentice, then placed in some office with a small salary; he has never been to a classical school or university, and yet his songs are so full of mature cultivation, so full of wit and the most refined irony, and there is such artistic perfection and masterly handling of the language, that he is the admiration, not only of France, but of all civilized Europe.
>
> But imagine this same Béranger—instead of being born in Paris, and brought up in this metropolis of the world—the son of a poor tailor in Jena or Weimar, and let him commence his career, in an equally miserable manner, in such small places, and ask yourself what fruit would have been produced by this same tree, grown in such a soil and in such an atmosphere.

I suppose I need not insist on the fact that as a focus of intellectual activity the London of Elizabeth bears no comparison to the Athens of Pericles. The Athenians were all, practically, inhabitants of one great town, and any man could meet with any other as often as he liked, while all came in daily contact with the great works of art that crowned the city. London, on the other hand, was hard to reach—how hard one may judge from the famous description of English roads in Macaulay's

* Conversation with Eckermann, May 3, 1827.

third chapter—and was not much of a place when you got there. It contained something like 150,000 people, of whom the great majority were ignorant artisans who must be classed, so far as culture is concerned, with the Athenian slaves.

Making due allowance for these things and assuming that the conditions other than race are about equal in the two cases, let us see if England can produce a list of men born within one century, which shall be other than ridiculous when set beside the one that Galton gives us from Athens. I choose the century beginning with 1550.

Athenians.	*Englishmen.*
Themistocles,	Cromwell,
Miltiades,	Sir Walter Raleigh,
Aristides,	Sir Philip Sidney,
Cimon,	Shakespeare,
Pericles,	Bacon,
Thucydides,	Ben Jonson,
Socrates,	Spenser,
Xenophon,	Milton,
Plato,	Bunyan,
Aeschylus,	Dryden,
Sophocles,	Locke,
Euripides,	Hobbes,
Aristophanes,	Jeremy Taylor,
Phidias.	Sir Isaac Newton.

Opinions will differ regarding these two lists; but few, I imagine, will go so far as to say that the Englishmen are outclassed.

It is not for me to praise Shakespeare, or Milton, or Cromwell, much less to depreciate Phidias or Sophocles. Some would say that to have produced Shakespeare was alone a sufficient title to greatness for any race, and enough to cast lasting doubt on all comparisons tending to make it appear less than others. Let the reader form his own opinion.

In such questions as these, where there is no definite criterion, we are necessarily more or less controlled by prejudice. In favor of the Englishmen there is the prejudice of race; in favor of the Greeks there is the prejudice of education. The writers of the latter people had a long start; they have been the school-books of Europe emerging from barbarism; they have grown with the growth of culture, and their fame is carried on by irresistible tradition. The fame of Shakespeare is still young, and it is only within the present century that he has come to be generally regarded as the peer of the great classic writers.

Anglo-Saxons of sensibility and culture regard Greek literature and art with an intensity of admiration which might be interpreted as a sense of their own inferiority. I would suggest, however, that this charm which the Greek spirit has for the northern races is the charm of difference rather than that of superiority. It is like the feeling of sex; just as there is something in what is womanly that appeals to men, and something in what is manly that appeals to women, so that which is Greek delights the modern nations without there being any question of greater or less in the matter at all. The Teutonic man, one may say, feels toward the spirit of his own race as toward a brother, but toward the Greek spirit as toward a mistress. This very capacity of admiring, and so assimilating, what is best in a different race is itself, perhaps, a title of greatness.

After all, were the Greeks an abler people than the Anglo-Saxon? Could they have advanced in liberty for a thousand years without falling into disorder? Could they have organized and maintained a commercial empire "greater than the Roman"? Could they have suppressed Napoleon and abolished the slave trade?

Such questions are interesting, perhaps, but quite unanswerable. In the meantime I imagine that most persons who consider the facts dispassionately will agree with me that even if we accept Galton's method of comparison, there is small foundation for his judgment "that the average ability of the Athenian race is, on the lowest possible estimate, very nearly two grades higher than our own—that is, about as much as our race is above that of the African Negro."

But it can be shown, I think, that this method, no matter how carefully we allow for differences of social organization, is still hopelessly fallacious. It can be satisfactorily tested, it seems to me, by examining the historical grouping of the eminent men produced by any one people, with a view to finding out whether they appear with such approximate regularity as would be expected if greatness is a function of race. If one thing is to be the criterion of another it must be shown to bear some reasonably definite relation to it. In Galton's argument it is assumed that we have an equation of two variable quantities, of which one being determined, namely the number of great men, we can determine the other, that is race ability. Now it is demonstrable that there are other unknown quantities entering into this equation which are not determined, and whose presence vitiates the reasoning.

The conspicuous fact that one generation may be rich in famous men and another, a little earlier or later, quite barren of them, does not entirely escape Galton; but he endeavors to account for it, as he apparently must under his theory, by a change in the race itself. Let us see how he does this in the case of the Athenians. In a paragraph already quoted, the rise of this people is explained as follows:

> Athens opened her arms to immigrants, but not indiscriminately, for her social life was such that none but very able men could take any pleasure in it; on the other hand, she offered attractions such as men of the highest ability and culture could find in no other city. Thus, by a system of partly unconscious selection, she built up a magnificent breed of human animals which . . . produced the following illustrious persons.

Now for the causes of the decline of this breed.

> We know, and may guess something more, of the reason why this marvelously gifted race declined. Social morality grew exceedingly lax; marriage became unfashionable, and was avoided; many of the more ambitious and accomplished women were avowed courtesans, and consequently infertile, and the mothers of the incoming population were of a heterogeneous class. In a small sea-bordered country, where emigration and immigration are constantly going on, and where the manners are as dissolute as were those of Greece in the period of which I speak, the purity of a race would necessarily fail. It can be, therefore, no surprise to us, though it has been a severe misfortune to humanity, that the high Athenian breed decayed and disappeared.

Now is this entirely plausible, or even consistent? Both the rise and the decline of the race are ascribed to the same cause, namely immigration. Certainly, then, some reason should be given for supposing that there was a radical change in the character of the immigration: but no such reason is given. Until something more definite and convincing than this is brought forward we must believe that the natural characteristics of a race are comparatively stable, and that it takes a long time, as a rule, to transform them into something quite different. Believing this we cannot explain the instances of rapid rise and decadence, of which history is full, by saying that they are due to changes in the breed.

[. . .]

We must also, I think, conclude that able races produce at all times a considerable number and variety of men of genius of whom only a few encounter those favorable conditions that enable them to achieve fame.

To make perfectly clear the grounds of this last inference let me suggest a comparison. Suppose one were following a river through a valley, and from time to time measuring its breadth, depth and current with a view to finding out how much water passed through its channel. Suppose he found that while in some places the river flowed with a swift and ample current, in others it dwindled to a mere brook and even disappeared altogether, only to break out in full volume lower down. Would he not be led to conclude that where little or no water appeared upon the surface the bulk of it must find its way through underground channels, or percolate invisibly through the sand? Would not this supposition amount almost to a certainty if it could be shown that the nature of the rock was such as to make the existence of underground channels extremely probable, and if in some cases they were positively known to exist? I do not see that the inference is any less inevitable in the case before us. We know that a race has once produced a large amount of natural genius in a short time, just as we know that the river has a large volume in some places. We see, also, that the number of eminent men seems to dwindle and disappear; but we have good reason to think that social conditions can cause genius to remain hidden, just as we have good reason to think that a river may find its way through an underground channel. Must we not conclude, in the one case as in the other, that what is not seen does not cease to be, that genius is present though fame is not?

There are reasons for believing that even where our river seems fullest a great part of its flow is underground. In the age of Elizabeth, for instance, there was a complete lack of those masters of painting and sculpture who made the chief glory of the age of Lorenzo de Medici. Yet later history has shown that the English people are by no means lacking in this sort of genius. The inference is that it was present but undeveloped.

The fact that genius can develop into greatness at some times and cannot at others is by no means inscrutable. The reasons for it can be indicated in a general way, though they are so complex that it is difficult to point out their precise application to various periods of history.

[. . .]

Since Galton includes distinguished oarsmen among his men of genius, I may be allowed at this point, to draw a comparison from the game of base-ball. It is as difficult for an American brought up in the western part of our country to become a good painter as it is for a Parisian to become a good base-ball player, and for similar reasons. Base-ball is a social institution with us; every vacant lot is a school, every boy an aspirant for success. The technique of the game is acquired in childhood, and every appearance of talent meets with enthusiastic appreciation. Hence we have many good players and a few great ones. Now it is probable that Frenchmen are from time to time born with a genius for this game, but how can it be developed? What chance do they have to achieve excellence or acquire fame? They probably remain in lifelong ignorance of their own possibilities. If the ambition did arise in one of them it would probably come too late for him to make up the lack of early training.

This somewhat humble illustration is believed to be well worthy of consideration by those who imagine that a social career can be independent of circumstances and the spirit of the time.

[. . .]

The main fact is that great success in any career calls for two things: natural ability, and a social mechanism to make this effective. Genius can reach high, as a rule, only when it stands on top of a culminating institution. When one looks off at the horizon of a rolling landscape he will notice two or three trees that seem to overtop all others. They seem to do so partly because they are really tall trees, and partly because they stand near the summit of the highest visible ridge. There may be higher trees in the valley—probably there are many equally high—but these do not appear. It is quite the same with men. The age of Elizabeth and the age of Lorenzo de Medici were, so to speak, natural elevations in the histories of England and Italy, resting upon which it was easy for genius to attain fame. I do not mean that they were superior, on the whole, to our own time, but they were more favorable to the development of certain sorts of ability. Individual faculty is real and powerful, and there is no greatness without it, but no man is tall enough to stand upright and fixed in the stream of history. He can at most swim a few strokes against or across it. "Who can separate his ship from the waves on which it is floating?"

I trust I have made clear my reasons for thinking that estimates of the worth of races based upon the number and grade of the eminent men they produce, have no scientific justification unless it be possible to eliminate those social conditions that have quite as much to do with the matter as race. That such elimination is usually impossible, I suppose all will admit. To show, in a general way, the power of historical forces is easy, but to take exact account of them, to predict their future operation, to show just how they differ in different times and countries, and how much must be allowed for that difference, is, in the present state of historical science, quite out of the question. If, however, cases can be found where two races mingle and compete in the same social order, and under conditions substantially the same, a valuable comparison might perhaps be made. Are there any such cases?

The negroes and the whites in the United States could not be so compared, as Galton justly remarks. Neither, for similar reasons, would it be possible to compare the older English stock of the same country with recent immigrants of other races. Perhaps no cases can be found in which the use of the method is more defensible than in the comparison of the ordinary English with the Scotch and the North-Country men, suggested by Galton, and the comparison between the Jews and other races carried out by Mr. Jacobs in the paper published by the Anthropological Institute.*

The question here is whether the peoples mentioned are really on an equality in respects other than race. It is commonly reported that the standard of education and individual freedom among the Lowland Scotch is considerably higher than it is in England. Galton says as much, and contrasts the well-being of the northern peasantry with "the draggled, drudged, mean look of the mass of individuals, especially of the women, that one meets in the streets of London and other purely English towns." Now to assume that this degradation is due to inferiority of race seems to me to be a begging of the whole question. Before doing that it should be shown that nurture and social conditions cannot thus degrade the members of a good race. I do not think it is

* *Journal*, Vol. xv, p. 351.

possible to show this, and I would cite the comparison of East and West End Jews, already referred to, as indicating the contrary.

If the comparison between English and Scotch were made at the time of Elizabeth it would seem to show that the English were a far superior race at that period, since Scotland was then conspicuously lacking in distinguished men.* If this lack was due to the backwardness of social development, how can we assume that the present apparent superiority of Scotland is not likewise due to social conditions, instead of to race? The men of the north may be "a fraction of a grade superior," but, if so, the fact needs further proof.

The author of the paper upon the ability of the Jews ascribes a great deal to their social conditions, which still differ much from those of the races with whom they mingle. Thus he explains their musical pre-eminence partly by "the home character of their religion, which necessarily makes music a part of every Jewish home." Again, "Persecution, when not too severe, has probably aided in bringing out their best powers; to a high-spirited race, persecution, when there is hope of overcoming it, is a spur to action."

Such comparisons, when made with as much thoroughness and caution as this one, are certainly interesting and valuable; and if they do not arrive at precise results they are no worse off in this respect than most social investigations.

On the whole it seems to me that the relation between genius and fame is fairly well represented by the comparison, suggested at the outset, of a farmer sowing mixed seeds in a furrow which traverses a great variety of ground. Here many come up and flourish, there none, and there again only those of a certain sort. The seed-bag is the race, the soil historical conditions other than race, the seeds genius, and the crop fame.

It is true that knowing so little as we do of the forces governing heredity and degeneration, we cannot be sure that the seeds are sown with anything like uniformity, that the amount of natural ability produced from a given stock is approximately constant. But this is certainly the simplest supposition, and it would seem reasonable to accept it until the contrary is shown.

---

* Lombroso. *The Man of Genius*, English translation, p. 154, makes a similar remark, ascribing the former deficiency of Scotch genius to religious intolerance.

THE NEGRO (1911)

Encyclopaedia Britannica

MENTALLY THE NEGRO is inferior to the white. The remark of F. Manetta, made after a long study of the negro in America, may be taken as generally true of the whole race: "the negro children were sharp, intelligent and full of vivacity, but on approaching the adult period a gradual change set in. The intellect seemed to become clouded, animation giving place to a sort of lethargy, briskness yielding to indolence." We must necessarily suppose that the development of the negro and white proceeds on different lines. While with the latter the volume of the brain grows with the expansion of the brainpan, in the former the growth of the brain is on the contrary arrested by the premature closing of the cranial sutures and lateral pressure of the frontal bone. This explanation is reasonable and even probable as a contributing cause; but evidence is lacking on the subject and the arrest or even deterioration in mental development is no doubt very largely due to the fact that after puberty sexual matters take the first place in the negro's life and thoughts. At the same time his environment has not been such as would tend to produce in him

---

This extract from the eleventh edition of the *Encyclopaedia Britannica* (1911) appeared under the entry for "Negro." It was written by Walter Francis Willcox, chief statistician, United States Census Bureau, and professor of social science and statistics at Cornell University.

the restless energy which has led to the progress of the white race; and the easy conditions of tropical life and the fertility of the soil have reduced the struggle for existence to a minimum. But though the mental inferiority of the negro to the white or yellow races is a fact, it has often been exaggerated; the negro is largely the creature of his environment, and it is not fair to judge of his mental capacity by tests taken directly from the environment of the white man, as for instance tests in mental arithmetic; skill in reckoning is necessary to the white race, and it has cultivated this faculty; but it is not necessary to the negro.

On the other hand negroes far surpass white men in acuteness of vision, hearing, sense of direction and topography. A native who has once visited a particular locality will rarely fail to recognize it again. For the rest, the mental constitution of the negro is very similar to that of a child, normally good-natured and cheerful, but subject to sudden fits of emotion and passion during which he is capable of performing acts of singular atrocity, impressionable, vain, but often exhibiting in the capacity of servant a dog-like fidelity which has stood the supreme test.

VII
TESTING AMERICA'S INTELLIGENCE

EUGENICS COMES TO AMERICA

Garland E. Allen

I N 1 8 8 3 the British naturalist and mathematician Francis Galton
(1822–1911) first introduced the term *eugenics* to the vocabulary of
science. According to Galton's lofty formulation, eugenics was "the
study of the agencies under social control that may improve or impair
the racial qualities of future generations, either physically or mentally." By 1911 the chief American advocate of eugenics, Charles B.
Davenport (1866–1944), had put it more bluntly; to him, eugenics was
no less than "the science of the improvement of the human race by
better breeding."[1]

Conceived as a scientifically grounded reform movement in an age
of social, political, and economic turbulence, eugenics looked to hered-

This research was supported by the National Science Foundation and the Charles Warren
Center for Studies in American History, Harvard University. I am grateful for the comments of Mark Adams, Randy Bird, Donald Fleming, Daniel J. Kevles, Kenneth Ludmerer, Jon Roberts, Barbara Rosenkrantz, and Stephen Thurnstrom.

[1] Francis Galton, *Inquiries into Human Faculty and Its Development* (New York: Dutton, 2nd
ed., n.d.): p. 17n.; quoted also on the frontispiece of the *Journal of Heredity*. Charles B.
Davenport, *Heredity in Relation to Eugenics* (New York: Henry Holt, 1911). p. 1.

Garland E. Allen is professor of biology at Washington University, St. Louis, and the
author of *Thomas Hunt Morgan* and *Life Science in the Twentieth Century*. This article is
excerpted from "The Eugenics Record Office at Cold Spring Harbor, 1910–1940: An
Essay in Institutional History," *Osiris*, II, 1986.

itary factors for the sources of such a vast array of human behavioral problems as alcoholism, feeblemindedness, rebelliousness—even criminality. Eugenicists also thought they had found the causes of many fundamental social problems in measurable hereditary defects. Eugenics as a social movement developed throughout most of the countries of Western Europe, but it enjoyed a particularly robust life in the United States. After 1900 the movement became, in the eyes of its American advocates, a major breakthrough in the application of rational, scientific methods to the problems of a complex urban and industrial society.

ALTHOUGH GALTON coined the term *eugenics* in 1883, by 1900 neither he nor his followers had been able to establish a serious eugenics movement in England. Both Galton and his disciple Karl Pearson (1857–1936) lacked a firm and workable theory of heredity. Their views, which were based on biometry, the statistical analysis of biological traits measured for large samples, encountered great difficulty when applied to individual families or lines of descent. With the rediscovery of Mendel's laws of heredity in 1900, however, the study of heredity in general and eugenics in particular found fertile ground, particularly in the United States. By 1910 most American biologists, except for a stalwart few, agreed that Mendel's theory could be applied to all sexually reproducing forms. The enthusiasm with which biologists—in the United States in particular—began to endorse the Mendelian scheme cannot be overemphasized. Here, for the first time, was what seemed to be a generalized, predictive, and experimentally verifiable concept of heredity that applied to *all* living forms, including human beings. Indeed, in the period 1900–1910 geneticists had concluded that several human traits follow a strictly Mendelian pattern of inheritance: red-green color blindness, the A-B-O blood groups, polydactyly (presence of short, stubby digits on the hands and feet), and several metabolic diseases or inborn errors of metabolism. A revolution in genetics had taken hold.[2]

---

[2] Much has been written in recent years about the history of Mendelian theory in the early decades of the century. Among the best general sources are L. C. Dunn, *A Short History of Genetics* (New York: McGraw-Hill, 1965); and E. A. Carlson, *The Gene: A Critical History* (Philadelphia: Saunders, 1966). For more detailed analyses of the first decades of genetics, see Garland E. Allen, *Thomas Hunt Morgan: The Man and His Science* (Princeton: Princeton University Press, 1978); and E. A. Carlson, *Genes, Radiation and Society: The Life and Work of H. J. Muller* (Ithaca, N.Y.: Cornell University Press, 1981).

The application of Mendelian theory to human beings armed eugenicists with a powerful analytical tool. Using pedigree analyses as the data from which possible Mendelian patterns of inheritance could be deduced, eugenicists in the United States began to study a wide variety of physical, mental, and moral traits in humans. Although American eugenicists did not adhere to the view, so common in England, that Mendelism and biometry were mutually exclusive, in practice most emphasized the Mendelian scheme. One of these early American supporters of Mendelism, and a champion of experimental biology, was Charles Benedict Davenport, under whose direction the Station for the Experimental Study of Evolution and the Eugenics Record Office were established at Cold Spring Harbor.

The establishment of the Eugenics Record Office (ERO) in 1910 at Cold Spring Harbor, Long Island (New York), was central to the development of eugenics in the United States. Associated with the larger Station for the Experimental Study of Evolution (SEE), the ERO provided both the appearance of sound scientific credentials and the reality of an institutional base from which eugenics work throughout the country, and even in Western Europe, could be coordinated. The ERO became a meeting place for eugenicists, a repository for eugenics records, a clearinghouse for eugenics information and propaganda, a platform from which popular eugenic campaigns could be launched, and a home for several eugenical publications. Moreover, the ERO was headed by two of the country's best-known eugenicists: C. B. Davenport, as director of both the SEE and the ERO, and Harry Hamilton Laughlin (1880–1943), as his deputy at the SEE and as superintendent of the ERO itself. Thus the ERO became a nerve center for the eugenics movement as a whole. When it closed its doors on 31 December 1939, it was clear that the movement as such no longer existed.

The ERO, whose life spans virtually the entire history of eugenics in the United States, provides an illuminating focus for historical study of the movement. Study of the ERO's activities also exposes the modern investigator to a representative cross section of the work and concerns of eugenicists throughout the world. Moreover, because its financial needs brought the ERO into direct contact with some of the individual philanthropists as well as the larger philanthropic foundations that were emerging in the first decades of this century, this study also provides historical perspective on the initiation and control of funding for scientific work during that period. In many ways, then, the ERO is a microcosm of the larger social macrocosm that was the American eugenics movement. It also provides a focus for exploring the relationship between the development of eugenics and the changing social, economic, and political life in the United States between 1900 and 1940.

To put the present study in perspective, however, I should emphasize that several other groups also played an important role in the development of the American eugenics movement—groups such as the American Breeders' Association (whose Eugenics and Immigration Committees were the first eugenics organizations in the country), the American Eugenics Society, the Eugenics Research Association, the Galton Society, the Institute of Family Relations, and the Race Betterment Foundation. The ERO, however, was the only major eugenics institution with a building, research facilities, and a paid staff. Although unique in having its own institutional base, it nevertheless could not have done as much without the existence of those other organizations. Another point to keep in mind is that the style and particular focus of the ERO's work was not typical of all aspects of the American eugenics movement. Although the ERO did provide a considerable amount of ideological direction, the American eugenics movement was not monolithic or highly organized. Many eugenicists would have preferred that the movement have more of a unified character, but this proved difficult to accomplish. Eugenicists came from all walks of life, though most were professional middle class or upper class. Often individualistic and independent, they tended to focus on their own projects and were generally not amenable to highly coordinated efforts. Although the ERO tried to provide nationwide coordination, in the long run there was little centralized organization or control. Despite the efforts of Charles Davenport and his staff, the ERO was probably far more effective as a clearinghouse and data repository than as an organizational force.

CHARLES BENEDICT DAVENPORT, who was to spearhead the American eugenics movement, was born in Brooklyn, of New England ancestry. He received an engineering degree from Brooklyn Polytechnic Institute in 1887 and an A.B. from Harvard College in 1889. He immediately enrolled in Harvard graduate school and received his Ph.D. in 1892, writing a thesis on morphology under

E. L. Mark (1847–1936). Davenport served as an instructor at Harvard until 1899, when he accepted an assistant professorship at the University of Chicago. There he remained until 1904, when he persuaded the Carnegie Institution of Washington to fund the Station for the Experimental Study of Evolution, with himself as director, at Cold Spring Harbor. Davenport remained director of the SEE, and of the Eugenics Record Office, from its founding in 1910 until his retirement in 1934. During this time he built both institutions into major research laboratories for the study of heredity and evolution—the SEE for the study of plants and nonhuman animals, the ERO for the study of human beings. A rigid and humorless man, Davenport was nonetheless well respected within the scientific community, both as a geneticist and as a statesman of science. He was a member of the National Academy of Sciences and the National Research Council, as well as secretary of the Sixth International Congress of Genetics (Ithaca, New York, 1932).[3]

Davenport's engineering background prepared him well to move from classical descriptive morphology into the quantitative and experimental study of heredity and evolution. Far more familiar with mathematics than most biologists of his era, he was among the first in the United States to appreciate the biometrical work of Galton and Pearson. Indeed, at Pearson's request he served as the American representative on the editorial board of the British biometrical journal *Biometrika*, of which Pearson was editor. Yet he was equally prepared to accept the experimental approach of the Mendelian theory. Beginning in the academic year 1892/93, Davenport taught a course entitled "Experimental Morphology" at Harvard (and later at Chicago), and he published a book by the same title in 1897 (revised, 1899). (Two of Davenport's students in that class were to become future leaders of both Mendelian genetics and eugenics: W. E. Castle, a long-time Harvard professor, and Herbert Spencer Jennings, for many years a protozoologist at Johns Hopkins.) Imbued with the rising tide of experimentalism that was so prominent in biology at the time, coupled with his own strong inclination to quantitative studies, Davenport was immediately receptive to the reports of Mendel's work by Carl Correns

[3] The standard biography of Davenport is Oscar Riddle, "Charles Benedict Davenport," *Biographical Memoirs of the National Academy of Sciences*, 1946, 25:75–110. This sketch contains a complete bibliography.

and Hugo De Vries in 1900.[4] In 1901 Davenport himself published one of the first papers on Mendelism in the United States.[5] He saw no dichotomy between Mendel's laws and biometrical thinking, though he realized early on that Mendel's notion of particulate, and therefore discontinuous, inheritance was not compatible with Galton's theories of continuous inheritance and regression.[6]

DURING HIS STAY at the University of Chicago two factors stimulated Davenport to seek funds for establishing an independent research laboratory. One was his own research, which focused at that time on large animals such as poultry and mice (as compared, for example, to insects) and thus required expanded facilities for care and breeding. For a while there was talk at Chicago of acquiring an experimental farm, but by 1902 Davenport was convinced that nothing would come of it and began looking for other alternatives. Coincidentally, the future of the summer school of the Brooklyn Institute of Arts and Sciences, held at a small summer marine laboratory at Cold Spring Harbor, was in doubt. Davenport, who had taught at the summer school since 1892, recognized Cold Spring Harbor as an ideal spot for the type of research station he envisaged. There would be room to expand animal care facilities, open space for experimental garden plots, facilities for housing a staff of caretakers and scientists, and plenty of marine organisms available for study. Never one to hesitate when an opportunity for funding, however remote, presented itself, in January 1902 Davenport approached the newly founded Carnegie Institution of Washington, established by the personal bequest of Andrew Carnegie.[7]

[4] Charles Rosenberg, "Charles Benedict Davenport and the Beginnings of Human Genetics," *Bulletin of the History of Medicine*, 1961, 35:266–276; see also A. H. Sturtevant, "The Early Mendelians," *Proceedings of the American Philosophical Society*, 1965, 109(4):199–204.

[5] C. B. Davenport, "Mendel's Law of Dichotomy in Hybrids," *Biological Bulletin*, 1901, 2:307–310.

[6] Pearson eventually asked Davenport to leave the editorial board of *Biometrika* because of a dispute between the two men over the interpretation of Wilhelm Johannsen's pure-line experiments. This was a rift in their personal and professional relationship that Davenport always regretted.

[7] Riddle, "Charles Davenport," pp. 80–81; see also C. B. Davenport, "Biological Experiment Station for Studying Evolution," *Yearbook of the Carnegie Institution of Washington*, 1902, 1:280.

Davenport sent his proposal to the Carnegie Institution's secretary, Charles Walcott, through an influential Chicago banker who agreed to act as an intermediary. The laboratory that Davenport proposed was to be for "the analyatic and experimental study of the causes of specific differentiation—of race change."[8] Convinced that the Darwinian theory of natural selection was hypothetical because it had not been demonstrated experimentally (that is, no new species had ever been produced by artificial selection, no matter how long or how rigorously selection was carried out), Davenport aimed to recast classical selection experiments in terms of the new Mendelian scheme. Intimately connected with this recasting was the problem of variation. On what types of variations (large, discontinuous or small, continuous) did selection act to produce new species? Did new variants breed true or, as Galton claimed, always regress toward the mean? Were Mendelian traits important to animal and plant adaptation, or were they, as some workers claimed, mostly trivial (such as the number of bristles on a fly's abdomen), in no way affecting an organism's fitness? Moreover, as Davenport was quick to recognize, such questions had an importance that extended beyond theoretical issues of evolution. A more thorough understanding of heredity, variation, and selection had enormous implications for agricultural breeding, an issue that was not lost on the Carnegie Institution's board, or on Andrew Carnegie himself. The board defined its purpose (in part) as sustaining "objects of broad scope that may lead to the discovery and utilization of new forces for the benefit of man." Indeed, just a few years later (1905) the Carnegie Institution was to make a substantial and ongoing commitment ($10,000 a year) to the work of Luther Burbank, specifically as an example of the application of scientific principles to practical problems.[9]

Davenport's initial proposal of 1902 was turned down by the Carnegie Institution of Washington, partly because the Board of Directors was engaged at that time in considerable debate over whether the CIW should fund research organizations or only individual researchers. By 1904, however, the board's Executive Committee had accommo-

[8] *Ibid.*
[9] Minutes of the Executive Committee, 3 Oct. 1902 and 12 Dec. 1905, Record Book, pp. 57 and 468–475. Carnegie Institution of Washington (CIW) Archives, Washington, D.C. I am indebted to Barry Mehler for gathering data and copies of material from these archives.

dated both views and determined to fund institutions as well as individuals provided that the researchers in the former worked cooperatively and in an organized manner. The CIW concluded that it could serve researchers best by helping them to *organize* their joint efforts: "In the field of research the function of the Institution is organization; to substitute organized for unorganized effort; to unite scattered individuals working independently, where it appears that such combination of effort will produce the best results; and to prevent needless duplication of work."[10] In this context, Davenport's second application was received more favorably, and on 12 December 1903 he was awarded a grant of $34,250, with fixed annual appropriations "to continue indefinitely, or for a long time." The "Station for the Experimental Study of Evolution" (SEE) was the name adopted for the facility at Cold Spring Harbor, and it was incorporated as the "Department of Experimental Biology of the Carnegie Institution of Washington," with the express purpose of studying "hereditary evolution, more particularly by experimental methods."[11] Edmund Beecher Wilson (1856–1939), a cytologist and chairman of the Zoology Department at Columbia University, was appointed as scientific adviser to Davenport in his work as director of the new research station.

No one could have agreed more than Davenport with the principles outlined by the Carnegie Executive Committee. He had always supported the notion of cooperation in research; more important, however, was his belief that for cooperation to occur an organizational base had to be developed. In his presidential address to the American Society of Naturalists given on 29 December 1907, Davenport emphasized that one of the features differentiating modern from ancient or medieval scientific work was its cooperative nature and thus its organization into societies, institutions, and multidisciplinary or international projects. However, he noted that there remained within the scientific community, especially among biologists, a strain of individualism that militated against cooperative programs and thus hampered research. Davenport reminded his fellow naturalists that the great natural history voyages of the nineteenth century, such as the *Challenger* expedition, were monuments to cooperative efforts; they would not have suc-

[10] Minutes of the Executive Committee. 3 Oct. 1902. Record Book, p. 56. CIW Archives.
[11] *Ibid.*

ceeded had individuals insisted on staking out their private research domains. Looking to the field of astronomy, he cited another example of cooperative effort whereby, beginning in 1887, eighteen observatories organized to produce a comprehensive photographic atlas of the heavens. Davenport urged that naturalists "should do well to adopt principles which have worked successfully in other fields of activity. In the modern commercial world one of the most important principles is cooperation."[12] The Station for the Experimental Study of Evolution was, in Davenport's mind, a perfect example of the spirit of cooperative research that could be fostered by successful organization.

THE SEE DEVELOPED into, and remained, a prestigious research institution. Today it is the Department of Genetics of the Carnegie Institution of Washington, with James D. Watson as its director. In the early decades of the century, highly qualified young investigators came to the station for varying periods to work on specific problems relating to heredity and evolution.[13] Davenport himself remained in complete administrative control. It was his kingdom. He administered it scrupulously, autocratically, and sometimes dictatorially, until his retirement in 1934 at the age of sixty-eight. The Carnegie Institution had invested not merely in a facility and a program for research but in one man and his vision of a new direction in biology.

Davenport's vision for the SEE was to bring together three areas of interrelated study: heredity, evolution, and cytology. Researchers were to employ experimental, quantitative, and, where feasible, mathematical methods. They would study heredity through carefully planned breeding experiments, the keeping of detailed, quantitative records of offspring of all crosses, and the analysis of the data by both biometrical and Mendelian means. They would examine evolution

---

[12] C. B. Davenport, "Cooperation in Research," *Science*, 8 Mar. 1907, 25(636):361–366.

[13] Among those who figured most prominently were George Harrison Shull (1904–1915), Roswell H. Johnson (1905–1908), A. F. Blakeslee (1915–1942), Ross A. Gortner (1909–1914), J. Arthur Harris (1907–1924), F. E. Lutz (1904–1909), and Oscar Riddle (1914–1945). In addition, a number of Associates—senior investigators who came to the SEE to give seminars, participate in research, and in general to keep the staff in touch with the latest developments—were appointed annually. Among the most prominent in this group were H. E. Crampton and E. B. Wilson of Columbia University, D. T. Mac-Dougal of the New York Botanical Garden, W. E. Castle and E. L. Mark of Harvard, and W. J. Moenkhaus of Indiana University.

through the quantitative study of variation in natural populations (following the methods of Galton and Pearson), as, for example, in Davenport's own work on populations of crabs in the waters around Cold Spring Harbor. They would also pursue selection experiments of the sort that Wilhelm Johannsen had initiated in Denmark (1899–1902) on pure lines of the bean *Phaseolus* and that W. E. Castle was to conduct some years later (1907–1914) on the piebald or "hooded" rat. The central issues of selection were, of course, the degree to which the results of selection can be maintained in a line after selection is relaxed and the possibility of creating new species by many generations of selection in a given direction. Researchers would bring in cytology as an adjunct to their studies, particularly heredity. The microscopic study of chromosomes as they relate to observed genetic differences was to become an important and novel part of Davenport's program: it was this aspect of his research that was picked up and developed so fully by the Morgan group at Columbia after 1910, using the common fruit fly *Drosophila*.

During the first years of the operation of the SEE, Davenport not only served as administrator but also carried out research on his own, studying heredity in poultry, mice, and horses. In this work he employed both biometrical and Mendelian analyses. At the same time he began to apply Mendelian analyses to human traits. With his wife, Gertrude Davenport, he wrote a paper on heredity and hair form in humans and several papers on the inheritance of skin color and other physical traits.[14] In 1910 he published the results of a lengthy study in which he explained for the first time the graded series of skin colors in black-white matings in terms of a polygenic inheritance—that is, several sets of genes interacting to produce what came to be called "quantitative inheritance."[15] At the same time he also applied the newly developed Mendelian concept of multiple alleles to the inheritance of human eye color.[16] Although not highly innovative, Davenport's work

[14] Gertrude C. Davenport and Charles B. Davenport, "Heredity of Hair Form in Man." *American Naturalist*, 1908, 42:341–349; C. B. Davenport, "Heredity of Some Human Physical Characteristics," *Proceedings of the Society for Experimental Biology and Medicine*, 1908, 5:101–102.
[15] C. B. Davenport, "Heredity of Skin Pigmentation in Man," *American Naturalist*, 1910, 44:642–672.
[16] Rosenberg, "Davenport" (cit. n. 4), p. 268.

was solid, and it earned him the respect of the rapidly growing community of Mendelian geneticists in the United States and abroad. By 1907 Davenport had already shown a strong interest in the inheritance of not only physical but also personality and mental traits in humans. Increasingly he believed that such traits were genetically determined and could be interpreted in Mendelian terms. Human heredity led naturally enough to questions of eugenics: What sorts of personality and social traits are inherited? What are their patterns of inheritance? And what are the best methods for maximizing the number of good traits and minimizing the number of bad traits within the population? Davenport was not unprepared to take an active interest in such questions. Through his earlier association with Galton and Pearson in England, he was already well aware of the eugenics ideal from both a scientific and a social point of view.

MORE DIRECTLY INFLUENTIAL in the development of Davenport's interest in eugenics was his involvement as a founding member of the American Breeders' Association (ABA). The brainchild of Assistant Secretary of Agriculture W. M. Hays in 1903, the ABA represented an attempt to form another of those cooperative networks—this time between academic biologists interested in heredity and practical breeders—about which both Davenport and the Carnegie Executive Committee waxed so euphoric. Hays envisioned for the Breeders' Association an "amicable union of practical breeders, who used records secured at the feeding trough, at the meat, butter, and wool scales, on the race track, and at the prize ring," with the more theoretical biologists who sought knowledge about heredity "by mathematical, mechanical, and other processes under which the facts concerning the relations of individuals and groups of individuals are compared."[17] Although the practical consequences of this union were not as directly realized as Hays and others had hoped, on one point both the breeders and their academic counterparts were in agreement: Mendel's laws of heredity provided the most important theoretical guide yet developed for the study of plant and animal heredity.

[17] W. M. Hays, "Address by the Chairman of Organizing Committee" *Report of the American Breeders' Association*, 1905, 1:9–15.

Among the most prominent of the ABA's forty-three appointed committees was the Eugenics Committee, formed in 1906 "to investigate and report on heredity in the human race" and "to emphasize the value of superior blood and the menace to society of inferior blood."[18] It was the first formal eugenics group in the United States. The chairman of the committee was David Starr Jordan (1851–1931), ichthyologist, evolutionist, and president of Stanford University. Other members of the committee included Alexander Graham Bell, Luther Burbank, Roswell H. Johnson, Vernon L. Kellogg, and William E. Castle. By 1908 Davenport, whose earliest involvements with the Breeders' Association were in the areas of agricultural breeding, poultry genetics, and heredity in racehorses, had shifted his attention mostly to eugenics.[19] For example, he was instrumental in expanding the scope of the Eugenics Committee's work and dividing it into ten subcommittees, each dealing with a specific issue (for example, deaf-mutism, criminality, hereditary insanity, feeblemindedness, epilepsy, and sterilization). Cleverly manipulating W. M. Hays's interest in making the ABA a broad-based coalition of practical breeders, genetics researchers, and agricultural businessmen, Davenport argued for increasing its popular support by including eugenics articles in its publication, the *Report of the American Breeders' Association*. After the reorganization into the American Eugenics Association in 1913, the *Report* became the *Journal of Heredity* and served as the major periodical in the United States for readable, popular papers on eugenics.

Davenport and Hays had more in common than their mutual interests in eugenics and the American Breeders' Association. Both were avid supporters of introducing methods of rational and scientific control into all areas of practical life, including the management of agriculture, research, and even the human germ plasm. In his address as chairman of the organizing committee of the ABA, Hays had argued that "the wonderful potencies in what we are wont to call heredity

---

[18] Barbara Kimmelman, "The American Breeders' Association: Genetics and Eugenics in an Agricultural Context, 1903–1913," *Social Studies in Science*, 1983, 13:163–204.

[19] See *ibid.*, pp. 183–189. The same point is made, with minor variations, by W. E. Castle in "The Beginnings of Mendelism in America," in *Genetics in the Twentieth Century*, ed. L. C. Dunn (New York: Macmillan, 1951), p. 66.

should be placed under the control and direction of man, as are the great physical forces of nature."[20]

Between 1902 and 1904, Davenport and Hays had carried on a lengthy correspondence regarding the prospect that the Carnegie Institution could be persuaded to fund a research laboratory for the study of heredity.[21] Hays, like Davenport, believed strongly in integrated, cooperative work organized for efficiency on a national scale. Hays's work, not only with the Breeders' Association and the U.S. Department of Agriculture but also in the country-life movement, was all aimed at integrating education, research, and agriculture on a national level.[22] Hays's address as chairman of the ABA organizing committee (delivered in 1903 and published in 1905) is strikingly similar to Davenport's speech on "cooperation and organization in research" (delivered in 1906 and published in 1907). The concepts of scientific management and control, of organization and development of research for the common good, permeated the writings and informed the activities of both men.

Although the American Breeders' Association served both to stimulate Davenport's interest in eugenics and to give him a forum for his own ideas on the subject, he soon realized that it would require another organization to develop eugenics on a national scale. The Eugenics Committee was a starting place, but it had neither significant funding nor, especially important in Davenport's eyes, an institutional base. Added to these problems was his growing rift with Hays over including the ABA's businessmen among its members and the society's lack of emphasis on research. Davenport therefore concluded that a separate organization, one devoted exclusively to eugenics investigation and education, would be desirable, and he naturally thought of

[20] W. M. Hays, "Address by the Chairman of the Organizing Committee" (cit. n. 17), pp. 9–10.

[21] See Kimmelman, "American Breeders' Association" (cit. n. 18), p. 184.

[22] For a discussion of the country-life movement, its history and values, see William L. Bowers, *The Country Life Movement in America, 1900–1920* (Port Washington, N.Y.: Kennikat Press, 1974). A more recent but more specialized discussion is David Danbom, "Rural Education Reform and the Country Life Movement, 1900–1920," *Agricultural History*, 1979, 53:462–474. Kimmelman discusses Hays's involvement in the country-life movement, showing just how integral it was to his vision of agriculture in general and the development of the ABA in particular.

locating any laboratory for the study of human heredity and eugenics in Cold Spring Harbor. As Davenport originally envisioned it, a eugenics institute would be administratively under his control but with the day-to-day supervision of research and operating details given over to a superintendent. Thus Davenport, while overseeing major organizational plans, still could devote most of his time to his research, which by 1910 had become almost wholly concerned with human genetics and eugenics. It was clear that he needed both additional facilities and personnel to get on with the growing work in human heredity, "its outlook so vast that . . . the Director . . . cannot cope with it alone."[23]

DAVENPORT'S FIRST STEP was to secure funding, without which nothing else could proceed. Ever the philanthropic entrepreneur, Davenport took advantage of two circumstances that led him directly to the doorstep of Mary Williamson Harriman. The first was the death of her husband, railroad magnate Edward Henry Harriman (b. 1848), in September 1909. Between 1880 and his death, Harriman had amassed a fortune, principally through his control of the Union Pacific, Southern Pacific, and Illinois Central railroads. Harriman's estate, estimated at approximately $70 million on his death, was left exclusively to his widow. Mrs. Harriman managed the estate for the next twenty-five years, turning over portions of it to her sons Averell and Roland as they reached majority and as her judgment allowed. In dealing with this fortune, Mary Harriman developed the principle of "efficient" giving—that is, philanthropy devoted to providing individuals with the opportunity to become more efficient members of society. Like her husband, she gave money to conservation groups (the Harrimans were both strong supporters of their friend John Muir), to hospitals, to the arts, and especially to charity organizations devoted to self-help for the poor. A cardinal principle in her philanthropy was to encourage cooperation and scientific planning in every aspect of society—from good government and urban landscaping to the care of the insane. She opposed the tendency toward individualism and competitiveness that she saw in early twentieth-century life, even though competitiveness had won her husband's fortune. From John Muir and C. Hart Merriam (director of the United States Biological Survey), she and

---

[23] Davenport's annual report, *Yearbook of the Carnegie Institution of Washington*, 1910, 9:85.

her husband gained an insight into the use of scientific principles to plan a more rational and orderly society—according to an order that existed so clearly in nature if human beings would only learn from it.[24]

Mary Harriman did not accept the foundation concept in philanthropy. She wanted to be in close touch with all the projects to which she gave money. She would not, in fact, give to any project with which she did not feel complete sympathy. Moreover, she particularly disliked the direction in which John D. Rockefeller, Jr., was taking the Rockefeller Foundation after 1910. Following an interview with Rockefeller on 9 March 1911, she wrote that for the first time she "saw the Rockefeller mask and heard their formulas." Indeed, she was later to complain when the Rockefeller Foundation engineered a takeover of the New York Bureau of Municipal Research Training School, which she had supported with the provision that the program would be altered according to guidelines set by the General Education Board. At a hearing of the U.S. Commission on Industrial Relations on the Rockefeller move, Mrs. Harriman stated: "Nothing has ever made me realize as does this what a grasp money has on this country."[25] Her style of philanthropy was of an older, more personalized sort, less national in scope than that of the rising foundations. Their aims were the same—social control—but the scale and the methods were quite different.

Within a few months after her husband's death, Mrs. Harriman received more than six thousand appeals for donations to many causes, the requests totaling over $247 million. One of those appeals came from Charles B. Davenport. For propriety's sake, Davenport held off initiating a move until February 1910, but then again, he had a special connection that gave him an edge over others. Davenport had taught Mrs. Harriman's daughter Mary in the summer of 1906 at the Biological Laboratory School of the Brooklyn Institute at Cold Spring Harbor,

[24] For more details than one could possibly care to know, the two-volume George Kennan biography, *E. H. Harriman* (Boston: Houghton-Mifflin, 1922), is adulatory but complete. A more manageable source is a short biography and appreciation of Mary Williamson Harriman: Persia Campbell, *Mary Williamson Harriman* (New York: Columbia University Press, 1960), with an introduction by Grayson Kirk. For the data summarized here, see *ibid.*, pp. 12–66, esp. 17–18.

[25] Entries from M. W. Harriman's diary, "following an interview . . . on 9 March, 1911": quoted in Campbell, *Mary Harriman*, pp. 24, 27.

and he found it very convenient to renew an old acquaintance.[26] His efforts were not misdirected: Mrs. Harriman was attracted to his project of studying hereditary social traits with a view toward solving social problems.

After several interviews and discussions, Davenport came away with an enthusiastic promise of support for what came to be known as the Eugenics Record Office, to be located at Cold Spring Harbor on a site next to the SEE. The site amounted to almost seventy-five acres and included a huge old mansion that had once been the country home of a wealthy New Yorker. Mrs. Harriman initially agreed to fund the complete operating expenses of the eugenics office for at least five years. This commitment included building a concrete, fireproof vault for storing eugenics records collected in the field and a main laboratory-office complex. The two building operations cost over $121,000. During the seven years that Mrs. Harriman was the major donor, she contributed an additional $246,000 in operating costs, including salaries, equipment, office furniture, and indexing facilities. Between 1910 and 1918, the so-called Harriman period in the history of the ERO, the total cost of all operations came to a little over $440,000.[27] During that time the relationship between Mrs. Harriman and Davenport, cordial from the beginning, developed into an almost daily ritual of communication. The correspondence between them, beginning in July 1910, records the extent to which Davenport presented his ideas, large and small, to her, explained his decisions, sought her advice, and submitted every major decision for her approval. As Davenport wrote on her death in 1932:

> For us at the Eugenics Office [*sic*] the things that counted most were her understanding of the needs of the work at a time when it was ridiculed by many and disesteemed by many oth-

---

[26] See Frances Hassencahl, "Harry H. Laughlin, 'Expert Eugenics Agent' for the House Committee on Immigration and Naturalization: (Ph.D. diss., Case Western Reserve Univ., 1969).

[27] See Harry H. Laughlin, "Notes on the History of the Eugenics Record Office, Cold Spring Harbor, Long Island, New York," mimeographed report compiled from official records of the ERO, Dec. 1939, pp. 5–6. Harry H. Laughlin Papers, Northeast Missouri State University (NMSU). Kirksville, Missouri.

ers. As she often said the fact that she was brought up among well bred race horses helped her to appreciate the importance of a project to study heredity and good breeding in man. Though she could turn a deaf ear to many appeals to the emotions, she had a lively sympathy for those things of whose lasting value she felt sure.[28]

In 1917 the Carnegie Institution of Washington agreed to take over responsibility for the annual operating expenses and future expansion of the ERO. At that time Mrs. Harriman transferred the ERO in its entirety to the CIW, with an additional endowment of $300,000, thus giving the ERO a financial independence that virtually none of the other departments of the Carnegie Institution enjoyed. The years from 1918 until the ERO was closed on 31 December 1939 are known as the Carnegie period. During that period the CIW spent approximately $25,000 per year in operating expenses. The Harriman period was one of expansion and growth; the Carnegie period, one of stabilization and eventual decline.

WITH FUNDS and space secured, Davenport turned to the search for a manager and planner for the ERO. The position of "superintendent," as it was called, required a person of scientific background, preferably someone who understood the principles and problems of heredity and had experience in practical breeding. It also required someone totally devoted to the eugenics cause, someone who could raise money among the wealthy, carry out educational programs, and promote a far-reaching vision of how eugenics could help to remake society. Many people have compared the advocates of eugenics to religious zealots, a comparison no doubt fostered by Francis Galton's references to the "religion of eugenics." In one sense Davenport was a preacher, and he was seeking someone of similar energy, devotion, and vision as his superintendent. This he found in the person of Harry Hamilton Laughlin (1880–1943), who was then teaching in the agriculture department of the State Normal School in Kirksville, Mis-

---

[28] Draft of a one-page eulogy, "Mrs. Harriman," in file, "Mrs. E. H. Harriman," Davenport Papers, American Philosophical Society (APS). Philadelphia.

souri.[29] Laughlin had first come to Davenport's attention in February 1907, when the young man had written to ask some questions about breeding chickens.[30] Noting Laughlin's interest in heredity, Davenport invited him to attend the Brooklyn Institute's summer course at Cold Spring Harbor in 1908. With their common interests in agricultural breeding and in heredity, Davenport and Laughlin hit it off well from the beginning. Both were highly energetic and serious about their work, utterly humorless and rigid in their approach to life, and totally dedicated to the cause of social reform through eugenics. For Laughlin, born in Oskaloosa, Iowa, the chance to study at an East Coast marine laboratory with a figure as well known as Davenport was the experience of a lifetime. Of that first summer, he wrote to Davenport: "I consider the six weeks spent under your instruction to be the most profitable six weeks that I ever spent."[31] Although not formally trained in biology or heredity, Laughlin was a quick learner, and his energy and enthusiasm for projects, usually on a grand scale, were boundless.

Although Laughlin wanted to return to Cold Spring Harbor for the summer course in 1908, his teaching duties made it impossible to be absent from Kirksville for another six-week period. Correspondence between Laughlin and Davenport continued regularly, however, during the next several years, concerned with topics such as filling out Mendelian information cards on students at Kirksville, winglessness in chickens, inheritance of redheadedness, and other genetic matters. Laughlin was particularly attentive in distributing all sorts of information cards on human traits to his students and in making sure the cards were completely and thoughtfully filled out.

Laughlin's thoroughness and energy impressed Davenport, and the possibility of a meeting suddenly arose when, in December 1908, Dav-

---

[29] Hassencahl's full-length study of the life and work of Harry Laughlin, which unfortunately has never been published, focuses particularly on Laughlin's lobbying activities. It contains a wealth of additional information on his other work, the ERO, and the Nazi *Rassenhygiene* movement. For a discussion of Laughlin's work as surveyed from his papers in Kirksville, see also Randy Bird and Garland Allen, "The J.H.B. Archive Report: The Papers of Harry Hamilton Laughlin," *Journal of the History of Biology*, Fall 1981, 14(2):339–353.

[30] Laughlin to Davenport, 25 Feb. 1907, Davenport Papers, APS.

[31] Laughlin to Davenport, 30 Mar. 1908, Davenport Papers, APS.

enport wrote to Laughlin that he would be journeying to Columbia, Missouri, the first week in January to attend the sixth annual meeting of the American Breeders' Association (6–8 January). Laughlin was ecstatic and immediately invited Davenport and his wife to visit Kirksville prior to the meeting.[32] Laughlin also hoped to attend the sessions himself, since he was now teaching "Nature Study and Agriculture," but he was not sure if the president of the Normal School would allow him to leave. The Davenports did visit the Laughlins in Kirksville, and Laughlin was able to attend the meeting in Columbia after all. Thus the two had the opportunity to discuss many facets of breeding. In Kirksville Davenport was induced to give two public lectures that aroused "great interest in the subject of heredity." For Laughlin, Davenport's visit was of special value because it gave a boost to his ongoing attempts to organize a scientifically based agriculture department. "It takes money to run a department like the one I want," he wrote. "In two or three years I will be able to show—I hope—an agricultural department worthy of the name."[33]

Little did Laughlin know that his plans would not materialize, but only because bigger things were in store for him. Davenport subsequently invited Laughlin to attend the 1910 summer course at Cold Spring Harbor, which included lectures and field trips related to eugenics. Then, in mid July, Davenport approached Laughlin about resigning from Kirksville and taking the job as superintendent. As Davenport wrote to Mrs. Harriman: "I was surprised to see how receptive he was of the idea. He said there would be no financial advantage but that, above all, he desired to go into this work. He made no conditions, even as to the length of appointment. I am more than ever satisfied that he is the man for us."[34] Laughlin accepted, returned with his wife Pansy to Missouri to straighten out their business affairs, and moved to the east in mid September 1910.

LAUGHLIN SET ABOUT organizing matters at Cold Spring Harbor as soon as he arrived. At first, because of a shortage of buildings on the new property, the ERO administrative quarters were located on

---

[32] Laughlin to Davenport, 15 Dec. 1908, Davenport Papers, APS.

[33] Laughlin to Davenport, 30 Jan. 1909, Davenport Papers, APS.

[34] Davenport to Mrs. Harriman, 1 Oct. 1910, Davenport Papers, APS.

the ground floor of the large home that had been the center of the former estate. The Laughlins lived on the part of the ground floor not occupied by the offices and on the second floor. Several record clerks, a groundskeeper, and two assistants lived on the third. A fireproof vault for eugenics records was added to the east side of the main house in 1911. The Eugenics Record Office opened its doors on 1 October 1910. Although Mrs. Harriman could not be present for the official opening, Davenport wrote her that it was "a red letter day."[35]

The Eugenics Record Office was organized with two general purposes: to carry out research on human heredity, especially the inheritance of social traits; and to educate laypersons about the importance of eugenic research and the implications of eugenic findings for public policy. The work of the ERO was to be strictly scientific, growing out of the experimental and biometrical studies of Davenport and the Station for the Experimental Study of Evolution.[36] To give the organization scientific credibility, Davenport set up a Board of Scientific Directors, consisting of, in addition to himself, Alexander Graham Bell, chairman; Lewellys F. Barker (professor of medicine, Johns Hopkins Medical School); William H. Welch, vice-chairman (dean, Johns Hopkins Medical School); Irving Fisher (professor of economics, Yale University); and E. E. Southard (a brilliant young psychiatrist at the Boston Psychopathic Hospital). Board members were required to attend meetings (they would be asked to resign if they missed more than two consecutively), which indicated that Davenport wanted the scientific advisers to be more than figureheads. Since minutes of meetings of the advisory board are not available, it is difficult to know how often these meetings were held or how seriously the advisers took their jobs. At any rate, Davenport did manage to assemble a prestigious group of advisers, including the dean of American medicine and medical reform (Welch) and one of the foremost inventors in the United States (Bell).[37]

---

[35] *Ibid.*

[36] Harry H. Laughlin, "The Eugenics Record Office at the End of Twenty-Seven Months Work," *Report of the Eugenics Record Office,* June 1913, No. 1, p. 1.

[37] Bell was interested in eugenics because of hereditary deafness in his own family and because he had always been fascinated with the breeding of sheep and other large domesticated animals.

In his first report, in 1913, Laughlin listed a number of the specific functions that the ERO was intended to perform. The following descriptions of these purposes give an indication of the scope of activities that Laughlin and Davenport envisaged.[38]

To serve eugenical interests as a repository and clearinghouse. First and foremost, the ERO was to become a data bank for information on human hereditary traits. This function was clearly one of research and was an extension of work already carried out through the Eugenics Committee of the ABA. The data would ultimately serve as the basis for analyzing the inheritance patterns of a wide variety of traits. As a clearinghouse and information repository, the ERO could also supply individuals with data about their family history if their families had participated in any of the studies. A newsletter, *Eugenical News*, contained short, nontechnical articles and items of information about eugenics research throughout the country.

To build up an analytical index of traits in American families. All data coming in to the ERO, from whatever source, were to be carefully indexed in accordance with a complex classification system known as *The Trait Book*, which Davenport had devised in 1910. *The Trait Book* listed all the human physical, physiological, and mental traits imaginable (and some that are hard to imagine)—rowdyism, moral imbecility, train-wrecking, and ability to play chess, to name but a few. It classified every trait by a numbering scheme akin to the Dewey Decimal System. The condition of harelip, for example, is classified as 623, where 6 indicates a condition of the nutritive system; 2, the mouth portion of the nutritive system; and 3, the specific mouth feature of harelip. Similarly, chess-playing ability is number 4598, where 4 signifies a mental trait; 5, general mental ability; 9, special game-playing ability; and 8, the specific game, chess. The ERO stored its information on such conditions in folders filed either by family name or by the case-worker who collected the information. This information was then indexed on 3 × 5 cards and cross-referenced in three ways: by family name, by number (for the trait), and by geographic locality. Thus an investigator could search out, for example, all the cases of harelip by going to the card drawer for the number 623, or all the references to a particular family by checking for its surname. Each card in the drawers

[38] Laughlin, "Eugenics Record Office" (cit. n. 36), pp. 2–21.

provided reference to the appropriate file folder or folders containing all the detailed information. By 1 January 1918, the ERO had accumulated 537,625 cards: there were nearly twice that many by the time the office closed in 1939. The information that was filed and catalogued at the ERO was organized into five main categories of traits: physical traits (e.g., stature, weight, eye and hair color, deformities), physiological traits (e.g., biochemical deficiencies, color blindness, diabetes), mental traits (e.g., intelligence, feeblemindedness, insanity, manic depression), personality traits (e.g., liveliness, morbundity, lack of foresight, rebelliousness, trustworthiness, irritability, missile throwing, popularity, radicalness, conservativeness, nomadism), and social traits (e.g., criminality, prostitution, inherited scholarship, alcoholism, patriotism, "traitorousness"). These groupings were not meant to be mutually exclusive since, for example, a personality trait could have more than one social manifestation. It was nonetheless the hope of Davenport, Laughlin, and others that, through such a detailed breakdown of traits into categories and subcategories, researchers could easily identify and follow the same traits through a wide variety of family lines.

To study the forces controlling and hereditary consequences of marriage-matings, differential fecundity, and survival migration. Today these studies, which include a considerable amount of sociological as well as biological information, would fall roughly under the heading of demography. From the start eugenicists were particularly concerned about the "differential fertility" issue—that is, about which groups in society were showing the higher and the lower birthrates.

To investigate the manner of inheritance of specific human traits. These studies were mainly straight-line applications of Mendelian principles to analyzing human genetic data. Thus eugenicists were interested in determining not only whether a trait was inherited but also whether it was dominant or recessive, whether it was sex-linked, the degree to which its expression might be influenced by environment, whether it was expressed early in life or was of late onset, and so forth. Investigations in this category involved constructing pedigree charts from raw data on families and deducing from the data what the pattern of heredity might be. (The obvious difficulties facing the eugenicist, especially in 1910–1920, in collecting enough reliable data to draw such conclusions are discussed in the original version of this paper.) In the analysis of inheritance patterns, ERO workers were advised and sometimes aided by members from the appropriate committee of the American Breeders' Association—for example, the Committee on Heredity of the Feebleminded, the Committee on the Heredity of Epilepsy, the Committee on Heredity of Deafmutism, the Committee on Heredity of Eye Defects, and the Committee on Heredity of Criminality.

To advise concerning the eugenical fitness of proposed marriages. Prospective marriage partners could visit or write to the ERO for what today might be called "genetic counseling." Drawing on as much of the individuals' family histories as possible, in conjunction with other data already in the files, ERO workers would discuss with the couple the probabilities of their children inheriting this or that trait and emphasize the importance of good mate selection in marriage. As Laughlin wrote:

> It is one of the cherished beliefs of the students of eugenics that when painstaking research has determined the manner of the inheritance of traits so that, upon examination of one's somatic traits and pedigree, something concerning his or her hereditary potentialities can be determined, social customs will make such hereditary potentialities marriage assets, valued along with—if not above—money, position and charming personal qualities. This belief is based not upon desire alone, but upon a few actual visits and letters from intelligent persons that come with increasing frequency to the Eugenics Record Office, asking for instructions for making a study of the eugenical fitness of a contemplated marriage.[39]

Laughlin noted that as of 22 January 1913 there were seventy-seven such requests on file at the ERO.

To train fieldworkers to gather data of eugenical import. The most reliable data on heredity could be collected, Laughlin noted, by fieldworkers who were trained to gather information in hospitals and asylums as well as in individual homes. Each summer the ERO ran a short training course for fieldworkers, including lectures by Laughlin, Davenport, and occasional guests on endocrinology, Mendelian heredity, Darwinian theory, elementary statistical methods, and eugenic leg-

[39] Laughlin, "Eugenics Record Office" (cit. n. 36), pp. 10–11.

islation. Students also became familiar with various mental tests (Binet, Yerkes-Bridges, army Alpha and Beta tests) and learned how to administer and interpret them. They memorized classifications of insanity, criminality, epilepsy, and skin and hair color and methods of anthropometrical measurement, with particular emphasis on cranial capacity. The course also involved field trips to nearby hospitals and institutions for mental defectives in New York—Kings Park Hospital for the Insane, Letchworth Village for the Feebleminded—and the receiving stations for immigrants at Ellis Island. To conclude the summer's training program each student produced a research project that involved collecting and analyzing eugenical data. The summer also had its lighter side, with clambakes, picnics, and boat trips. By 1917 the ERO had trained approximately 156 fieldworkers, 131 women and 25 men, among them 8 Ph.D.s and 7 M.D.s.

Those who completed the training program took up positions in various institutions. A few were retained as paid fieldworkers by the ERO. The majority were attached to state mental hospitals, insane asylums, or almshouses, with their salaries either paid wholly by those institutions or, more frequently, shared between the institution and the ERO. The fieldworkers' jobs involved taking family histories of patients within the institution to determine to what degree their conditions were hereditary. These linear studies, as they were called, would then be filed in large folders at the ERO, where they provided the basis for studies on the inheritance of mental deficiency, insanity, Huntington's chorea, and the like. Laughlin's records show that in the first three years (1910–1913) thirty-two fieldworkers amassed 7,639 pages of family case histories (text) and 800 pages of pedigree charts and averaged forty-six interviews per month.[40] The training program was carried out most extensively between 1910 and 1917; thereafter it tapered off somewhat but remained in operation until 1926. During the first seven years, funds for the training program came from the personal bequests of John D. Rockefeller, Jr., amounting to a total of $21,650.[41] From then on, for the duration of the program, funds came from the Carnegie Institution as part of the ERO's regular budget.

[40] *Ibid.*
[41] Harry H. Laughlin, "Notes on the History of the Eugenics Record Office," mimeographed report (Cold Spring Harbor, 1934), p. 5; original in the Laughlin Papers, NMSU.

To encourage new centers for eugenics research and education. Laughlin in particular conceived of the ERO as encouraging the formation of new groups and prompting existing organizations to take up eugenic studies within the context of their established programs. For example, he was quite active in getting the YMCA to take part in eugenical work (making available data on vital statistics of members as well as propagandizing eugenics ideals). He urged women's clubs to get involved and asked the director of the United States Census to include eugenics questions in the 1920 and subsequent censuses. He encouraged colleges to hold programs on eugenics, show eugenics films, teach eugenics courses, and take surveys of their student populations.

To publish the results of research and to aid in the dissemination of eugenic truths. A final specific function of the ERO was education. To Laughlin this included everything from showing films to publishing the results of research on human heredity, monographs on the status of relevant legislation, and analyses of public attitudes toward eugenic ideas. The ERO itself published a list of eugenics monographs, written by such investigators as Henry H. Goddard, Davenport, and Laughlin himself (a number of monographs came from his pen).[42]

BECAUSE EUGENICS claimed from the outset to be an objective and scientifically based program, to understand its general history and social impact it is important to see what type of research eugenicists pursued. While it is clearly beyond the scope of this study to examine these projects in depth, a few examples of work carried out at the ERO under the auspices of Davenport and Laughlin will show the style and flavor of eugenicists' scientific work. While the research interests and methods of analysis employed by Davenport and Laughlin are not necessarily representative of eugenics as a whole, they are nonetheless indicative of much of the work going on in the United States between 1910 and 1935.

The raw data from both individual family questionnaires and field-worker studies collected at the ERO during the years 1910–1939, as well as the index cards cross-referencing them, are now housed in the

---

[42] Laughlin, "Eugenics Record Office" (cit. n. 36), pp. 21–22.

basement of the Dight Institute of Human Genetics at the University of Minnesota in Minneapolis.[43] The vast bulk of the data (some ten filing cabinets) consists of individual questionnaires; the rest (some eight cabinets) consists of fieldworker studies of individual families. It is a testimony to the energy and dedication of the field and office workers that in the course of less than thirty years they accumulated, indexed, and cross-referenced such a monumental amount of material.

A quick perusal of the data collected by fieldworkers indicates that despite Davenport's and Laughlin's emphasis on rigorous, quantitative methodology, most of the data collected were of a subjective, impressionistic nature. One example will illustrate this point. The fieldworker Anna Wendt Finlayson carried out a study of the Dack family, descendants of two Irish immigrants in western Pennsylvania. She did no mental testing, and the data consist solely of "community reactions," a euphemism for "common gossip." The interviewer talked with family members, neighbors, and local physicians. The write-ups on two of the individuals, James Dack and William Dack, read as follows:

> *James Dack* (116) was commonly known as "Rotten Jimmy," the epithet was given because of the diseased condition of his legs, which were covered with chronic ulcers, although the term is said to have been equally applicable to his moral nature. He was a thief and general good-for-nothing, but neither shrewd nor cunning. His conversation quickly revealed his childlike mind.
>
> *William Dack* (12) was born in Ireland and came to the United States about 1815. He settled near a little town in the northern part of the soft coal district of Pennsylvania, which we will designate Bushville, and raised his children (9) in that vicinity. William died almost fifty years ago, but he is remembered by a few of the oldest settlers of the locality as a peculiar, silly old fellow who drank a good deal, stole sheep and household valuables from his neighbors, and did not seem to be very intelligent. He was mar-

---

[43] When Milislav Demerec, director of the SEE, wanted to clear out the old ERO building at Cold Spring Harbor in 1946, he put out a call to various organizations and individuals to see who would take the case studies, index cards, and back issues of *Eugenical News*. The only acceptance came from Sheldon Reed, director of the Dight Institute. I am grateful to Professor Reed for having preserved the material at that time and for his hospitality and guidance when I inspected the records in 1981.

ried twice, his first wife died in Ireland and we know nothing of her. She bore him one child. . . . William's second wife was (13) Mary Murphy. . . . An old resident of Bushville, now deceased, once stated to a woman who was interviewed by the writer that William and Mary were first cousins.[44]

Because there is no way to verify such information, it is of no value as objective data. Yet on the basis of that "evidence" the researchers drew up a pedigree chart indicating the presence of hereditary feeble-mindedness in the Dack family.

Slightly different problems are associated with the data processed from questionnaires sent out to families. In these cases the individual subjects recorded the data about themselves and their family members. These data are subject to the errors introduced when many different observers are involved in measuring the same quantity throughout a population. No two observers measure even the same item in the same way. The problem is obviously compounded when many different observers measure many different quantities. Even the data on height of individual family members (one item on the questionnaire) appear to be guesses, not actual measurements, for they often relate to relatives who are either geographically distant or deceased. In the collection of data known as the "Record of Family Traits," much of the information is secondhand, and none of it is quantitative. As Sheldon Reed, director emeritus of the Dight Institute in Minneapolis, has stated, most of the data collected by the ERO are worthless from a genetic point of view.[45]

Even if the raw data collected by ERO fieldworkers and others were considered reliable, their application in determining patterns of heredity was fraught with difficulties. The major method of analysis, of course, has always been the pedigree chart, but this involves two types of problems. First, many families have only a small number of children, statistically speaking, and thus the appearance, or especially the nonappearance, of a trait often says nothing about its actual mode of inheritance—for example, whether the trait is dominant, recessive,

---

[44] Anna Wendt Finlayson, "The Dack Family: A Study in Hereditary Lack of Emotional Control," *Bulletin of the Eugenics Record Office*, 1916, No. 15, pp. 6–7.
[45] Sheldon Reed, personal interview, 30 Oct. 1981, Minneapolis, Minn.

or sex-linked. Moreover, pedigree charts are often woefully incomplete—that is, many family members are not included, and thus what might look like a dominant trait (because it appears frequently) appears so only because data on other family members are missing. Second, and probably most critical, pedigree charts provide no way to separate genetically determined from environmentally determined phenotypes. The fact that musical ability, for example, appears repeatedly in the Hutchinson family pedigree says nothing about the actual inheritance of that trait in the genetic, as compared to the social, sense. The more a trait involves social, behavioral, or personality features, the less possible it is to separate genetic from environmental influences. Since eugenicists were far more interested in mental and personality traits than in clinical conditions, their pedigree charts were prone to such misinterpretation.

As an example of the simplistic generalizations in which eugenicists indulged, consider Davenport's study of the inheritance of *thalassophilia* ("love of the sea" or "sea-lust"). In 1919 Davenport published a book-length study, under the auspices of the Carnegie Institution of Washington, entitled *Naval Officers: Their Heredity and Development*. It was a study of why naval careers seemed to run in families. Davenport's explanation was genetic: in fact, he attributed this tendency to a single Mendelian gene! Here is how Davenport reasoned. Nomadism, the impulse to wander, was obviously hereditary because such racial groups as Comanches, Gypsies, and Huns were all nomadic. Searching individual family pedigrees, Davenport found recurrent examples of nomadism in the families of traveling salesmen, railroad workers, tramps, vagabonds, and boys who played hookey from school. Since the trait of nomadism showed up mostly in men, he concluded that it must be sex-linked and recessive, passing from mothers to half of their sons. Thalassophilia, a version of nomadism, is thus also genetically determined:

> Thus we see that thalassophilia acts like a recessive, so that, when the determiner for it (or the absence of a determiner for dislike) is in each germ-cell the resulting male child will have love of the sea. Sometimes a father who shows no liking for the sea . . . may carry a determiner for sea-lust recessive. It is theoretically probable that some mothers are heterozygous for love of the sea,

> so that when married to a thalassophilic man half of their children
> will show sea-lust and half will not.[46]

Davenport's method of argument was by analogy, not by direct evidence. Thus, he drew an analogy between thalassophilia and the inheritance of comb size in fowl: "It is possible . . . that the irresistible appeal of the sea is a trait that is a sort of secondary sex character in males in certain races, just as a rose comb is a male characteristic in some races of poultry."[47] By 1919 the inheritance pattern for rose comb was a well-established Mendelian trait. By making the comparison between human beings and poultry, Davenport assumed that superficial similarity in patterns of inheritance between two quite different species implied similarity in genetic causality. More important, he virtually discounted the effect of environmental factors in molding human behavioral traits.

Davenport's genetic determinism led to the obvious view that the source of a social problem was not environment but "bad genes." He urged philanthropists to donate their funds to eugenics, and not to charity, which would only perpetuate hereditary degeneracy. Accordingly, in a report to the Committee on Eugenics of the American Breeders' Association in 1909, Davenport insisted: "Vastly more effective than the million dollars to 'charity' would be ten million to eugenics. He who, by such a gift, should redeem mankind from vice, imbecility and suffering would be the world's wisest philanthropist."[48] In public and in private, Davenport belittled social reform. He apparently was fond of telling the parable of a man who found a bitter gourd and watered and tended it carefully to produce a delicious vegetable. That man was, Davenport claimed, like the trustee of a rehabilitation hospital for the insane. Poverty and lack of social or economic success were *de facto* the phenotypic expressions of genotypic inferiority. In 1912 he advised the National Conference of Charities and Corrections that social reform was futile since "the only way to secure innate

---

[46] C. B. Davenport, *Naval Officers: Their Heredity and Development* (Washington, D.C.: Carnegie Institution of Washington, 1919), p. 29.

[47] *Ibid.*, p. 28.

[48] C. B. Davenport, "Report of the Committee on Eugenics," *Rep. Amer. Breeders' Assoc.*, 1909, 6:94.

capacity is by breeding it."[49] To Davenport, the comparison between breeding humans and breeding strains of domesticated animals or plants was self-evident.

SINCE ONE of the expressed purposes of the ERO was education and the dissemination of "eugenical truths,"[50] it is not surprising to find that Laughlin (in particular) devoted considerable energy to publicity endeavors. One vehicle was the ERO's publication, *Eugenical News*, whose first volume was issued in 1916 with Davenport and Laughlin as editors. *Eugenical News* contained short, popular articles reporting on eugenics research, the menace of the feebleminded, differential fertility, the evils of race-crossing, and the like, as well as reviews of books on eugenics. The editorial board of the *News* remained substantially the same from 1916 through 1939, the only changes being the addition of Roswell H. Johnson for 1920–1929 and Morris Steggerda for 1932–1939. The tone of the *News* as a whole was overtly propagandistic, quite often with few facts and little or no presentation of data.

In addition to *Eugenical News*, the ERO helped to launch and guide through publication popular and semipopular works of other eugenicists who were not directly connected to the institute. Laughlin, for example, was a close personal friend of Madison Grant, a wealthy New York lawyer, conservationist, member of several public commissions, and author of one of the most racist, pro-Nordic tracts written during the period 1910–1920, *The Passing of the Great Race*. Laughlin met regularly with Grant in New York to discuss matters concerning the several eugenics organizations of which they both were members: the American Eugenics Society, the Eugenics Research Association, and later the Pioneer Fund. Grant regularly donated money to these organizations, as well as to specific ERO projects. Laughlin supported Grant in a variety of ways. When Grant was about to publish his second book, *Conquest of a Continent*, in 1932 (it was actually published in 1933),

---

[49] See Mark Haller, *Eugenics: Hereditarian Attitudes in American Thought* (New Brunswick, N.J.: Rutgers University Press, 1963), p. 65.

[50] See Laughlin, "Eugenics Record Office" (cit. n. 36), pp. 19–20, which lists among the ERO's purposes No. 9, "to encourage new centers of eugenics research and education" (p. 19), and No. 10, "to publish the results of researches and to aid in the dissemination of eugenical truths" (p. 20).

Laughlin went over the manuscript carefully and helped him to avoid some of the most blatant racial slurs.[51] Furthermore, Laughlin bid hard to encourage Yale to award Grant an honorary degree (Grant was a Yale alumnus, class of 1887). To Laughlin, presentation of an honorary degree by a prestigious university to one of the country's foremost eugenicists would provide a big shot in the arm for the movement in general and for the ERO, with which Grant was closely associated, in particular.

Through the ERO, Laughlin also organized a series of research and propaganda efforts, including a nationwide study of racial origins of inventiveness; a study of the hereditary lineage of aviators; a survey of the human resources of Connecticut, in which ancestry was studied in complete detail for the entire population of a small Connecticut town; a study of alien crime, organized in conjunction with Judge Harry Olson of the Municipal Court of the City of Chicago; and the distribution of defectives in state institutions by type of defect and by national and racial origins. He was also in close contact with Charles M. Goethe, a wealthy lumberman from Portland, Oregon, who gave considerable financial support to eugenics projects and was a great publicizer of eugenic ideals (Goethe also left his estate to the Dight Institute of Human Genetics in Minneapolis).[52] Laughlin supported and encouraged Goethe's plan to establish a "clinic on human heredity," a kind of eugenic counseling and birth control clinic that, despite all the effort, never materialized. The list could go on and on, but the point is this: using the ERO as an operational base, Laughlin developed and kept up a lively network of associations that served to gain financial and moral support for eugenics in general and the work of the ERO in particular. Furthermore, through his activities, Laughlin gave considerable organization and coordination to far-flung and conceptually diverse eugenics proj-

---

[51] See Madison Grant, *The Passing of the Great Race* (New York: Scribners, 1916); and Laughlin to Grant, 10 Nov. 1932, Laughlin Papers, NMSU. Laughlin told Grant he should strike from the manuscript the statement that "if the remainder of the Jews could be prevented from coming to the United States. . . ." As Laughlin remarked, "This has a tinge of 'Damn Jew' about it. It would, I believe, constitute a more forceful statement if it were pointed out that the United States has already one out of five of the world's Jews" (p. 2). Laughlin did not disagree with Grant in substance, only in form.

[52] Sheldon Reed, personal communication, 9 Nov. 1981.

ects in the United States and, somewhat later, throughout the Western Hemisphere.

Laughlin also helped to popularize eugenics through his ERO association. He loved exhibits. His correspondence is filled with plan after plan for exhibits at state fairs, genetics meetings, teachers' conferences, and the like. For example, in preparation for the Third International Congress of Eugenics at the American Museum of Natural History in New York in 1932, Laughlin sent out over one hundred letters asking for donations to mount a huge eugenics exhibit in one of the museum's largest halls. It was an ambitious exhibit, for which he finally raised sufficient funds. Laughlin used ERO secretarial and research help in preparing many of his projects, including exhibits. Without this sort of institutional support it would have been difficult, if not impossible, to carry out so many projects and integrate the activities of so many people.

Laughlin also used his institutional base at the ERO as a platform for political activity on behalf of eugenics. The two most notable examples are his research and testimony before the House Committee on Immigration and Naturalization and his effective lobbying for the passage of eugenical sterilization laws in various states. In 1924 the Johnson Act (also called the "Immigration Restriction Act") passed both houses of Congress, and by 1935 some thirty states had passed sterilization laws. Neither of these results can be attributed to Laughlin alone, but he was instrumental in both—perhaps more directly visible in his House testimonies than elsewhere. Laughlin brought forth reams of biological data to prove the genetic inferiority of southern European, central European, and Jewish people. His congressional testimony received wide press coverage, and a transcript was reprinted as part of the *Congressional Record*.

Laughlin's invitation to become the congressional "expert witness" came from Representative Albert Johnson, a rabidly anti-immigrant, antiradical, and anti-Communist journalist and editor from Washington State who had entered Congress in 1912 on a restrictionist platform. Laughlin, long interested in the immigration issue, had made the initial contact with Johnson and, along with Madison Grant, had established a close personal and professional relationship with him. One consequence was that in 1924 Johnson, who was not then even a member, was elected to the presidency of the Eugenics Research

Association.[53] As "eugenics expert," Laughlin received congressional franking privileges, and he used them to assemble vast amounts of data about the institutionalized alien and native stock. The Carnegie Institution of Washington in turn officially allowed Laughlin to use his secretarial staff at the ERO to help compile data and figures for the congressional testimony. Later the CIW would regret encouraging Laughlin in this overtly political role, but in the early and mid 1920s the directors had no objection.

The story of Laughlin's work as eugenics expert to the House Committee on Immigration and of his arguments in his major congressional hearings has been told in detail elsewhere.[54] What is striking in these testimonies is the strong racist and antiethnic feeling to which Laughlin, bolstered by charts and graphs, gave vent. Laughlin was already voicing distinctly anti-immigrant sentiment immediately after World War I; like Madison Grant, he now called for a "purification" of the good Nordic stock of the United States to free it from contamination by the "degenerate" sectors of Europe (according to Laughlin, eastern and southern Europe). Laughlin was particularly anti-Semitic, arguing that with respect to immigration "high-grade Jews are welcome, and low-grade Jews must be excluded." "Racially," he argued, "the country will be liberal if it confines all future immigration to the white race, then, within the white race, if it sets up differential numerical quotas which will admit immigrants in accordance not with external demand but on the basis of American-desired influence of such racial elements on the future seed-stock of America."[55] Laughlin further distinguished himself by devoting considerable research energy to showing that

[53] See Hassencahl, "Harry H. Laughlin" (cit. n. 26), pp. 206–208. Grant gave moral support to the committee but so far as we know did not appear before it in person: see *ibid.*, pp. 283, 293–300; and Kenneth Ludmerer, *Genetics and American Society: A Historical Appraisal* (Baltimore: Johns Hopkins Press, 1972), pp. 112–113.
[54] Ludmerer, *Genetics and American Society*, pp. 87–119; Hassencahl, "Harry H. Laughlin," pp. 161–312; and Garland E. Allen, "The Role of Experts in the Origin and Closure of Scientific Controversies: The Case of the American Eugenics Movement, 1910–1940," in *Scientific Controversies: Studies in the Resolution and Closure of Disputes Concerning Science and Technology*, ed. A. L. Caplan and H. T. Engelhard (New York: Cambridge University Press, 1987).
[55] Harry H. Laughlin, *Report of the Special Commission on Immigration and the Alien Insane* (submitted as a study of immigration control to the Chamber of Commerce of the State of New York, 16 Apr. 1934), pp. 17, 18.

recent immigrants and "aliens" were responsible for much of the crime committed in the United States between 1890 and 1920.[56]

In discussing the immigration issue, Laughlin was particularly disturbed by the specter of "race-crossing." He reported that a committee from the Eugenics Research Association had studied the matter and had failed to find a single case in history of two races living side by side and maintaining racial purity. Race mixtures, Laughlin said, are poor mixtures, referring for corroboration to a study on race-crossing in Jamaica in which Davenport was then engaged. Like W. E. Castle, Edward M. East, and other geneticists at the time who had agricultural interests, Laughlin compared human racial crossing with mongrelization in the animal world. The progeny of a cross between a racehorse and a draft horse, Castle once wrote, "will be useless as race horses and they will not make good draft horses. . . . For similar reasons, wide racial crosses among men seem on the whole undesirable."[57] Like Grant, Laughlin felt that immigrants from southern and eastern Europe, especially Jews, were racially so different from, and genetically so inferior to, the current American population that any racial mixture would be deleterious. Even after the phenomenon of "hybrid vigor" was known to be widespread, eugenicists conveniently explained it away by arguing that only a few of the offspring of any hybridization would really show increased vigor. The rest would be decidedly inferior.[58] Using statistics and data buttressed by analogies from agricultural breeding, Laughlin managed to provide a "scientific"

[56] See National Commission on Law Observance and Enforcement, *Report on Crime and the Foreign Born* (Washington, D.C.: U.S. Government Printing Office, 1931).

[57] C. B. Davenport, "Race Crossing in Jamaica," *Scientific Monthly*, 1982, 27:225–238. This was a summary of Davenport's lengthier study, carried out with Morris Steggerda, *Race Crossing in Jamaica* (Washington, D.C.: Carnegie Institution of Washington, 1929); and W. E. Castle, *Genetics and Eugenics* (Cambridge, Mass.: Harvard University Press, 1916), p. 233.

[58] See E. M. East and Donald F. Jones, *Inbreeding and Outbreeding* (Philadelphia: Lippincott, 1919). It is ironic that one of the coformulators of the notion of hybrid vigor, E. M. East, was also one of the eugenicists who tried to argue away the analogy to human racial crossing. In the final chapter of his book with Jones, East claims that because some human races are decidedly inferior to others, hybridization between races is not of general value unless the two races are equivalent in genetic endowment. East's argument is somewhat more complex because he admits that some hybridization can on occasion be a stimulus to further variability and thus to favorable new combinations of traits (see pp. 244 ff.).

rationalization in Congress for passage of a highly selective immigration restriction law. The effect of Laughlin's testimony, both on committee members and on the public (through newspaper accounts), was enormous.[59] The groups who were most restricted (Jews, Mediterraneans—particularly Italians—and people from Central Europe) were also the ones Laughlin claimed were the most biologically inferior.

With the immigration debates, the "old-style" eugenics movement hit its zenith. When the Johnson Act was passed in early 1924, Laughlin, Grant, and other eugenicists were euphoric.[60] Laughlin made good use of his position as superintendent of the ERO—not only in terms of the actual services his staff was able to render in preparing for the immigration testimony but also in terms of the prestige afforded by his title and by his association with the Carnegie Institution of Washington. Laughlin immediately aspired to even greater triumphs—advocating a Pan-American eugenics society, trying to convince the U.S. Census Bureau to use the 1930 Census to obtain eugenical data, drawing up model sterilization laws for all the forty-eight states, and presenting a plan to have American consulates in foreign countries perform eugenical tests on prospective immigrants before they left their native countries. None of these plans bore fruit. The eugenics movement began to take a new turn, losing some of the groundswell of support it had previously enjoyed from biologists, the wealthy elite, and the general public.

---

[59] Hassencahl, "Harry H. Laughlin" (cit. n. 26), pp. 282–283.
[60] Ludmerer, *Genetics and American Society* (cit. n. 53), p. 106.

THE PIONEERS OF IQ TESTING

Leon J. Kamin

> Terman was unapologetic about where he thought
> IQ comes from. He believed in the inheritance of
> IQ, at least to a considerable degree.
> —*Professor Richard Herrnstein, 1971*[1]

T HE FIRST USABLE INTELLIGENCE TEST was
developed in France by Alfred Binet in 1905. The basic facts are
known to everybody who has taken a college course in psychology, and
are available in any textbook. The French Minister of Public Instruction had commissioned Binet to develop a testing procedure that could
help to identify students whose academic aptitudes were so low as to
necessitate their placement in "special schools."

The test developed by Binet was very largely atheoretical. He
viewed it as a practical diagnostic instrument and was not concerned to
"make a distinction between acquired and congenital feeblemindedness."[2] Binet in fact prescribed therapeutic courses in "mental ortho-
pedics" for those with low test scores. His chapter on "The Training of
Intelligence" began with the phrase "After the illness, the remedy,"

Leon J. Kamin is professor of psychology at Northeastern University. He is author of *The Science and Politics of IQ*, from which this article is excerpted, and with R. C. Lewontin and Steven Rose of *Not in Our Genes*.

476

and his judgment on "some recent philosophers" who had given their "moral support" to the idea that "the intelligence of an individual is a fixed quantity, a quantity which one cannot augment" is clear: "We must protest and react against this brutal pessimism."[3]

With this orientation, it is perhaps as well that Binet died in 1911, before witnessing the uses to which his test was speedily put in the United States. The major translators and importers of the Binet test were Lewis Terman at Stanford, Henry Goddard at the Vineland Training School in New Jersey, and Robert Yerkes at Harvard. These pioneers of the American mental testing movement held in common some basic sociopolitical views. Their "brutal pessimism" took a very specific political form, manifested by their enthusiastic memberships in various eugenic societies and organizations. They arrived at the remarkable conclusion that the questions asked of children by the Binet test provided a fixed measure of "innate intelligence." The test could thus be used to detect the genetically inferior, whose reproduction was a menace to the future of the state. The communality of their views—and their divergence from Binet's—can best be illustrated by quotations from their early writings.

The Americanized "Stanford-Binet" test was published by Terman in a 1916 book.[4] The promise of the test was made explicit in the opening chapter:

> . . . in the near future intelligence tests will bring tens of thousands of these high-grade defectives under the surveillance and protection of society. This will ultimately result in curtailing the reproduction of feeble-mindedness and in the elimination of an enormous amount of crime, pauperism, and industrial inefficiency. It is hardly necessary to emphasize that the high-grade cases, of the type now so frequently overlooked, are precisely the ones whose guardianship it is most important for the State to assume.

Terman asserted that "there is no investigator who denies the fearful role played by mental deficiency in the production of vice, crime, and delinquency." The cause of mental deficiency—and by implication of crime—was transparently clear. "Heredity studies of 'degenerate' families have confirmed, in a striking way, the testimony secured by intelligence tests."

The test, in Terman's view, was particularly useful in the diagnosis of "high-grade" or "border-line" deficiency; that is, IQs in the 70–80 range. That level of intelligence

> is very, very common among Spanish-Indian and Mexican fami-
> lies of the Southwest and also among negroes. Their dullness
> seems to be racial, or at least inherent in the family stocks from
> which they come . . . the whole question of racial differences in
> mental traits will have to be taken up anew and by experimental
> methods. The writer predicts that when this is done there will be
> discovered enormously significant racial differences in general
> intelligence, differences which cannot be wiped out by any
> scheme of mental culture.
>
> Children of this group should be segregated in special classes.
> . . . They cannot master abstractions, but they can often be made
> efficient workers. . . . There is no possibility at present of con-
> vincing society that they should not be allowed to reproduce,
> although from a eugenic point of view they constitute a grave
> problem because of their unusually prolific breeding.[5]

The theme will reappear, so it is of interest to note that Terman did not draw a simple distinction between the white and the "col-ored" races. The "dull normals," with IQs between 80 and 90, were said to be "below the actual average of intelligence among races of western European descent. . . ." The "New Immigration" from southeastern Europe was already, by the time Terman wrote, a matter of considerable national concern. The distinction between the "races" of western and southeastern Europe was made forcefully by Madison Grant's influential *The Passing of the Great Race*,[6] and Ter-man's attribution of a high intelligence level to "races of western European descent" was clearly made in the light of concern over immigration policy.

Professor Terman's stern eugenical judgment fell, in any event, even-handedly on the very poor of all colors. Writing in 1917 under the heading "The Menace of Feeble-Mindedness," he observed that

> only recently have we begun to recognize how serious a menace
> it is to the social, economic and moral welfare of the state. . . . It

is responsible ... for the majority of cases of chronic and semi-chronic pauperism. . . .

... the feeble-minded continue to multiply ... organized charities ... often contribute to the survival of individuals who would otherwise not be able to live and reproduce. . . .

If we would preserve our state for a class of people worthy to possess it, we must prevent, as far as possible, the propagation of mental degenerates ... curtailing the increasing spawn of degeneracy.[7]

The violence of Terman's language stands in melancholy affirmation of Binet's earlier reproof to teachers of the "feeble-minded." "The familiar proverb which says: 'When one is stupid, it's for a long time' seems to be taken literally, without criticism, by some schoolmasters; those who disinterest themselves in students who lack intelligence; they have for them neither sympathy nor even respect, as their intemperance of language makes them say before these children such things as: 'This is a child who will never accomplish anything ... he is poorly gifted. . . .' Never! What a large word!"[8]

The views of Henry Goddard, who began to use the Binet test in 1908, did not differ in any important particular from those of Terman. The test data, to his mind, could be used to provide statistical support for the already demonstrated proposition that normal intelligence and "weak-mindedness" were the products of Mendelian inheritance. Perhaps the foremost of the "heredity studies of 'degenerate' families" cited by Terman was Goddard's lurid tracing of the family lines descended from one Martin Kallikak. With respect to the social menace of hereditary feeble-mindedness, Goddard had in 1912 predated Terman: ". . . we have discovered that pauperism and crime are increasing at an enormous rate, and we are led to pause and ask, 'Why?' Even a superficial investigation shows us that a large percentage of these troubles come from the feeble-minded."[9] The "troubles" had evidently caught the attention of alert social scientists who labored long before Professors Banfield[10] or Herrnstein.[11]

The sociopolitical views of the early mental testers are perhaps nowhere more clearly revealed than in Goddard's invited lectures at Princeton University in 1919. There Goddard discoursed on the new science of "mental levels." That new science made possible the accurate assessment of the mental levels both of children and of adults, and those levels had been fixed by heredity. The new science had generated data of profound social significance, and in particular, it invalidated the arguments of gentlemen socialists.

These men in their ultra altruistic and humane attitude, their desire to be fair to the workman, maintain that the great inequalities in social life are wrong and unjust. For example, here is a man who says, "I am wearing $12.00 shoes, there is a laborer who is wearing $3.00 shoes; why should I spend $12.00 while he can only afford $3.00? I live in a home that is artistically decorated, carpets, high-priced furniture, expensive pictures and other luxuries; there is a laborer that lives in a hovel with no carpets, no pictures, and the coarsest kind of furniture. It is not right, it is unjust." ... As we have said, the argument is fallacious. It assumes that that laborer is on the same mental level with the man who is defending him. ...

Now the fact is, *that workman* may have a ten year intelligence while you have a twenty. To demand for him such a home as you enjoy is as absurd as it would be to insist that every laborer should receive a graduate fellowship. How can there be such a thing as social equality with this wide range of mental capacity? The different levels of intelligence have different interests and require different treatment to make them happy. ...

As for an equal distribution of the wealth of the world that is equally absurd. The man of intelligence has spent his money wisely, has saved until he has enough to provide for his needs in case of sickness, while the man of low intelligence, no matter how much money he would have earned, would have spent much of it foolishly and would never have anything ahead. It is said that during the past year, the coal miners in certain parts of the country have earned more money than the operators and yet today when the mines shut down for a time, those people are the first to suffer. They did not save anything, although their whole life has taught them that mining is an irregular thing and that when they were having plenty of work they should save against the days when they do not have work. ...

These facts are appreciated. But it is not so fully appreciated that the cause is to be found in the fixed character of mental levels. In our ignorance we have said let us give these people one more chance—always one more chance.[12]

The progress from Binet's position is staggering. The feeble-minded, the paupers, and the unemployed coal miners now seem scarcely distinguishable. This is something more than the "brutal pessimism" protested by Binet. Whatever else we call it, this was a perversion of psychological "science." There are few more vivid examples of the subordination of science to political and economic ideology.

The point of view of the third major importer of Binet's test, Robert Yerkes, is sufficiently indicated by his 1917 appointment as chairman of the Committee on Inheritance of Mental Traits of the Eugenics Research Association. The relation of IQ to heredity and to economic factors is made clear in Yerkes' prescription for how "To make a true diagnosis of feeble-mindedness . . . never should such a diagnosis be made on the IQ alone. . . . We must inquire further into the subject's economic history. What is his occupation; his pay . . . we must learn what we can about his immediate family. What is the economic status or occupation of the parents? . . . When all this information has been collected . . . the psychologist may be of great value in getting the subject into the most suitable place in society. . . ."[13]

To be diagnosed as feeble-minded during this period, and to be assigned to a "suitable place," was not an enviable lot. There were few fine discriminations drawn, as we have seen, among the criminal, the poor, and the dull-witted. The public institutions to provide for such degenerates were in many states administered by a single official, the "Commissioner of Charities and Corrections." We catch some glimpses of the great value of mental testers to such institutions in the annual reports of Commissioner Wight to the Governor of the State of New Jersey. The commissioner's 1909 report, in discussing "the idiotic," indicated that "They are now in the families, or distributed among the almshouses, and county and State institutions. I find a number of families where there are two or more such imbeciles, suggesting increased necessity for a careful inquiry into causes."[14]

That careful inquiry was not long in forthcoming. Commissioner Wight's 1910 report contained for the first time a section headed "Research Work."

This is the name we give to the inquiry into heredity, habit, environment, etc., of criminals and defectives, to locate more definitely the primary cause of crime and dependency. The initiative of this important movement was taken by Prof. E. R. Johnstone and Dr. H. A. Goddard of the Training School for Feeble Minded Children ... The recent meeting of the Eugenic Section at Skillman ... was well attended by experts ... who seemed greatly interested in the results of our research work ... the investigations show that the union of drunken fathers, and feeble minded or epileptic mothers is rapidly increasing the number of imbeciles whom the State is expected to support. ...

I respectfully ask that a small appropriation be made to prosecute this research work, and send the facts out to the public.[15]

By 1911, having received his appropriation, Commissioner Wight was able to report the results of the research:

... enough has already been accomplished to demonstrate the fact of the transmission of criminal tendencies and mental and physical defect. ... How to remedy this is another matter. It may be done in part by a more rigid enforcement of the marriage laws, by a better control of the sale of liquor, cigarettes, and dopes known as soothing syrups. If the sterilization law of last winter shall be enforced it will also do much to prevent the evil.

... Blanks have been prepared to record such information concerning persons in custodial care as is deemed important in tracing the causes of crime and defectiveness, as they appear connected with heredity and environment. Under the indeterminate sentence act, the Court of Pardons is to determine the time of penal service between the minimum and maximum sentence, and it will be an important factor in settling the question of the fitness of the prisoner for parole if the Court should have his personal record and his family history before it.[16]

This was the social climate into which Terman, Goddard, and Yerkes introduced the intelligence test. The judgments of psychologists were to have social consequences even graver than the prohibition of soothing syrups. The measurement of the fixed mental level was to have a role in determining who was set free and who was jailed; and it was to aid in determining who was sufficiently fit to be allowed to reproduce. There is no record to the effect that the pioneers of American mental testing experienced the awe reported by the physicists who first split the atom.

The early history of testing in America fixed upon the Binet test an apparently indelible genetic interpretation. The hereditarian interpretation shared by Terman, Goddard, and Yerkes did not arise as a consequence of the collection of IQ data. Their involvement in the eugenics movement predated the collection of such data. There was, at the time they wrote, no quantitative genetics; there was in fact no tenable theory of how mental traits might be inherited. The notion that dependency, defectiveness, weak-mindedness, and other social ills were attributable to the genes was, in America, an idea whose time had come. We can trace the force of that idea—and its utter divorce from any meaningful scientific data—in the successful efforts of the eugenicists to enact sterilization laws. The rise of the mental testing movement coincided precisely in time with the passage of such laws by a large number of states. These sterilization laws, many of which—but not all—were never enforced, had two features in common. First, they were to be applied exclusively to inmates of publicly supported corrective or "charitable" institutions. Second, they asserted as a matter of fact that various forms of "degeneracy" were hereditarily transmitted.

The first reference which I have found to such a law was provided by Dr. Everett Flood in his 1898 article in the *American Journal of Psychology*, "Notes on the Castration of Idiot Children."[17] Dr. Flood indicated that "A castration bill was introduced into the Michigan Legislature providing for the castration of all inmates of the Michigan Home for the Feeble-Minded and Epileptic . . . also for that of all persons convicted for a felony for the third time." The Michigan bill seems not to have been passed, but it was in any event irrelevant to Dr. Flood's report on the therapeutic castration of 26 Massachusetts male children. Of these, "24 were operated on because of persistent epilepsy and masturbation, one for epilepsy with imbecility, and one for masturbation with weakness of mind."

The first bill actually passed by a legislature was in Pennsylvania. The year, ironically, was 1905, the year in which Binet first published his test. The bill was described as an "Act for the Prevention of Idiocy," but it was vetoed by Governor Pennypacker. Binet would have applauded with his whole heart the governor's veto message.

> These feeble-minded and imbecile children have been entrusted to the institutions by their parents or guardians for the purpose of training and instruction. It is proposed to experiment upon them; not for their instruction, but in order to help society in the future ... without their consent, which they cannot give. ... Laws have in contemplation the training and the instruction of the children. This bill assumes that they cannot be so instructed and trained. ... This mental condition is due to causes many of which are entirely beyond our knowledge. ...[18]

The first fully enacted law was passed by Indiana in 1907. The law's preamble, with slight modification, appeared repeatedly in sterilization laws subsequently passed by other states. The preamble stated very simply, "Whereas, heredity plays a most important part in the transmission of crime, idiocy, and imbecility."[19] This legislative fiat occurred before Terman and Goddard sketched out in detail the interrelations among crime, feeble-mindedness, and dependency. They were in large measure following the lead provided by the would-be behavior geneticists of the state legislatures.

The advancement of human behavior genetics seemed now to lie in the hands of politicians, and few could resist the temptation to contribute to science. To Indiana's list of traits in which "heredity plays a most important part" New Jersey added in 1911 "feeble-mindedness, epilepsy, criminal tendencies, and other defects."[20] The Iowa legislature in the same year provided for the "unsexing of criminals, idiots, etc." The "unsexing" provision, however, went beyond any valid eugenic need, and a scientifically sounder measure was adopted by Iowa in 1913. The new bill spelled out the "etc." of the 1911 law. The new measure provided for "The prevention of the procreation of criminals, rapists, idiots, feeble-minded, imbeciles, lunatics, drunkards, drug fiends, epileptics, syphilitics, moral and sexual perverts, and diseased and degenerate persons."[21]

Presumably the Supreme Court of the State of Washington had in mind the work of the pioneer mental testers when it upheld the Washington sterilization law on September 3, 1912. The court pointed out that "modern scientific investigation shows that idiocy, insanity, imbecility, and criminality are congenital and hereditary. . . . There appears to be a wonderful unanimity of favoring the prevention of their future propagation."[22]

The Attorney General of California, in upholding the California statute in 1910, succeeded in relating the views of the testers to a viable physiological theory. He wrote that

> Degeneracy is a term applied when the nervous or mental construction of the individual is in a state of unstable equilibrium. Degeneracy means that certain areas of brain cells or nerve centers of the individual are more highly or imperfectly developed than the other brain cells, and this causes an unstable state of the nerve system, which may manifest itself in insanity, criminality, idiocy, sexual perversion, or inebriety.* Most of the insane, epileptic, imbecile, idiotic, sexual perverts, many of the confirmed inebriates, prostitutes, tramps, and criminals, as well as habitual paupers, found in our county poor-asylums, also many of the children in our orphan homes, belong to the class known as degenerates. . . .[23]

Within seven years, Terman, at Stanford, was to write: "If we would preserve our state for a class of people worthy to possess it, we must prevent, as far as possible, the propagation of mental degenerates." The meek might inherit the kingdom of Heaven, but, if the views of the mental testers predominated, the orphans and tramps and paupers were to inherit no part of California. The California law of 1918 provided that compulsory sterilizations must be approved by a board including "a clinical psychologist holding the degree of Ph.D."[24] This was eloquent testimony to Professor Terman's influence in his home state.

The *Harvard Law Review* in December, 1912, grappled conscientiously with the implications of the findings of modern science. Discussing the constitutionality of sterilization laws, the *Review* observed that "Asexualization can only be justified in the case of born criminals

---

* This affliction has now been renamed. The term used by modern school systems is "minimal brain damage."

. . . born criminals who cannot be proved to be such must be granted immunity. However, there are probably some criminals whose degenerate character can be ascertained, and if a statute can be so drawn as to limit its operation to such as these it should be constitutional. . . . Larceny is common among born criminals. . . ."[25]

The scientific documentation offered by the mental testers that degeneracy and feeble-mindedness were heritable did not occur in a vacuum. Their views were responsive to social problems of the gravest moment. Their "findings" were politically partisan, and they had consequences. We can see clearly with hindsight how ludicrously beyond the bounds of science those views and "findings" extended. They fixed upon the succeeding generations of psychometricians, equipped with more sophisticated scientific tools, a clear predisposition toward a genetic interpretation of IQ data. That predisposition is still with us.

Though sterilization measures were fitfully enforced against the poor—most notably in California—they had no major impact on American society. There are, however, contemporary stirrings by advocates of sterilization. Thus, for example, a South Carolina obstetrician announced in 1973 that he would not take care of welfare mothers with three or more children unless they agreed to be sterilized. The rationale for this policy was not explicitly eugenic; instead, the physician expressed concern for the welfare burden assumed by taxpayers. The advocacy of sterilization as a policy measure does not necessarily imply a belief in the genetic determination of "undesirable" traits. This was made elegantly explicit by Reed and Reed in their massive 1965 study of mental retardation.[26] They concluded: "Few people have emphasized that where the transmission of a trait is frequently from parent to offspring, sterilization will be effective and it is irrelevant whether the basis for the trait is genetic or environmental." The belief in the heritability of IQ may thus merely have provided a convenient and "scientific" rationale for policies and laws which would have been enacted on other grounds.

The sterilization laws may have been largely dead letters, but in another sphere the mental testing movement was deeply involved in a major practical accomplishment. The findings of the new science were used to rationalize the passage of an overtly racist immigration law. The mental testers pressed upon the Congress scientific IQ data to demonstrate that the "New Immigration" from southeastern Europe was genetically inferior. That contribution permanently transformed American society. This disgraceful episode in the history of American psychology—one not without contemporary relevance—is the subject of the next section.

PSYCHOLOGY AND THE IMMIGRANT

> Were we set out on a sensible program regarding the immigrant, we should be led ultimately into an analogous one concerning the inferior stocks already extant in our population. Linking up these two programs with a sane educational policy we might look forward to a true national greatness. For who doubts that the contributors to a high culture must be of a high-minded race?
>
> —*Professor Kimball Young, 1922*[27]

THE UNITED STATES, until 1875, had no federal immigration law. The 1875 law, and all subsequent amendments until 1921, placed no numerical limitation on immigration. The first federal law simply listed a number of excluded classes of individuals. The 1875 list was modest—it barred coolies, convicts, and prostitutes.

The control over immigration developed slowly, and at first by the gradual addition of new excluded classes. There was also a "gentlemen's agreement" with Japan, and circuitous regulations having to do with the longitudes and latitudes from which immigration was debarred served to assure an appropriate racial balance. There were, however, no discriminations drawn among the various European countries which provided the bulk of immigration. Throughout the nineteenth century, the preponderance of immigration flowed from the countries of northern and western Europe.

The advances of psychology can be seen reflected in the changing terminology of the list of excluded classes. The 1882 immigration act debarred lunatics and idiots, and the 1903 law added epileptics and insane persons. By 1907, a differentiation had been made between "imbeciles" and "feeble-minded persons," both of which classes were excluded. The fullest development of modern mental science informed the law of 1917, which excluded "persons of constitutional psychopathic inferiority."

With the turn of the century, the "New Immigration" from south-eastern Europe began to assume massive proportions. The English, Scandinavian, and German stock which had earlier predominated was now outnumbered by a wave of Italian, Polish, Russian, and Jewish immigrants. The popular press and the literary magazines of the period were filled with articles questioning the assimilability of the new and exotic ethnic breeds. There arose a public clamor for some form of "quality control" over the inflow of immigrants. This at first took the form of a demand for a literacy test; but it could scarcely be doubted that the new science of mental testing, which proclaimed its ability to measure innate intelligence, would be called into the nation's service.

The first volunteer was Henry Goddard, who in 1912 was invited by the United States Public Health Service to Ellis Island, the immigrant receiving station in New York harbor. The intrepid Goddard administered the Binet test and supplementary performance tests to representatives of what he called the "great mass of average immigrants." The results were sure to produce grave concern in the minds of thoughtful citizens. The test results established that 83 percent of the Jews, 80 percent of the Hungarians, 79 percent of the Italians, and 87 percent of the Russians were "feeble-minded."[28] By 1917, Goddard was able to report in the *Journal of Delinquency* that "the number of aliens deported because of feeble-mindedness . . . increased approximately 350 percent in 1913 and 570 percent in 1914. . . . This was due to the untiring efforts of the physicians who were inspired by the belief that mental tests could be used for the detection of feeble-minded aliens. . . ."[29]

This accomplishment of the fledgling science won sympathetic attention from the Eugenics Research Association. That society's journal, *Eugenical News*, was edited by the biologist Harry Laughlin. Writing in his journal in 1917, under the heading "The New Immigration Law," Laughlin observed: "Recently the science of psychology has developed to a high state of precision that branch of its general subject devoted to the testing of individuals for natural excellence in mental and temperamental qualities. When the knowledge of the existence of this science becomes generally known in Congress, that body will then be expected to apply the direct and logical test for the qualities which we seek to measure. . . ."[30]

This appears to have been a relatively modest proposal, presumably pointing toward the use of mental tests in detecting would-be immigrants who fell into the debarred classes. There were, however, historical forces at work which were to catapult the science of mental testing to new levels of public acceptance, and which were to provide the scientists of the Eugenics Research Association with opportunities scarcely imaginable in early 1917. The United States was soon to enter the World War, and mental testing was to play a critical role in determining the ethnic and racial composition of the republic.

The president of the American Psychological Association when the country declared war was Robert Yerkes. The "point scale" version of the Binet test had been developed by Yerkes, and his views on the heritability of IQ were clearly formulated. They had led to his appointment to the Committee on Eugenics of the National Commission on Prisons, and to his chairmanship in 1917 of the Eugenics Research Association's Committee on Inheritance of Mental Traits. With the country mobilizing to prosecute the war, the APA, under Yerkes' leadership, suggested that the major contribution of psychologists might be the mass intelligence testing of draftees. The proposal was accepted by the military, and psychologists were commissioned in the Army's Sanitary Corps, under Major Yerkes. Their mission was to provide mental assessments, and hopefully to aid in the job classification of draftees.

The psychologists quickly developed a written group intelligence test—"Alpha"—which could easily be administered to large bodies of men. For "illiterates," a supplementary test—"Beta"—was designed. This test was "non-verbal," of the "performance" type. To accommodate non-English speakers, instructions were to be given to groups of men in pantomime. The work on test development was planned by a committee meeting at the Vineland Training School. The committee's membership included Terman, Goddard, and Yerkes.

The tests appear to have had little practical effect on the outcome of the war. They were not in fact much used for the placement of men. The testing program, however, generated enormous amounts of data, since some 2,000,000 men were given standardized IQ tests. The mental tests were very widely publicized. Public interest was doubtless excited by the finding that the "mental age" of the average white draftee was only 13.

Following the war, an intensive statistical analysis was performed on the scores of some 125,000 draftees. The results of this analysis, together with a detailed history of the testing program, were published in 1921 by the National Academy of Sciences, under Yerkes' editorship.[31] The publication of the data occurred in the same year in which Congress, as a temporary measure, first placed a numerical limitation on immigration.

The World War I data provided the first massive demonstration that blacks scored lower on IQ tests than did whites. That, however, was not a matter of pressing concern in 1921. The chapter in the Yerkes report with immediate impact was that on "Relation of Intelligence Ratings to Nativity." The chapter summarized IQ results for a total of 12,407 draftees who had reported that they were born in foreign countries. A letter grade, ranging from A through E, was assigned to each tested draftee, and the distribution of grades was presented separately for each country of origin. The results are reproduced from the Yerkes volume in Figure 1.

The style of the Yerkes volume was to refrain from editorial comment, and the discussion of Figure 1 was value-free. The chapter, edited in fact by Boring, observed: "The range of difference between the countries is a very wide one. . . . In general, the Scandinavian and English speaking countries stand high in the list, while the Slavic and Latin countries stand low . . . the countries tend to fall into two groups: Canada, Great Britain, the Scandinavian and Teutonic countries [as opposed to] the Latin and Slavic countries. . . ."[32]

These scientific data speedily became "generally known in Congress," with the considerable assistance of the scientists of the Eugenics Research Association, and of (by now) Colonel Yerkes, employed since after the war at the National Research Council in Washington. The flow of events may provide sustenance to those who entertain a conspiracy theory of history. The *Eugenical News* of 1918 had reported that in April of that year "a group of students of man" had gathered at the home of Professor Henry Fairchild Osborn to found the Galton Society. The original Charter Fellows were only nine in number, but provision was made for the election of further students up to a total of 25. The founder of the society, and its chairman, was Mr. Madison Grant, author of *The Passing of the Great Race*. The purpose of the Society had been made clear in a personal letter from Grant to Osborn, dated March 9, 1918. "My pro-

FIGURE 1. PERCENTAGE DISTRIBUTION OF LETTER GRADES IN INTELLIGENCE BY NATIVITY OF FOREIGN-BORN MEN IN DRAFT (FROM YERKES, 1921).

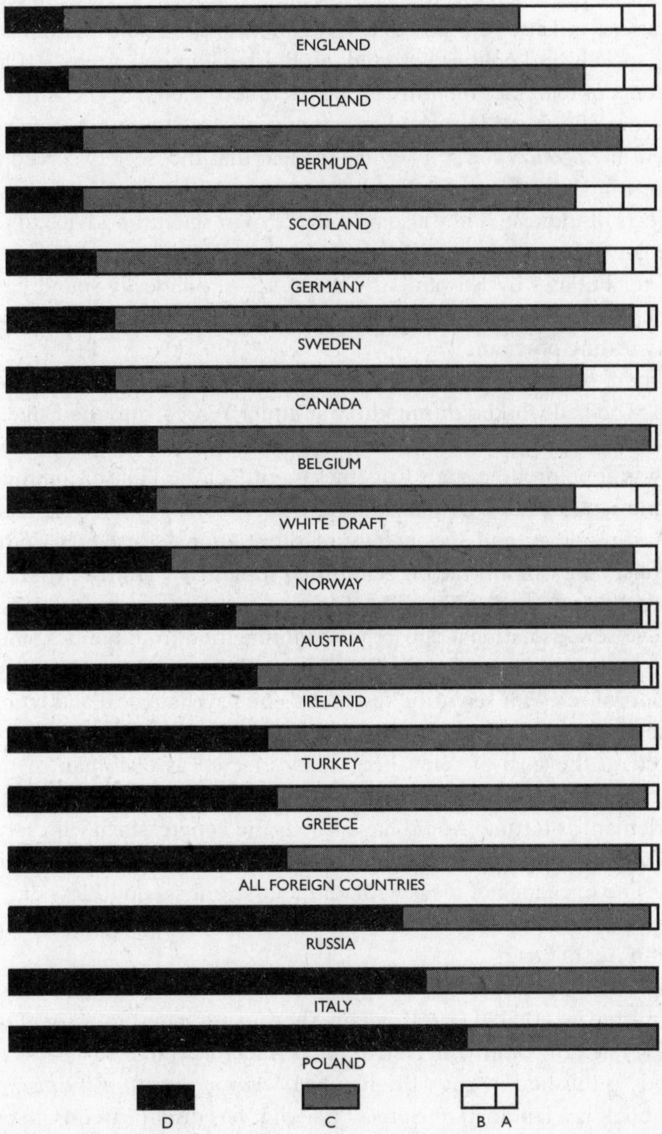

ENGLAND

HOLLAND

BERMUDA

SCOTLAND

GERMANY

SWEDEN

CANADA

BELGIUM

WHITE DRAFT

NORWAY

AUSTRIA

IRELAND

TURKEY

GREECE

ALL FOREIGN COUNTRIES

RUSSIA

ITALY

POLAND

D   C   B A

posal," Grant wrote, "is the organization of an anthropological society (or somatological society as you call it) here in New York City with a central governing body, self elected and self perpetuating, and very limited in members, and also confined to native Americans, who are anthropologically socially and politically sound, no Bolsheviki need apply."[33] These students of man met monthly in the Members' Room of the American Museum of Natural History. The minutes of some meetings were published in *Eugenical News*. They make clear that the Society served two major functions. The members read, and invited, scientific papers on subjects of interest. They also provided expert scientific advice to relevant government agencies. Psychology was ably represented among the Charter Fellows by Edward L. Thorndike—a politically sound native psychologist of the first rank, then serving as a consultant to Yerkes' Army testing program.

There occurred in 1920 a massive influx of experimental psychologists, who had worked during the war under Yerkes, into the Eugenics Research Association. The secretary of that association, Harry Laughlin, was appointed "Expert Eugenics Agent" of the House Committee on Immigration and Naturalization of the U.S. Congress. The Division of Anthropology and Psychology of the National Research Council established a Committee on Scientific Problems of Human Migration under Yerkes' leadership. The function of that committee was to remove serious national debate over immigration from politics, and to place it instead on a firm scientific basis. This was to be done by the support of relevant scientific research. The psychological and biological scientists of the Eugenics Research Association were equally committed to the goal of relevance. They elected as chairman of their association in 1923 the Honorable Albert Johnson. That honorable gentleman, as fortune would have it, was the congressman who served as chairman of the House Committee on Immigration and Naturalization. The exchange of ideas with eminent scientists doubtless did not impede Representative Johnson in his task of composing the Immigration Act of 1924.

The first research supported by the National Research Council's committee was that of Carl Brigham, then an assistant professor of psychology at Princeton University. The Princeton University Press had already published in 1923 Brigham's *A Study of American Intelligence*.[34] The book is a landmark of sorts. Though it has disappeared from contemporary reference lists, it can be argued that few works in the history of American psychology have had so significant an impact.

The book's foreword was composed by Yerkes, who "consented to write it because of my intense interest in the practical problems of immigration. . . ." The foreword declared that "Two extraordinarily important tasks confront our nation: the protection of the moral, mental, and physical quality of its people, and the re-shaping of its industrial system so that it shall promote justice and encourage creative and productive workmanship." Professor Brigham was said by Yerkes to have "rendered a notable service to psychology, to sociology, and above all to our lawmakers. . . . The author presents not theories or opinions but facts. It behooves us to consider their reliability and their meaning, for no one of us as a citizen can afford to ignore the menace of race deterioration or the evident relations of immigration to national progress and welfare."

The empirical contribution made by Brigham consisted of a reanalysis of the Army data on immigrant intelligence. The performance of Negro draftees was taken as a kind of bedrock baseline; fully 46 percent of the Poles, 42.3 percent of the Italians, and 39 percent of the Russians scored at or below the Negro average. The most original analysis, however, centered about the "very remarkable fact" that the measured intelligence of immigrants was related to the number of years that they had lived in America. This had been demonstrated by pooling the scores of immigrants from all countries, and then subdividing them into groups categorized according to the years of residence in America prior to being tested. This analysis indicated that foreigners who had lived in the country 20 years or more before being tested were every bit as intelligent as native Americans. Those who had lived in the country less than five years were essentially feeble-minded. To some analysts, this finding might have suggested that IQ scores were heavily influenced by exposure to American customs and language, but that was not the tack taken by Brigham.

"We must," Brigham declared, "assume that we are measuring native or inborn intelligence. . . ."[35] The psychologists had, after all, deliberately devised the Beta test to measure the genetically determined intelligence of the illiterate and the foreign-speaking. "The hypothesis of growth of intelligence with increasing length of residence may be identified with the hypothesis of an error in the method of measuring intelligence. . . ." That hypothesis was not likely to be congenial to a mental tester, and Brigham quickly disposed of it with a number of statistical and psychometric arguments. With this accomplished, "we are forced to . . . accept the hypothesis that the curve indicates a gradual deterioration in the class of immigrants examined in the army, who came to this country in each succeeding five year period since 1902."

Forced by the data to this conclusion, Professor Brigham was at no loss to provide a clarifying explanation—"the race hypothesis." He proceeded to estimate "the proportion of Nordic, Alpine and Mediterranean blood in each of the European countries," and to calculate the numbers of immigrants arriving from each country during each time period. These combined operations produced a sequential picture of the blood composition of the immigrant stream over time. There was thereby unearthed a remarkable parallelism; as the proportion of Nordic blood had decreased, and the proportions of Alpine and Mediterranean blood increased, the intelligence of the immigrants was deduced to have decreased. This is a nice example of the power of correlational analysis applied to intelligence data. There was no attempt by Brigham to discover whether, *within* each of the "races," measured intelligence had increased with years of residence in America. The conclusion reached by Brigham followed in the footsteps of the testing pioneers who had taught him his trade. He urged the abandonment of "feeble hypotheses that would make these differences an artifact of the method of examining" and concluded forthrightly that "our test results indicate a genuine intellectual superiority of the Nordic group. . . ."

The final two chapters of Brigham's book might fairly be described as reactionary. They pile together quotations from the racist ideologues of America and Europe with Brigham's own opinions. The quoted excerpts in the following sentence are in part Brigham's, and in part his quotations from Grant and others.

> The Nordics are . . . rulers, organizers, and aristocrats . . . individualistic, self-reliant, and jealous of their personal freedom . . . as a result they are usually Protestants. . . . The Alpine race is always and everywhere a race of peasants. . . . The Alpine is the perfect slave, the ideal serf . . . the unstable temperament and the lack of coordinating and reasoning power so often found among the Irish. . . . we have no separate intelligence distributions for the Jews. . . . our army sample of immigrants from Russia is at least

one half Jewish. . . . Our figures, then, would rather tend to disprove the popular belief that the Jew is intelligent . . . he has the head form, stature, and color of his Slavic neighbors. He is an Alpine Slav [pp. 182–3, 185, 189, 190].

The final paragraphs of the book raised the eugenic spectre of a long-term decline in the level of American intelligence as the consequence of continued immigration and racial mongrelization. "We must face a possibility of racial admixture here that is infinitely worse than that faced by any European country today, for we are incorporating the negro into our racial stock, while all of Europe is comparatively free from this taint. . . . The decline of American intelligence will be more rapid than the decline of the intelligence of European national groups, owing to the presence here of the negro."[36]

With national problems of this magnitude, nothing short of a radical solution seemed likely to be of much avail. From this stern logic, neither Professor Brigham nor his sponsor, Professor Yerkes, shrank. The final sentences of Brigham's book mean precisely what they say.

> The deterioration of American intelligence is not inevitable, however, if public action can be aroused to prevent it. There is no reason why legal steps should not be taken which would assure a continuously progressive upward evolution.
>
> The steps that should be taken to preserve or increase our present intellectual capacity must of course be dictated by science and not by political expediency. Immigration should not only be restrictive but highly selective. And the revision of the immigration and naturalization laws will only afford a slight relief from our present difficulty. The really important steps are those looking toward the prevention of the continued propagation of defective strains in the present population. If all immigration were stopped now, the decline of American intelligence would still be inevitable. This is the problem which must be met, and our manner of meeting it will determine the future course of our national life.

With this work behind him, Brigham moved on to the secretaryship of the College Entrance Examination Board. There he made further contributions to psychometric theory, and designed and developed the

Scholastic Aptitude Test, the primary screening instrument for admission to American colleges. By 1929 Brigham had been elected secretary of the American Psychological Association, and, after his death, the library building of Educational Testing Service was named in his honor.*

There is no record of the psychological community reacting with shock or outrage to Brigham's policy proposals. Perhaps none could be expected from a community in which Terman, Goddard, and Yerkes had helped to set an ideological tone—and which, in the year of publication of Brigham's book, had elected Lewis Terman president of the American Psychological Association. The review of Brigham's book in the 1923 *Journal of Educational Psychology* was probably representative of the psychology establishment's response: "The thesis is carefully worked up to by a logical and careful analysis of the results of the army tests . . . we shall certainly be in hearty agreement with him when he demands a more selective policy for future immigration and a more vigorous method of dealing with the defective strains already in this country."[37]

There now existed an alliance of scientific and political thinkers committed to "vigorous methods" in the solution of the nation's problems. The political usage of Brigham's book and of the Army data was immediate and intense. That branch of the subject of psychology "devoted to the testing of individuals for natural excellence" was to enlighten the Congressional assault on immigration to an extent that Harry Laughlin could not have fully appreciated early in 1917.

Francis Kinnicutt, of the Immigration Restriction League, testified to the U.S. Senate Committee on Immigration on February 20, 1923. He desired:

> to further restrict immigration from southern and eastern Europe
> . . . [since] the evidence is abundant . . . that . . . it is largely of a
> very low degree of intelligence. . . . A large proportion of this

---

* Professor Brigham, in 1930, retracted as incorrect his 1923 analysis of the Army IQ data. The retraction appears on page 165 of the *Psychological Review* of that year. The Immigration Act of 1924 had by then been in force for six years. Whether Professor Brigham's opinions about the character of Alpines and Mediterraneans changed is not known, and is not relevant.

immigration ... consists ... of the Hebrew elements ... engaged in the garment-making industry. ... some of their labor unions are among the most radical in the whole country. ... The recent Army tests show ... the intelligence of the Italian immigration ... is of a very low grade, as is also that of the immigration from Poland and Russia. All ... rank far below the average intelligence for the whole country. See *A Study of American Intelligence*, by Carl C. Brigham, published by the Princeton University Press.

This is the most important book that has ever been written on this subject ... Col. Robert M. Yerkes ... vouches for this book, and speaks in the highest terms of Prof. Carl C. Brigham, now assistant professor of psychology in Princeton University. This comes as near being official United States Army data as could well be had ... examine the different tables, which are very graphic and bring the facts out in a most clear way ... they had two kinds of tests, alpha and beta. ... They took the greatest care to eliminate the advantage which native Americans would otherwise have had. ...[38]

The chairman of the committee, Senator Colt, thanked Mr. Kinnicutt for having sent him a copy of Brigham's book, and asked him to leave the additional copy which he had brought with him, explaining "I think every member of the committee ought to read that book and then arrive at his own judgment in regard to it."

The views of Dr. Arthur Sweeney, on "Mental Tests for Immigrants," were made part of the appendix to the hearings of the House Committee on Immigration and Naturalization on January 24, 1923. Those hearings were chaired by Representative Albert Johnson, also chairman of the Eugenics Research Association. Dr. Sweeney had written:

We have been overrun with a horde of the unfit. ... we have had no yardstick. ... The psychological tests ... furnished us with the necessary yardstick. ... The Army tests ... revealed the intellectual endowment of the men. ... The tests are equally applicable to immigrants. ... All that is required is a staff of two or three trained psychologists at each port. ...

... See Memoirs of the National Academy of Sciences. ... We can not be seriously opposed to immigrants from Great Britain, Holland, Canada, Germany, Denmark, and Scandinavia. ... We can, however, strenuously object to immigration from Italy ... Russia ... Poland ... Greece ... Turkey. ... The Slavic and Latin countries show a marked contrast in intelligence with the western and northern European group. ... One can not recognize the high-grade imbecile at sight. ...

They think with the spinal cord rather than with the brain. ... The necessity of providing for the future does not stimulate them to continuous labor. ... Being constitutionally inferior they are necessarily socially inadequate. ... Education can be received only by those who have intelligence to receive it. It does not create intelligence. That is what one is born with. ... The D minus group can not go beyond the second grade. ... we shall degenerate to the level of the Slav and Latin races ... pauperism, crime, sex offenses, and dependency ... guided by a mind scarcely superior to the ox. ...

... we must protect ourselves against the degenerate horde. ... We must view the immigration problem from a new angle. ... We must apply ourselves to the task with the new weapons of science ... the perfect weapons formed for us by science. ... it is now as easy to calculate one's mental equipment as it is to measure his height and weight. The examination of over 2,000,000 recruits has tested and verified this standard. ... this new method ... will enable us to select those who are worthy and reject those who are worthless.[39]

Though Dr. Sweeney's remarks contain some infelicities of phrasing, they do not distort the views of the pioneers of mental testing. With disciples of this caliber pressing for vigorous action, there was no need for Professor Terman to abandon his duties as president of the American Psychological Association in order to testify before the Congress. Professor Boring's scholarly observation in the Memoirs of the National Academy of Sciences—"the Slavic and Latin countries stand low"—was done no serious violence by Dr. Sweeney's reference to "the level of the Slav and Latin races." There is nowhere in the records of the Congressional hearings—nowhere—a single remark by a single representative of the psychological profession to the effect that the results of the Army testing program were in any way being abused or misinterpreted. That program had been organized officially by the American Psychological Association under its then president, Robert Yerkes. The data not only came "as near being official United States Army data as could well be had," they came as near being official data of the psychological profession as could well be had. They reflected the almost universal belief, already established among psychologists, in the heritability of IQ scores, and in the potency of the testing methods developed by such scientists as Terman, Goddard, and Yerkes.

The psychologists failed to appear before the Congressional committees, but other patriotic thinkers carried their message for them. To be sure, in the case of the House Committee, chaired by the chairman of the Eugenics Research Association, it was carrying coals to Newcastle. There was an Alice-in-Wonderland quality to Representative Johnson's placing into the minutes of his hearing of January 10, 1924, the "Report of the Committee on Selective Immigration of the Eugenics Committee of the United States of America." The Eugenics Committee had been chaired by Brigham's patron, Madison Grant, author of *The Passing of the Great Race,* and founder, together with Thorndike, of the Galton Society. The Eugenics Committee included in its membership Harry Laughlin, Expert Eugenics Agent of the House Committee itself, and Representative Johnson, the House Committee's chairman.

The eugenic scientists had reported that "The country at large has been greatly impressed by the results of the Army intelligence tests . . . carefully analyzed by Lieut. Col. R. M. Yerkes, Dr. C. C. Brigham, and others. . . . with the shift in the tide of immigration . . . to southern and eastern Europe, there has gone a decrease in intelligence test scores. . . . The experts . . . believe that . . . the tests give as accurate a measure of intelligence as possible. . . . The questions . . . were selected with a view to measuring innate ability. . . . had mental tests been in operation . . . over 6,000,000 aliens now living in this country . . . would never have been admitted. . . . Aliens should be required to attain a passing score of, say, the median in the Alpha test. . . ."[40]

The chairman of the Allied Patriotic Societies of New York was also a student of the science of mental testing, and at the January 5, 1924 hearing Congressman Johnson placed his letter into the record: ". . . the bulk of the 'newer' immigration is made up of Italians, Hebrews, and Slavs. . . . During the war certain intelligence tests were made by our Army. . . . These tests threw considerable light on the mental qualities of the 'newer' . . . immigration . . . great care was taken to eliminate any advantage from speaking the English language. . . . The results . . . have been analyzed . . . particularly in the work of Prof. Carl Brigham, of Princeton . . . published by the Princeton University Press. . . . He worked under Colonel Yerkes. . . . Prof. Brigham's tables bring out certain very startling facts. . . . Professor Brigham figures out, moreover, that as many as 2,000,000 persons have been admitted . . . whose intelligence was nearer the intelligence of the average negro . . . than to the average intelligence of the American white."[41]

Professor Brigham's tables, and those published by the National Academy of Sciences, figured prominently in the extended lecture delivered to the Johnson Committee on March 8, 1924, by Dr. Harry Laughlin. The ubiquitous Dr. Laughlin was then employed as a "member of the scientific staff" of the Carnegie Institution. His position as Expert Eugenics Agent of the Johnson Committee had been supplemented by "an official appointment and credentials signed by the Secretary of Labor, authorizing me to go abroad as a United States immigration agent to Europe, to make certain scientific researches." Those researches concerned the biology of human migration. The chairman of the Johnson Committee carefully questioned his agent as to whether such problems "seem capable of being attacked by purely scientific methods without recourse to politics or contention." To this forthright question, agent-biologist Laughlin forthrightly replied, "Yes, sir. My province was that of a scientific investigator, and these problems were attacked in the purely scientific spirit."[42]

Scientist Laughlin proceeded to lecture on the "natural qualities of immigrants." There were, he said, some qualities which "American stock especially prized." They included truth-loving, inventiveness, industry, common sense, artistic sense, love of beauty, responsibility, social instinct, and the natural sense of a square deal. "Of course all of these elements are of a biological order. . . . It is possible to make biological studies of them. . . ."

This section of Laughlin's lecture was devoid of empirical data, and the mathematical precision and operationalism of his subsequent remarks on "natural intelligence" came as a refreshing contrast. The measurers of natural intelligence had obviously advanced their discipline beyond the point reached by the measurers of the natural sense of a square deal. "Many tests . . . are being developed by psychological research. Their purpose is to evaluate naked natural intelligence. . . . These examinations, as all members of the committee know, were conducted under the direction of Maj. Robert M. Yerkes. . . . The tests given were the best which the psychologists of the world had devised. . . ."

The proportions of Grade A through E men in the various countries were duly displayed in a series of charts, with appropriate credit to the National Academy of Sciences. These were supplemented by Laughlin's own tables, which equated various forms of intelligence test. The Congress was informed that those with a mental age below 9.5, or an IQ below 70, or a score on the Yerkes point scale or Alpha below 50, or a score on Beta below 40, or a score on Brigham's combined scale below 9.1, were D- or E men, who were described by the phrase "Cost of supervision greater than value of labor. Untrainable socially or economically." Statistician Laughlin calculated that the country already contained in its foreign-born white population 2,060,262 such men— not to mention another 4,287,573 D aliens, "Slow in adaptability; supervision needed." The number of admitted aliens deficient in a natural sense of a square deal was not calculated. Would such an estimate have been any more ludicrous than the quantifications of innate intelligence so maliciously provided to the Congress and the country by the pillars of American psychology?

The mental testers brought the facts not only to the Congress, but also to the thoughtful reading public. Their relevance to immigration policy was made entirely explicit. For example, Professor Kimball Young reported in the 1922 *Scientific Monthly*[43] that "general as well as specific abilities are transmitted by heredity" and that "special talents may actually turn out to be due to the presence of separate units in the germ plasm." The Ph.D. and M.A. theses of Terman's students at Stanford were cited to show that a group of 25 Italians had a median IQ of 84. Terman's student had written in her dissertation that "the tests are as accurate a judgment of the mental capacity of the low foreign element as of the American children." This conclusion was confirmed by the more massive scholarly work of a student at Columbia, who examined "500 cases each of Jewish, American, and Italian boys and 225 negro boys. . . . Italians who were thought by their teachers, principal, and neighborhood social workers to be laboring under no language handicap were found to be very inferior to the other three races." The surprisingly high performance of the blacks in this study was readily explained by Professor Young in a scholarly footnote: "The negroes were a much more highly selected group perhaps than the Italians. . . ."

The evidence, Professor Young indicated, pointed "conclusively to the fact that a continued deluge of this country of the weaker stocks of Europe will ultimately affect the average intelligence of the population. . . . these stocks are constantly sending out their tenacles [sic] into the higher biological strains. . . . We have of course the comparable problem of preventing the continuance of inferior lines in the present population. . . . The public opinion of this country needs arousing . . . immigration should be controlled. . . . It seems to me that there is not a better piece of service for the National Research Council than an attack upon this problem. . . . True, there remains after such a program, if it is ever accepted, the entire matter, noted already, of the inferior strains in the population now present in this country."

The Johnson-Lodge Immigration Act of 1924 was enacted after the conclusion of the congressional hearings. There had already been enacted, on a temporary basis, a 1921 law embodying the principle of "national origin quotas." The number of immigrants admitted from any given country in one year had been limited to 3 percent of the number of foreign-born from that country already resident in the United States, as determined by the census of 1910. The Johnson-Lodge Act established national origin quotas as a permanent aspect of immigration policy, and it reduced the quota to 2 percent; but most important, *the quotas were to be based on the census of 1890*. The use of the 1890 census had only one purpose, acknowledged by the bill's supporters. The "New Immigration" had begun after 1890, and the law was designed to exclude the biologically inferior D- and E peoples of southeastern Europe. The new law made the country safe for Professor Brigham's Nordics, but it did little for the safety of Alpines and Mediterraneans. The law, for which the science of mental testing may claim substantial credit, resulted in the deaths of literally hundreds of thousands of victims of the Nazi biological theorists. The victims were denied admission to the United States because the "German quota" was filled, although the quotas of many other Nordic countries were vastly undersubscribed. The Nazi theoreticians ultimately concurred with biologist Laughlin's assessment that, in the case of D- and E people, "Cost of supervision greater than value of labor."

The biological partitioning of the European land-mass by the Congress did much to place immigration policy on a firm scientific footing. There were, however, both scientific and political loose ends to be tidied up, and they did not escape the attention of the more ardent mental testers. Dr. Nathaniel Hirsch held a National Research Council Fellowship in Psychology at Harvard, under McDougall. The results of his research endeavor were published in the 1926 *Genetic Psychology Monographs*.

The intellectual inferiority of the immigrants had already been amply documented. To demonstrate conclusively its genetic origin, Hirsch gave intelligence tests to the American-born *children* of various immigrant groups. The children were to provide a clear test of the genetic hypothesis. They had attended American schools, they spoke the English language, but they carried their parents' genes. The data indicated that, for almost all groups, the children of immigrants were intellectually inferior.

The policy implications of his contribution did not escape Dr. Hirsch. While applauding the Immigration Act of 1924, he warned in the discussion section of his scientific treatise that

> that part of the law which has to do with the non-quota immigrants should be modified. . . . All mental testing upon children of Spanish-Mexican descent has shown that the average intelligence of this group is even lower than the average intelligence of the Portuguese and Negro children . . . in this study. Yet Mexicans are flowing into the country. . . .
>
> Our immigration from Canada . . . we are getting . . . the less intelligent of working-class people. . . . the increase in the number of French Canadians is alarming. Whole New England villages and towns are filled with them. The average intelligence of the French Canadian group in our data approaches the level of the average Negro intelligence.

Professor Hirsch then quoted the lament of an earlier observer:

> I have seen gatherings of the foreign-born in which narrow and sloping foreheads were the rule.... In every face there was something wrong—lips thick, mouth coarse ... chin poorly formed ... sugar loaf heads ... goose-bill noses ... a set of skew-molds discarded by the Creator.... Immigration officials ... report vast troubles in extracting the truth from certain brunette nationalities.[44]

Dr. Hirsch strove for and achieved a conceptual synthesis of psychological and biological principles: "The Jew is disliked primarily because despite physical, economic, and social differences among themselves, 'all Jews are Jews,' meaning that there is a psychobiological principle that unites the most dissimilar of types of this strange, paradoxical Natio-Race."

With so masterful a grasp of psychobiology, it was perhaps inevitable that Dr. Hirsch should turn his attention to the complicated problem of estimating the precise weights of heredity and environment in the determination of IQ. The results of this basic research, also supervised by McDougall, were published in a 1930 Harvard University Press book entitled *Twins*. Dr. Hirsch's interest in twins had been stimulated "in consequence of a suggestion made by President A. Lawrence Lowell of Harvard University." Hirsch deduced that "heredity is five times as potent" as environment. He concluded that "... there is no doubt that today many of the environmental agencies of civilization are contributing to 'The Decline of the West,' and that political wisdom can be garnered from a study of twins, and from other experimental studies of heredity and environment."[45]

The theme is recurrent. The academic seekers after truth pursue jointly the goals of political and scientific wisdom. Those who today investigate black-white differences in IQ, or whose concern for "The Decline of the West" prompts them to brood on IQ and the meritocracy, might do well to remember the colloquy between Representative Johnson and Expert Eugenics Agent Laughlin:

"The Chairman: Do all of these three problems seem capable of being attacked by purely scientific methods without recourse to politics or contention?

"Doctor Laughlin: Yes, sir. My province was that of a scientific investigator, and these problems were attacked in the purely scientific spirit."

There was a lively appreciation of the relation between science and politics expressed in the 1927 address of Frank L. Babbott to the Eugenics Research Association. Mr. Babbott explained to the assembled scientists that eugenics "has made its strongest appeal to me through its influence on immigration. . . . this is an indirect result of eugenics, but it comes as the natural development of research on the part of people like yourselves. It is possible that restriction of immigration would have come without the aid of our Society, but I doubt if it would have come so soon or so permanently if it had not been for the demonstration that men, like Dr. Laughlin, have been able to make to the Committee on Immigration. . . .

"The Eugenics Research Association began its work with the House Immigration Committee in 1920, and immediately took the whole question out of politics and placed it on a scientific or biological basis. . . . It was at this juncture that Dr. Laughlin was brought into the deliberations of the Committee. As one member of the Committee has said—he became their teacher and supplied them with arguments to meet the opposition. . . ."[46]

The contribution of the mental testers toward the formulation of national policies did not end in 1924. The meeting of the Galton Society on November 4, 1927, with Carl Brigham in the chair, opened with a report by Madison Grant that the Honorable Albert Johnson had requested suggestions from the Galton Society concerning the eugenical uses which might be made of the census of 1930. The Society suggested the collection of pedigree records detailing racial and family stocks, as well as the collection of mothers' maiden names. Further, it would be useful if all persons enumerated by the census were issued an official registration card. With this public business concluded, Professor Brigham introduced Dr. Harry Laughlin, who lectured to the students of man on "The Genetics of the Thoroughbred Horse."[47]

The Society, on April 5, 1929, adopted an official statement on the maintenance of immigration control. "The Galton Society appreciates the fact that the essential character of every nation depends primarily upon the inborn racial and family endowments of its citizens." Professors Thorndike and Brigham were present; the minutes do not record any disagreement.[48]

There is a moral to be drawn from this melancholy history. The immigration debate, together with its European victims,[49] is long since dead—but only to be replaced by a curiously similar issue. The major domestic issue of our own time, as our politicians remind us, is "the welfare mess." The welfare issue, like immigration, contains within itself a tangle of the most profound racial and economic conflicts. Today's psychometricians speak with voices more cultured than that of *Genetic Psychology Monographs* in 1926. There are some, however, who are again prepared to serve as teachers to the Congress, and to supply arguments to meet the opposition. These teachers once again assert that their effort is only to remove racial and economic conflicts from politics, and to place them on a firm scientific basis.

We see today that the psychologists who provided "expert" and "scientific" teaching relevant to the immigration debate did so on the basis of pitifully inadequate data. There is probably no living psychologist who would view the World War I Army data as relevant to the heritable IQ of European "races." There are few who now seem much impressed by the data on "Italians in America" summarized by Rudolf Pintner in his 1923 text, *Intelligence Testing*.[50] Professor Pintner had called attention to the "remarkable agreement in the median IQ for the Italian children" in six separate studies. That median IQ was 84, a full 16 points below the average American. There is probably no psychometrician today prepared to assert that that 16-point deficit was produced by inferior Italian IQ genes. That does not prevent the same mental testers from pointing gravely to the possible genetic significance of Professor Jensen's recent survey of the contemporary IQ literature. That survey led Jensen to report: "The basic data are well known: on the average, Negroes test about 1 standard deviation (15 IQ points) below the average of the white population, and this finding is fairly uniform across the 81 different tests of intellectual ability used in these studies. . . ."[51] This kind of finding, like Goddard's earlier report that 83 percent of Jewish immigrants were feeble-minded, cannot be ignored by thoughtful citizens.

There is, of course, the theoretical possibility that the genetic theorists are correct. Perhaps IQ *is* highly heritable; and perhaps differences between races, as well as among individuals, are in large measure due to heredity. There are serious scholars who have assumed this, and who have labored to adduce supporting evidence. Their data ought not to be ignored, and they deserve a careful scrutiny. That scrutiny is a scientific necessity, even though the social and political policies advocated by many hereditarian theorists are in no sense compelled or justified by the facts which they assert to be true.

NOTES

1. R. J. Herrnstein, *IQ in the Meritocracy* (Boston, Atlantic Monthly Press, 1973), p. 138.

2. A. Binet and T. Simon, "Sur la necessité d'établir un diagnostic scientifique des états inferieurs de l'intelligence," *L'année psychologique*, 11 (1905), 191.

3. A. Binet, *Les Idées modernes sur les enfants* (Paris, Flammarion, 1913), pp. 140–141.

4. L. M. Terman, *The Measurement of Intelligence* (Boston, Houghton Mifflin, 1916), pp. 6–7.

5. Ibid., pp. 91–92.

6. M. Grant, *The Passing of the Great Race* (New York, Scribner's, 1916).

7. L. M. Terman, "Feeble-minded Children in the Public Schools of California," *School and Society*, 5 (1917), 165.

8. Binet, *Idées*, pp. 140–141.

9. H. H. Goddard, "How Shall We Educate Mental Defectives?," *The Training School Bulletin*, 9 (1912), 43.

10. E. C. Banfield, *The Unheavenly City: The Nature and Future of Our Urban Crisis* (Boston, Little Brown, 1970).

11. Herrnstein, *IQ*.

12. H. H. Goddard, *Human Efficiency and Levels of Intelligence* (Princeton, Princeton University Press, 1920), pp. 99–103.

13. R. M. Yerkes and J. C. Foster, *A Point Scale for Measuring Mental Ability* (Baltimore, Warwick and York, 1923), pp. 22–25.

14. *Fifth Annual Report of the Department of Charities and Corrections, State of New Jersey* (Somerville, N.J., 1910), p. 14.

15. *Sixth Annual Report of the Department of Charities and Corrections, State of New Jersey* (Burlington, N.J., 1911), p. 23.

16. *Seventh Annual Report of the Department of Charities and Corrections, State of New Jersey* (Trenton, N.J., 1912), pp. 17–18.

17. E. Flood, "Notes on the Castration of Idiot Children," *American Journal of Psychology*, 10 (1898), p. 299.

18. H. H. Laughlin, *Eugenical Sterilization in the United States* (Chicago, Psychopathic Laboratory of the Municipal Court of Chicago, 1922), pp. 35–36.

19. Ibid., p. 15.

20. Ibid., p. 24.

21. Ibid., pp. 21–22.

22. Ibid., pp. 160–161.

23. Ibid., pp. 324–325.

24. Ibid., p. 60.

25. Ibid., pp. 123–124.

26. E. Reed and S. Reed, *Mental Retardation: A Family Study* (Philadelphia, Saunders, 1965), p. 77.

27. K. K. Young, "Intelligence Tests of Certain Immigrant Groups," *Scientific Monthly*, 15 (1922), 434.

28. H. H. Goddard, "The Binet Tests in Relation to Immigration," *Journal of Psycho-Asthenics*, 18 (1913), 105–107.

29. H. H. Goddard, "Mental Tests and the Immigrant," *Journal of Delinquency*, 2 (1917), 271.

30. *Eugenical News*, 2 (1917), 22.

31. *Psychological Examining in the United States Army*, ed. R. M. Yerkes (Washington, Memoirs of the National Academy of Sciences, 15, 1921).

32. Yerkes, *Psychological Examining*, p. 699. There are, at various points in the volume, references to the possibility that language handicaps *might* have depressed the scores of the foreign-born (e.g., p. 704).

33. M. Grant to H. F. Osborn, March 9, 1918, Davenport MSS, American Philosophical Society, Philadelphia.

34. C. C. Brigham, *A Study of American Intelligence* (Princeton, Princeton University Press, 1923). The Brigham research project supported by the National Research Council was devoted to the development of an "internationalized" test, presumably free of cultural and language bias. Whatever private reservations the NRC committee entertained about the fairness of the wartime tests, these were not expressed publicly, and did not influence the debate on the immigration law.

35. Ibid., p. 100.

36. Ibid., p. 210.

37. *Journal of Educational Psychology*, 14 (1923), 184–185.

38. *Hearing before the Committee on Immigration, United States Senate, February 20, 1923* (Washington, Government Printing Office, 1923), pp. 80–81.

39. *Hearings before the Committee on Immigration and Naturalization, House of Representatives, January 3, 4, 5, 22, and 24, 1923* (Washington, Government Printing Office, 1923), pp. 589–594.

40. *Hearings before the Committee on Immigration and Naturalization, House of Representatives, December 26, 27, and 31, 1923, and January 2, 3, 4, 5, 7, 8, 10, and 19, 1924* (Washington, Government Printing Office, 1924), p. 837.

41. Ibid., p. 580.

42. *Hearing before the Committee on Immigration and Naturalization, House of Representatives, March 8,* 1924 (Washington, Government Printing Office, 1924), pp. 1231–1284.

43. Young, *Tests,* pp. 418–425.

44. N. D. Hirsch, "A Study of Natio-Racial Mental Differences," *Genetic Psychology Monographs,* 1 (1926), 394–397.

45. N. D. Hirsch, *Twins: Heredity and Environment* (Cambridge, Harvard University Press, 1930), pp. 148–149.

46. *Eugenical News,* 12 (1927), 93.

47. Ibid., 172–173.

48. *Eugenical News,* 14 (1929), 71.

49. A. D. Morse, *While Six Million Died: A Chronicle of American Apathy* (New York, Random House, 1968).

50. R. Pintner, *Intelligence Testing: Methods and Results* (New York, Holt, 1923), pp. 351–352.

51. A. R. Jensen, "How Much Can We Boost IQ and Scholastic Achievement?" *Harvard Educational Review,* 39 (1969), 81.

BLACK INTELLECTUALS ON IQ TESTS

William B. Thomas

T HE PERIOD OF THE 1920s was an era of extensive research on mental differences. Psychologists were developing tests to differentiate individual abilities from those of other individuals belonging to the same milieu. Curiously, scores from these tests revealed a high incidence of low performance by blacks. To a large extent, American psychologists of the 1920s accepted uncritically this phenomenon and attributed its causes to the inherent mental inferiority of blacks.[1] A leading exponent of this hereditarian Weltanschauung, Lewis M. Terman wrote about blacks that "their dullness seems to be racial, or at least inherent in the family stock from which they came."[2] Similar conclusions were reached about the low test performance of southern and eastern European immigrants, following a massive testing program for the military in 1917.[3] Terman and his fellow hereditarians[4] believed that these differences could not be removed by any scheme of mental culture and were independent of the quality of schools, home environment, and the subject's disposition.[5]

William B. Thomas is a professor of education at the University of Pittsburgh, specializing in the history and sociology of education. His most recent works appear in the *American Educational Research Journal* and the *International Review of Social History*. His article appeared in *Teachers College Record*, Vol. 85, Spring 1984, as "Black Intellectuals, Intelligence Testing in the 1930s, and the Sociology of Knowledge."

The uncritical acceptance of this hereditarian perspective by white social scientists from leading universities caused black intellectuals to raise significant questions about conclusions extrapolated from test data. One was whether identifiable mental differences between racial groups were indeed irreversibly fixed and independent of the influences of social and economic inequality. A second concern was the ramifications that answers to this first question had for federal, state, and local policies affecting blacks and others of marginal status in the social order. In a campaign to undercut a rash of racist claims in the social sciences, these black intellectuals launched a polemic against those social scientists who had concluded that blacks were innately inferior.[6]

Understandably, one major concern they held in their challenges was the apparent inadequacy of their own verbal counteroffensive against experimental researchers of national renown. Historian Horace Mann Bond, therefore, marshaled the talents of every black intellectual to

> equip himself as an active agent against the insidious propaganda which, like its prototypes, seeks to demonstrate that the Negro is intellectually and physically incapable of assuming the dignities, rights and duties which devolve upon him as a member of modern society.[7]

Similarly, Joseph St. Clair Price, who later became dean at Howard University, urged that "if considerable progress is to be made in these investigations, the bulk of the research must be undertaken by Negroes."[8]

Despite these calls for blacks to enter the heated nature-nurture controversy raging around psychological testing, empirical studies by blacks on the mental differences of their racial group did not emerge in full force until the 1930s. In fact, when the National Society for the Study of Education called for scientific investigations on the nature-nurture issue for its 1928 edition, the black response to mental testing was conspicuously absent. This may have been due to several variables, which this article addresses briefly.

For now it is important to recognize that a group of social scientists did in fact become deeply involved in the research component of the controversy during the 1930s. The overall purpose of this article, then, is to focus on and examine the experimental research agenda and the conclusions of representative black social scientists studying the effects of environment on mental test scores. By juxtaposing their findings against those of hereditarians of the 1920s, I will illustrate a phenomenal paradigm shift between two opposing schools of thought, as described in Mannheim's *Ideology and Utopia*. On the one hand, blacks as environmentalists attempted to discredit the hereditarian view. They (1) assailed the causal validity of prevailing hereditarian studies; (2) pointed out methodological errors and abuses in the assumptions and administration of mental tests; and (3) developed alternative databases by administering the tests themselves. Significantly, hereditarian proponents modified some of their earlier inferences about the inherent inferiority of blacks and certain immigrant groups, even to the extent that some recanted and disclaimed their conclusions from the 1920s.

On the other hand, these black researchers instituted in black schools the same tests they had criticized earlier. These tests were used as scientific and objective mechanisms for sorting and selecting black youth for higher and lower prestige positions in the social order. By employing the tool that had been used to build a body of racist data, blacks were co-opted into an ironic legitimation of the testing instrument.

To understand the complexities of these paradoxical developments, it will be important first to explore briefly some of the variables leading to such a shift in views.

RESEARCH BARRIERS TO SCHOLARSHIP

UNTIL THE MID-1930S, blacks had remained peripheral to the dominant world of experimental psychological research. This has a number of implications for their relatively low visibility in the growing numbers of academic journals. Moreover, this may account for their polemical analysis of and assault against earlier mental testing data when an experimentally based counteroffensive may have been more appropriate for their purposes. An important consideration was that the few existing black social scientists attempted to contravene a psychological phenomenon of testing data interpretation principally from a nonempirical, sociological perspective. This fact calls attention to five problematic concerns they were facing in their historical mission to undercut racist assertions and conclusions made in the name of scientific empiricism.[9]

First, for the potential black researcher, there was "no ready and sympathetic outlet for the publications of the results of his investigations." According to Charles H. Thompson, it took a "considerable amount of stimulation to overcome the inertia and discouragement produced by these circumstances."[10] In fact, *The Crisis* and *Opportunity*, organs of the NAACP and the Urban League, respectively, were the two principal periodicals accessible to and encouraging of the qualitative research black social scientists offered in their critiques of intelligence testing. Outside of the scholarly *Journal of Negro History*, founded in 1916, these popular magazines for the black masses and those published by national, state, and local teacher associations were basically all that black scholars had for dissemination of their ideas.

Second, journals of the dominant culture may therefore have tended to overlook potential contributions of blacks because for so long blacks had been relegated to the limited spheres of defense psychology and propaganda for their racial group.[11] This possibility was exacerbated by what psychologist Francis C. Sumner charged was "the dominant community's unwillingness to accept the fact that blacks are capable of scholarly research."[12]

Third, black scholars' qualitative research did not conform to the rigorous norms of quantitative research that psychological journals, in particular, exacted from contributors. In fact, Bond noted that blacks had been an inert part of the intellectual life, and that through ignorance of the facts, had chosen to be silent rather than to expose their naiveté. "That time has passed," he went on to say. "No longer is there any justification for the silence of the educated Negro. Negroes must act through activity and investigation."[13]

A fourth explanation for this dearth of experimental research in testing by blacks was their lack of training as psychologists. Guthrie cited the existence of only two black psychologists with doctorates in the 1920s. They were Francis C. Sumner and Charles H. Thompson.[14]

A final and compelling factor mitigating the research visibility of blacks was their general isolation from centers of research and scholarship in the segregated South.[15] Having to rely on their employing institutions for whatever financial and administrative support they could muster, black social scientists were in some instances subject to administrative caprice. That is to say, teaching responsibilities often took precedence over research. To the extent that this was so, resources for research and an administrative commitment to sabbaticals, for example, were quite limited.[16]

Torn between conflicting goals of research and teaching, black scholars, according to Ralph Bunche, even more than whites, were

> subject to the munificence of the controlling wealthy groups in the population. . . . Whatever reorganization and reorientation of "Negro Education" is to be contemplated must meet the full approval of these controlling interests. . . . Most Negro schools tread very lightly in the purely academic fields of the social sciences. They cannot afford to take the risk of losing their financial support.[17]

In spite of the artificial social barriers these black scholars encountered, they were nevertheless able to launch a concerted attack against invidious claims by hereditarian social scientists. One avenue by which they overcame these impediments was through their alliances with white social scientists whose research offered these environmentalists a valuable database supportive of their world view.

BLACK-WHITE ALLIANCES

WHITE SOCIAL SCIENTISTS have been a vital component of black scholars' efforts to combat scientific racism. On such issues as mental differences between racial groups, liberal white intellectuals, northern and southern, were particularly important to the success of national conferences addressing the problems of black Americans. They brought scholarly credibility to the Annual Conference for Study of Negro Problems, begun in 1895 by W. E. B. Du Bois at Atlanta University. The list of scholars presenting their views and research at the twentieth conference in 1915 included cultural anthropologists Alexander F. Chamberlain (Clark University) and Franz Boas[18] (Columbia University), as well as anatomists and biologists. All of them spoke against scientific racism, which had even permeated their own universities.[19] By the end of the 1920s, this list of scholars had grown to include such notables as Herbert A. Miller (Ohio State University), Melville J. Herskovits (Northwestern), and Frank J. O'Brien (director of Psychological Clinic in Louisville, Kentucky).

Still under-represented in the field of differential psychology by the 1930s, blacks continued to employ the indigenous medium of popular and professional journals to disseminate the research of sympathetic white scholars. For example, Thomas R. Garth, an experimental psychologist at the University of Denver, discussed his views in "Eugenics, Euthenics, and Race" in a 1930 issue of *Opportunity*.[20] A second essay on race psychology was published in a 1934 issue of the *Journal of Negro Education*.[21] Similarly, Joseph Peterson of George Peabody College for Teachers challenged the naiveté of groups and individuals conducting mental testing research without adequate training.[22] In a similar vein, psychologist and anthropologist Otto Klineberg lent his perspective on environmentalism to the assault against hereditarianism. In his essay "The Question of Negro Intelligence," he charged that "as far as racial differences are concerned, drawing conclusions about the intelligence of two racial groups from the relative standing in intelligence tests, without taking full account of differences in education and background, is no longer a respectable procedure among psychologists."[23] While not totally eschewing notions that test results were based in part on heredity, he did assert that "any interpretations of these results must wait upon a complete analysis of the way in which culture enters into the determination of test performance."[24]

White social scientists also made their contribution to the integration of blacks into the dominant community of scholarship by teaching at black colleges as either guest or emeritus professors from their respective universities. Some examples of this collegial relationship were invitations to Fisk University by Charles S. Johnson to Robert Park (Chicago) and Edward B. Reuter (Iowa). Similarly, Howard W. Odum and Guy B. Johnson broke through the color barrier by inviting James Weldon Johnson, Langston Hughes, and John Hope, president of Atlanta University, to the University of North Carolina's Institute of Human Relations as guest speakers.[25]

Another way in which whites offered their support to black researchers was the protégé-mentor relationship formed when blacks entered northern and midwestern graduate universities to study the social sciences, and psychology in particular. An illustrative case was the lasting relationship between Martin D. Jenkins and Paul Witty at Northwestern University. Jenkins, who later became president of the then Morgan State College, wrote his dissertation on blacks of superior intelligence. His research spawned a number of jointly published articles in a number of reputable mainstream journals.[26] As an editor of *Educational Method,* Witty devoted a 1939 issue to the nature-nurture controversy, publishing an extensive essay by his former student on the intelligence of black youth.[27] As opportunities for graduate study became more prevalent for blacks through the largess of foundations, they were able to develop greater expertise in the social sciences. By the same token, they gained wider exposure to the dominant world of research and scholarship through academic journals. The net result was an apparent higher visibility and respectability, as black and white scholars now interacted on a collegial basis.

BLACK SOCIAL SCIENTISTS DON WHITE COATS OF SCIENCE

ENTERING A NEW PHASE of research, black scholars started with the assumption that factors other than innate mental differences accounted for the relatively lower test scores of blacks. Conducting empirical studies of mental testing, these blacks attempted to establish correlative or causative factors to explain test-score differences.

One aspect of research viewed such determinants as cultural, exemplified by home and school environments, parental educational and occupational levels, and places of birth and length of residence in northern communities. Black researchers reasoned that lower-scoring blacks seemed to be concentrated in the South. There they were subject to conditions of abject social and economic deprivation. There were also those blacks who had been recent migrants to the North. However, they too had not yet attained the benefits of educational and occupational advantages that more established and higher-achieving northern-born blacks had realized.

A second aspect of research took a long and considered look at heredity. The "mulatto hypothesis" led black researchers to examine test-score differences between lighter- and darker-complexioned blacks. Researchers also compared test-score differences between black males and females.

A third area of investigation was the possible influences of testing instruments on test data. Researchers therefore tested for the effects of establishing rapport with the subjects and of the subjects' familiarity with testing artifacts.

THE EFFECTS OF CULTURAL BACKGROUND ON INTELLIGENCE

IN 1916, Terman asked, "Is the place of the so-called lower classes in the social and industrial scale the result of their inferior mental endowment, or is their apparent inferiority mainly a result of their home and school training?"[28] To address this issue, black researchers, in concert with supportive white psychologists, set out to demonstrate that higher intelligence test and school-achievement scores would result from an acculturation process and improvement of environmental conditions. From this ameliorative perspective, they believed that lower-scoring blacks could indeed perform well on mental tests, which had been largely standardized on a northern, urban, middle-class population.

A representative researcher who investigated the effects of length of residence in northern cities and of socioeconomic status (SES) on test performance was Howard Hale Long. A master's student of G. Stanley Hall at Clark University (1916), Long wrote his dissertation at Harvard on the test performance of third graders. He correlated their test scores with that of their socioeconomic status.[29]

Building on the research of McAlpin,[30] Long attempted to establish the relation between intelligence scores and residence of pupils born outside of the District of Columbia (in southern states) and those born and reared in the District.[31] He administered to 4,684 first, third, and fifth graders the Kuhlmann-Anderson Test, which produced the data shown in Table 1.

TABLE 1. MEAN IQ SCORES OF FIRST, THIRD, AND FIFTH GRADERS BORN IN WASHINGTON, D.C., OR IN THE SOUTH

	GRADE 1A MEAN IQ	GRADE 3A MEAN IQ	GRADE 5A MEAN IQ
Entire population	93.35	95.71	92.72
Pupils born in D.C.	94.20	97.59	94.56
Pupils born outside of D.C.	91.35	91.61	89.19

These data indicated that first-, third-, and fifth-grade pupils born in the District scored approximately three, six, and four points higher, respectively, than those born outside the District. Long questioned the 3.39 and 3.03 differences between resident first and third graders and third and fifth graders, respectively. For an explanation of the decrease, he cited studies of rural white children by Jones,[32] who showed a decrease of approximately ten points from age ten to fourteen, and by Wheeler,[33] who showed a twenty-point decline from ages nine to fifteen. Long asserted that the lack of counteracting social-cultural support contributed greatly to the depression of IQ. That is, the decrease was roughly proportionate to the deficiency of environment. He saw this deprivation as progressive, theorizing that

> the social milieu necessary to maintain consistency of the IQ differs at different levels, and that the demand is for increasingly complex and rich environment. In very early childhood, the simple, underprivileged environment may be adequate. As the child becomes older, the same environment may cease to suffice, with the consequence that the IQ drops.[34]

Further examination of third and fifth graders selected and extracted from the total group of 4,684 showed that the average IQ varied only slightly after eight and one-half years of residence in the District; that the influences of the Washington environment on these migrant children was rather marked; and that the average IQ of black elementary school children born in Washington was 95.24, only 4.76 points below the average white elementary school child's score of 100. Granting the fairly equitable educational opportunity for blacks and whites in Washington, he perceived that discrepancies existed in vocational opportunities, wealth, and control of public affairs as major determinants for the difference.

A sequential analysis of the data in the preceding study focused on the correlation of intelligence and socioeconomic status of the native-born, third-grade black children in Washington.[35] In this investigation, Long compared test results from eight different intelligence and achievement tests, administered to the same pupils under controlled conditions. He then compared the results of the two groups from differing socioeconomic backgrounds to discover possible differential behavior with respect to these results. A major assumption underlying his study was that significant differences resulting from several tests administered to the same group of pupils are test differences, but significant differences resulting from the same test given to different groups are group differences.

His methodology consisted of selecting one hundred children for each of the two groups, Group 1 coming from underprivileged circumstances and Group 2 from better home conditions. He then administered the following tests to his third-grade subjects: Stanford-Binet; Pintner-Paterson Short Performance Scale; Dearborn A Intelligence; Kuhlmann-Anderson Intelligence; New Stanford Reading, Paragraph Meaning; New Stanford Reading, Word Meaning; New Stanford Arithmetic, Reasoning; New Stanford Arithmetic, Computation. Long's choice of the Stanford-Binet Test was based on its having been standardized at the ages corresponding to the third-grade pupils.

Shedding some light on the nature of the socioeconomic levels from which Groups 1 and 2 were drawn, Long presented the percentage distribution of parental occupation for each of these groups (see Table 2).

TABLE 2. PERCENTAGES OF OCCUPATIONAL DISTRIBUTION FOR PARENTS OF CHILDREN OF LOWER AND HIGHER SES AND IN GROUPS I AND II

OCCUPATION	% OF BLACK MALES IN D.C. WORKING IN THE OCCUPATION	% IN GROUP 1	% IN GROUP 2
Professional	3	1	11
Skilled	8	6	24
Semiskilled	24	21	29
Unskilled	65	72	37

The tests showed IQ averages of 97 for Group 1 and 112 for Group 2. Long also discovered that the differences in averages between four intelligence tests were not as great as had been supposed. Identifying the presence of thirty-four pupils having IQs of 120 or above, he examined the relationship between their scores and their fathers' occupations (see Table 3).

TABLE 3. CORRELATION OF PARENTAL OCCUPATION WITH IQ SCORES OF 34 PUPILS EARNING 20 OR ABOVE

	% OF CHILDREN WITH 120 OR ABOVE	AVERAGE IQ	NO. CHILDREN
Professional	17.6	137	6
Skilled	23.5	129	8
Semiskilled	35.3	127	12
Unskilled	11.8	124	4
Unknown	11.8	122	4

A significant phenomenon was that more than half of the gifted children whose parental occupations were known came from semi-skilled and unskilled occupations. The average IQ in these occupational classes decreased rapidly from the professional to the skilled group and then very gradually through the other classes, but, as he noted, the differences were so small that they depended on the consistency of the trend rather than on size for significance. These data made Long particularly cautious about making the usual inferences with reference to intelligence within socioeconomic categories, especially about those individuals from economically and culturally deprived circumstances.

INVESTIGATIONS by Long and others[36] reflect the vigorous interest black researchers had developed in intelligence testing. This group attempted to validate the correlative or causative effects of socioeconomic status and length of residence in the North and South on the intelligence-test performance of blacks. Often encountering statistical inconsistencies between their hypotheses and their findings about the effects of these variables, they were considerably circumspect in conclusions they drew from their data. Their research, when interpreted from their environmental perspective, suggested strongly that discrepancies in educational and occupational opportunities between northern and southern blacks were significant variables accounting for differences in test performance. Some black children from lower socioeconomic backgrounds in the North scored from average to very good on their tests. For these black researchers this was further evidence that when blacks were provided educational and occupational opportunities through an improved environment, they might even raise their scores.

REFUTING THE "MULATTO HYPOTHESIS"

THE SUPERIOR PERFORMANCE by some blacks was an enigma for hereditarians' categorical assertions that blacks as a racial group were innately and mentally inferior to whites. For an explanation they had turned to the "mulatto hypothesis." They claimed that "the light negroes were on the average 19.7 percent more intelligent than the dark negroes," due to their admixture of "white blood."[37] For some psychologists this was *prima facie* evidence that the closer so-called inferior groups approximated the "superior racial type," the more intelligent they became. That many black leaders had lighter complexions was further evidence of these claims.[38]

This concern over the effects of racial admixture had come to the very heart of the political questions of racial amalgamation and the preservation of racial purity. Evidence that lighter-skinned blacks scored higher on mental tests than did racial group members of darker hues was useful to some to validate their assumptions of the racial superiority of whites. Moreover, such claims might illustrate what happens to an "inferior type" when infused with "superior qualities." By the same measure, one might also have inferred from the data what happens to superior types when amalgamated with so-called inferior stock. Consequently, once established as scientific evidence, these data could be used in the political and social arenas to legitimize existing antimiscegenation legislation on the grounds that racial mixing would lead to the deterioration of the superior qualities of whites.

The mulatto hypothesis bore significance for black researchers in their vigilant campaign to debunk notions that nature was a greater factor than environment in setting a ceiling on intelligence. Yet another reason for their concern over superior intelligence among blacks was the intellectual's faith in higher-scoring blacks as the last hope for what Bond[39] and Long[40] termed "racial betterment."

Studying thirty exceptional black children in Chicago, selected from varying socioeconomic levels, Bond spearheaded undercutting the mulatto hypothesis.[41] Although not a psychologist, he administered the original Binet-Simon Test and correlated his data with those of Terman in his study of one thousand representative exceptional children.[42] Among five of his highest-scoring subjects, none of whom exhibited signs of white ancestry, Bond found a girl with an IQ of 142.

The possibility that darker-skinned black youth of superior intelligence existed piqued the interest of such psychologists as Martin D. Jenkins. His research attempted to ferret out such pupils, not only to demonstrate that they existed, but to show that their existence was no freak of nature. He suggested a special need for this area of research, as "no study dealing with the educational achievement of exceptional Negro children has yet been published."[43] With the aid of his adviser Paul Witty at Northwestern, Jenkins explored the mulatto hypothesis.

They assumed, based on extensive research, that there are "*differences between the races, and in sub-groups within each race, in test performance. There are no true racial differences in innate or inherited intelligence.*"[44] Jenkins and Witty, therefore, tested the validity of the theory that blacks who made the very highest scores on mental tests were those having a higher percentage of "white blood." Having identified from 8,145 children a total of 103 Chicago school children with an IQ of 120 or above, they compared the racial composition of 63 black children of superior intelligence from this group with that of 1,551 cases reported by Herskovits (see Table 4).

TABLE 4. RACIAL COMPOSITION OF 63 BLACK CHILDREN OF SUPERIOR INTELLIGENCE COMPARED WITH THAT OF 1,551 CASES REPORTED BY HERSKOVITS

CLASSIFICATION*	NUMBER	% OF SUPERIOR NEGRO CHILDREN IN STUDY BY JENKINS AND WITTY	% OF CLASSIFICATION IN HERSKOVITS'S POPULATION
N	14	22.2	28.3
NNW	29	46.1	31.7
NW	10	15.9	25.2
NWW	10	15.9	14.8

* N = no white ancestry; NNW = more Negro ancestry than white; NW = equal amount of Negro and white ancestry; NWW = more white ancestry than Negro.

Nearly one-half of the group of sixty-three was found in the more-Negro-ancestry-than-white classification and approximately one-fourth was found in the no-white-ancestry classification. In comparing the racial composition of black children of superior intelligence with that of the general American Negro population, the researchers noted that "an American 'Negro' may range from practically pure white to pure Negro. ... This group of Negro children of superior intelligence, however, constitutes a typical cross section in racial composition of the American Negro population."[45] Witty and Jenkins also found that twenty-eight of the subjects were "gifted" children, having IQs of 140 and above. The racial mixture of this group corresponded closely to that of the total group.

These and similar supporting data led the authors to conclude that intelligence-test performance was not conditioned by the relative proportion of Negro and white ancestry.

This investigation also drew conclusions from a case study Jenkins had done as part of his dissertation research in 1935.[46] It concerned a nine-year-old black girl whom he had discovered in one of the Chicago elementary schools and who had scored 200 on the Stanford-Binet. In the case study,[47] he had presented a genealogical account of her development. He showed, as Bond had in his 1927 study of an exceptional black girl, that no indications of white ancestry existed on either the maternal or paternal side. Moreover, he found that she had been exposed to museums and centers of culture, and that her home environment had nourished her ability and stimulated her attainment. He later asserted that the provenance of the girl's rare ability could be traced to a fortunate biological inheritance plus a fairly good opportunity for development, and that Negro blood was not always the limiting specter so universally proclaimed.

A second published phase of Jenkins's dissertation concerned itself with identifying the incidence of black children of superior intelligence in a segment of the school population in Chicago.[48] Teachers identified 539 children as "intelligent," and Jenkins administered an abbreviated form of the McCall Multi-Mental Scale to 512 of the nominees, of whom 127 scored above 119. When 103 of these pupils were tested with the Stanford-Binet, their scores ranged from 120 to over 200. Noting that the highest IQ score was obtained by a girl, Jenkins reported that no significant sex differences existed in IQ, the mean IQ for boys being 134.6 (Σ 10.8) and 133.9 for girls (Σ 13.0). Boys, however, manifested superiority in subject-matter attainment, the girls showing superiority to the boys in only two subtests of achievement, namely, spelling and language usage. He found further that while there was a relatively small percentage of children in this superior group who were born in the South (15.6 percent), not a single one had attended a southern school. Jenkins's use of the Sims Score Card for Socio-Economic Status disclosed that the collection of his subjects had come from schools of a somewhat higher socioeconomic level than that of the average black residential area in Chicago. The median educational levels of the fathers and mothers were 13.9 and 12.8 years of schooling, respectively, findings that correlated with those of Terman[49] and Witty.[50]

These data basically confirmed the earlier findings of Witty and Jenkins,[51] whose research at that time focused solely on the educational achievement of twenty-six black children ranging in age from six to thirteen, with IQs of 104 and above. They discovered that there were striking similarities between gifted blacks and other gifted groups. Concluding that their findings were limited to this group and those from a strictly comparable milieu, they also reported that the Stanford-Binet was a valid instrument for identifying potentially capable black pupils in the elementary school.

Jenkins[52] concluded further that the effective functioning of the individual was greatly enhanced when environmental conditions were optimum, and that blacks of superior intelligence emerged when these environmental conditions were propitious. Other significant conclusions were that Negro ancestry was not a limiting factor in psychometric testing, and that abstract mental tests did not measure factors of personality and motivation, which largely determined success in life.

RESEARCHERS such as Jenkins and other black psychologists,[53] studying the influences of racial admixture and gender on IQ scores, had developed a greater degree of testing sophistication than had blacks of the 1920s. These researchers found that racial admixture was not a factor in the attainment of higher test scores. Instead, children with above-average intelligence test scores came from homes of higher SES and attended urban schools having greater numbers of children from similar backgrounds. These youth also showed a greater educational superiority in their verbal skills, which these researchers believed were independent of school experiences. Such patterns conformed closely to those of other gifted children. In the matter of gender differences, there were large and reliable differences in verbal and numerical performances, females being favored on the verbal and males favored on the numerical.[54] These new data were potentially useful to black educators in making decisions about youth and for identifying the talented within the racial group.

EXAMINING THE EFFECTS OF TESTING METHODOLOGY ON INTELLIGENCE

A FEW BLACK RESEARCHERS acquired a particular interest in the effects of test familiarity and rapport between the examiner and the test subject. The earlier predictions of Pressey and Teter had cautioned:

> It may surely be questioned whether tests given by white examiners to colored pupils can give reliable data for a comparison of races. There may even be some doubt as to whether, with examiners of their own race, the reaction of colored children to the test situation would be quite the reaction of white children.[55]

Black researchers' reservations regarding the impact of rapport on test scores were largely speculative until they too began to conduct experiments to determine the validity of such opinions.

One black psychologist of this period who contributed to empirical studies on the effects of rapport was Herman G. Canady. Incorporating the results of his 1928 master's thesis written at Northwestern,[56] Canady's study[57] was one of the earlier assessments by black researchers of the importance of rapport in test administration. Testing the hypothesis that black children do not respond to white examiners as white children do, Canady administered the Stanford Revision of the Binet-Simon Intelligence Scale to forty-eight black and twenty-five white children attending elementary school in Evanston, Illinois. Twenty-three black and eighteen white children were tested first by a black examiner and then by a white examiner. The remaining twenty-five black and seven white children were tested by a white and then by a black examiner in order to measure the gains and losses of both groups of children. The interval between testing ranged from a day to a year.

Canady found that the average increase in IQ for black children was about the same as the average loss of the white children. Only four children in the combined black group gained more than ten IQ points under a black examiner, and only five children of the combined white group lost more than ten points. An average increase of six points in IQ was found for blacks tested by a black examiner and an average decrease of six points for the whites. Canady saw these fluctuations as haphazard rather than progressively upward or downward. He noted further that a change of ten points occurred in 18 percent of the combined groups. These figures seemed to correlate well with those in studies by Terman,[58] which showed on the average a change from the first IQ of about five points up or down, while a change of as much as ten points appeared in only 10–15 percent of all the cases. Holding that the IQ was not characteristic of the individual, Canady concluded that the group-for-group comparison of the performances of black and white subjects failed to reveal any differences that might legitimately be interpreted as due to the personal equation of the examiners.

Similarly, A. S. Scott,[59] Canady's colleague at West Virginia State College, set out to determine the effects of testing methodology on test-score validity by examining seventy-five black Florida high school students who had never before taken a standardized test. He administered the Army Alpha (Beta Form 6), the Otis Self-Administering Test of Mental Ability (Form A), Haggerty Intelligence (Delta 2), and Miller Mental Ability Test (Forms A and B) to randomly selected groups to determine the effects their familiarity with testing might have on their scores. Group 1 improved with practice and time by 8.25 points while Group 2 improved with practice and time 13.92 points. Group 1's average score on Miller Form A was 43.08; Group 2's was 40.28, a 2.8 difference. Over time and with no practice, Group 1's average score on Miller Form B rose to 51.33 while with practice Group 2's average score rose to 54.20, a 2.87 difference. Scott concluded from these data that there are decided advantages in taking standardized tests as a possible method for improving IQ test scores.

CONCLUSIONS by Canady suggested that concerns over possible negative effects of whites' administering tests to blacks and vice versa may have been unduly exaggerated. However, Canady was critical of the problems that arose from extrapolating data drawn from culturally biased exams. He contended that tests were applicable only to individuals of similar backgrounds and those on whom the tests had been standardized. Meanwhile, Scott allayed fears that blacks scored poorly due to factors other than their testing experiences. He concluded that pupils in schools in which tests were often administered had a distinct advantage over the ones who were unfamiliar with these new types of exams.

These and similar conclusions supportive of IQ tests as an educational tool generated an enthusiastic support for testing in black schools and colleges, which were now being affected by the entry of large numbers of pupils from diverse social and economic backgrounds.

WHITE SOCIAL SCIENTISTS RECANT THE HEREDITARIAN CLAIMS

PSYCHOLOGISTS of the 1920s who espoused a hereditarian perspective of mental differences had compiled a compendium of data on the innate inferiority of blacks to whites. Still influenced by Spencerian evolutionary theory, they tended to view their data from a morphological perspective, categorizing racial groups in a vertical hierarchy of "superior" and "inferior" types. This taxonomy categorically stereotyped blacks as inferior, to the detriment of the exceptions who did not conform to the stereotype. The development of scientific tools to quantify degrees of individual and group differences, therefore, greatly enhanced the interest in and prospect for influencing political decisions about blacks and certain immigrant groups on the basis of this "scientific evidence."

Conversely, blacks from all areas of the social sciences seemingly adopted the environmental world view, which placed responsibility for lower test scores of so many blacks on such variables as SES, the cultural bias of the tests, errors in test administration, and logical inconsistencies in assumptions about the subjects. Initially, their enthusiasm for environmental hypotheses was aimed at a reinterpretation of earlier research data supporting a conceptual ideology based on "superior" and "inferior" racial characteristics. Approaching their analyses from a horizontal slant, they inferred from research data that some blacks scored as well as many whites had scored, and some whites scored as poorly as many blacks had. They perceived that this overlapping stemmed more from the greater differences within the racial group than from differences between racial groups.

Significantly, as these social scientists were polarized in an ideological controversy over the effects of nature and nurture on intelligence-test scores, arguments on each side underwent major modification. This paradigm shift causes important questions to be raised in the sociology of knowledge. According to Mannheim, two or more socially determined modes of interpretation within the same society may come into conflict. Through mutual criticism, a new consensus emerges. As a result, "the outlines of the contrasting modes of thought are discovered . . . and later get to be the recognized mode of thinking."[60] These conflicts, Mannheim continues, which emerge in the criticisms, are the consequences of various positions of power within the same social structure.[61]

This suggests that while black environmentalists attempted to discredit hereditarians, exponents of the latter view modified their positions even to the point of recanting many of their conclusions from the 1920s. Meanwhile, as blacks entered powerful policymaking positions in education, they adopted some tenets of the hereditarian viewpoint. Several examples will illustrate these shifting positions and synthesis formation.

Brigham disclaimed earlier racist and nativist assumptions published in his 1923 book *A Study of American Intelligence*. He asserted that "comparative studies of various national and racial groups may not be made with existing tests . . . one of the most pretentious of these comparative racial studies—the writer's own—was without foundation."[62] In opting out of the hereditarian camp, he accused fellow psychologists of a "naming fallacy which easily enables them to slide mysteriously from the score in the test to the hypothetical faculty suggested by the name given the test."[63]

Similarly, Terman, who had held intelligence as constant and unaffected by nurture,[64] later acknowledged that IQ was subject to environmental influences and to errors resulting from inadequate sampling, personal qualities of the examiner, and standardization errors in the tests.[65]

Thompson showed a significant increase in the percentage of one hundred psychologists, thirty educators, and thirty-nine sociologists and anthropologists who now questioned previously accepted notions that test-score differences between racial groups represented actual differences in native mental ability.[66]

Not only were social scientists modifying their individual positions on mental tests, but in 1934 the Social Studies Commission of the American Historical Association was emphatic in its observation that "there seems to be no general agreement among students as to what it is that the test actually measures."[67] It went on to assert that any assumptions that tests are efficient guides for instruction in the social sciences are misconceptions, and that intelligence tests offer no "precise and positive guidance in determining whether a child with a given level of intelligence should be advised to enter a particular occupation or profession irrespective of his economic and cultural circumstances."[68]

BLACKS CO-OPTED INTO IRONIC TEST LEGITIMATION

AT THE OTHER END of the paradigm spectrum, blacks had gained a greater power base and social position in the research community. They had achieved more visibility in the dominant world of scholarship, and had earned, through philanthropic support, more doctorates in the social sciences, especially in psychology.[69] Their work had conformed to the prerequisites of quantitative research and analysis. With the rise in respectability of the study of blacks in American scholarship, and given new commitments from academic journals to publish their research about the racial group, black social scientists now approached the nature-nurture issues from new perspectives.

Long, one of the staunchest and most astute critics of Brigham and his conclusions, had gravitated toward a more sanguine view of heredity, mental differences, and the immense possibilities the tests offered.[70] As a high-level administrator for educational research in the public schools of Washington, D.C., he asserted:

> Today we witness a marked balance and sanity in scientific circles. It is believed that they are two sides of a whole and are functionally inseparable. Through all of the conflict of opinion and assertion, the scientist sees the tremendous importance of both nature and nurture. Notwithstanding their inseparableness, it cannot be gainsaid that nurture is the more fundamental of the

two. This would seem to be self-evident to anyone who has given study to this question.[71]

By accepting the premise that mental tests measured a quality called "intelligence," blacks were co-opted into a legitimation process. Under these terms, they now accepted even more than before the utilitarian value and predictive validity of mental tests as modern, scientific mechanisms of social control for sorting, selecting, and adjusting black youth for their place in a segregated social order. Social adjustment was to be accomplished through testing for curricula differentiation, for predicting the probable success individuals would meet in a given educational and occupational endeavor, and for objectively identifying strengths and weaknesses affecting the individual's academic and social adjustment.

This seemingly paradoxical institutionalization of mental testing in black schools suggests additional concerns in the sociology of knowledge. One compelling issue is the role that the changing power base of black social scientists played in concert with the consensus shift in paradigms. That is to say, intellectuals, an elite corps of scholars, have a special role in interpreting the world both to and for their societies, thereby enjoying what Mannheim termed "a monopolistic control over the moulding of that society's world view." He continues that they are also conditioned by the forces of this "organized collectivity." This means that those seeking access to this collectivity are bound by the modes of thought that sanction the epistemology and ways of knowing implicit in these modes of thought. Mannheim theorized further that these monopolistic intellectual enclaves are, however, subject to the rise of a free intelligentsia, characterized by its increasing recruitment from constantly varying social strata and life situations. This mode of thought of the new order is no longer subject to the regulations and sanctions of the closed order. Instead, in the throes of competing ideologies, in which the fundamental questioning of traditional "truths" begins, the almost unanimously accepted world view that had been artificially maintained through a "closed society" of intellectuals falls apart. With this liberation of the scholar, new ways of interpreting the world are gradually recognized.[72]

As these theoretical propositions are applied to the nature-nurture controversy, then, it is important to note that black social scientists had been peripheral to the centers of control in the dominant intellectual community. In their relatively powerless state, they had little access to national media for knowledge production and diffusion. However, when they gained, through foundation grants, greater opportunities for advanced studies in the social sciences and when they demonstrated their abilities to conform to the rigors of experimental research, for example, they qualified for entry into the intellectual circles formerly monopolized by white social scientists. At that time, the prevailing ideology among social scientists about racial differences was attached to a hereditarian *Weltanschauung*. By issuing into the community of scholars a contrasting and thereby competing ideology, or mode of thought, these black social scientists, with the assistance of whites espousing a similar and supportive world view, ingeniously challenged the traditional "truths" of the dominant intellectual community. Their activities were in part a factor in the reclassification of mental-test data in the minds of many white social scientists. It appears that while these whites were abandoning earlier claims on the influence of nature, blacks, having gained access to the scholarly community, adopted the intelligence test and some of the old assumptions on which it has been earlier administered and interpreted.

The consequences of this paradigm shift and power diffusion, whereby black scholars were co-opted to the "magic of scientism," proved problematic for some members of their own racial group. Significant to the paradigm and power shifts during the 1930s was an apparent agenda for blacks to build a black-controlled, bureaucratic educational superstructure. It would be a vehicle for increasing their influence over the education of blacks.[73]

This agenda, coupled with a southern drive for regional modernization,[74] coincided with new educational opportunities for black youth. In fact, in a major educational building program during the 1920s and 1930s, the number of public secondary schools for blacks had increased by a phenomenal 2,000 percent.[75] By as early as 1930, 79,388 black youth were already enrolled in public high schools in ten southern states.[76] As high schools became more available, increasing numbers of blacks maintained the traditional belief that education and individual achievement would yield greater benefits, diminishing the ascriptive emphasis on family status and race. However, the diverse population of blacks in secondary schools and land grant colleges provided an impetus to the spiritual interest black educators would have in mental testing as an objective method to sort out the "unfit."

Under these terms, black educators were concerned about the better-than-average students who were being subsumed by the large numbers of educationally deprived, lower-achieving pupils. This submerged group, they feared, would not assume the leadership positions to which they had reason to aspire.[77] The plaguing question now facing black *and* white educators[78] was how best to identify and separate this potential leadership class from the masses. For the answer, they turned to scientific empiricism. Illustratively, Ambrose Caliver, Senior Specialist in the Education of Negroes in the U.S. Office of Education, suggested that the application of science to education had moved toward the vanguard of social progress. He further asserted that "we are basing decisions on facts. This can free us from educational moguls. Perhaps the most significant contribution which science has made to our educational thinking is the creation of the concept of the controlling power of facts. . . . It seems therefore, that our only escape from the educational morass in which we find ourselves is more religiously to apply scientific methods in our educational procedures."[79]

Their enthusiasm was exponential. As advisors in their newly instituted graduate schools of education, for example, former mental-testing critics directed the research by elementary and secondary school teachers. As graduate students, these teachers correlated their pupils' achievement, their vocational and educational aspirations, and their personality with intelligence. Moreover, many of these novices to mental-testing research being conducted in their schools were aspiring educational guidance counselors, seeking training and certification in this relatively new profession in the South.[80]

Now situated in positions of educational policymaking, educators such as Horace Mann Bond, dean at Dillard University in Louisiana and once an outspoken opponent of the early research by some white psychologists upon blacks, wrote that

> we may not be getting inferior students into our colleges, but it is time we recognize the fact that our entrants do differ widely in the kind of preparations and abilities represented by such tests as the American Council Psychological Examination. I do not think

this is an occasion to develop a violent anger at intelligence testing, and to say that intelligence testing is "the bunk."[81]

Rhetorical statements by black educators about the "capacities,"
"abilities," "aptitudes," and "natural talents" of black youth are further compelling evidence that blacks had linked intelligence testing,
at least inferentially, to some form of native endowment. Moreover,
what some educators concluded about the "native capacities" of their
students may have been greatly influenced by their views on the age-
old Washington–DuBois debate. Central to this theme was the question of the ends to which blacks should be educated—in an industrial
or a classical tradition. Tragically, their answers to this question were
legitimized by blacks' lower scores on intelligence tests. Teacher
notions of blacks, documented by Frazier,[82] that "blood will tell" ironically ran counter to earlier posits by liberal whites who had asserted on
behalf of blacks that "we do not know just what it tells, nor which
blood it is which speaks."[83]

Progressive educator William A. Robinson, principal of Atlanta University Laboratory School, was acutely aware of such invidious conclusions levied against black youth by members of their own group when
he wrote:

> These men, who are consciously or unconsciously establishing
> their ideas in the thinking of boys and girls, have very little faith
> in the possibilities of Negroes in industry or business or profes-
> sions. They believe far more in the inherent inferiority and per-
> versity of Negro people than in the fact that, as human beings,
> they normally act like all other people and are worthy of equal
> consideration with other human beings. In other words, too many
> of us in Negro schools are accepting without much inner protest
> a deterministic and defeatist philosophy about a group with
> which they are connected and willy-nilly, we are indoctrinating
> our charges with our professional belief.[84]

The distinct conservatism and ideology of some educators'
responses to the social circumstances of their pupils were part and parcel of the power shift these educators had experienced. According to
Bond, such responses of an emerging intelligentsia indicated their

acceptance of "the tastes, ambitions, and viewpoints of the American middle class." Many, Bond noted, who had risen from the ranks of the poorer strata of society had "lost their orientation with the masses of their race . . . having no sympathy with the poor and the weak of their own people."[85] The case of intelligence-testing adoption appears to be a classic illustration of what Odum called "a conquered people dominating the culture of the conqueror."[86] As a manifestation of a social-class rift between the intelligentsia and the masses, black educators held a special interest in intelligence tests as explicit measurement tools and as implicit mechanisms of class distinction and social control. Data gleaned from these tests, which had now been validated by black researchers themselves,[87] aided in the identification and rigid classification, labeling, and sorting of young people whom test users were supposedly assisting.[88]

In conclusion, perhaps the greatest irony of all in this paradigm shift, and the ultimate co-optation of blacks as standard-bearers of a cultural mechanism alien to many of their pupils, was that these intelligence tests generated data that were used by southern attorneys attempting to thwart the 1954 desegregation efforts in *Brown* v. *Board of Education.*

Notes

1. See J. M. Whipple, ed., *Twenty-First Yearbook*, The National Society for the Study of Education (Bloomington, Ill.: Public School Publication Co., 1922); and Lewis M. Terman, ed., *Twenty-seventh Yearbook* (Bloomington, Ill.: Public School Publishing Co., 1928).

2. Terman, *Twenty-seventh Yearbook*, pp. 91–92.

3. Robert M. Yerkes, "Psychological Examining in the U.S. Army," *Memoirs of the National Academy of Science* 15 (1921): 705–42.

4. Paul Popenoe and Roswell Johnson, *Applied Eugenics* (New York: Macmillan, 1918); Henry H. Goddard, *Kallikak Family* (New York: Macmillan, 1919); Edward M. East, "Population," *Scientific Monthly* 10 (1920): 603–24; and Carl C. Brigham, *A Study of American Intelligence* (Princeton, N.J.: Princeton University Press, 1923).

5. Lewis M. Terman, *Intelligence Tests and School Reorganization* (New York: World Book, 1923), pp. 1–31.

6. William B. Thomas, "Black Intellectuals' Critique of Early Mental Testing: A Little Known Saga of the 1920s," *American Journal of Education* 90 (1982): 258–92.

7. Horace Mann Bond, "Intelligence Tests and Propaganda," *Crisis* 28 (1924): 61–64.

8. Joseph Price, "Negro-White Differences in Intelligence," *Opportunity* 7 (1929): 341–43.

9. The black response to twentieth-century studies on the inherent mental inferiority of blacks to whites had its roots deeply embedded in the eighteenth and nineteenth centuries. Benjamin Banneker wrote a defense of the mental capacities of blacks in a letter to Thomas Jefferson in 1792; George Lawrence, a free Negro, stated in 1813 that "vacuous must be the reasons of that man . . . who dared to assert that genius is confined to complexion"; James McCline Smith, a medical doctor responding to racist remarks by Secretary of State John C. Calhoun, pointed to the increasing numbers of blacks attending schools with whites, successfully pursuing their studies at schools such as Dartmouth and Oberlin Western Theological Seminary; and Martin Delany, also a medical doctor and the co-founder of Frederick Douglass's *North Star,* sought to ward off racist assertions in his somewhat nationalistic essay *The Conditions, Elevation, and Destiny of the Colored People of the United States* (1852) in which he discussed the black man's "dashing strides in national achievement, successful adventure, and unsurpassed enterprise" (cited in Herbert Aptheker, ed., *A Documentary History of the Negro People in the United States* [New York: Citadel Press, 1971], pp. 22–26, 57–59, 238–43, 326–27). The American Negro Academy, founded by Alexander Crummell on March 5, 1897, was one of the earlier successful attempts to organize black scholars in a concerted effort at racial uplift through scholarly methods. For more than a quarter of a century (1897–1924), the academy's Occasional Papers waged a battle in the intellectual arena in an attempt to meet the objectives the Academy had set forth, namely, the promotion of literature, science, and art; the fostering of higher education; and the defense of the Negro against vicious assaults. It launched its campaign by publishing a critical essay by Kelly Miller, professor at Howard University and subsequently dean of the College of Arts and Sciences. This essay was in response to Frederick Hoffman's 1896 publication *Race Traits and Tendencies of the American Negro,* a racist analysis about the innate inferiority of blacks and their ultimate extinction. See Alexander Crummell, *The American Negro Academy Occasional Papers* (New York: Arno Press, 1969).

10. Charles H. Thompson, "Why a Negro Journal of Education," *Journal of Negro Education* 1 (1932): 2–3.

11. See John H. Franklin, "The Dilemma of the American Negro Scholar," in *Soon One Morning,* ed. Herbert Hill (New York: Alfred Knopf, 1968), pp. 62–76; and Lionel B. Fraser, "The Dilemma of Our Colleges and Universities," *Opportunity* 15 (1937): 167–71.

12. Francis C. Sumner, "Environic Factors Which Prohibit Creative Scholarship among Negroes," *School and Society* 22 (1925): 294–96.

13. Bond, "Intelligence Tests," p. 64.

14. Robert Guthrie, *Even the Rat Was White* (New York: Harper & Row, 1976).

15. The problem existed not only along racial lines for blacks, but on a regional basis for whites, as manifested in the research conducted by Wilson Gee, director of the Institute for Research in the Social Sciences at the University of Virginia. His study, conducted for the Southern Regional Committee of the National Social Science Research Council, showed that educators in southern white colleges and universities also encountered the effects of scholarly deprivation. As black educators perceived their deprivation in racial terms and in relation to the larger dominant culture, so white southern educators saw theirs in contrast with university educators in the North and West. In writing of this deprivation, Gee noted that "throughout the country, and particularly in the South, there is a distressing lack of funds in the budgets for the universities and colleges allocated to the financing of research in the field of the social sciences. ... On the average, the Southern professor carries a teaching load approximately 30 percent greater than his Northern or Western colleague. ... This heavier teaching load reacts detrimentally upon the effectiveness of the teaching done in the South. Also, it operates severely to limit productive scholarly effort" (Wilson Gee, *Research Barriers in the South* [New York: The Century Co., 1932], pp. 165–69).

16. James Blackwell and Morris Janowitz, eds., *Black Sociologists: Historical and Contemporary Perspectives* (Chicago: University of Chicago Press, 1974).

17. Ralph Bunche, "Education in Black and White," *Journal of Negro Education* 5 (1936): 351–59.

18. Boas had a tempering effect on the unilinear, hereditarian view of racial differences. He advocated the "plasticity of human types," pointing out that differences between the two racial groups were insignificant when compared with the range of variability exhibited in each racial group itself. Citing, for example, the rapid development among "favorably situated social groups" of whites and retarded development among poorer whites, Boas concluded that these differentials did not sufficiently prove mental inferiority among the poorer group. If this was so, he reasoned, this analogy could stand for differences among social groups of blacks and between the two racial groups (Franz Boas, "The Race Problem," *Crisis* 1 [1910]: 22–25).

19. J. A. Bigham, ed., *Selected Discussion of Race Problems*, Publication #20 (Atlanta: Atlanta University, 1916).

20. Thomas Garth, "Eugenics, Euthenics, and Race," *Opportunity* 8 (1930): 206–07.

21. Thomas Garth, "The Problem of Race Psychology," *Journal of Negro Education* 3 (1934): 319–27.

22. Joseph Peterson, "Basic Considerations in Methodology in Race Testing," *Journal of Negro Education* 3 (1934): 403–10.

23. Otto Klineberg, "The Question of Negro Intelligence," *Opportunity* 9 (1931): 366–67.

24. Otto Klineberg, "Cultural Factors in Intelligence Test Performance," *Journal of Negro Education* 3 (1934): 478–83.

25. William B. Thomas, "Howard W. Odum's Social Theories in Transition: 1910–1930," *The American Sociologist* 16 (1981): 25–34.

26. Paul Witty and Martin D. Jenkins, "The Educational Achievement of a Group of Gifted Negro Children," *Journal of Educational Psychology* 25 (1934): 585–97; idem, "The Case Study of B, A Gifted Negro Girl," *Journal of Social Psychology* 6 (1935): 117–24; and idem, "Intra-Race Testing and Negro Intelligence," *Journal of Psychology* 1 (1936): 179–92.

27. Martin D. Jenkins, "The Intelligence of Negro Youth," *Educational Method* 19 (1939): 106–12.

28. Lewis M. Terman, *The Measurement of Intelligence* (New York: Houghton Mifflin, 1916), p. 19.

29. See Howard H. Long, "An Analysis of Test Results from Third Grade Children on the Basis of Socio-Economic Status" (Ph.D. diss., Harvard University, 1933). Long was no neophyte in the field of differential psychology or in critiques lodged against the discipline. In fact, he had been in the vanguard as a mental-testing critic in the early 1920s, when he challenged Carl C. Brigham's research data interpretation from Army Alpha. Long was sensitive to the importance of undercutting conclusions being drawn about the mental inferiority of southern and eastern Europeans, as such inferences, if unchallenged, could then be made of blacks as a racial group. He therefore pointed out several logical inconsistencies in Brigham's conclusions. According to Long, one of Brigham's failures, whether conscious or unconscious, was to give significant attention to the distinction between the average intelligence of northern and southern blacks (12.94 and 10.88 years mental age, respectively), as well as those of white draftees from Georgia, Louisiana, Alabama, and Mississippi. A second critical concern was Brigham's questionable statistical procedure of appealing to the normal curve of distribution of his data as a criterion of its validity. Brigham had estimated the proportion of Nordic, Alpine, and Mediterranean blood in each of the European groups. He had contended that in decrements of five, the percentage of Nordic blood in groups from Sweden, Norway, Scotland, and England ranged, respectively, from 100 to 80 percent. The percentage of Mediterranean blood in these same groups ranged from zero to 20, the English having the highest percentage. Ranking these groups in intelligence, Sweden ranked ninth, Norway tenth, Scotland third, and England first. To this inconsistency, Long responded, "Here is a strong indication of a high negative correlation between race and test scores. England, the most inferior of the white race, takes first rank in intelligence, according to Brigham, who concludes from his discussion that the nordic are markedly superior to the

rest of the white race, and that, of course, the Negro is out of the question. In fact, he views the introduction of the Negro into American institutions as one of the most sinister events in American history" (see Howard H. Long, "Our Bookshelf," *Opportunity* 1 [1923]: 222–23).

30. Alice McAlpin, "Changes in the Intelligence Quotients of Negro Children," *Journal of Negro Education* 1 (1932): 44–49.

31. Howard H. Long, "The Intelligence of Colored Elementary Pupils in Washington, D.C.," *Journal of Negro Education* 3 (1934): 205–22.

32. H. E. Jones, "A First Study of Parent-Child Resemblance in Intelligence," in *Twenty-seventh Yearbook*, ed. Lewis M. Terman (Bloomington, Ill.: Public School Publication Co., 1928), pp. 61–72.

33. L. Wheeler, "The Intelligence of East Tennessee Mountain Children," *Journal of Educational Psychology* 23 (1932): 351–70.

34. Long, "The Intelligence of Colored Elementary Pupils in Washington, D.C.," pp. 213–14.

35. Howard H. Long, "Test Results of Third-Grade Negro Children Selected on the Basis of Socio-Economic Status," *Journal of Negro Education* 4 (1935): 192–212.

36. See also Albert S. Beckham, "A Study of the Intelligence of Colored Adolescents of Different Socio-Economic Status in Typical Metropolitan Areas," *Journal of Social Psychology* 4 (1933): 70–90; Ambrose Caliver, *A Personnel Study of Negro College Students* (New York: Bureau of Publications, Teachers College, Columbia University, 1931); and Herman C. Canady, "The Intelligence of Negro College Students and Parental-Occupation," *American Journal of Sociology* 42 (1936): 388–89.

37. P. C. Young, "Intelligence and Suggestability in Whites and Negroes," *Journal of Comparative Psychology* 9 (1929): 339–59.

38. Edward B. Reuter, "The American Mulatto," *The Annals of the American Academy of Political and Social Sciences* 140 (1928): 36–43; Melville Herskovits, "On the Relation Between Negro-White Mixture and Standing in Intelligence Tests," *Pedagogical Seminary* 33 (1926): 30–42; and idem, "A Critical Discussion of the Mulatto Hypothesis," *Journal of Negro Education* 3 (1934): 389–402.

39. Horace Mann Bond, "Some Exceptional Negro Children," *Crisis* 34 (1927): 257–59.

40. Howard H. Long, "Our Above Average Children," *National Educational Outlook among Negroes* 2 (1938): 8–10.

41. Bond, "Some Exceptional Negro Children," pp. 257–59.

42. Terman, *The Measurement of Intelligence*.

43. Cf. Lillian S. Proctor, "A Case Study of Thirty Superior Colored Children of Washington, D.C." (Master's thesis, University of Chicago, 1929); and Janet Twillinger, "A Study of Negro Children, IQ Above 125" (Master's thesis, Teachers College, Columbia University, 1934).

44. Paul Witty and Martin D. Jenkins, "Intra-Race Testing and Negro Intelligence," *Journal of Psychology* 1 (1936): 179–92. Italics in original.

45. Ibid., p. 189.

46. Martin D. Jenkins, "A Socio-Psychological Study of Negro Children of Superior Intelligence" (Ph.D. diss., Northwestern University, 1935).

47. Witty and Jenkins, "The Case Study of B."

48. Martin D. Jenkins, "A Socio-Psychological Study of Negro Children of Superior Intelligence," *Journal of Negro Education* 5 (1936): 175–90.

49. Lewis M. Terman, *Genetic Studies of Genius* (Palo Alto: Stanford University Press, 1925).

50. Paul Witty, "A Study of 100 Gifted Children," *Bulletin*, University of Kansas 2 (1930): 7.

51. Witty and Jenkins, "The Educational Achievement of a Group of Gifted Negro Children."

52. Martin D. Jenkins, "The Mental Ability of the American Negro," *Journal of Negro Education* 8 (1939): 511–20.

53. See also Long, "Our Above Average Children," pp. 8–10; and Herman G. Canady, "Sex Differences in Intelligence Among Negro College Freshmen," *Journal of Applied Psychology* 22 (1938): 437–39.

54. Herman G. Canady, "Individual Differences and Their Educational Significance in the Guidance of the Gifted and Talented Child," *Quarterly Review of Higher Education Among Negroes* 5 (1937): 202–05.

55. S. L. Pressey and G. F. Teter, "A Comparison of Colored and White Children by Means of a Group Scale," *Journal of Applied Psychology* 3 (1919): 278.

56. Herman G. Canady, "The Effects of Rapport on the IQ: A Study in Racial Psychology" (M.A. thesis, Northwestern University, 1928).

57. Herman G. Canady, "The Effect of 'Rapport' on the IQ: A New Approach to the Problem of Racial Psychology," *Journal of Negro Education* 5 (1936): 209–19.

58. Lewis M. Terman, *The Intelligence of School Children* (New York: Houghton Mifflin, 1919), pp. 135–64.

59. A. S. Scott, "Effects of Familiarity with Standardized Intelligence Tests on Subsequent Scores," *The Bulletin of the National Association of Teachers in Colored Schools* 12 (1932): 12.

60. Karl Mannheim, *Ideology and Utopia* (New York: Harcourt, Brace & World, 1936), p. 253.

61. Ibid., p. 10.

62. Carl C. Brigham, "Intelligence Tests of Immigrant Groups," *Psychological Review* 37 (1930): 158–65.

63. Ibid., p. 159.

64. Lewis M. Terman, "The Influence of Nature and Nurture Upon Intelligence Scores," *Journal of Educational Psychology* 19 (1928): 362–73.

65. Lewis M. Terman, "Personal Reactions of the Committee," *Thirty-Ninth Yearbook* (Bloomington, Ill.: Public School Publishing, 1940).

66. Charles H. Thompson, "The Conclusions of Scientists Relative to Racial Differences," *Journal of Negro Education* 3 (1934): 494–512.

67. Monroe Work, ed., *Negro Yearbook, 1937–1938* (Tuskegee, Ala.: Tuskegee Institute Press, 1938), p. 146.

68. Ibid.

69. See Harry W. Greene, *Holders of Doctorates among American Negroes* (Boston: Meador Press, 1946).

70. Long, "Our Above Average Children," pp. 8–10.

71. Ibid., p. 8.

72. Mannheim, *Ideology and Utopia*, pp. 9–11.

73. A resolution adopted at the 1934 annual conference of the National Association of Teachers in Colored Schools held in Baltimore read: "As long as certain states in this American Union legalize the operation of a dual system of schools, so long as this Association demands that the school for Negro youth be under the immediate control and supervision of members of the Negro race" (see National Association of Teachers in Colored Schools, "Report of the Committee on Resolutions of the NATCS," *The Bulletin* 13 [1934]: 9).

74. See Howard W. Odum, *Southern Regions of the United States* (Chapel Hill, N.C.: University of North Carolina Press, 1936).

75. Work, *Negro Yearbook*, p. 166.

76. Horace Mann Bond, *The Education of the Negro in the American Social Order* (New York: Octagon Press, 1966), p. 206.

77. Cf. Ralph Bullock, "A Study of the Occupational Choices of Negro High School Boys," *Crisis* 37 (1930): 301–03; and Canady, "Individual Differences and Their Educational Significance in the Guidance of the Gifted and Talented Child," pp. 202–05.

78. The justification for and employment of intelligence tests in the southern educational setting of the 1930s were by no means confined to black schools. Margaret V. Cobb at the Institute of Educational Studies, Columbia University, had earlier voiced a similar concern over tracking, through testing, as applied to both blacks and whites in the South. Many of the white youth were of the same socioeconomic status as southern blacks. She noted that "it is obvious that large differences in the intelligence of the population in different states have very important implications for education. Since in some of southern states probably as many as 75 percent of the children cannot, or will not enter academic high schools, the problem of providing other and perhaps new types of training for children from 14 to 18 years of age is most acute in this part of the country" (see M. V. Cobb, "The Limits Set to Educational Achievement by Limited Intelligence," *Journal of Educational Psychology* 13 [1922]: 546–55).

79. Ambrose Caliver, "National Surveys and Education of Negroes," *The Bulletin*, National Association of Teachers in Colored Schools 12 (1933): 10–13.

80. Charles H. Thompson, "Vocational Guidance of Negroes," *Journal of Negro Education* 4 (1935): 1–4.

81. Horace Mann Bond, "The Liberal Arts College for Negroes: A Social Force," *A Century of Municipal Higher Education* (Chicago: Lincoln Printing, 1937), p. 361.

82. Franklin Frazier, *Negro Youth at the Crossways* (Washington, D.C.: American Council on Education, 1940), pp. 91–111.

83. Cited in Herbert Aptheker, ed., *A Documentary History of the Negro People in the United States* (New York: Citadel Press, 1971), p. 925.

84. William A. Robinson, "Vocational Guidance in the Negro Secondary School," *The Bulletin*, National Association of Teachers in Colored Schools 14 (1935): 32–35.

85. Bond, *Education of the Negro*, pp. 148–49.

86. Cited in William B. Thomas, "Howard W. Odum's Social Theories," p. 33.

87. See Witty and Jenkins, "The Educational Achievement of a Group of Gifted Negro Children," pp. 585–97.

88. William B. Thomas, "Guidance and Testing: An Illusion of Reform in Southern Black Schools and Colleges," in *Education and the Rise of the New South*, ed. Ronald K. Goodenow and Arthur O. White (Boston: G. K. Hall & Co., 1981), pp. 169–94.

THE MEASUREMENT OF INTELLIGENCE (1916)

Lewis M. Terman

*I*NTELLIGENCE TESTS *of retarded school children.* Numerous studies of the age-grade progress of school children have afforded convincing evidence of the magnitude and seriousness of the retardation problem. Statistics collected in hundreds of cities in the United States show that between a third and a half of the school children fail to progress through the grades at the expected rate; that from 10 to 15 per cent are retarded two years or more; and that from 5 to 8 per cent are retarded at least three years. More than 10 per cent of the $400,000,000 annually expended in the United States for school instruction is devoted to re-teaching children what they have already been taught but have failed to learn.

The first efforts at reform which resulted from these findings were based on the supposition that the evils which had been discovered could be remedied by the individualizing of instruction, by improved methods of promotion, by increased attention to children's health, and by other reforms in school administration. Although reforms along these lines have been productive of much good, they have neverthe-

Lewis M. Terman (1877–1956) was a Stanford University psychologist, best known for his revision and application of the Binet-Simon Intelligence Tests to army recruits and schoolchildren. Terman popularized the term IQ. This piece is excerpted from his *Measurement of Intelligence* (1916).

less been in a measure disappointing. The trouble was, they were too often based upon the assumption that under the right conditions all children would be equally, or almost equally, capable of making satisfactory school progress. Psychological studies of school children by means of standardized intelligence tests have shown that this supposition is not in accord with the facts. It has been found that children do not fall into two well-defined groups, the "feeble-minded" and the "normal." Instead, there are many grades of intelligence, ranging from idiocy on the one hand to genius on the other. Among those classed as normal, vast individual differences have been found to exist in original mental endowment, differences which affect profoundly the capacity to profit from school instruction.

We are beginning to realize that the school must take into account, more seriously than it has yet done, the existence and significance of these differences in endowment. Instead of wasting energy in the vain attempt to hold mentally slow and defective children up to a level of progress which is normal to the average child, it will be wiser to take account of the inequalities of children in original endowment and to differentiate the course of study in such a way that each child will be allowed to progress at the rate which is normal to him, whether that rate be rapid or slow.

While we cannot hold all children to the same standard of school progress, we can at least prevent the kind of retardation which involves failure and the repetition of a school grade. It is well enough recognized that children do not enter with very much zest upon school work in which they have once failed. Failure crushes self-confidence and destroys the spirit of work. It is a sad fact that a large proportion of children in the schools are acquiring the habit of failure. The remedy, of course, is to measure out the work for each child in proportion to his mental ability.

Before an engineer constructs a railroad bridge or trestle, he studies the materials to be used, and learns by means of tests exactly the amount of strain per unit of size his materials will be able to withstand. He does not work empirically, and count upon patching up the mistakes which may later appear under the stress of actual use. The educational engineer should emulate this example. Tests and forethought must take the place of failure and patchwork. Our efforts have been too long directed by "trial and error." It is time to leave off guessing and to acquire a scientific knowledge of the material with which we have to deal. When instruction must be repeated, it means that the school, as well as the pupil, has failed.

Every child who fails in his school work or is in danger of failing should be given a mental examination. The examination takes less than one hour, and the result will contribute more to a real understanding of the case than anything else that could be done. It is necessary to determine whether a given child is unsuccessful in school because of poor native ability, or because of poor instruction, lack of interest, or some other removable cause.

It is not sufficient to establish any number of special classes, if they are to be made the dumping-ground for all kinds of troublesome cases—the feeble-minded, the physically defective, the merely backward, the truants, the incorrigibles, etc. Without scientific diagnosis and classification of these children the educational work of the special class must blunder along in the dark. In such diagnosis and classification our main reliance must always be in mental tests, properly used and properly interpreted.

Intelligence tests of the feeble-minded. Thus far intelligence tests have found their chief application in the identification and grading of the feeble-minded. Their value for this purpose is twofold. In the first place, it is necessary to ascertain the degree of defect before it is possible to decide intelligently upon either the content or the method of instruction suited to the training of the backward child. In the second place, intelligence tests are rapidly extending our conception of "feeble-mindedness" to include milder degrees of defect than have generally been associated with this term. The earlier methods of diagnosis caused a majority of the higher grade defectives to be overlooked. Previous to the development of psychological methods the low-grade moron was about as high a type of defective as most physicians or even psychologists were able to identify as feeble-minded.

Wherever intelligence tests have been made in any considerable number in the schools, they have shown that not far from 2 per cent of the children enrolled have a grade of intelligence which, however long they live, will never develop beyond the level which is normal to the average child of 11 or 12 years. The large majority of these belong to the moron grade; that is, their mental development will stop somewhere between the 7-year and 12-year level of intelligence, more often between 9 and 12.

The more we learn about such children, the clearer it becomes that they must be looked upon as real defectives. They may be able to drag along to the fourth, fifth, or sixth grades, but even by the age of 16 or 18 years they are never able to cope successfully with the more abstract and difficult parts of the common-school course of study. They may master a certain amount of rote learning, such as that involved in reading and in the manipulation of number combinations, but they cannot be taught to meet new conditions effectively or to think, reason, and judge as normal persons do.

It is safe to predict that in the near future intelligence tests will bring tens of thousands of these high-grade defectives under the surveillance and protection of society. This will ultimately result in curtailing the reproduction of feeble-mindedness and in the elimination of an enormous amount of crime, pauperism, and industrial inefficiency. It is hardly necessary to emphasize that the high-grade cases, of the type now so frequently overlooked, are precisely the ones whose guardianship it is most important for the State to assume.

Intelligence tests of delinquents. One of the most important facts brought to light by the use of intelligence tests is the frequent association of delinquency and mental deficiency. Although it has long been recognized that the proportion of feeble-mindedness among offenders is rather large, the real amount has, until recently, been underestimated even by the most competent students of criminology.

The criminologists have been accustomed to give more attention to the physical than to the mental correlates of crime. Thus, Lombroso and his followers subjected thousands of criminals to observation and measurement with regard to such physical traits as size and shape of the skull, bilateral asymmetries, anomalies of the ear, eye, nose, palate, teeth, hands, fingers, hair, dermal sensitivity, etc. The search was for physical "stigmata" characteristic of the "criminal type."

Although such studies performed an important service in creating a scientific interest in criminology, the theories of Lombroso have been wholly discredited by the results of intelligence tests. Such tests have demonstrated, beyond any possibility of doubt, that the most important trait of at least 25 per cent of our criminals is mental weakness. The physical abnormalities which have been found so common among prisoners are not the stigmata of criminality, but the physical accompaniments of feeble-mindedness. They have no diagnostic significance except in so far as they are indications of mental deficiency. Without exception, every study which has been made of the intelligence level of delinquents has furnished convincing testimony as to the close relation existing between mental weakness and moral abnormality. Some of these findings are as follows:—

Miss Renz tested 100 girls of the Ohio State Reformatory and reported 36 per cent as certainly feeble-minded. In every one of these cases the commitment papers had given the pronouncement "intellect sound."

Under the direction of Dr. Goddard the Binet tests were given to 100 juvenile court cases, chosen at random, in Newark, New Jersey. Nearly half were classified as feeble-minded. One boy 17 years old had 9-year intelligence; another of 15½ had 8-year intelligence.

Of 56 delinquent girls 14 to 20 years of age tested by Hill and Goddard, almost half belonged either to the 9- or the 10-year level of intelligence.

Dr. G. G. Fernald's tests of 100 prisoners at the Massachusetts State Reformatory showed that at least 25 per cent were feeble-minded.

Of 1186 girls tested by Miss Dewson at the State Industrial School for Girls at Lancaster, Pennsylvania, 28 per cent were found to have subnormal intelligence.

Dr. Katherine Bement Davis's report on 1000 cases entered in the Bedford Home for Women, New York, stated that there was no doubt but that at least 157 were feeble-minded. Recently there has been established at this institution one of the most important research laboratories of the kind in the United States, with a trained psychologist, Dr. Mabel Fernald, in charge.

Of 564 prostitutes investigated by Dr. Anna Dwyer in connection with the Municipal Court of Chicago, only 3 per cent had gone beyond the fifth grade in school. Mental tests were not made, but from the data given it is reasonably certain that half or more were feeble-minded.

Tests, by Dr. George Ordahl and Dr. Louise Ellison Ordahl, of cases in the Geneva School for Girls, Geneva, Illinois, showed that, on a conservative basis of classification, at least 18 per cent were feeble-minded. At the Joliet Prison, Illinois, the same authors found 50 per cent of the female prisoners feeble-minded, and 26 per cent of the male prisoners. At the St. Charles School for Boys 26 per cent were feeble-minded.

Tests, by Dr. J. Harold Williams, of 150 delinquents in the Whittier State School for Boys, Whittier, California, gave 28 per cent feeble-minded and 25 per cent at or near the border-line. About 300 other juvenile delinquents tested by Mr. Williams gave approximately the same figures. As a result of these findings a research laboratory has been established at the Whittier School, with Dr. Williams in charge. In the girls' division of the Whittier School, Dr. Grace Fernald collected a large amount of psychological data on more than 100 delinquent girls. The findings of this investigation agree closely with those of Dr. Williams for the boys.

At the State Reformatory, Jeffersonville, Indiana, Dr. von Klein-Schmid, in an unusually thorough psychological study of 1000 young adult prisoners, finds the proportion of feeble-mindedness not far from 50 per cent.

But it is needless to multiply statistics. Those given are but samples. Tests are at present being made in most of the progressive prisons, reform schools, and juvenile courts throughout the country, and while there are minor discrepancies in regard to the actual percentage who are feeble-minded, there is no investigator who denies the fearful role played by mental deficiency in the production of vice, crime, and delinquency.

Heredity studies of "degenerate" families have confirmed, in a striking way, the testimony secured by intelligence tests. Among the best known of such families are the "Kallikaks," the "Jukes," the "Hill Folk," the "Nams," the "Zeros," and the "Ishmaelites."

The Kallikak family. Martin Kallikak was a youthful soldier in the Revolutionary War. At a tavern frequented by the militia he met a feeble-minded girl, by whom he became the father of a feeble-minded son. In 1912 there were 480 known direct descendants of this temporary union. It is known that 36 of these were illegitimates, that 33 were sexually immoral, that 24 were confirmed alcoholics, and that 8 kept houses of ill-fame. The explanation of so much immorality will be obvious when it is stated that of the

480 descendants, 143 were known to be feeble-minded, and that many of the others were of questionable mentality.

A few years after returning from the war this same Martin Kallikak married a respectable girl of good family. From this union 496 individuals have been traced in direct descent, and in this branch of the family there were no illegitimate children, no immoral women, and only one man who was sexually loose. There were no criminals, no keepers of houses of ill-fame, and only two confirmed alcoholics. Again the explanation is clear when it is stated that this branch of the family did not contain a single feeble-minded individual. It was made up of doctors, lawyers, judges, educators, traders, and landholders.[1]

The Hill Folk. The Hill Folk are a New England family of which 709 persons have been traced. Of the married women, 24 per cent had given birth to illegitimate offspring, and 10 per cent were prostitutes. Criminal tendencies were clearly shown in 24 members of the family, while alcoholism was still more common. The proportion of feeble-minded was 48 per cent. It was estimated that the Hill Folk have in the last sixty years cost the State of Massachusetts, in charitable relief, care of feeble-minded, epileptic, and insane, conviction and punishment for crime, prostitution, pauperism, etc., at least $500,000.[2]

The Nam family and the Jukes give equally dark pictures as regards criminality, licentiousness, and alcoholism, and although feeble-mindedness was not as fully investigated in these families as in the Kallikaks and the Hill Folk, the evidence is strong that it was a leading trait. The 784 Nams who were traced included 187 alcoholics, 232 women and 199 men known to be licentious, and 40 who became prisoners. It is estimated that the Nams have already cost the State nearly $1,500,000.[3]

Of 540 Jukes, practically one fifth were born out of wedlock, 37 were known to be syphilitic, 53 had been in the poorhouse, 76

---

[1] H. H. Goddard: *The Kallikak Family.* (1914.) 141 pp.
[2] Danielson and Davenport: *The Hill Folk.* Eugenics Record Office, Memoir No. 1. 1912. 56 pp.
[3] Estabrook and Davenport: *The Nam Family.* Eugenics Record Office. Memoir No. 2. (1912). 85 pp.

had been sentenced to prison, and of 229 women of marriageable age 128 were prostitutes. The economic damage inflicted upon the State of New York by the Jukes in seventy-five years was estimated at more than $1,300,000, to say nothing of diseases and other evil influences which they helped to spread.[4]

But why do the feeble-minded tend so strongly to become delinquent? The answer may be stated in simple terms. Morality depends upon two things: (*a*) the ability to foresee and to weigh the possible consequences for self and others of different kinds of behavior; and (*b*) upon the willingness and capacity to exercise self-restraint. That there are many intelligent criminals is due to the fact that (*a*) may exist without (*b*). On the other hand, (*b*) presupposes (*a*). In other words, not all criminals are feeble-minded, but all feeble-minded are at least potential criminals. That every feeble-minded woman is a potential prostitute would hardly be disputed by any one. Moral judgment, like business judgment, social judgment, or any other kind of higher thought process, is a function of intelligence. Morality cannot flower and fruit if intelligence remains infantile.

All of us in early childhood lacked moral responsibility. We were as rank egoists as any criminal. Respect for the feelings, the property rights, or any other kind of rights, of others had to be laboriously acquired under the whip of discipline. But by degrees we learned that only when instincts are curbed, and conduct is made to conform to principles established formally or accepted tacitly by our neighbors, does this become a livable world for any of us. Without the intelligence to generalize the particular, to foresee distant consequences of present acts, to weigh these foreseen consequences in the nice balance of imagination, morality cannot be learned. When the adult body, with its adult instincts, is coupled with the undeveloped intelligence and weak inhibitory powers of a 10-year-old child, the only possible outcome, except in those cases where constant guardianship is exercised by relatives or friends, is some form of delinquency.

Considering the tremendous cost of vice and crime, which in all probability amounts to not less than $500,000,000 per year in the

---

[4] R. L. Dugdale: *The Jukes*. (Fourth edition, 1910.) 120 pp. G. P. Putnam's Sons.

United States alone, it is evident that psychological testing has found here one of its richest applications. Before offenders can be subjected to rational treatment a mental diagnosis is necessary, and while intelligence tests do not constitute a complete psychological diagnosis, they are, nevertheless, its most indispensable part.

Intelligence tests of superior children. The number of children with very superior ability is approximately as great as the number of feeble-minded. The future welfare of the country hinges, in no small degree, upon the right education of these superior children. Whether civilization moves on and up depends most on the advances made by creative thinkers and leaders in science, politics, art, morality, and religion. Moderate ability can follow, or imitate, but genius must show the way.

Through the leveling influences of the educational lockstep such children at present are often lost in the masses. It is a rare child who is able to break this lockstep by extra promotions. Taking the country over, the ratio of "accelerates" to "retardates" in the school is approximately 1 to 10. Through the handicapping influences of poverty, social neglect, physical defects, or educational maladjustments, many potential leaders in science, art, government, and industry are denied the opportunity of a normal development. The use we have made of exceptional ability reminds one of the primitive methods of surface mining. It is necessary to explore the nation's hidden resources of intelligence. The common saying that "genius will out" is one of those dangerous half-truths with which too many people rest content.

Psychological tests show that children of superior ability are very likely to be misunderstood in school. The writer has tested more than a hundred children who were as much above average intelligence as moron defectives are below. The large majority of these were found located below the school grade warranted by their intellectual level. One third had failed to reap any advantage whatever, in terms of promotion, from their very superior intelligence. Even genius languishes when kept over-long at tasks that are too easy.

Our data show that teachers sometimes fail entirely to recognize exceptional superiority in a pupil, and that the degree of such superiority is rarely estimated with anything like the accuracy which is possible to the psychologist after a one-hour examination. *B. F.,* for example, was a little over 7½ years old when tested. He was in the third grade, and was therefore thought by his teacher to be accelerated in school. This boy's intelligence, however, was found to be above the 12-year level. There is no doubt that his mental ability would have enabled him, with a few months of individual instruction, to carry fifth or even sixth-grade work as easily as third, and without injury to body or mind. Nevertheless, the teacher and both the parents of this child had found nothing remarkable about him. In reality he belongs to a grade of genius not found oftener than once in several thousand cases.

Another illustration is that of a boy of 10½ years who tested at the "average adult" level. He was doing superior work in the sixth grade, but according to the testimony of the teacher had "no unusual ability." It was ascertained from the parents that this boy, at an age when most children are reading fairy stories, had a passion for standard medical literature and textbooks in physical science. Yet, after more than a year of daily contact with this young genius (who is a relative of Meyerbeer, the composer), the teacher had discovered no symptoms of unusual ability.

Teachers should be better trained in detecting the signs of superior ability. Every child who consistently gets high marks in his school work with apparent ease should be given a mental examination, and if his intelligence level warrants it he should either be given extra promotions, or placed in a special class for superior children where faster progress can be made. The latter is the better plan, because it obviates the necessity of skipping grades; it permits rapid but continuous progress.

The usual reluctance of teachers to give extra promotions probably rests upon three factors: (1) mere inertia; (2) a natural unwillingness to part with exceptionally satisfactory pupils; and (3) the traditional belief that precocious children should be held back for fear of dire physical or mental consequences. [. . .]

Are the inferior races really inferior, or are they merely unfortunate in their lack of opportunity to learn?

Only intelligence tests can answer these questions and grade the raw material with which education works. Without them we can never distinguish the results of our educational efforts with a given child from the influence of the child's original endowment. Such tests would have told us, for example, whether the much-discussed "wonder children," such as the Sidis and Wiener boys and the Stoner girl, owe their precocious intellectual prowess to superior training (as their parents believe) or to superior native ability. The supposed effects upon mental development of new methods of mind training, which are exploited so confidently from time to time (e.g., the Montessori method and the various systems of sensory and motor training for the feeble-minded), will have to be checked up by the same kind of scientific measurement.

In all these fields intelligence tests are certain to play an ever-increasing role. With the exception of moral character, there is nothing as significant for a child's future as his grade of intelligence. Even health itself is likely to have less influence in determining success in life. Although strength and swiftness have always had great survival value among the lower animals, these characteristics have long since lost their supremacy in man's struggle for existence. For us the rule of brawn has been broken, and intelligence has become the decisive factor in success. Schools, railroads, factories, and the largest commercial concerns may be successfully managed by persons who are physically weak or even sickly. One who has intelligence constantly measures opportunities against his own strength or weakness and adjusts himself to conditions by following those leads which promise most toward the realization of his individual possibilities.

All classes of intellects, the weakest as well as the strongest, will profit by the application of their talents to tasks which are consonant with their ability. When we have learned the lessons which intelligence tests have to teach, we shall no longer blame mentally defective workmen for their industrial inefficiency, punish weak-minded children because of their inability to learn, or imprison and hang mentally defective criminals because they lacked the intelligence to appreciate the ordinary codes of social conduct.

THE RISING TIDE OF COLOR (1920)

Lothrop Stoddard

O URS IS A SOLEMN MOMENT. We stand at a crisis—the supreme crisis of the ages. For unnumbered millenniums man has toiled upward from the dank jungles of savagery toward glorious heights which his mental and spiritual potentialities give promise that he shall attain. His path has been slow and wavering. Time and again he has lost his way and plunged into deep valleys. Man's trail is littered with the wrecks of dead civilizations and dotted with the graves of promising peoples stricken by an untimely end.

Humanity has thus suffered many a disaster. Yet none of these disasters were fatal, because they were merely local. Those wrecked civilizations and blighted peoples were only parts of a larger whole. Always some strong barbarians, endowed with rich, unspoiled heredities, caught the falling torch and bore it onward flaming high once more.

Out of the prehistoric shadows the white races pressed to the front and proved in a myriad ways their fitness for the hegemony of mankind. Gradually they forged a common civilization; then, when vouchsafed their unique opportunity of oceanic mastery four centuries ago, they spread over the earth, filling its empty spaces with their

Lothrop Stoddard (1883–1950) was a Massachusetts lawyer, author and follower of eugenics. His books include *The Revolt against Civilization* (1922) and *The Rising Tide of Color* (1920), from which this article is excerpted.

superior breeds and assuring to themselves an unparalleled para-
mountcy of numbers and dominion.

Three centuries later the whites took a fresh leap forward. The
nineteenth century was a new age of discovery—this time into the
realms of science. The hidden powers of nature were unveiled, incal-
culable energies were tamed to human use, terrestrial distance was
abridged, and at last the planet was integrated under the hegemony of
a single race with a common civilization.

The prospects were magnificent, the potentialities of progress
apparently unlimited. Yet there were commensurate perils. Towering
heights mean abysmal depths, while the very possibility of supreme
success implies the possibility of supreme failure. All these marvellous
achievements were due solely to superior heredity, and the mere maintenance of what had been won depended absolutely upon the prior
maintenance of race-values. Civilization of itself means nothing. It is
merely an effect, whose cause is the creative urge of superior germplasm. Civilization is the body; the race is the soul. Let the soul vanish,
and the body moulders into the inanimate dust from which it came.

Two things are necessary for the continued existence of a race: it
must remain itself, and it must breed its best. Every race is the result
of ages of development which evolves specialized capacities that make
the race what it is and render it capable of creative achievement.
These specialized capacities (which particularly mark the superior
races), being relatively recent developments, are highly unstable.
They are what biologists call "recessive" characters; that is, they are
not nearly so "dominant" as the older, generalized characters which
races inherit from remote ages and which have therefore been more
firmly stamped upon the germ-plasm. Hence, when a highly specialized stock interbreeds with a different stock, the newer, less stable,
specialized characters are bred out, the variation, no matter how great
its potential value to human evolution, being *irretrievably lost*. This
occurs even in the mating of two superior stocks if these stocks are
widely dissimilar in character. The valuable specializations of both
breeds cancel out, and the mixed offspring tend strongly to revert to
generalized mediocrity.

And, of course, the more primitive a type is, the more prepotent it is.
This is why crossings with the negro are uniformly fatal. Whites,
Amerindians, or Asiatics—all are alike vanquished by the invincible
pre-potency of the more primitive, generalized, and lower negro blood.

There is no immediate danger of the world being swamped by black blood. But there is a very imminent danger that the white stocks may be swamped by Asiatic blood.

The white man's very triumphs have evoked this danger. His virtual abolition of distance has destroyed the protection which nature once conferred. Formerly mankind dwelt in such dispersed isolation that wholesale contact of distant, diverse stocks was practically impossible. But with the development of cheap and rapid transportation, nature's barriers are down. Unless man erects and maintains artificial barriers the various races will increasingly mingle, and the inevitable result will be the supplanting or absorption of the higher by the lower types.

We can see this process working out in almost every phase of modern migration. The white immigration into Latin America is the exception which proves the rule. That particular migration is, of course, beneficent, since it means the influx of relatively high types into undeveloped lands, sparsely populated by types either no higher or much lower than the new arrivals. But almost everywhere else, whether we consider interwhite migrations or colored encroachments on white lands, the net result is an expansion of lower and a contraction of higher stocks, the process being thus a disgenic one. Even in Asia the evils of modern migration are beginning to show. The Japanese Government has been obliged to prohibit the influx of Chinese and Korean coolies who were undercutting Japanese labor and thus undermining the economic bases of Japanese life.

Furthermore, modern migration is itself only one aspect of a still more fundamental disgenic trend. The whole course of modern urban and industrial life is disgenic. Over and above immigration, the tendency is toward a replacement of the more valuable by the less valuable elements of the population. All over the civilized world racial values are diminishing, and the logical end of this disgenic process is racial bankruptcy and the collapse of civilization.

Now why is all this? It is primarily because we have not yet adjusted ourselves to the radically new environment into which our epochal scientific discoveries led us a century ago. Such adaptation as we have effected has been almost wholly on the material side. The no less sweeping idealistic adaptations which the situation calls for have not been made. Hence, modern civilization has been one-sided, abnormal, unhealthy—and nature is exacting penalties which will increase in severity until we either fully adapt or *finally perish.*

"Finally perish!" That is the exact alternative which confronts the white race. For white civilization is to-day conterminous with the white race. The civilizations of the past were local. They were confined to a particular people or group of peoples. If they failed, there were always some unspoiled, well-endowed barbarians to step forward and "carry on." But to-day *there are no more white barbarians.* The earth has grown small, and men are everywhere in close touch. If white civilization goes down, the white race is irretrievably ruined. It will be swamped by the triumphant colored races, who will obliterate the white man by elimination or absorption. What has taken place in Central Asia, once a white and now a brown or yellow land, will take place in Australasia, Europe, and America. Not to-day, nor yet to-morrow; perhaps not for generations; but surely in the end. If the present drift be not changed, we whites are all ultimately doomed. Unless we set our house in order, the doom will sooner or later overtake us all.

And that would mean that the race obviously endowed with the greatest creative ability, the race which had achieved most in the past and which gave the richer promise for the future, had passed away, carrying with it to the grave those potencies upon which the realization of man's highest hopes depends. A million years of human evolution might go uncrowned, and earth's supreme life-product, man, might never fulfil his potential destiny. This is why we to-day face "The Crisis of the Ages."

To many minds the mere possibility of such a catastrophe may seem unthinkable. Yet a dispassionate survey of the past shows that it is not only possible but probable if present conditions go on unchanged. The whole history of life, both human and subhuman, teaches us that nature will not condone disobedience; that, as I have already phrased it, "no living being stands above her law, and protozoön or demigod, if they transgress, alike must die."

Now we have transgressed; grievously transgressed—and we are suffering grievous penalties. But pain is really kind. Pain is the importunate tocsin which rouses to dangerous realities and spurs to the seeking of a cure.

As a matter of fact we are confusedly aware of our evil plight, and legion are the remedies to-day proposed. Some of these are mere quack nostrums. Others contain valuable remedial properties. To be sure, there is probably no *one* curative agent, since our troubles are complex and magic elixirs heal only in the realm of dreams. But one element should be fundamental to all the compoundings of the social pharmacopœia. That element is *blood*.

It is clean, virile, genius-bearing blood, streaming down the ages through the unerring action of heredity, which, in anything like a favorable environment, will multiply itself, solve our problems, and sweep us on to higher and nobler destinies. What we to-day need above all else is a changed attitude of mind—a recognition of the supreme importance of heredity, not merely in scientific treatises but in the practical ordering of the world's affairs. We are where we are to-day primarily because we have neglected this vital principle; because we have concerned ourselves with dead things instead of with living beings.

This disregard of heredity is perhaps not strange. It is barely a generation since its fundamental importance was scientifically established, and the world's conversion to even the most vital truth takes time. In fact, we also have much to unlearn. A little while ago we were taught that all men were equal and that good conditions could, of themselves, quickly perfect mankind. The seductive charm of these dangerous fallacies lingers and makes us loath to put them resolutely aside.

Fortunately, we now know the truth. At last we have been vouchsafed clear insight into the laws of life. We now know that men are not, and never will be, equal. We know that environment and education can develop only what heredity brings. We know that the acquirements of individuals are either not inherited at all or are inherited in so slight a degree as to make no perceptible difference from generation to generation. In other words: we now know that heredity is paramount in human evolution, all other things being secondary factors.

This basic truth is already accepted by large numbers of thinking men and women all over the civilized world, and if it becomes firmly fixed in the popular consciousness it will work nothing short of a revolution in the ordering of the world's affairs.

For race-betterment is such an intensely *practical* matter! When peoples come to realize that the *quality* of the population is the source of all their prosperity, progress, security, and even existence; when they realize that a single genius may be worth more in actual dollars than a dozen gold-mines, while, conversely, racial decline spells material impoverishment and decay; when such things are really believed, we shall see much-abused "eugenics" actually moulding social programmes and political policies. Were the white world to-day really convinced of the supreme importance of race-values, how long would it take to stop debasing immigration, reform social abuses that are killing out the fittest strains, and put an end to the feuds which have just sent us through hell and threaten to send us promptly back again?

Well, perhaps our change of heart may come sooner than now appears. The horrors of the war, the disappointment of the peace, the terror of Bolshevism, and the rising tide of color have knocked a good deal of the nonsense out of us, and have given multitudes a hunger for realities who were before content with a diet of phrases. Said wise old Benjamin Franklin: "Dame Experience sets a dear school, but fools will have no other." Our course at the dame's school is already well under way and promises to be exceeding dear.

Only, it is to be hoped our education will be rapid, for time presses and the hour is grave. If certain lessons are not learned and acted upon shortly, we may be overwhelmed by irreparable disasters and all our dear schooling will go for naught.

What are the things we *must* do promptly if we would avert the worst? This "irreducible minimum" runs about as follows:

First and foremost, the wretched Versailles business will have to be thoroughly revised. As it stands, dragon's teeth have been sown over both Europe and Asia, and unless they be plucked up they will presently grow a crop of cataclysms which will seal the white world's doom.

Secondly, some sort of provisional understanding must be arrived at between the white world and renascent Asia. We whites will have to abandon our tacit assumption of permanent domination over Asia, while Asiatics will have to forgo their dreams of migration to white lands and penetration of Africa and Latin America. Unless some such understanding is arrived at, the world will drift into a gigantic race-war—and genuine race-war means war to the knife. Such a hideous catastrophe should be abhorrent to both sides. Nevertheless, Asia should be given clearly to understand that we cannot permit either migration to white lands or penetration of the non-Asiatic tropics, and that for these matters we prefer to fight to a finish rather than yield to a finish—because our "finish" is precisely what surrender on these points would mean.

Thirdly, even within the white world, migrations of lower human types like those which have worked such havoc in the United States must be rigorously curtailed. Such migrations upset standards, sterilize better stocks, increase low types, and compromise national futures more than war, revolutions, or native deterioration.

Such are the things which simply *must* be done if we are to get through the next few decades without convulsions which may render impossible the white world's recovery.

These things will not bring in the millennium. Far from it. Our ills are so deep-seated that in nearly every civilized country racial values would continue to depreciate even if all three were carried into effect. But they will at least give our wounds a chance to heal, and they will give the new biological revelation time to permeate the popular consciousness and transfuse with a new idealism our materialistic age. As the years pass, the supreme importance of heredity and the supreme value of superior stocks will sink into our being, and we will acquire a true *race*-consciousness (as opposed to national or cultural consciousness) which will bridge political gulfs, remedy social abuses, and exorcise the lurking spectre of miscegenation.

In those better days, we or the next generation will take in hand the problem of race-depreciation, and segregation of defectives and abolition of handicaps penalizing the better stocks will put an end to our present racial decline. By that time biological knowledge will have so increased and the popular philosophy of life will have been so idealized that it will be possible to inaugurate positive measures of race-betterment which will unquestionably yield the most wonderful results.

Those splendid tasks are probably not ours. They are for our successors in a happier age. But we have our task, and God knows it is a hard one—the salvage of a shipwrecked world! Ours it is to make possible that happier age, whose full-fruits we shall never see.

Well, what of it? Does not the new idealism teach us that we are links in a vital chain, charged with high duties both to the dead and the unborn? In very truth we are at once sons of sires who sleep in calm assurance that we will not betray the trust they confided to our hands, and sires of sons who in the Beyond wait confident that we shall not cheat them of their birthright.

Let us, then, act in the spirit of Kipling's immortal lines:

"Our Fathers in a wondrous age,
Ere yet the Earth was small,
Ensured to us an heritage,
And doubted not at all
That we, the children of their heart,
Which then did beat so high,
In later time should play like part
For our posterity.

Then, fretful, murmur not they gave
So great a charge to keep,
Nor dream that awestruck Time shall save
Their labor while we sleep.
Dear-bought and clear, a thousand year
Our fathers' title runs.
Make we likewise their sacrifice,
Defrauding not our sons."[1]

---

[1] Rudyard Kipling, "The Heritage." Dedicatory poem to the volume entitled "The Empire and the Century" (London, 1905), the volume being a collaboration by prominent British writers.

THE MENTAL AGE OF AMERICANS (1922)

Walter Lippmann

A STARTLING BIT of news has recently been unearthed and is now being retailed by the credulous to the gullible. "The *average* mental age of Americans," says Mr. Lothrop Stoddard in *The Revolt Against Civilization*, "is only about fourteen."

Mr. Stoddard did not invent this astonishing conclusion. He found it ready-made in the writings of a number of other writers. They in their turn got the conclusion by misreading the data collected in the army intelligence tests. For the data themselves lead to no such conclusion. It is impossible that they should. It is quite impossible for honest statistics to show that the average adult intelligence of a representative sample of the nation is that of an immature child in that same nation. The average adult intelligence cannot be less than the average adult intelligence, and to anyone who knows what the words "mental age" mean, Mr. Stoddard's remark is precisely as silly as if he had written that the average mile was three-quarters of a mile long.

Walter Lippmann (1889–1974) was a journalist and critic. In 1958 he received a special Pulitzer Prize citation. His books include *A Preface to Politics* (1913) and *The Good Society* (1937). This article and the following piece are two of six essays he wrote for *The New Republic* on IQ testing. "The Mental Age of Americans" appeared in the issue of October 25, 1922, and "A Future for the Tests" in the issue of November 29, 1922, of *The New Republic*.

The trouble is that Mr. Stoddard uses the words "mental age" without explaining either to himself or to his readers how the conception of "mental age" is derived. He was in such an enormous hurry to predict the downfall of civilization that he could not pause long enough to straighten out a few simple ideas. The result is that he snatches at a few scarifying statistics and uses them as a base upon which to erect a glittering tower of generalities. For the statement that the average mental age of Americans is only about fourteen is not inaccurate. It is not incorrect. It is nonsense.

Mental age is a yardstick invented by a school of psychologists to measure "intelligence." It is not easy, however, to make a measure of intelligence and the psychologists have never agreed on a definition. This quandary presented itself to Alfred Binet. For years he had tried to reach a definition of intelligence and always he had failed. Finally he gave up the attempt, and started on another tack. He then turned his attention to the practical problem of distinguishing the "backward" child from the "normal" child in the Paris schools. To do this he had to know what was a normal child. Difficult as this promised to be, it was a good deal easier than the attempt to define intelligence. For Binet concluded, quite logically, that the standard of a normal child of any particular age was something or other which an arbitrary percentage of children of that age could do. Binet therefore decided to consider "normal" those abilities which were common to between 65 and 75 percent of the children of a particular age. In deciding on these percentages, he thus decided to consider at least 25 percent of the children as backward. He might just as easily have fixed a percentage which would have classified 10 percent of the children as backward, or 50 percent.

Having fixed a percentage which he would henceforth regard as "normal," he devoted himself to collecting questions, stunts, and puzzles of various sorts, hard ones and easy ones. At the end he settled upon fifty-four tests, each of which he guessed and hoped would test some element of intelligence; all of which together would test intelligence as a whole. Binet then gave these tests in Paris to 200 school children who ranged from three to fifteen years of age. Whenever he found a test that about 65 percent of the children of the same age could pass he called that a Binet test of intelligence for that age. Thus a mental age of seven years was the ability to do all the tests which 65 to 75 percent of a small group of seven-year-old Paris schoolchildren had shown themselves able to do.

This was a promising method, but of course the actual tests rested on a very weak foundation indeed. Binet himself died before he could carry his idea much further, and the task of revision and improvement was then transferred to Stanford University. The Binet scale worked badly in California. The same puzzles did not give the same results in California as in Paris. So about 1910, Professor L. M. Terman undertook to revise them. He followed Binet's method. Like Binet he would guess at a stunt which might indicate intelligence, and then try it out on about 2,300 people of various ages, including 1,700 children "in a community of average social status." By editing, rearranging, and supplementing the original Binet tests he finally worked out a series of tests for each age which the average child of that age in about one hundred Californian children could pass.

The puzzles which this average child among one hundred Californian children of the same age about the year 1913 could answer are the yardstick by which mental age is measured in what is known as the Stanford Revision of the Binet-Simon scale. Each correct answer gives a credit of two months' mental age. So if a child of seven can answer all tests up to the seven-year-old tests perfectly, and cannot answer any of the eight-year-old tests, his total score is seven years. He is said to test "at age," and his "intelligence quotient" or "IQ" is unity or 100 percent. Anybody's IQ can be figured, therefore, by dividing his mental age by his actual age. A child of five who tests at four years' mental age has an IQ of 80 ($\frac{4}{5} = .80$). A child of five who tests at six years' mental age has an IQ of 120 ($\frac{6}{5} = 1.20$).

The aspect of all this which matters is that mental age is simply the average performance with certain rather arbitrary problems. The thing to keep in mind is that all the talk about "a mental age of fourteen" goes back to the performance of eighty-two California school children in 1913–1914. Their success and failures on the days they happened to be tested have become embalmed and consecrated as the measure of human intelligence. By means of that measure writers like Mr. Stoddard fix the relative values of all the peoples of the earth and of all social classes within the nations. They don't know they are doing this, however, because Mr. Stoddard at least is quite plainly taking everything at second hand.

However, I am willing for just a moment to grant that Mr. Terman in California has worked out a test for the different ages of a growing child. But I insist that anyone who uses the words "mental age" should remember that Mr. Terman reached his test by seeing what the average child of an age group could do. If his group is too small or is untypical, his test is in the same measure inaccurate.

Remembering this, we come to the army tests. Here we are dealing at once with men all of whom are over the age of the mental scale. For the Stanford-Binet scale ends at "sixteen years." It assumes that intelligence stops developing at sixteen, and everybody sixteen and over is therefore treated as "adult" or as "superior adult." Now the adult Stanford-Binet tests were "standardized chiefly on the basis of results from 400 adults of moderate success and of very limited educational advantages" and also thirty-two high school pupils from sixteen to twenty years of age. Among these adults, those who tested close together have the honor of being considered the standard of average adult intelligence.

Before the army tests came along, when anyone talked about the average adult he was talking about a few hundred Californians. The army tested about 1,700,000 adult men. But it did not use the Binet system of scoring by mental ages. It scored by a system of points which we need not stop to describe. Naturally enough, everyone interested in mental testing wanted to know whether the army tests agreed in any way with the Stanford-Binet mental-age standard. So by another process, which need also not be described, the results of the army tests were translated into Binet terms. The result of this translation is the table which has so badly misled poor Mr. Stoddard. This table showed that the average of the army did not agree at all with the average of Mr. Terman's Californians. There were then two things to do. One was to say that the average intelligence of 1,700,000 men was a more representative average than that of 400 men. The other was to pin your faith to the 400 men and insist they gave the true average.

Mr. Stoddard chose the average of 400 rather than the average of 1,700,000 because he was in such haste to write his own book that he never reached page 785 of *Psychological Examining in the United States Army,* the volume of the data edited by Major Yerkes.* He would have found there a clear warning against the blunder he was about to commit, the blunder of treating the average of a small number of instances as more valid than the average of a large number.

But instead of pausing to realize that the army tests had knocked the Stanford-Binet measure of adult intelligence into a cocked hat, he wrote his book in the belief that the Stanford measure is as good as it ever was. This is not intelligent. It leads one to suspect that Mr. Stoddard is a propagandist with a tendency to put truth not in the first place but in the second. It leads one to suspect, after such a beginning, that the real promise and value of the investigation which Binet started is in danger of gross perversion by muddleheaded and prejudiced men.

---

* "For norms of adult intelligence, the results of the Army examinations are undoubtedly the most representative. It is customary to say that the mental age of the average adult is about sixteen years. This figure is based, however, upon examinations of only 62 persons. . . . This group is too small to give very reliable results and is furthermore probably not typical." *Psychological Examining in the United States Army,* p. 785.

The reader will note that Major Yerkes and his colleagues assert that the Stanford standard of adult intelligence is based on only sixty-two cases. This is a reference to page 49 of Mr. Terman's book on the Stanford Revision of the Binet-Simon Scale. But page 13 of the same book speaks of 400 adults being the basis on which the adult tests were standardized. I have used this larger figure because it is more favorable to the Stanford-Binet scale.

It should also be remarked that the army figures are not the absolute figures but the results of a "sample of the white draft" consisting of nearly 100,000 recruits. In strictest accuracy, we ought to say then that the disagreement between army and Stanford-Binet results derives from conclusions drawn from 100,000 cases as against 400.

If these 100,000 recruits are not a fair sample of the nation, as they probably are not, then in addition to saying that the army tests contradict the Stanford-Binet Scale, we ought to add that the army tests are themselves no reliable basis for measuring the average American mentality.

A FUTURE FOR THE TESTS (1922)

Walter Lippmann

H OW DOES IT HAPPEN that men of science can presume to dogmatize about the mental qualities of the germplasm when their own observations begin at four years of age? Yet this is what the chief intelligence testers, led by Professor Terman, are doing. Without offering any data on all that occurs between conception and the age of kindergarten, they announce on the basis of what they have got out of a few thousand questionnaires that they are measuring the hereditary mental endowment of human beings. Obviously, this is not a conclusion obtained by research. It is a conclusion planted by the will to believe. It is, I think, for the most part unconsciously planted. The scoring of the tests itself favors an uncritical belief that intelligence is a fixed quantity in the germplasm and that, no matter what the environment, only a predetermined increment of intelligence can develop from year to year. For the result of a test is not stated in terms of intelligence, but as a percentage of the average for that age level. These percentages remain more or less constant. Therefore, if a child shows an IQ of 102, it is easy to argue that he was born with an IQ of 102.

There is here, I am convinced, a purely statistical illusion, which breaks down when we remember what IQ means. A child's IQ is his percentage of passes in the test which the average child of a large group of his own age has passed. The IQ measures his place in respect to the average at any year. But it does not show the rate of his growth

566

from year to year. In fact, it tends rather to conceal the fact that the creative opportunities in education are greatest in early childhood. It conceals the fact, which is of such far-reaching importance, that because the capacity to form intellectual habits decreases as the child matures, the earliest education has a cumulative effect on the child's future. All this the static percentages of the IQ iron out. They are meant to iron it out. It is the boast of the inventors of the IQ that "the distribution of intelligence maintains a certain constancy from five to thirteen or fourteen years of age, *when the degree of intelligence is expressed in terms of the intelligence quotient.*"* The intention is to eliminate the factor of uneven and cumulative growth, so that there shall be always a constant measure by which to classify children in classrooms.

This, as I have pointed out, may be useful in school administration, but it can turn out to be very misleading for an unwary theorist. If instead of saying that Johnny gained thirty pounds one year, twenty-five the next, and twenty the third, you said that measured by the average gain for children of his age, Johnny's weight quotients were 101, 102, 101, you might, unless you were careful, begin to think that Johnny's germplasm weighed as much as he does today. And if you dodged that mistake, you might nevertheless come to think that since Johnny classified year after year in the same position, Johnny's diet had no influence on his weight.

The effect of the intelligence quotient on a tester's mind may be to make it *seem* as if intelligence were constant, whereas it is only the statistical position in large groups which is constant. This illusion of constancy has, I believe, helped seriously to prevent men like Terman from appreciating the variability of early childhood. Because in the mass the percentages remain fixed, they tend to forget how in each individual case there were offered creative opportunities which the parents and nurse girls improved or missed or bungled. The whole more or less blind drama of childhood, where the habits of intelligence are formed, is concealed in the mental test. The testers themselves become callous to it. What their foot rule does not measure soon ceases to exist for them, and so they discuss heredity in schoolchildren before they have studied the education of infants.

* *Stanford Revision of Binet-Simon Scale*, p. 50.

But of course, no student of human motives will believe that this revival of predestination is due to a purely statistical illusion. He will say with Nietzsche that "every impulse is imperious, and, as *such*, attempts to philosophize." And so behind the will to believe he will expect to find some manifestation of the will to power. He will not have to read far in the literature of mental testing to discover it. He will soon see that the intelligence test is being sold to the public on the basis of the claim that it is a device which will measure pure intelligence, whatever that may be, as distinguished from knowledge and acquired skill.

This advertisement is impressive. If it were true, the emotional and the worldly satisfactions in store for the intelligence tester would be very great. If he were really measuring intelligence, and if intelligence were a fixed hereditary quantity, it would be for him to say not only where to place each child in school, but also which children should go to high school, which to college, which into the professions, which into the manual trades and common labor. If the tester could make good his claim, he would soon occupy a position of power which no intellectual has held since the collapse of theocracy. The vista is enchanting, and even a little of the vista is intoxicating enough. If only it could be proved, or at least believed, that intelligence is fixed by heredity, and that the tester can measure it, what a future to dream about! The unconscious temptation is too strong for the ordinary critical defenses of the scientific methods. With the help of a subtle statistical illusion, intricate logical fallacies and a few smuggled obiter dicta, self-deception as the preliminary to public deception is almost automatic.

The claim that we have learned how to *measure hereditary intelligence* has no scientific foundation. We cannot measure intelligence when we have never defined it, and we cannot speak of its hereditary basis after it has been indistinguishably fused with a thousand educational and environmental influences from the time of conception to the school age. The claim that Mr. Terman or anyone else is measuring hereditary intelligence has no more scientific foundation than a hundred other fads—vitamins and glands and amateur psychoanalysis and correspondence courses in will power—and it will pass with them into that limbo where phrenology and palmistry and characterology and the other Babu sciences are to be found. In all of these, there was some admixture of primitive truth which the conscientious scientist retains long after the wave of popular credulity has spent itself.

So, I believe, it will be with mental testing. Gradually, under the impact of criticism, the claim will be abandoned that a device has been invented for measuring native intelligence. Suddenly it will dawn upon the testers that this is just another form of examination, differing in degree rather than in kind from Mr. Edison's questionnaire or a college entrance examination. It may be a better form of examination than these, but it is the same sort of thing. It tests, as they do, an unanalyzed mixture of native capacity, acquired habits and stored-up knowledge, and no tester knows at any moment which factor he is testing. He is testing the complex result of a long and unknown history, and the assumption that his questions and his puzzles can in fifty minutes isolate abstract intelligence is, therefore, vanity. The ability of a twelve-year-old child to define pity or justice and to say what lesson the story of the fox and crow "teaches" may be a measure of his total education, but it is no measure of the value or capacity of his germplasm.

Once the pretensions of this new science are thoroughly defeated by the realization that these are not "intelligence tests" at all nor "measurements of intelligence," but simply a somewhat more abstract kind of examination, their real usefulness can be established and developed. As examinations they can be adapted to the purposes in view, whether it be to indicate the feeble-minded for segregation, or to classify children in school, or to select recruits from the army for officers' training camps, or to pick bank clerks. Once the notion is abandoned that the tests reveal pure intelligence, specific tests for specific purposes can be worked out.

A general measure of intelligence valid for all people everywhere at all times may be an interesting toy for the psychologist in his laboratory. But just because the tests are so general, just because they are made so abstract in the vain effort to discount training and knowledge, the tests are by that much less useful for the practical needs of school administration and industry. Instead, therefore, of trying to find a test which will with equal success discover artillery officers, Methodist ministers, and branch managers for the rubber business, the psychologists would far better work out special and specific examinations for artillery officers, divinity school candidates, and branch managers in the rubber business. On that line they may ultimately make a serious contribution to a civilization which is constantly searching for more successful ways of classifying people for specialized jobs. And in the meantime the psychologists will save themselves from the reproach of having opened up a new chance for quackery in a field where quacks breed like rabbits, and they will save themselves from the humiliation of having furnished doped evidence to the exponents of the New Snobbery.

A STUDY OF AMERICAN INTELLIGENCE (1923)

Carl C. Brigham

T HE QUESTION of the differences that may exist between the various races of man, or between various sub-species of the same race, or between political aggregations of men in nationality groups may easily become the subject of the most acrimonious discussion. The anthropologists of France and Germany, shortly after the close of the Franco-Prussian war, fought another national war on a small scale. It is difficult to keep racial hatreds and antipathies out of the most scholarly investigations in this field. The debate becomes especially bitter when mental traits are discussed. No one can become very indignant on finding his race classified by its skull dimensions, stature, or hair color, but let a person discover the statement that his race is unintelligent or emotionally unstable, and he is immediately ready to do battle.

Until recent years we have had no methods available for measuring mental traits scientifically, so that the literature on race differences consists largely of opinions of students who are very apt to become biased, when, leaving the solid realm of physical measurements, they enter the more intangible field of estimating mental capacity.

Carl C. Brigham (1890–1943) was a psychology professor at Princeton University. He is author of *Two Studies in Mental Tests* (1917) and *A Study of American Intelligence* (1923), from which this piece is excerpted.

Gradually, however, various investigators using more or less refined psychological measurements commenced to assemble a body of data that will some day reach respectable proportions. The status of the psychological investigations of race differences up to 1910 has been admirably summarized by Woodworth.[1] Since 1910, we have witnessed in this country a remarkable development in methods of intelligence testing, and these methods have been applied to the study of race differences. Scattered investigations report and compare the intelligence scores of children of white, negro, or Indian parentage, and sometimes the scores of various nationality or nativity groups. The results of these investigations are, however, almost impossible to correlate, for they have been made by different methods, by different measuring scales, on children of a wide variety of chronological ages, and above all, on comparatively small groups of subjects, so that conclusions based on the studies have no high degree of reliability.

For our purposes in this country, the army mental tests give us an opportunity for a national inventory of our own mental capacity, and the mental capacity of those we have invited to live with us. We find reported in Memoir XV of the National Academy of Sciences[2] the intelligence scores of about 81,000 native born Americans, 12,000 foreign born individuals, and 23,000 negroes. From the standpoint of the numbers examined, we have here an investigation which, of course, surpasses in reliability all preceding investigations, assembled and correlated, a hundred fold. These army data constitute the first really significant contribution to the study of race differences in mental traits. They give us a scientific basis for our conclusions.

When we consider the history of man during the half million years which have probably elapsed since the time of the erect primate, *Pithecanthropus*, the temporary political organizations, such as Greece, Rome, and our modern national groups, become of minor importance compared with the movements of races and peoples that have occurred. The tremendous expansion of the Alpine race at the end of the Neolithic and the beginning of the Bronze Period, the submer-

---

[1] R. S. Woodworth. *Racial Differences in Mental Traits,* Science, New Series, Vol. 31, pp. 171–186.
[2] *Psychological Examining in the United States Army.* Edited by Robert M. Yerkes. Washington: Government Printing Office, 1921, 890 pp.

gence of this race by the Nordics in the 2000 years preceding the Christian era, and the subsequent peaceful re-conquest of Eastern Europe by the Alpine Slavs from the Dark Ages on, represent an historical movement in comparison with which the Great World War of 1914 resembles a petty family squabble.

If the history of the United States could be written in terms of the movements of European peoples to this continent, the first stage represents a Nordic immigration, for New England in Colonial times was populated by an almost pure Nordic type. There followed then a period of Nordic expansion. The next great movement consisted of the migrations of Western European Mediterraneans and Alpines from Ireland and Germany, a movement which started about 1840, and which had practically stopped by 1890. Since there is a considerable proportion of Nordic blood in Ireland and Germany, we should not regard the original Nordic immigration as a movement which stopped suddenly, but merely as having dwindled to two-fifths or one-half of the total racial stock coming here between 1840 and 1890. The third and last great movement consisted of migrations of the Alpine Slav and the Southern European Mediterraneans to this continent, a movement that started about 1890, and which has not yet ceased. Running parallel with the movements of these European peoples, we have the most sinister development in the history of this continent, the importation of the negro.

[. . .]

Our figures, then, would rather tend to disprove the popular belief that the Jew is highly intelligent. Immigrants examined in the army, who report their birthplace as Russia, had an average intelligence below those from all other countries except Poland and Italy. It is perhaps significant to note, however, that the sample from Russia has a higher standard deviation (2.83) than that of any other immigrant group sampled, and that the Alpine group has a higher standard deviation than the Nordic or Mediterranean groups (2.60). If we assume that the Jewish immigrants have a low average intelligence, but a higher variability than other nativity groups, this would reconcile our figures with popular belief, and, at the same time, with the fact that investigators searching for talent in New York City and California schools find a frequent occurence of talent among Jewish children, The able Jew is popularly recognized not only because of his ability, but because he is able and a Jew.

Our results showing the marked intellectual inferiority of the negro are corrobated by practically all of the investigators who have used psychological tests on white and negro groups. This inferiority holds even when a low intellectual sampling of whites is made by selecting only those who live in the same environment, and who have had the same educational opportunities. Professor Ferguson,[3] who has studied the problem most carefully, concludes that in general 25% of the negroes exceed the median white. Our figures show a greater difference than he estimates, less than 12% of the negroes exceeding the average of the native born white draft. Professor Ferguson also estimates that 20% of pure negroes, 25% of negroes three quarters pure, 30% of the true mulattoes, and 35% of the quadroons equal or exceed the average score of *comparable* whites.

The discrepancies between data from various investigators as to the *amount* of difference between negroes and whites probably result from different methods of selecting whites. If we compare negroes only to those whites who live in the same neighborhood, and who have had the same educational opportunities, our differences are smaller than those obtained by comparing samples of the entire white and negro populations.

Some writers would account for the differences found between white and negro by differences of educational opportunity alone. The army tests showed the northern negro superior to the southern negro, and this superiority is attributed to the superior educational opportunities in the North. The educational record of the negro sample we are studying shows that more than half of the negroes from the southern States did not go beyond the third grade, and only 7% finished the eighth grade, while about half of the northern negroes finished the fifth grade, and a quarter finished the eighth grade. That the difference between the northern and southern negro is not entirely due to schooling, but partly to intelligence, is shown by the fact that groups of southern and northern negroes of *equal schooling* show striking differences in intelligence.

The superior intelligence measurements of the northern negro are due to three factors: first, the greater amount of educational opportunity, which does affect, to some extent, scores on our present intelli-

[3] G. O. Ferguson. *The Mental Status of the American Negro.* Scientific Monthly, 1921, pp. 12, 533–543.

gence tests; second, the greater amount of admixture of white blood; and, third, the operation of economic and social forces, such as higher wages, better living conditions, identical school privileges, and a less complete social ostracism, tending to draw the more intelligent negro to the North. It is impossible to dissect out of this complex of forces the relative weight of each factor. No psychologist would maintain that the mental tests he is now using do not measure educational opportunity to some extent. On the other hand, it is absurd to attribute all differences found between northern and southern negroes to superior educational opportunities in the North, for differences are found between groups of the same schooling, and differences are shown by beta as well as by alpha.

At the present stage of development of psychological tests, we can not measure the actual *amount* of difference in intelligence due to race or nativity. We can only prove that differences do exist, and we can interpret these differences in terms that have great social and economic significance. The intellectual superiority of our Nordic group over the Alpine, Mediterranean, and negro groups has been demonstrated. If a person is unwilling to accept the race hypothesis as developed here, he may go back to the original nativity groups, and he can not deny the fact that differences exist.

When our methods of measuring intellectual capacity have been perfected, we will be in a position to determine quantitatively the amount of race differences. Rough group tests of the type we are now using will indicate the fact that differences exist. However, while scientists are perfecting their methods of examining, it would be well for them to perfect their logic at the same time. Particularly misleading and unsound is the theory that disregards all differences found between racial groups unless the groups have had the same educational and environmental opportunities.

This theory in its most extreme form is set forth by Garth[4] as follows:

The elements in a study of racial mental similarities or differences must be these: (1) Two so-called races R_1 and R_2, (2) an

[4] T. R. Garth, *White, Indian and Negro Work Curves.* Journal of Applied Psychology, 1921, 5, 14–25.

equal amount of educational opportunity, E, which should include social pressure and racial patterns of thought, and (3) psychological tests, D, within the grasp of both racial groups. We should have as a result of our experiment R_1 E D equal to, greater than, or less than R_2 E D. In this experiment the only unknown elements should be R_1 and R_2. If E could be made equal the experiment could be worked.

This element of educational opportunity—nurture, is the one causing most of the trouble in racial psychology as an uncontrollable element. It does not offer quite so much difficulty in the study of sex differences, yet it is there only in smaller degree than in racial differences, and as it is controlled the "sex differences" tend to disappear. Since this element of education, or nurture, cannot be eliminated it would be safer to take for comparison such racial groups as have had as nearly the same educational opportunity as is possible having any disparity of this sort well in mind when we interpret the results of the experiment. Having done this, we first take the complete distributions on the scale of measurement for the groups as statements of the true facts of the case, race for race. We then combine these distributions into a total distribution of accomplishment of all the races taken together to see if we have multimodal effects. Should we find these effects we may conclude that we have evidence of types, or racial types, and there should in this case be one mode for each racial group. But should the combined distribution for the several racial groups reveal only one mode we may conclude that the test reveals no types—no real racial differences but rather similarities. (p. 16.)

If intelligence counts for anything in the competition among human beings, it is natural to expect that individuals of superior intelligence will adjust themselves more easily to their physical and social environment, and that they will endow their children not only with material goods, but with the ability to adjust themselves to the same or a more complex environment. To select individuals who have fallen behind in the struggle to adjust themselves to the civilization their race has built as typical of that race is an error, for their position itself shows that they are, for the most part, individuals with an inferior hereditary endowment.

In the same way, our educational institutions are themselves a part of our own race heritage. The average negro child can not advance through an educational curriculum adapted to the Anglo-Saxon child in step with that child. To select children of equal education, age for age, in the two groups, is to sample either superior negroes or inferior whites.

The scientific problem is that of eliminating from the tests used as measuring instruments those particular tests which demonstrably measure nurture, and to measure, with genuine tests of native intelligence, random or impartial samples from each race throughout the entire range of its geographical and institutional distribution.

[...]

Our immigration figures show a very decided shift from the Nordic in favor of the Alpine. The immigration between 1820 and 1890 probably never contained more than 50% or 60% Nordic blood, and prior to 1820 there was very little immigration. The earliest settlers were almost pure Nordic types, and we may assume the existence by 1820 of a race as predominantly Nordic as that of England. This recent change was, of course, reflected in the cross section of the foreign born population taken at 1910, and which constitutes the basis of our present immigration act restricting immigration to 3% of the nationals then resident here. A rough estimate of the racial composition of the quotas from various countries admissable under the new law shows about 35% Nordic blood, 45% Alpine blood and 20% Mediterranean blood in the annual stream of approximately one-third of a million that may enter.

There can be no doubt that recent history has shown a movement of inferior peoples or inferior representatives of peoples to this country. Few people realize the magnitude of this movement or the speed with which it has taken place. Since 1901, less than a single generation, it may be estimated that about 10,000,000 Alpine and Mediterranean types have come to this country. Allowing for the return of one-third or three-eighths of these, and using our army estimates of intellectual ability, this would give us over 2,000,000 immigrants below the average negro.

We may consider that the population of the United States is made up of four racial elements, the Nordic, Alpine, and Mediterranean races of Europe, and the negro. If these four types blend in the future into one general American type, then it is a foregone conclusion that this future blended American will be less intelligent than the present native born American, for the general results of the admixture of higher and lower orders of intelligence must inevitably be a mean between the two.

If we turn to the history of races, we find that as a general rule where two races have been in contact they have intermingled, and a cross between the two has resulted. Europe shows many examples of areas where the anthropological characteristics of one race shade over into those of another race where the two have intermixed, and, indeed, in countries such as France and Switzerland it is only in areas that are geographically or economically isolated that one finds types that are relatively pure. The Mongol-Tatar element in Russia is an integral part of the population. The Mediterranean race throughout the area of its contact with the negro has crossed with him. Some of the Berbers in Northern Africa show negroid characteristics, and in India the Mediterranean race has crossed with the Dravidians and Pre-Dravidian negroids. The population of Sardinia shows a number of negroid characteristics. Turn where we may, history gives us no great exception to the general rule that propinquity leads to opportunity and opportunity to intermixture.

In considering racial crosses, Professor Conklin[5] states that

> It is highly probable that while some of these hybrids may show all the bad qualities of both parents, others may show the good qualities of both and indeed in this respect resemble the children in any pure-bred family. But it is practically certain that the general or average results of the crossing of a superior and an inferior race are to strike a balance somewhere between the two. This is no contradiction of the principles of Mendelian inheritance but rather the application of these principles to a general population. The general effect of the hybridization of races can not fail to lead to a lowering of the qualities of the higher race and a raising of the qualities of the lower one. (pp. 50–51.)

And as to the possibility of a cross between races in the future, Professor Conklin writes:

[5] Edwin G. Conklin. *The Direction of Human Evolution.* New York, 1921, 247 pp.

Even if we are horrified by the thought, we cannot hide the fact that all present signs point to an intimate commingling of all existing human types within the next five or ten thousand years at most. Unless we can re-establish geographical isolation of races, we cannot prevent their interbreeding. By rigid laws excluding immigrants of other races, such as they have in New Zealand and Australia, it may be possible for a time to maintain the purity of the white race in certain countries, but with constantly increasing intercommunications between all lands and peoples such artificial barriers will probably prove as ineffectual in the long run as the Great Wall of China. The races of the world are not drawing apart but together, and it needs only the vision that will look ahead a few thousand years to see the blending of all racial currents into a common stream. (p. 52.)

If we frankly recognize the fact that the crossing of races in juxtaposition has always occurred in the past, what evidence have we that such crosses have had untoward consequences? Our own data from the army tests indicate clearly the intellectual superiority of the Nordic race group. This superiority is confirmed by observation of this race in history. The Alpine race, according to our figures, which are supported by historical evidence, seems to be considerably below the Nordic type intellectually. However, our recruits from Germany, which represents a Nordic-Alpine cross, are about the same as those from Holland, Scotland, the United States, Denmark, and Canada, countries which have on the whole a greater proportion of Nordic blood than Germany. Again, the Nordic and Alpine mixture in Switzerland has given a stable people, who have evolved, in spite of linguistic differences, a very advanced form of government. The evidence indicates that the Nordic-Alpine cross, which occurred in Western Europe when the Nordics overwhelmed the Alpines to such an extent that the type was completely submerged and not re-discovered until recently, has not given unfortunate results.

This evidence, however, can not be carried over to indicate that a cross between the Nordic and the Alpine Slav would be desirable. The Alpines that our data sample come for the most part from an area peopled largely by a branch of the Alpine race which appeared late and radiated from the Carpathian Mountains. It is probably a different branch of the Alpine race from that which forms the primitive substratum of the present population of Western Europe. Our data on the Alpine Slav show that he is intellectually inferior to the Nordic, and every indication would point to a lowering of the average intelligence of the Nordic if crossed with the Alpine Slav. There can be no objection to the intermixture of races of equal ability, provided the mingling proceeds equally from all sections of the distribution of ability. Our data, however, indicate that the Alpine Slav we have imported and to whom we give preference in our present immigration law is intellectually inferior to the Nordic type.

The Mediterranean race at its northern extension blends with the Alpine very considerably, and to a less extent with the Nordic. At the point of its furthermost western expansion in Europe it has crossed with the primitive types in Ireland. Throughout the area of its southern and eastern expansion it has crossed with negroid types. In this continent, the Mediterranean has crossed with the Amerind and the imported negro very extensively. In general, the Mediterranean race has crossed with primitive race types more completely and promiscuously than either the Alpine or the Nordic, and with most unfortunate results.

We must now frankly admit the undesirable results which would ensue from a cross between the Nordic in this country with the Alpine Slav, with the degenerated hybrid Mediterranean, or with the negro, or from the promiscuous intermingling of all four types. Granted the undesirable results of such an intermingling, is there any evidence showing that such a process is going on? Unfortunately the evidence is undeniable. The 1920 census shows that we have 7,000,000 native born whites of mixed parentage, a fact which indicates clearly the number of crosses between the native born stock and the European importations.

The evidence in regard to the white and negro cross is also indisputable. If we examine the figures showing the proportion of mulattoes to a thousand blacks for each twenty year period from 1850 to 1910, we find that in 1850 there were 126 mulattoes to a thousand blacks, 136 in 1870, 179 in 1890 and 264 in 1910. This intermixture of white and negro has been a natural result of the emancipation of the negro and the breaking down of social barriers against him, mostly in the North and West. In 1850, the free colored population showed 581 mulattoes to a thousand blacks as against 83 in the slave population. At each of the four censuses (1850, 1870, 1890 and 1910) the South, where the social barriers are more rigid than elsewhere, has returned the smallest proportion of mulattoes to a thousand blacks. The 1910 census showed 201 in the South, 266 in the North and 321 in the West, and the West has returned the highest proportion at each of the censuses except 1850.

We must face a possibility of racial admixture here that is infinitely worse than that faced by any European country to-day, for we are incorporating the negro into our racial stock, while all of Europe is comparatively free from this taint. It is true that the rate of increase of the negro in this country by ten year periods since 1800 has decreased rather steadily from about 30% to about 11%, but this declining rate has given a gross population increase from approximately 1,000,000 to approximately 10,000,000. It is also true that the negro now constitutes only about 10% of the total population, where he formerly constituted 18% or 19% (1790 to 1830), but part of this decrease in percentage of the total population is due to the great influx of immigrants, and we favor in our immigration law those countries 35% of whose representatives here are below the average negro. The declining rate of increase in the negro population from 1800 to 1910 would indicate a correspondingly lower rate to be expected in the future. From 1900 to 1920 the negro population increased 18.4%, while the native born white of native parents increased 42.6%, and the native born white of foreign parents increased 47.6%. It is impossible to predict at the present time that the rate of infiltration of white blood into the negro will be checked by the declining rate of increase in the negro blood itself. The essential point is that there are 10,000,000 negroes here now and that the proportion of mulattoes to a thousand blacks has increased with alarming rapidity since 1850.

According to all evidence available, then, American intelligence is declining, and will proceed with an accelerating rate as the racial admixture becomes more and more extensive. The decline of American intelligence will be more rapid than the decline of the intelligence of European national groups, owing to the presence here of the negro. These are the plain, if somewhat ugly, facts that our study shows. The deterioration of American intelligence is not inevitable, however, if public action can be aroused to prevent it. There is no reason why legal steps should not be taken which would insure a continuously progressive upward evolution.

The steps that should be taken to preserve or increase our present intellectual capacity must of course be dictated by science and not by political expediency. Immigration should not only be restrictive but highly selective. And the revision of the immigration and naturalization laws will only afford a slight relief from our present difficulty. The really important steps are those looking toward the prevention of the continued propagation of defective strains in the present population. If all immigration were stopped now, the decline of American intelligence would still be inevitable. This is the problem which must be met, and our manner of meeting it will determine the future course of our national life.

WHAT THE ARMY "INTELLIGENCE"

TESTS MEASURED (1924)

Horace M. Bond

O NE OF THE MOST INTERESTING phenomena of the last century was the attempt made by certain thinkers to establish race differences upon the unquestioned basis of biological and psychological fact. It was an epoch in the history of thought by no means peculiar to its times; for, wherever man in his diverse racial types has cause to congregate, there will be found the proponents of a self assumed superior group dogmatizing and belittling the accomplishments, the abilities, and the very humanity itself, of the race whose peculiar cast of form or feature may have aroused the unreasoning prejudices of the masses.

It is not too far fetched to see in the designation of the Hebrew tribes as the "Chosen people" an example of this self perpetuating propaganda; and it is certain that the ironic words of Molière, when mouthed by the ecclesiastical supporters of slavery in this country, represent a rather primitive desire to justify the iniquitous custom of

Horace Mann Bond (1904–1972), an educator, was a president of Lincoln University and dean at Atlanta University; he is author of *The Education of the Negro in the American Social Order* (1934), *The Search for Talent* (1959), and other works. This essay appeared in *Crisis*, July 1924.

enslaving Africans on the ground that they, after all, were not wholly human; "It is impossible to pity them; their skin is so black and their features are so irregular!" And, when Biblical justification for inhuman practices began to lose its authority, it was but natural that the proponents of racial superiority should shift their ground to the rapidly rising natural sciences.

Gobineau and Galton and Spencer, with the assistance of faulty anthropometric measurements, meaningless criteria of judgment, and absolutely gratuitous conclusions, for a time were successful in bolstering up this man of straw, and presenting him to the public as an authenticated and scientific reality. Better instruments, closer attention to accuracy of observation and interpretation, and a new realization of the significance of the culture of the so-called "inferior" races, all served to reduce the assumed differences to a significant nonentity, and Woodworth summarizes the status of investigations into racial differences up to 1910 with the conclusion that, if any such differences really existed, neither the anthropologist nor the psychologist had devised any methods for their accurate and authoritative estimation.

The result of the widely accepted teachings of Spencer and his co-workers, however, was to create a widespread sentiment which religiously depended upon the belief in racial differences, even after the scientific nature of any such differences had been discredited. Such men as Ripley, Grant, and Stoddard represent this "hang-over" from the hectic days of the birth of the "Super-Man" idea, and their influence has been such as to amount to a coterie of devout and implicit followers, seeking eagerly in the obscure muck of unfounded assumption for the food with which to sustain a boundless Ego.

Such was the status of racial differences during the first decade of the Twentieth Century. This decade, however, was to witness the birth of a new instrument of psycho-physical research; and the next was to see the almost amazing spread of the underlying idea and its unquestioned acceptance on the part of many reputable psychologists and educators. Working in a Paris Laboratory devoted to the treatment of sub-normal cases, Alfred Binet had for a long time seen that the treatment afforded the mentally incompetent in the Parisian schools was neither equable nor efficient. He saw the desirability for the evolution of some criteria by which the hopelessly under-average cases might be separated from the normal cases, and given the special care and supervision which their unfortunate condition warranted. The ability to compete successfully with one's fellows in the world of affairs he called Intelligence; and though he had no means for estimating the extent nor the underlying nature of this ability, yet, for the practical purposes of the psychiatrist, and in a narrower sense the demands of the schoolman in need of a coarse yard-stick for classification immediate and tentative, the work of Binet is valuable and noteworthy.

Binet, unfortunately, died in 1911, before he could fully impress upon his disciples the need and the necessity for caution in the use of his method, which might well, as he himself pointed out in a letter to one of his confreres, become a double-edged sword in the hands of the extremist or biased observer. The Binet system was transported to America, and immediately met with the widest possible success in its diffusion and acceptance as a valuable contribution to the methodology of modern Pedagogy.

Professor Terman, of Stanford University, California, was responsible for the next step in the extension of the new scale in America, and the Stanford Revision is now the standard for all comparative endeavors in this field. It is almost amusing to note that Professor Terman, while recognizing the influence of social status upon the results of his tests, yet is one of the strongest in assuming the mental inferiority of certain racial types which are manifestly handicapped in their range of social impressions.

At the time of America's entry into the war, heroic measures were determined upon to whip the great mass of unprepared and undisciplined men into shape, preparatory to use on the Western Front. With this end in view, certain psychologists were called to Washington to devise tests which could be used in the grading of ability in the performance of certain rudimentary tasks in the limits of a small time allotment, believing that such tests would afford the quickest, if not perhaps the most efficient, means for the separation of the feeble-minded from the great mass of normal draftees, and the selection of the non-commissioned officers who were needed to officer the vast army in process of preparation.

The result of the work of this group of Psychologists is embodied in the since famous Alpha and Beta tests; Alpha, a test for literates, and Beta, a test for illiterates and foreign speaking draftees. The makers of this scale were under no illusions as to what they were testing, or at least their initial utterances gave no indication of any such intimations, even if they possessed them. They were at all times willing to accept the words of Stern; who said: "It must be remembered that no series of tests, however skillfully selected it may be, does reach the innate intellectual endowment, stripped of all complications, but rather this endowment in conjunction with all of the influences to which the examinee has been subjected up to the moment of the testing."

The Alpha Army Tests were given to large numbers of men, and data was accumulated and tabulated which shows the scores of 103,500 white recruits and 19,000 Negroes. It is on the basis of these results, particularly, that many extreme and misleading conclusions have been made, leading to grave and dangerous misunderstandings on the part of the public. It was on the basis of these tests that the army investigators concluded that the average mental age of the white draft was 13.1 years; and that the average mentality of the Negro soldier, and consequently the average Negro, granting that the army cross section was typical, to be that of a child of 10.4! It is on the basis of these tests that the Nordic races have been granted the heaven-sent mental superiority over South Europeans which entitles them to entry into this country; that a prominent College president and pulpit orator of the East justifies the policy of segregation in the public schools; and that one observer bewails the fact that "There seems to be no immediate possibility of convincing the public of the necessity for preventing the reproduction of these groups."

All of these conclusions would be amusing were they not positively dangerous. They have given to the professional race-hatred agitator a semblance of scientific justification for his mouthings, and, in the writings of popular and ill-informed publicists, they are rapidly moulding a public opinion in support of the most reactionary and inequable measures of general policy and welfare.

Let us re-examine the reasonableness of the stand taken by these discoverers of native and inherent intelligence, by means of a number of tests which admittedly cannot be divorced from environmental influences. In the beginning, we have seen that no one dares define Intelligence; and besides this, no one even boasts of having an objective evidence as to its presence or absence. Our tests are also faulty, for, while the intention is the measurement of Intelligence, we are measuring environment, and assuming that by this secondary method we are attaining the original end. Such an assumption is valid only when the experiences of the group under consideration are the experiences of all; when the environment of the most lowly is the mutual background of the number made the subject of investigation; and when the test has been so devised that it minimizes the effect of environment and renders such effect void and unimportant.

The proponents of the Alpha Army Tests, as well as those other adaptations of the original Binet scale utilized in the measurement of intellectual capacity, assume that the typical resident of the United States possessed the background sufficient to enable the tests to be applied to him with fairness and efficiency of comparison of the results. They assume that the minimum of experience possessed by a Negro from the horribly inefficient schools of the far South places him on a plane of equality, for purposes of comparison, with the graduate of the highly standardized grammar school systems of California or the District of Columbia. They assume that the experience gained by a Negro living in the slums of Memphis is sufficient to warrant comparison with the product of the proudest scions of Malden or of Beverly Hills.

Manifestly, if the assumption outlined above is correct and scientific, an arrangement of the scores of the whites should show no deviation which might correspond to societal conditions from which the respective representatives of the given group were drawn. Evidently, if instruments for psycho-physical research are to justify themselves as simon pure calipers of native and inherent mental ability, the white youth, scion of the Anglo-Saxon stock of Georgia, should score just as highly as the white youth, the scion of the Anglo-Saxon stock of Oregon; and the Negro youth of Mississippi should score just as highly as the Negro youth from the District of Columbia or from Illinois.

Let us examine the results of the Alpha Army Tests in their relation to environmental and geographical conditions, and see in what light they stand; for, if racial differences and norms are to be deduced from these tests, they must be free from the influence of a superior or an inferior environment.

Perhaps the most outstanding evidence of civic consciousness and advancement is to be found in the development of a representative and efficient school system; and it is certain that the school life of the children of this nation is a fundamental index to their environmental surroundings at their most impressive and formative periods. It is impossible for the layman to estimate the worth of respective school systems, because his criteria are uncertain and his methods at best are lacking the scientific method. Fortunately, we are not forced, for the purposes of this comparison, to rely upon the views of an untrained and uninformed observer; for there is a reliable index as to the comparative efficiency of the various state school systems throughout our land. Leonard P. Ayers, with all of the perspective of trained and authoritative educational methods, and with the resources of the Russell Sage Foundation, issued in 1918 "An Index Number for State School Systems." This report, the result of careful and intensive research, ranks the states in the order of their educational advancement on the basis of the following points:

1. Salary paid teachers
2. Number of school children in state
3. Number of children attending school for a reasonable period
4. Length of school term
5. Requirements for teachers
6. Amount of state funds appropriated for purpose of education per capita school child
7. Number of high schools and students in them
8. Normal school facilities for teacher training
9. Amount of supervision.

With these considerations in mind, it is evident that a very good cross section of the school systems of our states could be sampled, and thus the Ayers index is invaluable from the standpoint of comparison.

Statistics show that the average draftee was 26 years of age at the time of his induction into the service; and thus it would be reasonable to suppose that the average soldier was of school age during the period 1900–1910.

In order to obtain as fair a comparison as possible, the scores of all Negro draftees was eliminated; the standing of the states, then, represents the relative standing of the white representatives alone of the respective states.

According to the median score of the soldiers, the states, eliminating those whose figures include manifest inaccuracies, as in the case of New Jersey, ranked in the Alpha Army Test as follows:

RANK OF STATES IN ALPHA (WHITE RECRUITS)

STATE	ALPHA MEDIAN SCORE	INDEX
Oregon	79.85	1
Washington	79.15	2
District of Columbia	78.75	3
California	78.11	4
Wyoming	77.60	5
Idaho	73.40	6
Connecticut	72.30	7
Utah	72.25	8
Massachusetts	71.50	9
Colorado	69.65	10
Montana	68.51	11
Wisconsin	68.35	12
Pennsylvania	68.30	13
Vermont	67.40	14
Ohio	66.75	15
Nebraska	66.05	16
Maine	64.85	17
Nevada	64.55	18
New York	64.50	19
Iowa	64.45	20
Minnesota	64.00	21
Illinois	63.70	22
Michigan	63.30	23
Kansas	63.00	24
Rhode Island	62.85	25
New Hampshire	61.70	26
New Mexico	60.00	27
Missouri	59.50	28
Florida	59.35	29
South Dakota	58.15	30
North Dakota	57.00	31
Virginia	56.45	32
Indiana	56.05	33
Maryland	56.00	34
West Virginia	55.55	35
Texas	50.80	36
Delaware	50.00	37
South Carolina	47.35	38

Tennessee	47.25	39
Alabama	45.20	40
Louisiana	45.03	41
North Carolina	43.10	42
Georgia	42.12	43
Arkansas	41.55	44
Kentucky	41.50	45
Mississippi	41.25	46

Comparison was made by means of the Pearsonian Coefficient of Correlation. Without going into a technical exposition of his time-moment formula, it is sufficient to remember that 1.00 is considered evidence of perfect correlations or relationship existing between two groups; and that any correlation above .50 is considered as highly suggestive of a relationship existing which cannot be explained by the laws of casual distribution.

STATE RANK IN ALPHA STANDING
CORRELATED WITH AYERS INDEX FOR 1900 (WHITE RECRUITS)

STATE RANK IN AYERS INDEX FOR 1900 STATE	RANK	RANK IN ALPHA SCORE	RANK	D	D²
Massachusetts	1	71.50	9	8	64
New York	2	64.50	19	17	289
Dist. of Columbia	3	78.75	3	0	0
California	4	78.11	4	0	0
Connecticut	5	72.30	7	2	4
Rhode Island	6	62.85	25	19	361
Nevada	7	64.55	18	11	121
Colorado	8	69.65	10	2	4
Montana	9	68.51	11	2	4
Utah	10	72.25	8	2	4
Ohio	11	66.75	15	4	16
Illinois	12	63.70	22	10	100
Washington	13	79.15	2	11	121
Pennsylvania	14	68.30	13	1	1
Indiana	15	56.05	33	18	324
Nebraska	16	66.05	16	0	0
Michigan	17	63.30	23	6	36

Maryland	18	56.00	34	16	256
Vermont	19	67.40	14	5	25
Minnesota	20	64.00	21	1	1
North Dakota	21	57.00	31	10	100
Iowa	22	64.45	20	2	4
Wisconsin	23	68.35	12	11	121
South Dakota	24	58.15	30	6	36
New Hampshire	25	61.70	26	1	1
Maine	26	64.85	17	9	81
Oregon	27	79.85	1	26	676
Wyoming	28	77.60	5	23	529
Missouri	29	59.50	28	1	1
Kansas	30	63.00	24	6	36
Delaware	31	50.00	37	6	36
Idaho	32	73.40	6	26	676
West Virginia	33	55.55	35	2	4
Kentucky	34	41.50	45	11	121
New Mexico	35	60.00	27	8	64
Texas	36	50.80	36	0	0
Florida	37	59.35	29	8	64
Tennessee	38	47.25	39	1	1
Virginia	39	56.45	32	7	49
Louisiana	40	45.03	41	1	1
Georgia	41	42.12	43	2	4
Arkansas	42	41.55	44	2	4
Mississippi	43	41.22	46	3	9
South Carolina	44	47.35	38	6	36
Alabama	45	45.20	40	5	25
North Carolina	46	43.10	42	4	16

r (Coefficient of Correlation) equals r = .7403 = Sigma D^2 = 4326

For 1900 the correlation of the states, in the relative efficiency of their school systems, with the rank of the white draftee in Alpha, was .7403; a striking correlation which cannot be explained as due to chance. It is interesting to note that of the eleven Southern States, which occupied the eleven bottom positions in the educational standing, Florida possessed a median score of 59, just 20 less than the median score of the district of Columbia; in other words, the whites of Florida made the median score equivalent to the mentality of a 13 year old child, while the whites from the District of Columbia made scores equivalent to the mentality of a 15 year old child; an increment of two years! Are we to conclude from this result that the whites of Florida are inferior in intelligence to the whites of the District of Columbia?

Let us examine an even more startling implication of this standing. The median score of the white soldiers from the states of Mississippi, Kentucky, Arkansas, and Georgia, averaged within .9 of 41. This, according to the Stanford scale upon which Negro intellect has been damned and discounted, would give the mental age of the soldiers from these states as being that of a twelve and a half year old child. This, when compared to the median mental age of the white soldiers from the states of Washington, California, Oregon, and the District of Columbia, would mean that the average mentality of the white inhabitants of the first named groups was 3 years less than that of the last named group. Again, are the exponents of intelligence tests as discriminators of racial differences prepared to assert that the white population of Arkansas is inherently and racially the inferior of the whites of another section of the United States? With the vagaries of the Helena atrocities way fresh in mind, one is almost prepared to grant the claim of the Intelligence testers if it will imply the natural inference as to the intellect of the typical participant in that massacre.

We have confined the above comparison to the white draftees in order to investigate the claims for racial differences. Certainly, if Lothrop Stoddard, Madison Grant, and McDougall are correct in their hypothesis that the Nordic, or North European stock, which comprised our early immigration, is superior to the Southern European, or more recent immigration, the representatives of such communities as Georgia and South Carolina, with the purest racial stock of the so-called Nordic branch now existent in America, would be superior to any other section showing the infiltration of Foreign and South European stock. Yet a comparison of these states with states showing a large infiltration of races from Southern Europe shows that the Southern States, as in other classifications, are low in intelligence rankings.

It is thus an evident fact that either one of two factors may explain the low rank of the Southern States in intelligence rankings of their white citizenry; either the racial stock of these states is distinctly inferior to the whites of other sections of the country, or the rank in the Alpha Army Tests is dependent upon environmental conditions as reflected in the efficiency of school systems and other criteria of cultural advancement. For there exist other standards of comparison which give the same results: A recent investigator, commenting on the correlation existing between Alpha standing and literacy, says: "Using literacy, a basic index to the distribution of cultural opportunity, and correlating with Alpha rank, a coefficient results amounting to .64."*

CORRELATIONS OF ALPHA STANDING WITH OTHER RANKINGS

Alpha with Ayers Index Rating for 1890	.6825
Alpha with Ayers Index Rating for 1910	.8251
Alpha with Ayers Index Rating for 1918	.7973
*Alpha with per cent of Literacy	.640
*Alpha with Average Wage for Farm Labor	.830
*Alpha with per cent of Urban Population	.620

The average wage for farm laborers was arranged in order by states and the rank correlated with Alpha. This comparison yielded a correlation of .83; a striking similarity in view of the fact that the Negroes tested during the war were rural farm laborers to the extent of 60 per cent of the total.

Brigham, one of the most pronounced dogmatists as to the inferiority of the Negro, who refers to his importation as the most "sinister event in the history of America," recognizes the fact that the northern Negro scored notably higher than the southern Negro in the Alpha tests. Mr. Brigham, however, would ascribe this to the fact that "The most energetic and progressive Negroes have migrated northward, leaving their duller and less accomplished fellows in the South." While this view is amusing when the opinion of the typical Southerner concerning the Negro migrant is considered, one wonders how Mr. Brigham squares the facts of southern white deficiency with his theory?

However, not to be outdone, Mr. Brigham made a comparison of northern and southern Negroes who had had the same schooling, and triumphantly announced the fact that the same discrepancy was present. A commentator in *Opportunity* clearly exposes the fallacy of such treatment by inquiring, "By what measuring rod did Mr. Brigham find the wretched schools of the South to be equal to the northern schools in all particulars?"

* H. A. Alexander, *School and Society*, Vol. XVI. No. 405.

RANGE OF IQS

THE EFFECT OF SOCIAL STATUS ON THE DISTRIBUTION OF INTELLIGENCE QUO-
TIENTS (NATIVE WHITE CHILDREN)

SOCIAL STATUS	50 TO 59.9	60 TO 69.9	70 TO 79.9	80 TO 89.9	90 TO 109.9	110 TO 119.9	120 TO 129.9	130 TO 139.9	140 AND ABOVE	TOTAL
Very Superior	0	0	1	0	6	4	6	3	4	24
Superior	0	0	0	0	12	17	14	4	1	48
Average	0	1	3	2	41	16	10	2	1	76
Inferior	1	3	5	9	23	1	0	1	0	43

There is but one answer to those who would base theories of racial inequalities upon the results of the Alpha Army Tests; and that is the indisputable truth that Alpha measures environment, and not native and inherent capacity. Instead of furnishing material for the racial propagandists and agitators, it should show the sad deficiency of opportunity which is the lot of every child, white or black, whose misfortune it is to be born and reared in a community backward and reactionary in cultural and educational avenues of expression.

There are others who would certify the results of other investigations as demonstrating the lack of intelligence on the part of Negroes.* Terman, in the investigation which he made while revising the original Binet scale, found that the advancement made by children coming from homes classified as Inferior, amounted to what is, at the age of 14, an equivalent of 2 years. The Negroes were in practically all cases drawn from the group classified as from Inferior homes; yet Terman states that he has found "a racial dullness in the case of Negroes, Mexicans, and Indians."

In the case of the white children, Mr. Terman states that the children of the lower classes rank lower, not because of any handicap in social experience, but because their parents are of inferior mentality as reflected by their menial and un-remunerative employments. "Common observation would itself suggest that the social class to which the family belongs depends less on chance than on the parents' native qualities of intellect and character."

---

* Carl Brigham, *A Study of American Intelligence*.

Does the social environment of the typical Negro family depend on native qualities of intellect and character? Does the intellect and character of the Negro parent of Chicago determine whether his child will have the recreational facilities, the clean streets, the uncrowded neighborhood, the cultured associates, of some such locality as Hyde Park, as compared with the crowded and deadly conditions of the "black belt"? Does the intellect and character of the Negro parent of Atlanta determine whether his child will have a full day of teaching or a half one; libraries and museums to elevate the mind, or backyards and soiled alleys to learn the elements of crime and vice? Does the intellect and character of the Negro father of the South determine whether his child shall attend a 9 months school, with well paid and well prepared teachers, or some dilapidated shack, with 3 or 4 months of mediocre teaching at the hands of an inadequately paid and careless teacher? If these conditions of environment are free and open to the Negro, without fear, favor, or the hint of prejudice as we find it even in northern schools, we may admit the plausibility of Mr. Terman's contention, while deploring it from the standpoint of democratic principles; but until that time, let no conclusions be drawn to the demerit and under-rating of a race discriminated and segregated, in opportunity and outlook.

Miss Arlitt made a study of several hundred children of a New York neighborhood.* She too attempted to compare the different race groups, taking into consideration the race level. When she came to compare the scores made by the white children of Superior homes with the scores of the Negro children from a superior social status, she was at a loss, for there were none of the latter level to warrant comparison! When compared as to social status within the white group alone, she found that "the median IQs for the four groups (Very Superior homes, Superior, Average, and Inferior) were respectively 92, 107, 118.7, and 125.9, or a difference of 33.9 points between children of inferior and superior social status, of the same race and attending the same grades in the same schools."

Of the Negro children tested by Miss Arlitt, 93 per cent were from homes classified as inferior from the standpoint of social advantages.

---

* Ada H. Arlitt, "On the Need for Caution in Establishing Race Norms," *Journal of Applied Psychology*, Vol. V, No. 2.

These children made a median score of 85; and this score is the same which Terman found to be the average for the Negro children whom he tested.

In considering this question, it is well that we should bear in mind the conclusions of Miss Arlitt. She states that "No study of racial differences which fails to take into consideration the social status of the groups tested can be considered valid."

Yet, this is exactly what Terman, Brigham, and others have attempted to do in evaluating norms predicating the intellectual inferiority of various racial groups. They have forgotten, as we have intimated, that the intelligence tests, so-called, do not measure intelligence; they have neglected the fact that the intelligence tester, according to Colvin, must realize that "We never measure inborn intelligence; we always measure acquired intelligence, but we infer from differences in acquired intelligence, differences in native endowment when we compare individuals in a group who have had common experiences and note the differences in the attainment of these individuals."

In what way, then, have the individuals, who saw in the intelligence tests an instrument for evaluating racial difference, erred? They have assumed that the groups which they compared had a common background of experience, while a careful analysis of the fact would have shown that variation among social classes will explain the phenomena they ascribed to inherent intelligence.

There are numberless other investigations which tend to show the validity of the above conclusion. Binet, the father of tests, found that the children of the poor wards of Paris scored from one to two years below the level of the children of an aristocratic private school in Brussels; Stern found that the children of the Vorsschule, the class type of school for the children of the German higher social orders, were distinctly above the ratings made by the children attending the Volksschule in Breslau; and William F. Book, in a statewide investigation of the High Schools of Indiana, found that the poorer southern section of the state ranked very much lower than the richer and industrial north.

This is the position of the twentieth-century prototype of Gobineau in his attempt to provide a scientific basis for the prejudices of an unreasoning race-hatred. Instead of the mountain which they loudly asserted to exist, the observed differences have dwindled into a mole hill of insignificant and ill-defined dimensions. The supremacy of the Nordic dwindles when we find a state like South Carolina, whose people can trace their stock almost entirely to England and Northern Europe, making a median mental age of 12 years; while such a state as California or Connecticut, with from 15 to 30 per cent of foreign born of South European extraction, averages a median mental age of 15. And the boasted superiority of the white over the Negro stock does not seem so impressive when the Negroes of Illinois make a score of 47.35, while the whites of at least four Southern States were making a score of 41.

RANK OF WHITE RECRUITS OF SOUTHERN STATES COMPARED WITH MARKS OF NEGRO RECRUITS OF NORTHERN STATES

SOUTHERN STATES—MEDIAN SCORES OF WHITE RECRUITS	
Mississippi	41.25
Kentucky	41.50
Arkansas	41.55
Georgia	42.12

NORTHERN STATES—MEDIAN SCORES OF NEGRO RECRUITS	
Illinois	47.35
New York	45.02
Ohio	49.50
Pennsylvania	42.00

With these facts in mind, it is impossible for anyone to make any conclusions which do not recognize these facts:

(1) The Alpha Army Tests are very accurate measures of opportunity for experience and education.

(2) The Alpha Army Tests were proposed to select in a very short time large numbers of officers, and to segregate the mentally unfit. In this task they were reasonably successful; but, once this task completed, their usefulness is at an end save for the avowed testing of education and environment.

(3) All tests so far devised and given have shown differences in social degrees of rating; and all so-called racial difference can be resolved into social differences.

If these conclusions are kept in mind, there is no reason but that the intelligence test in time may come to be a very valuable addition to the pedagogical methodology of modern practice. As a valuable instrument of classification, and as a remedy of the classic faults of teachers' judgment, they may well bring about a revolution in the schools of tomorrow.

But for those who would make them the fetishes of an impossible race cleavage—who would make them the shibboleth which would determine the right of a race to higher avenues of expression and advancement, the words of Thomas Garth, prominent psychologist, must be recommended: "The elements in a study of racial mental similarities or differences must be these—(1) two so-called races, R_1, and R_2; (2) an equal amount of educational opportunity, E, which should include social pressure and racial patterns of thought; and (3) psychological tests D, within the grasp of both racial groups. We should have as a result of our experiment, R_1 E D equal to, greater than, or less than R_2 E D. In this experiment the only unknown elements should be R_1 and R_2. If E could be made equal, the experiment could be worked."*

Has any investigator yet equalized E?

* White, Indian, and Negro Work Curves, *Journal of Applied Psychology*, Vol. V, No. 1; Thomas R. Garth.

VIII
THE RETURN OF THE REPRESSED

IQ

Richard J. Herrnstein

T HE MEASUREMENT of intelligence forced its way into
America's public consciousness during World War I, when almost
two million soldiers were tested by the Army and categorized as "alpha"
and "beta" for literates and illiterates respectively. The lasting effect of
that innovation has not been the surprise at learning that the average
American soldier had an intelligence equal to that of a thirteen-year-old,
or that artillery officers were substantially brighter than medical officers,
or any of the myriad other statistical curiosities. Even if those facts are
still as true as they were in 1918, the lasting effect has been the mere use
of the tests and their serious consideration by responsible people. For
intelligence tests, and the related aptitude tests, have more and more
become society's instrument for the selection of human resources. Not
only for the military, but for schools from secondary to professional, for
industry, and for civil service, objective tests have cut away the traditional grounds for selection—family, social class, and, most important,
money. The traditional grounds are, of course, not entirely gone, and
some social critics wonder if they do not lurk surreptitiously behind the
scenes in our definition of mental ability.

The late Richard J. Herrnstein was professor of psychology at Harvard University, and the
co-author (with Charles Murray) of *The Bell Curve*. This piece is excerpted from his article which originally appeared in the *Atlantic Monthly* in September 1971.

But at least on the face of it there is a powerful trend toward "meritocracy"—the advancement of people on the basis of ability, either potential or fulfilled, measured objectively.

Lately though, the trend has been deplored, often by the very people most likely to reap the benefits of measured intellectual superiority. More than a few college professors and admissions boards and even professional testers have publicly condemned mental testing as the basis for selection of people for schools or jobs. The IQ test, it is said with fervor, is used by the establishment to promote its own goals and to hold down the downtrodden—those non-establishment races and cultures whose interests and talents are not fairly credited by intelligence tests. These dissenting professors and testers are naturally joined by spokesmen for the disadvantaged groups. We should, these voices say, broaden the range of humanity in our colleges (to pick the most frequent target) by admitting students whose low college entrance examination scores might otherwise have barred the way. For if the examinations merely fortify an arbitrarily privileged elite in its conflict with outsiders, we must relinquish them. The ideals of equality and fraternity must, according to this view, take precedence over the self-interest of the American–Western European middle class.

The issue is intensely emotional. It is almost impossible for people to disagree about the pros and cons of intelligence testing and long avoid the swapping of oaths and anathema. Yet should not the pros and cons be drawn from facts and reason rather than labels and insults? For example, is it true that intelligence tests embody only the crass interests of Middle America, or do they draw on deeper human qualities? Is the IQ a measure of inborn ability, or is it the outcome of experience and learning? Can we tell if there are ethnic and racial differences in intelligence, and if so, whether they depend upon nature of nurture? Is there only one kind of intelligence, or are there many, and if more than one, what are the relations among them? If the tests are inadequate— let us say, because they overlook certain abilities or because they embody arbitrary cultural values—how can they be improved? For those who have lately gotten their information about testing from the popular press, it may come as a surprise that these hard questions are neither unanswerable nor, in some cases, unanswered. The measurement of intelligence is psychology's most telling accomplishment to date. Without intending to belittle other psychological ventures, it may be fairly said that nowhere else—not in psychotherapy, educational reform, or consumer research—has there arisen so potent an instrument as the objective measure of intelligence. No doubt intelligence testing is imperfect, and may even be in some sense imperfectible, but there has already been too much success for it to be repudiated on technical grounds alone. If intelligence testing is to change, it must change in light of what is known, and more is known than most might think.

[. . .]

The problem with nature and nurture is to decide which—inheritance or environment—is primary, for the IQ is exclusively the result of neither one alone. Advocates of environment—the clear majority of those who express themselves publicly on the subject—must explain why IQs usually stay about the same during most people's lives and also why high or low IQs tend to run in families. Those facts could easily be construed as signs of a genetic basis for the IQ. The usual environmentalist answer argues that IQs remain the same to the extent that environments remain the same. If you are lucky enough to be wellborn, then your IQ will show the benefits of nurturing, which, in turn, gives you an advantage in the competition for success. If, on the other hand, you are blighted with poor surroundings, your mental growth will be stunted and you are likely to be stuck at the bottom of the social ladder. By this view, parents bequeath to their children not so much the genes for intelligence as the environment that will promote or retard it.

In one plausible stroke the environmentalist arguments seem to explain, therefore, not only the stability of the IQ but also the similarity between parents and children. The case is further strengthened by arguing that early training fixes the IQ more firmly than anything we know how to do later. And then to cap it off, the environmentalist may claim that the arbitrary social barriers in our society trap the underprivileged in their surroundings while guarding the overprivileged in theirs. Anyone who accepts this series of arguments is unshaken by Jensen's reminder that compensatory education has failed in the United States, for the answer seems to be ready and waiting. To someone who believes in the environmental theory, the failure of compensatory education is not disproof of his theory, but rather a sign that we need more and better special training earlier in a person's life.

To be sure, it seems obvious that poor and unattractive surroundings will stunt a child's mental growth. To question it seems callous.
But even if it is plausible, how do we know it is true? By what evidence
do we test the environmentalist doctrine? The simplest possible
assessment of the inherited factor in IQ is with identical twins, for only
environmental differences can turn up between people with identical
genes. In an article recently published in the periodical *Behavior Genetics*, Professor Jensen surveys four major studies of identical twins who
were reared in separate homes. Most of the twins had been separated
by the age of six months, and almost all by the age of two years. The
twins were Caucasians, living in England, Denmark, and the United
States—all told, 122 pairs of them. The overall IQ of the 244 individuals was about 97, slightly lower than the standard 100. Identical twins
tend to have slightly depressed IQs, perhaps owing to the prenatal
hazards of twindom. The 244 individuals spanned the range of IQs
from 63 to 132, a range that brackets most of humanity—or to be more
precise, 97 percent of the general population on whom intelligence
tests have been standardized.

Being identical twins, the pairs shared identical genetic endowments, but their environments could have been as different as those of
random pairs of children in the society at large. Nevertheless, their IQs
correlated by about 85 percent, which is more than usual between
ordinary siblings or even fraternal twins growing up together with their
own families. It is, in fact, almost as big as the correlations between the
heights and weights of these twins, which were 94 percent and 88 percent respectively. Even environmentalists would expect separately
raised twins to look alike, but these results show that the IQs match
almost as well. Of course if the environment alone set the IQ, the correlations should have been much smaller than 85 percent. It would,
however, be rash to leap to the conclusion that the 85 percent correlation is purely genetic, for when twins are placed into separate homes,
they might well be placed into similar environments. The children had
been separated not for the edification of psychologists studying the
IQ, but for the weighty reasons that break families up—illness,
poverty, death, parental incapacity, and so on—and the accidents of
separation may not have yielded well-designed experiments. Some of
the pairs were no doubt raised by different branches of the same family, perhaps assuring them considerable environmental similarity anyway. In such cases, the correlation of 85 percent would not be purely

genetic, but at least partly environmental. Fortunately for our state of knowledge, one of the four studies examined by Jensen included ratings of the foster homes in terms of the breadwinner's occupation. Six categories sufficed: higher professional, lower professional, clerical, skilled, semiskilled, unskilled. Now, with this classification of homes, we know a little about whether the twins were raised in homes with a similar cultural ambience. To the extent that the environment in a home reflects the breadwinner's occupation, the answer is unequivocally negative, for there was literally no general correlation in the occupational levels of the homes into which the pairs were separated. At least for this one study—which happened to be the largest of the four—the high correlation in IQ resulted from something besides a social-class correlation in the foster homes, most likely the shared inheritance.

Twins raised apart differ on the average by about seven points in IQ. Two people chosen at random from the general population differ by seventeen points. Only four of the 122 pairs of twins differed by as much as seventeen points. Ordinary siblings raised in the same household differ by twelve points. Only nineteen of the 122 twin pairs differed by as much as that. And finally, fraternal twins raised in the same home differ by an average of eleven points, which was equaled or exceeded by only twenty-three of the 122 pairs. In other words, more than four times out of five the difference between identical twins raised apart fell short of the average difference between fraternal twins raised together by their own parents. At the same time, those separated twins were not so similar in schoolwork. Identical twins raised together resemble each other in both IQ and school grades. When twins are separated, their IQs remain quite close, but their grades diverge. It seems that school performance responds to the environment substantially more than does the IQ, although neither one is solely the outcome of either nature or nurture.

The comparison between IQ and grades was one theme of Jensen's controversial earlier article, "How Much Can We Boost IQ and Scholastic Achievement?," which appeared in the winter of 1969 in the *Harvard Educational Review*, Jensen answered the title's rhetorical question about IQ with a scholarly and circumspect form of "not very much." The article is cautious and detailed, far from extreme in position or tone. Not only its facts but even most of its conclusions are familiar to experts. The failure of compensatory education was the occasion for the article, which served especially well in assembling many scattered but pertinent items. Jensen echoes most experts on the subject of the IQ by concluding that substantially more can be ascribed to inheritance than environment. Since the importance of inheritance seems to say something about racial differences in IQ that most well-disposed people do not want to hear, it has been argued that Jensen should not have written on the subject at all or that the *Harvard Educational Review* should not have, as it did, invited him to write on it.

Some of Jensen's critics have argued that because environment and inheritance are intertwined, it is impossible to tease them apart. The criticism may seem persuasive to laymen, for nature and nurture are indeed intertwined, and in just the way that makes teasing them apart most difficult. For intelligence—unlike, for example, skin color—the main agents of both nature and nurture are likely to be one's parents. One inherits skin color from one's parents, but the relevant environment does not come directly from them but from sun, wind, age, and so on. For skin color, resemblance to parents signifies (albeit not infallibly) inheritance; for intelligence, resemblance is ambiguous. Nevertheless analysis is possible even with IQ, as Jensen and his predecessors have shown. The most useful data for the purpose are the correlations between IQ and kinship, as exemplified by the twin studies, which set genetic similarity high and environmental similarity low. Foster children in the same home define the other extreme of kinship and environment. If environment had no bearing at all on intelligence, then the IQs of such unrelated children should correlate slightly at most (and only to the extent caused by a special factor to be mentioned shortly). In contrast, if environment were all, then the correlation should approach the value for natural siblings. Actually, the IQs of foster children in the same home correlate by about 24 percent (less than half the value for natural siblings). However, even the correlation of 24 percent cannot be credited entirely to the children's shared environment. Bear in mind that adoption agencies try to place "comparable" children in the same home, which means that there is more than just their common surroundings making them alike. Suppose, for example, that adoption agencies tried to put children with similar hair color in any given family. They could check on the natural parents, and perhaps even on the grandparents, and make a reasonable guess about the baby's eventual hair color. The foster children in a given home would then often have similar hair color; they would be unrelated by blood, but the similarity would be more genetic than environmental. By trying for a congenial match between foster child and foster parents—in appearance and in mental ability—adoption agencies make the role of environment look more important than it probably is.

In between foster siblings and identical twins come the more familiar relations, and these too have been scrutinized. If intelligence were purely genetic, the IQs of second cousins would correlate by 14 percent and that of first cousins by 18 percent (the reasons for those peculiar percentages are well beyond the scope of this article, so they are offered without proof). Instead of 14 percent and 18 percent, the actual correlations are 16 percent and 26 percent—too large for genetic influences alone, but in the right range. Uncle's (or aunt's) IQ should, by the genes alone, correlate with nephew's (or niece's) by a value of 31 percent, the actual value is 34 percent. The correlation between grandparent and grandchild should, on genetic grounds alone, also be 31 percent, whereas the actual correlation is 27 percent, again a small discrepancy. And finally for this brief survey, the predicted correlation between parent and child, by genes alone, is 49 percent, whereas the actual correlation is 50 percent using the parents' adult IQs and 56 percent using the parents' childhood IQs—in either case too small a difference to quibble about. Parents and their children correlate about as well whether the children are raised at home or by a foster family, which underscores the relative unimportance of the environment.

The foregoing figures are lifted directly out of Jensen's famous article, figures that he himself culled from the literature of intelligence testing. The measurements say that (1) the more closely related by blood two people are, the greater the correlation between their IQs and (2) the correlations fall in the right range from the purely genetic standpoint. By evaluating the total evidence, and by a procedure too technical to explain here, Jensen concluded (as have most of the other experts in the field) that the genetic factor is worth about 80 percent and that only 20 percent is left to everything else— the social, cultural, and physical environment, plus illness, prenatal factors, and what have you.

JENSEN'S TWO PAPERS leave little doubt about the heritability of IQ among North American and Western European whites, whom most data on the subject describe. In fact, there is little dispute on this score, even among those who object vigorously to this work. It is the relation between heritability and racial differences that raises the hackles. Given the well-established, roughly fifteen-point black-white difference in IQ, the argument is whether the difference arises in the environment or the genes. If intelligence were entirely genetic, then racial differences would be genetic simply because they could be due to nothing else. Conversely, if the genes were irrelevant, then the racial difference would have to be due to the environment, again because there would be no alternative. As it is, IQ reflects both a person's genes and his environment. The racial issue really poses the nature-nurture question all over again, but this time for a particular finding—the higher scores of whites over blacks on IQ tests.

In general—not just for the racial issue—the question of nature and nurture boils down to the study of variation. Granted that IQs vary among people, to what extent does the variation correlate with the differences in their surroundings on the one hand and with the differences in their genetic makeup on the other? No one disputes the existence of all three kinds of variation—in IQ, environment, and inheritance—only their interconnections. In effect, the environmentalist is saying that among a group of people, the various IQs reflect the various surroundings more or less without regard to the genes. In contrast, the nativist is saying the reverse—that different IQs reflect different genetic endowments rather than different environments. The study of quantitative genetics contrives to answer such riddles, and so a brief didactic excursion is in order. But instead of starting the lesson with IQ, let us consider a trait which we are not emotionally committed to to begin with.

Suppose we wanted to know the heritability of skin color. We would not need science to tell us that dark or fair complexions run in certain families or larger groups. Nor must we be told that nongenetic elements also enter in, as when a person is tan from the sun or pale with illness or yellow from jaundice or red with rage or blue with cold. The task of quantitative genetics is to come up with a number that says how large a role inheritance plays in the total amount of variation in skin color that we see in a particular group of people at a particular time. If the number is large, then skin color is largely heritable; if very small, then the heritability is negligible. If the number is large, then there will be marked family resemblances: if small, then members of given families will be no more alike than unrelated people. To convey such information, the number must reflect which group of people we choose to study. Consider first the United States, with its racial and ethnic diversity. Much skin variation here is related to ancestry, whether black, white, yellow, red, or Mediterranean, Nordic, Alpine, or some blend. Family resemblances in skin color are quite strong in America, so the heritability should come out large. Now contrast this with an isolated village in Norway, full of Scandinavians with generations of pale-skinned ancestors. In the Norwegian town, whatever little variation there is in skin color is likely to be environmental, due to the circumstances of life rather than to the accident of inheritance. As regards skin color, children will be no more like their parents than their nonrelatives, so heritability should come out low.

The hardest thing to grasp about heritability is that it says something about a trait in a population as a whole, not about the relation between particular parents and their offspring. Skin color turns out to be more heritable in the United States than in Norway, even though the physiological mechanisms of inheritance are surely the same. In the Norwegian town, a swarthy father and mother (who probably got that way from exposure to the weather) are likely to have children as fair-skinned as their neighbors. In the American town, however, it is more likely that the swarthiness of swarthy parents is genetic and will be passed on to the children. Although heritability is not the strictly physiological concept that laymen imagine it to be, it is uniquely useful for talking about the nature-nurture question, for it tells us whether traits run in families within a broader population of individuals.

The technical measure of heritability is a number between 0 and 1.0 that states how much of the variation in a trait is due to genetic factors. How it is calculated need not detain us here. It is enough to know that a heritability of .5 means (omitting some technical complexities) that the variation is due half to genetic factors and half to other factors; a heritability of .2 means that only a fifth of the variation is genetic, and so on. Some actual heritabilities of traits in animals may be helpful. In piebald Holstein cattle, for example, the amount of white in the fur has a heritability of about .95, a value so high that it is almost right to say the environment plays no role here. In contrast, milk yield has a heritability of only .3. White in the fur, therefore, breeds more true than milk production. In pigs, the thickness of body fat has a heritability of .55, while the litter size has a heritability of only .15.

Now back to IQ and the racial issue. Using the procedures of quantitative genetics, Jensen (and most other experts) estimates that IQ has a heritability between .80 and .85, but this is based almost entirely on data from whites. We may, therefore, say that 80 to 85 percent of the variation in IQ among whites is due to the genes. Because we do not know the heritability for IQ among blacks, we cannot make a comparable statement for them. But let us simply assume, for the sake of discussion, that .8 is the heritability for whites and blacks taken together. What could we say about the racial difference in IQ then? The answer is that we could still say nothing positive about it. Recall that the concept of heritability applies to a population as a whole. All we could say is that the differences between people, on the average and without regard to color, are 80 percent inherited. But within this broad generality, particular differences could and would be more or less inherited. Take, for example, the differences in IQ between identical twins. Even with the average heritability equal to .8, all twin differences have to be totally environmental, since their genes cannot differ. Or conversely, consider the differences between foster children in a given foster family. Because they are growing up in the same home, their IQ differences could easily be relatively more genetic than those of people taken at random. When this line of reasoning is applied to a racial (or ethnic) difference in IQ, the only proper conclusion is that we do not know whether it is more genetic, less genetic, or precisely as genetic as implied by a heritability of .8.

Jensen notes that we lack a good estimate of the heritability of intelligence among blacks. Although there are scraps of evidence for a genetic component in the black-white difference, the overwhelming case is for believing that American blacks have been at an environmental disadvantage. To the extent that variations in the American social environment can promote or retard IQ, blacks have probably been held back. But a neutral commentator (a rarity these days) would have to say that the case is simply not settled, given our present stage of knowledge. To advance this knowledge would not be easy, but it could certainly be done with sufficient ingenuity and hard work. To anyone who is curious about the question and who feels competent to try to answer it, it is at least irritating to be told that the answer is either unknowable or better not known, and both enjoinders are often heard. And there is, of course, a still more fundamental issue at stake, which should concern even those who are neither curious about nor competent to study racial differences in IQ. It is whether inquiry shall (again) be shut off because someone thinks society is best left in ignorance.

Setting aside the racial issue, the conclusion about intelligence is that, like other important though not necessarily vital traits, it is highly heritable. It is not vital in the sense that it may vary broadly without markedly affecting survival, although it no doubt affects one's lifestyle. Does it do us any practical good to know how heritable intelligence is? We are not, for example, on the verge of Galton's vision of eugenics, even though we now have the mental test that he thought was the crucial prerequisite. For good or ill, and for some time to come, we are stuck with mating patterns as people determine them for themselves. No sensible person would want to entrust state-run human breeding to those who control today's states. There are, however, practical corollaries of this knowledge, more humble than eugenics, but ever more salient as the growing complexity of human society makes acute the shortage of high-grade intellect.

Heritability is first and foremost the measure of breeding true, useful for predicting how much of some trait the average offspring in a given family will have. For example, to predict the IQ of the average offspring in a family:

1. Average the parents' IQ's.
2. Subtract 100 from the result.
3. Multiply the result of (2) by .8 (the heritability).
4. Add the result of (3) to 100.

Thus, given a mother and father each with IQs of 120, their average child will have an IQ of 116. Some of their children will be brighter and some duller, but the larger the family, the more nearly will the average converge onto 116. With parents averaging an IQ of 80, the average child will have an IQ of 84. The formula predicts something the experts call "regression toward the mean," the tendency for children to be closer to the general population average (in this case, IQ 100) than their parents. And in fact, *very bright* parents have children who tend to be merely *bright*, while *very dull* parents tend to have them merely *dull*. The amount of regression for a trait depends on the heritability—with high heritability, the regression is smaller than with low.

Also, for a given trait the regression is greater at the extremes of a population than at its center. In other words, ordinary parents are more like their children (on the average) than extraordinary ones (whether extraordinarily high or low). All of these characteristics of the "generation gap" follow directly and completely from the simple formula given above. Thus, when the parents average 120, the regression effect is only four IQ points, but if they averaged 150, the regression effect would be ten points. In comparison, height, with its heritability of .95, would show smaller regression effects than IQ, since the multiplier in step 3 of the formula is closer to 1.0. But even so, very tall parents tend to have children who are merely tall, and very short parents tend to have them merely short. As long as the heritability of a trait falls short of 1.0, there is some regression effect.

Intelligence may be drifting up or down for environmental reasons from generation to generation, notwithstanding the high heritability. Height, for example, is said to be increasing—presumably because of diet and medicine—even with its .95 heritability. We can easily tell whether there has been a change in height, for the measures are absolute, and there is the tangible evidence of clothing, furniture, coffins, and the skeletons themselves. For intelligence, however, we have no absolute scales, only relative ones, and the tangible remains of intelligence defy interpretation. But if height has changed, why not intelligence? After all, one could argue, the IQ has a heritability of only .8, measurably lower than that of height, so should be even more amenable to the influence of the environment. That, to be sure, is correct in principle, but the practical problem is to find the right things in the environment to change—the things that will nourish the intellect as well as diet does height. The usual assumption, that education and culture are crucial, is running into evidence that the physical environment—for example, early diet—might be more important. In fact, the twin studies that Jensen surveyed showed that the single most important environmental influence on IQ was not education or social environment, but something prenatal, as shown by the fact that the twin heavier at birth usually grew up with the higher IQ.

Suppose we do find an environmental handle on IQ—something, let us say, in the gestating mother's diet. What then? Presumably society would try to give everyone access to the favorable factor, within the limits of its resources. Intelligence would increase accordingly. But that would not end our troubles with IQ. Recall that heritability is a measure of relative variation. Right now, about 80 percent of the variation in IQ derives from the genes. If we make the relevant environment much more uniform (by making it as good as we can for everyone), then an even larger proportion of the variation in IQ will be attributable to the genes. The average person would be smarter, but intelligence would run in families even more obviously and with less regression toward the mean than we see today. It is likely that the mere fact of heritability in IQ is socially and politically important, and the more so the higher the heritability.

THE SPECTER of Communism was haunting Europe, said Karl Marx and Friedrich Engels in 1848. They could point to the rise of egalitarianism for proof. From Jefferson's "self-evident truth" of man's equality, to France's "*égalité*" and beyond that to the revolutions that swept Europe as Marx and Engels were proclaiming their *Manifesto*, the central political fact of their times, and ours, has been the rejection of aristocracies and privileged classes, of special rights for "special" people. The vision of a classless society was the keystone of the Declaration of Independence as well as the *Communist Manifesto*, however different the plan for achieving it.

Against this background, the main significance of intelligence testing is what it says about a society built around human inequalities. The message is so clear that it can be made in the form of a syllogism:

1. If differences in mental abilities are inherited, and
2. If success requires those abilities, and
3. If earnings and prestige depend on success,
4. Then social standing (which reflects earnings and prestige) will be based to some extent on inherited differences among people.

The syllogism has five corollaries, which make it more relevant to the future than to the past or present.

(a) As the environment becomes more favorable for the development of intelligence, its heritability will increase, as the preceding section showed. Regardless of whether this is done by improving educational methods, diet for pregnant women, or whatever, the more advantageous we make the circumstances of life, the more certainly will intellectual differences be inherited. And the greater the heritability, the greater the force of the syllogism.

(b) All modern political credos preach social mobility. The good society should, we believe, allow people to rise (and, by implication if not by frank admission, fall) according to their own efforts. The social barriers of the past—race, religion, nationality, title, inherited wealth—are under continuous assault, at least in principle. The separation of church and state, the graduated income tax, the confiscatory inheritance tax, the laws against discrimination and segregation, the abolition of legal class and caste systems all manifest a desire to accelerate movement on the social ladder. The standard wisdom of our time avows that people should be free of "unfair" impediments and divested of "unfair" advantages in all their endeavors. But the syllogism becomes more potent in proportion to the opportunities for social mobility, for it is only when able and energetic individuals can rise and displace the dull and sluggish ones that there can be sorting out of people according to inherited differences. Actual social mobility is blocked by innate human differences after the social and legal impediments are removed.

(c) It was noted earlier that there are many bright but poor people even in affluent America. The social ladder is tapered steeply, with far less room at the top than at the bottom. The obvious way to rescue the people at the bottom is to take the taper out of the ladder, which is to say, to increase the aggregate wealth of society so that there is more room at the top. This is, of course, just what has been happening since the Industrial Revolution. But one rarely noted by-product of poverty is that it minimizes the inherited differences between classes by assuring that some bright people will remain at the bottom of the ladder. As the syllogism implies, when a country gains new wealth, it will tend to be gathered in the hands of the natively endowed. In other words, the growth of wealth will recruit for the upper classes precisely those from the lower classes who have the edge in native ability. Whatever else this accomplishes, it will also increase the IQ gap between upper and lower classes, making the social ladder even steeper for those left at the bottom.

(d) Technological advance changes the marketplace for IQ. Even if every single job lost in automating a factory is replaced by a new job someplace else in a new technology, it is more than likely that some of those put out of the old jobs will not have the IQ for the new ones. Technological unemployment is not just a matter of "dislocation" or "retraining" if the jobs created are beyond the native capacity of the newly unemployed. It is much easier to replace men's muscles with machines than to replace their intellects. The computer visionaries believe that their machines will soon be doing our thinking for us too, but in the meantime, backhoes are putting ditchdiggers out of work. And the ones who stay out of work are most likely the ones with the low IQs. The syllogism implies that in times to come, as technology advances, the tendency to be unemployed may run in the genes of a family about as certainly as bad teeth do now.

(e) The syllogism deals manifestly with intelligence. The invention of the intelligence test made it possible to gather the data necessary to back up the three premises. However, there may be other inherited traits that differ among people and contribute to their success in life. Such qualities as temperament, personality, appearance, perhaps even physical strength or endurance, may enter into our strivings for achievement and are to varying degrees inherited. The meritocracy concerns not just inherited intelligence, but all inherited traits affecting success, whether or not we know of their importance or have tests to gauge them.

The syllogism and its corollaries point to a future in which social classes not only continue but become ever more solidly built on inborn differences. As the wealth and complexity of human society grow, there will be precipitated out of the mass of humanity a low-capacity (intellectual and otherwise) residue that may be unable to master the common occupations, cannot compete for success and achievement, and are most likely to be born to parents who have similarly failed. In Aldous Huxley's *Brave New World*, it was malevolent or misguided science that created the "alphas," "gammas," and the other distinct types of people. But nature itself is more likely to do the job or something similar, as the less well-known but far more prescient book by Michael Young, *The Rise of the Meritocracy*, has depicted. Young's social-science-fiction tale of the antimeritocratic upheavals of the early twenty-first century is the perfect setting for his timely neologism, the word "meritocracy." The troubles he anticipated, and that the syllogism explains, have already caught the attention of alert social scientists, like Edward Banfield, whose book *The Unheavenly City* describes the increasingly chronic lower class in America's central cities. While Sunday supplements and popular magazines crank out horror stories about genetic engineering (often with anxious but self-serving testimonials from geneticists), our society may be sorting itself willy-nilly into inherited castes. What is most troubling about this prospect is that the growth of a virtually hereditary meritocracy will arise out of the successful realization of contemporary political and social goals. The more we succeed in achieving relatively unimpeded social mobility, adequate wealth, the end of drudgery, and wholesome environment, the more forcefully does the syllogism apply.

Are there alternatives short of turning back to social rigidity, poverty, drudgery, and squalor? The first two premises of the syllogism cannot sensibly be challenged, for they are true to some extent now and are likely to become more so in time. The heritability of intelligence will grow as the conditions of life are made more uniformly wholesome: intelligence will play an increasingly important role in occupational success as the menial jobs are taken over by machines. The one even plausible hope is to block the third premise by preventing earnings and prestige from depending upon successful achievement. The socialist dictum. "From each according to his ability, to each according to his needs," can be seen as a bald denial of the third premise. It states that, whatever a person's achievement, his income (economic, social, and political) is unaffected by his success. Instead, the dictum implies, people will get what they need however they perform, but only so long as they fulfill their abilities. Those in power soon discover that they must insist on a certain level of performance, for what the dictum neglects is that "ability" is, first of all, widely and innately variable, and secondly, that it expresses itself in labor only for gain. In capitalist countries, the gain is typically in material wealth, but even where the dictum rules (if such places exist), social and political influence or relief from threat would be the reward for accomplishment. Human society has yet to find a working alternative to the carrot and the stick. Meanwhile, the third premise assures the formation of social classes.

Classlessness is elusive because people vary and because they compete for gain—economic and otherwise. The tendency to respect, honor, remunerate, and perhaps even envy people who succeed is not only ingrained but is itself a source of social pressure to contribute to one's limit. Imagine, for example, what would happen if the gradient of gain were inverted by government fiat. Suppose bakers and lumberjacks got the top salaries and the top social approval, while engineers, physicians, lawyers, and business executives got the bottom. Soon thereafter, the scale of IQs would also invert, with the competition for the newly desirable jobs now including people with the highest IQs. (For simplicity's sake, only IQ is mentioned, but there may be, and no doubt are, other factors that contribute to success, for recall that IQ is only necessary, not sufficient.) The top IQs would once again capture the top of the social ladder. But no government (let alone people themselves) is likely to conduct such an experiment, for it is not a sensible allocation of a scarce resource like high-grade intelligence. Nor could a government long equalize the gains from all occupations. It was noted before that the premium given to lawyers, doctors, engineers, and business managers is not accidental, for those jobs are left to incompetents at our collective peril. There are simply fewer potentially competent physicians than barbers. The gradient of occupations is, then, a natural measure of value and scarcity. And beneath this gradient is a scale of inborn ability, which is what gives the syllogism its unique potency.

It seems that we are indeed stuck with the conclusion of the syllogism. The data on IQ and social-class differences show that we have been living with an inherited stratification of our society for some time. The signs point to more rather than less of it in the future, assuming that we are not plunged back into a state of primeval poverty by some cataclysm or do not turn back to rigidly and arbitrarily privileged classes. Recall that regression toward the mean depends upon the heritability and that improving the environment raises the heritability. The higher the heritability, the closer will human society approach a virtual caste system, with families sustaining their position on the social ladder from generation to generation as parents and children are more nearly alike in their essential features. The opportunity for social mobility across classes assures the biological distinctiveness of each class, for the unusual offspring—whether more or less able than his (or her) closest relatives—would quickly rise above his family or sink below it, and take his place, both biologically and socially, with his peers.

If this is a fair picture of the future, then we should be preparing ourselves for it instead of railing against its dawning signs. Greater wealth, health, freedom, fairness, and educational opportunity are *not* going to give us the egalitarian society of our philosophical heritage. It will instead give us a society sharply graduated, with ever greater innate separation between the top and the bottom, and ever more uniformity within families as far as inherited abilities are concerned. Naturally, we find this vista appalling, for we have been raised to think of social equality as our goal. The vista reminds us of the world we had hoped to leave behind—aristocracies, privileged classes, unfair advantages and disadvantages of birth. But it is different, for the privileged classes of the past were probably not much superior biologically to the downtrodden, which is why revolutions had a fair chance of success. By removing arbitrary barriers between classes, society has encouraged the creation of biological barriers. When people can freely take their natural level in society, the upper classes will, virtually by definition, have greater capacity than the lower.

The measurement of intelligence is one of the yardsticks by which we may assess the growing meritocracy, but other tests of human potential and performance should supplement the IQ in describing a person's talents, interests, skills, and shortcomings. The biological stratification of society would surely go on whether we had tests to gauge it or not, but with them a more humane and tolerant grasp of human differences is possible. And at the moment, that seems our best hope.

THE DIFFERENCES ARE REAL

Arthur R. Jensen

I N 1969, in the appropriately academic context of *The Harvard Educational Review* I questioned the then and still prevailing doctrine of racial genetic equality in intelligence. I proposed that the average difference in IQ scores between black and white people may be attributable as much to heredity as environment. Realizing that my views might be wrongly interpreted as conflicting with some of the most sacred beliefs of our democracy, I emphasized the important distinction between individual intelligence and the average intelligence of populations. Moreover, I presented my research in a careful and dispassionate manner, hoping that it would stimulate rational discussion of the issue as well as further research.

Much to my dismay, however, my article set off an emotional furor in the world of social science. Amplified by the popular press, the furor soon spread beyond the confines of academia. Almost overnight I became a *cause célèbre*, at least on college campuses. I had spoken what Joseph Alsop called "the unspeakable." To many Americans I had thought the unthinkable.

Arthur R. Jensen is professor emeritus of educational psychology at the University of California, Berkeley. He is author of *Genetics and Education, Bias in Mental Testing,* and other works. This essay appeared in *Psychology Today,* December 1973.

FOR THE PAST three decades the scientific search for an explanation of the well-established black IQ deficit has been blocked largely, I feel, by fear and abhorrence of racism. In academic circles doctrinaire theories of strictly environmental causation have predominated, with little or no attempt to test their validity rigorously. The environmentalists have refused to consider other possible causes, such as genetic factors. Research into possible genetic influence on intelligence has been academically and socially taboo. The orthodox environmental theories have been accepted not because they have stood up under proper scientific investigation, but because they harmonize so well with our democratic belief in human equality.

The civil-rights movement that gained momentum in the 1950s "required" liberal academic adherence to the theory that the environment was responsible for any individual or racial behavioral differences, and the corollary belief in genetic equality in intelligence. Thus, when I questioned such beliefs I, and my theories, quickly acquired the label "racist." I resent this label, and consider it unfair and inaccurate.

SINCE THE HORRORS of Nazi Germany, and Hitler's persecution of the Jews in the name of his bizarre doctrine of Aryan supremacy, the well-deserved offensiveness of the term "racism" has extended far beyond its legitimate meaning. To me, racism means discrimination among persons on the basis of their racial origins in granting or denying social, civil or political rights. Racism means the denial of equal opportunity in education or employment on the basis of color or national origin. Racism encourages the judging of persons not each according to his own qualities and abilities, but according to common stereotypes. This is the real meaning of racism. The scientific theory that there are genetically conditioned mental or behavioral differences between races cannot be called racist. It would be just as illogical to condemn the recognition of physical differences between races as racist.

When I published my article in 1969, many critics confused the purely empirical question of the genetic role in racial differences in mental abilities with the highly charged political-ideological issue of racism. Because of their confusion, they denounced my attempt to study the possible genetic causes of such differences. At the same time, the doctrinaire environmentalists, seeing their own position threatened by my inquiry, righteously and dogmatically scorned the genetic theory of intelligence.

Thankfully, the emotional furor that greeted my article has died down enough recently to permit sober and searching consideration of the true intent and substance of what I actually tried to say. Under fresh scrutiny stimulated by the controversy, many scientists have reexamined the environmentalist explanations of the black IQ deficit and found them to be inadequate. They simply do not fully account for the known facts, in the comprehensive and consistent manner we should expect of a scientific explanation.

FIRST OF ALL, it is a known and uncontested fact that blacks in the United States score on average about one standard deviation below whites on most tests of intelligence. On the most commonly used IQ tests, this difference ranges from ten to twenty points, and averages about fifteen points. This means that only about 16 percent of the black population exceeds the test performance of the average white on IQ tests. A similar difference of one standard deviation between blacks and whites holds true for 80 standardized mental tests on which published data exist.

A difference of one standard deviation can hardly be called inconsequential. Intelligence tests have more than proved themselves as valid predictors of scholastic performance and occupational attainment, and they predict equally well for blacks as for whites. Unpleasant as these predictions may seem to some people, their significance cannot be wished away because of a belief in equality. Of course, an individual's success and self-fulfillment depends upon many characteristics *besides* intelligence, but IQ does represent an index, albeit an imperfect one, of the ability to compete in many walks of life. For example, many selective colleges require College Board test scores of 600 (equivalent to an IQ of 115) as a minimum for admission. An average IQ difference of one standard deviation between blacks and whites means that the white population will have about seven times the percentage of such potentially talented persons (i.e., IQs over 115) as the black population. At the other end of the scale, the fifteen-point difference in average IQ scores means that mental retardation (IQ below 70) will occur about seven times as often among blacks as among whites.

The IQ difference between blacks and whites, then, clearly has considerable social significance. Yet the environmentalists dismiss this difference as artificial, and claim it does not imply any innate or genetic difference in intelligence. But as I shall show, the purely environmental explanations most commonly put forth are faulty. Examined closely in terms of the available evidence, they simply do not sustain the burden of explanation that they claim. Of course, they may be *possible* explanations of the IQ difference, but that does not necessarily make them the *most probable*. In every case for which there was sufficient relevant evidence to put to a detailed test, the environmental explanations have proven inadequate. I am not saying they have been proven 100 percent wrong, only that they do not account for *all* of the black IQ deficit. Of course, there may be other possible environmental explanations as yet unformulated and untested.

THE GENETIC HYPOTHESIS on the other hand, has not yet been put to any direct tests by the standard techniques of genetic research. It must be seriously considered, however, for two reasons: (1) because the default of the environmentalist theory, which has failed in many of its most important predictions, increases the probability of the genetic theory; (2) since genetically conditioned physical characteristics differ markedly between racial groups, there is a strong *a priori* likelihood that genetically conditioned behavioral or mental characteristics will also differ. Since intelligence and other mental abilities depend upon the physiological structure of the brain, and since the brain, like other organs, is subject to genetic influence, how can anyone disregard the obvious probability of genetic influence on intelligence?

Let us consider some of the genetically conditioned characteristics that we already know to vary between major racial groups: body size and proportions; cranial size and shape; pigmentation of the hair, skin and eyes; hair form and distribution; number of vertebrae; fingerprints; bone density; basic-metabolic rate; sweating; consistency of ear wax; age of eruption of the permanent teeth; fissural patterns on the surfaces of the teeth; blood groups; chronic diseases; frequency of twinning; male-female birth ratio; visual and auditory acuity; color blindness; taste; length of gestation period; physical maturity at birth. In view of so many genetically conditioned traits that do differ between races, wouldn't it be surprising if genetically conditioned mental traits were a major exception?

ONE ARGUMENT for the high probability of genetic influence on the IQ difference between blacks and whites involves the concept of *heritability*. A technical term in quantitative genetics, heritability refers to the proportion of the total variation of some trait, among persons within a given population, that can be attributed to genetic factors. Once the heritability of that trait can be determined, the remainder of the variance can be attributed mainly to environmental influence. Now intelligence, as measured by standard tests such as the Stanford-Binet and many others, does show very substantial heritability in the European and North American Caucasian populations in which the necessary genetic studies have been done. I don't know of any geneticists today who have viewed the evidence and who dispute this conclusion.

No precise figure exists for the heritability of intelligence, since, like any population statistic, it varies from one study to another, depending on the particular population sampled, the IQ test used, and the method of genetic analysis. Most of the estimates for the heritability of intelligence in the populations studied indicate that genetic factors are about twice as important as environmental factors as a cause of IQ differences among individuals.

I do not know of a methodologically adequate determination of IQ heritability in a sample of the U.S. black population. The few estimates that exist, though statistically weak, give little reason to suspect that the heritability of IQ for blacks, when adequately estimated, should differ appreciably from that for whites. Of course the absence of reliable data makes this a speculative assumption.

What implication does the heritability *within* a population have concerning the cause of the difference *between* two populations? The fact that IQ is highly heritable within the white and probably the black population does not by itself constitute formal proof that the difference between the populations is genetic, either in whole or in part. However, the fact of substantial heritability of IQ within the populations does increase the *a priori* probability that the population difference is partly attributable to genetic factors. Biologists generally agree that, almost without exception throughout nature, any genetically conditioned characteristic that varies among individuals within a subspecies (i.e., race) also varies genetically between different subspecies. Thus, the substantial heritability of IQ within the Caucasian and probably black populations makes it likely (but does not prove) that the black population's lower average IQ is caused at least in part by a genetic difference.

What about the purely cultural and environmental explanations of the IQ difference? The most common argument claims that IQ tests have a built-in cultural bias that discriminates against blacks and other poor minority groups. Those who hold this view criticize the tests as being based unfairly on the language, knowledge and cognitive skills of the white "Anglo" middle class. They argue that blacks in the United States do not share in the same culture as whites, and therefore acquire different meanings to words, different knowledge, and a different set of intellectual skills.

HOWEVER COMMONLY and fervently held, this claim that the black IQ deficit can be blamed on culture-biased or "culture-loaded" tests does not stand up under rigorous study. First of all, the fact that a test is culture-*loaded* does not necessarily mean it is culture-*biased*. Of course, many tests do have questions of information, vocabulary and comprehension that clearly draw on experiences which could only be acquired by persons sharing a fairly common cultural background. Reputable tests, called "culture-fair" tests, do exist, however. They use nonverbal, simple symbolic material common to a great many different cultures. Such tests measure the ability to generalize, to distinguish differences and similarities, to see relationships, and to solve problems. They test reasoning power rather than just specific bits of knowledge.

Surprisingly, blacks tend to perform relatively better on the more culture-loaded or verbal kinds of tests than on the culture-fair type. For example, on the widely used Wechsler Intelligence Scale, comprised of eleven different subtests, blacks do better on the culture-loaded subtests of vocabulary, general information, and verbal comprehension than on the nonverbal performance tests such as the block designs. Just the opposite is true for such minorities as Orientals, Mexican-Americans, Indians, and Puerto Ricans. It can hardly be claimed that culture-fair tests have a built-in bias in favor of white, Anglo, middle-class Americans when Arctic Eskimos taking the same tests perform on a par with white, middle-class norms. My assistants and I have tested large numbers of Chinese children who score well above white norms on such tests, despite being recent immigrants from Hong Kong and Formosa, knowing little or no English, and having parents who hold low-level socioeconomic occupations. If the tests have a bias toward the white, Anglo, middle-class, one might well wonder why Oriental children should outscore the white Anglos on whom the tests were originally standardized. Our tests of Mexican-Americans produced similar results. They do rather poorly on the culture-loaded types of tests based on verbal skills and knowledge, but they do better on the culture-fair tests. The same holds true for American Indians. All these minorities perform on the two types of tests much as one might expect from the culture-bias hypothesis. Only blacks, among the minorities we have tested, score in just the opposite manner.

THOSE WHO TALK of culture bias should also consider that all the standard mental tests I know of are color blind, in that they show the same reliability and predictive validity for blacks and whites. In predicting scholastic achievement, for example, we have found that several different IQ tests predict equally well for blacks and whites. College-aptitude tests also predict grades equally well for blacks and whites. The same equality holds true for aptitude tests which predict job performance.

We have studied culture bias in some standard IQ tests by making internal analyses to see which kinds of test items produce greater differences in scores between blacks and whites. For example, we made such an item-by-item check of the highly culture-loaded Peabody Picture Vocabulary Test, on which blacks average some fifteen points lower than whites. The PPVT consists of 150 cards, each containing four pictures. The examiner names one of the pictures and the child points to the appropriate picture. The items follow the order of their difficulty, as measured by the percentage of the children in the normative sample who fail the item.

TO ILLUSTRATE the sensitivity of this test to cultural differences in word meanings, we compared the performance of white schoolchildren in England with children of the same age in California. Although the two groups obtained about the same total IQ score, the

California group found some culture-loaded words such as "bronco" and "thermos" easy, while the London group found them difficult. The opposite occurred with words like "pedestrian" or "goblet." Thus the difficulty of some items differed sharply depending on the child's cultural background. A similar "cultural" bias shows up when comparing the performance of boys and girls, both black and white. Though boys and girls score about equally well over all, they show significant differences in the rank order of item difficulty; specific items, e.g. "parachute" versus "casserole" reflect different sexual biases in cultural knowledge.

Yet when we made exactly the same kind of comparison between blacks and whites in the same city in California, and even in the same schools, we found virtually no difference between the two groups in the order of items when ranked for difficulty, as indexed by the percent failing each item. Both groups show the same rank order of difficulty, although on each item a smaller percentage of blacks give the correct answer. In fact, even the differences between adjacent test items, in terms of percent answering correctly, show great similarity in both the black and white groups.

If this kind of internal analysis reflects cultural bias between different national groups, and sexual bias *within* the same racial group, why does it not reflect the supposed bias *between* the two racial groups? If the tests discriminate against blacks, why do blacks and whites make errors on the same items? Why should the most and least common errors in one group be the same as in the other?

Another way internal analysis can be used to check for bias involves looking for different patterns of item intercorrelations. For example, if a person gets item number 20 right, he may be more likely to get, say, item 30 right than if he had missed item 20. This follows because the test items correlate with one another to varying degrees, and the amount of correlation and the pattern of intercorrelations should be sensitive to group differences in cultural background. Yet we have found no significant or appreciable differences between item intercorrelations for blacks and whites.

In summary, we have found no discriminant features of test items that can statistically separate the test records of blacks and whites any better than chance, when the records are equated for total number correct. We could do so with the London versus California groups, or for sex differences within the same racial group. Thus, even when using the PPVT, one of the most culture-loaded tests, black and white performances did not differ as one should expect if we accept the culture-bias explanation for the black IQ deficit. I consider this strong evidence against the validity of that explanation.

WHAT ABOUT SUBTLE influences in the test situation itself which could have a depressing effect on black performance? It has been suggested, for example, that a white examiner might emotionally inhibit the performance of black children in a test situation. Most of the studies that have attempted to test this hypothesis have produced no substantiation of it. In my own study in which 9,000 black and white children took a number of standard mental and scholastic tests given by black and white examiners, there were no systematic differences in scores according to the race of the examiners. What about the examiner's language, dialect, or accent? In one study, the Stanford-Binet test, a highly verbal and individually administered exam, was translated into black ghetto dialect, and administered by a black examiner fluent in that dialect. A group of black children who took the test under these conditions obtained an average IQ score less than one point higher than the average IQ score of a control group given the test in standard English.

TO TEST THE POPULAR notion that blacks do poorly on IQ tests because they are "verbally deprived," we have looked at studies of the test performances of the most verbally deprived individuals we know of: children born totally deaf. These children do score considerably below average on verbal tests, as expected. But they perform completely up to par on the nonverbal culture-fair type of tests. Their performances, then, turn out to be just the opposite of the supposedly verbally deprived blacks, who score higher on the verbal than on the nonverbal tests.

If one hypothesizes that the black IQ deficit may be due to poor motivation or uncooperative attitudes of blacks in the test situation, then one must explain why little or no difference in scores occurs between blacks and whites on tests involving rote learning and memory. Such tests are just as demanding in terms of attention, effort and persistence but do not call upon the kinds of abstract reasoning abilities that characterize the culture-fair intelligence tests. We have devised experimental tests, which look to pupils like any other tests, that minimize the need for reasoning and abstract ability and maximize the role of nonconceptual learning and memory. On these tests black and white children average about the same scores. Therefore, the racial difference clearly does not involve all mental abilities equally. It involves mainly conceptual and abstract reasoning, and not learning and memory.

Another factor often cited as a possible explanation for the black IQ deficit is teacher expectancy—the notion that a child's test score tends to reflect the level of performance expected by his or her teacher, with the teacher's expectation often based on prejudice or stereotypes. Yet numerous studies of teacher expectancy have failed to establish this phenomenon as a contributing factor to the lower IQ scores of blacks.

TO TEST THE ENVIRONMENTALIST hypothesis, we have examined the results of those tests that most strongly reflect environmental sources of variance, and they turn out to be the very tests that show the least difference between blacks and whites in average scores. The greatest difference in scores between the two racial groups occurs on the tests we infer to be more strongly reflective of genetic variance. If the cultural-environmental hypothesis were correct, just the opposite would be true.

IN AN ATTEMPT to disprove the genetic hypothesis for the black IQ deficit, environmentalists frequently cite studies that compare IQs of socioeconomically matched racial groups, and find considerably less difference in test scores than the usual 15-point difference between races. Here we have a good example of the "sociologist's fallacy." Since whites and blacks differ in average socioeconomic status (SES), the matching of racial groups on SES variables such as education, occupation and social class necessarily means that the black group is more highly selected in terms of whatever other traits and abilities correlate with SES, including intelligence. Therefore the two groups have been unfairly matched in terms of IQ.

Those who cite the socioeconomic matching studies also fail to take account of the well-established genetic difference between social classes, which invalidates their comparison. For example, when the two races are matched for social background, the average skin color of the black group runs lighter in the higher SES groups. This difference indicates that genetic characteristics do vary with SES. Thus, SES matching of blacks and whites reduces the IQ difference not only because it controls for environmental differences, but because it tends to equalize genetic factors as well.

A HOST of other environmental variables don't behave as they ought to according to a strictly environmentalist theory of the black IQ deficit. For example, on practically all the socioeconomic, educational, nutritional and other health factors that sociologists point to as causes of the black-white differences in IQ and scholastic achievement, the American Indian population ranks about as far below black standards as blacks do below those of whites. The relevance of these environmental indices can be shown by the fact that within each ethnic group they correlate to some extent in the expected direction with tests of intelligence and scholastic achievement. Since health, parental education, employment, family income, and a number of more subtle environmental factors that have been studied are all deemed important for children's scholastic success, the stark deprivation of the Indian minority, even by black standards, ought to be reflected in a comparison of the intelligence and achievement-test performance of Indians and blacks. But in a nationwide survey reported in the Coleman Report, in 1966, Indians scored *higher* than blacks on all such tests, from the first to the twelfth grade. On a nonverbal test given in the first grade, for example, before schooling could have had much impact, Indian children exceeded the mean score of blacks by the equivalent of 14 IQ points. Similar findings occur with Mexican-Americans, who rate below blacks on socioeconomic and other environmental indices, but score considerably higher on IQ tests, especially on the nonverbal type. Thus the IQ difference between Indians and blacks, and between Mexican-Americans and blacks, turns out opposite to what one would predict from purely environmental theory, which of course, assumes complete genetic equality for intelligence. No testable environmental hypothesis has as yet been offered to account for these findings.

WHAT ABOUT malnutrition, another factor frequently cited by the environmentalists to disprove the genetic hypothesis? Malnutrition has indeed been found to affect both physical and mental development in a small percentage of children in those areas of the world that suffer severe protein deficiencies: India, South America, South Africa, and Mexico. But few blacks in the United States show any history or signs of severe malnutrition, and I have found no evidence that the degree of malnutrition associated with retarded mental development afflicts any major segment of the U.S. population.

Nor do I know of any evidence among humans that maternal malnutrition, by itself, can have pre- or postnatal effects on a child's mental development. The severe famine in the Netherlands during the last years of World War II provided an excellent case study of such a possibility. Thousands of men conceived, gestated, and born during the period of most severe famine, were later tested, as young adults, on Raven's Standard Progressive Matrices, a nonverbal reasoning test. Their scores did not differ significantly from the scores of other Dutch youths of the same age who had not been exposed to such maternal nutritional deprivation.

If further research should definitely establish the existence of genetically conditioned differences in intelligence between certain races, what would be the practical implications? It would take several articles to consider the question adequately, but the only morally tenable position in human relations would remain unchanged: that all persons should be treated according to their own individual characteristics, and not in terms of their group identity. Let me stress that none of the research I have discussed here allows one to conclude anything about the intelligence of any individual black or white person.

Equality of rights and opportunities is clearly the most beneficial condition for any society. Acceptance of the reality of human differences in mental abilities would simply underline the need for equality of opportunity in order to allow everyone to achieve his or her own self-fulfillment. In order to take account and advantage of the diversity of abilities in the population, and truly to serve all citizens equally, the public schools should move beyond narrow conceptions of scholastic achievement. They should offer a much greater diversity of ways for children of whatever aptitude to benefit from their education.

I HAVE TRIED to emphasize the uncertainty of our knowledge of the causes of race differences in mental abilities. I do not claim any direct or definite evidence, in terms of genetic research, for the existence of genotypic intelligence differences between races or other human population groups. I have not urged acceptance of a hypothesis on the basis of insufficient evidence. I have tried to show that the evidence we now have does not support the environmentalist theory, which, until quite recently, has been accepted as scientifically established. Social scientists have generally accepted it without question, and most scientists in other fields have given silent assent. I have assembled evidence which, I believe, makes such complacent assent no longer possible, and reveals the issue as an open question, calling for much further scientific study.

MOST OF THE SCIENTISTS and intellectuals with whom I have discussed these matters in the past few years see no danger in furthering our knowledge of the genetic basis of racial differences in mental or behaviorial traits. Nor do they fear general recognition of genetic differences in such traits by the scientific world, if that should be the eventual outcome of further research. They do see a danger in politicizing a basically scientific question, one that should be settled strictly on the basis of evidence.

Most of the attempts to politicize the issue, I have found, come from the radical left. True liberals and humanists, on the other hand, want to learn the facts. They do not wish to expend their energies sustaining myths and illusions. They wish to face reality, whatever it may be, because only on the level of reality can real problems be effectively confronted. This means asking hard questions, and seeking the answers with as much scientific ingenuity and integrity as we can muster. It means examining all reasonable hypotheses, including unpopular ones. It means maintaining the capacity to doubt what we might most want to believe, acknowledging the uncertainties at the edge of knowledge, and viewing new findings in terms of shifting probabilities rather than as absolute conclusions.

DIFFERENCES ARE NOT DEFICITS

Theodosius Dobzhansky

T HE DOCTRINE that all men are created equal is widespread in much of the modern world. We take equality for granted in American tradition, spell it out in the Declaration of Independence, but the idea frequently bogs down in misunderstanding and apparent contradictions. Equality is often confused with identity, and diversity with inequality.

Even some reputable scientists claim biology demonstrates that people are born unequal. This is sheer confusion; biology proves nothing of the sort. Every person is indeed biologically and genetically different from every other. Even identical twins are not really identical; they are recognizably separate persons who may engage in different occupations and achieve unequal socioeconomic status. But this phenomenon is biological diversity, which has nothing to do with human inequality.

Human equality and inequality are sociological designs, not biological phenomena. Human equality consists of equality before the law, political equality and equality of opportunity. These are human rights that come from religious, ethical or philosophical premises, not from

Theodosius Dobzhansky (1900–1975), a Russian-born American geneticist, taught in California and New York; he was well-known for his research on *Drosophila* and his writings on genetics and evolution. This essay appeared in *Psychology Today*.

genes. The United Nations recognized this fact in its 1952 UNESCO statement on race: "Equality of opportunity and equality in law in no way depend, as ethical principles, upon the assertion that human beings are in fact equal in endowment."

We may grant equality to all members of the human species or to only a small segment of the population, but we cannot brush away genetic diversity; it is an observable fact. And later in this article I will indicate how a society of equality of opportunity is most propitious for human self-fulfillment.

The reader may question whether genetic diversity has a social significance. At first thought, the answer seems to be no. With the exception of some pathological variants, one's form of enzyme or blood group seems to make no difference socially but genes may have effects that modify several characteristics. One cannot rule out the possibility that apparently neutral genetic variants may produce physiological or mental changes. For example, some scientists claim that B, A and O blood groups have something to do with resistance to plague, smallpox and syphilis respectively. The validity of this claim is still under scrutiny.

It has been established, however, with varying degrees of certainty, that many human traits which unquestionably matter to their possessors and to society, are genetically conditioned. Intelligence, personality, and special abilities are all susceptible to modification by genetic as well as environmental factors. And recent sensational and inflammatory pronouncements about the genetic basis for racial and socioeconomic differences in IQ make mandatory a critical consideration of the subject.

THE UNDERPINNINGS of human intelligence are still somewhat unclear. The most extreme environmentalists say we enter the world with a blank slate upon which circumstance writes a script. Strict hereditarians, on the other hand, believe that parental genes dictate our abilities.

A moderate form of the blank-slate doctrine appeals to many social scientists, who believe we are born with essentially equal potentialities, and become different primarily through upbringing, training and social position. They say that cultural and socioeconomic differences can explain the disparity in intelligence scores between races and classes.

Even a tempered view of genetic predisposition is distasteful in a competitive society. It seems hardly fair that some persons should start life with an advantage over others, and particularly repugnant to think that one race or class is superior to another. But dislike of a theory does not prove or disprove anything.

A third, and more likely, explanation exists for individual and group differences in IQ. Both environment and genetic conditioning may be at work. In this explanation, the bone of contention is not environment versus heredity, but how much environment and how much heredity.

For a clear understanding of the matter, we must define what we mean by IQ. An intelligence quotient is not a measure of the overall quality or worth of an individual. Someone with a high IQ may be vicious, selfish, lazy and slovenly, while someone with a lower score may be kind, helpful, hard-working and responsible. Even psychologists disagree about the mental and psychophysical traits an IQ test measures. Sir Cyril Burt was one of those who claimed that "we may safely assert that the innate amount of potential ability with which a child is endowed at birth sets an upper limit to what he can possibly achieve at school or in afterlife." He believed IQ measures this supposedly innate ability. Others deny that intelligence testing provides any valid information, and see it merely as a device that the privileged use to maintain their status over the less advantaged. Further, there is always the danger that IQ tests are biased in favor of the race, social class, or culture of those who devised the tests. Certainly all existing intelligence tests fall short of being culture-free or culture-fair.

IT IS UNDENIABLE, however, that there are significant statistical correlations between IQ scores and success in schooling, advances in the existing occupational structure, and prestige in Western societies.

Researchers have also securely established that *individual* differences in scores are genetically as well as environmentally conditioned. The evidence comes from more than 50 independent studies in eight countries. But how much of this variation is due to genetics, or heritability as scientists call it, is unknown. The best estimates come from studies on twins and other close relatives reared together and apart. Arthur Jensen has carefully reviewed these data, and his analysis has indicated that approximately 80 percent of individual differences in

IQ are inherited. This degree of heritability is high compared to the genetic components of other traits in different organisms. It is much higher than that of egg production in poultry or yield in corn, yet animal and plant breeders have substantially improved these characteristics through genetic selection. In insects, artificial selection has induced spectacular changes for traits that are only half as genetically conditioned as human IQ.

Because people misunderstand the significance of the high heritability of IQ, we should clarify what it does and does not mean. To begin with, it does not mean that genes alone condition IQ. A possessor of certain genes will not necessarily have a certain IQ. The same gene constellation can result in a higher or lower score in different circumstances. Genes *determine* the intelligence (or stature or weight) of a person only in his particular environment. The trait that actually develops is *conditioned* by the interplay of the genes with the environment. Every person is unique and nonrecurrent, and no two individuals, except identical twins, have the same genes.

MARIE SKODAK and Harold M. Skeels showed the influence of environment on IQ in their study of identical twins raised together and apart. They found a consistently lower IQ correlation between twins raised apart compared to that between twins reared together. Because identical twins have identical genes, the greater IQ differences in twins raised apart, compared to those reared together, must be due to their different environments.

Now let us consider people in general rather than a particular person. Genes really determine reaction ranges for individuals with more or less similar genes. Genetic traits emerge in the process of development as one's genetic potential is realized. Similar genes may have different effects in unlike environments, and dissimilar genes may have similar effects in like environments.

But it is not useful to say that genes determine the upper and lower limits of intelligence, since existing environments are endlessly variable and we constantly add new ones. To test the reactions of a given gene constellation in all environments is obviously impossible. For example, how could one discover the greatest height I could become in some very propitious environment, or the shortest stature I could have in another environment and still remain alive? It is even more far-fetched to forecast stature in environments that may be engineered in the future, perhaps with the aid of some new growth hormone.

More importantly, heritability is not an intrinsic property of IQ, but of the population in which it occurs. Consideration of limiting cases makes this obvious. If we had a population of genetically identical persons, all individual differences in IQ would be environmentally determined. There would be *no* genetic influence affecting the *differences* in IQ that developed among them. Alternately, if all members of the population lived in the same environment, all IQ differences would be genetic. Therefore, we must confine our estimates of the heritability of IQ to the population under study and to the time we collected the data.

WHEN WE LOOK at estimates of heritability, we must keep in mind the genetic and environmental uniformity or heterogeneity of the population studied. Most of the information on IQ comes from studies on white, middle-class populations. The most abundant data pertain to research on twins and siblings raised together. Children in the same family do not grow up in identical environments, but their surroundings are certainly more alike on the average than those across socioeconomic classes or races. Estimating heritability of IQ differences in one population is beset with pitfalls. Cross-racial and cross-class research is even more difficult.

Scientists have documented differences in average IQ for various socioeconomic classes. This is neither surprising nor unexpected, since we know that educational and other opportunities are unequal for members of different social classes. Burt summarized data on 40,000 parents and their children in England. He gathered information on higher professional, lower professional, clerical, skilled, semiskilled and unskilled workers. Fathers in the higher professional category had an average IQ of about 140. This score was about 85 for the unskilled laborers. Children's average IQs ranged from about 121 for the higher professional group to about 93 in the unskilled sample. The children of the high professionals scored lower than their fathers while the children of the unskilled workers scored higher than their fathers. This is the well-known phenomenon called regression toward the mean. Regardless of whether the IQ differences between occupational classes are mainly genetic or environmental, children do not fully inherit the superior or inferior performance of their parents.

THE SITUATION is analogous with human races. Researchers have found a consistent ten to twenty point disparity in average IQ scores between blacks and whites in the U.S. And because races, unlike socioeconomic groups, are usually physically recognizable, this disparity is often blamed on inferior black genes. But persons who belong to different races, whether they live in different countries or side by side, do not always have equal opportunities for mental development. Nobody, not even racists, can deny that living conditions and educational opportunities are disparate in races and classes.

After psychologist Arthur Jensen explicitly recognizes that heritability of individual differences in IQ cannot be used as a measure of average heritability across populations, he tries to do just that. In fairness to Jensen, he presents a detailed analysis of the environmental factors that could account for the discrepancy, but then he concludes that none of these factors or their combinations can explain the difference in average black and white IQ scores. He appeals to studies which try to equate black and white environments by comparing populations of equal socioeconomic status. This diminishes the IQ difference between the two races, but it does not erase the difference. Jensen takes this as evidence that a strong genetic component is operating. I remain unconvinced.

W. F. Bodmer and L. L. Cavalli-Sforza have pointed out the inadequacies of equating similar socioeconomic status with similar total environment. In their words: "It is difficult to see, however, how the status of blacks and whites can be compared. The very existence of a racial stratification correlated with a relative socioeconomic deprivation makes this comparison suspect. Black schools are well known to be generally less adequate than white schools, so that equal number of years of schooling certainly do not mean equal educational attainments. Wide variation in the level of occupation must exist within each occupational class. Thus one would certainly expect, even for equivalent occupational classes, that the black level is on the average lower than the white. No amount of money can buy a black person's way into a privileged upper-class white community, or buy off more than two hundred years of accumulated racial prejudice on the part of the whites . . . It is impossible to accept the idea that matching for status provides an adequate, or even substantial, control over most important environmental differences between blacks and whites."

THE CONTROVERSY over the relative influence of nature and nurture on racial differences in IQ has grown hotter since scientists documented the high heritability of *individual* IQ. Racists try to gain maximum propaganda mileage from this fact, but the different race and class *averages* may be less genetically conditioned than individual variations in IQ.

Sandra Scarr-Salapatek shows evidence of this proposition in her study of twins in Philadelphia schools. She attacks the presumption that the influence of genetics and environment is simply additive, and suggests that the two factors may operate dependently and in different ways. She hypothesizes that genetic differences show up more in persons who mature in favorable surroundings, but remain hidden or unused in individuals from adverse or suppressive environments. If her assertion is correct, the heritability of IQ should be lower among disadvantaged groups (both social and racial) than among privileged classes. On the other hand, if genetic and environmental influences simply add together, heritability should be uniform in all groups.

Scarr-Salapatek tested the two hypotheses in her study of intelligence and scholastic-aptitude test data on 1,521 pairs of twins attending public schools in Philadelphia. She compared test scores across races and across socioeconomic levels and found that differences between upper and lower class blacks were much smaller (5.3 points) than those between whites of similar classes (16.1 points). More importantly, for both blacks and whites, test scores varied more among advantaged than among disadvantaged children. She concludes: "From studies of middle-class white populations, investigators have reached the conclusion that genetic variability accounts for about 75 percent of the total variance in IQ scores of whites. A closer look at children reared under different conditions shows that the percentage of genetic variance and the mean scores are very much a function of the rearing conditions of the population. A first look at the black population suggests that genetic variability is important in advantaged groups, but much less important in the disadvantaged. Since most blacks are socially disadvantaged, the proportion of genetic variance in the aptitude scores of black children is considerably less than that of white children . . ."

Scarr-Salapatek's work lends further support to the possibility that we can explain at least a part of racial and socioeconomic differences in IQ with environmental reasons. But nothing I have said excludes the possibility that there is also a genetic component in such differences. We simply don't know. The available data are inadequate to settle the question.

SUPPOSE for the sake of argument, that the average intelligence of some class or race is lower than the average for other classes or races in the environments that now exist. This still would not justify race and class prejudice, since one could still induce important changes in manifested intelligence by intensive care and tutoring of children. Perhaps it may even be possible to nullify or to reverse the disparity of group averages by altering environments and practices of child rearing.

We have seen that individual variability within classes and races is both genetically and environmentally conditioned. This is true of IQ as well as scholastic aptitude and achievement. We should keep in mind that IQ is not a unitary trait determined by a single gene, but rather it is a composite of numerous genetic components. IQ surely is not the only genetically conditioned trait. Less detailed but still substantial evidence suggests that many personality characteristics and special abilities, from mathematics to music, have genetic components. It is accurate to say that whenever a variable human trait, even an apparently learned habit such as smoking, has been studied genetically, some genetic conditioning has come to light. In any case, genetic conditioning, no matter how strong, does not preclude improvement by manipulation of the environment, as we have shown in our discussion of race, class and IQ.

Let us return to my original thesis that we can maximize the benefits of human diversity in a society where all individuals have truly equal opportunities. It is utterly unlikely that the incidence of all genetically conditioned traits will remain uniform throughout all socioeconomic classes. While genes for a particular trait, such as IQ, eyesight or stature, may be more common in class A than in class B, this does not mean that all A persons and no B individuals will possess these genes. Since only gene frequencies are involved, an individual's potentialities are determined by his own genetic endowment, not by his class or race. So only in a society of equal opportunity for all, regardless of race or class, will every individual have a chance to use his fullest potential.

Scholastic ability and achievement are important determinants of social mobility in a society with equality of opportunity. Schools and universities are principal ladders for socioeconomic rise. Insofar as achievement is genetically conditioned, social mobility is in part a genetic process. In *Genetics and Sociology*, Bruce K. Eckland writes "... talented adults rise to the top of the social hierarchy and the dull fall or remain on the bottom. Therefore, as the system strives to achieve full equality of opportunity, the observed within-class variance among children tends to diminish while the between-class variance tends to increase on selective traits associated with genetic differences." Some may be chagrined to learn that increasing equality of opportunity *increases,* rather than decreases, genetic differences between socioeconomic classes. But I intend to show that if we had true equality of opportunity, the classes as we know them now would no longer exist.

WE CAN MAXIMIZE the benefits of human diversity without creating a meritocracy in which the genetic elite concentrate in the upper socioeconomic classes. With anything approaching full equality, those most genetically and environmentally fit for each trade, craft or profession will gravitate to that occupation. But these aggregations of genetic aptitudes will not result in socioeconomic classes or castes. I believe they will develop into new social phenomena, barely foreshadowed at present.

These aptitude aggregations will differ from our present socioeconomic classes primarily by their fluidity. Aggregations will gain new members who are not descended from old members. These gains will be offset by losses of some of the progeny of old members who will join other occupational groups. Some gains and losses may come to pass when individual occupations become more or less attractive or socially important. Others will be genetically conditioned and hence genetically significant. They result from the segregation of trait genes and must not be frustrated by the impulses of parents either to make their offspring follow in their own occupational footsteps, or to propel them to more privileged job categories.

But it is unlikely that every member of, say, the musicians aggregation, would have the gene for music, even if such a gene really existed.

More likely the genetic basis of musical talent is a constellation of several genes, and possibly of different genes in different persons. Some children in the group will lack this genetic predisposition toward musical talent, and move on to other aggregations. Conversely, some talented musicians will be born in other aggregations, and will pass into the aggregation of musicians. This is to some extent analogous to present social-class mobility, but it is more closely tied to human genetics. While socioeconomic mobility is only vertical, aggregate mobility is horizontal and vertical.

Genes for various aptitudes exist in all social strata and professional aggregations, but propinquity and assortive mating will greatly increase the number of marriages between individuals who carry genes for similar aptitudes. This will not necessarily yield a bumper crop of geniuses, but it enhances the possibility.

It is not surprising that not everybody welcomes the prospect of equality. Even a few biologists have concocted horrendous tales of its genetic consequences. They say equality has drained the lower classes of genetic talents, and only worthless dregs remain. We can dispel this fantasy by pointing out that a former untouchable is a cabinet minister in India's government, and that after most of the aristocracy was destroyed during the Russian revolution, able individuals from the former lower classes took over the functions of government.

On the other hand, it may not seem realistic to envisage an entire society consisting of elite aggregations. Maybe one large aggregate will be left with no particular aptitudes. To this I can only say that I agree with Scarr-Salapatek. Differences between humans "can simply be accepted as differences and not as deficits. If there are alternate ways of being successful within the society, then differences can be valued variations on the human theme regardless of their environment or genetic origins." We must not brand people or professions as elite or common. To complement equality of opportunity we need equality of status. Manual labor is not intrinsically inferior to intellectual labor, even though more of us may be more adept at the former than at the latter. The presence of rare abilities need not detract from appreciation of more common ones. Though this may be hard to accept for individuals who grew up in a class society, I feel it is ethically desirable. Moreover, history is moving in this direction.

JENSEN AND EDUCATIONAL DIFFERENCES

Carl Bereiter

I N T H E S E D E C A D E S common sense does not know what to make of human inequality. For millennia inequality was viewed as part of the natural order, with nature's differences and society's differences harmoniously coordinated. That view has collapsed, but no other coherent view has come to take its place. Common sense recognizes naturally occurring ability differences, but it has never assimilated the Mendelian model, which offers an integrative explanation of both similarities and differences as these relate to both genetic and environmental effects. Instead, common sense has tended to attribute similarities mainly to heredity and differences mainly to the environment, a fundamentally incoherent model which, however, works fairly well on a day-to-day basis. A model that attributes human differences mainly to the environment is also, of course, compatible with egalitarian social programs, including progressive educational programs.

The thrust of Jensen's work, as I see it, has been toward establishing a more coherent model of ability differences in the minds of educated people. It has not been sufficient, of course, simply to expound

Carl Bereiter teaches at the Ontario Institute for Studies in Education (Toronto). He is author of *The Psychology of Written Composition* and other books. This article appeared in *Arthur Jensen: Consensus and Controversy* (1987), edited by Sohan and Celia Modgil.

a scientifically more adequate model. Too much is at stake morally. Whatever the excesses some of Jensen's critics may have gone to, they have been correct in their intuition that any change in the way we view ability differences is a potential threat to the worldwide drive toward social equality.

Jensen's massive research program has not succeeded in installing a different model of human differences in the common understanding. Indeed, common sense in the last two decades may have slipped farther away from a coherent model, and Jensen's work may only have lessened the slide. But common sense is bound to change. For educators, and I trust for many other social agents, Jensen has provided an indispensable scientific basis for reconceptualizing differences in human intelligence. It remains, however, for someone to reveal to us a way of thinking about human differences that is morally as well as scientifically coherent. Jensen has not accomplished this, but much less so have his critics. Intelligence and social equality are both too important to the survival of civilization for us to persist much longer with models that require us to ignore one in order to conceive of the other.

In this chapter I make no pretense of revealing a "morally as well as scientifically coherent way of thinking about human differences." But I do hope my remarks will be seen as contributing to the purpose. Jensen's work is often seen as damaging to hopes that education can play a significant role in promoting social equality. Partly this is true in that he has confronted educators with evidence that ability differences have deeper roots than many had supposed. Partly it is false and rests on misinterpretations of his research. And partly, I believe, it reveals some limitations in Jensen's own approach to the issues of education and inequality. The focus of the chapter is on sorting out these three aspects of the implications of Jensen's work.

THE TITLE of the paper that rocked education. "How Much Can We Boost IQ and Scholastic Achievement?" was actually a misnomer. The title should have been "How Much Can We Reduce Inequality in IQ and Scholastic Achievement?" As critics were quick to point out (e.g., Crow, 1969), and as Jensen readily acknowledged, heritability is largely irrelevant to the question of how much intelligence and achievement in school subjects can be improved. On the other hand, heritability is highly relevant to the question of how much education and other environmental factors can be expected to reduce individual and group differences.

Confusion between the issues of improvability and equalizability has sapped much of the educational significance of discussions about heredity and mental abilities. To argue that intelligence cannot be improved amounts to arguing that education is impossible. The responses of educationally oriented psychologists to Jensen's "IQ and Scholastic Achievement" paper tended to give passing assent to the role of heredity in individual differences and then to focus on the improvability of intelligence (e.g., Bloom, 1969; Hunt, 1969). The improvability of intelligence remains a significant scientific issue (cf. Detterman and Sternberg, 1982), and Jensen's recent work on mental speed is relevant to it. But it is not the right issue to discuss in relation to Jensen's work on heritability.

Jensen's main point about heritability and individual differences can be conveyed by simple arithmetic. If the heritability of IQ is taken to be .70, then getting rid of *all* the variance due to environment would reduce the variance of IQ by 30 percent—from 256 to 179. But this would reduce the standard deviation of IQ only from 16 to 13.4 points (the square roots of the preceding numbers). This is a significant reduction, to be sure, but one not likely to be noticeable at the classroom level. Changing the heritability estimate to .60 or .80 does not substantially alter the picture. At the same time, however, a heritability of .60 to .80 allows plenty of room for significant *increases* in individual or mean IQ: every standard deviation of relevant improvement in the environment should produce a gain of 7 to 10 points. But except through some strange inversion, whereby the environments of high-IQ children were degraded while those of low-IQ children were raised, there is no way within the arithmetic presented here that the improvability of IQ can be translated into a major equalization of IQ.

Apart from simply ignoring it, there are several ways of countering the discouraging spectacle of genetically determined educational inequality. One may argue for a radically lower estimate of the heritability of intelligence or deny that individual differences are as great as they appear (arguing on grounds of bias or invalidity of intelligence tests).

An alternative is to shift the focus from intelligence to its outcomes. This was the main practical message of Jensen's original "IQ and

Scholastic Achievement" article. The argument Jensen advanced there was that, since scholastic achievement shows lower heritability than IQ, the prospects for ameliorating educational inequality are better if educators focus on promoting achievement rather than on raising IQ. Although the conclusion is one that Jensen has continued to argue for, the original argument was weak and he did not sustain it for long. In the first place heritability ratios for school achievement, although somewhat lower than for IQ, are still high enough that equalizing environments would not substantially reduce inequality.

A more practical objection, however, is that improvements in the quality of education typically aim at helping students "realize their potential," which very likely means increasing individual differences. The lower heritability of school achievement may reflect, among other things, faulty instructions, which results in a number of bright children failing to master academic skills. Alleviating such deficiences of the education system could be expected to increase the correlation of school achievement with IQ and hence increase its heritability.

FROM AN EDUCATIONAL STANDPOINT the essence of Jensen's work on group differences can be summed up by the subtitle of one of his articles—"The Differences Are Real" (1973c). Although his notoriety comes from having suggested that racial and group differences in IQ might have a genetic component, his research has not pursued that issue. From a practical educational standpoint it is of no immediate importance whether group differences in test scores are wholly a consequence of environmental factors or whether they are due in some degree to genetic factors. What does matter, however, is whether test score differences represent real differences in aptitude and acquired knowledge or whether they are just artifacts—reflections of test wiseness, test bias, and the like.

The tendency to dismiss test score differences as meaningless has been very strong throughout the "Jensen debate." Whole books have been published largely devoted to this way of dismissing evidence on group differences—for instance. Richardson, Spears and Richards (1972) and Senna (1973). I have been amazed to find educators taking this sort of argument seriously. Their daily experience should have convinced them that differences in reading achievement, for instance, were at least as great as those indicated by test scores. A likely reason for the widespread appeal of the "damn the tests" movement has been that people feel they can participate in it without any technical knowledge. Genetic arguments are intimidating to the nonspecialist. But there is a tradition of nonspecialist criticism of tests (e.g., Hoffmann, 1962), which requires little more than ingenuity in thinking up alternative correct answers to test items.

In actuality, of course, it does require technical knowledge to evaluate tests. What a test measures and whether it is biased against one type of examinee or another are not questions that can be answered by inspection of the items. Against the various claims of invalidity and bias that have had so much appeal to nonspecialists. Jensen has mounted impressive psychometric evidence. *Educability and Group Differences* (1973a) and *Bias in Mental Testing* (1980) are *tours de force* in which every argument against the validity of test score differences takes a battering. One need not concede every point to Jensen in order to acknowledge the main point he has been trying to make, which is that the test scores indicate genuine deficits of some significant kind being frequent among minority students.

It is easy enough to understand why educators should wish to avoid acknowledging that "the differences are real." It smacks of racism and defeatism, even if only indirectly; and it inevitably leads to a question that is very difficult to handle, especially when it comes from a parent: "Why don't our children do as well?" But what are the consequences of not acknowledging the reality of group differences?

From what I have seen in American schools, where problems have been most acute, the consequence of denying group differences has been to foster the very thing egalitarians have feared most—unequal schools. In the vast experiment with compensatory education methods carried out through the Follow Through program, the net effect of compensatory education tended slightly toward the negative (Stebbins et al., 1977). That is, disadvantaged children in the special programs tended to do slightly less well than comparable children who did not receive special treatment. Although the aggregate effect was slight, its tendency was toward an increase in inequality.

The only compensatory education program credited with generally positive results was the Direct Instruction model, which was the one that most clearly treated the children as having learning deficits that needed to be overcome. This is not to say that the other models took a Panglossian attitude toward the disadvantaged child. In some measure the full range of problems was recognized by all the educators involved. But in the less successful models the emphasis was on services or experiences that the children lacked, on the need of the school to adapt to the cultural background of the children, and on general principles of child development. Valid as these concerns might be, they have a certain head-in-the-sand quality when one is talking about children who are entering the second grade and not one of them can read or when one is talking about a high-school class for the university-bound where the teaching is done by lecture and films because the textbook (a standard high-school text) is judged too difficult for most of the students.

I am suggesting that failure to recognize group differences results in accommodating to those differences. Whatever is typical of the group defines the normal expectation. The curricula of schools serving minority students become geared to low levels of literacy, low levels of learning and thinking skills, and low expectations of future achievement. Such curricula may be defensible as necessary interim measures on the way toward educational equality (cf. Stanley, 1971), but even then it would seem that intelligent planning of such curricula should be based on a recognition of facts rather than on dismissal of comparative data.

It must be made clear that the issue is not use versus non-use of standardized tests. Standardized tests can be helpful in making gross assessments of educational needs and in evaluating the success of remedial programs. But the facts are often evident without testing. Furthermore, tests can easily be made to hide unpleasant facts. One school district I know of is busy creating local norms for a standardized reading test, with different norms for different parts of the district. The justification is that socioeconomic and cultural differences within the district are so vast that one set of norms cannot be appropriate for all children. This justification was put forward by my informant as self-evident. As Jensen's research makes its way into the understanding of school people, it should start to become clear to them that such a justification is not self-evident at all, and that it should be used with extreme caution because of its separatist implications.

THE MOST HOPEFUL argument that Jensen developed in "IQ and Scholastic Achievement" grew out of his distinction between

Level I and Level II abilities. He said, "I am reasonably convinced that all the basic scholastic skills can be learned by children with normal Level I learning ability, provided the instructional techniques do not make *g* (i.e., Level II) the *sine qua non* of being able to learn" (1969a, p. 117). More generally put, the argument was that there must be alternative ways of learning things, which make use of different strengths.

The underlying idea here is Cronbach's (1957) of aptitude-by-treatment interactions. It is a programmatic rather than a theoretical idea, pointing to the possibility that if we study different kinds of students under different kinds of educational treatments, we may discover ways of matching students to treatments that are substantially more effective than giving all students the treatment that is best on the average. To the extent that such a program is successful, it should be possible to achieve a degree of equalization of learning outcomes without the need for an equalization of abilities. After examining the evidence, however, Jensen began to be less optimistic about the promise of this approach, reporting that he could find "very little evidence of pupil X type of instruction interaction in the realm of learning school subjects or for complex learning in general" (1969b, p. 236).

A few years later Jensen (1976) was avowedly negative about the possibilities of discovering ways to make learning less dependent on *g*, chiding me for excessive optimism, when originally it was I who chided him (Bereiter, 1969). Let us see if we can sort out the matters of substance that underlie these shifting sentiments.

Jensen's original assertion that all the basic scholastic skills could be taught to children with adequate Level I abilities can still be taken as roughly valid. Although functional illiteracy continues as a serious problem in the English-speaking nations, there is substantial evidence that the basics of literacy can be taught to children of low IQ (Becker, 1977). Recent research on cognitive strategy instruction also indicates that such children can learn to achieve reasonably high levels of comprehension as well (Palincsar and Brown, 1984). The prevailing methods of reading instruction, however, illustrate what is meant by making learning unnecessarily dependent on *g*. Students are left to figure out the confusing English phonetic code with little help; and the help they get is usually remote from the reading process, consisting of after-the-fact lessons on phonics that require children to make their own translations of "theory" into practice (Chall, 1983).

Recent research on children's mathematics difficulties shows even more strikingly that children's Level I abilities are not being used to full advantage. In a detailed comparison of the mathematical knowledge of children who were either normal or backward in elementary mathematics, Russell and Ginsburg (1984) found that the only outstanding difference between the two groups was in knowledge of number facts. This should come as a surprise to those who believe that the schools are specialized for the production of rote learning. A look at the standard approach to teaching number facts removes the mystery, however. Children do pages and pages of simple addition, subtraction, and multiplication exercises, which provide abundant practice for those who have already learned the relevant number facts, but do nothing whatever to teach them to those who have not. Here it seems that children do not need intelligence in order to figure out the material to be learned but they need it in order to mobilize their own effective strategies for learning the material. Since such strategies are not taught either, it is only the more fortunately endowed children who pick them up. Although I do not know of specific evidence on the teachability of number facts, there is evidence that carefully conceived instruction can upgrade achievement not only in the mechanics of elementary mathematics but also in problem-solving (Dilworth and Warren, 1980).

Many educators would dispute the preceding assertions, arguing either that existing educational practices are not as bad as I have painted them or that the results of experimental programs are not as encouraging. If they are right, then the prospects for improving the lot of low achievers are poor indeed. But for the sake of argument let us grant the more hopeful prospect that I have sketched and see where it leads as far as inequality is concerned.

The points I have been making all deal with the improvability of scholastic achievement, not with reduction of individual differences. It might seem, however, that number facts are number facts—there are only so many of them that people normally learn, just as there are only so many letter-sound correspondences to learn—and therefore instructional improvements that enable more children to master these elements ought to reduce inequality. For those particular elements, yes. But for achievement in general it is a different matter. In my experience any instructional innovation that puts certain skills within the reach of previously failing children also makes it possible for the more successful children to acquire those skills at an earlier age. The result-ing acceleration can easily increase the spread of differences.

A FAIRLY LARGE PORTION of research on child development is devoted to studying correlations between child-rearing conditions and practices on one hand and developmental outcomes such as IQ and achievement on the other (Scott-Jones, 1984). There is also a con-tinuous translation of this research into guides for parents, which often focus on raising the child's IQ. This body of research rests on a premise that virtually all the researchers recognize as shaky: the premise that antecedent conditions found to correlate with developmental out-comes cause those outcomes. Behavioral genetics provides a set of alternative premises that are, seemingly by common consent, simply ignored in most child development research (Plomin, DeFries and Loehlin, 1977). One such premise, for instance, is that parenting behavior and school achievement are different manifestations of the same genetic characteristics being expressed in parents and their off-spring.

Jensen has not involved himself in child-rearing issues the way some other genetically oriented psychologists have done (cf. Scarr and McCartney, 1983). He can hardly be faulted for this, but in not involv-ing himself with the complexities of cognitive development he has, it seems to me, lent support to a view of intelligence development that is not much different from that of naive environmentalists. Intelli-gence, Jensen says (1973b, p. 89), "is the result of a large number of genes each having a small additive effect." Substitute "environmental factors" for "genes" and you have the naive environmentalist theory. Include both and you have the prevailing textbook view. What all the views have in common is the notion of a lot of little undifferentiated items having an additive effect.

In practical educational terms, what is wrong with these addi-tive models is that they provide no basis for the creative pursuit of heredity-environment interactions. I have already noted Jensen's dis-enchantment with aptitude-treatment interaction research (which I share). But ATI research has been mostly a blind groping for existing environmental variants that might interact strongly with individual characteristics. Existing variants in child-rearing and educational prac-tices are unlikely to interact strongly with individual differences because in order to achieve their status as existing variants they had to have evolved through use with a variety of children. The potential interactions, if there ever were any, would have been averaged out before the treatment conditions came to the attention of ATI researchers.

There remains, however, a realm of almost totally unexplored possibilities of child-rearing and educational practices designed to compensate for specific genetic lacks. Suppose, to take a simple example, that some children's intellectual development is hampered by the fact that they are not very curious. Now to say that the child's lack of curiosity is itself a sign of low intelligence is no more helpful than to say that the child's lack of curiosity is due to a dull environment. It might be more productive as a working hypothesis to suppose that the child's lack of curiosity is one element in having low intelligence. It is an element that may have both genetic and environmental causes, but it is not the whole of intelligence and so it might be possible to overcome or compensate for it by other intellectual resources available to the child.

Such an approach to compensating for handicaps has been quite effective in the treatment of deficits caused by brain injury (Luria, 1963), and there is no a priori reason to suppose it could not be effective in dealing with the normal run of deficits affecting intelligence. The basic idea is that it should be possible for people with rather differently constituted brains to achieve functionally equivalent intelligence. This probably already happens incidentally, but we do not know how to make it happen. If we did, we would have some hope of generating hereditary-environment interactions that were both beneficial and equalizing in their effect.

To speculate on the possibility of as yet undiscovered strong interactions between heredity and educational treatments may seem dilatory, given the urgent problems of educational inequality. But it should not for that reason be taken lightly. Such interactions appear to be the only hope there is for education to effect major reductions in intellectual differences, and therefore the search for them deserves to be a high priority, no matter how uncertain the outcome. It is important, therefore, that the model of educational differences we carry forward should be a heuristically valuable model, guiding research along the most promising channels. Additive effect models, whether hereditarian, environmentalist, or eclectic, with or without interaction terms, may give a good fit to existing data, but they offer little guidance to exploration.

THE INEQUALITY to which we have been referring and which has been the object of Jensen's empirical research is inequality on various score scales that are presumed to have equal intervals. Thus if everyone increases by six IQ points or by three-tenths of a grade equivalent, we say that there has been no reduction in inequality. But equality and inequality of score scales is only of interest insofar as it relates to equality and inequality in real-world outcomes, and real-world outcomes often exhibit discontinuities. Reading test scores, for instance, are continuously distributed, but an important discontinuity is recognized between a level of reading ability that is adequate for everyday needs (functional literacy) and a level that is not. At a lower range many reading experts would recognize another discontinuity between a level of ability at which students can figure out unfamiliar words and a level at which they can only recognize a particular set of words. Similarly, with respect to general intelligence, there are commonly recognized discontinuities that have to do with being able or unable to handle regular school work and being able or unable to get along without custodial care.

The implication of these discontinuities or threshold effects is that an educational treatment that increased everyone's test scores by the same amount might nevertheless produce a significant change in the spread of differences as far as real-life outcomes are concerned. This would be the case, for instance, if the gain moved a significant number of students above the threshold of functional literacy who would otherwise have remained below it. Gains of this kind, unlike the gains I speculated about in the preceding section, are within the grasp of current educational technology and may soon be within practical reach as well.

I do not think this point should be regarded as a mere footnote to the immense literature on individual differences in aptitudes and achievement. This literature commands attention outside the psychometric laboratories precisely because it speaks to real-world issues of competence and its outcomes. Yet throughout the individual differences literature the metrics used tend to be those of convenience rather than those that would tell us about an individual's chances of making it into a university, of earning a living wage, of being able to figure unit prices or even to understand what a unit price is, and so on (cf. Bereiter, 1973). There are substantial practical reasons why psychometricians must confine most of their work to relating one score scale to another. But at the end of the line, where conclusions of great social import are set out for the rest of the world to ponder, there ought at least to be more explicit notice taken of the artificial nature of the variables that have gone into the research. Jensen is certainly no more remiss than others in this regard; but because he has tackled more important social issues than others, such as issues of racial and social group differences, the responsibility seems greater of making sure that findings expressed in terms of score means and standard deviations, of regression lines and variance accounted for, are not casually translated into pronouncements about the human condition.

REFERENCES

Becker, W. C. (1977) "Teaching reading and language to the disadvantaged: What we have learned from field research," *Harvard Educational Review*, 47, pp. 518–43.

Bereiter, C. (1969) "The future of individual differences," *Harvard Educational Review*, 39, pp. 310–18.

Bereiter, C. (1973) "Review of inequality: A reassessment of the effect of family and schooling in America by C. Vencks et al.," *Contemporary Psychology*, 18, pp. 401–3.

Bloom, B. S. (1969) "Letter to the editor," *Harvard Educational Review*, 39, pp. 419–21.

Chall, J. (1983) *Learning to Read: The Great Debate*, 2nd ed., New York, McGraw-Hill.

Cronbach, L. J. (1957) "The two disciplines of scientific psychology," *American Psychologist*, 12, pp. 671–84.

Crow, J. F. (1969) "Genetic theories and influences: Comment on value of diversity," *Harvard Educational Review*, 39, pp. 301–9.

Detterman, D. K. and Sternberg, R. S. (1982) *How and How Much Can Intelligence Be Increased*, Norwood, N.J., Ablex.

Dilworth, R. P. and Warren, L. M. (1980) *An Independent Investigation of Real Math: The Field-Testing and Learner Verification Studies*, LaSalle, Ill., Open Court.

Hoffmann, B. (1962) *The Tyranny of Testing*, New York, Collier Books.

Hunt, J. McV. (1969) "Has compensatory education failed? Has it been attempted?" *Harvard Educational Review*, 39, pp. 278–300.

Jensen, A. R. (1969a) "How much can we boost IQ and scholastic achievement," *Harvard Educational Review*, 39, pp. 1–123.

Jensen, A. R. (1969b) "Reducing the heredity-environment uncertainty," *Harvard Educational Review*, 39, pp. 449–83; reprinted in (1969) "Environment, heredity, and intelligence," *Harvard Educational Review*. Reprint Series No. 2. pp. 209–43.

Jensen, A. R. (1973a) *Educability and Group Differences*, London, Methuen; New York, Harper and Row, pp. xiii + 407.

Jensen, A. R. (1973b) *Educational Differences*, London, Methuen, pp. xiii + 462.

Jensen, A. R. (1973c) *Genetics and Education*, London, Methuen: New York, Harper and Row, pp. vii + 379.

Jensen, A. R. (1976) "Equality and diversity in education," in Ashline, N. F., et al. (Eds), *Education, Inequality, and National Policy*, Lexington, Mass., Lexington Books, pp. 125–36.

Jensen, A. R. (1980) *Bias in Mental Testing*, New York, The Free Press.

Luria, A. R. (1963) *Restoration of Function after Brain Injury*, New York, Pergamon.

Palincsar, A. S. and Brown, A. L. (1984) "Reciprocal teaching of comprehension-fostering and monitoring activities." *Cognition and Instruction*, 1, pp. 117–75.

Plomin, R., DeFries, J. C. and Loehlin, J. C. (1977) "Genotype-environment interaction and correlation in the analysis of human behavior," *Psychological Bulletin*, 84, pp. 309–22.

Richardson, K., Spears, D. and Richards, M. (Eds) (1972) *Race, Culture and Intelligence*, Harmondsworth, Penguin.

Russell, R. L. and Ginsburg, H. P. (1984) "Cognitive analysis of children's mathematics difficulties," *Cognition and Instruction*, 1, pp. 217–44.

Scarr, S. and McCartney, K. (1983) "How people make their own environments: A theory of genotype-environment effects," *Child Development*, 54, pp. 424–35.

Scott-Jones, D. (1984) "Family influences on cognitive development and school achievement." *Review of Research in Education*, 11, pp. 259–304.

Senna, C. (Ed.) (1973) *The Fallacy of IQ*, New York, The Third Press.

Stanley, J. C. (1971) "Predicting college success of the educationally disadvantaged." *Science*, 171, pp. 640–7.

Stebbins, L. B., St. Pierre, R. G., Proper, E. C., Anderson, R. B. and Cerva, T. R. (1977) *A Planned Variation Model, Vol. IV-A, Effects of Follow Through Models*, Washington, D.C., U.S. Office of Education.

SCIENCE OR SUPERSTITION?

David Layzer

A NUMBER of years ago, when high school teachers in North Carolina were being paid a starting salary of $120 per month, I happened to ask a member of that state's legislature whether he considered this to be an adequate salary. "Certainly," he said, "they're not worth any more than that." "How do you know?" I asked. "Why, just look at what they're paid." Circular reasoning? I think not. Our views on salary and status reflect our basic assumptions concerning the individual and his relation to society. One possible assumption is that society should reward each of its members according to his needs and contributions. Another is that society has a fixed hierarchic structure and each individual gravitates inevitably toward the level where he belongs. My question was based on the first assumption, the legislator's reply on the second.

The idea that, by and large, we get what we deserve—that there is a preordained harmony between what we are and what we achieve—was an essential ingredient in the Calvinist doctrine of New England's Puritan settlers. What really mattered to them was not, of course, how well they did in this world but how well they would do in the next.

David Layzer is the Donald L. Menzel Professor of Astrophysics at Harvard University. A German translation of his revised *Cosmogenesis: The Growth of Order in the Universe* has just been published by Insel Verlag. This article originally appeared in *Cognition: International Journal of Cognitive Science* (1972).

The first was important only insofar as it provided a clue to the second. Although Calvinism's other-worldly orientation has long since gone out of fashion, its underlying social attitudes persist and continue to play an important part in shaping our social, educational, and political institutions. Because we still tend to interpret wealth and power as tokens of innate worth (and poverty and helplessness as tokens of innate worthlessness), we tend to believe that it is wicked to tamper with "natural" processes of selection and rejection (Thou shalt not monkey with the Market), to erect artificial barriers against economic mobility (downward or upward), or to penalize the deserving rich in order to benefit the undeserving poor.

Not unnaturally, such attitudes have always appealed strongly to the upwardly mobile and those who already inhabit society's upper strata. Besides, they offer a convenient rationalization for our failure to cope with, or even to confront, our most urgent social problem: the emergence of a growing and self-perpetuating lower class, disproportionately Afro- and Latin-American in its ethnic composition, excluded from the mainstream of American life and alienated from its values, isolated in rural areas and urban ghettos, and dependent for the means of bare survival on an increasingly hostile and resentful majority. Faced with this problem, many people find it comforting to believe that human nature, not the System, is responsible for gross inequalities in the human condition. As Richard Nixon has said, "Government could provide health, housing, means, and clothing for all Americans. That would not make us a great country. What we have to remember is that this country is going to be great in the future to the extent that individuals have self-respect, pride, and a determination to do better."

Although such attitudes are deeply ingrained, increasing numbers of Americans are beginning to question their validity. The System may be based on eternal moral truths, but in practice it seems to be working less and less well; and one of the eternal moral truths does, after all, assert that practical success is inner virtue's outward aspect. Yet the quality of life in America is deteriorating in many ways, not only for the downwardly mobile lower class (who, according to Mr. Nixon, are not trying hard enough) but also for the upwardly mobile middle class (who are already trying as hard as they can). In these circumstances any argument that lends support to the old, embattled attitudes is bound to arouse strong emotional responses both among those who recognize a need for basic social reform and among those who oppose it.

JENSENISM

THIS MAY HELP to explain the furor generated by the publication, in a previously obscure educational journal, of a long scholarly article provocatively entitled, "How Much Can We Boost IQ and Scholastic Achievement?" (Jensen, 1969). Very little, concludes the author—because differences in IQ largely reflect innate differences in intelligence. Children with low IQs, he argues, lack the capacity to acquire specific cognitive skills, namely, those involved in abstract reasoning and problem solving. Such children should be taught mainly by rote and should not be encouraged to aspire to occupations that call for higher cognitive skills.

What is true of individuals could also well be true of groups, continues Jensen: differences between ethnic groups in average performance on IQ tests probably reflect average differences in innate intellectual capacity. Jensen does not shirk the unpleasant duty of pointing out that this conclusion has an important bearing on fundamental questions of educational, social and political policy:

> Since much of the current thinking behind civil rights, fair employment, and equality of educational opportunity appeals to the fact that there is a disproportionate representation of different racial groups in the various levels of educational, occupational and socioeconomic hierarchy, we are forced to examine all the possible reasons for the inequality among racial groups in the attainments and rewards generally valued by all groups within our society. To what extent can such inequalities be attributed to unfairness in society's multiple selection processes? . . . And to what extent are these inequalities attributable to really relevant selection criteria which apply equally to all individuals but at the same time select disproportionately between some racial groups because there exist, in fact, real average differences among the groups—differences . . . indisputably relevant to educational and occupational performance?

The contention that IQ is an index of innate cognitive capacity is of course not new, but it has not been taken very seriously by most biologists and psychologists. Jensen's article purports to put it on a sound scientific basis. In outline, his argument runs as follows. IQ test scores represent measurements of a human trait which we may call intelligence. It is irrelevant to the argument that we do not know what intelligence "really is." All that we need to know is that IQ tests are internally and mutually consistent and that IQ correlates strongly with scholastic success, income, occupational status, etc. We can then treat IQ as if it was a metric character like height or weight, and use techniques of population genetics to estimate its "heritability." In this way we can discover the relative importance of genetic and environmental differences as they contribute to differences in IQ. Such studies show, according to Jensen, that IQ differences are approximately 90 percent genetic in origin.

Jensen's 123-page article is largely devoted to fleshing out this argument and developing its educational implications. Jensenism has also been expounded at a more popular level: in Great Britain by H. J. Eysenck (1971) and in America by R. J. Herrnstein (1971). While Eysenck's main concern is to stress the genetic basis of differences between ethnic groups, Herrnstein is more concerned with the social and political implications of Jensenism. He argues that the more successful we are in our efforts to equalize opportunity and environment, the more closely will the structure of society come to reflect inborn differences in mental ability. Thus "our present social policies" must inevitably give rise to a hereditary caste system based largely on IQ. Indeed, the lowest socioeconomic classes already consist of people with the lowest IQs. Since, according to Jensen, IQ is essentially genetically determined, Herrnstein's argument implies that the current inhabitants of urban ghettos and depressed rural areas are destined to become the progenitors of a hereditary caste, its members doomed by their genetic incapacity to do well on IQ tests to remain forever unemployed and unemployable, a perpetual burden and a perpetual threat to the rest of society.

Many of Jensen's and Herrnstein's critics have accused them of social irresponsibility. In reply, Jensen and Herrnstein have invoked the scholar's right to pursue and publish the truth without fear or favor. Besides, they point out, we cannot escape the consequences of unpleasant truths either by shutting our eyes to them or by denouncing them on ideological grounds. But how firmly based are these "unpleasant truths"?

The educational, social, and political implications of Jensen's doctrine justify a careful examination of this question. It is easy to react emotionally to Jensenism, but teachers and others who help to shape public attitudes toward education and social policy cannot allow themselves to be guided wholly by their emotional responses to this issue.

There is another reason why Jensen's technical argument repays analysis. It exemplifies—almost to the point of caricature—a research approach that is not uncommon in the social sciences. Taking the physical sciences as their putative model, the practitioners of this approach eschew metaphysical speculation and work exclusively with hard, preferably numerical, data, from which they seek to extract objective and quantitative laws. Thus Jensen deduces from statistical analyses of IQ test scores that 80 percent of the variance in these scores is attributable to genetic differences. By exposing in some detail the logical and methodological fallacies underlying Jensen's analysis, I hope to draw attention to the weaknesses inherent in the "operational" approach that it exemplifies.

The Irrelevance of Heritability

JENSEN'S CENTRAL CONTENTION, and the basis for his and Herrnstein's doctrines on education, race, and society, is that the heritability of IQ is about .8. This means that about 80 percent of the variation in IQ among (say) Americans of European descent is attributable to genetic factors. Other authors have made other estimates of the heritability of IQ—some higher, some considerably lower than .8. In the following pages I shall try to explain why all such estimates are unscientific and indeed meaningless. But before we embark on a discussion of heritability theory and its applicability to human intelligence, it is worth noticing that, even if Jensen's central contention were meaningful and valid, it would not have the implications that he and others have drawn from it. Suppose for the sake of the argument that IQ was a measure of some metric trait like height, and that it had a high heritability. This would mean that under prevailing developmental conditions, variations in IQ are due largely to genetic differences between individuals. It would tell us nothing, however, about what might happen under different developmental conditions. Suppose—to take a more concrete example than IQ—that a hypothetical population of first-graders raised in identical environments has been taught to read by method A. Measured differences in their reading ability will then be attributable largely to genetic differences. If method B had been used instead of method A, the differences in reading ability would still have been attributable largely to genetic factors, but both the individual scores on a test of reading ability and even their rank order might have been quite different, since it is well known that different methods of teaching reading suit different children. Thus, *the heritability of such scores tells us nothing about the educability of the children being tested.* To conclude, as Jensen and Herrnstein have done, that children with low IQ's have a relatively low capacity for acquiring certain cognitive skills is to assume either that these skills cannot be taught at all or that, insofar as they can be taught, they have been taught equally well to all children.[1]

What does the alleged high heritability of IQ imply about genetic differences between ethnic groups? The answer to this question is unequivocal: nothing. Geneticists have been pointing out for well over half a century that it is meaningless to try to separate genetic and environmental contributions to measured differences between different stocks bred under different developmental conditions.[2] Between ethnic groups, as between socioeconomic groups, there are systematic differences in developmental conditions (physical, cultural, linguistic, etc.) known to influence performance on IQ tests substantially. Since we have no way of correcting test scores for these differences, the only objectively correct statement that can be made on this subject is the

---

[1] Richard C. Lewontin (1970) has drawn attention to an ironical aspect of this assumption: "Jensen's article puts the blame for the failure of his science [educational psychology] not on the scientists but on the children. According to him, it is not that his science and its practitioners have failed utterly to understand human motivation, behavior and development but simply that the damn kids are ineducable. . . . Jensen proposes . . . that, in the terms of his metaphor, fallen bridges be taken as evidence of the unbridgeability of rivers. The alternative explanation, that educational psychology is still in the seventeenth century, is apparently not part of his philosophy."

[2] A beautiful extended example illustrating this point is given by Lewontin (1970). See also Waddington (1957), pp. 92–94, who quotes an exceptionally clear argument by Hogben (1933).

following: "The reported differences in average IQ tell us nothing whatever about any average genetic differences that may exist. On the data, black genetic superiority in intelligence (or whatever it is that IQ tests measure) is neither more nor less likely than white superiority."[3] If we ultimately succeed in building a color-blind society, then and only then will we be able to estimate, in retrospect, how great the systematic effects of racial prejudice really were. As S. L. Washburn (quoted by Lerner [1968]) has said,

> I am sometimes surprised to hear it stated that if Negroes were given an equal opportunity, their IQ would be the same as the whites'. If one looks at the degree of social discrimination against Negroes and their lack of education, and also takes into account the tremendous amount of overlapping between the observed IQs of both, one can make an equally good case that, given a comparable chance to that of the whites, their IQs would test out ahead. Of course, it would be absolutely unimportant in a democratic society if this were to be true, because the vast majority of individuals of both groups would be of comparable intelligence, whatever the mean of these intelligence tests would show.

To sum up, even if Jensen's considerations of the heritability of IQ were meaningful and valid, they would have no direct bearing on the question of educability or on the issue of genetic differences between ethnic groups. Their apparent relevance is a result of semantic confusion. In ordinary usage, when we speak of a highly heritable trait we mean one that is largely inborn. In genetics, however, a trait can have high heritability either because its expression is insensitive to environmental variation or because the range of relevant environmental variation happens to be small. Jensen and Herrnstein apparently assume that the first of these alternatives is appropriate for IQ. But the available experimental evidence, some of which is cited later in this article, shows that IQ scores are in fact highly sensitive to variations in relevant developmental conditions.

---

[3] Herrnstein appears to have misunderstood this point: he writes that the reported differences between ethnic groups could be "more genetic, less genetic, or precisely as genetic as implied by a heritability of .8."

Science and Scientism: A Question of Methodology

THE THEORY of heritability, some elementary aspects of which are described below, was developed by geneticists within a well-defined biological context. The theory applies to metric characters of plants and animals—height, weight, and the like. To apply this theory to human intelligence, Jensen and the authors whose work he summarizes must assimilate intelligence to a metric character and IQ to a measurement of that character. Most biologists would, I think, hesitate to take this conceptual leap. Jensen, however, justifies it on the following philosophical grounds:

> Disagreements and arguments can perhaps be forestalled if we take an operational stance. First of all, this means that probably the most important fact about intelligence is that we can measure it. Intelligence, like electricity, is easier to measure than to define. And if the measurements bear some systematic relationships to other data, it means we can make meaningful statements about the phenomenon we are measuring. There is no point in arguing the question to which there is no answer, the question of what intelligence *really* is. The best we can do is obtain measurements of certain kinds of behavior and look at their relationships to other phenomena and see if these relationships make any kind of sense and order. It is from these orderly relationships that we gain some understanding of the phenomena.

The "operational stance" recommended by Jensen is thought by many social scientists to be the key ingredient in the "scientific method" as practiced by physical scientists. This belief is mistaken. The first and most crucial step toward an understanding of any natural phenomenon is not measurement. One must begin by deciding which aspects of the phenomenon are worth examining. To do this intelligently, one needs to have, at the very outset, some kind of explanatory or interpretive framework. In the physical sciences this framework often takes the form of a mathematical theory. The quantities that enter into theory—mass, electric charge, force, and so on—are always much easier to define than to measure. They are, in fact, completely—if implicitly—defined through the equations that make up the theory.

Once a mathematical theory has been formulated, its predictions can be compared with observation or experiment. This requires appropriate measurements. The aspect of scientific measurements that nonscientists most often fail to appreciate is that they always presuppose a theoretical framework. Even exploratory measurements, carried out before one has a definite theory to test, always refer to quantities that are precisely defined within a broader theoretical context. (For example, although we do not yet have a theory for the origin of cosmic rays, we know that such a theory must involve the masses, energies, momenta and charges of cosmic-ray particles. In designing apparatus to measure these quantities, physicists use well-established mathematical theories that describe the behavior of fast particles under a wide variety of conditions.) The theoretical framework for a given set of measurements may be wrong, in which case the measurements will ultimately lead to inconsistencies, but it must not be vague. In short, significant measurements usually grow from theories, not vice versa. Jensen's views on scientific method derive not from the practice of physical scientists but from the philosophical doctrine of Francis Bacon (1561–1626), who taught that meaningful generalizations emerge spontaneously from systematic measurements.

These considerations apply equally to biology, where mathematical theories do not yet occupy the commanding position they do in the physical sciences. The following criticism by C. H. Waddington (1957) of *conventional* applications of the heritability theory is illuminating:

> . . . There has been a tendency to regard a refined statistical analysis of incomplete experiments as obviating the necessity to carry the experiments further and to design them in more penetrating fashion. For instance, if one takes some particular phenotypic character such as body weight or milk yield, one of the first steps in an analysis of its genetic basis should be to try to break down the underlying physiological systems into a number of more or less independent factors. Are some genes affecting the milk yield by increasing the quantity of secreting tissue, others by affecting the efficiency of secretion, and others in still other ways?

These views contrast sharply with those of Jensen and Herrnstein, who believe in the possibility of discovering meaningful relations between measurable aspects of human behavior without inquiring too closely into the biological or psychological significance of that behavior. In this way they hope to avoid "metaphysical" speculation. This is an admirable objective. But it not so easy to operate without a conceptual framework. As we shall see, what Jensen and Herrnstein have in fact done is not to dispense with metaphysical assumptions but to dispense with stating them. Such a policy is especially dangerous in the social sciences, where experimental verification of hypotheses is usually difficult or impossible. As Gunnar Myrdal has wisely pointed out, the failure of the social sciences to achieve the same degree of objectivity as the natural sciences can be attributed at least as much to a persistent neglect on the part of social scientists to state and examine their basic assumptions as to the complexity of the phenomena they deal with.

The operational approach not only spares Jensen the task of trying to understand the nature of intelligence. It also enables him to draw an extremely powerful conclusion from statistical analyses of IQ test scores:

Regardless of what it is that our tests measure, the heritability tells us how much of the variance in these measurements is due to genetic factors.

Because this assertion holds the key to Jensen's entire argument, we shall analyze it in some detail.

HERITABILITY

IN THE STATEMENT just quoted, Jensen uses the term *heritability* in a specific technical sense that must be elucidated before the statement can be analyzed. Suppose that we have measured an individual character like height or weight within a given population. The two most fundamental statistical properties of a character are its *mean* and its *variance*. The mean is the average of the measurements; the variance is the average of the squared differences between the individual measurements and the mean. The variance is the most convenient single measure of the spread of individual measurements within a population. Now, this spread results partly from genetic and partly from nongenetic causes. *But this does not mean, nor is it true in general, that a definite fraction of the spread, as measured by the variance, can be attributed to genetic factors and the rest to nongenetic factors.* The variance splits up into separate genetic and nongenetic parts only if the variable part of each measurement can be expressed as the sum of *statistically independent* genetic and nongenetic contributions—that is, only if variations of the relevant genetic and nongenetic factors contribute additively and independently to the character in question. (A criterion for statistical independence will be given later.) In this case the genetic fraction or percentage of the variance is called the heritability.

Characters like eye color and blood type, which are entirely genetically determined, have heritability 1. In general, however, the heritability of a character depends on the population considered and on the range of relevant nongenetic factors. Reducing this range always increases the heritability because it increases the relative importance of the genetic contribution to the variance.

It is not easy to find realistic examples of metric characters affected independently by genetic and nongenetic factors. Human height is a possible, though not a proven, example, provided we restrict ourselves to ethnically homogeneous populations. Giraffe height, on the other hand, is a counterexample, since a giraffe's nutritional opportunities may depend strongly on his genetic endowment. Human weight is another counterexample: on a given diet one person may gain weight while another loses weight.

Let us suppose, however, that we have reason to believe that variations of a given character are in fact the sum of independent genetic and environmental contributions. To calculate the heritability we need to be able to estimate either the genetic or the environmental contribution to the variance. This can be done if, for example, the population contains a large number of split pairs of one-egg twins. By a split pair I mean one whose members have been separated since birth and reared in randomly selected, statistically uncorrelated environments. All observable differences between such twins are environmental in origin, and the environmental differences are, by assumption, representative of those between individuals selected at random from the reference population. If, in addition, the genotypes of the twins are representative of those in the population as a whole, then, using elementary statistical techniques one can derive separate estimates for the genetic and environmental contributions to the variance of any metric character that satisfies the assumptions of additivity and independence. The same calculations serve to check these assumptions.

If a suitably representative population of split twin-pairs is not available, one can cary out a similar but slightly more complicated analysis using pairs of genetically related individuals. In this case, however, one needs to know what degree of statistical correlation between the genetic contributions to a given character results from a given degree of genetic relationship. This information is available only for relatively simple characters such as those studied by Mendel in his classic experiments. For most characters of interest to students of animal genetics, the necessary information must be supplied by admittedly oversimplified theoretical considerations. Where human characters are concerned, the fact that mating patterns are both uncontrolled and nonrandom introduces a further source of uncertainty into the calculation.

Although geneticists can often carry out carefully controlled experiments involving known variations in genetic and environmental factors, the lack of reliable theoretical information concerning the genetic basis of complex characters makes the concept of heritability less useful than one might at first sight suppose. In poultry, for example, the heritabilities of such economically important characters as adult body weight, egg weight, shell thickness, etc., have been repeatedly estimated. Yet for most such characters the estimates span a considerable range—sometimes as great as 50 percent (Lerner, 1968). Again, estimates of milk yield in dairy cattle range from 25 percent to 90 percent. This spread does not result from random errors in individual estimates but from the fact that different methods, which in theory ought to be equivalent, yield systematically different heritability estimates. As Waddington (1957) has remarked in a similar context, "The statistical techniques available [for the analysis of heritability], although imposing and indeed intimidating to most biologists, are in fact very weak and unhandy tools."

The assumption that genetic and environmental factors contribute additively and independently to a phenotypic character is, on general grounds, highly suspect. From a purely mathematical point of view, additivity is an exceedingly special property. Moreover, a character that happens to have this property when measured on one scale would lose it under a nonlinear transformation to a different scale of measurement. Additivity is therefore a plausible postulate only when there exists some specific biological justification for it. For complex animal characters there is little reason to expect additivity and independence to prevail. On the contrary, such characters usually reflect a complicated developmental process in which genetic and environmental factors are inextricably mingled.

It is easy enough to produce more general mathematical models in which genetic and environmental factors contribute nonadditively and nonindependently to the expression of a character. The difficulty with such models is that they are too flexible to be useful. The available statistical data do not suffice to evaluate the parameters needed to specify the model. Thus in the absence of a deeper understanding of the genetic and developmental factors affecting complex animal characters, the theory of heritability must operate within a severely restricted range.

IQ as a Measure of Intelligence

WE ARE NOW READY to analyze the key assertion quoted earlier: "Regardless of what it is that our tests measure, the heritability tells us how much of the variance of these measurements is due to genetic factors." Implicit in this statement are two distinct assumptions: that IQ is a phenotypic character having the mathematical structure (additivity and independence of the genetic and environmental contributions) presupposed by the theory of heritability; and that—assuming this condition to be fulfilled—the heritability of IQ can be estimated from existing data. Now, the IQ data that Jensen and others have analyzed were gathered in eight countries and four continents, over a period of fifty years, by investigators using a wide variety of mental tests and testing procedures. Geneticists and other natural scientists who make conventional scientific measurements under controlled conditions know from bitter experience how wayward and recalcitrant, how insensitive to the needs and wishes of theoreticians, such measurements can be. Their experience hardly leads one to anticipate that the results of mental tests constructed in accordance with unformulated, subjective and largely arbitrary criteria possess the special mathematical structure needed to define heritability. It is difficult to imagine how this happy result could have been achieved except through the operation of collective serendipity on a scale unprecedented in the annals of science. Nevertheless, let us examine the case on its merits.

At the very outset we have to ask, is IQ a valid measure of intelligence? Jensen and Herrnstein assure us that it is. "The most important fact about intelligence is that we can measure it," says Jensen, while Herrnstein remarks that the "objective measurement of intelligence" is psychology's "most telling accomplishment." I find these claims difficult to understand. To begin with, the "objective measurement" does not belong to the same *logical category* as what it purports to measure. IQ does not measure an individual phenotypic character like height or weight; it is a measure of the rank order or relative standing of test scores in a given population. Thus the statement "A has an IQ of 100" means that half the members of a certain reference population scored lower than A on a certain set of tests and half scored higher. "B has an IQ of 115" means that 68 percent of the reference population scored lower than B and 32 percent higher, and so on. (IQ tests are so constructed that the frequency distribution of test scores in the reference population conforms as closely as possible to a normal distribution—the familiar bell-shaped curve—centered on the value of 100 and having a half-width or standard deviation [the square root of the variance] of 15 points.) To call IQ a measure of intelligence conforms neither to ordinary educated usage nor to elementary logic.

One might perhaps be tempted to dismiss this objection as a mere logical quibble. If IQ itself belongs to the wrong logical category to be a measure of intelligence, why not use actual test scores? One difficulty with this proposal is the multiplicity and diversity of mental tests, all with equally valid claims. (This is part of the price that must be paid for a strictly "operational" definition of intelligence.) Even if one were to decide quite arbitrarily to subscribe to a particular brand of mental test, one would still need to administer different versions of it to different age groups. An appearance of uniformity is secured only by forcing the results of each test to fit the same Procrustean bed (the normal distribution). But this mathematical operation cannot convert an index of rank order on tests having an unspecified and largely arbitrary content into an "objective measure of intelligence." Even Burt (1956), a convinced hereditarian whose work forms the mainstay of Jensen's technical argument, recognized this difficulty. "Differences in this hypothetical ability [intelligence]," he wrote, "*cannot* be directly measured. We can, however, systematically observe relevant aspects of the child's behavior and record his performances on standardized tests; and in this way we can usually arrive at a reasonably reliable and valid estimate of his 'intelligence' in the sense defined." (Emphasis added. Earlier in the paper cited above, Burt defines intelligence as "an innate, general, cognitive factor.") Burt's conviction that intelligence cannot be directly or objectively measured—a conviction bred by over half a century of active observation—profoundly influenced his practical approach to the problem. In assessing children's intelligence, Burt and his assistants used group tests, but also relied heavily on the subjective impressions of teachers. When a discrepancy arose between a teacher's assessment and the results of group tests, the child was retested individually, if necessary more than once. Burt's final assessments may be "reliable and valid," as he claims, but they are certainly not objective, nor did he consider them to be so.

TQ AND TENTACLE LENGTH

THE FACT that IQ cannot, for purely logical reasons, be an objective measure of intelligence (or of any other individual characteristic) does not automatically invalidate Jensen's arguments concerning heritability. Rank order on a mental test could still be, as Burt suggested, an *indirect* measure of intelligence. To illustrate this point, suppose that members of a superintelligent race of octopuses, unable to construct rigid measuring rods but versed in statistical techniques, wished to measure tentacle length. Through appropriate tests of performance they might be able to establish rank order of tentacle length in individual age groups. By forcing the frequency distribution of rank order in each group to fit a normal distribution with mean 100 and standard deviation 15, they would arrive at a TQ (tentacle quotient) for each octopus. In all probability, differences in TQ would turn out to be closely proportional to differences in actual tentacle length within a given age group, though the factor of proportionality would vary in an unknown way from one group to another. Thus our hypothetical race of octopuses would be able to *infer* relative tentacle length within an age group from information about rank order. This inference evidently hinges on the assumption that tentacle length, which the octopuses cannot measure directly, is in reality normally distributed within each age group.

SOME TACIT ASSUMPTIONS UNMASKED AND ANALYZED

SIMILARLY, the *inference* that IQ is a measure of intelligence depends on certain assumptions, namely: (a) that there exists an underlying one-dimensional, metric character related to IQ in a one-to-one way, as tentacle length is related to TQ, and (b) that the values assumed by this character in a suitable reference population are normally distributed.

If these assumptions do not in themselves constitute a theory of human intelligence, they severely restrict the range of possible theories. Once again we see that the "operational stance," though motivated by a laudable desire to avoid theoretical judgments, cannot in fact dispense with them. The choice between a theoretical approach and an empirical one is illusory; we can only choose between explicit theory and implicit theory. But let us examine the assumptions on their own merits.

The first assumption is pure metaphysics. Assertions about the existence of unobservable properties cannot be proved or disproved; their acceptance demands an act of faith. Let us perform this act, however—at least provisionally—so that we can examine the second assumption, which asserts that the underlying metric character postulated in the first assumption is normally distributed in suitably chosen reference populations. Why normally distributed? A possible answer to this question is suggested by a remark quoted by the great French mathematician Henri Poincaré: "Everybody believes in the [normal distribution]: the experimenters because they think it can be proved by mathematics, the mathematicians because it has been established by observation." Nowadays both experimenters and mathematicians know better. Generally speaking, we should expect to find a normal frequency distribution when the variable part of the measurements in question can be expressed as the sum of many individually small, mutually independent, variable contributions. This is thought to be the case for a number of metric characters of animals such as birthweight in cattle, staple length of wool, and (perhaps) tentacle length in octopuses. It is not the case, on the other hand, for measurements of most kinds of skill or proficiency. Golf scores, for example, are not likely to be normally distributed because proficiency in golf does not result from the combined action of a large number of individually small and mutually independent factors.

What about mental ability? Jensen and Herrnstein believe that insight into its nature can be gained by studying the ways in which people have tried to measure it. Jensen argues that because different mental tests agree moderately well among themselves, they must be probing a common factor (Spearman's *g*). Some tests, says Jensen, are "heavily loaded with *g*," others not so heavily loaded. Thus *g* is something like the pork in cans labeled "pork and beans."

Herrnstein takes a less metaphysical line. Since intelligence is what intelligence tests measure, he argues, what needs to be decided is what we *want* intelligence tests to measure. This is to be decided by "subjective judgment" based on "common expectations" as to the "instrument." "In the case of intelligence, common expectations center around the common purposes of intelligence testing—predicting success in school, suitability for various occupations, intellectual achievement in life." Thus Herrnstein defines intelligence "instrumentally" as the attribute that successfully predicts success in enterprises whose success is commonly believed to depend strongly on . . . intelligence. That is, intelligence is what is measured by tests that successfully predict success in enterprises whose success is commonly believed to depend strongly on what is measured by tests that successfully predict success in enterprises whose success is commonly believed to depend strongly on . . .

Whatever the philosophical merits of the definitions offered by Jensen and Herrnstein, they afford little insight into the question at hand: Does intelligence depend on genetic and environmental factors in the manner required by heritability theory? In other words, is the heritability of intelligence a meaningful concept? To pursue this question we must go outside the theoretical framework of Jensen's discussion.

INTELLIGENCE DEFINED; COGNITIVE DEVELOPMENT

MANY MODERN WORKERS believe that intelligence can usefully be defined as information-processing ability. As a physical scientist, I find this definition irresistible. To begin with, it permits us to distinguish as many qualitatively different kinds of information as we may find it useful to do. Moreover, because information is a precisely defined mathematical concept, there is no obvious reason why it should not be possible to devise practical methods for reliably measuring the ability to process it. (In its broadest sense information-processing involves problem-solving as well as the extraction and rearrangement of data.) Whether or not such tests would be accurate predictors of "success" I do not know. They could, however, be usefully employed in assessing the effectiveness of teachers, educational procedures, and curricula.

Information-processing skills, like other skills, are not innate, but develop over the course of time. What is the nature of this development? Consider such complex skills as skiing or playing the piano. In order to acquire an advanced technique one must acquire in succession a number of intermediate techniques. Each of these enables one to perform competently at a certain level of difficulty, and each must be thoroughly mastered before one can pass to the next level. The passage to a higher level always involves the mastery of qualitatively new techniques. Through systematic observations carried out over half a century with the help of numerous collaborators, Jean Piaget (1952) has demonstrated that basic cognitive structures also develop in this way, and he has traced the development of a great many of these structures in meticulous detail. Each new structure is always more highly organized and more differentiated than its predecessor. At the same time it is more adequate to a specific environmental challenge. The intermediate stages in the development of a given structure are not rigidly predetermined (there are many different ways of learning to read or ski or play the piano), nor is the rate at which an individual passes through them, but in every case cognitive development follows two basic rules (Piaget 1967): "Every genesis emanates from a structure and culminates in another structure. Conversely, every structure has a genesis."

Cognitive development may be compared to the building of a house. Logic and the laws of physics demand that the various stages be completed in a definite order: the foundations before the frame, the frame before the walls, the walls before the roof. The finished product will depend no doubt on the skill of the builder and on the available materials, but it will also reflect the builder's intentions and the nature of the environmental challenge. Similarly, although cognitive development is undoubtedly strongly influenced by genetic factors, it represents an adaptation of the human organism to its environment and must therefore be strongly influenced by the nature of the environmental challenge. Thus we may expect cultural factors to play an important part in shaping all the higher cognitive skills, for the environmental challenges that are relevant to these skills are largely determined by cultural context.

GENETIC-ENVIRONMENTAL INTERACTION

IF INTELLIGENCE, or at least its potentially measurable aspects, can be identified with information-processing skills and if the preceding very rough account of how these skills develop is substantially correct, then it seems highly unlikely that scores achieved on mental tests can have the mathematical properties that we have been discussing—properties needed to make "heritability of IQ" a meaningful concept. The information-processing skills assessed by mental tests result from developmental processes in which genetic and nongenetic factors interact continuously. The more relevant a given task is to an individual's specific environmental challenges, the more important are the effects of this interaction. Thus a child growing up in circumstances that provide motivation, reward and opportunity for the acquisition of verbal skills will achieve a higher level of verbal proficiency than his twin reared in an environment hostile to this kind of development. Even if two genetically unlike individuals grow up in the same circumstances—for example, two-egg twins reared together—we cannot assume (as Jensen, Herrnstein, and other hereditarians usually do) that the relevant nongenetic factors are the same for both. If one twin has greater verbal aptitude or is more strongly motivated to acquire verbal skills (usually the two factors go together), he will devote more time and effort to this kind of learning than his twin. Thus differences between scores on tests of verbal proficiency will not reflect genetic differences only, but also—perhaps predominantly—differences between the ways in which the genetic endowments of the twins have interacted with their common environment.

One might be tempted to classify these interactive contributions to developed skills as genetic, on the grounds that they are not purely environmental and that the genetic factor in the interaction plays the active role. In technical discussions, however, common sense must accommodate itself to definitions and conventions laid down at the outset. If we redraw the line that separates genetic and nongenetic factors we must formulate a new theory of inheritance; if we wish to use the existing theory we must stick to the definitions that it presupposes.

[. . .]

THE HYPOTHESIS OF FIXED MENTAL CAPACITY

SO FAR we have been chiefly concerned with the arguments by which Jensen and other hereditarians have sought to establish the high heritability of IQ. We have seen that these arguments do not hold water. In the first place, the "heritability of IQ" is a pseudo-concept like "the sexuality of fractions" or "the analyticity of the ocean." Assigning a numerical value to the "heritability of IQ" does not, of course, make the concept more meaningful, any more than assigning a numerical value to the sexuality of fractions would make *that* concept more meaningful. In the second place, even if we had a theory of inheritance that could be applied to IQ test scores, we could not apply it to the correlation data employed by Jensen. A scientific theory, like a racing car, needs the right grade of fuel. Jensen's data are to scientific data as unrefined petroleum is to high-test gasoline. Jensen and Herrnstein would have us believe that we can gain important insights into human intelligence and its inheritance by subjecting measurements that we do not understand to a mathematical analysis that we cannot justify. Unfortunately, many people appear to be susceptible to such beliefs, which have their roots in a widespread tendency to attribute magical efficacy to mathematics in almost any context. The perennial popularity of astrology is probably an expression of this tendency. Astrology is based, after all, on hard numerical data, and the success and internal consistency of its predictions are customarily offered as evidence for its validity. The most important difference between astrology and the Jensen-Herrnstein brand of intellectual Calvinism is not methodological but philosophical; one school believes that man's fate is written in the stars, the other that it runs in his genes.

Jensen's and Herrnstein's central thesis is that certain cognitive skills—those involving abstract reasoning and problem solving—cannot be taught effectively to children with low IQs. From this thesis and from it alone flow all the disturbing educational, social, and political inferences drawn by these authors. If social and educational reforms could raise the general level of mental abilities to the point where people with IQs of 85 were able to solve calculus problems and read French, rank order on mental tests would no longer seem very important. It is precisely this possibility that Jensen's argument seeks to rule out. For if only a small fraction of the difference in average IQ between children living in Scarsdale and in Bedford-Stuyvesant can be attributed to environmental differences it seems unrealistic to expect environmental improvements to bring about substantial increases in the general level of intelligence.

Now, even if Jensen's theoretical considerations and his analysis of data were beyond reproach, they would afford a singularly indirect means of testing his key thesis. The question to be answered is whether appropriate forms of intervention can substantially raise (a) the rate at which children acquire the abilities tested by IQ tests and/or (b) final levels of achievement. This question can be answered experimentally, and it has been. Since we do not yet know precisely what forms of intervention are most effective for different children, negative results (such as the alleged failure of compensatory education) carry little weight. On the other hand, all positive results are relevant. For if IQ can be substantially and consistently raised—by no matter what means—it obviously cannot reflect a fixed mental capacity.

The professional literature abounds in reports of studies that have achieved striking positive results. Several of these are cited by Scarr-Salapatek (1971a) in a critical review of recent hereditarian literature. In one extended study,

> the Milwaukee Project, in which subjects are ghetto children whose mothers' IQs are less than 70, intervention began soon after the children were born. Over a four-year period Heber has intensively tutored the children for several hours every day and has produced an enormous IQ difference between the experimental group (mean IQ 127) and a control group (mean IQ 90).

Has intensive tutoring engendered in these ghetto children a previously absent "capacity" for abstract reasoning and problem solving?

In a study published in 1949 and frequently cited in the psychological literature, Skodak and Skeels compared the IQs of adopted children in a certain sample with those of their biological mothers, whose environments were systematically poorer than those of the adoptive mothers. They found a 20 point mean difference in favor of the children, although the rank order of the children's IQs closely resembled that of their biological mothers.

Many tests have shown that blacks living in the urban north score systematically higher on IQ tests than those living in the rural south. For many years hereditarians and environmentalists debated the interpretation of this finding. The environmentalists attributed the systematic IQ difference to environmental differences, the hereditarians to selective migration (they argued that the migrants could be expected to be more energetic and intelligent than the stay-at-homes). The environmental interpretation was decisively vindicated in 1935 by O. Klineberg, who showed that the IQs of migrant children increased systematically and substantially with length of residence in the north. In New York (in the early 1930s) migrant black children with eight years of schooling had approximately the same average IQ as whites. These important findings were fully confirmed by E. S. Lee (1951), who fifteen years later repeated Klineberg's experiment in Philadelphia. Additional studies bearing on IQ differences between ethnic groups are reviewed and analyzed by L. Plotkin (1971).

Teachers and therapists who work with children suffering neuropsychiatric disorders (including emotional and perceptual disturbances) regularly report large increases in their tested IQs. One remedial reading teacher of my acquaintance works exclusively with "ineducable" children. So far she has not had a single failure; every one of her pupils has learned to read. And reading, of course, provides the indispensable basis for acquiring most of the higher cognitive skills.

The Hypothesis of Unlimited Educability

THAT THE GROWTH of intelligence is controlled in part by genetic factors seems beyond doubt. The significant questions are "What are these factors?" "How do they operate?" "How do they interact with noncognitive and environmental factors?" Experience suggests that children differ in the ease with which they acquire specific kinds of cognitive skills as well as in the intensity of their cognitive drives or appetites. But cognitive appetites, like other appetites, can be whetted or dulled. Nor are aptitude and appetite the only relevant factors. Everyone can cite case histories in which motivation has more than compensated for a deficit in aptitude. There are excellent skiiers, violinists, and scientists who have little natural aptitude for any of these activities. None of them will win international acclaim, but few of them will mind. I know of no theoretical or experimental evidence to contradict the assumption that everyone in the normal range of intelligence could, if sufficiently motivated, and given sufficient time, acquire the basic cognitive abilities demanded by such professions as law, medicine, and business administration.

Once we stop thinking of human intelligence as static and predetermined, and instead focus our attention on the growth of cognitive skills and on how the interaction between cognitive, noncognitive, and environmental factors affects this growth, the systematic differences in test performance between ethnic groups appear in a new light. Because cognitive development is a cumulative process, it is strongly influenced by small systematic effects acting over an extended period. Information-processing ability grows roughly in the same way as money in a savings account: the rate of growth is proportional to the accumulated capital. Hence a small increase or decrease in the interest rate will ultimately make a very large difference in the amount accumulated. Now, the "cognitive interest rate" reflects genetic, cultural, and social factors, all interacting in a complicated way. Membership in the Afro-American ethnic group is a social factor (based in part on noncognitive genetic factors) that, in the prevailing social context, contributes negatively to the cognitive interest rate. The amount of the negative contribution varies from person to person, being generally greatest for the most disadvantaged. But there is no doubt that it is always present to some extent. In these circumstances we should expect to find exactly the kind of group differences that we do find. I think it is important to take note of these differences. They are valuable indices of our society's persistent failure to eradicate the blight of racism.

It may be that the assumption of unlimited educability will one day be shown to be false. But until then, it could usefully be adopted as a working hypothesis by educators, social scientists, and politicians. We have seen that the widely held belief in fixed mental capacity as measured by IQ has no valid scientific basis. As a device for predicting scholastic success (and thereby for helping to form the expectations of teachers, parents and students), as a criterion for deciding that certain children should be excluded from certain kinds of education, and as a lever for shifting the burden of scholastic failure from schools and teachers to students, the IQ test has indeed been, in Herrnstein's words, "a potent instrument"—potent and exceedingly mischievous.

Admirers of IQ tests usually lay great stress on their predictive power. They marvel that a one-hour test administered to a child at the age of eight can predict with considerable accuracy whether he will finish college. But, as Burt and his associates have clearly demonstrated, teachers' subjective assessments afford even more reliable predictors. This is almost a truism. If scholastic success is to be predictable, it must be reasonably consistent at different age levels (otherwise there is nothing to predict). But if it is consistent, then it is its own best predictor. Johnny's second-grade teacher can do at least as well as the man from ETS. This does not mean that mental tests are useless. On the contrary, sound methods for measuring information-processing ability and the growth of specific cognitive skills could be extremely useful to psychologists and educators—not as instruments for predicting scholastic success but as tools for studying how children learn and as standards for assessing the effectiveness of teaching methods.

CONCLUSIONS

TO WHAT EXTENT are differences in human intelligence caused by differences in environment, and to what extent by differences in genetic endowment? Are there systematic differences in native intelligence between races or ethnic groups? Jensen, Herrnstein, Eysenck, Shockley, and others assure us that these questions are legitimate subjects for scientific investigation; that intelligence tests and statistical analyses of test results have already gone a long way toward answering them; that the same techniques can be used to reduce still further the remaining uncertainties; that the results so far obtained clearly establish that differences in genetic endowment are chiefly responsible for differences in performance on intelligence tests; that reported differences in mean IQ between Afro- and Euro-Americans may well be genetically based; and that educational, social and political policy decisions should take these "scientific findings" into account. We have seen, however, that the arguments put forward to support these claims are unsound. IQ scores and correlations are not measurements in any sense known to the natural sciences, and "heritability estimates" based on them have as much scientific validity as horoscopes. Perhaps the single most important fact about human intelligence is its enormous and as yet ungauged capacity for growth and adaptation. The more insight we gain into cognitive development, the less meaningful seems any attempt to isolate and measure differences in genetic endowment—and the less important. In every natural science there are certain questions that can profitably be asked at a given stage in the development of that science, and certain questions that cannot. Chemistry and astronomy grew out of attempts to answer the questions, How can base metals be transmuted into gold? How do the heavenly bodies control human destiny? Chemistry and astronomy never answered these questions, they outgrew them. Similarly, the development of psychology during the present century has made the questions posed at the beginning of this paragraph seem increasingly sterile and artificial. Why, then, are they now being revived? Earlier in this article I suggested that a combination of cultural, historical and political factors tempts us to seek easy "scientific" solutions to hard social problems. But this explanation is incomplete. It leaves out a crucial psychological factor: once we have acquired a skill we find it hard to believe that it was not always "there," a latent image waiting to be developed by time and experience. The complex muscular responses of an expert skier to a difficult trail are, to him, as instinctive as a baby's reaction to an unexpected loud noise. For this reason the doctrine of innate mental capacity exercises an intuitive appeal that developmental accounts can never quite match. This however, makes it all the more important to scrutinize critically the logical, methodological and psychological underpinnings of that doctrine.

References

Burt, C. (1966) The genetic determination of differences in intelligence: A study of monozygotic twins reared together and apart. *Brit. J. Psychol.*, 57 (1 and 2), 137–153.

Burt, C. and Howard, M. (1956) The multifactorial theory of inheritance and its application to intelligence. *Brit. J. stat. Psychol.*, 9, 95–131.

Deutch, M. (1969) Happenings on the way back to the forum. *Harvard educ. Rev.*, 39, 423–557.

Erlenmeyer-Kimling, L. and Jarvik, L. F. (1964) Genetics and intelligence. *Science*, 142, 1477–1479.

Eysenck, H. J. (1971) *The IQ Argument, Race Intelligence and Education*. New York, The Library Press.

Fehr, F. S. (1969) Critique of hereditarian accounts. *Harvard educ. Rev.*, 39, 571–580.

Herrnstein, R. J. (1971) II. *The Atlantic Monthly*, 228, 43–64.

Jensen, A. R. (1969) How much can we boost IQ and scholastic achievement? *Harvard educ. Rev.*, 39, 1–123.

Juel-Nielsen, N. and Mogensen, A. (1959) Uniovular twins brought up apart. *Acta Genetica*, 7, 430–433.

Klineberg, O. (1935) *Negro Intelligence and Selective Migration*. New York, Columbia University Press.

Lee, E. S. (1951) Negro intelligence and selective migration: A Philadelphia test of the Klineberg hypothesis. *Amer. soc. Rev.*, 16, 227–233.

Lerner, I. M. (1968) *Heredity, Evolution and Society*. San Francisco, W. H. Freeman and Company.

Lewontin, R. C. (1970) Race and intelligence. *Bulletin of the Atomic Scientists*, March, 2–8.

Newman, H. H., Freeman, F. N., and Holzinger, K. J. (1937) *Twins: A Study of Heredity and Environment*. Chicago. Chicago University Press.

Piaget, J. (1952) *The Origins of Intelligence in Children*. New York, International Universities Press.

Piaget, J. (1967) *Six Psychological Studies*. New York, Random House.

Plotkin, L. (1971) Negro intelligence and the Jensen hypothesis. *The New York Statistican*, 22, 3–7.

Roe (1953) *The Making of a Scientist*. New York, Dodd, Mead and Company.

Scarr-Salapatek, S. (1971) Unknowns in the IQ equation. *Science*, 174, 1223–1228.

Scarr-Salapatek, S. (1971) Race, social class and IQ. *Science*, 174, 1285–1295.

Shields, J. (1962) *Monozygotic Twins*. London, Oxford University Press.

Skodak, M. and Skeels, H. (1949) A final follow-up study of 100 adopted children. *J. genet. Psychol.*, 75, 85.

Waddington, C. H. (1957) *The Strategy of the Genes*. London, Allen and Unwin.

FURTHER READING

The literature on IQ, class, and race is vast. *The IQ Debate*, the first item listed here, describes some 400 items from the 1970s and 1980s. The following is a partial listing of recent books.

Aby, Stephen H., with Martha J. McNamara, *The IQ Debate: A Selective Guide to the Literature* (New York: Greenwood Press, 1990).

Bannister, Robert C., *Social Darwinism: Science and Myth in Anglo-American Social Thought* (Philadelphia: Temple University Press, 1979).

Barkan, Elazar, *Retreat of Scientific Racism: Changing Concepts of Race in Britain and the United States Between the World Wars* (New York: Cambridge University Press, 1991).

Blacker, C. P., *Eugenics: Galton and After* (Westport, Conn.: Hyperion Press, 1987).

Blum, Jeffrey M., *Pseudoscience and Mental Ability: The Origins and Fallacies of the IQ Controversy* (New York: Monthly Review Press, 1978).

Buss, Allan R., ed., *Psychology in Social Context* (New York: Irvington Publishers, 1979).

Chapman, Paul Davis, *Schools as Sorters: Lewis M. Terman, Applied Psychology, and the Intelligence Testing Movement, 1890–1930* (New York: New York University Press, 1988).

Chase, Allan, *The Legacy of Malthus: The Social Costs of the New Scientific Racism* (New York: Alfred A. Knopf, 1977).

Darrough, Masako N., and Robert H. Blank, eds., *Biological Differences and Social Equality: Implications for Social Policy* (Westport, Conn.: Greenwood Press, 1983).

Degler, Carl N., *In Search of Human Nature: The Decline and Revival of Darwinism in American Social Thought* (New York: Oxford University Press, 1991).

Eckberg, Douglas Lee, *Intelligence and Race: The Origins and Dimensions of the IQ Controversy* (New York: Praeger, 1979).

Ehrlich, Paul R., and S. Shirley Feldman, *The Race Bomb: Skin Color, Prejudice, and Intelligence* (New York: Quadrangle/New York Times Books, 1977).

Eysenck, H. J., *The IQ Argument: Race, Intelligence, and Education* (New York: Library Press, 1971).

Eysenck, H. J., and Leon Kamin, *The Intelligence Controversy* (New York: John Wiley, 1981).

Fancher, Raymond E., *The Intelligence Men: Makers of the IQ Controversy* (New York: Norton, 1985).

Flynn, James R., *Race, IQ, and Jensen* (Boston: Routledge & Kegan Paul, 1980).

———, *Asian Americans: Achievement Beyond IQ* (Hillsdale, NJ: Lawrence Erlbaum, 1991).

Forrest, D. W., *Francis Galton: The Life and Work of a Victorian Genius* (New York: Taplinger, 1974).

Gould, Stephen Jay, *The Mismeasure of Man* (New York: Norton, 1983).

Haller, Mark H., *Eugenics: Hereditarian Attitudes in American Thought* (New Brunswick, N.J.: Rutgers University Press, 1984).

Joseph, André, *Intelligence, IQ, and Race: When, How, and Why They Became Associated* (San Francisco: R&E Research Associates, 1977).

Kamin, Leon J., *The Science and Politics of IQ* (Potomac, Md.: Lawrence Erlbaum Associates, 1974).

Kevles, Daniel J., *In the Name of Eugenics: Genetics and the Uses of Human Heredity* (New York: Alfred A. Knopf, 1985).

Kühl, Stefan, *The Nazi Connection: Eugenics, American Racism, and German National Socialism* (New York: Oxford University Press, 1994).

Loehlin, John C., Gardner Lindzey, and J. N. Spuhler, *Race Differences in Intelligence* (San Francisco: W. H. Freeman, 1975).

Lewontin, R. C., Steven Rose, and Leon J. Kamin, *Not In Our Genes: Biology, Ideology and Human Nature* (New York: Pantheon, 1984).

McLaren, Angus, *Our Own Master Race: Eugenics in Canada, 1885–1945* (Toronto: McClelland & Stewart, 1990).

Mensh, Elaine, and Harry Mensh, *The IQ Mythology: Class, Race, Gender, and Inequality* (Carbondale: Southern Illinois University Press, 1991).

Minton, Henry L., *Lewis M. Terman: Pioneer in Psychological Testing* (New York: New York University Press, 1988).

Montagu, Ashley, ed., *Race and IQ* (New York: Oxford University Press, 1975).

Pickens, Donald K., *Eugenics and the Progressives* (Nashville: Vanderbilt University Press, 1968).

Richardson, Ken, and David Spears, eds., *Race and Intelligence: The Fallacies behind the Race-IQ Controversy* (Baltimore: Penguin Books, 1972).

Scarr, Sandra, *Race, Social Class, and Individual Differences in IQ* (Hillsdale, N.J.: Lawrence Erlbaum Associates, 1981).

Schiff, Michel, and Richard Lewontin, *Education and Class: The Irrelevance of IQ Genetic Studies* (Oxford: Clarendon Press, 1986).

Schorr, Lisbeth B., *Within Our Reach: Breaking the Cycle of Disadvantage* (New York: Anchor Press, 1988).

Seligman, Daniel, *A Question of Intelligence: The IQ Debate in America* (New York: Birch Lane, 1992).

Smith, J. David, *Minds Made Feeble: The Myth and Legacy of the Kallikaks* (Rockville, Md.: Aspen Publication, 1985).

———, *The Eugenic Assault on America: Scenes in Red, White, and Black* (Fairfax, Va.: George Mason University Press, 1992).

Snyderman, Mark, and Stanley Rothman, *The IQ Controversy, the Media and Public Policy* (New Brunswick, N.J.: Transaction Books, 1988).

Sokal, Michael M., ed., *Psychological Testing and American Society, 1890–1930* (New Brunswick, N.J.: Rutgers University Press, 1987).

Stevenson, Harold W., and James W. Stigler, *The Learning Gap: Why Our Schools are Failing and What We Can Learn from Japanese and Chinese Education* (New York: Summit Books, 1992).

Taylor, Howard F., *The IQ Game: A Methodological Inquiry into the Heredity-Environment Controversy* (New Brunswick, N.J.: Rutgers University Press, 1980).

Tobach, Ethel, and Harold M. Proshansky, eds., *Genetic Destiny: Race as a Scientific and Social Controversy* (New York: AMS Press, 1976).

Tucker, William H., *The Science and Politics of Racial Research* (Urbana: University of Illinois Press, 1994).

Wolf, Theta H., *Alfred Binet* (Chicago: University of Chicago Press, 1973).

PERMISSIONS ACKNOWLEDGMENTS

Grateful acknowledgment is made to the following for permission to reprint previously published material:

Garland E. Allen: "The Eugenics Record Office at Cold Spring Harbor, 1910–1940," published in *Osiris,* 2 (1986), pp. 225–250. Reprinted by permission of Garland E. Allen.

The American Prospect: Article by Howard Gardner from the Winter 1994 issue of *The American Prospect.* Copyright © New Prospect, Inc. Reprinted by permission.

Elizabeth Austin: "Brains, Brawn, and Black Babies" from the October 27, 1994 issue of *Chicago Tribune.* Reprinted by permission of Elizabeth Austin.

Ciarán Benson: "Ireland's Low IQ: A Critique of the Myth" by Ciarán Benson. Reprinted by permission of Ciarán Benson.

Carl Bereiter: "Jensen and Educational Differences" in *Arthur Jensen: Consensus and Controversy,* published by Falmer Press. Reprinted by permission of Carl Bereiter.

Douglas Besharov: "Race and IQ: Stale Notions," originally published in *The Washington Post,* October 23, 1994. Reprinted by permission of Douglas Besharov.

The Boston Globe: "A High Ignorance Quotient," a *Boston Globe* editorial published August 10, 1994. Reprinted courtesy of *The Boston Globe.*

Peter Brimelow: "For Whom the Bell Tolls" by Peter Brimelow. Originally published in *Forbes* (October 24, 1995). Reprinted by permission.

Business Week: Book review by John Carey from the November 7, 1994 issue of *Business Week* and "In America IQ Is Not Destiny" from the October 31, 1994 issue. Reprinted by permission. Copyright © 1994 by McGraw-Hill, Inc.

Buffalo News: "IQ Debate Leads Nowhere," an editorial from the October 21, 1994 issue of *Buffalo News.* Reprinted by permission.

Margaret Chon: "False Flattery Gets Us Nowhere" by Margaret Chon originally appeared in *New York Newsday,* October 28, 1994. Reprinted by permission of Margaret Chon.

The Christian Science Monitor: "The Bellicose Curve" (editorial, October 28, 1994). Copyright © 1994 The Christian Science Publishing Society. All rights reserved. Reprinted by permission from the editorial page of *The Christian Science Monitor.*

Tom Christie: "An IQ Furor? So What!" by Tom Christie. Reprinted by special permission of Tom Christie.

Chronicle Features: "Bell Curve Tolls Revival of Racism" by Cynthia Tucker. All rights reserved. Reprinted by permission of Chronicle Features, San Francisco, California.

E. J. Dionne: "Race and IQ: Stale Notions" from the October 18, 1994 issue of *The Washington Post.* Reprinted by permission of *The Washington Post.*

The Economist Surveys: "How Clever Is Charles Murray?" from the October 22, 1994 issue of *The Economist Surveys.* Copyright © 1994 by The Economist Newspaper Group, Inc. Further reproduction prohibited. Reprinted by permission.

Elsevier Science Publishers B.V.: "Science or Superstition?" by David Layzer from *Cognition* (1972). Reprinted by permission.

Emerge: "Straightening Out the Bell Curve" by Appiah and Washington (*Emerge,* December–January 1994–95). Copyright © 1994 by *Emerge: Black America's Newsmagazine.* Reprinted by permission.

Lawrence Erlbaum Associates, Inc.: Pages 5–32 from *The Science and Politics of IQ* by Leon J. Kamin. Reprinted by permission of Lawrence Erlbaum Associates, Inc.

The Estate of Horace Mann Bond: "What the Army "Intelligence" Tests Measured" by Horace Mann Bond from *Opportunity,* July 1924. Reprinted by permission of the Estate of Horace Mann Bond. All rights reserved.

Stephen J. Gould: "Curveball" by Stephen J. Gould. Originally published in the November 28, 1994 issue of *The New Yorker.* Copyright © 1994 by Stephen J. Gould. Reprinted by permission.

Richard J. Herrnstein: "IQ" by Richard J. Herrnstein from the September 1971 issue of the *Atlantic Monthly* magazine. Reprinted with permission by the estate

The New York Times: "The Bell Curve Agenda" (editorial, October 24, 1994), "In America: Throwing a Curve" by Bob Herbert (October 27, 1994), "You're Smart If You Know What Race You Are" by Steven A. Holmes (October 23, 1994), "Anti-Social Science?" by Jim Holt (op-ed, October 19, 1994), "Books of the Times/It's a Grim Message . . ." by Peter Passell (October 27, 1994), "Editorial Notebook: The Scientific War on the Poor" by Brent Staples (October 28, 1994), "Lessons Beyond the Bell Curve" by Christopher Winship (November 15, 1994). Copyright © 1994 by The New York Times Company. Reprinted by permission.

Richard E. Nisbett: "Warning! Dangerous Curves Ahead" by Richard Nisbett. Copyright © 1994 by Richard E. Nisbett. Reprinted by permission of Richard E. Nisbett.

North America Syndicate: Column by Carl Rowan. Copyright © 1994. Reprinted with special permission of North American Syndicate.

Nell Irvin Painter: "A History of Genes as Social Destiny" by Nell Irvin Painter (*Miami Herald*, October 23, 1994). Reprinted by permission.

The Philadelphia Inquirer: "Bell Curve Doesn't Deserve the Fuss" by David M. Kutzik (November 1, 1994). Reprinted by permission.

The Progressive: "Intellectual Brown Shirts" by Adolph Reed (December 1994). Reprinted by permission from *The Progressive*, 409 East Main Street, Madison, WI 53703.

Psychology Today: "The Differences Are Real" by Arthur R. Jensen and "Differences Are Not Deficits" by Theodosius Dobzhansky from the December 1973 issue of *Psychology Today*. Reprinted with permission from *Psychology Today* magazine. Copyright © 1973 by Sussex Publishers, Inc.

Gary Earl Ross: "The Insidiousness of the Bell Curve" by Gary Earl Ross. Copyright © 1994 by Gary Earl Ross. Reprinted by permission.

Irving Louis Horowitz and *Society:* "The Rushton File: Racial Comparisons and Media Passions" by Irving Louis Horowitz. In *Society*, January–February 1995, Volume 32, Number 2, pp. 7–17. Copyright © Transaction. Reprinted by permission.

Barry Sautman: "Theories of East Asian Superiority" by Barry Sautman. Copyright © Barry Sautman. Reprinted by permission of Barry Sautman.

John Sedgwick: "The Mentality Bunker" by John Sedgwick. Originally published in the November 1994 issue of *GQ*. Copyright © 1994 by John Sedgwick. Reprinted by permission of John Sedgwick.

Scientific American: "For Whom the Bell Curve Really Tolls" by Tim Beardsley (January 1995). Reprinted by permission.

Michael Stern: "Exploring the Bell Curve Furor" by Michael Stern. Copyright © 1994 by Michael Stern. All rights reserved. Reprinted by permission of Michael Stern.

St. Louis Post-Dispatch: "Charles Murray's Dead End Curve," editorial from the October 29, 1994 issue of the *St. Louis Post-Dispatch*. Reprinted by permission.

Straight Arrow Publishers, Inc.: "Professors of Hate" by Adam Miller, from the October 20, 1994 issue of *Rolling Stone*. Copyright © 1994 by Straight Arrow Publishers Company, L.P. All rights reserved. Reprinted by permission.

David Suzuki: "IQ Debate" by David Suzuki. Reprinted by permission.

Teacher's College Record and William B. Thomas: "Black Intellectuals: Intelligence Testing in the 1930s and the Sociology of Knowledge" by William B. Thomas (*Teacher's College Record*, Spring 1984, pp. 477–500). Reprinted by permission.

The Times of London: "Racism and the Barmy Laird of Nigg" by Magnus Linklater (November 23, 1994). Reprinted by permission.

USA Today: "Living Proof That Author of 'Bell Curve' Is Wrong" by DeWayne Wickham from the October 24, 1994 issue of *USA Today*. Copyright © 1994 by Gannett Co., Inc. Reprinted with permission.

The Wall Street Journal: "Black Academic Environment" by Hugh Pearson, November 23, 1994. Copyright © 1994 Dow Jones & Company, Inc. Reprinted by permission of *The Wall Street Journal*.

Mike Walter: "Word Problems to Take Your Mind Off the Bell Curve" by Mike Walter. Reprinted by permission of Mike Walter.

The Washington Monthly: "The Case Against the Bell Curve" by Greg Easterbrook (December 1994). Copyright © 1994 by The Washington Monthly Company. Reprinted by permission of *The Washington Monthly*, 1611 Connecticut Avenue, N.W., Washington, D.C., 20009; (202) 462-0128.

The Washington Post Writer's Group: "Is IQ Really Everything?" by William Raspberry (October 12, 1994) and "Why Can't We Count People One by One?" by Charles Krauthammer (October 23, 1994). Reprinted by permission.

Ellen Willis: Article from the November 15, 1994 issue of *The Village Voice.* Copyright © 1994 by Ellen Willis. Reprinted by permission.

INDEX